SECURITY AND PRIVACY IN THE AGE OF UNCERTAINTY

IFIP – The International Federation for Information Processing

IFIP was founded in 1960 under the auspices of UNESCO, following the First World Computer Congress held in Paris the previous year. An umbrella organization for societies working in information processing, IFIP's aim is two-fold: to support information processing within its member countries and to encourage technology transfer to developing nations. As its mission statement clearly states,

> *IFIP's mission is to be the leading, truly international, apolitical organization which encourages and assists in the development, exploitation and application of information technology for the benefit of all people.*

IFIP is a non-profitmaking organization, run almost solely by 2500 volunteers. It operates through a number of technical committees, which organize events and publications. IFIP's events range from an international congress to local seminars, but the most important are:

- The IFIP World Computer Congress, held every second year;
- Open conferences;
- Working conferences.

The flagship event is the IFIP World Computer Congress, at which both invited and contributed papers are presented. Contributed papers are rigorously refereed and the rejection rate is high.

As with the Congress, participation in the open conferences is open to all and papers may be invited or submitted. Again, submitted papers are stringently refereed.

The working conferences are structured differently. They are usually run by a working group and attendance is small and by invitation only. Their purpose is to create an atmosphere conducive to innovation and development. Refereeing is less rigorous and papers are subjected to extensive group discussion.

Publications arising from IFIP events vary. The papers presented at the IFIP World Computer Congress and at open conferences are published as conference proceedings, while the results of the working conferences are often published as collections of selected and edited papers.

Any national society whose primary activity is in information may apply to become a full member of IFIP, although full membership is restricted to one society per country. Full members are entitled to vote at the annual General Assembly, National societies preferring a less committed involvement may apply for associate or corresponding membership. Associate members enjoy the same benefits as full members, but without voting rights. Corresponding members are not represented in IFIP bodies. Affiliated membership is open to non-national societies, and individual and honorary membership schemes are also offered.

SECURITY AND PRIVACY IN THE AGE OF UNCERTAINTY

IFIP TC11 18th International Conference on Information Security (SEC2003)
May 26–28, 2003, Athens, Greece

Edited by

Dimitris Gritzalis
Athens University of Economics and Business
Greece

Sabrina De Capitani di Vimercati
University of Milan
Italy

Pierangela Samarati
University of Milan
Italy

Sokratis Katsikas
University of the Aegean
Greece

SPRINGER SCIENCE+BUSINESS MEDIA, LLC

Library of Congress Cataloging-in-Publication Data

A C.I.P. Catalogue record for this book is available from the Library of Congress.

Security and Privacy in the Age of Uncertainty
Edited by Dimitris Gritzalis, Sabrina De Capitani di Vimercati, Pierangela Samarati, and Sokratis Katsikas

DOI 10.1007/978-0-387-35691-4

Originally published by Kluwer Academic Publishers in 2003
MyCopy version of the original edition 2003

Printed on acid-free paper.
www.springer.com/mycopy

Contents

Preface

This volume contains the papers selected for presentation at the 18th IFIP International Information Security Conference (IFIP/SEC-2003) and at the associated Workshops. The Conference and Workshops were held on 26-28 May 2003, in Athens, Greece, and hosted by the Athens Chamber of Commerce and Industry.

In response to the call for papers, 121 papers were submitted to the main conference track. These papers were evaluated on the basis of their significance, novelty, and technical quality. Each paper was reviewed by at least three members of the Programme Committee. The Program Committee meeting was held electronically. Of the papers submitted, 33 were selected for presentation at the conference (an acceptance rate of 27%). This volume contains also 18 short papers selected with a similar process by the Workshop Committees from additional papers submitted to their Workshops.

An event like this just does not happen; it depends on the volunteering efforts of a lot of individuals, as well as on the support of the local co-organizers and of the sponsoring institutions. There is a long list of people who volunteered their time and energy to put together the conference and workshops and who deserve special thanks. We thank Bart De Decker, Simone Fisher-Hübner, Kai Rannenberg, Jan Verschuren and Matt Warren, for chairing the Workshop committees. We also thank all the members of the program committees, and the external reviewers for their hard work in the paper evaluation and Sabrina De Capitani di Vimercati who collated this volume. We are grateful to the local co-organizing institutions (the Athens Chamber of Commerce and Industry, the Athens University of Economics and Business, and the University of the Aegean) as well as to the main sponsors of the Conference (Citibank, and Ernst & Young). We are also grateful to the people whose hard work ensured a smooth organization process. Among them we would like to mention Nickolas Kyrloglou, Maria Karyda, Dimitris Lekkas, Sia Vagena.

Last, but certainly not least, our thanks go to the members of TC-11 of IFIP, who gave us the opportunity to organize this event, to all the authors who submitted papers, and to all the attendees. We hope you find the programme stimulating.

Dimitris Gritzalis, Athens University of Economics and Business
(General Chair)

Pierangela Samarati, Università di Milano
Sokratis Katsikas, University of the Aegean
(Program Chairs)

IFIP/Sec'03 Conference Committees

Conference Chairs

General Chairs: *Dimitris Gritzalis*, Athens University of Economics and Business (AUEB), Greece

Program Chairs: *Pierangela Samarati*, University of Milan, Italy
Sokratis Katsikas, University of Aegean, Greece

Program Committee

Gail-Joon Ahn, The University of North Carolina at Charlotte, USA
Helen Armstrong, Curtin University, Australia
Vijay Atluri, Rutgers University, USA
Walter Caelli, Queensland University of Technology, Australia
Sabrina De Capitani di Vimercati, University of Milan, Italy
Bart De Decker, Katholieke Universiteit Leuven, Belgium
Yves Deswarte, LAAS-CNRS, France
Michel Dupuy, SGDN/DCSSI/CERTA, France
Mahmoud T. El-Hadidi, Cairo University, Egypt
Jan Eloff, Rand Afrikaans University, South Africa
Csilla Farkas, University of South Carolina, USA
Steven Furnell, University of Plymouth, UK
Stefanos Gritzalis, University of the Aegean, Greece
Sushil Jajodia, George Mason University, USA
Evangelos Kiountouzis, AUEB, Greece
Spyros Kokolakis, University of the Aegean, Greece
Kwok-Yan Lam, PrivyLink, Singapore
Peng Liu, The Pennsylvania State University, USA
Luigi V. Mancini, University of Rome, Italy
Juha E. Miettinen, Sonera, Finland
György Papp, VRAM Communication, Hungary
Ahmed Patel, University College Dublin, IR
Guenther Pernul, University of Essen, Germany
Francesco Pinciroli, Politecnico di Milano, Italy
Hartmut Pohl, ISIS, Germany

Reinhard Posch, Graz University of Technology, Austria
Sihan Qing, Chinese Academy of Sciences, China
Kai Rannenberg, Microsoft, United Kingdom
Indrajit Ray, Colorado State University, USA
Ravi Sandhu, George Mason University, USA
Corey D. Schou, Idaho State University, USA
E. Eugene Schultz, University of California-Berkeley Lab., USA
Gene Spafford, Purdue University, USA
Diomidis Spinellis, AUEB, Greece
Sebastiaan H. von Solms, Rand Afrikaans University, South Africa
Rossouw von Solms, Port Elizabeth Technikon, South Africa
Leon Strous, Bank of Netherlands, The Netherlands
Vijay Varadharajan, Macquire University, Australia
Jan Vershuren, TNO-EIB, The Netherlands
Josef Vyskoc, VaF, Slovakia
Tatjana Welzer, University of Maribor, Slovenia
Louise Yngstrom, University of Stockholm, Sweden

Referees
Thodoris Balopoulos, University of the Aegean, Greece
Erik de Vink, Eindhoven University of Technology, The Netherlands
Bert den Boer, TNO-EIB, The Netherlands
Rutger Coolen, TNO-FEL, The Netherlands
Roberto Di Pietro, Univeristy of Rome, Italy
Fredj Dridi, University of Essen, Germany
Marjan Druzovec, University of Maribor, Slovenia
Antonio Durante, Univeristy of Rome, Italy
Mariki M. Eloff, University of South Africa, South Africa
Lothar Fritsch, Goethe University Frankfurt, Germany
James Frost, Idaho State University, USA
Vaibhav Gowadia, University of South Carolina, USA
John Iliadis, University of the Aegean, Greece
Alessandro Mei, Univeristy of Rome, Italy
Dina Kambouraki, Greek Data Protection Authority, Greece
Costas Lambrinoudakis, University of the Aegean, Greece
Torsten Priebe, University of Essen, Germany
Heiko Rossnagel, Goethe University Frankfurt, Germany
Sankardas Roy, George Mason University, USA
Victoria E. Skoularidou, AUEB, Greece
Andrei Stoica, University of South Carolina, USA
Suzan Thompson, TNO-EIB, The Netherlands

IFIP/Sec'03 Workshop Program Committees

Workshop on Information Security Management

Matt Warren, Deakin University, Australia (Chair)
Steven Furnell, Plymouth University, UK
William Hutchinson, Edith Cowan University, Australia
Rossouw von Solms, Port Elizabeth Technikon, South Africa

Workshop on Privacy and Anonymity Issues in Networked and Distributed Systems

Bart De Decker, K.U.Leuven, Belgium (Co-Chair)
Els Van Herreweghen, IBM Research Lab, Switzerland (Co-Chair)
Sabrina De Capitani di Vimercati, University of Milan, Italy
Yves Deswarte, LAAS-CNRS, Toulouse, France
Hannes Federrath, University of Berlin, Germany
Simone Fischer-Hübner, Karlstad University, Sweden
Urs Gattiker, EICAR, Aalborg University, Denmark
Keith Martin, Royal Holloway, University London, UK
Refik Molva, EurÈcom, France
Andreas Pfitzmann, University of Dresden, Germany
Peter Ryan, University of Newcastle, UK
Pierangela Samarati, University of Milan, Italy
Vitay Shmatikov, SRI International, USA

Workshop on Small Systems Security

Jan Verschuren, TNO-EIB, The Netherlands (Chair)
Joan Daemen, Proton World, Belgium
Jan Eloff, Rand Afrikaans University, South Africa
Pieter Hartel, University of Twente, The Netherlands
Jaap-Henk Hoepman, Catholic University of Nijmegen, The Netherlands
Les Labuschagne, Rand Afrikaans University, South Africa

Piet Maclaine Pont, Mullpon vof, The Netherlands
Bart Preneel, Catholic University of Leuven, Belgium
Erik de Vink, Eindhoven University of Technology, The Netherlands

Workshop on Security and Control of IT in Society

Simone Fischer-Hübner, Karlstad University, Sweden (Co- Chair)
Kai Rannenberg, Goethe University Frankfurt, Germany (Co-Chair)
Dagmar Brechlerova, CUA, Czech Republic
Arslan Brömme, University of Magdeburg, Germany
Roger Clarke, Xamax Pty, Australia
Giovanni Iachello, Georgia Inst. of Technology, USA
Rik Kaspersen, Vrije Universiteit Amsterdam, The Netherlands
Martin Latzenhofer, T-Mobile Austria & University of Vienna, Austria
Richard Sizer, BCS, UK
Suzana Stojakovic-Celustka, UZI VRH, Croatia
Jozef Vyskoc, VaF, Slovakia
Gunnar Wenngren, FOI - SDRA, Sweden
Albin Zuccato, Karlstad University, Sweden

TRUST MEDIATION FOR DISTRIBUTED INFORMATION SYSTEMS

Brian Toone, Michael Gertz, Premkumar Devanbu
Department of Computer Science, University of California, Davis
{toone, gertz, devanbu}@cs.ucdavis.edu

Abstract: Distributed information systems are increasing in prevalence and complexity as we see an increase in the number of both information consumers and information providers. Applications often need to integrate information from several different information providers. Current approaches for securing this process of integration do not scale well to handle complex trust relationships between consumer applications and providers. *Trust mediation* is a technique we introduce to address this problem by incorporating a model for representing trust into a framework for retrieving information in a distributed system. Our model for representing trust uses a type system by which data from a source is labeled with a trust type based on qualities of the data itself or the information source(s) providing the data. With this model we develop algorithms to perform static analysis of data queries to infer how the result of the data query can be trusted. We describe an enhanced mediation framework using this inference technique that enables the mediator to govern the flow of information to match intended trust policies in large distributed information systems, even when information may originate from many heterogeneous sources.

Key words: Trust mediation, trust model, scalable information security, data integration

1. INTRODUCTION

This paper is concerned with *trusted, distributed information systems*, where clients pose questions that can only be answered by combining information from several different sources. If clients plan to use this information in ways critical to their business or property, how can they gain confidence in the information to be retrieved and used? Information relevant to a client query may occur in multiple sources of variable quality and/or access costs. The following settings illustrate the dimensions of this problem.

- Consider an investor attempting to decide whether to invest money in a business. She may need information about the market the business sells into: revenue/sales information about the company; stock price history; qualifications of the management team; and (given current events) possible criminal history and/or financial misdeeds of the other major stakeholders.

- A doctor with a large, changing, and ethnically diverse set of patients, confronted with a client presenting unusual symptoms, may wish to know: the past history of the patient; types of congenital problems members of the client's ethnic group are known to have; and drugs that have undesirable interactions with the medication the patient currently uses.

- A user desiring to install a new piece of software may want to know: if any software currently installed on his machine will induce a library version conflict [1]; the set of known defects and vulnerabilities in the new software; what other libraries and packages he needs to download to use the new software.

In the above settings, we see a large, potentially diverse set of users, interacting with many different information sources. In addition, there is a strong need for *trust* in the retrieved information; incorrect information may lead to service disruptions, or loss of life and/or property. A trusted distributed information system, then, provides clients with not just answers, but answers from trustworthy sources. There are several challenges to the proper design of a trusted distributed information system:

Scaling Trust Relationships Trust, as a social construct is at its core a pairwise relationship between a *trustor* and a *trustee*. The natural extension of this to information processing, where each client attempts to develop a trust relationship with an information source, leads to a quadratic scaling problem with m clients and n sources. We desire a solution that manages this scaling problem.

Diversity of Trust Clients may have different criteria by which they choose to assign trust to information sources. Brand names, ratings by bureaus, perceived commitment to information acquisition, investment in processing and networking capability, may all be factors. We desire an approach that does not inhibit diverse bases for trust relationships.

Trust Composition As illustrated above, a typical client query may require a diversity of information, which in turn may imply a diversity of sources that may not be uniformly trusted. In the presence of differing trust levels, the architecture should be able to compose information at different trust levels, and still give the client an indication of the trustworthiness of the computed answer. If it were not possible to develop uniform rules to combine information at different trust levels, then the client would have to manage this in an ad-hoc and inherently non-scaleable fashion.

Our paper makes several contributions to these problems. First, we introduce the *trust mediation* architecture, which introduces the notion of trust into traditional mediated architectures. This architecture separates the concern of providing trust ratings into separate elements, thus providing a means of scaling the management of trust relationships. Second, the architecture uses a flexible, open notion of *trust types* which allows "trust" to be defined in different ways in different contexts. Finally, for specific, and (we believe) intuitively appealing and important contexts, we provide a formal *static trust typing* system which allows types for queries to be inferred, even before the queries are evaluated; query types are inferred based on trust ratings for primitive relations provided by elements of the trust mediation architecture.

The paper is organized as follows: Section 2 discusses related work. Section 3 gives an overview of our conceptual framework for implementing the trust management component and outlines our formal model for representing the trust that is being managed by our framework. Then in Section 4 we describe our algorithms for processing trust, which forms the core of the trust-enhanced mediation component. Finally, in Section 5 we summarize our approach and describe future work.

2. RELATED WORK

Trust mediation has been studied extensively under the name *secure mediation*, addressing the problem of managing client credentials to ensure that a mediator does not violate information source security policies when integrating data to satisfy client queries [2-6]. We address an orthogonal problem of ensuring that data integrated from multiple sources meets client requirements in terms of trustworthiness of the sources used to provide information. In [7], a model is described for secure mediation that somewhat resembles our approach to trust mediation. The model includes the notion of "characterizing properties" assigned by trusted authorities to client and source entities. We take a similar approach except we establish "trust types" and "trust requirements" akin to their notion of "characterizing properties".

In addition, we establish mediation algorithms that take into account the interaction of properties when considering the trustworthiness of the result of data integrated from multiple, differently trusted sources. Secure mediation research does not typically address such interaction because security in this context is related to *independent* access by clients to multiple sources. Because the trustworthiness of sources is not considered, one only has to address the properties of a single client when determining whether access to sources should be allowed. This is not the case for trust mediation, where we consider different levels of trustworthiness when integrating data from multiple sources simultaneously.

To a certain extent our proposed framework for trust mediation resembles the concept of utilizing data quality information to improve data integration [8]. In our approach, however, we present a decoupled architecture for assigning and managing trust information. Our proposed architecture provides better scalability to account for trust relationships between clients and large numbers of heterogeneous sources.

Trust management is a major component of our framework. PGP [9] is a way of managing trust via certificate chains. Policymaker [10] is an example of a general purpose framework for trust management. When applied to our environment, it is subject to both trust scalability and trust diversity problems.

3. TRUST MEDIATION

This section describes our framework for trust mediation. Trust mediation can be divided into two functional components: trust management and trust-enhanced mediation. *Trust management* describes the process of maintaining some quantitative or qualitative measure of trust relationships among trustors and trustees. The *trust-enhanced mediation* component uses trust metadata to govern information flow to clients from sources. We address each of these components, in turn, in Section 3.1 and 3.2.

3.1 Conceptual Architecture

We build our trust mediation framework by extending the infrastructure typical of a mediated query system (MQS) (see, e.g., [11] for an overview). Multiple heterogeneous sources supply information to multiple clients. A mediator or collection of mediators connects clients to sources by integrating information from sources to satisfy client queries. Figure 1a shows the query/response interaction among components in a typical MQS. Lighter arrows indicate queries. Darker arrows indicate responses.

Figure 1b highlights the many trust relationships in a typical MQS. The dashed arrows in Figure 1b point from trustor to trustee. For example, clients trust the mediator to decompose submitted queries correctly (t_{decomp}) and to integrate information returned from sources correctly (t_{comp}). Clients also trust sources to provide correct, reliable information. Conversely, sources trust clients to use data in a non-malicious way ($t_{gooduse}$). In a competitive market model where multiple mediators may exist, mediators trust sources to provide correct ($t_{correct}$), reliable ($t_{reliable}$) information because incorrect information reflects poorly on the mediator.

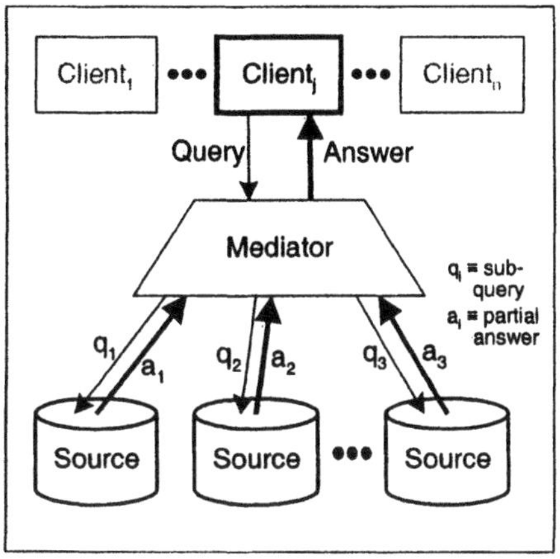

Figure 1a. Mediated Query System (MSQ) component interactions.

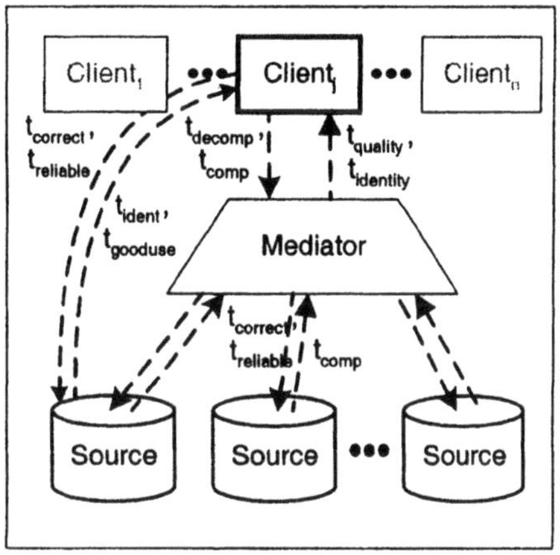

Figure 1b. Implicit trust relationships in a MQS. Arrows point from trustor to trustee.

Our framework for trust mediation provides a mechanism to specify and take these trust relationships into account in the design of a MQS. Depending on the type of information sources, however, specifying and accounting for every trust relationship shown in Figure 1b may be unnecessary to achieve the desired characteristics of a trustworthy distributed information system. For example, a system where information providers exist in the public domain obviates the need for analysis of the trustworthiness of clients. Clients cannot misuse the system to obtain access to restricted information because no such provider exists. Similarly, the trustworthiness of mediators can be assumed when the mediator exists within the same administrative and security domains as clients accessing the system. For simplicity, we will assume that the trustworthiness of mediators and clients is either irrelevant or handled outside of our trust mediation framework – e.g. use existing secure mediation techniques such as those found in [7].

With many clients and numerous information sources, mediators now are in the untenable position of tracking a quadratically growing number of trust relationships in addition to their normal data integration tasks. Therefore, we propose to separate the concern of "trust management". It is not feasible to program the mediator with a different global schema for each client to satisfy individual trust requirements. Figure 2 shows a high level view of our approach. *Trust authorities* analyze sources and assign trust ratings based on precise trust definitions. A trust authority may be an actual external entity such as the Better Business Bureau or a conceptual component consisting of a network of clients willing to share their expertise and experience interacting with a source in order to establish a trust rating for a source. Whatever the implementation, ratings assigned by trust authorities are stored in a *trust broker*, which the mediator accesses during processing of client queries.

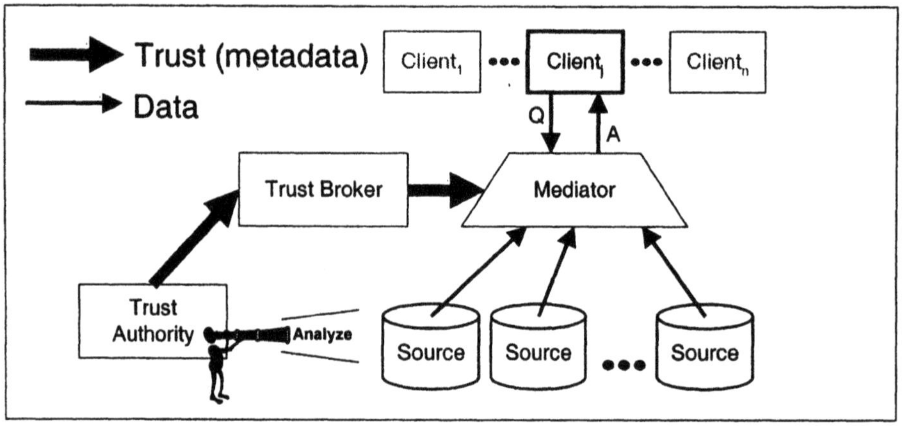

Figure 2. Conceptual architecture for trust mediation.

The operation of our architecture begins when clients submit queries to a mediator. Clients may also attach trust requirements to the submitted queries. The mediator determines multiple query plans for the client query based on the global (mediated) schema. It is important to note here that multiple query plans exist because data may be duplicated in several sources. Recall that the trustworthiness of these sources may be different and thus the result of query plan execution may not be identical as is typical in a mediated query system. This is accounted for by the client through the specification of trust requirements. To select a query plan for execution, the mediator processes the trust ratings stored in the trust broker for the sources specified in each query plan. The result of this processing step is trust ratings for the integrated data that would be returned to the client for each executed query plan. The trust processing algorithm we present for performing this static analysis of query plans to determine trustworthiness of the integrated result is detailed in Section 4. Operation of the framework continues as the mediator executes a query plan whose trust rating satisfies the client trust requirements. The retrieved data is then sent to the client. The mediator notifies the client if no query plan satisfies the client trust requirements.

3.2 Trust Model for Trust Mediation

Before describing the details of assigning trust ratings, formulating trust requirements, and processing trust, we present in this section our model for representing trust. We describe more clearly the notion of trust we use for trust mediation by defining the relationship that exists when a trustor trusts a trustee. Our notion of trust is based on expectations similar to those expressed in [12], where trust is defined as "a belief in the system characteristics, specifically belief in the competence, dependability and security of the system, under conditions of risk." We adapt this definition for our setting:

Definition 1. *Trust* in the context of distributed information systems is the belief held by a trustor that expectations will be met regarding specific observable attributes of a trustee and/or the information the trustee provides.

In the framework that we have presented, trust authorities act on behalf of clients (trustors) to evaluate and establish trust ratings for information sources (trustees) according to this definition of trust. To accommodate a real distributed information system where clients may trust information in multiple ways depending on its intended use, we add granularity to our definition by introducing the notion of a *trust type.*

Definition 2. A *trust type* specifies the attributes and expected values of those attributes, which are measured to decide whether a trustee is trusted.

Definition 2 gives us the ability to define precisely what it means for a trustor to trust a trustee. The attributes specified in a trust type could be related to the information source or, alternatively, to the information content – even at the granularity of actual data values. The four example trust types given in Figure 3 take this latter approach.

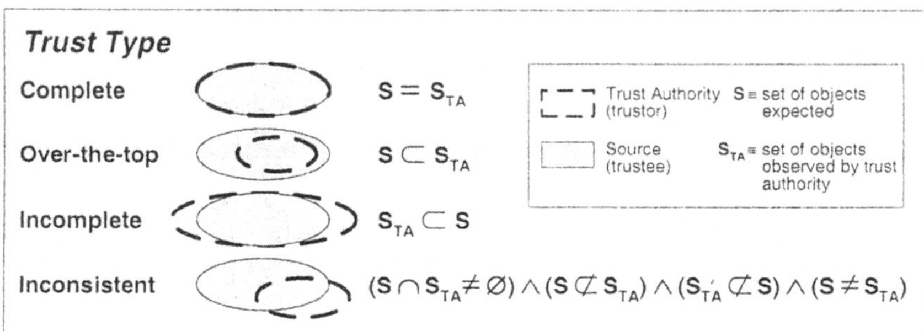

Figure 3. Four example trust types with definitions using set notation.

The trust type "complete" indicates that the trustor (e.g., trust authority) believes that the trustee (e.g., information source) will provide exactly the complete set of relevant objects as indicated by the Venn diagram. Likewise, the trust type "incomplete" indicates a trust authority believes that, when queried, an information source will provide only a subset of relevant objects; but not the complete set. The trust type "over-the-top" indicates a belief that an information source will provide at least one irrelevant object in addition to the complete set of relevant objects. Lastly, an information source trusted according to the "inconsistent" trust type is believed to be capable of providing at least one relevant object. The trustor, however, believes that the "inconsistent" information source will not be able to provide the complete set of relevant objects and will also provide at least one irrelevant object.

To see the applicability of these example trust types to a distributed information system, consider a client medical application which queries for medications to treat a disease. Obviously, the client would be satisfied by a "complete" answer that returns all relevant medications. Depending, however, on the intended use for the information (i.e., the type or severity of disease), the client may be willing to settle for an "incomplete" answer if the cost for retrieving a "complete" answer is significantly higher.

The example trust types in Figure 3 require a trust authority to know a complete data set in order to assign a rating. Despite having such knowledge, a trust authority may not be configured to answer client queries for information directly. Recall that the trust authority may only be conceptual –as described previously where the trust authority consisted of a set of clients sharing their experiences interacting with sources. This conceptual trust authority cannot answer queries; it can only assign trust ratings based on collective knowledge of what the information source should contain.

Trust type definitions are established for a specific application domain. There are a variety of ways this can be accomplished: a distributed information systems (or mediator, i.e., value-added mediation) design team may create relevant trust type definitions for the application domain along with the appropriate inference rules for trust mediation. Trust authorities and clients use these definitions to assign trust ratings and specify trust requirements. Alternatively, trust authorities may independently develop trust types and publish these definitions for clients to use when specifying trust requirements. The systems designer would be responsible for developing the appropriate inference rules for the given trust types, which would then be used in our trust mediation algorithm as discussed in Section 4.

Once trust type definitions have been established, trust authorities analyze sources to observe the values of the properties specified in a particular trust type definition. Figure 4 gives an overview of this process. The analysis process could involve a general review of the qualities of the information source or utilize a series of key query probes to determine the consistency of the probe result with expected values according to the trust type definition. If the analysis matches the values specified in the trust type definition, the trust authority labels the source with the corresponding trust type and records this trust rating in the trust broker. A *trust rating*, then, is a trust type assigned to a source by a trust authority indicating that the source can be trusted according to that particular trust type. Multiple trust authorities may assign different trust ratings to identical sources if the technique used to evaluate sources differs among trust authorities.

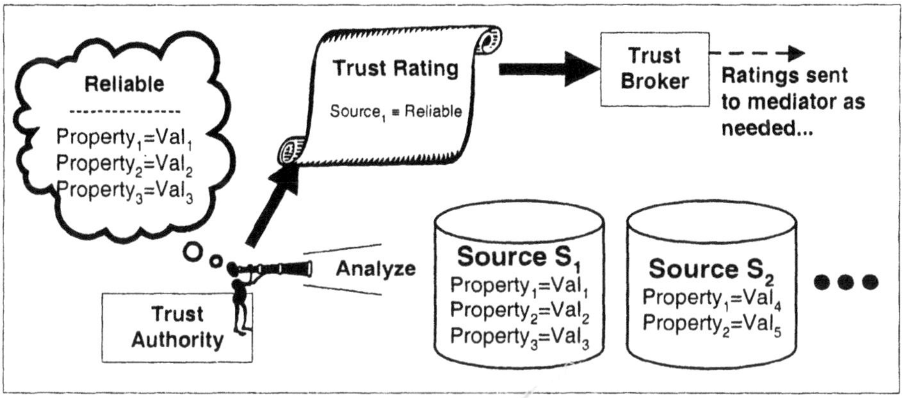

Figure 4. Overview of trust rating assignment process.

We handle this potential inconsistency by assuming that trust authorities agree upon a rating before it is stored in the trust broker. Even if we relax this assumption, we could alter our mediation algorithm to take a pessimistic or optimistic approach to resolving inconsistencies. In the example shown in Figure 4, a trust authority analyzes two sources $\mathbf{S_1}$ and $\mathbf{S_2}$ using the trust type "reliable". In $\mathbf{S_1}$, values of the relevant properties match exactly those given by the trust type definition. In $\mathbf{S_2}$, the values do not match exactly. Therefore, the trust authority assigns a trust rating of "reliable" to $\mathbf{S_1}$ only and sends this rating to the trust broker. The trust authority may continue to evaluate these sources and other sources using different available trust type definitions.

4. ALGORITHM FOR TRUST MEDIATION

We now describe the algorithm that the mediator uses to combine trust requirements and trust ratings during the processing of client queries. Using the trust typology described in the previous section, we employ a technique for performing static trust typing of the query plan analogous to static typing in programming languages. In a statically typed programming language, the type of the result of an operation can be calculated statically by examining the types of the operands and applying a set of type inference rules to the operation. We take the same approach for our trust mediation algorithm. The operations of interest are the operations of a typical mediator query plan, i.e., the relational algebra. All query plans can be specified in terms of these operations. Therefore, we have developed a set of inference rules for these basic operations which can be applied recursively to the operations specified in a query plan in order to calculate the trust type of the result. It is important to note that the operations of the relational algebra have well-defined semantics in terms of set theory. Defining trust types using set theory allows us to prove soundness of our algorithms by demonstrating that trust type labeling applied to the result of an integration operation produces the same trust rating as inferred statically from the input ratings.

Recall the basic operation of our framework. A client formulates both a query based on the mediated schema and a meta-query (trust requirements) using published trust type definitions and sends both to the mediator. The mediator formulates one or more query plans based upon the global schema and then applies our algorithm for trust mediation to the query plan selected for exection to determine the trust rating for the result without having to execute the query plan. Consider generic query plan:**qp** = operand$_1$ *op* operand$_2$.

The operands can be sources (relations) or the result of nested query plans that produce some portion of the total answer for the client query. Our trust mediation algorithm applied to **qp** follows:

```
trust_mediation algorithm (qp){
  if operand1 is a source
    let t_operand1 = trust rating for source (look up in trust broker)
  else // operand must be a nested query plan
    let t_operand1 = trust_mediation algorithm (operand1)

  if operand2 is a source
    let t_operand2 = trust rating for source (look up in trust broker)
  else // operand must be a nested query plan
    let t_operand2 = trust_mediation algorithm (operand2)

  return inference_rule(op, t_operand1, t_operand2)
}
```

The last step of the mediation algorithm shown above is a simple table lookup indexed by the operation and operand ratings. Table 1 gives example inference rules along with abbreviated soundness proofs. For example, Inference Rule #1 states that if source $\mathbf{S_1}$ has a trust rating of "complete" (C) and source $\mathbf{S_2}$ has a trust rating of "complete" (C), the result of an intersection operation using $\mathbf{S_1}$ and $\mathbf{S_2}$ will also have a trust rating of "complete". The intuition behind the proof is that the trust rating for the result of the integration operation, if calculated a posteriori given the trust type definition for "complete" shown in Figure 3, will be identical to that produced by our inference rule. To demonstrate completeness, we have developed a complete set of axioms for each of the operations and for each combination of trust rating for the input relations which are included in [13]. For brevity here, we include the entire set of rules in [13]. We claim that they are easily derived from the definitions of trust types and relational algebra operators.

Table 1. Sample inference rules and abbreviated soundness proofs.

Inference Rule	*Proof*	
Inference Rule #1: $\dfrac{S_1{:}C\ ,\ S_2{:}C}{S_1 \cup S_2{:}C}$	1. $S_1 = S_{1,TA}$	"Def. of complete"
	2. $S_2 = S_{2,TA}$	"Def. of complete"
	3. $\{S_1 \cup S_2\}=\{S_{1,TA} \cup S_{2,TA}\}$	"Def. of union"
	4. $S_1 \cup S_2$ is *C*.	"Def. of complete"
Inference Rule #2: $\dfrac{S_1{:}C\ ,\ S_2{:}O}{S_1 - S_2{:}C \text{ or } I}$	1. $S_1 = S_{1,TA}$	"Def. of completef"
	2. $S_{2,TA} \subset S_2$	"Def. of over-the-top"
	3. $\{S_1 - S_2\} \subseteq \{S_{1,TA} - S_{2,TA}\}$	"Def. of difference"
	4. $S_1 - S_2$ is *C* or *I*.	"Def. of complete, incomplete"

Consider again a medical scenario. A client application queries a mediator for non-interacting disease medications. Source S_1, rated complete, provides chemotherapy medications. Source S_2, rated complete, provides non-chemotherapy medications. Source S_3, rated over-the-top, provides drug interaction data. To respond to the client query, the mediator generates the query plan **qp** to produce answer **A:** $\mathbf{A = (S_1 \cup S_2) - S_3}$. Applying our inference algorithm, even without performing the query, the mediator can conclude that the data will either be *complete* or *incomplete.* If the client application were interested giving initial advice to a patient, an incomplete result might be acceptable. But if the client application is being used by a doctor who has a patient that has tried many medications unsuccessfully, the doctor needs a complete result. In most cases, an over-the-top result would be unacceptable as potential for harm through drug interactions could be life-threatening. Based on the particular client trust requirement specified, the mediator can decide whether to incur the expense of executing the query plan or inform the client that an answer is not possible with the specified trust requirements.

5. CONCLUSIONS AND FUTURE WORK

In this paper we introduced a framework for managing trust relationships between clients and information sources. We have shown our type-inference style approach for analysis of information sources whereby trust ratings are used to derive a cumulative trust rating for the result of a query. As with static typing, this inference is performed prior to query evaluation, which allows a mediator to determine if the result of a query will satisfy client trust requirements, without committing to the expense of query evaluation. We are currently developing a prototype of our trust type inference engine using Prolog. We are using the Amzi! Logic Server which provides necessary tools for embedding Prolog in Java [14]. Our goal for this prototype is to demonstrate the feasibility and benefits of deployment into Willow – a distributed information system for survivability through reconfiguration [15]. Future work will focus on enhancements to our trust model to accommodate additional trust types and inference rules.

Acknowledgements

Brian Toone's work was supported in part by a United States Department of Education Government Assistance in Areas of National Need (DOE-GAANN) grant #P200A980307. Michael Gertz and Premkumar Devanbu gratefully acknowledge support from the NSF ITR Program, Grant No. 0085961. This material is also based in part upon work sponsored by SPAWAR and the Defense Advanced Research Projects Agency under Contract Number N66001-00-8945. The content of the information does not necessarily reflect the position or the policy of the Government and no official endorsement should be inferred.

References

[1] P. Devanbu, "The ultimate reuse nightmare: honey, I got the wrong DLL," in Proc. of the 5th Symposium on Software Reusability (SSR '99), 1999, ACM pp. 178-180.

[2] J. Biskup, U. Flegel, and Y. Karabulut, "Secure mediation: requirements and design," in Proc. Int'l Working Conf. on Database Security.: DBSec 1999, Kluwer pp. 127-40.

[3] S. Dawson, S. Qian, and P. Samarati, "Providing security and interoperation of heterogeneous systems," Distributed and Parallel Databases, vol. 8, pp. 119-45, 2000.

[4] Y. Karabulut, "Credential management for secure mediators," presented at 11th GI-Workshop Grundlagen von Datenbanken, Thüringen, Germany, 1999.

[5] K. S. Candan, S. Jajodia, and V. S. Subrahmanian, "Secure mediated databases," in the 12th Int'l Conf. on Data Engineering, IEEE Computer Society 1996, pp. 28-37.

[6] S. Dawson, S. Qian, and P. Samarati, "Secure interoperation of heterogeneous systems: a mediator-based approach," in the IFIP 14th Int'l Conf. on Information Security, 1998.

[7] J. Biskup and Y. Karabulut, "A hybrid PKI model with an application for secure mediation," in Proc. of 16th Annual IFIP WG11.3 Working Conference on Data and Application Security, July 2002.

[8] F. Naumann, U. Leser, and J. C. Freytag, "Quality-driven integration of heterogeneous information systems," in Proc. of the 25th Int'l Conf. on VLDB, Morgan Kaufmann, 1999.

[9] S. Garfinkel, PGP: pretty good privacy. O'Reilly & Associates, 1995.

[10] M. Blaze, J. Feigenbaum, and J. Lacy, "Decentralized trust management," in IEEE Symposium on Security and Privacy, IEEE Computer Society, 1996.

[11] R. Domenig and K. R. Dittrich, "An overview and classification of mediated query systems," SIGMOD Record, vol. 28 no. 3, pp. 63-72, 1999.

[12] A. Kini and J. Choobineh, "Trust in electronic commerce: definition and theoretical considerations," in 31st Hawaii Int'l Conf. on System Sciences, IEEE Computer Soc., 1998.

[13] B. Toone, "Inference rules for trust mediation," Dept. of Comp. Sci., Univ. of Calif. Davis, http://wwwcsif.cs.ucdavis.edu/~toone/research/trust/inference.html, 2002.

[14] M. Kroening, "Java meets Prolog for advisors, analysts and agents," PC AI, vol. 10, pp. 27-31, 1996.

[15] J. Knight, et. al., "The willow survivability architecture," in Proceedings of the Information Survivability Workshop, IEEE Computer Society, 2001.

CONCERNING ENTERPRISE NETWORK VULNERABILITY TO HTTP TUNNELLING

C. Daicos and G.S. Knight
Dept of Electrical and Computer Engineering, Royal Military College of Canada

Abstract: It has been understood for some time that arbitrary data, including the communications associated with malicious backdoors and Trojan horses, can be tunnelled by subverting the HTTP protocol. Although there are a number of demonstration programs openly available, the risks associated with this vulnerability have not been characterised in the literature. This research investigates the nature of the vulnerability and the efficacy of contemporary network defence strategies such as firewall technology, intrusion detection systems, HTTP caching and proxying, and network address translation. All of these techniques are quite easily circumvented by HTTP tunnelling strategies. This vulnerability is serious for most enterprise environments today. The use of some Internet services is considered to be a requirement for business operations in many organisations. Even with very strict firewall rule sets and layered defence architectures, legitimate web traffic originating from within the protected network is often allowed. Web traffic also forms a large portion of the traffic crossing network boundaries, which makes the HTTP protocol an attractive target for subversion. This research explores techniques that may be used to hide malicious traffic in what seems to be legitimate HTTP traffic originating from within the protected network. The covert channel provides external control of a computer on the protected network from a machine anywhere on the Internet. The techniques explored by this project are used in parallel research projects to detect such malicious tunnel traffic and validate new intrusion detection technology.

1. INTRODUCTION

The purpose of this research is to investigate and characterise the security risk presented by HTTP tunnels in an enterprise network environment. HTTP tunnels are an important class of network vulnerability for which there has been little formal treatment in the literature. This is the case even though the basic mechanisms of HTTP tunnelling have been understood for some time. Open-source demonstration programs for the UNIX environment are available [HTTPT, RWWW] and in the Windows environment there are commercial ventures [HTC, TotalRC] that provide software and gateway services to individuals who wish to circumvent the firewall protecting their host network. It is common for users of peer-to-peer networking applications such as Morpheus and Gnutella to use HTTP tunnels to access the Internet after their network administrator has blocked access at the firewall to the normal ports these programs communicate on.

In many enterprise environments today access to the World Wide Web is considered to be a requirement for the network's support to enterprise operations. This is the case for many business organisations, and includes commercial, government and military networks. The messages sent to request a specific web page, and the web page returned, can contain covert information. This channel for covert information can be used to signal commands to a backdoor/Trojan horse program inside a protected network. This can give the outside attacker control of an internal enterprise computer. The covert channel can be used to modify, delete, or steal sensitive information from the internal enterprise computer. The well-known backdoor Back Orifice 2000 [BO2K] has a communication mode that uses an HTTP tunnel to penetrate the target network's firewall.

HTTP tunnelling is a current exploitable vulnerability of enterprise networks and precludes organisations from providing Internet access for many sensitive networks. The current intrusion detection sensor technology and firewalls provide little support for preventing or detecting such covert channels.

This paper describes an investigation of covert HTTP tunnels that included the development of a proof-of-concept application that was used to penetrate the security perimeter of several networks. The work also tries to anticipate the next generation of covert HTTP tunnels that will use obscuring techniques to hide the tunnel traffic more effectively in the background noise of the legitimate HTTP traffic [RFC2068] being carried on the network. HTTP tunnels are an important class of network vulnerability and it is expected that the risk associated with such tunnels will be a major driver of research in computer system configuration validation, and intrusion detection technology.

The techniques and proof-of-concept application resulting from this research are being used as test generators in parallel research projects to detect malicious tunnel traffic and validate new intrusion detection technology.

Section 2 of the paper provides some background on the simple use of HTTP tunnels to penetrate a network firewall. Section 3 demonstrates how a tunnel can penetrate a network with a more robust security architecture. Ways in which tunnels can be made more covert and harder to detect are presented in section 4. Section 5 provides a discussion about research strategies that might be useful in defeating covert HTTP tunnels, and concluding remarks are provided in the last section of the paper.

2. HTTP TUNNELING

2.1 Subverting the HTTP Protocol

Consider a location on the Internet described by the following URL:

```
http://anysite.com:80/
```

A client request method is a method issued to an HTTP server by an HTTP client that declares its intentions. The client methods include GET (retrieve a page), POST (client provides content to a server), PUT, CONNECT, etc. [Won00]. An example of a message that a web browser might send to the machine anysite.com when asked to retrieve a web page from this resource is:

```
GET / HTTP/1.1
Accept: image/gif, image/jpeg, */*
Accept-Language: en-us
Accept-Encoding: zip
User-Agent: Mozilla/4.0
Host: anysite.com
Connection: Keep-Alive
```

This is the Request Header. The first line of this request "GET / HTTP/1.1" requests a document at / from the server. The "1.1" is the version of the HTTP protocol in use by the browser. The name of the document requested in a GET message (just a '/' in this example) is a data field that is totally controlled by the sender of the message. It can be almost anything.

Given a request like the one above, the web server looks for the resource (e.g. web page) associated with requested name and returns it to the sender of the message, preceding it with some header information in its response. The resource associated with the URL depends on how the server is implemented. It could be a static file or it could be dynamically generated. In this case, the server might return:

```
HTTP/1.1 200 OK
Date: Mon, 06 Nov 2001 20:21:35 GMT
Server: Apache/1.3.6 (Unix)
Last-Modified: Fri, 03 Nov 2001 12:00:09 GMT
Accept-Ranges: bytes
```

```
Content-length: 1000
Connection: Close
Content-Type: text/html

<html> ...
```

The above text is called the response header and the part with the HTML code (two carriage returns below the header) is the body.

To create the covert HTTP tunnel, information can be encoded in the name strings of the client's GET messages and in the bodies of the responses from the server. The concept behind the mechanism described below is quite general; where specific detail is provided it is for the case of the application developed by the researchers.

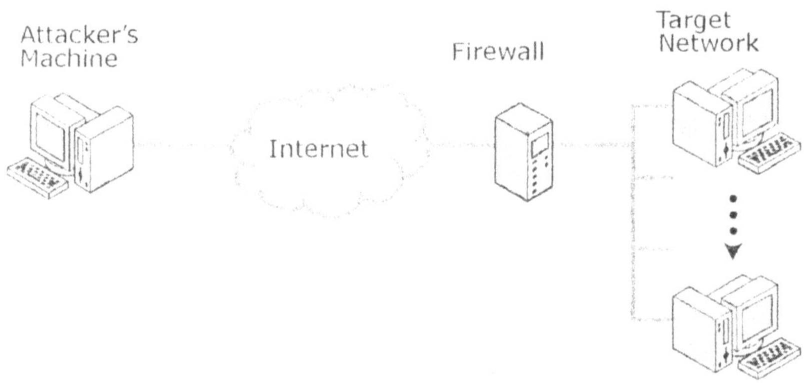

Figure 1 – A Simple Network Architecture

Specifically consider the case described by Figure 1, which can be used to describe an *HTTP reverse tunnel.* To illustrate the capabilities of the reverse tunnel assume that a machine on the target network is running a malicious program (the client) that will communicate with an attacker (the server) somewhere on the Internet, in violation of the security policy of the network. How this program first establishes itself on the machine is not within the scope of the discussion. Network computers can become compromised by viruses, removable media, during the movement of laptop computers between trusted and untrusted environments, or by legitimate users either wittingly or unwittingly installing unauthorised programs. Also assume that firewall on target network runs a highly restrictive rule set and that the only outbound communication allowed is HTTP GET requests. The only inbound communication allowed is the response messages from web servers.

The client code behaves like a very simple web browser. Once executed on the target machine, it calls "home" to the server program by issuing a simple GET request whose header might look like this:

```
GET /some_sub_dir/index.html HTTP/1.1
User-Agent: Mozilla/4.0
Host: 123.109.117.215
Connection: Keep-Alive
```

The IP specified in the "Host" field of the request header is the IP of the attacker's computer. The sub-directory specified as the requested resource in the GET field may not be a directory listing at all, but acts as a code-word to the server program on the outside that a covert client is calling home. The server program on the attacker's computer, which is listening on port 80 will receive the request from the target machine and return a confirmation embedded in the body of an innocuous-looking web page; just as if it was serving up a page about news, sports, or weather:

```
HTTP/1.1 200 OK
Date: Mon, 06 Nov 2001 20:21:35 GMT
Server: Apache/1.3.6 (Unix)
Last-Modified: Fri, 03 Nov 2001 12:00:09 GMT
Accept-Ranges: bytes
Content-length: 1000
Connection: Close
Content-Type: text/html

<html>
<body>
normal-looking HTML here ...
IDENTIFIER TAG =Confirmed
...
</body></html>
```

Once the target machine on the inside of the firewall has received the acknowledgement, it issues a new GET request every few seconds. The attacker can respond to any one of these requests with a web page containing an encoded command to be executed on the client machine. If no data is returned from the attacker's machine, the Trojan client simply times out and retries after some set period of time.

When it retrieves a page with a system command embedded in the body of the HTML (indexed by some string or keyword) like this:

```
<html>
<body>
normal-looking HTML here ...
SYS_COMMAND=dir c:\secret_files\*.doc
...
</body></html>
```

The target machine executes that command on the target system, parses the output from the standard output into a series of strings that are then embedded in a series of GET requests. These GET requests are received on the HTTP port of the attacking machine, and the strings from each request are reassembled to display the output from the results of the system command executed on the compromised machine.

2.2 Matching a Legitimate Protocol

The power and stealth of this exploit lies in the fact that the connection is *one way*. Unlike some existing exploits that establish a *two-way* connection on obscure or redirected ports, or attempt to use port 80 to connect directly to a telnet or ssh server, commands in this reverse tunnel scheme are only piped to the target machine *when it asks for them*.

The reverse tunnel described here is different from a popular tool known as "httptunnel" [HTTPT]. Httptunnel tunnels through a firewall from the inside out like a reverse tunnel, but it has no automatic client initiation. It requires modification to redirect data at the endpoints, and it uses client methods like POST and PUT to do file transfers, which are more easily recognisable in the packet stream.

With all signalling initiated by the client, and with all the details of the transfer buried or even encrypted inside the body of an innocent looking web page, the stream of data becomes hard to distinguish from the normal traffic produced by real web browsers on the network.

3. HTTP TUNNELING AND NETWORK DEFENCES

Now consider the more robust security architecture of the system illustrated in figure 2. The firewall and its rule set are similar to the last example. In this case however, the firewall is also performing network address translation (NAT). The entire target network is running in a private address space so that an individual machine address is not routable from a remote Internet machine. The only machine on the target network that is visible to the Internet is the firewall, and it does not accept any unsolicited inbound traffic (only responses to HTTP GET messages). The traffic flowing by the firewall is being monitored by an intrusion detection system (IDS). The IDS will alarm the network administrator if it recognises the signature of an intruder in the traffic in-bound to, or out-bound from, the network. A caching HTTP proxy server vets all HTTP traffic on this network. In this configuration no network web browser communicates directly with a web server on the Internet. Web browsers may only communicate with the proxy server. The proxy server opens a separate new connection with the outside Internet web server on behalf of the internal web browser and passes requested web pages back to the browser. The proxy matches the return traffic with the requests and ensures that only pages that were actually requested are passed back through to the client. The use of the HTTP proxy is password protected.

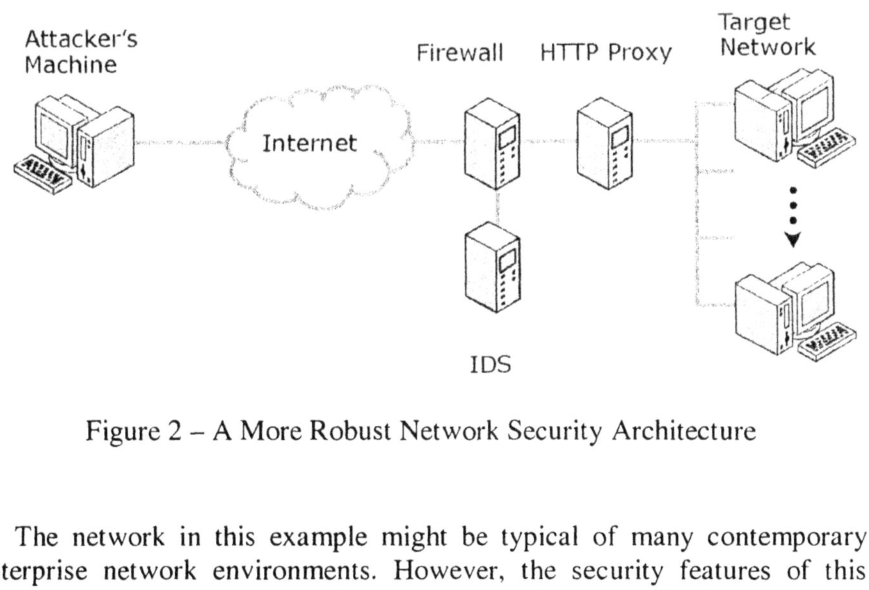

Figure 2 – A More Robust Network Security Architecture

The network in this example might be typical of many contemporary enterprise network environments. However, the security features of this network do not substantially change the operation and effectiveness of the HTTP reverse tunnel. Recall, the tunnel information is carried in the name of the resource requested and in the content of the web page returned. These fields are not changed in transit through the security perimeter. In the proof-of-concept tunnel application some additional features were employed to provide a password when required and additional header lines were required to route the request through the HTTP proxy. These modifications were minor and predictable. The information required (e.g. proxy's address, password) is available on the machine that has been compromised by the tunnel client software. It is also possible that the tunnel client software can subvert the legitimate web browser on the target machine. This would make it very difficult to differentiate legitimate user initiated web traffic and traffic associated with the covert tunnel.

Although several well-known HTTP tunnelling programs can be detected by a signature-based IDS, this is not the case in general. The IDS usually detects a keyword string that is unique to the control of communication by the tunnel's information coding scheme. This kind of signature-based detection is not useful in the general case were the attacker is using a unique application, or is obscuring or encrypting the communication. The IDS/firewall can also detect/block traffic to well-known HTTP tunnel gateways. But, an attacker is not obliged to operate from a well-known HTTP tunnel gateway. The attacking machine could be at any address on the Internet.

The proof-of-concept tunnel application was successfully trialed against several test networks and live enterprise networks that included the security features described above. The application was designed to be deployed on Windows 2000 machines. The tunnel provides a command shell and basic ftp-like services. The client is written in C++ and the server is a GUI-based application written in Visual Basic.

4. OBSCURING HTTP TUNNELS

The majority of traffic crossing the firewall in many large enterprise networks is HTTP traffic. Sometimes web traffic is the only traffic of any appreciable volume to cross the network perimeter. This makes HTTP an attractive target for abuse. The HTTP tunnel traffic is hidden in the large volume of background noise provided by the legitimate HTTP traffic being carried on the network. The authors anticipate a new generation of covert HTTP tunnels that will use obscuring techniques to hide the tunnel traffic more effectively.

It is expected that creating and detecting tunnels will be an evolution of measure and counter-measure. The tunnel builder will strive to provide tunnel communications that are better and better matches to legitimate HTTP traffic (measure). The intrusion detection community will identify means to separate normal HTTP traffic from anomalous traffic that may indicate malicious use of the protocol (counter-measure).

The following techniques are measures that can be used to obscure a covert tunnel.

4.1 Non-Friendly Client Access

The attacker would not consider it desirable for any client to be able to pull down the synthetic web pages from the tunnel's server program. Only actual covert tunnel clients should be able to request the "special" web pages that constitute the tunnel. In the event that a system administrator would like to check the content of the web pages that a suspicious computer is requesting, she should not be able to observe any questionable HTML. Cutting off access completely to unfriendly clients is suspicious, so clients that cannot be identified are served a page of daily updated sports scores or something similar. Serving "404 page not found" errors is also a possibility.

4.2 System Header and Operating Camouflage

As stated earlier, the header for a GET request from any given web browser will look something like this:

```
GET / HTTP/1.1
Accept: image/gif, image/jpeg, */*
Accept-Language: en-us
Accept-Encoding: zip
User-Agent: Mozilla/4.0
Host: anysite.com
Connection: Keep-Alive
```

If configured properly, an HTTP proxy or firewall can scan these headers and reject them based on a ruleset that disallows unregistered or misconfigured browsers to access the internet. To circumvent this, the tunnel client can scan the infected system for recognisable browsing processes, and compile a header to exactly match the User-Agent, Accept-Language, and most other fields.

4.3 Concurrent Activity

By setting the exploit to run only when another web-client process is active would avert suspicion when analyzing HTTP traffic during off-hours.

4.4 Asynchronous Communication

The response time of early remote-shell prototypes communicating through reverse-HTTP tunnels was hampered by the inability to transmit data the moment it was available. Because communication is always client-initiated, the server side of the covert channel is forced to wait for a subsequent GET from the client before it can send information. This model generates many unnecessary connections, and requires that response time be a function of polling frequency. Asynchronous communication without polling is possible. For example, consider the behaviour of web browsers when attempting to load a large page on a slow connection. When a large number is specified in the `Content-length` header of the page served, the web browser is obligated to wait expectantly for the remainder of the data. Major browsers have a timeout of between two and four minutes. If in that time the server has more data to send, it simply sends it through the already open connection. Conversely, if during this period the user wishes to terminate the connection and reload the page, the browser tears down the connection, establishes a new one, and issues a new GET.

We can mimic the above behaviour to make data transfer on a reverse tunnel asynchronous. This allows for real time interaction with a remote shell. By specifying random large numbers in the `Content-length` header of a response to a GET, a connection can be left open for a two-minute window. If in that time there is another command to execute, it is sent immediately through the open connection. Upon command execution, the client will reset the existing connection, establish a new one, and issue a new GET with the results. In this way, asynchronous communication is established without violating the behaviour expected of a web browser.

4.5 Reverse Tunnel Traffic Encoding

GET strings are becoming longer and longer as companies continually add more functionality to their websites with Common Gateway Interface (CGI) programs, and proprietary html-like formats such as .ASP, .CFM, and others. It is not uncommon to see very long GET strings.

A reverse tunnel can exploit this fully by parsing the information being sent back to the attacker computer into strings formatted with the same conventions observable in the Internet applications. For example, a request string when logging on to a hotmail server might be:

```
http://lc2.law13.hotmail.passport.com/cgi_bin/loginerr?
curmbox=F000000001&a=20d9351fd99bfbdd66c9715defff8069&e
rror=4&sec=no&reauth=&id=2&fs=1&cb=_lang%253dEN&ct=1008
617408&_lang=EN&domain=hotmail%2ecom&utf8=0
```

A request string encoded by a tunnel might be:

```
http://119.124.155.107/p99377/rnad.srf?lc=4105&Pd=6528&
ru=htQr_7982626_1265_shx%3fmsu%3d_673kkd/clo2230005=%3f
```

```
C%nQs%3d1%26msnruend%3d1&tw=1000000&kv=2&cbid=6528&ts=_
5&da=passport.c?%%om&r=20.0248.1&t=pf=9bf547478 5dbfb620
f5925b718cbc965
```

It is fair to say that the requests look similar. The first one is from a legitimate Hotmail session, whereas the second contains the first 200 characters of a file named "Draft Earnings Forecast Q3 2002" and is destined for an attacker's machine. An observer would likely notice nothing special about this traffic, and current firewalls cannot detect the difference. They would allow it to pass unhindered.

The Reverse Tunnel's server responses of course, are easier to hide. Since the server can embed its response in a pile of HTML, it is nearly impossible to trace.

Keyword searches or body scans on traffic can be eluded by basic encoding and steganographic techniques used to hide the data in transit. For example, GET requests might be base64 encoded, and limited to 512 byte lengths, while server responses are base64 encoded and embedded in HTML, or encoded in some standard image format.

5. DEFEATING HTTP TUNNELS

As has been demonstrated by the research, HTTP tunnelling is a current exploitable vulnerability of enterprise networks. To manage the risks associated with such tunnels, one must either detect the traffic or lock down the internal network such that the tunnel client cannot establish itself. Both alternatives provide open research opportunities.

The current generation of security perimeter defences and IDSs offer little protection from a tunnel once it is established. We believe that HTTP tunnel traffic encoding will make it difficult for signature-based IDSs to mitigate the threat. Anomaly-based intrusion detection technologies may be better suited to this problem. If the anomaly-based malicious use sensor can characterise the legitimate web traffic on the enterprise network, then traffic that differs from this norm can be flagged as malicious and subject to special analysis. This is the motivation for development of the proof-of-concept tunnel application described in this paper. The application will serve as a test bed to generate test and validation traffic to be used in research into new anomaly-based detection technology.

An alternative to monitoring and detecting established tunnels is to control the configuration of the enterprise network tightly enough to ensure that covert code cannot be run on the internal systems. Again, the current generation of operating systems seems to have difficulty offering adequate protection. Integrity checking applications and system configuration validation techniques can be used to detect and prevent the compromise of network computing platforms.

6. CONCLUSION

The Reverse Tunnel is a serious threat to computer security, with obvious applications in computer espionage. The magnitude of this threat is almost wholly derived from the fact that it targets a well-known protocol on a well-known port that is easy to exploit, expensive to fix, and far too useful to terminate. This makes for an exploit whose variations will likely continue to be a threat for a long time.

The HTTP protocol and the network components that implement and secure it have no real way of differentiating between legitimate and offending traffic. Contemporary network defence strategies such as firewall technology, intrusion detection systems, HTTP caching and proxying, and network address translation are not effective in detecting and preventing covert HTTP tunnels. It is expected that creating and detecting tunnels will be an evolution of measure and counter-measure. To manage the risks associated with such tunnels, one must either detect the traffic or lock down the internal network such that the internal tunnel client cannot become established.

REFERENCES

[BO2K] Sourceforge, Back Orifice 2000, http://bo2k.sourceforge.net/

[HTC] HTTP-Tunnel Corporation, http://www.http-tunnel.com

[HTTPT] Httptunnel, http://www.nocrew.org/software/httptunnel.html

[RFC2068] Hypertext Transfer Protocol -- HTTP/1.1, http://www.ietf.org/rfc/rfc2068.txt

[RWWW] Reverse WWW Tunnel Backdoor (rwwwshell), http://www.securiteam.com/tools/5WP08206KU.html

[Smi00] Smith, J.C., Covert Shells, http://rr.sans.org/covertchannels/covert_shells.php, 2000.

[TotalRC] TotalRC, http://www.totalrc.net

[Won00] Wong, Clinton. *HTTP Pocket Reference*. O'Reilly & Associates, Sebastopol, Californian, 2000.

PROVIDING VOICE PRIVACY OVER PUBLIC SWITCHED TELEPHONE NETWORKS

[2]Mohamed Sharif and [1,2]Duminda Wijesekera
{msherif|dwijesek}@gmu.edu
[1]Center for Secure Information Systems,
[2]Department of Information and Software Engineering,
George Mason University, MS 4A4, Fairfax, VA 22030-4444

Abstract: The public telephone network has been evolving from manually switched wires carrying analog encoded voice of the 19th century to an automatically switched grid of copper-wired, fiber optical and radio linked portions carrying digitally encoded voice and other data. Simultaneously, as our security consciousness increases, so does our desire to keep our conversations private. Applied to the traffic traversing the globe on the public telephone network, privacy requires that our telephone companies provide us with a service whereby unintended third parties are unable to access other's information. However, existing public telephone network infrastructures do not provide such a service. This paper proposes a security architecture that provides end-to-end voice privacy and authentication services within the boundaries of the existing public telephone network infrastructures. Proposed architecture uses public key cryptography for authentication and key distribution, and symmetric key cryptography for voice privacy. This work is a part of an on going project on securing telecommunication system architectures and protocols.

Key words: Public Switched Telephone Network (PSTN), Signaling System 7 (SS7), Certificate Authority (CA), ANSI-41 (IS-41), Global System for Mobile Communications (GSM), Secure Telephone Unit Third Generation (STU III)

1 INTRODUCTION

Wired or wireless voice communication, otherwise known as telephony plays an important role in our society. By lifting the handset of the telephone and dialing a series of numbers we can reach any other telephone in the world. However, as things stand today, an eavesdropper can easily monitor supposedly private telephone conversations. Thus, telephone calls need to be protected against eavesdropping. Existing security architectures in wire-line and wireless telephone infrastructures comes short of providing end-to-end voice privacy as well as authentication for subscribers. Thus, the main objective of this paper to describe an architecture that provides end-to-end voice privacy at the application layer with minimum modification to existing public telephone network infrastructures. Voice privacy is achieved by encrypting voice signals between two end telephones using symmetric keys and a one-time encryption key. This one-time encryption key is used to prevent replay attacks. We also propose imposing an authentication mechanism for telephone subscribers and telephones that are to be used for secure communications. Proposed authentication technique uses public key cryptography and provides authentication center(s) the assurance that the telephone set and the user at the other end of the connection are what they claim to be. We show how to integrate our proposed key distribution services on public telephone grids.

Our proposed architecture for secure telephony will be implemented at the *application service elements* (ASE) layer of the *Signal System 7 (SS7)* protocol model, where exiting security architectures and other advanced intelligent network services in the wire-line and wireless network are being implemented. Proposed architecture takes advantage of information sharing taking place between the telephone companies to facilitate wire-line and wireless call processing.

The rest of the paper is organized as follows. Section 2 summarizes related work involved with the security of wire-line and wireless telephone networks. Section 3 provides a detail description of the proposed security architecture. Section 4 describes how to integrate the proposed security architecture with PSTN. Finally, Section 7 concludes the paper.

2 RELATED WORK

Telephone services have been improving from old hand switched analog encoded telephones to current day advance intelligent network applications. However the security in wire-lines, otherwise known as *public switched telephone network* (PTSN) is still a major concern. Currently, PTSN does not have a system to protect against unauthorized eavesdropping of conversations. That is not to say there is no way to conduct secure telephone conversation in PSTN. There are several secure telephones that provide protection againt eavesdropping in PSTN. These secure telephones are design to work only as dedicated pairs through public telephone network infrastructure and use predetermined symmetric keys. In addition, most of these secure phones address only the confidentiality part of the security services and not other security services such as authentication, authorization, and non-repudiation. An example of such a secure phone is STU III, discussed next.

2.1 Secure Telephone Unit: Third Generation (STU III)

Secure telephones widely used in the intelligence community, commonly known as *secure telephone unit third generation (STU III)*, was developed by the National Security Agency (NSA) in 1987 [20]. It uses symmetric keys to encrypt voice messages. These keys are downloaded and stored in the telephone unit. STU III has an in-built key management system for customizing and downloading keys. Obtaining a STU III requires NSA's permission.

2.2 Wireless Networks

Wireless communications are more susceptible to eavesdropping than wire-line (Public Switch telephone Network) communication, because readily available radio scanners can easily monitor radio signals [6,19]. Because wireless signals are sent over the air using insecure radio channels, eavesdroppers can not only monitor the conversation but also obtain mobile station information such as Mobile Identification numbers. Once this information is known, it can be used to create a clone. Due to mobile station cloning, Wireless telephone industry is loosing millions of dollars every year [13,21]. In order to address these security issues, the wireless industry started to implement authentication to protect against cloning and confidentiality (voice privacy) to protect against eavesdropping.

Authentication and confidentiality for wireless network are defined in ANSI-41 (IS-41) and *Global System for Mobile Communications (GSM)* standards. Both IS-41 and GSM security are based on symmetric key cryptographic techniques where a secret key is shared between the mobile station and the authentication center in the network. Details of IS-41 and GSM security appear on [3,5,6,9]. Both IS-41 and GSM security addresses the issue of wireless telephone cloning, but do not offer end-to-end voice privacy or subscriber authentication.

3 PROPOSED SECURITY ARCHITECTURE

The proposed security architecture consists of *certificate authorities (CA)*, *authentication centers (AC)* and telephone sets with cryptographic capabilities on top of the existing public telephone network infrastructure as shown in Figure 1.

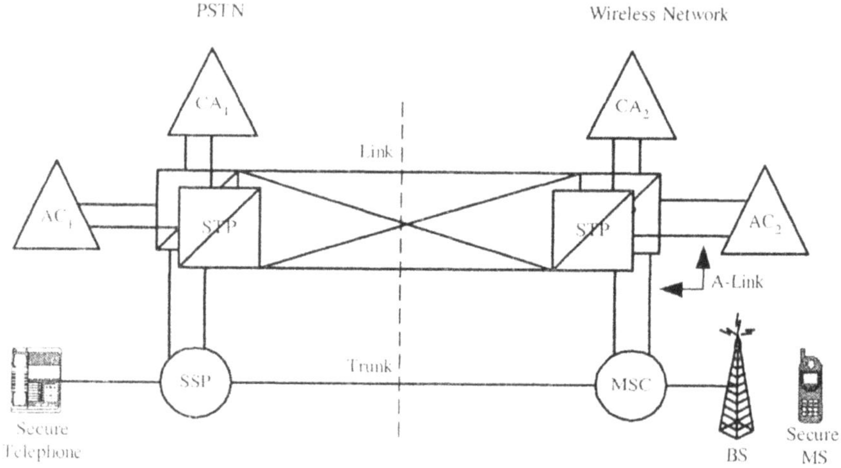

Figure 1. Secure Network Architecture

The CA and AC are to be implemented at the *application service element (ASE)* of the SS7 protocol model. CA is responsible for generating public/private keys, creating digital certificate of public keys, and storing the digital certificates in the publicly available database as well as interfacing with other CA's in the public telephone network. In addition, it is responsible for maintaining the *certificate revocation list (CRL)*, which contains the list of compromised and expired keys. A digital certificate is a record that binds the telephone's public key to the telephone number and is signed by the CA of the telephone company, which is providing the privacy services.

AC is responsible for generating and distributing the encryption keys, and authenticating telephones and subscribers. It is also responsible for maintaining the authentication database, which contains subscriber profiles. Subscriber's profile contains the subscriber identification with corresponding password as well as other information. AC interfaces with other AC's in the public telephone network to service roaming subscribers.

Proposed security enhancements assume that every telephone company establishes a *certificate authority (CA)* and every CA cross-certifies with other CA's in the telephone network. This cross-certification is only valid for the connection process, and allows a telephone or AC in one telephone company's domain to communicate securely with other telephones or AC's in a different telephone company's domain. We now describe authentication services in detail.

3.1 Authentication

The proposed security architecture uses public key cryptography to achieve authentication. The CA of the telephone company generates the public/private key pair and the digital certificate of the AC. It stores the digital certificate of the AC in the CA's database which is publicly available, and stores AC's public/private key pair in a secure file in the AC server.

Whenever a subscriber requests a telephone service, the CA generates the public/private key pair and a digital certificate of the telephone set. It stores the digital certificate of the telephone in the telephone's profile as well as in the CA's database. Then, the CA installs the telephone's public/private key pair and AC's public key in the telephone set. The telephone's profile contains other information in addition to public/private key pairs such as the telephone location, the subscriber, billing information etc. It can be stored in the *line information database (LIDB)* for PSTN telephones and in the *home location register (HLR)* for the wireless phone. The telephone's public/private key pair is unknown to the subscriber. When a private key of the telephone set is compromised, the CA will revoke the digital certificate of the telephone set and store it in the CRL as well as in the telephone's profile. Then it generates a new key pair.

When the subscriber requests privacy service, the subscriber will have to selects an ID and password pair, and the AC stores them in subscriber's profile. The subscriber's profile can be stored in the authentication database in the AC. A subscriber, who subscribes to the privacy service, can use any secure telephone to get voice privacy service. There are two types of authentication taking place in the proposed architecture: system (device) authentication and subscriber authentication. System authentication is used to authenticate the telephone set and the AC, and the subscriber authentication is used to authenticate the subscriber who is requesting a provicy service.

3.1.1 System Authentication

Either the telephone or the AC can initiate the system authentication and it is transparent to the subscriber. However, it will be mostly used by the AC to authenticate the telephone as illustrated in Figure 2. The following steps describe the telephone set authentication process:

1. The AC generates a random number (R), and it encrypts R with AC's private key (K^*AC) using the encryption algorithm (E) to obtain signed R (S_{AC}), which is the digital signature of the AC. [i.e. $S_{AC}=E_{K^*AC}(R)$].
2. The AC sends S_{AC} to the telephone set over the control channel of the digital subscriber lines and voice channel of the analog lines.
3. When the telephone set receives S_{AC}, it decrypts S_{AC} with AC's public key KAC using the decryption algorithm D to recover R,

[i.e. $R = D_{KAC}(S_{AC}) = D_{KAC}(E_{K*AC}(R))$].

4. The telephone set performs the same process as step 1 to sign the decrypted R, [i.e. $S_T = E_{K*T}(R)$], and then sends S_T to the AC.
5. When the AC receives S_T, it performs the same process as step 3 to decrypt the original R, [i.e. $R = D_{KT}(S_T) = D_{KT}(E_{K*T}(R))$]

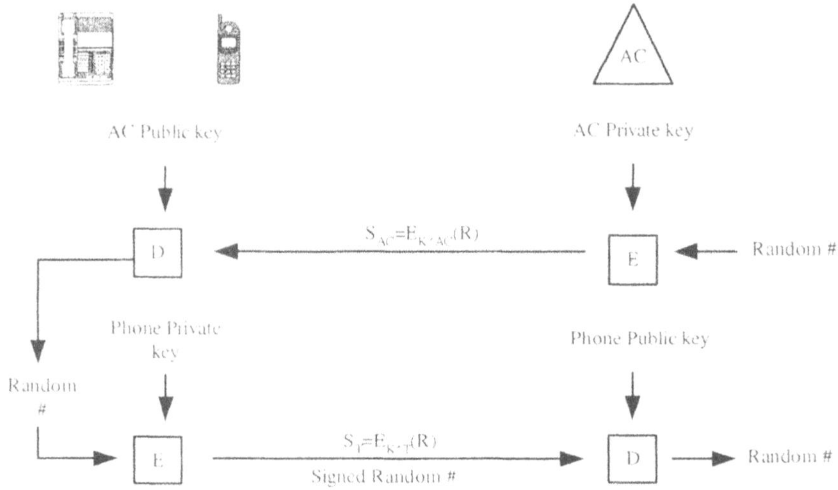

Figure 2. The System Authentication Process

This process provides the AC the assurance that the random number response came from the telephone. Now, the telephone set is allowed to receive services from the network.

3.1.2 Subscriber Authentication

When the caller requests a privacy service, the AC initiates the subscriber authentication process as illustrated in Figure 3, and The following steps describes subscriber authentication process:

1. The subscriber requests the secure connection, and in response, the *interactive voice response (IVR)* at the end office instruct the subscriber to enter the subscriber's ID and password (ID&P) pair over the voice channel.
2. Once the subscriber enters the ID&P, the telephone encrypts the ID&P with AC's public key (KAC) using the encryption algorithm E to obtain encrypted ID&P say C, [i.e. $C = E_{KAC}(ID\&P)$] and sends C to the AC over the control channel of the digital subscriber lines and voice channel of the analog lines.

3. When the AC receives C, it decrypts C with AC's private key K*AC using the decryption algorithm D to recover *ID&P*, [i.e. $ID\&P = D_{K*AC}(C) = D_{K*AC}(E_{KAC}(ID\&P))$].

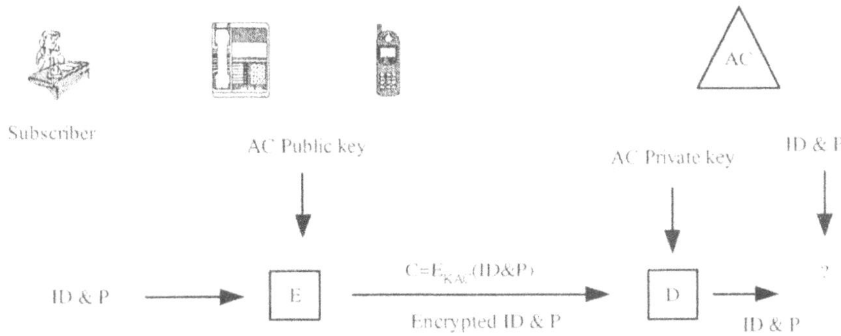

Figure 3. The Subscriber Authentication Process

The AC verifies the ID&P received with the ID&P in the authentication database. If verified to be correct, the calling subscriber is allowed to receive the privacy service, and is denied otherwise. Once the calling subscriber is authenticated, the AC authenticates the called subscriber using the same process.

3.2 Voice Privacy

Voice privacy is achieved by encrypting the voice signals between the two end telephones using a symmetric key algorithm as illustrate in Figure 4. Voice encryption starts when the telephone and subscriber are authenticated, at the caller's end and the called subscriber accepted the privacy service request. The following steps describes voice encryption process:

1. The AC generates the encryption key K_E, and encrypts it with the corresponding telephone's public key KMS using the encryption algorithm E to obtain encypted K_E, say C1 and C_2. Then, it sends C_1 and C_2 to telephone 1 (MS1) and telephone 2 (MS2) respectively over the control channel of the digital subscriber lines and voice channel of the analog lines. [i.e. $C_1 = E_{KMS1}(K_E)$, $C_2 = E_{KMS2}(K_E)$]
2. When each telephone set receives the encrypted K_E, it decrypts with its private key K*MS using the decryption algorithm D to recover K_E, [i.e. $K_E = D_{K*MS1}(C_1) = D_{K*MS1}(E_{KMS1}(K_E))$], and uses it to encrypt/decrypt the voice signals using a *secret key encryption and decryption (E &D)*

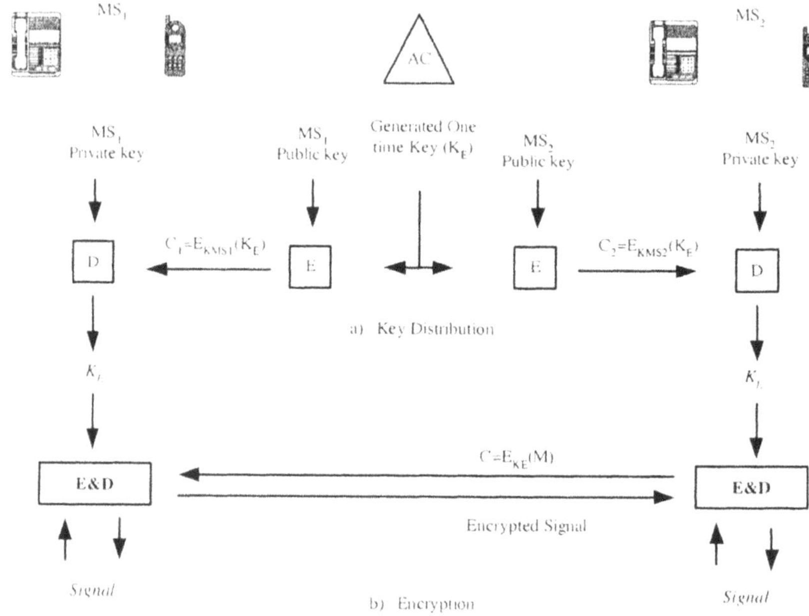

Figure 4. Voice Privacy in the Secure Architecture

This key K_E is only valid during the call in progress, and destroyed once the call is terminated.. If K_E is compromised during the call and the call is on an analog subscriber line the call must be disconnected. If K_E is compromised during the call and the call is on digital subscriber line, the AC will generate a new K_E and sends to the telephone over the control channel. Once the telephone receives the new key K_E, it destroys the compromised key and uses the new key. We are working on the process of compromised encryption key, and we will describe it in our next paper.

4 PROVIDING VOICE PRIVACY AS A SERVICE WITHIN THE PSTN

In PSTN, call processing involves setting up, monitoring, and releasing the connection as well as managing other features related to the call. The signaling protocol is responsible for the call processing. Figure 5 shows the typical signaling messages between two telephones on analog line in the PSTN. The signaling message between the telephone and *Sercvice Switching Point (SSP)* at the end office is subscriber signaling, and the signaling messages within the PSTN are *ISDN User Part (ISUP)* for connection setup and *Trasnaction Capabilities Applications Part (TCAP)* for features related connection setup such as subscriber authentication, 800 number translation, etc. In Figure 5, the broken lines represent secure messages and solid lines represent normal messages. The following call process assumes that subscriber S_1 requests privacy call, S_2 accepts the privacy call, and S_2 hangs up first.

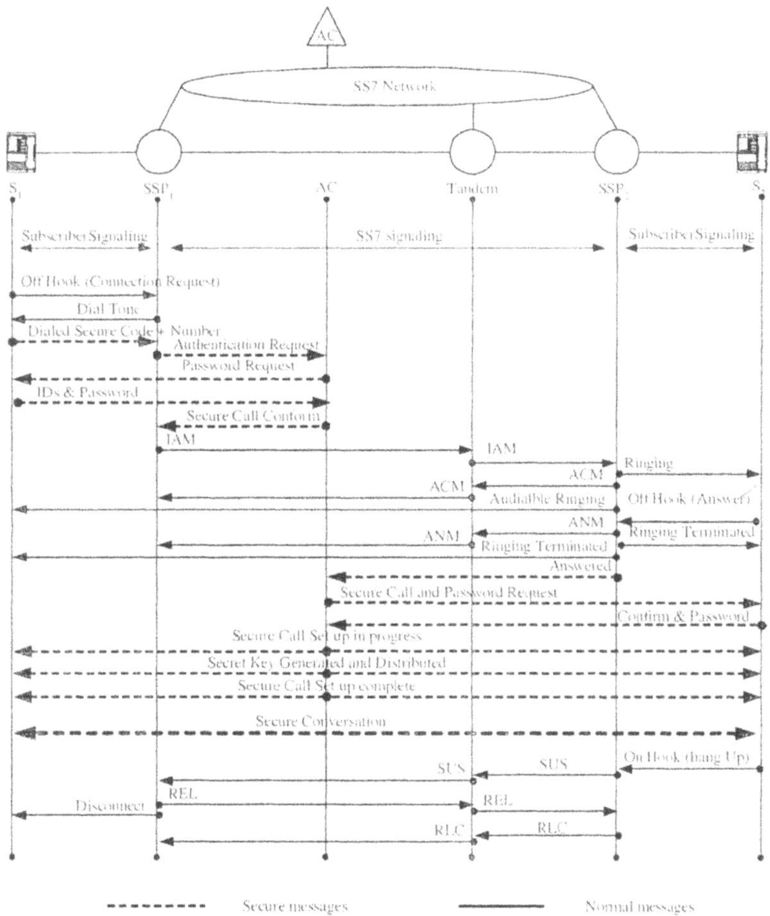

Figure 5. Typical Privacy Service Call Processing in PSTN

When S_1 lifts (Off-hook) the handset of the telephone, SSP_1 interprets off-hook as a request for service and responds with a dial tone to S_1. Then, S_1 dials the secure connection code and S_2's number. SSP_1 waits until all the numbers have been dialed and then examines and decides to route the call to the tandem, and to request for S_1's ID and password. Then, SSP_1 sends request for S_1's ID & password and S_2's ID to the S_1 via *interactive voice response (IVR)* message. While SSP_1 is waiting the response from S_1, it identifies an available trunk, and sends *Initial Address Message (IAM)* to the tandem via SS7 network. IAM is an ISUP message and contains the information required for the tandem to setup the requested connection. Once SSP_1 receives the encrypted S_1's ID, S_1's password, and S_2's ID from S_1, it forwards it to the authentication center (AC) using an appropriate TCAP message. The connection process continues, If and only if the AC authenticates the S_1.

When the tandem receives the IAM, it examines the IAM and determines that it needs to forward the request to SSP_2. The tandem identifies an available trunk, generates another IAM, and sends it to SSP_2 via the SS7 network. When SSP_2 receives the IAM, it examines the IAM, and determines the status of S_2. If S_2 is busy, it sends a R*elease (REL)* message to SSP_1 via SS7 and releases the trunk for another call. REL is another ISUP message. Upon receiving the REL, SSP_1 sends a busy signal to S_1. However, if S_2 is available, SSP_2 sends *Address Complete Message (ACM)* to the tandem via the SS7 network, and the tandem forwards it to SSP_1. The ACM is an ISUP message, and informs SSP_1 that SSP_2 is ringing the S_2 and the requested trunk is reserved. SSP_2 sends the ringing tone to S_2 and S_1 through the trunk.

When S_2 answers the telephone, SSP_2 sends an *Answer (ANM)* message to the tandem, and a TCAP message to AC via the SS7 network. The ANM is an ISUP message that informs SSP_1 that S_2 has answered the call. When the tandem received the ANM, it sets up the forward path of the trunk between the tandem and SSP_2, and forwards the ANM message to SSP_1. Upon the receipt of ANM, SSP_1 sets up the forward path of the trunk between itself and the tandem. Finally, SSP_2 stops sending the ringing tone to S_1. The AC sends the privacy service and ID & password request to S_2 via IVR. If S_2 does not accept it or responds with incorrect ID & password, then S_1 is given a choice to continue as a normal connection or to terminate the connection. If S_2 responds with correct ID & password, then the AC announces the key generation and distribution (for detail, see previous section). Once S_1 and S_2 receive the encryption/decryption key, the secure conversation between S_1 and S_2 starts.

Figure 5 assumes that S_2 hangs up first and then SSP_2 generates and sends a *Suspend (SUS)* message to the tandem, which forwards it to SSP_1. When SSP_1 receives the SUS message, it starts a SUS timer and waits to receive an on-hook signal from S_1, a R*esume (RES)* message from SSP_2, or the SUS timer to expire. If a RES message arrives from SSP_2, the connection continues to be active. If an on-hook signal arrives from S_1 or the SUS timer expires, SSP_1 destroys the encryption key, sends a *Release (REL)* message to the tandem via the SS7 network, and releases the trunk. Upon the receipt of the REL message, the tandem releases the trunk, and sends a REL message to SSP_2 via SS7 network. When the SSP_2 receives the REL message, it destroys the encryption key and sends a *Release Complete (RCL)* message to the SSP_1

through the tandem. The RCL message means that the SSP_2 has released the trunk at its end.

5 CONCLUSIONS

We have described an architectural enhancement necessary to provide end-to-end voice privacy at the application layer of the SS7 protocol model with minimum modification to existing public telephone networks. Voice privacy is achieved by encrypting voice signals between the two end telephones using a symmetric key algorithm and one-time encryption key. The latter key is used to prevent replay attacks. In addition, we have described an authentication process for subscribers and telephones. The authentication techniques provide the AC the assurance that the telephone set and the subscriber at the other end of the connection are what they claim to be. Finally, we described how to integrate our proposed voice privacy service with the PSTN and wireless network. Our ongoing work addresses performance issues and an efficient PKI infrastructure suitable for the SS7 network. The summary of the comparison between the proposed security architecture and the existing security architectures in public telephone network is given in Table 1.

Table 1. Comparison between the proposed and existing security architectures

	Proposed Security Architecture	IS-41 Security	GSM Security	STU III [20]
Devices Authentication	Yes	Yes	Yes	No
Subscriber Authentication	**Yes**	**No**	**No**	**No**
Voice Privacy between the telephone and SSP or MSC	Yes	Yes	Yes	Not Applicable
End-to-End Voice Privacy	**Yes**	**No**	**No**	**Yes**
One time encryption key	Yes	Not Always	Not Always	Not Always

NOTES

This research is partly supported by NSF under grant CCR-0113515, Center for Secure Information Systems at GMU and Prof. S. Jajodia

REFERENCES

1. Berman, R. K. and Brewster, J. H., "Perspective on the AIN Architecture", IEEE Communications Magazine, 31, No. 2, February 1992.
2. Black, U., "ISDN and SS7", Prentice Hall PTR, Upper Saddle River, New Jersey, 1997.
3. Bosse, J. G. von, "Signaling IN Telecommunication Networks", John Wiley & Sons, New York, 1998.
4. Baum, M. S. and Ford, W., "Secure Electronic Commerce", Prentice Hall PTR, Upper Saddle River, New Jersey, 1997.
5. Carne, E. B., "Telecommunications Primer, Second Edition", Prentice Hall PTR, Upper Saddle River, New Jersey, 1999.
6. Chlamtac, I., and Lin, Y., "Wireless and Mobile Network Architectures", John Wiley & Sons, New York, 2001.
7. Chow, M., "Understanding Telecommunications: Systems, Networks and Applications", Volume 1, Andan Publisher, Holmdel, New Jersey, 2000.
8. Douskalis, B., "IP Telephony", Prentice Hall PTR, Upper Saddle River, New Jersey, 2000.
9. Gallagher, M. D. and Snyder, R. A., "Wireless Telecommunications Networking with ANSI-41", Second Edition, McGraw-Hill, New York, 2001.
10. Modarressi, A. R., and Skoog, R. A., "Signaling System No. 7: A Tutorial", IEEE Communications Magazine, pp. 19-35, July 1990.
11. Noll, A. M., "Introduction to Telephones and Telephone Systems", Third Edition, Artech House, Boston, 1998.
12. Rappaport, T. S., "Wireless Communications", Prentice Hall PTR, Upper Saddle River, New Jersey, 2002.
13. Rose, G., "Authentication and Security in Mobile Phones", http://people.qualcomm.com/ggr/QC/AUUG99AuthSec.pdf
14. Russell, T., "Signaling System # 7", Second Edition, McGraw-Hill, New York, 1998.
15. Schneier, B., "Applied Cryptography", Second Edition, John Wiley & Sons, New York, 1996.
16. Scourias, J., "Overview of the Global System for Mobile Communications", http://ccnga.uwaterloo.ca/~jscouria/GSM/gsmreport.html.
17. Stallings, W., "ISDN: An Introduction", Macmillan Publishing Company, New York, 1989.
18. Stallings, W., "Cryptography and Network Security", Second Edition, Prentice Hall PTR, Upper Saddle River, New Jersey, 1999.
19. Tanenbaum, A. S., "Computer Networks" third Edition, Prentice Hall PTR, Upper Saddle River, New Jersey, 1996.
20. Department of Defense Security Institute, "STU-III Handbook for Industry", http://www.tscm.com/STUIIIhandbook.html, February 1997.
21. ISAAC security research group, "GSM Cloning", http://www.isaac.cs.berkeley.edu/isaac/gsm-faq.html, http://www.isaac.cs.berkeley.edu/isaac/gsm.html.

A MULTI-PARTY NON-REPUDIATION PROTOCOL FOR EXCHANGE OF DIFFERENT MESSAGES

Jose Antonio Onieva*, Jianying Zhou*
Mildrey Carbonell**, Javier Lopez**

Abstract Non-repudiation is a security service that provides cryptographic evidence to support the settlement of disputes. In this paper, we introduce the state-of-the-art of multi-party non-repudiation protocols, and analyze the previous work where one originator is able to send the same message to many recipients. We propose a new multi-party non-repudiation protocol for sending different messages to many recipients. We also discuss the improvements achieved with respect to the multiple instances of a two-party non-repudiation protocol, and present some applications that would benefit from them.

Keywords: non-repudiation, fair exchange, group communications

1. Introduction

During the last years the impressive growth of the Internet and more generally of open networks has created several security-related problems. Non-repudiation is one of them. Non-repudiation must ensure that no party involved in a protocol can deny having participated in a part or the whole of the protocol. Therefore, a non-repudiation protocol must generate cryptographic evidence to support dispute resolution. In case a dispute arises, an arbitrator must be able to resolve it using the evidence generated and transferred during the non-repudiation protocol.

Non-repudiation is especially important in electronic commerce to protect customers and merchants. It must not be possible for the merchant to claim that he sent the electronic goods when he did not. In the same way, it must not be possible for the customer to deny having received the goods. Evidence should be collected to resolve this type of

*Institute for Infocomm Research, 21 Heng Keng Mui Terrace, Singapore 119613. onieva@i2r.a-star.edu.sg, jyzhou@i2r.a-star.edu.sg

**Computer Science Department, E.T.S. Ingenieria Informatica, University of Malaga, Spain, 29071 - Malaga. mildrey@crypto.lcc.uma.es, jlm@lcc.uma.es disputes arisen between participating entities in an electronic commerce scenario.

An important requirement of non-repudiation services is fairness with which neither party can gain an advantage by quitting prematurely or otherwise misbehaving during a protocol [10]. In other words, either all participating entities obtain all the messages and the evidence needed, or none of them obtains items expected (i.e., the messages for the recipients and evidence of receipt for the originators).

Several solutions to fair non-repudiation have been developed [6]. Some of them use a *Trusted Third Party* (TTP) that plays the role of an intermediary between the participating entities. The major disadvantage of this approach is the communication bottleneck created at the TTP. Nevertheless, Zhou and Gollmann presented a protocol [9] where the TTP intervenes during each execution as a "low weight notary" rather than as an intermediary. Other solutions use an off-line TTP, assuming that participating entities have no malicious intentions and the TTP does not need to be involved unless there is an error in the protocol execution. This is called the *optimistic approach*. There are also solutions that eliminate the TTP's involvement. However, they need a strong requirement: all involved parties must have the same computational power.

Some work about multi-party scenarios in a related topic, such as *fair exchange*, where entities have to exchange items between them without loss of fairness, exists [3, 2, 4, 8]. The research towards a generalization of non-repudiation, where multiple entities may participate in the consecutive non-repudiation protocols, has not been sufficiently undertaken. Markowitch and Kremer extended the non-repudiation scenarios to allow one originator to send the same message to multiple recipients in a general non-repudiation protocol [5, 7]. In this paper, we extend their multi-party non-repudiation protocols by allowing one originator to send different messages to multiple recipients.

In this paper we classify the multi-party scenarios into two types. The first is called *SOMR-M* (simple origin, with many recipients, for exchange of the same message). The second is called *SOMR-M_i* (simple origin, with many recipients, for exchange of different messages). The two-party non-repudiation approaches could be used to provide solutions to both types of scenarios, thus creating multiple encrypted messages with different keys. However, as we will see in this paper, it is a better solution for a transaction scenario with a low-weight TTP to store only one key k by the TTP for every protocol run.

The remainder of the paper is organized as follows: In section 2 we describe the first multi-party non-repudiation protocol designed by Kremer and Markowitch. In section 3 we present a new protocol which allows different messages to be transferred to the intended recipients. In section 4 we compare the complexity between our new multi-party protocol and n-instance of a two-party protocol. In section 5 we show typical application scenarios of our approach as well as a specific adaptation of our protocol. The following basic notation is used throughout the paper.

- x, y : concatenation of messages x and y
- u_P : the public key of user P
- $S_P(X)$: digital signature of user P over message X
- $E_K(X)$: encryption of message X with key K
- $h(X)$: hash function
- f : a flag indicating the purpose of a message
- $\leftrightarrow$: fetch operation

2. A Fair Multi-Party Non-repudiation Protocol with Same Message

In this section, we review the extension by Kremer et al. [5] of a low weight notary protocol [9] for multi-party purposes. This SOMR-M protocol supports a one-to-many scenario with the same message.

2.1 Additional Notation

Some useful notation in the protocol description is:

- $X \Rightarrow \prod$: multicast from entity X to the set $\prod$
- M : message being sent from the originator to the recipients
- k : key being selected by the originator O
- $c = E_k(M)$: message encrypted with k
- $l = h(M, k)$: label of message M and key k
- t : a timeout chosen by O, before which the TTP has to publish some information
- R : set of intended recipients
- R' : set of recipients that replied to the originator with the evidence of receipt
- $E_{R'}(k)$: a group encryption scheme that encrypts k for the group R'
- $EOO = S_O(feoo, R, l, t, c)$: evidence of origin
- $EOR_i = S_{R_i}(feor, O, l, t, c)$: evidence of receipt of each R_i
- $Sub_k = S_O(fsub, R', l, t, E_{R'}(k))$: evidence of submission of the key to the TTP
- $Con_k = S_{TTP}(fcon, O, R', l, t, E_{R'}(k))$: evidence of confirmation of the key by the TTP

2.2 Group Encryption

Group encryption [1] is used to encrypt the message k for the recipients R' in the Kremer-Markowitch protocol. It is based on a public-key encryption scheme and on the Chinese remainder theorem. This method is generic as it can use any public-key cryptosystem.

- Let u_{R_i} and v_{R_i} be the public and private keys of R_i, respectively (i corresponds with all parties that belong to R').
- Each recipient of R' receives a random integer $P_i < E_{u_{R_i}}(k)$ such that all P_i are pair-wise relatively prime (when choosing randomly large primes or multiplications of distinct primes for example, the probability of obtaining two numbers that are not relatively primes is negligible).
- O computes $X \equiv E_{u_{R_i}}(k) \ mod \ P_i$. As all of P_i are prime integers, using the Chinese remainder theorem, only one solution is obtained from this equation. Hence, $E_{R'}(k) \equiv X$. Each recipient R_i can obtain k by computing $X \equiv E_{u_{R_i}}(k) \ mod \ Pi$ using her private key v_{R_i}.

2.3 The Protocol

The Kremer-Markowitch protocol is as follows.

1. $O \Rightarrow R$: $feoo, R, l, t, c, EOO$
2. $R_i \rightarrow O$: $feor, O, R_i, l, EOR_i$ where each $R_i \in R$
3. $O \rightarrow TTP$: $fsub, R', l, t, E_{R'}(k), Sub_k$
4. $R'_i \leftrightarrow TTP$: $fcon, O, R', l, E_{R'}(k), Con_k$ where each $R'_i \in R'$
5. $O \leftrightarrow TTP$: $fcon, O, R', l, E_{R'}(k), Con_k$

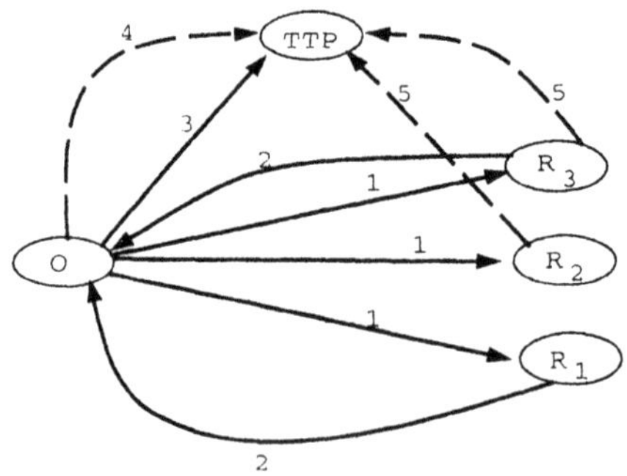

Figure 1. Protocol SOMR-M

The protocol in figure 1 uses the same key k for each recipient R_i, such that, an encrypted message c, evidence EOO, Con_k, Sub_k are generated for each protocol run. This solution claims to disclosure the key only to those recipients (R' ∈ R) that send evidence of receipt in order to achieve fairness. The solution uses a public-key group encryption scheme $E_{R'}(k)$, such that only those included in R' will be able to access to the key k.

This protocol broadcasts a message among several entities. Nevertheless, it is not possible to send different messages to different recipients. In that way no personal and confidential messages can be sent to these parties without loss of privacy.

3. A Fair Multi-Party Non-repudiation Protocol with Different Messages

To the best of our knowledge, the SOMR-M_i scenario (Simple Origin Multiple Recipients with i different messages) has not been reported in the literature yet. We propose a new protocol that extends the Kremer-Markowitch SOMR-M protocol to eliminate the restriction on the exchange of the "same-message". In other words, personal and confidential messages could be sent to multiple entities.

It is important to realize that the use of the same key by multiple recipients could be justified in several ways. Basically, this depends on the application, which is specifically discussed in section 5. Sending messages (same or different) to several recipients could mean a single transaction in a specific application. Therefore, it would be better to store the same key and evidence in the TTP record for every protocol run. In those types of applications, the storage and computation requirements of the TTP are reduced and it will be easy to distinguish between different transactions, regardless of how many entities involved.

In this extension, the use of the same key for all users creates a new problem that did not appear in the SOMR-M protocol. As messages are different, when the same key is used for encryption, and after the key k is published, any recipient will be able to read the messages destined to the other recipients (by eavesdropping the messages that are transmitted between O and R). In this section we propose a solution to this problem.

Let R be the group of recipients and M_i the different plain messages that O wants to send to each R_i, with i ∈ $\{1..|R|\}$. A random value n_i is generated for each recipient R_i. Let

$v_i = E_{u_{R_i}}(n_i)$ be the encryption of n_i with R_i's public key

$k_i = k \ xor \ n_i$ be a key for each R_i

$c_i = E_{k_i}(M_i)$ be the encrypted message with a key k_i for each R_i

3.1 Additional Notation

Some useful notation in the protocol description is:

- $X \Rightarrow \prod$: multicast from entity X to the set $\prod$
- M_i : message being sent from the originator O to the recipient R_i
- k : key being selected by O
- $c_i = E_{k_i}(M_i)$: encrypted message for R_i
- $l_i = h(M_i, k)$: label of message M_i
- t : a timeout chosen by O, before which the TTP has to publish some information
- R : set of intended recipients
- R' : set of recipients that replied to the originator with the evidence of receipt
- L' : labels of all the messages being sent to R'
- $E_{R'}(k)$: a group encryption scheme that encrypts k for the group R'
- $EOO_i = S_O(feoo, R_i, l_i, t, v_i, u_{R_i}, c_i)$: evidence of origin
- $EOR_i = S_{R_i}(feor, O, l_i, t, v_i, u_{R_i}, c_i)$: evidence of receipt of each R_i
- $Sub_k = S_O(fsub, R', L', t, E_{R'}(k))$: evidence of submission of the key to the TTP. In this case (R',L') denotes concatenation of R_i with corresponding l_i
- $Con_k = S_{TTP}(fcon, O, R', L', t, E_{R'}(k))$: evidence of confirmation of the key by the TTP

3.2 The Protocol

Here, we describe the protocol:

1. $O \Rightarrow R_i$	:	$feoo, R_i, l_i, t, v_i, c_i, EOO_i$
2. $R_i \rightarrow O$	:	$feor, O, l_i, EOR_i$ where each $R_i \in R$
3. $O \rightarrow TTP$	:	$fsub, R', L', t, E_{R'}(k), Sub_k$
4. $R'_i \leftrightarrow TTP$	:	$fcon, O, R', L', E_{R'}(k), Con_k$ where each $R'_i \in R'$
5. $O \leftrightarrow TTP$	:	$fcon, O, R', L', E_{R'}(k), Con_k$

The protocol works in the following way.

Step 1: O sends to R_i the evidence of origin corresponding to the encrypted message c_i, together with v_i. In this way, R_i has the encrypted message as well as n_i. There is no breach of fairness if the protocol stops at step 1 because c_i cannot be obtained without key k.

Step 2: Some entities (or all of them) send evidence of receipt of c_i back to O. Again, there is no breach of fairness if the protocol stops.

Step 3: O sends k and Sub_k to the TTP in order to obtain Con_k from the TTP at step 5. As we assume that the communication channel between O and the TTP is not permanently broken, O will be eventually able to send k and Sub_k to the TTP in exchange for Con_k. The key k is encrypted using a group encryption scheme where the group of users is R'. Hence, only those entities belonging to R' will be able to decrypt and extract the key.

Step 4: Each recipient R_i fetches $E_{R'}(k)$ and Con_k from the TTP. They will obtain k_i by computing the expression: k xor n_i. Also, they save Con_k as the evidence to prove that k originated from O.

Step 5: O fetches $E_{R'}(k)$ and Con_k from the TTP and saves it as the evidence to prove that k is available to R'.

3.3 Dispute Resolution

Two kinds of disputes can arise: repudiation of origin and repudiation of receipt. Repudiation of origin arises when a recipient R_i claims having received a message M_i from an originator O who denies having sent it. Repudiation of receipt arises when the originator O claims having sent a message M_i to a recipient R_i who denies having received it.

Repudiation of Origin. If O denies sending M_i, R_i can present evidence EOO_i and Con_k plus $(R_i, t, u_{R_i}, v_i, c_i, n_i, k, E_{R'}(k), M_i, R', L')$ to the arbitrator. The arbitrator will check:

- $v_i = E_{u_{R_i}}(n_i)$
- $k_i = k$ xor n_i
- $c_i = E_{k_i}(M_i)$
- $l_i = h(M_i, k)$
- O's signature EOO_i
- TTP's signature Con_k

Repudiation of Receipt. If R_i denies receiving M_i, O can present evidence EOR_i and Con_k plus $(t, u_{R_i}, v_i, c_i, n_i, k, E_{R'}(k), M_i, R', L')$ to the arbitrator. The arbitrator will check:

- R_i belongs to R'
- $v_i = E_{u_{R_i}}(n_i)$
- $k_i = k$ xor n_i
- $c_i = E_{k_i}(M_i)$
- $l_i = h(M_i, k)$
- R_i's signature EOR_i
- TTP's signature Con_k

Hence, all possible disputes can be resolved if any of the entities misbehaves during the protocol, using the generated and stored evidence as well as an arbitrator that checks the validity of the evidence.

4. Complexity Comparison

We compare our approach with the one where an n-instance of a two-party protocol [9] is used in order to send messages to the intended parties. The complexity of the computation of three principal entities participated in the protocol is analyzed, using an operation comparison. For this comparison we will use the following basic operations:

- signature generation and verification
- generation of random numbers
- asymmetric encryptions and decryptions
- modular equation computation
- store and fetch operations

Depending on which algorithm is chosen for each of these operations, the bit complexity (as well as the bandwidth requirements) of each of the participating entity will change, although the relation going between them remains.

SOMR-M_i vs. extension of n-instanced two-party protocol. We denote:

$|R| = N$
$|R'| = N'$ (with $N' \leq N$)
$>$ greater
$\gg$ much greater

Hence we can see in table 3 the TTP's computation complexity is reduced when it is generalized to multiple entities. This extension can be used when no overload is possible for the TTP with multiple participating entities, and in scenarios where it is better that the TTP stores only one entry per transaction. Since communicating entities will usually pay for the TTP services, we achieve a more efficient and cheaper TTP service. In addition, we can see in tables 1 and 2 that O's computation complexity is reduced too while R_i's is slightly increased.

5. Applications

Our approach fits better in shopping scenarios (i.e. O is a custom and R_i are merchants). Here we present a possible scenario:

n-instanced two-party		SOMR-M_i
Evidence of origin EOO_i	$=$	**Evidence of origin EOO_i**
N signatures.		N signatures.
Generation of k_i	$\approx$	**Generation of n_i plus k**
Evidence of submission Sub_{k_i}	$\gg$	**Sub_k**
N' signatures.		1 signature.
$E_{u_{R_i}}(k_i)$ Encrypted key k_i	$\ll$	**$E_{R'}(k)$ Encrypted key k plus $E_{u_{R_i}}(n_i)$**
N' encryption operations with each public key.		N' random numbers P_i. N' encryption operations with each public key. Compute equation $X \equiv E_{u_{R_i}}(k_i) \ mod \ P_i \rightarrow \Theta(\lg n)$. N encrypt operations with each public key (v_i).
N fetches operations of Con_{k_i}	$\gg$	**One fetch operation**

Table 1. ORIGINATOR'S COMPUTATION COMPLEXITY

n-instanced two-party		SOMR-M_i
Evidence of receipt EOR_i	$=$	**Evidence of receipt EOR_i**
Fetch k and Con_{k_i}	$=$	**Fetch k and Con_k**
Obtain k_i	$<$	**Obtain k plus n_i**
Decrypts $E_{u_{R_i}}(k_i)$.		compute equation $X \equiv E_{u_{R_i}}(k_i) \ mod \ P_i$. Decrypt $E_{u_{R_i}}(k_i)$. Decrypt $E_{u_{R_i}}(n_i)$.

Table 2. $R_i'S$ COMPUTATION COMPLEXITY

n-instanced two-party		SOMR-M_i
Store N' keys	$\gg$	**Store only one key**
Generation of N' evidences Con_{k_i}	$\gg$	**Generation of only one evidence Con_k**

Table 3. TTP'S COMPUTATION COMPLEXITY

Suppliers and customers. In B2B scenarios, we can usually find established relations between companies, such that some of them play the role of suppliers and the others apply for supplies. Frequently, these companies need to stock up vast amounts of products. For example, an electronic equipment producer has to apply for cables, metals, sockets, etc. and send an order to various suppliers. These suppliers do not mind who of them supplies the order received; in other words, they can cooperate. Typically, in these scenarios, collusion between suppliers is not a usual matter.

We can classify the orders destined to N suppliers that supply similar or different products. Figure 2 shows a scenario with one customer (C1) and four suppliers (Si), where C1 sends two requests, one for suppliers 1, 2, and 3, and the other for suppliers 1, 3 and 4.

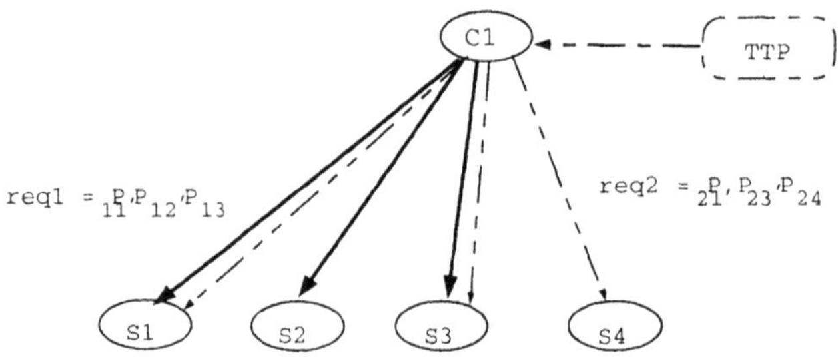

Figure 2. Customers and suppliers

One-to-many protocols using the same key offer a more efficient solution than the one with an n-instantiated two-party protocol. Each transaction (order) is registered in the TTP with a key plus the evidence of this key.

Actually, B2B architecture is growing fast on Internet. It can accelerate the business process among customers and suppliers, and increase the participation of suppliers, products, and on-line supplies (i.e. software, music files, etc...). Obviously, this architecture has stronger security requirements than B2C architecture in that it usually involves high amounts of money. Some solutions have been developed, most of them are based on the *Virtual Private Network* (VPN) that provides secure connection between customers and suppliers.

We can find a good example in the *Automotive Network eXchange*[1] (ANX) . The ANX network is used for mission critical business transactions by leading international organizations and net markets in aerospace, automotive, chemical, electronics, financial services, healthcare, logistics, manufacturing, transportation and related industries. Through a global standard that assures the highest levels of security and quality, the ANX network offers connected customers the most reliable multi-vendor extranet and Virtual Private Network services available today.

[1] http://www.anx.com

If SOMR-M_i is designed over a VPN, it may use the secret session keys managed by the VPN, and there is no need to generate the random numbers and send the encrypted random numbers to the recipients. Thus, we can reduce the operation complexity of the originator and recipients (see table 4 and 5). If it is not possible to use the secret session keys (due to the limitation on the random numbers being used in the group encryption scheme), the originator only needs to generate n_i for each entity and send them to the recipients through a confidential channel provided by the VPN. That means n_i need not be encrypted with R_i's public key, thus the operation complexity of the originator and the recipients is also reduced.

n-instanced two-party		SOMR-M_i
Evidence of origin EOO_i	=	**Evidence of origin EOO_i**
N signatures.		N signatures.
Generation of k_i	$\gg$	**Generation of only one key k**
Generation of N random numbers.		Generation of only one number.
Evidence of submission Sub_{k_i}	$\gg$	**Sub_k**
N' signatures.		1 signature.
$E_{u_{R_i}}(k_i)$ Encrypted key k_i	$<$	**$E_{R'}(k)$ Encrypted key k**
N' encryption operations with each public key.		N' random numbers P_i. N' encryption operations with each public key. Compute equation $X \equiv E_{u_{R_i}}(k_i) \ mod \ P_i \rightarrow \Theta(\lg n)$.
N fetches operations of Con_{k_i}	$\gg$	**One fetch operation**

Table 4. ORIGINATOR'S COMPUTATION COMPLEXITY

n-instanced two-party		SOMR-M_i
Evidence of receipt EOR_i	=	**Evidence of receipt EOR_i**
Fetch k and Con_{k_i}	=	**Fetch k and Con_k**
Obtain k_i	$\approx$	**Obtain k**
Decrypts $E_{u_{R_i}}(k_i)$.		compute equation $X \equiv E_{u_{R_i}}(k_i) \ mod \ P_i$. Decrypt $E_{u_{R_i}}(k_i)$.

Table 5. $R_i'S$ COMPUTATION COMPLEXITY

6. Conclusions and Future Work

The research on non-repudiation protocols with multiple entities is still in its initial stage. Although many two-party solutions that can be instantiated for multi-party scenarios have been developed, more efficient and adapted solutions are needed.

In this paper, we analyzed the previous work on multi-party scenarios where one originator sends a message to multiple recipients. We suggested an improvement that allows the originator to send different messages to the recipients. This is the further generalization of a two-party fair non-repudiation protocol, which also reduces the computation complexity compared with the n-instanced two-party protocol. We identified applications for B2B scenarios that could make use of our protocol, and explained how these applications would benefit from it.

Further reducing the recipient's operation complexity could be carried out in a future work. It is also possible to extend our idea of SOMR-M_i to an *optimistic* multi-party fair non-repudiation protocol [7]. Other topologies and scenarios with multiple entities participating in a non-repudiation protocol will be studied as well.

References

[1] G. Chiou and W. Chen. *Secure broadcasting using the secure lock.* IEEE Transaction on Software Engineering, Vol. 15, No. 8, August 1989.

[2] M. Franklin and G. Tsudik. *Secure group barter: multi-party fair exchange with semi-trusted neutral parties.* Proceedings of Financial Cryptography 1998, Lecture Notes in Computer Science 1465, February 1998.

[3] N. Gonzalez-Deleito and O. Markowitch. *An optimistic multi-party fair exchange protocol with reduced trust requirements.* Proceedings of 4th International Conference on Information Security and Cryptology (ICISC 2001), Lecture Notes in Computer Science 2288, Seoul, Korea, December 2001.

[4] J. Kim and J. Ryou. *Multi-party fair exchange protocol using ring architecture model.* Japan-Korea Joint Workshop on Information Security and Cryptology, January 2000.

[5] S. Kremer and O. Markowitch. *A multi-party non-repudiation protocol.* Proceedings of SEC 2000: 15th International Conference on Information Security, IFIP World Computer Congress, pages 271-280, Beijing, China, August 2000.

[6] S. Kremer, O. Markowitch and J. Zhou. *An intensive survey of non-repudiation protocols.* Computer Communications, 2002.

[7] O. Markowitch and S. Kremer. *A multi-party optimistic non-repudiation protocol.* Proceedings of 3rd International Conference on Information Security and Cryptology (ICISC 2000), Lectures Notes in Computer Science vol. 2015, pages 109-122, Seoul, Korea, December 2000.

[8] O. Markowitch and S. Saeednia. *Optimistic fair-exchange with transparent signature recovery.* Proceedings of Financial Cryptography 2001, Lecture Notes in Computer Science, February 2001.

[9] J. Zhou and D. Gollmann. *A fair non-repudiation protocol.* Proceedings of the IEEE Symposium on Security and Privacy, pages 55-61, Oakland, California, May 1996.

[10] J. Zhou. *Non-repudiation in electronic commerce.* Computer Security Series, Artech House, 2001.

ESTABLISHING CHAIN OF EVIDENCE AS A BASE FOR NON-REPUDIATION SERVICES

Jing-Jang Hwang[a], Min-Hua Shao[b], Soushan Wu[c]
[a]*Department of Information Management, Chang Gung University, 259 Wen-Hwa 1st Road, Kwei-Shan, Tao-Yuan, Taiwan 333, R.O.C.*
[b]*Institute of Information Management, National Chiao Tung University, 1001 Ta Hsueh Road, Hsinchu, Taiwan 300, R.O.C.*
[c]*College of Management, Chang Gung University, 259 Wen-Hwa 1st Road, Kwei-Shan, Tao-Yuan, Taiwan 333, R.O.C.*

Abstract: Disputes are inevitable in business. Disputes in the real world are resolved in various ways. Similarly, in the virtual world, there is a variety of non-repudiation services as defined in the ISO/IEC standards [5, 6, 7, 8]. Whatever actions are taken, evidence is the key to the successful conduct of these services. These previous works usually define the concept of non-repudiation services using a single piece of evidence, which fails to describe the causality of an event completely. In business, no activity is atomic, and evidence therefore does not exist as an atomic piece. Rather, evidence exists in the form of a series of relevant pieces of evidence. That is, we must consider a series of activities—formed onto a cycle of value transfers. This paper introduces a chain-of-evidence concept to electronic commerce as a basis for the refinement of the pertinent international standards. The chain of evidence can be analyzed and derived from the cyclic model of value transfers. From information security and information processing perspectives, this paper aims to provide a better evidence-management methodology as the first step to be taken in settling any disputes. As a result, we expect that the research will contribute a theoretical basis for non-repudiation services in the practical world.

Key words: evidence management, cycle of value transfers, non-repudiation services, disputes resolution, electronic commerce

1. INTRODUCTION

Disputes are inevitable in business, and the resolution of such disputes is necessary in electronic commerce just as it is in any other form of commerce. Disputes cannot be resolved unless the evidence underlying the dispute has been previously recorded. Non-repudiation services establish evidence. Non-repudiation services for open systems such as the Internet are one type of security services defined in ISO/IEC standards. Pertinent standards include ISO/IEC 10181-4 [5], 13888-1 [6], 13888-2 [7], and 13888-3 [8], which deal with general concepts of evidence and which define the system framework and some mechanisms for non-repudiation services. The goal of non-repudiation services is to generate, collect, maintain, make available, and validate irrefutable evidence concerning a claimed event or action in order to resolve disputes about the occurrence of the event or action. As stated in the standards themselves, and in the academic literature [3, 10, 12, 13, 14], they define the concept of using a single piece of evidence according to a particular event or action. Given that in business, and in electronic commerce in particular, no activity is atomic, we must consider a series of activities, rather than an isolated instance. It follows that evidence does not exist as an atomic piece. Rather, it exists in the form of relevant pieces of related evidence. In this paper, we take the chain-of-evidence concept, as originally conceived for law-enforcement purposes, and adapt it to non-repudiation services, with a view to supplementing the above-mentioned international standards, which are, as noted above, based on the presumption of a static state of evidence. A chain of evidence must be identified and organized, such that each piece of evidence stored in a computer somewhere can be traced, and its accountability established in any given event or action. Evidence accountability is the future basis on which disputes can be resolved.

Since a composite transaction consists of a sequence of events, the evidence chain derived from these events will be helpful in gaining a clear picture of what has transpired. A business transaction is not complete until a series of activities involving value transfers has been successfully conducted. The series of activities presents a cycle of value transfers, and the closing of the cycle simultaneously produces a concluded transaction. Two events—payment in monetary terms and delivery of goods—form a minimum value-transfers cycle, although the cycle normally involves a longer series of events. Asokan et al. [2] defined the concept of value transfers in a general payment model, which was proposed by Pfitzmann and Waidner [9]. However, Asokan et al.'s works put much emphasis on movement of monetary value only. Recently, under pressure from the need for cost reductions in business-to-consumer (B2C) transactions, other types of value transfers (for example, the delivery of goods or services) have come under scrutiny. But, it appears that most electronic payment systems cannot be tightly coordinated with logistic activities, which must be conducted through separate distribution channels. Therefore, a complete transaction cycle must combine movement of monetary value with separate delivery of purchased-object value. In summary, the main purpose of a chain of evidence is to enhance evidence accountability by examining the series of activities formed as a value-transfer cycle.

The remainder of this paper is organized as follows. Section 2 clarifies disputes resolution in a non-repudiation process. Section 3 provides a redefinition of the transactional cycle. Based upon this cycle, the concept of chain-of-evidence is developed in Section 4. Finally, Section 5 concludes the paper with a discussion of our approach.

2. DISPUTES-RESOLUTION PHASE IN A NON-REPUDIATION PROCESS

To illustrate how the concepts of the chain of evidence and the value-transfer cycle assist dispute resolution, Fig. 1 presents a procedure for handling the dispute-resolution phase of a non-repudiation process. Discussion on that is outside the scope of the pertinet standards [5]. The procedure consists of four steps: (i) stating the claim; (ii) collecting evidence; (iii) arbitrating in the dispute; and (iv) deciding on the fact. First, the claim-stating step indicates what activities are investigated and who may get involved. Value transfers associated with these activities can be determined. These value-transfer activities are significant in establishing the context of the dispute. The next step is evidence collection. The primary challenge of this task is how to collect all relevant evidence effectively. The chain of evidence acts as a 'clue map' to provide a guide to necessary information. The map indicates events, interested parties, relevant documents, and the time and place of pertinent occurrences. By analyzing the interested parties, the ISO/IEC 10181-4 document defines some roles involved in a non-repudiation system, including the evidence subject, the evidence generation requester, the evidence user, the evidence generator, the evidence verifier, and one or more trusted third parties in the evidence-generation phase; and the plaintiff, the defendant, and the agreed adjudicators in the dispute-resolution phase. Generally, the type of role played by various entities depends on the cryptographic techniques employed. In the case of B2C market transactions, the possibility of involving trusted third parties in existing application systems is decreased by transaction costs and difficulties in implementation efficiency. In addition, to accord with legal restraints and the validity of evidence, most application systems employ digital signature techniques to provide non-repudiation evidence. The evidence subjects, for the most part, act as the evidence generators, and the evidence users are also the evidence verifiers. Third, in the dispute-arbitration step, the arbitration criterion is determined by the non-repudiation policy. The policy can include the following items [5]: (i) rules for the generation of evidence; (ii) rules for the verification of evidence; (iii) rules for the storage of evidence; (iv) rules for the use of evidence; and (v) rules for adjudication. After arbitration, the last step is to announce the decision, indicating the truth or existence of something.

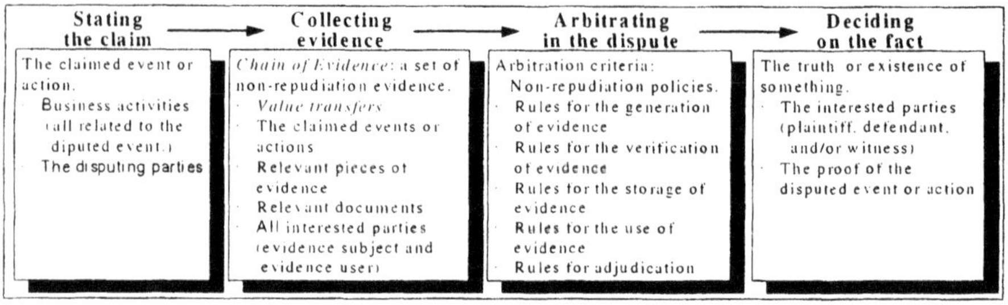

Figure 1. Dispute-resolution procedure

3. VALUE-TRANSFER CYCLE

The section demonstrates value transfers in a business transaction and shows how to form a whole cycle of value transfer. Pfitzmann and Waidner [9] indicated that one of the major distinctions among payment systems is the point at which there is money transfer between the payment initiator and the receiver. The basic function of these payment systems is to provide value transfer among different players. Generally, the basic set of players involved in the payment transaction is made up of the payer, the payee, and the financial institutions (including the issuer interacting with the payer and the acquirer interacting with the payee). Value transfers between the issuer and the acquirer occur in proprietary banking systems, which are outside the scope of the generic payment service [1]. In the study of on-line payment and that of dispute resolution, the word *bank* often signifies various types of financial institutions. For the purpose of dispute expression about transfers between payer or payee and bank, Asokan et al. [2] defined three types of value transfers based upon the work of Pfitzmann and Waidner. These three types of value transfer are: (i) value subtraction; (ii) payment; and (iii) value claim. The three value transfers, taken together, fully sketch the profile of the payment service in a transaction. A partial view of the payment service involves a subset of the players, and their interaction is an instance of what is defined as a 'primitive transaction'. The 'primitive transaction' of *value subtraction* is to convert 'real value' into electronic value. Normally, a bank and a payer engage in a value subtraction. In other words, the payer allows the bank to remove real value from the payer's account. In a *payment*, the players involved in the transaction are a payer and a payee. The payer moves electronic value to the payee. Then the payee requests the bank to convert electronic value into real value in the primitive transaction of a *value claim.*

However, these three primitive transactions of monetary value transfer portray only a part of a usual composite transaction. In the past few years, the development of global B2C markets has been held up by insufficient support of distribution channels. Business transactions are conducted online, but with inadequate logistics services. Many disputes arise from the product-delivery service. Due to this, customers can be more or less reluctant to proceed to the purchase phase and complete a transaction on the Internet. According to a survey of the means of on-line payment polled by ActiveMedia research group, a majority (56 percent) of Internet shoppers prefer off-line payment (such as telephone, fax, or account transfer) to on-line payment. To help overcome the challenge of consumer concerns regarding delivery, business alliances between Internet retailers (especially 'pure' virtual stores) and off-line distributors, so-called 'click-and-brick' alliance or 'B2B2C', can be very effective to support the overall transaction—including payment and delivery services. No activity in business is independent of others and the successful conducting of a series of activities usually brings about a completed business transaction. The series of business activities thus also involve a cycle of value transfers. The cyclic model should comprise at least two types of value—the movement of monetary value and the ownership of purchased-object value transfer form the essence of a value transfer cycle (as illustrated in Fig. 2). In Fig. 2, a solid line represents the movement of monetary value whereas a dotted line shows the delivery of purchased-object value, with the direction of the arrowhead reflecting the direction of value transfers between parties. The movement of monetary value is defined in the work of Asokan et al. [2] as noted above. With regard to the delivery of purchased-object value, an intermediary agent, called a delivery authority (DA), is usually involved in the distribution process. One or more DAs, trusted by the seller and the buyer, provide delivery services in accordance with the terms of the sale and the nature of the purchased object. The delivery can precede, follow, or accompany the exchange of monetary value. Considering the overall distribution process, we define three type of value transfers—(i) value submission; (ii) value transport; and (iii) purchased-object delivery. These three constitute the ownership value transfer. The *purchased-object delivery* is initiated from the buyer as specifying shipping method along with payment, but is transferred from the seller to the buyer often later than the successful transfer of monetary value. The players involved in a *value submission* are the payee and a DA. That is, the payee consigns goods or services to the DA in accordance with the sales agreement. The DA is responsible for delivery to the intended recipient on time. The players involved in a *value transport* are a DA and a payer.

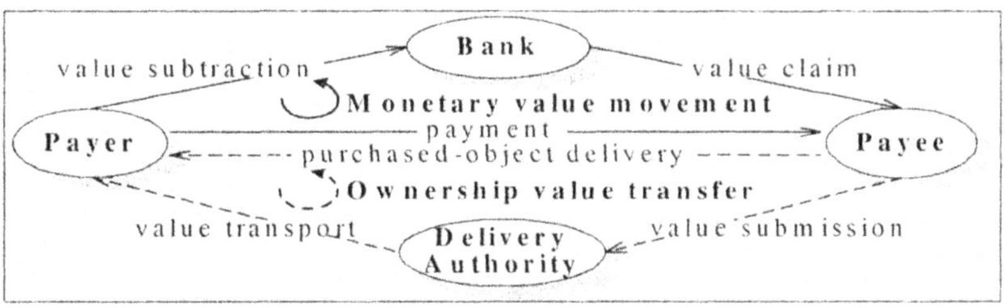

Figure 2. A cycle of value transfers for a typical business-to-consumer transaction

4. EVIDENCE MANAGEMENT

The section introduces the concept of a chain of evidence to reinforce evidence accountability in ISO/IEC standards. Particularly, we show how to begin from a cycle of value transfers and then obtain the evidence chain.

4.1 Non-repudiation services

There are four types of exchanges between the buyer and the seller in a typical commercial transaction. These are: (i) information enquiry and response; (ii) agreement on the terms and conditions of the sale and payment; (iii) payment instructions provided by the buyer; and (iv) shipment and delivery of the items acquired done by the seller. The transferring or receiving of messages during these exchanges can be regarded as a commitment, and can be recorded as evidence. The protection of such digital evidence against injury depends on cryptographic techniques. Both symmetric (secret-key) and asymmetric (public-key) cryptographic techniques can be used for non-repudiation. Technically speaking, there are three particular forms of evidence [5]: (i) digital signatures using public key techniques; (ii) secure envelopes and (iii) security tokens both using secret key techniques. Functionally speaking, the ISO/IEC 13888-1 standard defines four main types of document demanded for non-repudiation services, all related to the transfer of messages between the two communicating parties. They are: (i) proof of origin; (ii) proof of delivery; (iii) proof of submission; and (iv) proof of transport. The *proof of origin*, notated as Non-Repudiation of Origin (NRO), is intended to prevent foul play on the part of the sender in the form of denial of being both the creator of a message and the sender of that message. The *proof of delivery*, notated as Non-Repudiation of Delivery (NRD), itself contains (a) proof of receipt and (b) proof of knowledge simultaneously. The first of these, proof of receipt, is notated as Non-Repudiation of Receipt (NRR), and is intended to prevent a recipient's foul play in the form of denial of having received a message. The second of these, proof of knowledge, is notated as Non-Repudiation of Knowledge (NRK), and means that the recipient is aware of the content of the message. The *proof of* submission, notated as Non-Repudiation of Submission (NRS), means that the delivery authority was commissioned to transmit the purchased object for the seller but, in most case, wasn't well aware of the content of the object. The *proof of transport*, notated as Non-Repudiation of Transport (NRT), is intended to prevent the delivery authority's false denial of having delivered the purchased object to the intended recipient. The last two proofs, NRS and NRT, cover the cases in which one or more delivery authorities are involved in transfer of the purchased object between a sender and a recipient. Furthermore, if two or more delivery authorities participate in a delivery order, NRS is also suitable for evidence that proves the transmission of the object between them.

As a whole, there are at least four roles involved in a non-repudiation system during a cycle of value transfers: (i) the payer; (ii) the payee; (iii) banks; and (iv) the delivery authority. The role of the delivery authority (DA) in this paper is rather different from that in the ISO standards defined for non-repudiation services. DA in these ISO documents is a third party trusted by the sender who delivers digital data from the sender to the receiver—as in the cases of Internet service providers, B2B exchanges, and e-marketplaces. Furthermore, the DA in a value-transfer cycle provides services in the delivery of physical or information goods. FedEx is a classic example.

4.2 Chain of evidence

Non-repudiation services establish one piece of evidence regarding a particular event or action. One piece of evidence offers information that can be used to prove the occurrence or non-occurrence of an event or action, but does not necessarily establish the truth of that event or action. Once each piece of evidence is generated, the next step is to provide for its accountability of each event or action within the transaction. Evidence accountability is the conjunction of technical and managerial factors. On the technical side, the validity of each piece of evidence can be examined or ensured through cryptography techniques. With respect to management factors, the key point is how to make a conjunction with every piece of evidence stored in a computer somewhere, in order to draw a map of the evidence. A map of evidence presents clues as to the overall truth of a situation, and is therefore useful in evidence collection in the dispute-resolution phase. Only by clarifying the causality of an event can the truth be ascertained. Evidence generation usually goes along with a specific event or action that has taken place. So, a set of gathered evidence will reflect a sequence of business activities named a cycle of value transfers. Consequently, the map of evidence in this paper is defined as a 'chain of evidence'. The chain-of-evidence concept was originally introduced by Welch [11], where it served as a means of tracing accountability by law-enforcement agencies in their conduct of criminal investigations. The detailed items in the chain of evidence include such matters as who obtained the evidence, where and when the evidence was obtained, who secured the evidence, and who has control or possession of the evidence.

A chain of evidence, as applied to a business transaction, must be obtained from a cycle of value transfers. Any event or action can trigger various business activities, or value transfers, at any given time. To identify value transfer in every phase of the transaction, it is first necessary to identify the relevant event or action. In the following, we consider a specific set of events or actions, all of which are related to specific non-repudiation services in connection with evidence purpose, the derivative documents, and the interested parties. Generally, a specific set of events or actions is common to similar properties or functions of many electronic transaction systems for electronic commerce. We now define a 'primitive event' as an abstract of a specific set of events or actions for a general B2C transaction. The above procedure of establishing a chain of evidence is depicted in Fig. 3.

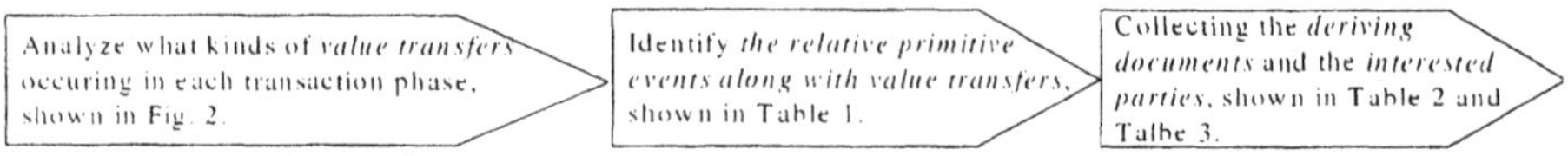

Figure 3. The procedures for establishing a chain of evidence

The detailed treatment of the primitive events is according to a cycle of value transfers. With respect to the primitive events for monetary value movement, Pfitzmann and Waidner [9] have defined some interface events for digital payment systems. Although interface events and primitive events are not identical in views, we will make their efforts fit for our works. In particular, there are three standard input interface events—*pay*, *receive*, and *allow*. The pay event is initiated, or consented to, by a buyer in making a payment; the receive event is an input by the merchant who responds to the pay event from a buyer; the allow event is an input by the buyer's bank which checks his or her account of external money to ensure that there is enough to make an electronic payment. In addition, the major output events are the following: *deduct*, *add*, *paid*, and *received*. The deduct event gives the buyer's bank notice to deduct the authorized money from his or her account; the add event notifies the merchant's bank to add the authorized money to the merchant's account; the paid event and the received event indicate to the buyer and the merchant, respectively, that an authorized payment has been fulfilled. In effect, the paid event is the successful culmination of the allow event and the deduct event. The received event must take another event into consideration. This is the liquidate event, in which the merchant makes a 'capture' request to the merchant's bank. Thus the received event is not complete until both the liquidate event and the add event have been accomplished. Therefore, we do not consider "paid" and "received" as primitive events, and do not include these in Table 1.

With respect to the composite event of purchased-object value delivery, we define six basic primitive events according to the overall distribution process. These six events are all concerned with the generation of evidence during the ownership of purchased-object delivery. They are: (i) the *submit* event (in which the merchant commissions the delivery authority to provide shipment service of the purchased object); (ii) the *undertake* event (which signals the delivery authority to accept the commission); (iii) the *shipping-to* event (which is an input by the buyer that chooses shipping method and preference for the purchased objects, e.g. goods or services); (iv) the *shipping-from* event (which is the corresponding input by the merchant); (v) the *delivery* event (by which the delivery authority transports the purchased object to the intended recipient); and (vi) the *obtain* event (which signals that the buyer has received the purchased object). By analyzing these primitive events, we clarify the relation of value transfers further, as shown in Table 1.

Table 1. The relation between the primitive events and value transfers.

Value transfers		Primitive events
Monetary Value Movement	Value Subtraction	Allow
		Deduct
	Payment	Pay
		Receive
	Value Claim	Liquidate
		Add
Ownership Value Transfer	Value Submission	Submit
		Undertake
	Purchased-object Delivery	Shipping-from
		Shipping-to
	Value Transport	Deliver
		Obtain

As far as monetary value movement is concerned, either the deduct event or the allow event can launch a primitive transaction of value subtraction. A primitive transaction of payment is connected with either the pay event or the receive event. A primitive transaction of value claim is related to the liquidate event or the add event. With respect to ownership value transfer, a primitive transaction of value submission is related to the submit event or the undertake event. A primitive transaction of purchased-object delivery is in connection with the shipping-from event or the shipping-to event. Either the delivery event or the obtain event can launch a primitive transaction of value transport. In particular, depending on the specific situation some primitive events will turn into a composite event, which is formed with other primitive events. For example, in view of monetary value transfer by means of credit card, the pay event and the receive event, respectively, is a composite event; the pay event is the successful fulfillment of the allow event and the deduct event, and further, the receive event is the successful fulfillment of the liquidate event and the add event. By contrast, the pay event and the receive event are primitive events as payment by remittance or credit transfers.

Evidence is generated on the data describing the occurrence event along with value transfers. Therefore, the primitive events are the key intermediaries in linking a series of business activities with every piece of evidence. Documents derived from these events can be classified as various types of evidence, according to the purpose of each. In the meantime, the interested parties in a chain of evidence take most account of the evidence subject and the evidence user. The evidence subject whose involvement in an event or action is established by evidence [5], and the entity is also the event initiator. The evidence user, who uses non-repudiation evidence, is usually in opposition to the evidence subject, and the entity is also the event claimant. Therefore, the interested parties engaging in the event—consisting of the event initiator and the event claimant—are recognized. This shows a chain of evidence must be identified in order to trace the accountability of each event along the cycle. In order to distinguish the notation about evidence purpose defined by ISO/IEC 13888-1 standard from our suggestion, the chain of evidence for a typical B2C transaction is divided into two tables upon value transfers. Table 2 shows the evidence chain associated with monetary value transfers, and the other one—ownership value transfer—is depicted in Table 3. These primitive events are continued from table 1, and each of their derivative documents is a general name of transactional information. The notation about evidence purpose is according to specific non-repudiation service and then in conjunction with value transfers upon the primitive event occurred. Specifically, the non-repudiation services all related to the transfer of messages over network in the pertinent standards [4, 5, 6, 7]. Considering monetary value movement is covered in the case, a part of notation for evidence purpose uses two types of non-repudiation evidence—NRO and NRR—in the ISO/IEC 13888-1 standard.

Table 2. A chain of evidence associated with monetary value transfers.

Primitive Event	Derivative Document	Evidence Purpose (Defined by ISO/IEC 13888-1)	the Interested Parties	
			Event Initiator	Event Claimant
Allow	Payment Instruction	NRO_Value Subtraction	Payer	Bank
Deduct	Payment Authorization	NRR_Value Subtraction	Bank	Payer
Pay	Purchase Order	NRO_Payment	Payer	Payee
Receive	Confirmation and Invoice	NRR_Payment	Payee	Payer
Liquidate	Capture Claim	NRO_Value Claim	Payer	Bank
Add	Capture Acceptance	NRR_Claim	Bank	Payer

As regards the ownership of purchased-object, especially physical object, value transfers, non-repudiation evidence can be filled in with moderate difficulty given previous standards or other literature. In view of this, we suggest the *proof of purchased-object delivery*, notated as Non-Repudiation of Purchased-object Delivery (NRPD), as a solution of evidence purpose for ownership value transfer. The non-repudiation of purchased-object service covers the case regarding the product, such as the possession of goods or services, shipping preference, and so on. For example, the service is intended to protect against a holder's false denial of having agreed shipping method and/or possessed the product.

Table 3. A chain of evidence associated with ownership value transfer.

Primitive Event	Derivative Document	Evidence Purpose (Suggested by the authors)	the Interested Parties	
			Event Initiator	Event Claimant
Submit	Consignment Receipt	NRPD_Value Submission	DA	Payee
Undertake				
Shipping-from	Shipping Agreement	NRPD_Purchased-object Delivery	Payee	Payer
Shipping-to			Payer	Payee
Delivery	Acknowledgement Receipt	NRPD_Value Transport	Payer	DA / Payee
Obtain				

In the case of an electronic transaction environment, we define nine main types of evidence and their derivative documents from the primitive events in a cycle of value transfers. The descriptions are as follows: (i) The document of *payment instruction* prepares non-repudiation evidence of a value subtraction primitive transaction, notated as NRO_Value Subtraction. It indicates the occurrence of the allow event. The initiator of the allow event is the payer, and the allow event claimant is the bank. (ii) The document of *payment authorization* offers non-repudiation evidence of a value subtraction primitive transaction, notated as NRR_Value Subtraction. It proves the occurrence of the deduct event. The event initiator is the bank, and the payer is the event claimant. (iii) The *purchase order* offers non-repudiation evidence of a payment primitive transaction, notated as NRO_Payment. The document is toward the accountability of the pay event. The payer is the event initiator and the payee is the event claimant. (iv) The *confirmation and invoice* offers non-repudiation evidence of a payment primitive transaction, notated as NRR_Payment. It traces the occurrence of the receive event. The payee is the event initiator and the payer is the event claimant. (v) The *capture claim* document offers non-repudiation evidence of a value claim primitive transaction, notated as NRO_Value Claim. It aims to account for the liquidate event. The payee is the event initiator and the bank is the event claimant. (vi) The *capture acceptance* document offers non-repudiation evidence of a value claim primitive transaction, notated as NRR_Value Claim. It testifies that the add event has taken place. The bank is the event initiator and the payee is the event claimant. (vii) The *consignment receipt* provides for non-repudiation evidence of a value submission primitive transaction, notated as NRPD_Value Submission. In the case in which the delivery authority provides evidence to the merchant (payee), the event initiator is the delivery authority and the event claimant is the merchant. (viii) The *shipping agreement* regarding the product delivery, such as shipping method and preference, provides non-repudiation evidence of a primitive transaction of ownership transfer. Due to the exchange of the agreement between the buyer (payer) and the merchant, this document, as notated NRPD_Purchased-object Delivery, can be used to account for two events—the shipping-to event and the shipping-from event. For the shipping -to event, the buyer is the event initiator and the merchant is the event claimant; and further, as regards the shipping-from event, the merchant is the event initiator and the buyer is the event claimant. (ix) The *acknowledgement receipt* provides non-repudiation evidence of a value transport primitive transaction, notated as NRPD_Value Transport. In the case in which the recipient acknowledges to the delivery authority and the merchant that the purchased object has been duly received, the event initiator is the recipient and the event claimant is the delivery authority and the merchant.

5. CONCLUSIONS

Even if a transaction is concluded successfully, there can be subsequent disputes about what happened during the transaction. Having observed that it is a common practice to operate non-repudiation services in traditional markets, but not in the electronic marketplace, we have attempted to propose a better evidence-management model as an appropriate basis for disputes resolution in electronic commerce. In reviewing previous research efforts, including the international standards, it is apparent that non-repudiation services deal essentially with single pieces of evidence. Each piece of evidence can provide information to account for a claimed event or action, but it is quite limited in attempting to learn about the total context. Only if evidence is viewed in conjunction with business activities will the context of the occurrence of the event be clarified. For this purpose, we introduce the chain-of-evidence concept into the idea of a non-repudiation service, in order to associate it with a series of activities. We also show a cycle of value transfers that presents a series of activities to form a whole business transaction. Consequently, a chain of evidence can trace accountability of each event along the cycle. The main contribution of the present paper is to establish chain of evidence in order to work for the betterment of non-repudiation services for electronic commerce.

ACKNOWLEDGEMENTS

Part of this research was funded by the National Science Council of Taiwan under the contract of NSC 91-2416-H-182-209-, while the first author of this article was working at National Chiao Tung University.

REFERENCE

[1] Abad Peiro J.L, Asokan N., Steiner M., Waidner M., Designing a generic payment service, *IBM Systems Journal* 37 (1), 1998.

[2] Asokan N., Herreweghen E.V., Steiner M., Towards a framework for handling disputes in payment systems, *3rd USENIX Workshop on Electronic Commerce*, Sep. 1998, pp. 1– 28.

[3] Coffey T. and Saidha P., Non-repudiation with mandatory proof of receipt, Computer Communication Review (26:1), Jan. 1996, pp. 6– 14.

[4] ISO/IEC 10181-1. *Information technology—open systems interconnection—security frameworks for open system: overview*, 1996.

[5] ISO/IEC 10181-4. *Information technology—open systems interconnection—security frameworks for open system: non-repudiation framework*, 1997.

[6] ISO/IEC 13888-1. *Information technology-security techniques-non-repudiation part 1:general*, 1997.

[7] ISO/IEC 13888-2. *Information technology—security techniques—non-repudiation part 2: mechanisms using symmetric techniques*, 1997.

[8] ISO/IEC 13888-3. *Information technology—security techniques—non-repudiation part 3: mechanisms using asymmetric techniques*, 1997.

[9] Pfitzmann B., Waidner M., Properties of payment systems: general definition sketch and classification, *IBM Research*, Research Report RZ 2823, May 1996, pp. 1– 28.

[10] Schneider S., Formal analysis of a non-repudiation protocol, *Proceedings of 11th IEEE Computer Security Foundations Workshop*, 1998, pp. 54– 65.

[11] Welch T., *Handbook of information security management*, In M. Krause and H.F. Tipton (Eds.), Boca Raton, Fla.: Auerbach, 1999.

[12] You C.H., Zhou J. and Lam K.Y., On the efficient implementation of fair non-repudiation, *Computer Communication Review* (28:5), Oct. 1998.

[13] Zhou J., Evidence and non-repudiation, *Journal of Network & Computer Applications*, Jul. 1997.

[14] Zhou J. and Gollmann D., An efficient non-repudiation protocol, *Proceedings of 10th IEEE Computer Security Foundations Workshop*, 1997, pp. 126– 132.

SECURING XML-BASED MULTIMEDIA CONTENT

Ernesto Damiani
Dipartimento di Tecnologie dell'Informazione
Università di Milano, Crema, Italy
damiani@dti.unimi.it

Sabrina De Capitani di Vimercati
Dipartimento di Tecnologie dell'Informazione
Università di Milano, Crema, Italy
decapita@dti.unimi.it

Abstract Multimedia content delivery applications are becoming widespread thanks to increasingly cheaper access to high bandwidth networks. Also, the pervasiveness of XML as a data interchange format has given rise to a number of standard formats for multimedia, such as SMIL for multimedia presentations, SVG for vector graphics, VoiceXML for dialog, and MPEG-21 for video. Innovative programming paradigms (such as the one of Web services) rely on the availability of XML-based markup and metadata in the multimedia flow in order to customize and add value to multimedia content distributed via the Net.

In this paper, we present a general access control model for multimedia information that allows for expressing complex filtering conditions on a wide range of properties of multimedia data. Access control policies' syntax and enforcement is illustrated by applying the model to some of XML-based multimedia data formats for multimedia.

Keywords: Access Control, XML multimedia formats

1. Introduction

Multimedia information (such as free text, audio, video, images and animations) is of paramount importance for human-computer interaction in a number of application fields, such as entertainment, distance learning, collaboration, and others. Multimedia data have been available for a long time over nearly all transport infrastructures, and are now becoming even more widespread thanks to the increasingly cheaper access to high bandwidth networks. However, the importance of complementing binary multimedia data with descriptive metadata in the form of XML tagging has been fully realized only recently. XML-based standard formats for multimedia representation such as SMIL [8]and VoiceXML [9]make the internal structure of multimedia flows available to a variety of consumer applications and devices. More ambitious efforts, such as MPEG-21, are aimed at achieving the same results for video. Intelligent applications like search indexes, topic maps or browsable directories can use XML tagging and auxiliary metadata to identify the structural or semantics-related components of multimedia flows, such as keywords, key frames, audiovisual summaries, semantic concepts, color histograms, shapes, as well as recognized speech. XML formats are paving the way to a new generation of applications even in more traditional fields such as image processing. For instance, raster graphical formats (e.g., `GIF` or `JPEG`) have severe limitations, inasmuch they do not carry any information that can be queried, re-organized, or searched through. *Scalable Vector Graphics* (SVG) [7]is an XML-based language for describing two-dimensional vector and mixed vector/raster graphics that works well across platforms, across output resolutions and color spaces. Also, SVG cleanly specifies the image structure, allowing applications to process data at a finer level of granularity. The wealth of semantics- and structure-related information carried by new XML-based multimedia formats suggests that the time has come to enrich traditional, coarse-grained access control models with a number of new concepts that are specific to the nature and meaning of multimedia data. In our approach, all semantics-related and structural components of multimedia data, such as a room in the vector-based map of a building or a range in the frequency spectrum of an audio clip are considered first-class citizens when writing fine-grained access and fruition policies for multimedia. An interesting consequence of using XML for writing our fine-grained access policies is that XML elements used to refer to multimedia components inside policies can be mapped to XML tags and metadata in the data flow. Policy-to-data mapping can be customized to the particular XML-based multimedia format under discussion, achieving fast and effective enforcement either via data filtering or even by encryption. In this paper, we use some popular XML-based formats for multimedia to illustrate our approach, showing fine-grained access and fruition policies referring to specific components of the multimedia data, and discussing how they can be efficiently enforced via on-line data transformation.

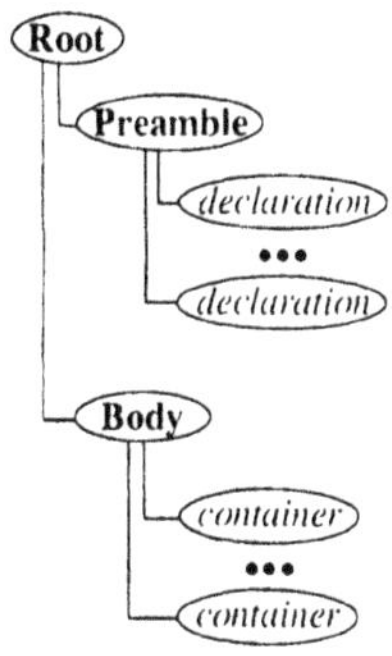

Figure 1. General structure of an XML-based multimedia document

2. Preliminaries

We now describe the document abstraction model on which our approach is based and give some preliminary concepts that will be used throughout the paper. Specifically, we consider the general problem of protecting multimedia data associated with XML-based metadata formats, such as SVG [7] for vector graphics, VoiceXML [9] for dialog, and SMIL [8] for creating interactive multimedia presentations. XML-based metadata formats for multimedia differ in terms of the type of binary data they organize and represent; however, they do share a common structure and semantics. As depicted in Figure 1, XML-based documents attached to multimedia data follow the same general structure of all XML-based documents. They include a root element (e.g., <`svg`> for SVG documents and <`vxml`> for VoiceXML documents), a *preamble*, and a *body*. The preamble of an XML-based multimedia document usually includes one or more *declarations*, whose scope is the whole document. Such declarations are delimited by a pair of start and end tags. For instance, the preamble of a VoiceXML document may contain: `meta` elements, for specifying meta information; `var` and `script` elements, for defining variables and scripts, respectively; `property` elements, for setting property values; `catch` elements, for handling events; and `link` elements, for defining links.[1] The body of a multimedia document includes a number of *top-level container* elements. In our model, a top-level container element is used for *grouping together* multiple semantically related XML elements. For instance, in a SVG document representing the map of a building, graphical elements used for drawing individual rooms are nested into a suitable container element. Examples of containers are ele-

[1] For the sake of conciseness, here we give a sketchy description of XML-based multimedia data formats; W3C recommendations [7–9]contain complete specifications.

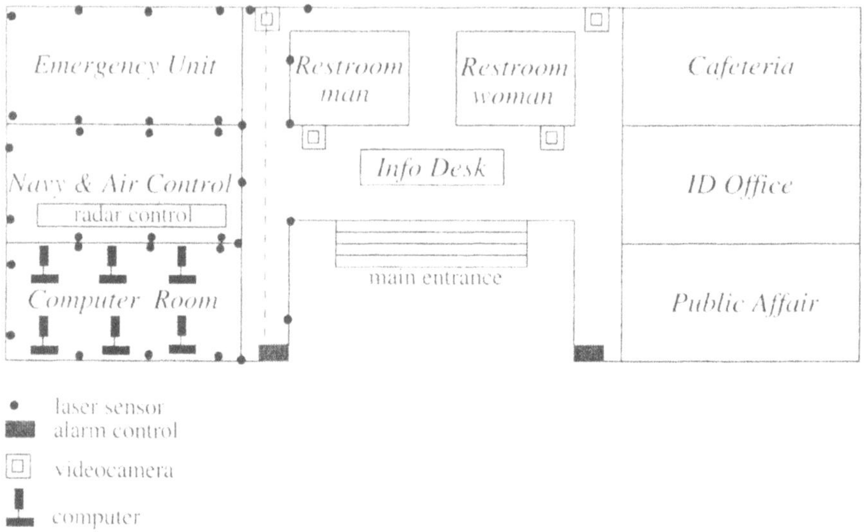

Figure 2. Rendering of a sample SVG document showing the map of a Department of Defense

ment `g` for SVG documents, elements `form` and `menu` for VoiceXML documents, as well as SMIL `layout` and `region` elements. More precisely, SVG element `g` delimits a set of related graphical elements, VoiceXML elements `form` and `menu` represent two different types of dialogs while SMIL `layout` and `region` elements enclose `Layout Modules`.[2] While differing in their vocabulary, all XML-based representations of multimedia content follow a common pattern where a (top-level) container element contains other container elements and so on, down to an arbitrary depth. This nested structure is indeed not surprising, as XML element containment straightforwardly models the spatial or temporal dependencies which are typical of multimedia data. Each element may have its own properties, modeled by XML attributes. All container elements in the document can be uniquely identified including the special attribute `id`.

2.1 Running examples

In the remainder of this paper we refer our examples to to two instances of multimedia documents: a SVG document showing the map of an hypothetical *Department of Defense* (see Figure 2) and a VoiceXML document (see Figure 3) providing a *quote service*. The SVG docu-

[2]SMIL modules can be further grouped into `profiles`.

```
<?xml version="1.0" encoding="ISO-8859-1"?>
<vxml version="1.0">
  <noinput> Welcome to Quote Service Inc. </noinput>
  <form id="Quote">
    <field name="OriginZip">
      <prompt>
        What is the origin ZIP code?
      </prompt>
      <grammar src="string.grxml"/>
    </field>
    <field name="DestinationZip">
      <prompt>
        What is the destination ZIP code?
      </prompt>
      <grammar src="string.grxml"/>
    </field>
    <field name="Weight">
      <prompt>
        What is the weight?
      </prompt>
      <grammar src="string.grxml"/>
    </field>
    <field name="CorporateCode">
      <prompt>
        What is your corporate discount code?
      </prompt>
      <grammar src="string.grxml"/>
    </field>
    <field name="ServiceType">
      <prompt>
        What kind of service do you want?
        You can choose from <enumerate/>
      </prompt>
      <option dtmf="1" value="48h"> 48-hours </option>
      <option dtmf="2" value="24h"> 24-hours </option>
      <option dtmf="3" value="OverN"> Overnight </option>
    </field>
  </form>
```

Figure 3. A simple VoiceXML document

ment displays department layout, that is, offices location and control equipment location. Figure 4(a) illustrates a tree-based representation of the document rendered in Figure 2, reporting the types associated with the `group` elements composing its body. In particular, the body is a group element whose identifier is `deptdefense`; its sub-elements are `main_entrance`, `public_area`, and `private_area` (our sample document defines one group for each of them). Group `public_area` includes `cafeteria`, `IDoffice`, two `restroom` instances, `info_desk`, and `public_affair` office. Each of the latter elements, in turn, is composed of a graphical representation (i.e., `rectRoom`, `rectRest` and `rectInfo` definitions), and a `name`.

Group `private_area` includes `emerg_unit`, `n&acontrol`, `computer_room`, four `videocamera` instances, eight `laser_sensor` instances, and two `alarm_control` instances. Like groups in the `public_area`, each of the group in the `private_area` includes a graphical representation, a name, and possibly some additional groups. For instance, group `computer_room` contains six instances of the `computer` object (called a *symbol* in SVG terminology). The VoiceXML document in Figure 3 describes an application to get quotes for international deliveries. In particular, a user of this service can specify the ZIP code

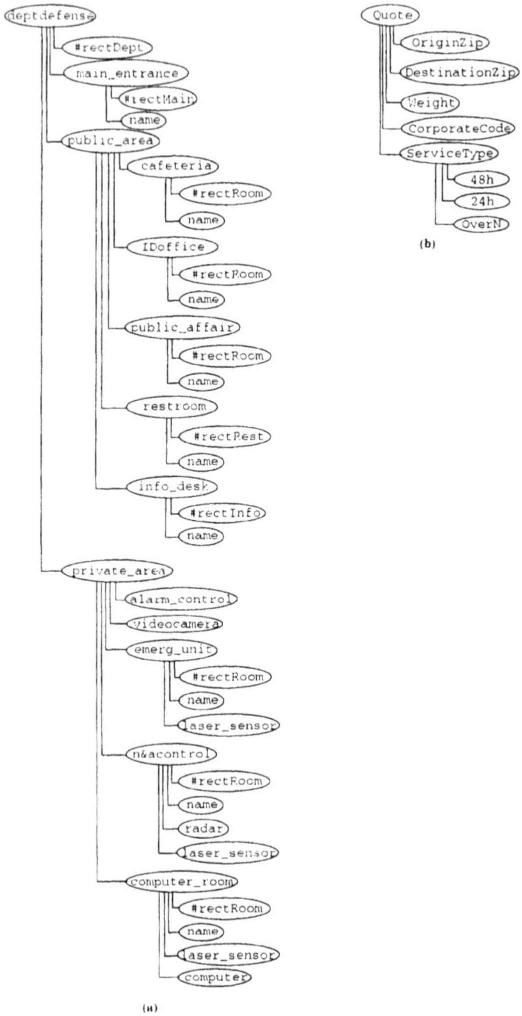

Figure 4. Tree-based graphical representation of the SVG document rendered in Figure 2 (a) and of the VoiceXML document in Figure 3 (b)

of the origin and destination, the parcel's weight, a corporate code, and then can select a service type. Figure 4(b) illustrates a tree-based representation of the VoiceXML document in Figure 3.

3. An access control model for multimedia

We illustrate our model and the main components of our XML-based authorizations. Access authorizations are *rules* that state which actions performed on multimedia data are to be allowed (or denied). Basically,

```
<user_profile id='Alice'>
   <name value='AliceDoo'/>
   <group value='SecurityOfficer'/>
   <address value='Univerity Dr.'/>
   <job value='head'/>
   <level value='senior'/>
</user_profile>
```

```
<user_profile id='Bob'>
   <name value='Bob'/>
   <group value='Administration'/>
   <address value='Manchester Rd'/>
   <citizenship value='EU'/>
   <job value='doctor'/>
</user_profile>
```

Figure 5. An example of user profiles

each authorization has three components: the entity (*subject*) against which access must be controlled; the *object* to be protected; and the *action* being authorized (or denied). Note that for simplicity, here we limit ourselves to `read` authorizations.[3] We are now ready to describe subjects and objects of our access rules and to provide implementation guidelines.

Subjects

In the Web services programming paradigm, where XML-based multimedia documents are released for distribution, it is crucial to provide a simple and, at the same time, highly expressive language for defining authorization subjects. Also, in such an environment the ability to access an object often depends on characteristics (attributes) of the requestor such as age, citizenships, field-of-specialization, membership to groups [2–3], and on his/her role rather than on his/her identity. Our approach addresses both traditional and role-based access control by supporting *XML profiles*. Intuitively, for each user or role, a *profile* specifies the values of properties on which the access control model can express conditions. When dealing with traditional access control, profiles can be straightforwardly exploited for supporting information about *user groups* and *user identity*. As usual, *groups* are sets of users hierarchically organized: they can be nested and need not be disjoint [6]. Note that, in order to allow for specifying authorizations based on user and groups, user-group hierarchies needs to be explicitly defined and be accessible during policy enforcement. We model user profiles as semi-structured documents which can be referenced within policies, for instance, by means of path expressions [11]. XPath expressions are an handy tool to define a mapping between elements denoting subjects

[3]Note that supporting other actions does not complicate the authorization model and can be regulated by allowing (or not allowing) access to the corresponding element

inside our policies and subject properties in XML user profiles.[4]. An *XPath expression* is a sequence of element names or predefined functions separated by character / (slash) and is used to identify a *node-set* (i.e., a set of elements and attributes) within an XML document. For instance, XPath expression `user_profile//[.//group[@value = 'SecurityOfficer']` returns elements `user_profile` selected within profiles of users who belong to group `SecurityOfficer`. With respect to profiles in Figure 5, this XPath expression would return the profile of user `Alice`. Authorization subjects are defined as XML elements as follows:

```
<subject>
  <group value=''group_id''/>
  <role value=''role_id''/>
  <subj-expr value=''xpath-expr1''/>
  ...
  <subj-expr value=''xpath-exprn''/>
</subject>
```

where *group_id* is the group identifier, *role_id* is the role identifier, and $xpath\text{-}expr_1 \ldots xpath\text{-}expr_n$ are path expressions that can evaluate the user's profile. For instance, the authorization subject

```
<subject>
  <group value=''Administration''>
  <subj-expr value=''user_profile/citizenship[@value="EU"]''>
</subject>
```

denotes European citizens that are members of group `Administration`.

Objects

In our model, any XML element in the multimedia document can be an authorization object. Of course, XPath expressions are an effective way to specify the XML elements to which an authorization applies [5]. However, XPath expressions are only one of the possible ways that can be used to identify authorization objects. Our model allows policy writers to refer to XML elements by using their *identifiers* (XML `id` attributes) or, if applicable, their *type* (attribute `typeElement`.[5]) Notations `id.value1` and `type.value2` are used to denote elements whose identifier and type is `value1` and `value2`, respectively. Also, we use a predefined function `perimeter()` to identify the shape (i.e., the drawing

[4] Of course, specialized mappings could be defined to map subjects to XML-based information sources about requestors other than our profiles, such as standard SAML assertions [1]For the sake of simplicity, we do not deal with the technicalities of such mappings in this paper.

[5] Attribute `typeElement` is specific of our model.

Predicates	Semantics
`inside(obj)`	It returns the object in the authorization rule if it is inside an element whose identifier, type, or name is *obj*
`together_with(obj)`	It returns the object in the authorization rule if it is a child of an element together with an object whose identifier, type, or name is *obj*
`number_of(obj,n)`	It returns the object in the authorization rule if there are *n* instances of the object whose identifier, type, or name is *obj*

Table 1. Multimedia predicates

instructions) of an element (referenced via its identifier or type). Function `parameter()` is also used to identify parameters provided by users when they submit their access request and represented in the multimedia document.

In order to provide additional expressive power and flexibility, our model also allows specifying *object conditions* that identify a set of objects satisfying specific properties. Such conditions are expressed in the form of *multimedia predicates.* Table 1 illustrates multimedia predicates together with their semantics. Authorization objects are defined as XML-elements of the form:

<object>
<refer value='*object-id*$_1$ ... *object-id*$_n$'/>
<cond>*pred-expr*</cond>
</object>

where *object-id*$_1$ ... *object-id*$_n$ are the object identifications and *pred-expr* is a boolean expression of multimedia predicates. For instance, the following authorization object:

<object>
<refer value='type.laser_sensor'/>
<cond>`inside(id.computer_room)`</cond>
</object>

denotes all the laser sensor that are inside the computer room.

3.1 Implementation Guidelines

Our enforcement algorithm exploits the tree structure (DOM representation [10]) of XML documents. More specifically, our enforcement is based on a tree labeling. The enforcement algorithm evaluates all *applicable authorizations* at once and translates them into labels associated with nodes of the tree, namely, elements and attributes of the documents. These labels consist of the authorization subject identity and the sign of the authorization. They are then propagated along the XML tree (see [4]for more details). Finally, all subtrees rooted at a node with a negative label or subtrees whose nodes are all unlabeled are discarded.

From the implementation point of view, tree labeling may be performed equally well programmatically (e.g., writing Java code) or using the XPath query engine of a server-side XSL transformer before releasing the multimedia data to the client. For instance, all the `laser_sensor` groups of our SVG example can be easily selected via a single XPath, namely `root/.../g[@type='laser_sensor']`. It should however be noted that predicates of our model (e.g., `inside`, `number_of` and `together_with`) limit the scope of labeling and may introduce a performance burden on the enforcement algorithm, as they require linear scanning the XPath result node-set. Their execution goes as follows: for each node in the node set retrieved by the main XPath query identifying potential objects, an auxiliary XPath query is executed to extract all the node's siblings and check whether they satisfy the predicate; if this is the case, the current node gets labeled, otherwise it does not. On the other hand, single unnamed objects must be labeled by following the unique XPath leading to each of them. After labeling has been completed, the transformation phase will be performed on all nodes having a `sign` attribute; again, XSLT or Java code can be used.

4. Examples of multimedia data protection

Next, we present some examples of protection requirements and illustrate how they can be expressed in our model. We assume that `User` is the root of the user-group hierachy and that `SecurityOfficer` is a its sub-group. Also, subscribers to the quote service are not maintained at the system, and therefore handled with *credentials* stating the ability of the requestor to play the role of `Subscribers` or `FidelitySubscribers`. The letters between brackets identify the authorizations in Figure 6 expressing the requirements.

SVG document.

- Everybody can see the content of any room in the public area. **[s1]**

- Only members of the `SecurityOfficer` group whose job description is 'controller' can see the laser sensors and alarm controls. **[s2]**

- Everybody can see the perimeter of any room in the private area. **[s3]**

Rule	Subject	Object	Sign
[s1]	<subject> <group value=‘Users’/> </subject>	<object> <refer =‘id.public_area’/> </object>	+
[s2]	<subject> <group value=‘SecurityOfficer’/> <subj-expr value= “job[@value= “controller”]” > </subject>	<object> <refer = ‘type.laser_sensor type.laser_control’/> </object>	+
[s3]	<subject> <group value=‘Users’/> </subject>	<object> <refer =‘//g’/> <cond>inside(id.private_area)</cond> </object>	+
[v1]	<subject> <role value=‘Subscribers’/> </subject>	<object> <refer =‘id.Quote’/> </object>	+
	<subject> <role value=‘Subscribers’/> </subject>	<object> <refer =‘parameter(CorporateCode)’/> </object>	-
	<subject> <role value=‘FidelitySubscribers’/> </subject>	<object> <refer =‘parameter(CorporateCode)’/> </object>	+
[v2]	<subject> <group value=‘Users’/> </subject>	<object> <refer =‘//ServiceType/24h //ServiceType/OverN’/> </object>	-

Figure 6. Example of authorization rules

VoiceXML document.

- All subscribers can get quotes *but*, but a corporate discount code can be issued only if a valid fidelity card (e.g., a credential) is attached to the request. **[v1]**
- Individual users can place orders for 48-hour service only (fast deliveries are not accepted through this interface). **[v2]**

5. Conclusions

We have presented a general yet powerful technique for fine-grained feature protection of XML-based multimedia formats. While our technique was originally aimed at controlled dissemination of multimedia information representing confidential or sensitive data (e.g., information about industrial plants or transportation and utility networks), other interesting potential applications of our feature protection technique are currently under discussion. XML-based standard multimedia formats, in particular graphical formats, are considered by many the natural successors of current proprietary formats for high volume distribution of graphical content, such as Macromedia Flash. High-volume distribution of graphics over the Internet presents a host of problems of its own, mainly related to digital rights management. Interestingly, however, some intellectual property-related protection problems can be straightforwardly mapped into our model. For instance, it is customary distribution graphics not to include information about layers, scenes, and other authoring-specific information, leaving only essential content for fast download and, more importantly, for theft prevention. Experience has shown that regardless of its low-level format, graphics whose semantics information has been stripped out is less easily hacked and modified by unauthorized persons. This issue promise to be an interesting extension point of the proposal presented in this paper.

References

[1] Advancing SAML, an XML-based security standard for exchanging authentication and authorization information. http://www.oasis-open.org/committees/security/.

[2] P. Bonatti, E. Damiani, S. De Capitani di Vimercati, and P. Samarati. An access control system for data archives. In *16th International Conference on Information Security*, Paris, France, June 2001.

[3] P. Bonatti, E. Damiani, S. De Capitani di Vimercati, and P. Samarati. A component-based architecture for secure data publication. In *17th Annual Computer Security Applications Conference*, New Orleans, Louisiana, December 2001.

[4] E. Damiani, S. De Capitani di Vimercati, E. Fernandez-Medina, and P. Samarati. An access control system for SVG documents. In *Proc. of the Sixteenth Annual IFIP WG 11.3 Working Conference on Data and Application Security*, King's College, University of Cambridge, UK, July 2002.

[5] E. Damiani, S. De Capitani di Vimercati, S. Paraboschi, and P. Samarati. A fine-grained access control system for XML documents. *ACM TISSEC*, 2002.

[6] S. Jajodia, P. Samarati, M.L. Sapino, and V.S. Subrahmanian. Flexible support for multiple access control policies. *ACM TODS*, 26(2):18–28, June 2001.

[7] World Wide Web Consortium. *Scalable Vector Graphics (SVG) 1.0 Specification*, September 2001. http://www.w3.org/TR/SVG.

[8] World Wide Web Consortium. *Synchronized Multimedia Integration Language (SMIL 2.0)*, August 2001. http://www.w3.org/TR/smil20.

[9] World Wide Web Consortium. *Voice Extensible Markup Language (VoiceXML) Version 2.0*, April 2002. http://www.w3.org/TR/voicexml20.

[10] World Wide Web Consortium (W3C). *Document Object Model (DOM) Level 1 Specification Version 1.0*, October 1998. http://www.w3.org/TR/REC-DOM-Level-1.

[11] World Wide Web Consortium (W3C). *XML Path Language (XPath) 2.0*, December 2001. http://www.w3.org/TR/xpath20.

SECURE AUDIT LOGGING WITH TAMPER-RESISTANT HARDWARE

Cheun Ngen Chong, Zhonghong Peng and Pieter H Hartel
Universiteit Twente, Enschede, The Netherlands.
{chong, zhong, pieter}@cs.utwente.nl

Abstract Secure perimeter schemes (e.g. DRM) and tracing traitor schemes (e.g. watermarking, audit logging) strive to mitigate the problems of content escaping the control of the rights holder. Secure audit logging records the user's actions on content and enables detection of some forms of tampering with the logs. We implement the Schneier and Kelsey's secure audit logging protocol [6], strengthening the protocol by using tamper-resistant hardware (an iButton) in three ways: Firstly, our implementation of the protocol works offline as well as online. Secondly, we use unforgeable timestamps to increase the possibilities of fraud detection. Lastly, we generate the authentication keys, core security of Schneier and Kelsey's protocol on the iButton to alleviate the possibilities of malicious client generating the bad keys. We provide a performance assessment of our implementation to show under which circumstances the protocol is practical to use.

1. Introduction

Digital content is so easily distributed, and dissociated from the meta-data that describes owner, terms and conditions of use etc. that copyright infringement is rife. Secure perimeter schemes such as digital rights management (DRM) alleviate the problem in some cases [2] but most (if not all) DRM systems are vulnerable to attacks. The raw content can then be redistributed, severely damaging the interests of the rights holder. Tracing traitor schemes trace leaks of content to the users who can be identified, and ultimately whose behaviour can be recorded as evidence. Many techniques exist to rediscover the identity and thence the rights on the content, such as cryptography, digital fingerprinting, watermarking etc. In this paper, we assume that users can be identified, and we concern ourselves with the issue of gathering information on the user's behaviour.

Secure audit logging records the actions of a user on an item of content and does so in a manner that allows some forms of tampering with the log to be detected. We implement the Schneier and Kelsey secure audit logging protocol [6], using tamper-resistant hardware (TRH). For brevity in the sequel, we refer to Schneier and Kelsey [6] as "SK".

An audit log is an important tool to detect and to comprehend damages of a computer or network system caused by intrusions, defects or accidents. An audit log contains descriptions of noteworthy events. In our DRM experiment audit logs are generated in the user's personal computer (PC). The PC is a hostile environment (untrusted domain) because of its vulnerability against various malicious attacks. Therefore, the audit logs require protection to ensure integrity.

SK involves two parties: an untrusted machine and a trusted machine. The untrusted machine is not physically secure or sufficiently tamper-resistant. SK makes the audit logs survive the adversary's attacks. In other words, SK renders audit logs impossible for an adversary to *undetectably* view, forge and delete even after the untrusted machine is compromised by the adversary. Furthermore, the audit logs record all the actions performed by the adversary, including her attempts to compromise the untrusted machine.

The comment by SK that "the trusted machine may typically be thought of as a server in a secure location, or implemented in various ways, which includes a tamper-resistant token" has inspired us to use tamper-resistant hardware (TRH) as the trusted machine for secure logging. The TRH (or the trusted machine) we use is a Java iButton (*www.ibutton.com*) for the following reasons:

1 The iButton contains a programmable tamper-evident real time clock. The real time clock keeps time in $\frac{1}{256}$ second increments.

2 The iButton supports efficient implementations of common cryptographic algorithms.

3 The iButton version 1.1 provides up to 6kB non-volatile RAM, the more expensive version 2.2 contains approximately 134kB non-volatile RAM.

We use the iButton as a trusted device to aid in the audit log creation in the manner proposed by SK. An iButton is too small to store a log of any useful size in a cost effective manner: A typical PC contains 40GB storage, i.e. around $300,000$ times more than the iButton.

Our DRM system has the usual Client/Server architecture. The Client is a user with her PC, which represents the untrusted domain. The Server is a trusted environment where content and license are stored.

When the Client accesses the content piecemeal from the Server (e.g. by streaming), the latter is able to protect the content to some extent because the Client's actions can be monitored. However, when the Client downloads the content to the PC's non-volatile storage to accesses the content offline (i.e. disconnected from the Server), the Server is not able to monitor the Client's behaviour. We propose using secure audit logging with TRH to bring the security of offline DRM to the level of online DRM. The main contributions of this paper are:

1 To implement SK embedded in several auxiliary protocols and with the iButton, to support security of offline DRM.

2 To evaluate the performance of the implementation; thus investigating whether the iButton can be used effectively.

3 To strengthen SK by making sure that some of its security assumptions are valid by virtue of using the iButton. We generate core secrets and timestamps on the iButton instead of the untrusted PC.

To the best of our knowledge ours is the first attempt to implement SK and the first endeavour to analyse the performance of SK in general, and SK with iButton in particular.

A weakness of any system, which relies on TRH to coerce an untrusted Client into specific behaviour, is that the user may simply sever the connection between the Client and the TRH. We suggest a number of ways to discourage the Client from such behaviour: (1) The Server is designed so that it insists on the iButton being present to authenticate and authorize the Client; (2) Organizational policy (e.g. in a corporate intranet) is used to enforce the use of the iButton. In both cases users are provided an incentive to maintain communication with the iButton: *no iButton means no content.*

The main problem with audit logging is that at some stage a dishonest user may cheat by disabling the audit logging functionality of the DRM application at the Client. She is able to deny any actions she has performed during the offline period without evidences in the log.

At this point, the protection offered by DRM is weak on PCs but potentially stronger on consumer electronics appliances. The reason for this weakness is that PCs are open and programmable, whereas Consumer electronics appliances are more tamper-resistant than PCs and therefore somewhat more difficult to hack the DRM application. Therefore, the dishonest user will find it much harder to bypass a CE device (the Client) audit logging mechanism. The audit logging mechanism is able to record all the user's actions, including her attempts to tamper with the audit logs.

The remainder of this paper is divided into sections as follows: Section 2 describes related work. Section 3 explains SK using the iButton. Section 4 discusses concisely the refinement we have made of SK. Section 5 gives our performance analysis on the implementation. Finally, section 6 concludes this paper also mentioning future work.

2. Related Work

Shapiro and Vingralek [8] survey several mechanisms to manage the persistent state in a DRM system, including protected digital content, audit trail, content usage counts and decryption keys. One of the mechanisms they mention is secure audit logging. The two secure audit logging methods they cite are Bellare and Yee as well as Schneier and Kelsey.

Bellare and Yee [1] (BY) propose a scheme to construct audit logs which possess the forward integrity property: The keys are altered on a regular basis by feeding different secret values to a family of pseudorandom functions that generate the MACs over the entire log entries. If an adversary is able to compromise the current MAC key, it is unfeasible for her to deceive the historical entries generated because she is not able to fabricate the MAC keys for previous log entries. "Forward integrity" can be viewed as an integrity analogue of "forward secrecy" [5]. A protocol possesses the forward integrity property if a compromise of long-term keys does not compromise the past keys. BY maintains the audit logs on untrusted machines.

Schneier and Kelsey [6] (SK) uses a linear hash chain [4] to link the entire audit log entries so that some forms of tampering can be detected. The hash-chain is constructed by hashing each previous hash value of each log entry, concatenating with some other values. SK provides a complete secure audit logging protocol, from the log creation to log verification and viewing. A trusted machine is needed during log file creation but not at every log entry creation. The untrusted machine needs to communicate with the trusted machine from time to time to create new log file and to validate log files. Similar to BY, SK shares the "forward integrity" property, but SK uses a collusion-resistant hash function to generate the keys for MACs generation of each log entry.

SK and BY share a security weakness. If an adversary is able to compromise the untrusted machine at time t, i.e. obtains the key at time t, she is able to forge the log entry at time t. SK and BY are able to make illicit deletion of audit logs detectable. However, they are not able to *prevent* unauthorized removal of complete audit logs. Both

SK and BY reckon that the deletion of log entries cannot be prevented by using cryptographic methods, but only by using write-only hardware such as CD-ROM, or paper printout.

3. The Protocols

Figure 1 illustrates the protocols in our secure audit logging method. SK1 and SK2 are from SK. The others, P1 and P2 are our own protocols.

SK1 creates and closes an audit log. We focus on the technical details of the protocol and refer the reader to Reference [6] for the motivations behind the protocol and other details. We use the notations listed in Reference [6] to describe our protocols.

SK2 verifies and displays the audit logs to the Verifier. We have changed slightly the SK Verifier in that it does not store the Client's log file locally. The Verifier reads and verifies the log file remotely from the Server. In other words, the log file is stored securely in the Server, and the cryptographic processes are operated at the Server. Similar to SK1, Reference [6] elaborates this protocol.

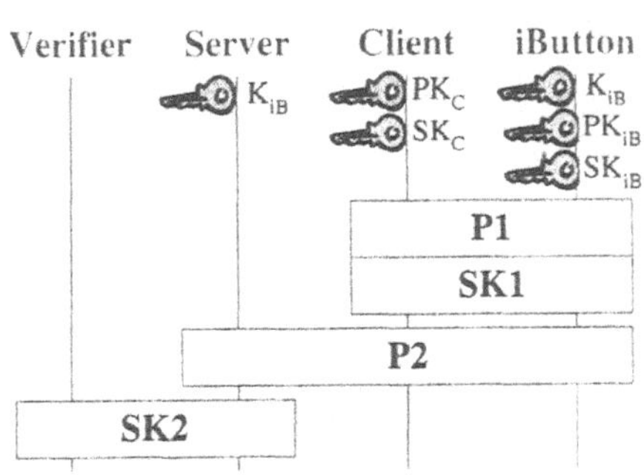

Figure 1. Overview of the secure audit logging method.

The Client and the iButton own different sets of key pairs. PK_C and SK_C are the public key and private key of the Client, respectively. PK_{iB} and SK_{iB} are the public key and private key of the iButton, respectively. The iButton and the Server share a secret key, K_{iB}. The public/private keys and the shared secret key are preloaded on the iButton before it is deployed.

We have made some assumptions that we believe to be reasonable while implementing the protocols. The main reason is to facilitate the implementation of SK in the resource constrained iButton.

1 Without restricting generality, there is only *one* Verifier, *one* Server, *one* Client and *one* iButton in the audit logging process. There is only *one* audit log file created from the process.

2 If the iButton is removed from the iButton reader halfway through an instruction then the log file is closed abnormally with a reason stated in the log.

3.1 P1

P1 generates the authentication keys, A_j and to generate the timestamp, d_j for recording the log entry. We have refined SK1 by deciding that the iButton should generate the keys and timestamps, as can be seen in Figure 2.

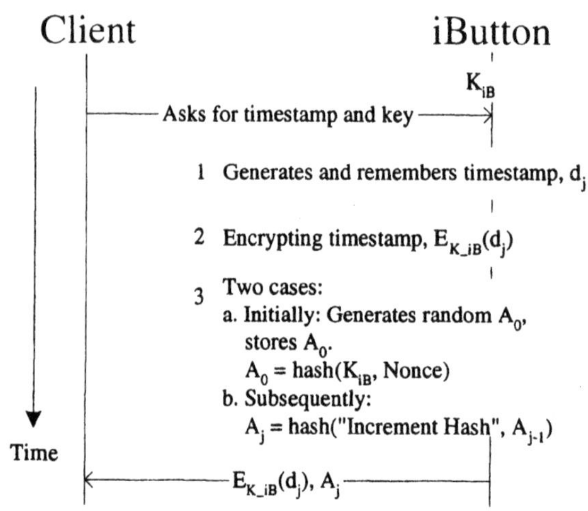

Figure 2. The P1 protocol for generating the initial authentication key A_0 and timestamp d from the iButton.

We improve SK1 to the extent that A_0, which represents the core security of SK1, and the timestamps are generated in a trusted subdomain. A fresh nonce, *Nonce* is generated and stored on the iButton. The purpose of *Nonce* is to ensure the freshness of the initial authentication key. The generated nonce is concatenated with the key, K_{iB}. Thereby, the initial authentication key cannot be generated by a malicious Client because she does not know the *Nonce* and K_{iB}.

We use the iButton real-time clock to generate the timestamps. We encrypt the timestamps generated using the key, K_{iB} shared between the iButton and the Server. By doing so, the timestamps cannot be manufactured by the Client (who does not have access to K_{iB}).

The Client first requests an encrypted timestamp and an authentication key from the iButton for the current log entry. The iButton generates the timestamp using its real-time clock and encrypts the time stamp with the iButton secret key, K_{iB}. The iButton then remembers the first timestamp, i.e. the timestamp for the initialisation log entry, with type *"LogFileInitializationType"* and also the last timestamp, for the close log entry, with type *"NormalCloseType"* or type *"AbnormalCloseType"*. We will come back to this in section 4.

The iButton then generates a random key, as the initial authentication key, A_0 if it is the first log entry the Client constructs; otherwise, the iButton hashes the previously existing authentication key, A_{j-1} concatenated with a message to generate the next authentication key, A_j. The iButton stores the initial authentication key, A_0 and current authentication key, A_j for generating subsequent keys, A_{j+1}. After finishing the generations, the iButton sends the encrypted timestamp and the authentication key back to the Client.

3.2 P2

P2 synchronizes the iButton clock to the Server clock, which is a trusted clock. P2 also sends the log file maintained at the Client and the corresponding initial authentication key on the iButton to the Server, as shown in Figure 3. The Server and the iButton share a secret symmetric key, K_{iB}, which is used to encrypt the data exchanges between the iButton and the Server (and also the timestamps) from the Client.

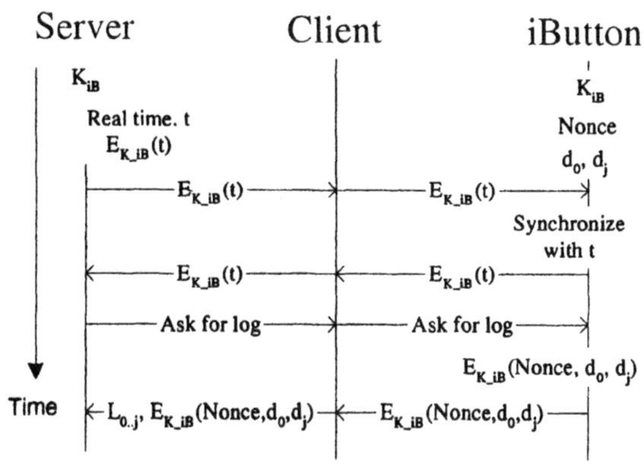

Figure 3. The P2 protocol of synchronizing the iButton real-time clock and sending audit logs to the Server.

The Server encrypts its current time with K_{iB}, and sends the encrypted time to the iButton for time synchronization. The iButton then decrypts the message and adjusts its real time according to the received time. Once the time is synchronized, the iButton sends back the accepted encrypted time to the Server as an indication that the time is synchronized.

After the clock synchronization, the Server sends a request message to the Client asking for the available log file. The Client forwards the request to the iButton. The iButton sends the encrypted *Nonce* (the secret used to generate the initial authentication key), as well as initialisation timestamp, d_0 and close timestamp, d_j to the Server via the Client. At the same time, the Client sends the available log file (corresponds to the ID_{log} of *Nonce*) to the Server. In the DRM system, P2 is transparent to the Client.

4. SK Refinement

We have refined SK by introducing two auxiliary protocols, P1 and P2. P1 lets the trusted iButton instead of the untrusted client generate the authentication keys and the timestamps. The iButton remembers the timestamps for initialization and closing of the log. Additionally, the Client only possesses the encrypted timestamp from the iButton for audit logging, i.e. the integrity and confidentiality of the timestamps are ensured. P2 enables the iButton to transfer the encrypted initial authentication key and stored timestamps using the shared secret key with the Server. In other words, P2 is able to guarantee the integrity of the initial authentication key and the timestamps during the transmitting process.

As pointed out by Schneier and Kelsey [6], [7], there is a security weakness in SK. If an adversary is able to compromise the Client by getting hold of the key A_t, directly after it has been generated at time t, the adversary is able to falsify the log entry at time t. The adversary is also able to create more counterfeit log entries and remove some log entries. The Verifier is not able to detect the frauds because the adversary is able to construct another "truthful" hash-chain and MAC over the entire log entries using the compromised authentication key.

In our refinement of SK, by using encrypted timestamps, we are able to detect some of the aforementioned frauds. If the adversary wishes to create more log entries, she has to obtain the cooperation of the iButton to generate valid timestamps. The adversary does not have the right key, so she cannot fabricate arbitrary timestamps herself. The adversary can reuse genuine encrypted timestamps, but the verifier will notice missing or duplicate time stamps, or time stamps that are presented out of order. The adversary will also be caught truncating the log file when the time of truncation does not match the time of the last transaction remembered by the iButton. In case of tampering, the user can be held responsible for the entire period between the log initialization time and close time.

We now present a concrete example of the difference between the original SK and our version as shown in Figure 4. An adversary, who owns a protected document and an associated license, starts the content renderer on the Client. The first log entry, initialization log, is then generated. Subsequent log entries are generated when she turns to other pages of the document. At time t_4, the adversary successfully steals the key A_4. She does not stop browsing the document, but keeps reading until time t_{10}. She closes the document at time t_{11} and so the log file is closed. She wants to deny the fact that she has viewed the document from t_4 till t_{10}. Instead the adversary wants the Verifier to believe that she has viewed the document until t_3. The adversary would wish to do so for example when she is charged on a pay-per-view basis. The adversary thus removes the log entries from t_4 onwards, and creates a false close log entry using timestamp t_4. As she possesses the key A_4, she is able to construct a valid hash-chain and forge the MACs for this fraudulent log. In our version of SK, the Verifier is able to detect the forgery because the iButton remembers the log closing time (t_{11}), which in the scenario above does not match t_4. The original SK protocol does not detect this situation.

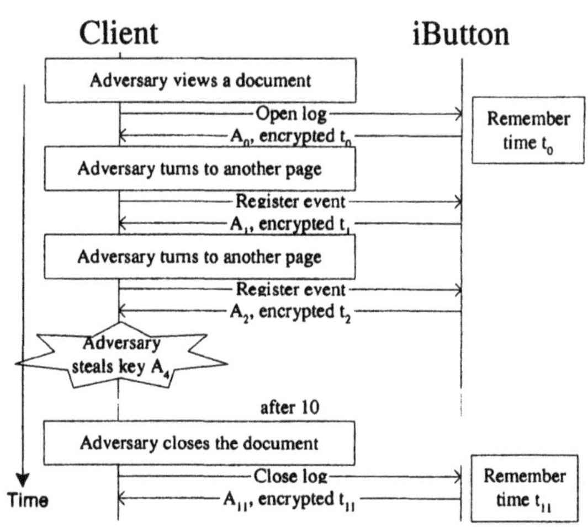

Figure 4. An adversary views a protected document and steals the key at time $t = 4$, during the logging process.

Suppose that the Client cheats by using key A_4 instead of A_{11} to close the log file. The next time the client connects to the server to get new content she will need the cooperation of the iButton to authenticate herself. This gives the iButton the chance to present the latest key A_{11} to the server, and so the cheating Client will be found out.

Using encrypted time stamps improves the security of the protocol but weaknesses remain. For example if after a perfectly legitimate run of the protocols the user starts viewing the content using an application that does not log any actions, then this will not be noticed.

5. Performance Analysis

We are interested to know how the iButton affects the performance of the Client during audit logging. This allows us to determine if the iButton is practical for secure audit logging in a DRM system. We have run several performance tests on the implementation. We have used a PC machine Pentium III 800MHz with 256MB RAM as the Client machine for performing the tests.

We have measured the time for creating different numbers of log entries, from 1 to 10 on the Client. The graph is nearly a straight line. Generating 1 log entry takes approximately 1 minute.To explore why it takes roughly 1 minute to generate only 1 log entry, we have measured the time spent for performing cryptographic operations on the iButton. We believe that the cryptographic operations are the main causes to the long time taken for generating log entries.

We read the start time on the iButton right before the iButton starts the calculation under investigation. We read the stop time on the iButton once it stops the process. The time taken is the value of deducting the start time from the stop time. The result is then transmitted back to the Client. As only time with seconds-precision is available on the iButton (the software does not provide access to the $\frac{1}{256}$ second accuracy of the hardware clock), we have run the process repeatedly on the iButton, dividing the time measures by the number of repetition. We take the average value of 20 measurements as our final value using the standard deviation as error margin.

We evaluate the time spent for encrypting/decrypting a message of various size in bytes (from 8 to 128) using the 64-bit key DES algorithm on the iButton. We realize that the times are around 200 ms for large message (size bigger than 128 bytes). We measure the time spent for hashing a message of sizes range from 8 to 128 bytes using the SHA1 message digest algorithm. The time spent for hashing 56 bytes is almost double the time spent for hashing 48 bytes. This is due to the message padding to 64 bytes [3]. We also measure the time consumed for encrypting a message of sizes from 8 bytes to 128 bytes, using 128-bit public key of RSA algorithm; and decrypt using the corresponding private key on the iButton. The RSA encryption takes averagely 25 seconds, while 22 seconds are needed for RSA decryption. We measure the time needed to sign a message using SHA1 and RSA and to verify the signed message. It takes 4 to 5 seconds to sign a message on the iButton, but it takes 5 to 6 seconds to verify the signature.

We do a back of the envelope calculation to confirm the measurement on the log entry generation time we obtain. The iButton takes less than 1 second for generating the timestamp and authentication key, i.e. to complete the protocol P1. The cryptographic operations on the iButton, as mentioned earlier consume most time. RSA private key decryption and public key encryption take approximately 24 seconds and 20 seconds, respectively. DES encryption and decryption need about 0.1 second, respectively. Signature generation and verification require roughly 5 seconds and 4 seconds respectively. These values are taken according to the size of the message we have used.

To conclude our performance analysis, as it takes about 1 minute just to generate 1 log entry, the iButton is not practical to be used in a system that requires frequent logging. However, if the system only logs the main events, such as playing a 4-minute song, reading an eBook, and other content access taking a longer time, we believe that the iButton is practical. Note that in our system logging overlaps with the actual content rendering.

For logging frequent events, we believe that we could use iButton as a bootstrap device for ensuring the trustworthiness of the first audit log entry, and we could do the subsequent log entries creation for frequent events without the presence of the iButton. This issue remains open for future investigation.

6. Conclusions and Future Work

We propose using secure audit logging in a DRM system where the Client is not permanently online. This allows the Server to obtain knowledge of the Client's behaviour during offline periods. We implement the Schneier and Kelsey (SK) secure audit logging protocol, using tamper-resistant hardware (an iButton) as the SK trusted machine.

The performance evaluation reveals that it takes about 1 minute for generating 1 log entry. We reckon that this is not practical for a system that requires frequent logging but feasible for a system that only needs to log the main events such as playing a 4-minute song. To make the iButton implementation also practical for recording more frequent events in future work we intend to use the current implementation recursively:

one entire log on the untrusted PC would then correspond to one log entry that involves the iButton. The performance could also be improved dramatically using a more powerful iButton.

The main problem with all secure audit logging protocols is that if a log entry at time t is compromised, then none of the log entries after time t can be trusted. Our use of securely encrypted time stamps can solve this problem in some (but not all) cases. We believe that we can improve the security further by asking the iButton to do a little more work. This remains open for future work.

Acknowledgement

We like to thank Dr. Jaap-Henk Hoepman for his valuable comments on this paper.

References

[1] Mihir Bellare and Bennet S. Yee. Forward integrity for secure audit logs. Technical report, UC at San Diego, Dept. of Computer Science and Engineering, November 1997. http:// citeseer.nj.nec.com/ bellare97forward.pdf.

[2] Cheun N. Chong, René van Buuren, Pieter H. Hartel, and Geert Kleinhuis. Security attribute based digital rights management. In *Joint Int. Workshop on Interactive Distributed Multimedia Systems/Protocols for Multimedia Systems (IDMS/PROMS)*, pages 339–352. Springer-Verlag, Berlin, November 2002.

[3] FIPS-PUB-180-1. Secure hash standard. Technical report, US Departmenet of Commerce/NIST, Washington D. C., United Stats, April 1995.

[4] Leslie Lamport. Password authentication with insecure communication. In *Communications of the ACM*, volume 24, pages 770–772. ACM Press, November 1981.

[5] Alfred J. Menezes, Paul C. Van Oorschot, and Scott A. Vanstone. *Handbook of Applied Cryptography*, chapter 12. CRC Press, 2001. ISBN: 0-8493-8523-7.

[6] Bruce Schneier and John Kelsey. Cryptographic support for secure logs on untrusted machines. In *The 7th USENIX Security Symposium Proceedings*, pages 53–62. USENIX Press, January 1998.

[7] Bruce Schneier and John Kelsey. Secure audit logs to support computer forensics. In *ACM Transactions on Information and System Security*, volume 2, pages 159–176. ACM Press, May 1999.

[8] William Shapiro and Radek Vingralek. How to manage persistent state in DRM systems. In *Proceedings of the ACM Workshop in Security and Privacy in Digital Rights Management*, November 2001. http://www.star-lab.com/sander/spdrm/papers.html.

PCMHoDC

A Scheme to Protect Copyright & Modification History of Digital Contents

HeeJae Park and Jong Kim
Department of Computer Science and Engineering
Pohang University of Science and Technology (POSTECH)
San 31, Hyoja-dong, Nam-gu, Pohang, Kyungbuk, South Korea
E-mail: {myphj,jkim}@postech.ac.kr

Abstract: Nowadays, protecting digital contents becomes important because it is easy to copy them and hard to distinguish the copy from the original one. As the Internet becomes wider and faster, digital contents are distributed illegally wider and faster than ever. Much research is conducted on preventing illegal distribution and on developing new protection technologies, such as digital watermarking, digital right management, etc. But these technologies are mainly used for commercial and business purposes. Moreover, these technologies are based on the assumption that digital contents will not be modified after being distributed by the contents owner.

In this paper, we propose a new scheme to protect against the illegal distribution of modifiable digital contents. The proposed scheme also manages modification history and the copyright information of modified digital contents. The proposed scheme assumes that the system is composed of server, client, and application that manages modification history. The application exists in the client side and has a secret key. Any legal user receives encrypted digital contents from the server via this application, but cannot place decrypted contents into storage. If a user has distributed his digital contents and his private key to others, our scheme can determine who has distributed them. We compare our scheme with previous technologies such as simple encryption method, digital watermarking, digital right management, and secure file system, and show that the proposed scheme has better characteristics.

Key words: Copyright protection, management of modification history, modifiable digital contents.

1. INTRODUCTION

Unlike analogue contents, digital contents, which are represented only by 0 and 1, enables us to achieve a high quality reproduction of original contents. However, digital contents are easy to copy, difficult to distinguish a copy from an original, and hard to protect the copyrights of their creators. Moreover, as the Internet becomes faster and more widespread, illegal copies and distribution occurs more than ever. Although the method of distributing encrypted digital contents to prevent unauthorized copy from illegal users is widely used, it cannot protect the case that a legal user decrypts the encrypted contents and redistributes them as decrypted forms. Therefore, lawsuits about infringements of the copyright of digital contents such as image, audio, video contents, and software programs occur frequently and these litigations of illegal copies show that digital contents have demerits as well as merits.

Methods of protecting the copyright of digital contents have been studied recently. Digital watermarking [1, 15] and digital right management (DRM) [4, 16] belong to them. Digital watermarking technology, firstly applied to multimedia contents such as image, audio, and video files, enables the creators of digital contents to place their copyright information in the contents itself. Digital watermarking studies are expanded to text documents and software programs, but since everyone can view watermarked contents without restriction, this technique does not proactively protect against illegal distribution. Another approach is digital right management (DRM), an integrated technology that guarantees the security of the contents in each step of creation, distribution, and storage. This technique supplies not only the copyright information of digital contents like watermarking techniques, but also mechanisms to prevent the viewing of the contents. A well-known example of using DRM technique is "Windows Media Player" developed by Microsoft [4, 10].

However, DRM focuses only on creation and distribution of the contents but not on their modification. It means that it is impossible to manage the copyright of contents that are modified many times by several people.

In this paper, we propose a scheme, called PCMHoDC, that manages the copyright information of modifiable contents. The proposed scheme manages the modification history and the copyright information of modified digital contents. The proposed scheme assumes a system composed of server, client, and application that manages the modification history. The application exists in the client side and has a secret key. Any legal user receives encrypted digital contents from the server via this application, but cannot place a decrypted one into storage. If a user has distributed his digital contents and his private key to others, our scheme can identify him.

The rest of this paper is organized as follows. In Section 2, we explain the design goals and the system architecture of PCMHoDC. In Section 3, we explain the data formats for digital contents, their communication protocol, and the characteristics of PCMHoDC. We present the previous related works and compare the proposed scheme with them in Section 4. Finally, we summarize in Section 5.

2. DESIGN GOALS AND SYSTEM ARCHITECTURE OF PCMHoDC

In this section, we first present the design goals of PCMHoDC. Next, we show the system architecture and assumptions for PCMHoDC.

2.1 Design Goals

We set three goals related to the protection of modifiable contents, as shown below.

(G1) Authenticated users must be able to cooperate for making digital contents and all participating users must have their copyright.

(G2) Users must be able to modify the contents and must be able to claim the copyright of his modification.

(G3) Secure contents should not be shown to the right-less user and if this occurs, it must be able to identify the illegal distributor.

2.2 The System Architecture and Assumptions

The proposed system architecture is a server-client structure as shown in Figure 1. Assumptions for the server, the MMAP, and a user are as follows.

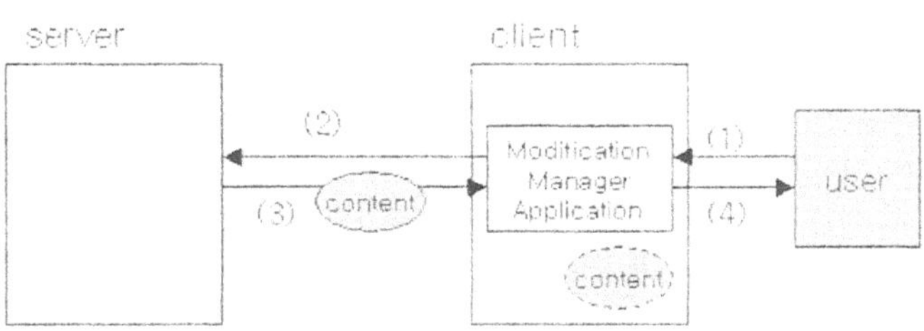

Figure 1: System architecture.

A. Server

- The server does not destruct or remove the contents, and does not distribute them illegally.

- The server encrypts contents with a secret key that the MMAP knows.
- The server has a private key and a public key, and the private key is never disclosed.

B. Modification Manager Application Program (MMAP)

- The server distributes the MMAP to users and users install this MMAP in the client. The MMAP has a secret key unknown to outside of the program by hiding the key in the program itself. This is done by the method of hiding functions [6] or by the data (indistinguishable) obfuscation used for the software protection [7].
- The MMAP stores contents only in the form received from the server. When a user modifies contents, the MMAP sends their modified blocks to the server and receives new version.

C. User

- A user has a private key and a public key and must hide the private key from the public.
- A user can use all resources of client he is connected to.
- A user requests contents to the server, reads and modifies them via the MMAP.

2.3 Notations

- $H(v)$: the hash value of v.
- K_{AppSec} : the secret key of modification manager application program.
- $K_{ser(pr)}$, $K_{ser(pu)}$: a private key and a public key of server, respectively.
- $K_{usr(pr)}$, $K_{usr(pu)}$: a private key and a public key of a user, respectively.
- C_{server} : the form of contents stored in the server
- C_{send} : the form of contents when transmitted.
- C_{client} : the form of contents stored in the client.
- M : the last version of contents.
- $M(i)$: the ith modified block. Let M_i represent the contents after the ith modification. Then $M(i)$ means the difference between M_{i-1} and M_i.
- $CR_{M(i)}$: the copyright information for the ith modified block. The user making $M(i)$ encrypts the hash value of $M(i)$ and sequence number i of the modified block together with his private key. When the user usrA makes $M(i)$,

$$CR_{M(i)} = K_{usrA(pr)}\{H(M(i)), i\}$$

- D_{id} : the digital contents identifier.
- U_{info} : the information about a specific user.

3. PCMHoDC: PROTECTING COPYRIGHT & MODIFICATION HISTORY OF DIGITAL CONTENTS

In order to maintain the copyright and modification history of digital contents, we propose the data formats of digital contents and communication protocols between the server and the MMAP. Then we explain the characteristics of the proposed scheme.

3.1 The data formats of digital contents

Original contents are stored unencrypted in the server, since it is assumed that the server does not distribute contents illegally. However, when contents are transmitted to a client or stored in the client side, they must be encrypted in order to avoid illegal distribution. So, digital contents have two formats, encrypted and unencrypted.

A. The contents format stored in the server

The server must have contents' identifier, last modified version, modified blocks, and the copyright information of all modified blocks.

- $C_{server} = D_{id} \cdot M \cdot M(n) \ldots M(1) \cdot CR_{M(n)} \ldots \cdot CR_{M(1)}$

The server stores all contents in the above format. When a user requests them, the server encrypts them and sends them to the user.

B. The contents format transmitted to the client or stored in the client

When a user requests the contents, the server encrypts them with the user's public key, and only that user decrypts them with his private key. After decrypting, a user can know who has modified each part of the contents by seeing the modification information of all modified blocks. There are two methods for receiving the modification information based on when the server sends this to the client.

One method is that the server sends the contents only and does not send the related modification information until a user requests it. Another is that the server sends the contents and modification information simultaneously. While the former has shorter time for viewing the contents, the latter is more effective for viewing the modification information. Table 1 shows C_{send} and C_{client} of each method.

In order to identify the user distributing the contents illegally, user information (U_{info}) is included in the message C_{send}. Also, the hash value of the contents is included to check the alteration of the digital contents and their modification information.

Table 1: The transmission and storing format of digital contents.

		Method1(Contents only)	Method2(Together)
C_{send}	Transmission of contents	$E_{K(AppSec)}\{E_{K(usr(pu))}\{K\},U_{info},D_{id}\} \cdot E_K\{M \cdot H(M)\}$	$E_{K(AppSec)}\{E_{K(usr(pu))}\{K\}, U_{info},D_{id}\} \cdot E_K\{M \cdot M(n)...M(1) \cdot CR_{M(n)}...CR_{M(1)} \cdot H(M)\}$
	Transmission of modification information	$E_{K(AppSec))}\{E_{K(usr(pu))}\{K\},U_{info}, D_{id}\} \cdot E_K\{M(n)...M(1) \cdot CR_{M(n)}...CR_{M(1)} H(M)\}$	
C_{client}		Both of the above	The above

3.2 Communication protocols

A user can make and register any contents to the server and request to delete them from the server. And, a user can read and modify the contents by interacting with the server. Therefore, communication protocols between the server and a user must be specified for contents protection when a user wants to register, read, modify, and delete digital contents. These communication protocols must be accomplished under the encrypted mode with their private keys and public keys for security management.

A. When a user requests digital contents for reading.

Figure 2 shows the communication protocol when a user requests digital contents for reading. Each step is described in detail.

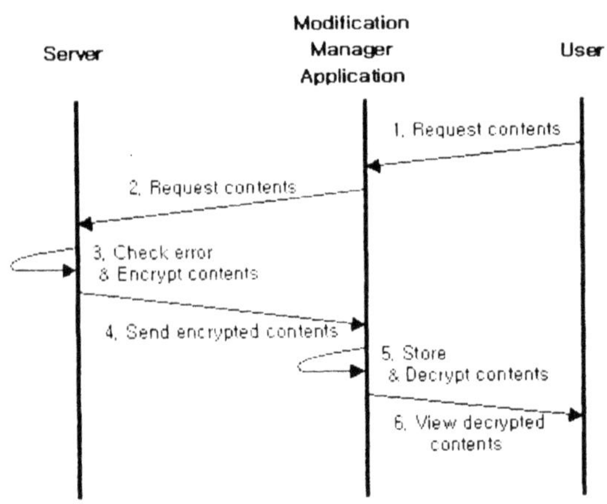

Figure 2: Communication protocol for a user's reading request.

1. A user requests specific contents to an MMAP. He gives his own private key and the identifier of the requesting contents (D_{id}).
2. The MMAP requests the contents to the server.
3. The server sends an error message to the MMAP in the following cases:
   a) The requesting user is not included in the reading list.

   b) The requesting MMAP is an illegal copy.
   c) The requested contents do not exist in the server.
4. If there exists no error, the server makes the message C_{send} and returns it to the requesting MMAP.
5. The MMAP stores the received, encrypted contents and decrypts them.
6. The MMAP shows the decrypted contents to the user.

B. When a user modifies digital contents.

Figure 3 shows the communication protocol when a user wants to modify digital contents. Each step is described in detail.

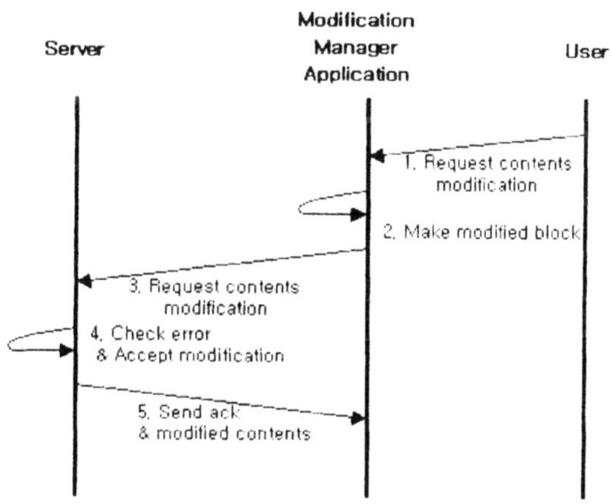

Figure 3: Communication protocol for a user's modification request.

1. A user requests the modification of the contents to the MMAP.
2. The MMAP makes the modified block (M(n+1)) based on the difference between the modified version and the previously received version. It calculates the hash value of this modified block and then makes the copyright information by encrypting the hash value and sequence number (n+1) with the user's private key ($CR_{M(n+1)}=K_{usr(pr)}\{H(M(n+1)), (n+1)\}$).
3. The MMAP encrypts M(n+1) and $CR_{M(n+1)}$ with the server's public key and sends it to the server.
4. After the server checks if the user has the right to modify the contents, it is changed from $C_{server}= M\cdot M(n)...M(1)\cdot CR_{M(n)}...CR_{M(1)}$ to $M\cdot \mathit{M(n+1)}M(n)...M(1)\cdot \mathit{CR_{M(n+1)}}\, CR_{M(n)}...CR_{M(1)}$.
5. The server notifies the MMAP whether the contents are modified successfully and sends their new version to the MMAP.

C. When a user creates new contents.

A user sends new contents to the server by using the same modification protocol shown in Figure 3. At this time, he attaches the list of users with their rights to read and modify. The server maintains the list and uses it to check the right of another user.

D. When a user requests to delete existing contents.

When the server receives the request to delete contents from the user who have created them, it broadcasts the deletion messages to all users who modified the contents previously. If there is no objection message against it, the server deletes them.

3.3 Characteristics

A. Only legal users can read contents.

The contents are always transmitted and stored in the encrypted form, C_{send} and C_{client}. Since the server sends the contents only to legal users by encrypting with the public key of that user, no one except for the requesting user can see the contents, copyright, and their modification information.

B. The copyright and modification information of digital contents is always managed.

The server stores the copyright and modification information together with the contents as unencrypted because of the assumption that it cannot be cracked. However, it would pose a problem if someone modifies the modification information of contents and distributes it. Therefore, when contents are distributed from the server, it is important to detect the altering of modification information, as well as to keep the contents as encrypted. We consider two cases, shown in Table 1.

In the first method, the server encrypts the modification information together with the contents and distributes in the following data format.

- $E_{K(AppSec)}\{E_{K(usr(pu))}\{K\},U_{info},D_{id}\}\cdot E_K\{M\cdot M(n)\ldots M(1)\cdot CR_{M(n)}\ldots CR_{M(1)}\cdot H(M)\}$

In the above data format, since a user cannot know the random key K as long as the MMAP does not leak its secret key and the key K, he cannot modify the part $E_K\{M\cdot M(n)\ldots M(1)\cdot CR_{M(n)}\ldots CR_{M(1)}H(M)\}$. If a user changes the modification information maliciously, the MMAP can detect it by checking the hash value.

Another method is to encrypt the contents and the modification information separately. In this method, the server distributes the contents and the modification information in the following formats, respectively.

- $E_{K(AppSec)}\{E_{K(usr(pu))}\{K\},U_{info},D_{id}\}\cdot E_K\{M\cdot H(M)\}$

- $E_{K(AppSec)}\{E_{K(usr(pu))}\{K\},U_{info},D_{id}\}\cdot E_K\{M(n)\ldots M(1)\cdot CR_{M(n)}\ldots CR_{M(n)}\cdot H(M)\}$

The MMAP checks the hash value H(M) whenever it receives the modification information. If a malicious user changes it, the hash value is also changed, and so the MMAP can detect the alteration.

If the MMAP detects the illegal alteration of the modification information, all it has to do is to request the modification information to the server again.

C. Illegal distributor can be found.

Under the assumption that the secret key of MMAP is secure, non-authorized users can view the contents only when an authorized user gives his own private key to them. The proposed scheme has the mechanism of identifying this illegal sharing. The MMAP notifies the user information to the server whenever it requests to read digital contents. The requested digital contents are encrypted with a random key that is again encrypted with the user's public key. Hence, the user's private key is required to see the encrypted contents. If a non-authorized user's reading is detected, the illegal distributor can be determined easily since the user information (U_{info}) is found by the MMAP, by decrypting the contents.

D. It is impossible to modify contents in behalf of another.

We can consider two possibilities.

- When a user wants to modify contents in behalf of another.

  In order for a user to modify contents, he must send the modified block and its modification information, which are encrypted with his private key, to the server. But as a user does not expose his private key, any user cannot encrypt the modification block with another user's private key. Even the replay attack, re-sending the same modified block and the same modification information to the server by eavesdropping, cannot succeed since the server checks the sequence number.

- When the server wants to modify contents in behalf of a user.

  The server may be the dangerous place because contents are stored as unencrypted. It does not destruct any contents, but it may modify some contents as if a user performed the modification. However, the server cannot make M(i) and $CR_{M(i)}$ directly because he does not know a user's private key. The replay attack, using a stored modified block and the matched modification information, can be detected by the sequence number in the copyright information $CR_{M(i)}$ in the client side.

4. RELATED WORKS AND COMPARISON

Similar works related to the proposed scheme are the revision control system, encryption method, digital watermarking, DRM, and secure file system.

First, the revision control system (RCS) has the advantage that it eases the cooperation for modifying contents and controlling the modification history of the contents, and so the study on the revision control via the WWW is proposed recently [8]. However, in RCS, the user who modified the contents cannot have a right to his work and the contents are easy to be disclosed because of no encryption.

The simple encryption method can be used to keep contents secret when transmitting them. Although it enables to distribute the contents and the modification information securely, it does not protect a legal user from distributing the contents in the decrypted form.

Digital watermarking is the technique that inserts special invisible copyright information into the contents itself [1, 2, 3, 15]. In this method, the owner is guaranteed the ownership of the contents, but everyone can view contents because they are distributed without encryption.

Digital right management is the integrated technique that guarantees the right, confidence, security, and the integrity of contents [4, 5, 10, 14, 16]. But this only targets the creation and distribution of contents and does not support modifiable contents.

The techniques of secure file systems support the encryption in file system layer so that only legal users can see the file. Examples are the cryptographic file system [11], capability file names [12], and strong security for distributed file systems [9]. However, re-writing contents to another non-secure file system can make these systems useless.

Table 2: The data formats of other techniques.

	C_{server}	C_{send}	C_{client}
RCS	$M(1)\cdot M(2)\cdot\ldots\cdot M(n)$	$M(1)\cdot M(2)\cdot\ldots\cdot M(n)$	$M(1)\cdot M(2)\cdot\ldots\cdot M(n)$
Encryption Method	M	$E_{K(usr(pu))}\{M\}$	M
Digital Watermarking	M	$M\cdot CR_M$	$M\cdot CR_M$
DRM	M	$E_K\{M\}$	$E_K\{M\}$
Secure File System	$E_K\{M(1)\cdot M(2)\cdot\ldots\cdot M(n)\}$	$M(1)\cdot M(2)\cdot\ldots\cdot M(n)$	$E_K\{M(1)\cdot M(2)\cdot\ldots\cdot M(n)\}$
Bakker's method [13]	M	M	M

Bakker proposed a system preventing illegal distribution in a peer-to-peer environment [13]. This system traces the distribution of all the files in the globe distribution network and when the uploaded software turns out to be illegal, the system deletes all the files uploaded by that user and bans that user from uploading files. But this system cannot show the owner and the modification information of digital contents.

The data formats of these schemes are summarized in Table 2. RCS manages modified information at any time, and encryption method uses the contents encryption in transmission. Digital watermarking method distributes the contents inseparable from the copyright information, DRM distributes the contents as encrypted and secure file system manages modified information and encrypts it, but reveals the contents as unencrypted when transmitting.

Table 3 shows the comparison of our model with related works. Our scheme has the above four characteristics needed for protecting modifiable digital contents. The encryption method and secure file system have the capability that only legal users can read. The watermarking technique can manage copyright information and digital right management with only these two characteristics. The modification history can be managed in a revision control system. In Bakker's method, only the characteristic of finding the illegal distributor is supported.

Table 3: Comparison with related works.

	Capability that only legal user can read	Management of copyright	Management of modified history	Finding the illegal distributor
Proposed Idea	O	O	O	O
Revision Control System	X	X	O	X
Encryption Method	O	X	X	X
Digital Watermarking	X	O	X	X
DRM	O	O	X	X
Secure File System	O	X	X	X
Bakker's method [13]	X	X	X	O

5. CONCLUSIONS

In the paper, we proposed a scheme, called PCMHoDC, to protect the copyright and modification history of modifiable digital contents. We have shown the architecture, the data format of digital contents, and the communication protocols in order to manage the copyright and modification information. Based on the server-client architecture, we have given the role of protecting the modification to the modification manager application program (MMAP), that guarantees to store contents as encrypted and to show decrypted contents to a user. The server has the role of storing original and modified digital contents. The proposed scheme has more viable characteristics in protecting modifiable digital contents than any other related works like revision control system, digital watermarking, digital right management, or secure file system, etc.

ACKNOWLEDGEMENTS

This research is supported in part by the Ministry of Information & Communication of Korea, under the "Support Project of University Information Technology Research Center (ITRC)" supervised by KIPA.

REFERENCES

1. M. D. Swanson, M. Kobayashi and A. H. Tewfik, "Multimedia Data-Embedding and Watermarking Technologies," Proceedings of the IEEE, Vol. 86, No. 6, JUNE 1998.
2. J. Brassil, S. Low, N. Maxemchuk, L. O'Gorman, "Electronic Marking and Identification Techniques to Discourage Document Copying," IEEE J. Select. Areas Commun., vol. 13, pp 1495-1504, Oct 1995.
3. Http://www.watermarkingworld.org/webring.html
4. Http://www.microsoft.com/windows/windowsmedia/drm.asp
5. Http://cryptome.org/ms-drm-os.htm
6. T. Sander and C. F. Tschudin, "On software protection via function hiding," Lecture Notes in Computer Science, 1525:111–123, 1998.
7. Boaz Barak, Oded Goldreich, Russell Impagliazzo, Steven Rudich, Amit Sahai, Salil Vadhan, Ke Yang, "On the (Im)possibility of Obfuscating Programs," * Advances in Cryptology - CRYPTO `01, vol. 2139 of Lecture Notes in Computer Science, pp. 1-18, August 19-23, 2001.
8. Jurgen Reuter, Stefan U. Hngen, James J. Hunt, and Walter F. Tichy, "Distributed Revision Control Via the World Wide Web," In Proc. Sixth Intl. Workshop on Software Configuration Management, Berlin, Germany, March, 1996.
9. Ethan Miller, *et.al.*, "Strong Security for Distributed File Systems," the 20th International Performance, Computing, and Communications Conference (IPCCC2001).
10. Microsoft Digital Media Division, "Security Overview of Windows Media Rights Manager," September 2001.
11. Matt Blaze, "A Cryptographic File System for Unix," 1st ACM Conference on Communications and Computing Security, pages 9-16, November 1993.
12. Jude T.Regan and Christian D. Jensen, "Capability file names: Separating authorization from user management in an internet file system," In Proceedings of the 10th USENIX Security Symposium, pages 221-233, The USENIX association, August 2001.
13. A. Bakker, M. van Steen, and A. Tanenbaum, "A Law-Abiding Peer-to-Peer Network for Free-Software Distribution," In Proc. Int'l Symp. Network Computing and Applications, Cambridge, MA, Feb. 2002. IEEE.
14. Http://www.intertrust.com/main/research/whitepapers/IDCUnderstandingDRMSystems.pdf
15. C.I. Podilchuk and E.J. Delp, "Digital watermarking: Algorithms and applications," IEEE Signal Processing Magazine, vol. 18, no. 4, pp. 33–46, July 2001.
16. F. Hartung and F. Ramme, "Digital Rights Management and Watermarking of Multimedia Contents for M-Commerce Applications," IEEE Communications Magazine, vol. 38, no. 11, pp. 78-84, Nov. 2000, Invited paper.

USING KEYSTROKE ANALYSIS AS A MECHANISM FOR SUBSCRIBER AUTHENTICATION ON MOBILE HANDSETS

N.L. CLARKE*, S.M. FURNELL*, B. M. LINES* and P.L. REYNOLDS**

**info@network-research-group.org*
Network Research Group
Department of Communication and Electronic Engineering
University of Plymouth
PLYMOUTH
PL4 8AA
United Kingdom
Tel: +44 1752-233520   Fax: +44 1752-233520

*** Orange Personal Communications Services*
Bradley Stoke
BRISTOL
United Kingdom

Key words: Keystroke Analysis, User Authentication, Biometrics, Mobility.

Abstract: The next few years will witness the widespread introduction of third generation mobile networks, completing the transition from the purely telephony devices of the first generation analogue networks, into a multimedia mobile communications tool. The ability of these new handsets to store and access sensitive information such as financial records, digital certificates and company records in association with a large handset penetration (864 million subscribers) makes them a desirable target for impostors. The authentication technique for current mobile phones has many weaknesses from a technological and subscriber perspective, and as such non-intrusive and stronger subscriber authentication techniques are required. This study investigates the plausibility of one such technique that of keystroke analysis, comparing and contrasting a number of pattern recognition and neural network based approaches to classification. It was found that neural network-based approaches performed substantially better than the pattern recognition-based approaches with false acceptance and false rejection rates of 3.2%.

1. INTRODUCTION

The mobile communications sector has witnessed substantial growth in recent years with global mobile subscribers forecasted to rise from 864m in 2002 [1] to 1,848m by 2004 [2]. However, in parallel with this rise in ownership there has been a rise in mobile related abuse, with over 700,000 handsets stolen from subscribers in 2001, in the UK [3]. It can be conjectured that the more advanced capabilities of third generation handsets with their ability to pay for products using micro-payments and digital money, surf the internet, buy and sell stocks, transfer money and manage bank accounts will make the handsets even more desirable targets. Current authentication for handsets is achieved through a PIN (Personal Identification Number) approach, which relies heavily on the user to ensure its validity. For example, the subscriber should not use the default setting, tell other people, or write it down. Apart from the technological arguments, a recent survey into attitudes and opinions of mobile phone subscribers found that 45% of respondents thought the PIN to be inconvenient and did not use the facility [4]. The findings also demonstrated the user's awareness of the security implications, with 81% of respondents in support for more security.

Approaches to the verification of an identity can be achieved in one of three ways. Something the user *knows, has* or *is* [5]. The first approach is a secret-knowledge technique identical to the PIN and will therefore be just as inconvenient. The second is based on the user having to carry a token. However, due to the very nature of a mobile handset it is likely to remain within the handset permanently and thus diminished any security the token would provide (for example, subscriber's use of the SIM). The last approach, commonly termed as biometrics, is based on some unique characteristic feature of a person and includes physiological characteristics such as, fingerprints and hand geometry and behavioural traits such as a person's voice and signature. Another behavioural biometric is keystroke analysis which measures the typing characteristic of a user. In this context it has a number of advantages including a keypad that already resides on the device and the possible non-intrusive application of the technique thereby reducing user inconvenience. This paper will compare and contrast the performance of a number of pattern recognition and neural network approaches to solving the problem of keystroke analysis on a mobile handset keypad.

2. KEYSTROKE ANALYSIS

The principal concept behind keystroke analysis is the ability of the system to recognise patterns, such as characteristic rhythms, during keyboard interactions. In particular, this study utilises the time between two successive keystrokes (known as a digraph pair) and is referred to as the inter-keystroke latency. Classification is achieved by comparing an input sample against a reference template for the claimed user and given sufficient similarity the input sample is deemed to have come from the authorised user. The reference template is securely acquisitioned from the user when they enrolled on the system initially. However this template matching process gives rise to a characteristic performance plot between the two main error rates governing biometrics, the False Acceptance Rate (FAR), or the rate at which an impostor is accepted by the system, and the False Rejection Rate (FRR), or the rate at which the authorised user is rejected from the system. A third error rate known as the Equal Error Rate (EER) is used as a comparative measure between biometric techniques and equates to the mean value of the FAR and FRR [6].

A significant amount of prior research has been conducted in this domain, dating back to the 1980s. However, all of these studies have focused upon alphabetic inputs from a standard PC keyboard. Little work to date has considered the application of keystroke analysis to a mobile handset keypad, which has obvious tactile and interoperability differences. A previous feasibility study by the authors [7] has demonstrated promising results. However, the classification algorithm was an un-optimised neural network classifier. It is the aim of this paper to present a number of classification algorithms, including optimised neural network configurations, in order to define the most appropriate classifier for this particular problem.

3. CLASSIFICATION ALGORITHMS

Previous researchers have utilised a number of pattern recognition approaches such as linear and non-linear distance techniques [8], z-tests [12] and Bayesian classifiers [16], with more recent research efforts focussing on the use of neural network approaches [14-16]. A number of these techniques were selected on the basis of providing a broad range of classification techniques and this section will give a brief outline of them. For more detailed information and analysis of the techniques refer to references [8, 12, 18-22].

- *Mean & Standard Deviation Algorithm.*

  This is a traditional pattern recognition algorithm [8], based on the assumption that users keystroke latencies for a given digraph pair will be similar within an acceptable tolerance. A mean and standard deviation is calculated from the user's reference profile for the most regular digraph pairs which is used in comparing against an unseen input vector. If a sufficient number of digraph pair keystroke latencies reside within the tolerance envelope then the user is deemed to be the authorised user, if not, then an impostor.
- *Z-Test*

  The z-test is a statistical hypothesis test which can be used to establish whether an input vector comes from a particular sample population or not. The test assumes the sample size is large, so that the central limit theorem applies and we can use the normal distribution and assume that the sample standard deviation is an estimate of the population standard deviation. The null and alternative hypotheses are defined as:

  Null Hypothesis, H_0:
  Reference Profile Mean, μ_x = Input Vector Mean, μ_o
  Alternative Hypothesis, H_1:
  Reference Profile Mean, $\mu_x \neq$ Input Vector Mean, μ_o

  The z-test investigation is a two-tailed test and will vary the level of significance, α in order to determine the most efficient level in terms of the performance rates.
- *Euclidean Distance Algorithm*

  The Euclidean distance algorithm is a linear minimum distance technique that computes the Euclidean distance between an input vector and reference profile. If the distance is within a predefined tolerance level then the input vector is deemed to have come from the authorised user, if not then an impostor. The Euclidean distance is calculated using:

  $\| x - m_k \|$ Where x = input vector; m_k = reference profile

  Here $\| u \|$ is called the norm of the vector u and corresponds to different ways of measuring distance. The Euclidean metric is calculated using:

  $$\| u \| = (u_1^2 + u_2^2 + u_3^2 + \dots u_d^2)^{\frac{1}{2}}$$

- *Mahalanobis Distance Algorithm*

  The Mahalanobis distance algorithm is a non-linear minimum distance technique which uses the same mechanism as the Euclidean algorithm but with a difference technique for measuring the distance. The Mahalanobis metric is calculated using:

$$r^2 = (x - m_x)^T C^{-1} (x - m_x)$$

  In principal the non-linear problem solving abilities of the Mahalanobis classifier should provide better decision boundaries and improve the performance over the Euclidean algorithm.

- *Feed-Forward Multi-Layered Perceptron (FF MLP) Neural Network*

  A FF MLP utilising a backpropagation training algorithm are best known for their pattern associative properties. Patten associative networks work by training the network to respond in a certain way given a certain input sample and backpropagation training is mathematically proven to converge towards the most optimal results [20]. However great care needs to be taken to ensure the training data is representational of the problem the network is to solve.

  Unfortunately FF MLP networks have no rules governing what the network parameters need to be given a certain complexity of classification problem. As such trial and error approaches are often utilised in order to achieve the most desirable performance rates.

- *Radial Basis Function (RBF) Neural Network*

  RBF networks are very similar mathematically to MLP networks in that they both provide techniques for approximating arbitrary non-linear functional mappings between multi-dimensional spaces. An advantage of RBF over FF MLP is their ease of implementation with only two network parameters to define, i.e., the mean sum-squared error and the spread of the radial basis neurons. The network works on the principle of transforming the input space into a higher dimensionality in the likelihood that it will be more linearly separable [20].

- *Generalised Regression Neural Network (GRNN)*

  GRNNs are another network topology often used for function approximation tasks and have a similar network paradigm to the RBF networks. GRNNs are again useful because of their ease of implementation and in particular their speed of training. A potential disadvantage is the one-to-one mapping of training vectors to radial basis neurons resulting in a large and computationally complex network with large training datasets.

- *Learning Vector Quantisation (LVQ) Neural Network*
  LVQ networks are a supervised version of vector quantisation [22] designed for adaptive pattern classification. The network paradigm utilises a competitive layer which will automatically learn to classify input samples similar to an unsupervised clustering technique, however the LVQ network also has a mechanism to transform the competitive layer classes into target classifications defined by the user. This technique was used with notable success in [16].

Each of the classification techniques implements an identical mechanism for the evaluation of valid and impostor input samples, so that a fair comparison of the approaches can be achieved. The correct or false acceptance of a user is based not on the success or failure of individual digraphs but on a complete input sample.

4. EXPERIMENTAL PROCEDURE

The eventual application of keystroke analysis to a mobile phone would ideally authenticate a user by monitoring their use of the phone, during activities such as the entry of telephone numbers, use of the menu system, and composition of text messages. However, the objective at this stage is to investigate a number of classification techniques rather than to provide a complete solution to the problem. As such, the initial study has been confined to two types of data, namely:

1. Entry of a fixed four-digit number, analogous to the PINs used on many current systems.
2. Entry of a fixed eleven-digit number, analogous to the telephone numbers in which you would enter on a handset.

A total of sixteen test subjects were asked to enter the data for both sets of data thirty times. Twenty of these inputs were utilised in the generation of the reference profile, with the remaining ten used as validation samples. The pattern classification tests were performed with one user acting as the valid authorised user, whist all the other users are acting as impostors. A specially written application was used to collect the sample data.

A standard numerical keypad on a PC keyboard was not deemed to be an appropriate means of data entry, as it differs from a mobile handset in terms of both feel and layout, and users would be likely to exhibit a markedly different style when entering the data. As such, the data capture was performed using a modified mobile phone handset, interfaced to a PC through the keyboard connection.

5. RESULTS

An analysis of the input data allows an insight into the complexities of successfully authenticating a person from a single input vector of latency values. The problem is that latency vectors observed from a single user may incorporate a fairly large spread of values and as such do not exist on clearly definable classification regions. Figure 1 illustrates some similar and dissimilar input vectors as an indication of the difficulties the pattern classification techniques have in discriminating between users.

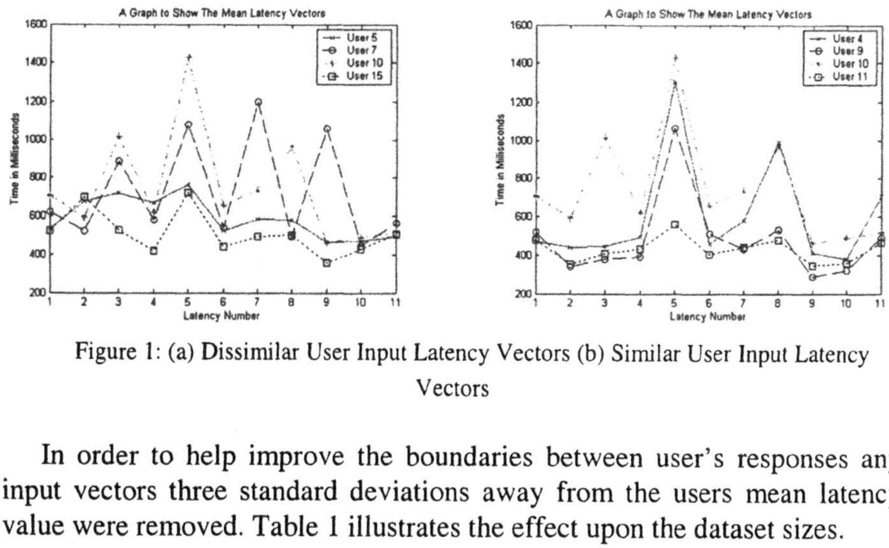

Figure 1: (a) Dissimilar User Input Latency Vectors (b) Similar User Input Latency Vectors

In order to help improve the boundaries between user's responses any input vectors three standard deviations away from the users mean latency value were removed. Table 1 illustrates the effect upon the dataset sizes.

Input	Original # of Samples	Modified # of Samples	Training Dataset Size	Validation Dataset Size
4-Digit	30	26	18	8
11-Digit	30	21	14	7

Table 1: Training & Validation Dataset

Figures 2 and 3 illustrate the results of the comparison of the various classification techniques. The most successful pattern recognition technique with the 4-digit input was the Euclidean technique, with an EER of 14.2%, followed by the mean and standard deviation algorithm, with an EER of 17.7%. Conversely, with the 11-digit input, the mean and standard deviation algorithm performed most successfully with an EER of 17.9%, followed by the Euclidean technique with an EER of 21.2%. The worst classifier with both the 4-digit and 11-digit inputs was the Mahalanobis algorithm, with EERs of 19.3% and 28.7% respectively. This is somewhat unusual as the Mahalanobis distance algorithms performance was significantly inferior to its linear distance (Euclidean) counterpart. Re-testing both the Euclidean and Mahalanobis algorithms with the validation dataset replaced with the training dataset found that the performance of the Mahalanobis algorithm superseded the Euclidean as would be expect due to the non-linear boundaries it can form. The fact it does not perform as well using the validation dataset would suggest the more general boundaries produced by the Euclidean technique are more appropriate to the complete dataset, indicating the training dataset may not be as representative as required.

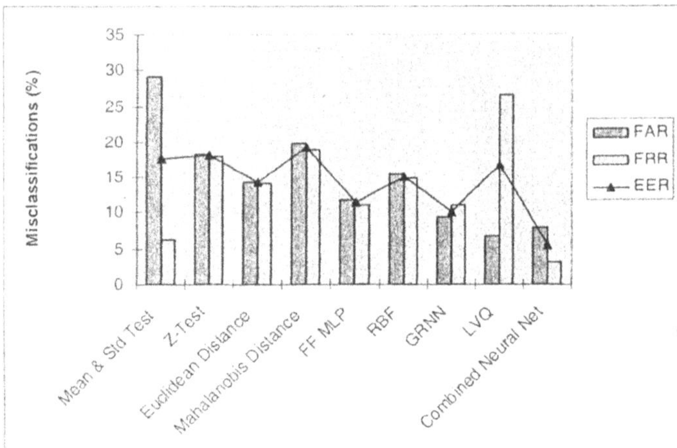

Figure 2: Classification Results for the 4-Digit Input

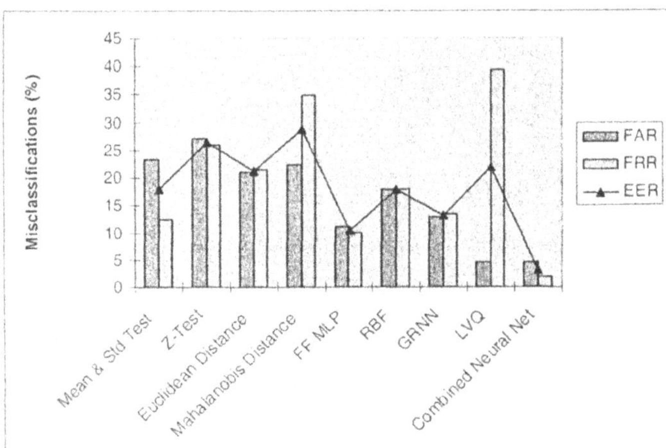

Figure 3: Classification Results for the 11-Digit Input

Overall it was the neural network based approaches that performed best, significantly improving the performance rates. The GRNN was most successful with the 4-digit input achieving a EER of 10.1%, followed by the FF MLP with an EER of 11.3%. Conversely again this role was reversed with the 11-digit input, as the FF MLP was the most successful, obtaining an EER of 10.4%, with the GRNN achieving an EER of 13.1%.

Analysis showed that individual user's performance varied with the different neural network techniques, with some users performing better on one than another. As such a combined neural network technique was created using the best result achieved by each user in any of the neural based techniques, resulting in the classifier achieving an EER of 5.5% and 3.2% with the 4-digit and 11-digit inputs respectively – by far the best result achieved thus far.

As both the 4-digit and 11-digit inputs represent a static keystroke analysis approach, in that they discriminate users based on a identical input string, an extension to the investigation was sought that provided a dynamic approach, in order to gauge the viability. As such 16 participants entered 50 random telephone numbers, which after outliers were removed decreased to 38 (26 for training and 12 for validation). A larger dataset was utilised so that more training data was available due to the more difficult task of discriminating users based on varying input vectors. The results, as would be expected, show the performance of the classification algorithms to be far poorer than the static-based techniques, with the best performance being achieved by the feed-forward MLP with an EER of 24.8%. Using the combined neural network technique the EER reduces to 16.1%.

6. DISCUSSION

The investigations have shown the ability for classification algorithms to correctly discriminate between users with a relatively good degree of success, with neural network approaches performing significantly better than their pattern recognition counterparts. The general performance of the 4-digit input vector, (analogous to the PIN) suggests that the entering of a PIN number on a mobile handset has a quite unique dialling pattern, perhaps due to user's previous experience of having to enter such short sequences on a regular basis. Classification algorithms typically find verification simpler when the input vector is larger, as it will typically contain more discriminative information. Overall, this was not the case, with the 4-digit input outperforming the 11-digit input, suggesting that although the user's entry of a fixed 11-digit number is more consistent than for a variable series of numbers, it is not as fluid as the 4-digit PIN input.

From an analysis of the classification algorithms, it is clear that some of the individual network performances experienced 40%+ false acceptance and false rejection rates. This would indicate two problems. Firstly, a user's input varies too considerably from input to input for even a static keystroke analysis technique to prove useful, or secondly, the classifier may not be sensitive enough to the users' data. Both of these problems could be counteracted as the user enters more and more data to the classification engine. However, this error rate is currently unsatisfactory in a mobile operator context and further developments will need to monitor the individual error rates not only the average. Conversely, a number of classifiers (particularly the neural network based techniques) experienced a number of users achieving an FAR and FRR of 0%, reiterating the ability for user's keypad interactions to be discriminative.

Although the static-based classifiers were relatively successful, any effective implementation of keystroke analysis would depend on the ability to provide dynamic-based classification in order to provide non-intrusive, ad hoc authentication. Although the results for dynamic-based classification have been poor in comparison with a static approach they are nevertheless encouraging, especially considering the small datasets with which the classifier was trained and validated. It may also be possible to improve dynamic authentication performance by utilising the more static elements of a varying input such as the area code of a telephone number, thereby reducing the number of varying telephone numbers that could be entered.

The mutually exclusive relationship that exists between the false acceptance and false rejection mean that it would be unlikely for both error rates to achieve near 0% simultaneously [23]. Therefore, the study suggests the best implementation of a keystroke analysis authentication technique would be as a larger hybrid authentication algorithm, involving two or more non-intrusive biometric authentication techniques, such as utilising voice recognition during a voice call, and facial recognition during a video conference.

7. CONCLUSIONS & FUTURE WORK

The implementation employed in this study has focussed on the feasibility of a keystroke analysis technique using a number of classification algorithms. Although neural network approaches have clearly outperformed the traditional pattern recognition techniques, the variability of the results in and between the neural network approaches means that much scope remains for fine tuning the networks – especially if larger and more representative input data were made available, with a larger group of participants. In particular, the most successful algorithm implemented in this study was the combined neural network, but the use of such a technique in practicality is difficult, as training the user iteratively on a wide spread of networks is computational intense and time consuming. In order for this technique to be of any practical relevance it would be necessary to develop an algorithm for analysing a user's input data and (dependant on its complexity) decide which network was most relevant.

This study used keypad interactions exclusively linked with dialling numbers. However the use of mobile handsets for data services such as SMS (Short Message Service) messaging, and other mobile related interactions such as the menu system, opens the possibility of authenticating a user by other means such as the way in which they type words and characters. Additionally, recent research has shown that using classification algorithms that utilise both the inter-keystroke time and hold-time (the time taken to press and release a single key) has more distinct and thus discriminative information than the traditional inter-keystroke timings used in this study [16, 24].

8. REFERENCES

[1] Cellular Online. September 2002. www.cellular.co.za

[2] Giussani, B. 2001. Roam – Making Sense of the Wireless Internet. Random House Business Books, London, UK.

[3] BBC. 2002. "Huge surge in mobile phone thefts", BBC News Report, 8th January 2002. http://news/bbc.co.uk/hi/english/uk/newsid_1748000/1748258.htm

[4] Clarke, N.L., Furnell, S.M., Rodwell, P.M. and Reynolds, P.L. 2002. "Acceptance of subscriber authentication methods for mobile telephony devices". Computers & Security, vol. 21, no.3, pp. 220-228.

[5] Wood, H.M. 1978. "The Use of Passwords for controlling the Access to Remote Computer Systems and Services". Computers & Security, vol. 3.

[6] Ashbourn, J. 2000. *Biometric. Advanced Identity Verification. The Complete Guide*. Springer.

[7] Clarke, N.L., Furnell, S.M., Lines, B., Reynolds, P.L. 2002. "Subscriber Authentication for Mobile Phones using Keystroke Dynamics". Proceedings of the Third International Network Conference (INC 2002), Plymouth, UK. pp.347-355.

[8] Umphress D., Williams, G. 1985. "Identity Verification through Keyboard Characteristics". International Journal of Man-Machine Studies, vol. 23, pp. 263-273.

[9] Leggett, J., Williams, G. 1987. "Verifying Identity via Keystroke Dynamics". International Journal of Man-Machine Studies, vol. 28, pp 67-76.

[10] Joyce, R., Gupta, G. 1990. "Identity Authorisation Based on Keystroke Latencies". Communications of the ACM, 33(2): 168-176.

[11] Brown, M., Rogers, J. 1993. "User Identification via Keystroke Characteristics of Typed Names using Neural Networks". International Journal of Man-Machine Studies, vol. 39, pp 999-1014.

[12] Napier, R., Laverty, W., Mahar, D., Henderson, R., Hiron, M., Wagner, M. 1995. "Keyboard User Verification: Toward an Accurate, Efficient and Ecologically Valid Algorithm". International Journal of Human-Computer Studies, vol.43, pp 213-222.

[13] Monrose, R., Rubin, A. 1999. "Keystroke Dynamics as a Biometric for Authentication". Future Generation Computer Systems, 16(4) pp 351-359.

[14] Cho, S., Han, C., Han D., Kin, H. 2000. "Web Based Keystroke Dynamics Identity Verification Using Neural Networks". Journal of Organisational Computing & Electronic Commerce, vol. 10, pp 295-307.

[15] Obaidat, M., Macchairolo, D. 1994. "A Multilayer Neural Network System for Computer Access Security". IEEE Transactions on Systems, Man, and Cybernetics, vol. 24, no. 5, pp. 806-813.

[16] Obaidat M., Sadoun, B. 1997. "Verification of Computer Uses Using Keystroke Dynamics". IEEE Transactions on Systems, Man, and Cybernetics – Part B: Cybernetics, vol. 27, no. 2, pp.261-269.

[17] Ord, T., Furnell, S. 2000. "User Authentication for Keypad-Based Devices using Keystroke Analysis". MSc Thesis, University of Plymouth, UK.

[18] Triola, M. 1998. *Elementary Statistics (7th Edition)*. Addison Wesley.

[19] Hogg, R., Ledolter, J. 1989. *Engineering Statistics*. Macmillan Publishing.

[20] Bishop, M. 1995. *Neural Networks for Pattern Classification*. Oxford University Press.

[21] Haykin, S. 1999. *Neural Networks: A Comprehensive Foundation (2nd Edition)*. Prentice Hall.

[22] Kohonen, T. 1997. *Self Organising Maps*. Springer.

[23] Cope, B. 1990. "Biometric Systems of Access Control". Electrotechnology, April/May: 71-74.

[24] Robinson, J., Liang, V., Chambers, J., MacKenzie, C. 1998. "Computer User Verification Using Login String Keystroke Dynamics". IEEE Transactions on Systems, Man, and Cybernetics – Part A: Systems and Humans, vol. 28, no.2, pp. 236-241.

INTRODUCING PKI TO ENHANCE SECURITY IN FUTURE MOBILE NETWORKS

Georgios Kambourakis, Angelos Rouskas and Stefanos Gritzalis
Department of Information and Communication Systems Engineering, University of the Aegean, Samos 83200, Greece

Abstract Current wireless network standards perform user authentication, signaling and data encryption, as well as message integrity protection, by utilizing only symmetric key methods. However, as mobile networks are evolving into full-IP and the communication is envisaged to change from second generation (2G) person-to-person model to fourth generation (4G) machine-to-machine model, there is greater demand to provide more flexible, reconfigurable and scalable security mechanisms that can advance in a many-to-many trust relationship model. Employing public key methods in many-to-many schemes drops the requirement for a secure channel to transfer keys between two communication parties, thus providing the appropriate scalability to the whole system. With a large number of different network technologies and operators, expected in the future mobile communications environment, that should frequently and seamlessly interwork with each other, and a constantly increasing population of communication parties, capturing the full benefits of open channel key transfers and scaling public key methods requires Public Key Infrastructure (PKI). In this paper, we discuss and investigate different ways to take advantage of a proposed PKI system. From the network side, we investigate how PKI can provide future inter/intra mobile core network security, while from the user's perspective we present solutions that far enhance authentication procedures and end-to-end communication model trust. We show that PKI offers the appropriate framework to overcome symmetric key based security inefficiencies, providing powerful solutions to protect both network core signaling and user's data from potential intruders.

Keywords: PKI; Mobile Networks; IKE; Network Domain Security; SSL/TLS; IPsec

1. INTRODUCTION

An identified security weakness in 2G systems is the absence of security in the core network. Originally, this was not a problem, since 2G networks were closed networks with very little interworking among different 2G operators and between 2G operators and the Internet. Nevertheless, in a future wireless communication environment, like 3G and beyond, that will require frequent interworking of many different network technologies and providers, there will also be a greater need for advanced security protection. Moreover, the introduction of IP, used not only for signaling traffic, but also for user traffic, as the network layer in the GPRS backbone network and later in the UMTS network domain, raises further reasons to worry about. The introduction of IP states not only a shift towards packet switching, but also a shift towards completely open and easily accessible networks. From a security point of view, a whole new set of threats and risks must be faced. For example, in next generation systems the protection of the core network signaling protocols will be a clear and essential requirement.

The adaptation of Public Key Infrastructure elements in future wireless networks will substitute long-term symmetric key relationships, with a flexible, reconfigurable and scalable public key based mechanism. This will not only provide the appropriate level of inter/intra operator trust, but it will also offer solutions that far enhance user-to-network confidence and end-to-end security options.

The rest of this paper is organized as follows. In Section 2, we provide an overview of the current 3G-inter/intra security options and explain how PKI can adapt to existing architecture. In Section 3, we propose and analyze some solutions that can be implemented, to provide inter/intra operator trust, user-to-network and end-to-end security by taking advantage of PKI. Finally, the paper is concluded in Section 4.

2. EXISTING 3G CORE NETWORK SECURITY AND PKI

2.1 Overview of 3G Inter/Intra network Security

Global Mobile System (GSM) and Universal Mobile Telecommunication System (UMTS) networks (Figure 1), use Mobile Application Part (MAP) protocol for the exchange of signaling messages between network Elements (NEs). User profile exchange, authentication, and mobility management are performed using MAP. MAP runs typically over the Signaling System Number 7 (SS7) protocol stack.

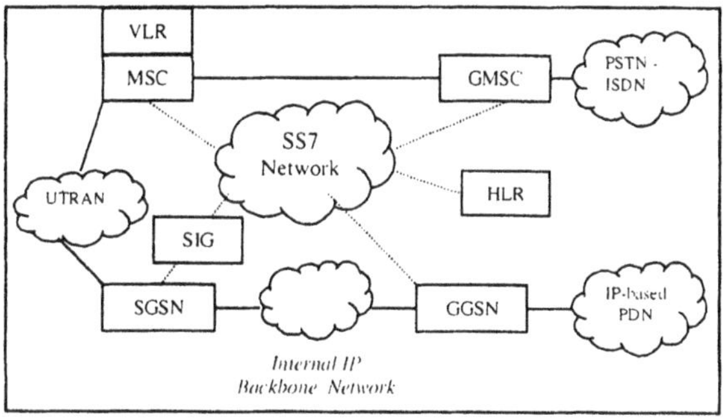

Figure 1. UMTS Architecture

3GPP has also defined a mechanism for protecting the MAP protocol at the application layer [1], [2]. MAP may also be protected at the network layer when IP is used as the transport protocol. However, when internetworking with networks using SS7-based transport is necessary, protection at the application layer shall be used. For this reason a new protocol header has been developed to protect MAP messages, much in the same way as the Encapsulating Security Payload (ESP) protocol protects IP packets. This new protocol is called MAPsec. While MAP runs over SS7, MAPsec and Internet Key Exchange (IKE) always run over IP (Figure 2). Therefore, it is assumed that nodes implementing MAPsec always have IP connectivity in addition to SS7 connectivity [2]. In the 3GPP architecture MAPsec is typically running between two different network operators, and the same Security Associations (SAs) are shared by a number of NEs. The necessary MAPsec-SAs between networks are negotiated between the respective Key Administration Centers (KACs) of the networks.

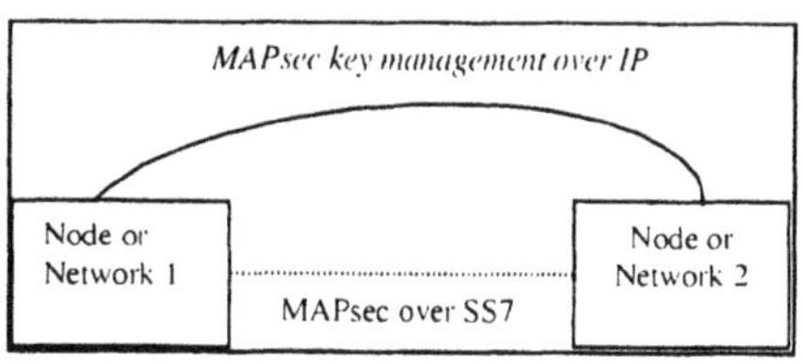

Figure 2. Architecture for MAPsec Security

On the other hand, for native IP protocols, as in the GPRS backbone network [3], security shall be provided at the network layer. The security protocols to be used are the IETF defined IPsec suite [4]. The UMTS network domain control plane is sectioned into security domains, which typically coincide with operator borders. The borders between the security domains are protected by Security Gateways (SEGs) as shown in Figure 3.

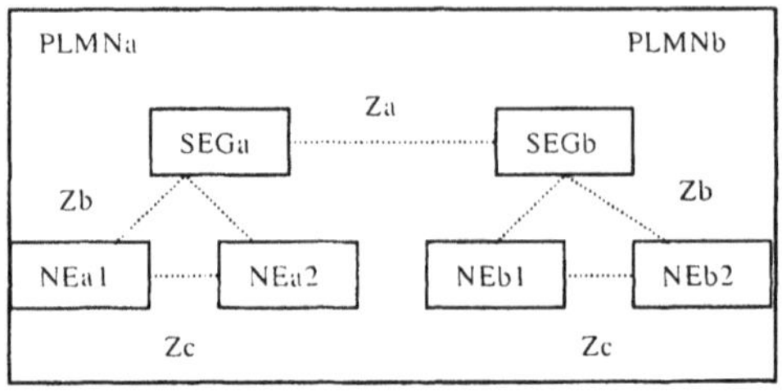

Figure 3. Network Domain architecture for IP-based protocols. (Dashed lines represent IKE connections)

All network domain traffic shall pass though a SEG before entering or leaving the security domain. Taking that into account, Network Domain Security (NDS)/IP will only support tunnel mode IPsec SAs, ESP and main mode. SEGs shall offer capabilities for secure storage of long term keys used for IKE authentication, so NDS/IP will only support Internet Security Association and Key Management Protocol (ISAKMP) SAs with pre-shared keys [5].

Only the inter-security domain SA IKE negotiations over the Za interface shall be mandatory, while the Zb interface is optional. Concluding, there is normally no NE-to-NE interface for NE belonging to different security domains.

2.2 Adding PKI to mobile networks

As we already mentioned, proposals and technical specifications for core network security in 3G, are based on IPsec. Agreements on keys and security associations are carried out on a bilateral basis between operators. Taking into account that the number of network elements of each operator increases and that the interworking between a high number of networks of different technologies will be more intense, a more scalable solution would be to replace those relationships with a PKI [6], [7]. So secure communications can be achieved without having to generate and distribute long-term secret keys.

Comparing an asymmetric key system with a symmetric one, we note the following:

- The number of keys needed in a symmetric key system with n network elements communicating with each other is $O(n^2)$. On the other hand, in a public cryptosystem, the corresponding need for keys is $O(n)$. Therefore, when n increases, the costs in terms of key generation and distribution associated with the introduction of a new network element are quite different. In the symmetric model, we need to establish n new secret keys, while in the asymmetric case we only need 2 new keys (private + public) for any new network element.

- Pre-shared secrets are a rather inflexible way to provide authentication. A properly designed PKI, which supports digital certificates, will offer more dynamic, flexible and scalable mechanisms to issue certificates for new network elements and to revoke certificates that are no longer valid.
- One basic requirement and assumption in both GSM and UMTS, is that the Home Environment (HE) has to trust the Serving Network (SN), e.g. for the Authentication and Key Agreement (AKA) procedure. However, in future systems, where many different technologies, owned by different network operators, must frequently and seamlessly interwork, this is no longer the case. By introducing a Trusted Third Party (TTP) the requirement for bilateral trust is reduced.
- PKI can be used for authentication and symmetric key encapsulation and transport procedures, while derived symmetric session keys can be used to support confidentiality. Thus, we can by-pass the known public key cryptosystem disadvantages of key lengths and computational load.
- From the user scope, the implementation of public key algorithms in Mobile Stations (MSs) had been considered to be resource demanding. However, the increased processing requirements of IP capable terminals have driven towards high power computational platforms, which are now becoming ordinary in wireless devices. In addition, advanced standards such MExE and WAP have also moved forward to introduce public key methods. This development strengthens the assertion that PKI has become an acknowledged component of standards that deal with many-to-many, complex relationships.

Furthermore, as IP-based networks are introduced to serve a large variety of applications, that may involve many and different network/service operators, complex and flexible communication relationships are necessary, which in turn demand a complex trust model. In many cases, the communication parties may not have pre-arranged security agreements. So, in order unknown partners perform mutual authentication and establish session keys, a public key based digital signature that is supported by a PKI will satisfy security needs. For example, a Session Initiation Protocol (SIP) registration server, either proxy or redirect [3], may not share any symmetric key with the User Equipment (UE). Instead, a digital signature may be an appropriate way to authenticate the proxy server.

Certainly, the support of asymmetric key services by a wireless network requires the adaptation of some PKI elements, which are not necessarily part of the speculated network core. Figure 4 depicts the necessary PKI elements that should be included in the UMTS architecture.

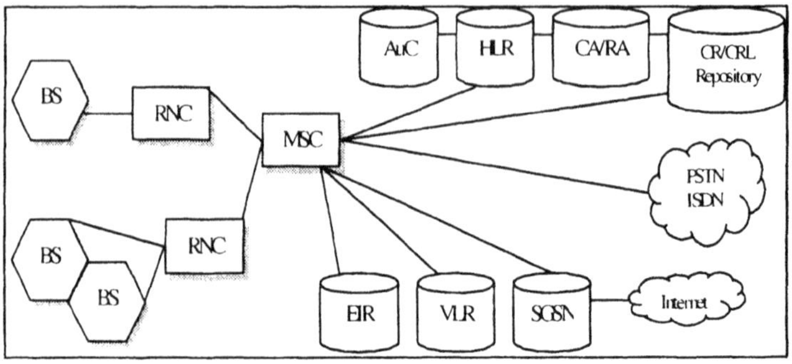

Figure 4. UMTS architecture and PKI

More specifically, we assume the following:

- There is some sort of Certification Authority (CA/RA) per Public Land Mobile Network (PLMN) operator, which issues and revokes certificates. A Registration Authority (RA) can offload the CA with certain functions i.e. establish and confirm identities of a new network element, generate keying material, perform certain key/certificate life cycle functions etc.
- There is one-at-least digital certificate database, which stores all the digital certificates and is being managed by the PLMN's CA.
- There is one at least revoked certificates database (CRL-database), which is being managed by the PLMN's CA and is accessible from all network elements that belong to the mobile network core.
- Web servers or FTP servers can be used to store certificates and CRLs. Certificate revocation can be periodic or Online Certificate Status Protocol (OCSP) based [8].
- CAs, which belongs to different PLMN's issue (off-line) cross-reference certificates for inter-PLMN trust relationships [8]. For example in the case of two PLMNs with the corresponding certification authorities CA_a & CA_b, CA_a issues $Cert(CA_a)CA_a$[1] (the root certificate) and $Cert(CA_b)CA_a$. Respectively, CA_b issues $Cert(CA_b)CA_b$ and $Cert(CA_a)CA_b$.
- Cross-Reference certificates are cached in local Security Gateways SEGs (which probably implement firewall policies among other things) on the borders of IP security domains. Every PLMN can use one or more SEG, in order to balance inter network traffic.
- Every network element possesses a key pair (private + public), and the corresponding digital certificate (intra-operator trust). NE's private key and the public key of the local CA are stored locally in a secure manner.
- If we are planning to extend PKI usage to the user, primarily for authentication and symmetric key encapsulation, we can assume the following:

---

[1] Cert(X)y = Public key certificate of X with format X.509v3 (or subset) issued by Y.

- The USIM-4G smart card should be a crypto-card with good pseudo-random (or random) generation capabilities and in-built crypto accelerator chip.
- Every subscriber possesses a key pair and his private key is stored in his USIM-4G card. The keys are associated with the user at registration time.
- Furthermore, the USIM-4G card is pre-loaded with all the CA's public keys, which exist in the particular PLMN.

3. PROPOSED PKI SOLUTIONS

3.1 PKI-based Intra/Inter Future Network Domain Security

With network domain security we mainly mean secure communications between network elements. Thus, by introducing a PKI to a future wireless network we can use powerful protocols to protect signaling and user traffic both between inter-network and intra network elements.

Three connections have to be protected as shown in Figure 3:

1. Za or SEG-to-SEG (inter-operator security),
2. Zb or SEG-to-NE (intra-operator security) and
3. Zc or NE-to-NE (intra-operator security).

One candidate for this task is IPsec [9], and IKE in particular. As we already mentioned, 3GPP currently uses pre-shared secrets for IKE phase I. This means that each NE has to be configured with a password that is associated with the remote system's IP address being authenticated. Note, however, that the keys to be used for encryption and authentication (SKEYID_*), after the completion of phase I, have been generated solely based on the peer's IP address [10]. So, in scenarios where the IP address is dynamic, the responder cannot maintain pre-shared secrets indexed by an IP address that may not be known at that time. Remote access solutions are an example where the initiator's IP address may be different for each connection (road-warrior cases) [9]. Additionally, the main drawback in pre-shared secret key authentication is the lack of a secure and scalable mechanism for exchanging pre-shared secret keys. That is appropriate only in a rather small-scale environment with a restrained number of systems, in which the set of peers is known in advance. However, if a pre-shared secret key is compromised, there is no universal method to alert the peer and launch a replacement.

An alternative solution based on PKI, can overcome these shortcomings. According to this, IKE is used for key exchange over the Za, Zb and Zc interfaces, while the authentication could be based on digital signatures with certificates instead of pre-shared secrets. The sequence of messages for this procedure is shown in Figure 5.

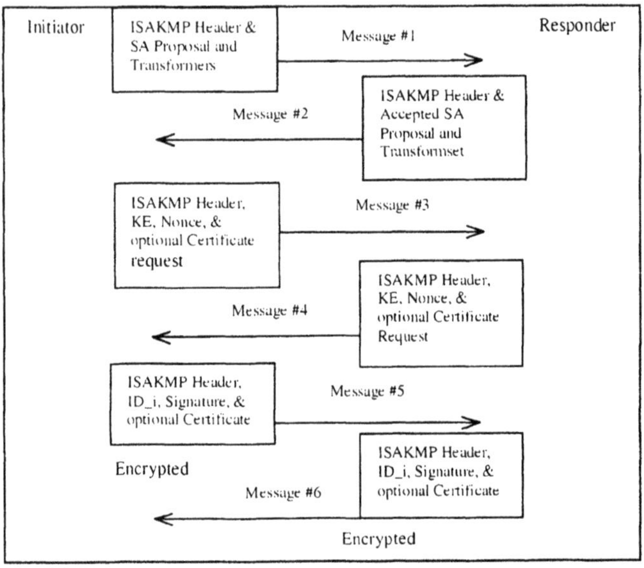

Figure 5. Main mode with digital signature

We note that, in such a case, the keys to be used for encryption and message authentication are generated based solely on the peer's nonce and Diffie-Hellman key value (SKEID = prf[2] (Nonce_i | Nonce_r, DH_Key). For system authentication, a certificate request can be included to obtain the public key of the peer if the initiator does not already have it. The peer must have the other's public key to validate the signature and authenticate the peer in the third exchange (messages 5 & 6). Also, the use of certificates in such a scheme provides for non-repudiation [8], [10].

Another solution, which benefits by the incorporation of PKI, is the use of SSL/TLS to protect communications between security gateways and probably between NEs. SSL/TLS is a flexible, session-oriented protocol that provides security at the transport layer, a higher layer in the TCP/IP stack than IP [11]. SSL/TLS has many of the advantages of IPsec and the successful introduction of the protocol in the wired Internet has proved its usability and effectiveness. Likewise, SSL/TLS can be part of an all-IP mobile environment. In this context, we provide below a short description of

[2] Pseudo random function

the necessary SSL/TLS handshake protocol message exchanges between SEGa and SEGb, to protect the borders of different operators.

1. SEGa, acting as a client, initiates the connection with a Hello message, which contains SEGa's security options and a session ID.
2. SEGb, acting as a server, replies with its Hello message. If SEGb support cryptographic and compression methods common to SEGa, those are included in its message. Otherwise, the connection is terminated. In addition, SEGb sends its 32-bit random number and a session ID. If the latter is equal to SEGa's session ID it is implied that the parties are going to use security parameters agreed on a previous session (this is the session resumption option, which considerably speeds-up the overall process [11]. Otherwise, SEGb generates a fresh session ID number denoting a new connection.
3. SEGb sends its digital certificate to SEGa, along with the appropriate cross-certificate, in a certificate chain and requests SEGa's certificate, concluding its part of negotiation with a HelloDone Message.
4. Once SEGb's certificate and cross-certificate have been validated, SEGa generates a pre-master secret, encrypts it using SEGb's public key and sends the encapsulated key to SEGb.
5. SEGb validates SEGa's certificate chain and decrypts the pre-master secret by using its private key.
6. Both parties convert the pre-master secret into master secret. The master key will be used for ciphering and MAC computations.
7. SEGa and SEGb send CipherSpec + Finished messages to each other. Note that the finished messages are cryptographically and integrity protected making use of previously negotiated parameters.

3.2 PKI and wireless network user benefits

From the user's side, a PKI can support the appropriate reconfigurable infrastructure, which offers great flexibility and scalability in an all-IP wireless environment. In this way, we can provide for authentication and end-to-end security solutions, which far enhance the user's trust, in a continuously evolving environment.

It is still a common misbelief, that mobile devices are not ready for "hungry", in terms of memory and processing power, public key computations. However, that is partially true, since contemporary wireless devices are featuring advanced architectures with StrongArm processors up to 206MHz, memory capacities of 64MB RAM and 32MB ROM, support for java applications and strong operating systems which can support a variety of applications and protocols. Besides that, these trends has also driven smart cards toward more advanced architectures, all the way to where we are beginning to see 32-bit RISC-based ARM processors in smart cards.

These cards based on such modern chips from companies like Atmel and Infineon are just appearing in the market, and they can effectively store and protect the subscriber's private key, generate good pseudo-random values and take over of symmetric key (un)wrapping functions [8]. The mobile's device processor can efficiently carry out the rest of the calculations, needed by protocols like IPsec and SSL/TLS. Last but not least, wireless network speed is continuously increasing, thus offering the necessary bandwidth.

In an IP-enabled mobile device with the aforesaid characteristics, IPsec, can effectively secure authentication and user traffic, therefore, providing a secure end-to-end channel (Figure 6). Once again, IKE with authentication based on digital certificates will be used instead of pre-shared secrets. Road-warrior cases can also be effectively authenticated using this scheme.

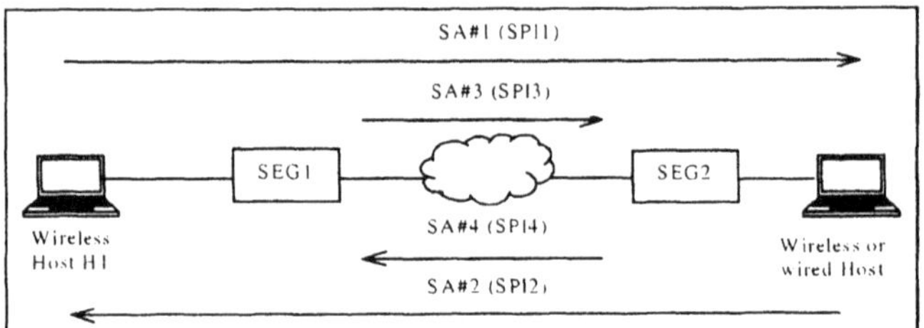

SA#	Src Addr	Dest Addr	IPsec Protocol	SPI	Mode
1	H1	H2	AH	SPI1	Transport
2	H2	H1	AH	SPI2	Transport
3	SEG1	SEG2	ESP	SPI3	Tunnel
4	SEG2	SEG1	ESP	SPI4	Tunnel

Figure 6. Nested headers for end-to-end IPsec protection

For example, consider the following scenario:

"A business employee has IPsec-based Virtual Private Network (VPN) client software installed on his laptop, which is connected to his wireless network provider, via his mobile phone. Also assume that the employee is roaming to a foreign (serving) network. When he connects, he is being authenticated by IKE sending its digital certificate and receiving Visitor Location Register's (VLR) certificate and cross-reference certificate. When IPsec's SAs have been created, VPN client filters the traffic, watching for IP packets destined to the employee's head office. It allows any traffic not going to the head office to pass unprotected. When however the client spots a packet that is addressed to the head office intercepts it. It then uses IPsec services to transmit the packet securely and to assure that all traffic back from the head office to him is also secure".

The first thing that the VPN client does is to establish a bi-directional IPsec Security Association (SA) with the head office server. IKE (ISAKMP) [12] defines the framework how the VPN client and server set up security associations. It does however require the use of digital signatures within the authentication section. This means that the VPN client and server must have IPsec public key certificates to be able to establish a security association.

Taking into account the aforesaid technological trends, SSL/TLS can similarly provide for user authentication and end-to-end security. Until now performance considerations in using SSL/TLS in a resource-constrained environment drove wireless designers to choose a different, incompatible and insecure gateway oriented security protocol for their mobile clients, like in the case of WAP [13], [14]. Provided that it is possible to develop a usable, in terms of performance, implementation of SSL for a handheld device, we can employ a more secure, flexible and reconfigurable Authentication and Key Agreement (AKA) procedure for 4G systems [16]. The ASPeCT project [17] has demonstrated that public-key authentication is possible and GSM and UMTS applications can coexist on a single smart card. A recent study has also shown the feasibility of SSL/TLS in handheld wireless devices [18].

Moreover, the PLMN capability to pre-load an asymmetric key pair in the USIM-4G card combined with public key infrastructure, allows the CAs to publish temporary certificates (attributes or service certificates) [8], which will admit the user access to specific time-limited services and resources [19]. To be more specific, we present the following scenario:

"The user applies to the serving network to provide him a specific time-limit service and signs his request with his private key, which is stored in the USIM-4G. The request is forwarded to the local CA, which checks its validity and then publishes -on the fly- a temporary signed by it certificate, which specifically designates the service type and its expiration time. The certificate is forwarded back to the user, who can use it correspondingly in a SSL/TLS protected channel, communicating with the provider of the specific service. One of the advantages of these certificates having a short life, is that they will not usually need to be revoked and will therefore not need to be included in any CRL. They may also not require revocation if they are issued in respect of a pre-paid subscription service. This mechanism can also support non-repudiation services."

4. CONCLUSIONS

As users rush to adopt IP technology and want mobile access to IP networks, they also become aware of the need for security features and protection of their privacy. The constantly increasing population of users expects from wireless operators to provide features that will protect their data while in transit, safeguard their billing and customer information, and offer availability and quality comparable to that of the wired services. Thus, more flexible, dynamic and scalable mechanisms are necessary in order to support on-demand services and all-IP end-to-end solutions in a many-to-many trust model integrated with the Internet environment. In this paper, we proposed several alternative procedures based on PKI infrastructure introduced in the mobile network architecture for providing future inter/intra mobile core network security, enhancing authentication procedures and end-to-end communication model trust. We showed that PKI offers the appropriate framework to overcome symmetric key based security inefficiencies, providing powerful solutions to protect both network core signaling and user's data from potential intruders.

5. REFERENCES

[1] 3GPP Technical Specification, MAP Application Layer Security, (TS 33.200 v. 5.0.0), March 2002

[2] J.Arko, R. Blom, "The MAP Security Domain of Interpretation for Internet Security Association and Key Management Protocol", <draft-arkko-map-doi-07.txt>, May 2002.

[3] Wisely, D., Eardley, P., & Burness, L., *IP for 3G*, Wiley, 2002.

[4] Kent, S. & Atkinson, R., *Security Architecture for the Internet Protocol*, RFC 2401, Nov. 1998.

[5] 3GPP Technical Specification, IP Network Layer Security, (TS 33.210 v.5.1.0), June 2002

[6] 3GPP TSG, "Using PKI to provide network domain security", Discussion Document S3-010622 SA WG3 Security – S3#21, Nov. 2001.

[7] 3GPP TSG, "Security Services using Public Key Cryptography", Discussion Document S3z000025 SA WG3 Security – S3#15bis, Nov. 2000.

[8] Duane, N. & Brink, J., *PKI Implementing and Managing E-Security*, Berkeley, RSA press, 2001

[9] Frankel, S., *Demystifying IPsec Puzzle*, Artech House, 2001.

[10] Tiller, J., A Technical Guide to IPsec Virtual Private Networks, Auerbach CRC Press, 2000.

[11] Thomas S., *SSL and TLS essentials*, New York, Wiley, 2000.

[12] Maughan, D., et al, Internet Security Association and Key Management Protocol (ISAKMP), RFC 2408, Nov. 1998.

[13] Khare R., "W* Effect Considered Harmful", IEEE Internet Computing, Vol. 3, no 4, pp.82-92, July/Aug. 1999.

[14] WAP forum WAP-217-WPKI, "Wireless Application Protocol Public Key Infrastructure Definition", April 2001, www.wapforum.org/what/technical.htm.

[15] 3GPP Technical Specification, 3G Security Architecture, (TS 33.102 v.4.3.0), December 2001.

[16] Kambourakis G., Rouskas A., & Gritzalis S., "Using SSL/TLS in Authentication and Key Agreement Procedures of Future Mobile Networks", In the Proc. of the 4th IEEE Int'l Conf. on Mobile and Wireless Comm. Networks. (MWCN), pp. 152-156, 2002.

[17] ASPeCT Project, *Securing the future of Mobile Communications*, http://www.esat.kuleuven.ac.be/cosic/aspect, 1999.

[18] Gupta V. & Gupta S., "Securing the Wireless Internet", IEEE Communications Magazine, Vol 39, no 4, pp. 69-74, Dec. 2001.

[19] 3GPP TSG, "Support of certificates in 3GPP security Architecture", Discussion Document S3-010353 SA WG3 Security – S3#19, July 2001.

A TIME DRIVEN METHODOLOGY FOR KEY DIMENSIONING IN MULTICAST COMMUNICATIONS*

Roberto Di Pietro, Luigi V. Mancini, and Alessandro Mei
Dipartimento di Informatica, Università di Roma "La Sapienza",
Via Salaria 113, 00198-Roma, Italy.
{dipietro, mancini, mei}@dsi.uniroma1.it

Abstract This work considers the key management for secure multicast in the Logical Key Hierarchy (LKH) model, and proposes a methodology to establish the minimal key length that guarantees a specified level of confidentiality. We reach such a result by analyzing and extending the threat model to the confidentiality of the multicast information. For this extended threat model, we present a methodology that takes into account the following parameters: (1) the required lifetime of the information confidentiality; (2) the level of the key in the LKH model; (3) the dynamics of the multicast group, that is the eviction rate of the users. From these rationales we develop an analytical model that, for each level, derives the appropriate key length, that is the minimal length that assures the desired degree of confidentiality under the hypotheses in the threat model. Finally, for a specific instance of the LKH model, we describe a numerical example that shows the saving that can be achieved in terms of the key lengths.

Keywords: key management protocol, time driven methodology, threat model, secure multicast, reliable multicast, efficient multicast.

1. Introduction

Many emerging applications (for instance pay per view TV, stock option bid), are based upon a group communication model. In particular, they require message delivery from one or more authorized senders to a large number of authorized receivers. This model is available on the Internet, where multicast communication has been successfully imple-

*This work was partially supported by the EU IST-2001-34734 EYES project and by the Italian MIUR under the WEB-MINDS project.

mented to provide an efficient, best effort delivery service to large groups of users Dee88. The deployment of network applications requiring group communication will accelerate in coming years. Thus, security is an important concern to enable the adoption and diffusion of the multicast paradigm.

Cryptographic techniques should prevent unauthorized users from accessing the content of delivered messages. As a result, securing group communications, that is, providing confidentiality, authenticity, and integrity of messages delivered between group members, is a critical issue. In this paper, message confidentiality is assured by using simple and efficient private key techniques for group data encryption. Note that, although group communications using sophisticated cryptographic techniques are proposed in the literature STW98, our choice is motivated by the fact that asymmetric cryptography requires much more resources to decrypt messages Sch96, thus depleting the level of service perceived by the users.

Confidentiality is among the main requirements we consider: only authorized users should decrypt a multicast message, even though this message is broadcast over a geographical region. The confidentiality requirement can be translated in the context of secure multicast into the following four requirements on key distribution: (1) Non-group Confidentiality: users that were never part of the group should not have access to any key that can decrypt any multicast data sent to the group; (2) Forward Confidentiality: users deleted from the group at some time t do not have access to any key used to encrypt data after t, unless they are authorized to join again the group; (3) Collusion Freedom: no subset of deleted users should be able to decrypt future group communications, even by sharing the keys they had before deletion; (4) Backward Confidentiality: a user added at time t should not have access to any key used to encrypt data before t while the user was not part of the group.

This paper focuses on key distribution schemes for secure group communications. In particular, we focus our efforts on an efficient use of the bandwidth available to the center. The available bandwidth is one of the most valuable resources affecting the management of group dynamics ASW00; CMN99. To reduce the bandwidth used by management messages, we derive a model in which the length of the encryption keys is reduced with respect to the current solution in literature, while not affecting the overall security of the model.

We provide a methodology to select the bit length of the encryption keys in the LKH model. In particular, we provide: (1) a threat model for information confidentiality in multicast communications; (2) an analytical model which supports the following results: (a) the length of the encryption keys can be set accordingly to the parameters indicated in the threat model and the key level in the LKH hierarchy; (b) such a key length is shorter than the key length from current literature, without weakening the security level enforced by the standard model; (c) the key length decreases as the number of users in the system increases; (d) our methodology achieves savings in the number of bits to be broadcast of the order of $\Theta(\log^2 n)$ with respect to current re-keying schemes (see Section 1.5), and these savings are remarkable in real-world numerical examples as well. Reducing the key length in the LKH model, reduces the re-keying completion time, enhance the reliability of the key transmission and reduces the storage requirement for the users.

In Section 1.2, we describe the multicast communication model assumed in this paper, while in Section 1.3 we define the threat model. In Section 1.4 we first derive an analytical methodology, and then we show a numerical example. In section 1.5 we describe related work in the field. Finally, Section 1.6 contains some concluding remarks.

2. Multicast Model

2.1 The LKH Model

We assume the LKH model described in WGL00 (*key graph model*). That is, there is a multicast group $\mathcal{M} = \{u_1, .., u_n\}$, which is a dynamically changing subset of all possible users. The set can change according to the eviction of a user from the group, or according to a new user joining the group. We assume there is a super user, called *the center*, which can send a message to the multicast group that can be received by all members of $\mathcal{M}$. The message is sent over an insecure channel, therefore the same message can be received by other entities not belonging to $\mathcal{M}$. To enforce the privacy of data, we can assume available to the users in $\mathcal{M}$ and to the center a cryptographic module, based on symmetric key cryptography. In the following, when the center needs to send a message m to $\mathcal{M}$, the center will compute $m' = E_k(m)$ and then will broadcast to the group $\mathcal{M}$ the message. The key k, shared by all users and the center is the session key. A join occurs when a new user u_j is added to $\mathcal{M}$, while a deletion occurs when a user u_e is evicted from $\mathcal{M}$.

The *key graph* requires to build up a tree of auxiliary keys (in the following *key graph tree*), whose leaves are the private key of the users in $\mathcal{M}$. Each user has to store the keys that are on the leaf-root path. Within this framework, an excellent trade-off between the *per user* required storage, and efficiency in the number of message required is achieved.

Referring to this model, we will adopt the following terminology: (1) the siblings of a user u_i in the key graph is the set of users that share

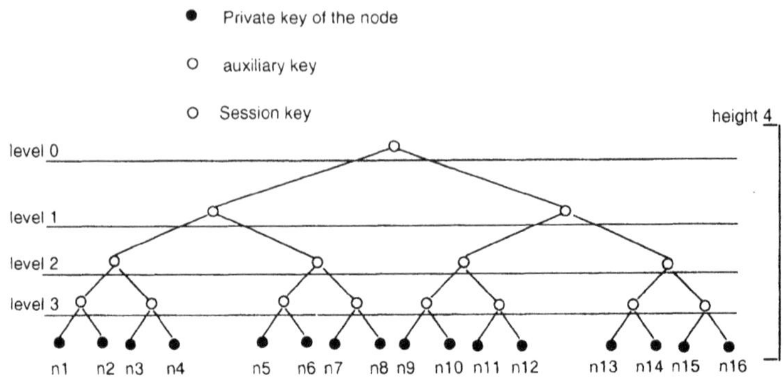

Figure 1. Notation and terminology employed in the following.

with the user u_i the same parent; (2) we will assume, unless otherwise specified, that the number of the users in the key graph is exactly $n = |\mathcal{M}| = b^h$, where b is the ariety of the key graph. This assumption (that is, the key graph is perfectly balanced) does not affect the generality of our findings, but simplifies the presentation; (3) the root of the key graph (that is the session key) is located at height 0, while its leaves are at height h; (4) the user to be excluded from the multicast group will be denoted by u_e. In Figure 1 an example of such a key tree. Note that the relevant literature in the field assumes that all keys in the key graph tree have the same bit length.

In the following, we assume, without loss of generality, that $b = 2$. That is, the key graph we consider is a binary tree. However, the same kind of results hold for an arbitrary tree ariety.

2.2 Security in the LKH Model

When the session key has to be changed due to the occurrence of an eviction, all users need to change the auxiliary keys shared with the evicted user u_e. Indeed, employing one of these keys to encrypt any message would result in a violation of the privacy, since the encryption key is hold by u_e, which could correctly decrypt the message. When a join occurs, the newly joined user u_j receives the appropriate sequence of auxiliary keys from the center. The center encrypts such messages *via* the private key of u_j, which is known only by the center and u_j himself.

It has been shown in CGI+99; YLZL01 that the most complex re-keying operation is an eviction, and in the following we will deal with this kind of re-keying operation. Moreover, a re-keying operation due to a join can be performed according to an optimal algorithm described in WCS+99.

3. The Threat Model and its Implication

Information confidentiality is a time related property. Indeed, information usually requires to be protected from unauthorized access for a certain period of time only, after which it is not worth securing that information any longer. For instance, stock quotes may need to be protected for, say, twenty minutes. After such a period, this information can be assumed to be publicly known, and there is no point in assuring its confidentiality. We refer to the period during which it is worth securing a given information as its *lifetime* (LL). A first ingredient to the definition of the lifetime of a piece of information is the period t_d for which the manager of the multicast group desires this information to be confidential. In general, $LL \leq t_d$, as it is worthless to enforce confidentiality beyond t_d. However, LL and t_d are usually different. For instance, even though a broker in the stock market could desire to keep stock quotes confidential for one hour, after twenty minutes this information is uncovered by many different sources. Hence, while t_d is equal to 60 minutes, the *lifetime* cannot be more than 20 minutes.

Given the goal of enforcing confidentiality of a piece of information throughout its lifetime, it is important to define the capabilities of the attackers. In the next section, we will describe the threat model for multicast communications in a dynamic group of users.

3.1 The Threat Model

Our threat model assumes that an enemy has the capability of intercepting all the communications between the center and the multicast group. That is, the enemy is able to eavesdrop all the encrypted payload traffic, as well as the management traffic. The management traffic is the set of communications which do not carry payload information, like re-keying messages. However, we limit the adversary to be passive, that is the adversary cannot inject forged messages in the communication channel. This assumption is coherent with our goal to preserve information confidentiality.

We extend such a threat model by taking into account the behavior of the currently legitimate users, as well as the behavior of the evicted users. As for the legitimate users, we assume that a legitimate user does not leak any information he holds. This assumption is congruent with the relevant literature of the field (see Section 1.5). Indeed, to discourage any legitimate user from disclosing its keys, a tracing traitor scheme

NNL01; BPS00 can be applied. Note that such a solution does not prevent a legitimate user to leak its keys, but can deter users from such a malicious behavior since the leaking user can be traced and prosecuted.

As for evicted users, we assume that each evicted user can have a malicious behavior. In particular, we adopt the conservative assumption that a coalition of evicted users can cooperate to recover the new keys employed by the center to securely communicate to the group. Moreover, we assume that as soon as a user u_e is evicted from the multicast group, u_e can disclose all the previous received information.

4. Choosing the Key Length

Even without knowing the key used to encrypt a message, the attacker can recover its plain text. The time required by this operation is related to the encryption mechanism and the length of the encryption key. A number of techniques aimed at recovering the plain text from the cypher text exist Sch96, but their analysis is out of the scope of this paper.

These techniques are available to the attacker (an evicted user as well as an external entity). Given his computational capabilities, it is possible to find out the time required by the attacker to recover from the cypher text the corresponding plain text. We assume that this time depends exponentially with the key length, that is, adding one bit to the encryption key yields a message requiring twice as much time to be broken.

4.1 The Session Key

The session key protects the payload. Therefore, its bit length should be related to the confidentiality requirements of the payload, that is, its lifetime. A first upper bound on the lifetime of the payload can be given by the manager of the multicast service. Parameter t_d measures how long the information sent is desired to be protected. However, this is not the only factor. Note that, once a legitimate user is evicted from the multicast group, we are not guaranteed that the same user does not leak either the past session key or the payload itself to the public. Consequently, there is no point in protecting past payload held by an evicted user, since we can assume this payload to be compromised. The above remarks can be summarized in the following statement, where t_e refers to the time interval between one eviction and the next one.

Statement 1. *The lifetime LL of the payload depends on the desired level of confidentiality t_d of the information as well as on the frequency of the evictions t_e of the users in the multicast group, according to the formula $LL = min\{t_d, t_e\}$.*

The session key has to resist from malicious attacks for time LL. Assuming that the kind of an attacker we are willing to stop is capable of breaking an s bit key in time t_q, the length of the session key k_0 should be set to:

$$|k_0| = s + \lceil \log(LL/t_q) \rceil. \tag{1}$$

The above discussion does not hold any more when considering an auxiliary key in the key graph tree. Take, as an example, one of the two keys at level 1. Such a key is not changed at every user eviction, and, when it is not changed, is used to multicast the new session key. It is thus intuitive that this key should be stronger than the session key, since it has to resist for a longer time interval.

Statement 2. *The length of an auxiliary key in the key graph tree depends on the desired level of confidentiality t_d of the payload, as well as on the frequency of the evictions t_e of the users in the multicast group, and on the position of the key in the key graph tree.*

¿From the above discussion it follows that the length of the keys in the LKH model does not need to be the same for all the keys in the tree. In the next section, we will show an analytical model to formalize the above discussion.

4.2 The Auxiliary Keys

In the following, we assume that the eviction probability of every single user u_i is exponentially and independently distributed with parameter λ. That is, the probability that user u_i is evicted within time t is given by: $\mathcal{P}(u_i \leq t) = 1 - e^{-\lambda t}$. Note that, due to the exponential law properties, the probability that at least one eviction occurs from the multicast group $\mathcal{M}$ within a period t is given by: $\mathcal{P}(\mathcal{M} \leq t) = 1 - e^{-n\lambda t}$. On the average, one user is evicted every $t_e = 1/(n\lambda)$ time, which is the expectation of an exponentially distributed random variable with parameter $n\lambda$.

Consider an intermediate key $k_{i,j}$, where i is the level and j is the position within the level from left to right in the key graph tree. Let $S_{k_{i,j}}$ be the set of users sharing key $k_{i,j}$. Key $k_{i,j}$ can be considered as the root of a subtree having $|S_{k_{i,j}}| = 2^{h-i}$ leaves. When an eviction occurs, the probability that the evicted user u_e belongs to the set $S_{k_{i,j}}$, for all $i \in [0 \ldots h-1]$ and for all $j \in [0 \ldots 2^{h-i} - 1]$, is given by:

$$\mathcal{P}(u_e \in S_{k_{i,j}}) = \frac{|S_{k_{i,j}}|}{n} = \frac{2^{h-i}}{n}; \tag{2}$$

that is the position of u_e is uniformly distributed over the leaves of the key graph. ¿From Equation (2), we can derive the following straightforward fact.

Fact 1. *For any two keys $k_{i,j1}$ and $k_{i+1,j2}$ the probability that the evicted user u_e holds key $k_{i,j1}$ is twice the probability that u_e holds key $k_{i+1,j2}$.*

The above framework allows to set a probabilistic methodology for choosing the length of each key in the key graph according to our threat model. Note that, in our model, assuming that all the keys have the same length $L_{\max}$ is counterintuitive. Indeed, the lower the level of a key, the higher the number of users sharing that key and therefore the higher is the probability of that key to be changed due to an eviction. For instance, consider the root key: at each eviction such a key is renewed. Consequently its lifetime is shorter than all other keys, and its length can be reduced as follows without compromising in any way the confidentiality of the protocol.

¿From Fact 1, keys at level i, with $i \in [0 \ldots h-1]$, should be asked to be $L_{\min} + i$ bits long, where $L_{\min} = |k_0|$. Hence, the total number of bits on a leaf-root path to broadcast when an eviction occurs is:

$$\sum_{i=0}^{h-1} |k_i| = \sum_{i=0}^{h-1} (L_{\min} + i) = hL_{\min} + \sum_{i=0}^{h-1} i = hL_{\min} + \frac{(h-1)h}{2} \tag{3}$$

Therefore, the keys of maximal length are those at level $h-1$, whose length is $L_{\max} = L_{\min} + (h-1)$ bits.

Now focus on the standard key graph, in which all the keys are of equal length. We want to investigate what key length assures the same level of confidentiality provided by our methodology. It is easy to realize that the length of all the keys must be at least $L_{\max}$. Indeed, choosing a shorter length weakens the keys at highest levels, and thus compromises the strength of the whole scheme. For a standard re-keying operation, when all keys have the same length $L_{\max}$, the total number of bits of the keys to be changed is:

$$\sum_{i=0}^{h-1} |k_i| = \sum_{i=0}^{h-1} L_{\max} = hL_{\max}. \tag{4}$$

Thus the fraction of bits saved employing our methodology is given by:

$$\left(hL_{\max} - \left(hL_{\min} + \frac{h(h-1)}{2}\right)\right) / hL_{\max} = \frac{h-1}{2L_{\max}}. \tag{5}$$

Note that the saving in the number of bits increases as the number of users in the system increases.

4.3 A Numerical Example

In this subsection we show with a numerical example the possible savings that can be achieved in the key length by adopting our methodology. In this example, the system is characterized as follows:

- the multicast group consists of $n = 2^{16} = 65,536$ users;
- each user leaves $\mathcal{M}$ according to the exponential law of parameter $\lambda = 1/180$, where time is measured in days. This essentially means that each user belongs to the multicast group for 180 days on the average;
- the desired confidentiality lifetime of the information t_d is equal to 15 days;
- to recover 20 bits of plain text from 20 bits of cypher text, without any knowledge of the encryption key, the attacker takes 10 seconds.

¿From these hypotheses, a user is evicted from $\mathcal{M}$ approximately every 238 seconds on the average. According to the threat model, the lifetime can be computed as the minimum between the desired period of confidentiality and the eviction rate, that is LL is equal to 238 seconds. Consequently, key $k_{0,0}$ should be $20 + \lceil \log(238/10) \rceil = 25$ bits long. According to Fact 1, all keys $k_{i,j}$, for all $i \in [1 \ldots h-1]$ and $j \in [0 \ldots 2^i - 1]$, should be $25 + i$ bits long. Therefore the total length of all keys to be changed when an eviction occurs is, by Equation 3, equal to $hL_{\max} - (h-1)h/2 = 520$ bits. Note that a re-keying operation within the classical LKH model would have required, by Equation 4, $hL_{\max} = 16 * (25 + 15) = 640$ bits. The saving achieved is equal to the 18.75%. Indeed, by Equation 5, $(h-1)/2L_{\max} = 15/(2 * 40) = 18.75$.

4.4 Comparison

In this subsection, we show the gain that can be achieved by employing our methodology with respect to the other protocols in the literature. We refer to the protocol proposed in this paper as Time Driven Key Dimensioning (TDKD). For a detailed comparison of current protocols, not including TDKD, see PMJ02. Due to room limitation, we show the total number of bits sent by the center in case of a single user eviction and a single user join only (see Table 1). With K, we refer to the size of the key of maximal length L_{max} in bits, and with I to the user ID ($\log n$ bits long).

Model	Join: message size			Leave:Multicast Message size
	Join unic.	Sibling unic.	Multicast	
LKH++	$(h+1)K$	0	$K+I$	$I+(h-1)K$
EHBT	$(h+1)K$	I	hI	$I+hK$
ELK	$(h+1)K$	I	0	$I+h(n_1+n_2)$
OFT	$(h+1)K$	$I+2K$	$(h+1)K$	$I+(h+1)K$
LKH+	$(h+1)K$	$I+K$	hI	$I+2hK$
TDKD	$h(K-\frac{h-1}{2})$	0	$K+I$	$I+h(K-\frac{h-1}{2})$

Table 1. Comparison of messages size for a single user joining or leaving $\mathcal{M}$.

5. Related work

The Logical Key Hierarchy (LKH) model was introduced in HH99; WHA99; WGL00 to manage multicast group within a framework of security and efficiency. In WCS$^+$99 a protocol is proposed called LKH+. The performances achieved by LKH+, as for the join of new users, improve on WGL00. Indeed, the keys to be refreshed, instead of being encrypted with their respective children's keys, are refreshed by hashing.

The OFT protocol MS98; BMS02 requires each re-keying message to carry just $\log n$ keys instead of $2\log n$ as in the basic LKH model. The ELK protocol PST01 focuses on reliable and secure multicast for large groups, providing a periodic re-keying scheme. The ELK protocol is similar to OFT, but ELK employs pseudo random functions to build and manipulate the keys in the tree. In RMH01, the use of the old keys to create or update the new keys saves information to be transmitted to the users when a membership change occurs.

In PMJ02, protocol LHK++ is introduced. This protocol takes advantage of: (1) the set of information the users share that can be used to locally generate the new keys; (2) the set of keys that the users logically share from a certain point onward in the LKH, and that allows the users to compute locally their path to the root employing a one-way hash function. In this way, it has been shown how to reduce of 50% the bandwidth required by the center for unicast communications to perform group set-up, and to deal with mass join. Moreover, this approach allows to save more than 50% of the computations required by the center in mass evictions and requires less computations on the user device than the other solutions.

About reliability in multicast communication, the protocol proposed by Yang et al. YLZL01 uses proactive FEC in which parity packets are transmitted along with payload packets in each FEC block. An interesting approach proposed by some works KCWP00; TSPL01 is to send the key updates in the same stream as data packets. The main advantage is that key updates are synchronized with the encrypted data, and a separate protocol is not needed for reliable key delivery.

6. Concluding Remarks

In this paper, we have described a methodology to establish the key length of the encryption keys in the LKH model. In particular, we have developed an analytical model, based on a threat model for information confidentiality in multicast communications, that proves the length of the encryption keys can vary according to: (1) the eviction rate of the user in the multicast group; (2) the level in the key graph tree at which the logical key is placed; (3) the desired level of confidentiality. Note that our model provides two properties: first, reducing the length of the encryption keys does not weaken the security of the LKH model; second, the length of the key decreases as the number of users in the system increases. Reducing the keys length in LKH reduces the re-keying completion time, enhances the reliability of the key transmissions and reduces the storage requirement for the users.

References

[ASW00] M. Abdalla, Y. Shavitt, and A. Wool. Key management for restricted multicast using broadcast encryption. *IEEE/ACM Transaction on Networking*, 8(4), 2000.

[BMS02] D. Balenson, D. McGrew, and A. Sherman. Key management for large dynamic groups: One-way function trees and amortized initialization. Internet draft, IETF, June 2002.

[BPS00] Omer Berkman, Michal Parnas, and Jiri Sgall. Efficient dynamic traitor tracing. In *Symposium on Discrete Algorithms*, pages 586–595, 2000.

[CGI+99] R. Canetti, J. Garay, G. Itkis, D. Micciancio, M. Naor, and B. Pinkas. Multicast security: a taxonomy and some efficient constructions. In *Proceedings of IEEE INFOCOM'99: Conference on Computer Communications*, 1999.

[CMN99] R. Canetti, T. Malkin, and K. Nissim. Efficient communication-storage tradeoffs for multicast encryption. In Springer-Verlag, editor, *Advances in Cryptology, EUROCRYPT 1999*, volume 1592 of *Lecture Notes in Computer Science*, 1999.

[Dee88] S. E. Deering. Multicast routing in internetworks and extended LANs. *Computer Communication Review*, 18(4), 1988. ACM SIGCOMM '88 Symposium: Communications Architectures and Protocols.

[HH99] H.Harney and E. Harder. Logical key hierarchy protocol. Internet draft, IETF, April 1999.

[KCWP00] M. Kandansky, D. Chiu, J. Wesley, and J. Provino. Tree-based reliable multicast (tram). IETF Internet Draft, 2000.

[MS98] D. A. McGrew and A. T. Sherman. Key establishment in large dynamic groups using one-way function trees. Technical Report 0755, TIS Labs at Network Associates, Inc., Glenwood, MD, May 1998.

[NNL01] Dalit Naor, Moni Naor, and Jeff Lotspiech. Revocation and tracing schemes for stateless receivers. *Lecture Notes in Computer Science*, 2139:41–62, 2001.

[PMJ02] R. Di Pietro, L. V. Mancini, and S. Jajodia. Efficient and secure keys management for wireless mobile communications. In *Proceedings of the second ACM international workshop on Principles of mobile computing*, pages 66–73. ACM Press, 2002.

[PST01] A. Perrig, D. Song, and D. Tygar. ELK, a new protocol for efficient large-group key distribution. In *Proc. of 2001 IEEE Symposium on Security and Privacy*, pages 247–262, 2001.

[RMH01] S. Rafaeli, L. Mathy, and D. Hutchison. EHBT: an efficient protocol for group key management. *Lecture Notes in Computer Science*, 2233:159–171, 2001.

[Sch96] B. Schneier. *Applied Cryptography: Protocols, Algorithms and Source Code in C.* John Wiley & Sons, 1996.

[STW98] M. Steiner, G. Tsudik, and M. Waidner. CLIQUES: A protocol suite for key agreement in dynamic groups. In *Proceedings. 18th IEEE International Conference on Distributed Computing Systems*, 1998.

[TSPL01] W. Trappe, Jie Song, R. Poovendran, and K.J.R. Liu. Key distribution for secure multimedia multicasts via data embedding. In *Proc. of IEEE ICASSP 2001*, pages 1449–1452, 2001.

[WCS+99] M. Waldvogel, G. Caronni, D. Sun, N. Weiler, and B. Plattner. The versakey framework: Versatile group key management. *IEEE Journal on Selected Areas in Communications*, 17(9):1614–1631, September 1999.

[WGL00] C. K. Wong, M. Gouda, and S. S. Lam. Secure group communications using key graphs. *IEEE/ACM Transaction on Networking*, 8(1), 2000.

[WHA99] D. Wallner, E. Harder, and R. Agee. Key management for multicast: Issues and architectures. RFC 2627, June 1999.

[YLZL01] Y. R. Yang, X. S. Li, X. B. Zhang, and S. S. Lam. Reliable group rekeying: a performance analysis. In *Proc. of the 2001 conference on applications, technologies, architectures, and protocols for computer communications*, pages 27–38. ACM Press, 2001.

A FLEXIBLE CATEGORY-BASED COLLUSION-RESISTANT KEY MANAGEMENT SCHEME FOR MULTICAST

Claudiu Duma, Nahid Shahmehri, Patrick Lambrix

Department of Computer and Information Science, Linköpings universitetet, Sweden
{cladu, nahsh, patla}@ida.liu.se

Abstract: Current key management schemes for multicast provide either no resistance to collusion or perfect resistance to collusion. However, resistance to collusion is achieved at the expense of efficiency in terms of the number of transmissions and the number of keys that are used. We argue that applications may have certain assumptions regarding the users and their access to the multicast channel that may be used to provide a larger choice for balancing efficiency against resistance to collusion.

Starting from a user categorization, based on the accessibility to the multicast channel, we formalize the collusion requirement. Different user categorizations give different degrees of collusion resistance and we show that the existing work has focused on special cases of user categorizations. Further, we propose and evaluate a flexible key management strategy for the general case where the accessibility relation defines the order of exclusion of the categories. The theoretical and experimental results show that our scheme has good performance regarding transmissions and keys per controller.

Key words: multicast, security, key management, collusion, efficiency, category-based

1. INTRODUCTION

IP Multicast provides an efficient way for one-to-many communication. Unfortunately, IP Multicast is inherently insecure. Data is transmitted in plain text and is accessible to any hostile party that has access to the communication channel. Assurance on the secrecy of the multicasted data can be provided by encrypting all transmitted data with a secret key available only to sender and to authorized receivers. We call this secret key, the session key. The group of authorized receivers can be very dynamic, new users are included into the group while others leave due to, for instance, expiration of their subscription. Every time the group of authorized receivers changes, the secret session key shared by that group must be updated accordingly. This process is called re-keying and it must be carried out in a secure and scalable way.

Due to the large number of group members the scalability of the key management scheme is crucial. The requirements are in terms of minimizing the number of transmissions required to re-key as well as the storage requirements (number of keys) for each receiver user and for the group controller.

The security requirements for re-keying are usually in terms of backward and forward access control. Backward access control refers to the impossibility of a newly joined user to gain access to previous session keys. Forward access control refers to the impossibility of a former group member that has been excluded to gain access to future session keys. A third requirement, resistance to collusion, refers to the impossibility of a coalition of two or more excluded members to gain access to future session keys by combining their keying material. This requirement is usually implicitly treated by the previous work in multicast security. Moreover, it usually takes extreme forms. Either no resistance to collusion, or the opposite, perfect resistance to collusion is provided. The resistance to collusion is achieved at the expense of efficiency. However, applications may have certain assumptions regarding members and accessibility to the multicast channel. Based on this we argue that adequate key management schemes can be designed to balance the given collusion constraints against efficiency.

Starting from a user categorization based on the accessibility to the multicast communication channel we formalize the collusion requirement. Different configurations of categories give different constraints on collusion. We show that "no resistance to collusion" and "perfect resistance to collusion" are special cases of our more general collusion requirement and they can be specified by configurations of categories and their relationships. Further, we give a key management strategy for the general case. We assess the efficiency and compare with the referenced work.

2. KEY TREE SCHEMES AND COLLUSION

As shown by the existing work in multicast security the key management schemes based on a logical tree arrangement of the auxiliary keys bring good balance between storage requirements and the number of transmissions [15, 16, 17]. The idea is to recursively partition the multicast group into subgroups, and assign auxiliary keys to these subgroups. Whenever a user leaves the multicast group the controller uses these auxiliary keys to re-key the remaining users on a subgroup basis by using a minimum number of subgroups covering all non-excluded users. Because the auxiliary keys are actually used to encrypt other keys, they are sometime called Key Encryption Keys [15, 16]. In this paper we use the term auxiliary keys and we refer to the tree arrangement as the auxiliary key tree or just the key tree.

We categorize the key tree schemes based on the properties of their key arrangement. In particular, we make the distinction between the unique keys scheme (UKS) and the reuse keys scheme (RKS):

- In the UKS all keys in the auxiliary key tree are distinct;
- In the RKS, not all the keys are distinct, but for a partition factor of 2 each level of the tree will introduce only two new auxiliary keys.

Logical tree distribution of auxiliary keys reduces the communication overload when re-keying. As shown in [18] the lower bound complexity for re-keying communication when the group key is encrypted using only one key is O(logN). This is a property of UKSs, such as the Logical Key Hierarchy (LKH) [15, 16, 17], One-Way Function Tree (OFT) [11] or One-Way Function Chain (OFC) [3], providing perfect resistance to collusion. More efficient results are achieved by reusing auxiliary keys among different groups of users and encrypting the group key with a combination of these keys (e.g. XOR-ing the keys). This way ad-hoc groups can be created which usually cover more users than the groups pre-established by the key tree. The Boolean Function Minimization (BFM) [4] and the Flat [15] schemes fall in this category. However, the RKS is susceptible to collusion attacks. In [4] it is suggested to artificially increase the key tree such that the probability of collusion would decrease. However, such a solution may not be satisfactory for applications that have certain requirements regarding collusion. The collusion requirement and its formalization are the subject of the next section.

3. COLLUSION REQUIREMENT

As a step towards a definition of collusion we introduce the notion of categories. We say that users belonging to the same category have the same accessibility to the multicast group. A binary accessibility relation is defined on the set of categories, reflecting the fact that users from one category have access to at least all sessions that users of another category have access to, and maybe more. The collusion requirement of a certain application can be defined as a specific configuration of the categories and of the accessibility relation. We introduce the following notation:

- U is the set of users and N is the total number of users.
- C is the set of accessibility categories and M is the total number of categories.

- The function users: $C \rightarrow \wp(U)$, where users(c) gives all the users of category c. We assume that a user can belong to only one category, therefore: $\forall\, c_1, c_2 \in C: c_1 \neq c_2 \rightarrow users(c_1) \cap users(c_2) = \varnothing$.
  Users with the same accessibility belong to the same accessibility category. All users need to belong to a category, that is $\bigcup_{i=1,M} users(c_i) = U$.
- $\prec \subseteq C \times C$, a reflexive partial order, is the accessibility relation on categories reflecting the relative access to the multicast communication the users from one category have compared to users from another category. If $c_1 \prec c_2$, then users from c_2 can access at least all sessions that users from c_1 have access to.
- $E \subseteq C$ the set of excluded categories.

With the above notation we define the collusion requirement as follows: *No coalition of users from a subset I of excluded categories,* $I \subseteq E$, *can gain access to future session keys unless* $\exists c \in C \setminus E, \exists c' \in I: c \prec c'$.

In other words, a coalition of users from a subset I of excluded categories can gain access to future session keys only if there is a category in I that can access more than a not yet excluded category.

An example scenario that can be modeled by our definition of collusion is the software delivery [7, 8] where users can be categorized according to how much they buy. Some users could buy only the initial software product, while others could subscribe to a certain number of updates and future versions. This would correspond to a "buy more" total order, as observed in [8]. However, software can split in different version branches (e.g. separating features) or merge different tools into one single software product. Also, users could subscribe for more than one product or more than one branch of the same product. Therefore a more general model of this scenario is the partial order, as proposed in this paper. We observe that this order also intuitively relates to the order in which users are excluded from the group of authorized receivers. Although our accessibility relation generalizes the buy more from [8], it is not limited only to that scenario, but it can model any situation where the exclusion order is known or can be inferred.

3.1 Discussion

According to our definition, the collusion requirement for an application depends solely on the configuration of the category set C and of the accessibility relation $\prec$. We discuss a number of possible configurations.

1. $C = \{c\}$ and $\prec = \{<c,c>\}$. All users are in one category. This case corresponds to applications that have no constraints with respect to collusion. Solutions for this case such as BFM and Flat reuse auxiliary keys and achieve best efficiency.
2. $C = \{c_1, c_2, \ldots c_M\}$ and $\prec$ is a total order. Categories are defined. In this case the controller knows exactly the order in which the categories will be excluded. The solution proposed in [8] addresses this case by using BFM with a special arrangement of users such that users from "buy less"

categories can not collude over users from "buy more" categories. Although the number of keys is kept low, the solution imposes too strict constraints regarding the maximum cardinality of each category.

3. $C = \{c_1, c_2, \ldots c_M\}$ and $\prec$ is a reflexive partial order. This is the general case. The controller knows that some order exists among some of categories, where other categories are incomparable. Special solutions do not exist.
4. $C = \{c_1, c_2, \ldots c_M\}$ and $\prec = \{<c_i, c_i>\}_{i=1, M}$. In this case the controller cannot make any assumption regarding the order the categories are going to be excluded. Leaving the multicast group happens in an undeterministic manner. No prior knowledge is available about how much access one category has compared to another. Special solutions do not exist.
5. $C = \{c_1, c_2, \ldots c_M\}$, $M = N$, $users(c_i) = \{u_i\}$ and $\prec = \{<c_i, c_i>\}_{i=1, M}$. This is a special configuration of the previous case where each category directly maps to a user. Again, leaving the multicast group happens in an undeterministic manner. The collusion requirement can be rewritten as *no coalition of excluded users can get access to future session keys.* This is the most common requirement in the existing work for securing multicast. Although solutions for this case provide perfect resistance to collusion, this comes at an expense on efficiency.

In the next section we propose a key management strategy for the general case of collusion, which takes into consideration the existence of different categories of users. We show that our solution is more efficient in terms of transmissions, than the solutions for case 5, which has been the premise for most of the work in securing multicast.

4. SOLUTION STRATEGY

We consider a centralized architecture, where one group controller manages the users' access to the group communication channel. The controller initiates all the sessions, generates and distributes the keys, maintains information about the categories, and accordingly removes and adds users and categories from the multicast channel. Although the central controller can be a potential performance bottleneck, this architecture is more desirable in systems where one party must retain the control such as in multicast software delivery [7, 8]. Methods of replication can be used to unload the controller. For other systems such as GPS that use one-to-many unidirectional satellite communication it is hard if not impossible to use a decentralized architecture.

We assume that *categories are excluded based on the accessibility relation* and we formulate the requirement that is used in the design of our solution:

(i) $\forall c, c' \in C : c \in E \wedge c' \prec c \rightarrow c' \in E$; *(ii) No coalition of users from excluded categories can gain access to future session keys.*

This requirement implies the collusion requirement but maps better to operations performed by the controller and is therefore more helpful when approaching the solution. In particular, the $\prec$ relation can be mapped to the knowledge the controller has regarding the order in which the categories must be excluded. Our new problem is then to find a mechanism to exclude a category when the order of exclusion is known, where the exclusion must have perfect resistance to collusion.

To illustrate and exemplify the solution we use the graph representation of the partial order relation $\prec$, e.g. figure 1.a, and call it the categories accessibility graph (CAG). The CAG is obtained from the diagraph of $\prec$ by eliminating all length one cycles, implied by the reflexive property, and all the arcs implied by the transitivity property. The result is a non-transitive and non-reflexive diagraph where the nodes stand for categories and an arc $A \leftarrow B$ corresponds to the relation $A \prec B$ between the categories A and B. In the remainder we talk about categories and nodes representing them interchangeably.

We start from the observation that if $A \prec B$ (or $A \leftarrow B$ in CAG) then whenever node A has to be re-keyed node B will also need to be re-keyed. Therefore we introduce the propagation principle: *if $A \prec B$ then give node B the keys that are used for re-keying A*. This will assure that whenever A is re-keyed B is also re-keyed, without the need to specifically re-key B and its ancestors.

However this will not solve the case when category A must leave the group while B, together with its ancestors, remain in the group. Therefore: *if $A \prec B$ then B must have at least one key that is not known to A*. This key will be used to re-key B when A leaves. Again we can apply the first principle for the ancestors of B, so that the key of B is given to its ancestors too.

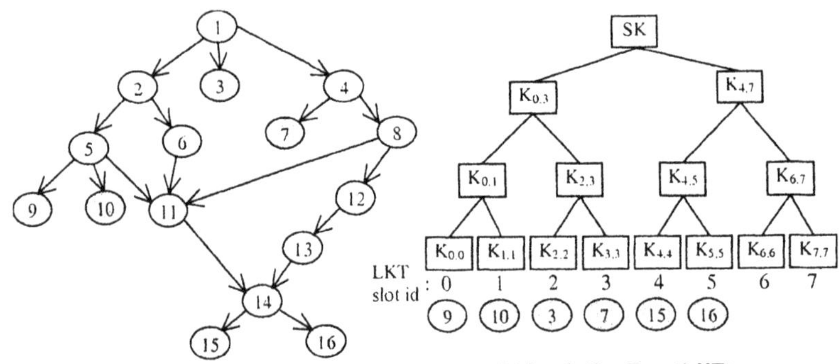

a) Categories Accessibility graph (CAG) b) Leafs Key Tree (LKT)

Figure 1. LKT corresponding to the CAG

We also make the observation that at any time any of the leaf nodes can un-deterministically be excluded, independent of the exact branches where they are situated. For the leaf nodes we use a unique key scheme, particularly the LKH key arrangement, and construct the key tree corresponding to the leaf nodes in CAG, naming it the leafs key tree (LKT). We refer to keys in LKT using the notation from [15]. A key $K_{m,n}$ denotes that the key is shared by all nodes with the slot identifier i such that $m \leq i \leq n$.

Figure 1 shows an example CAG and its corresponding LKT. In this case node 9 will be given the session key SK and the auxiliary keys $K_{0,3}$ $K_{0,1}$ and $K_{0,0}$. Following the propagation principle these keys will also be given to nodes 5, 2, and 1. Moreover, node 5 has a key known only to it and its ancestors.

Each leaf node A in the CAG receives the session key SK and a set of auxiliary keys from LKT, corresponding to the node's slot identifier:

$$keys_{LKT}(A) = SK \cup \{K_{m,n} \mid m \leq i \leq n \ \wedge i = LKTslotid(A)\}.$$

Each interior node B has a key K_B. Further if $A \prec B$, then all the keys of A are given also to B. In general the key assignment is:

$$keys(X) = \begin{cases} K_X \bigcup\limits_{y \in descendants_{CAG}(X)} keys(Y), \text{if } X \notin leafs_{CAG} \\ keys_{LKT}(X), \text{if } X \in leafs_{CAG} \end{cases} \tag{1}$$

where $leafs_{CAG}$ is the set of leaf nodes in CAG and $keys_{LKT}$ as defined above.

The re-keying algorithm to exclude a leaf node X from CAG is:

Step 1. Exclude node X from the LKT following the algorithm for exclusion in the LKH as in [15, 16, 17]. This assures that all leafs, except for the excluded leaf will get the new session key SK^{new}. When removing node 9, for instance, nodes 10, 3, 7, 15 and 16 will be re-keyed. Since their ancestors know the keys of these nodes, the ancestors will also be able to decrypt these messages and learn the new auxiliary keys as well as the new SK^{new}.

Step 2. Further two cases are distinguished:

Step 2.1. No new nodes become leafs in CAG. In this case all the remaining nodes have been re-keyed. Go to step 3.

Step 2.2. New nodes become leafs in CAG. Since these nodes have no other descendants than the one that is excluded they cannot be re-keyed. In figure 1.a, when removing node 14 (assuming that nodes 15 and 16 were removed earlier) nodes 11 and 13 will become leafs. In this case each new leaf in CAG must be included in the LKT and re-keyed. Two subcases follow:

Step 2.2.1. The LKT has enough free slots (unused key leafs) to accommodate the new leafs. Go to step 2.3.

Step 2.2.2. The LKT doesn't have enough free slots. In this case LKT must be expanded. LKT grows with one or more levels such that it accommodates all the newcomers. To grow the LKT with one level, for instance, the controller generates a new root key SK^{new} for the LKT. The old LKT will be the left sub-tree starting from the new SK^{new}. That is, the SK becomes the $K_{0,2^{d}-1}$, where d is the depth of the initial LKT. The SK^{new} is conveyed to the old members of the tree by encrypting it with the old SK and multicasting to the group. Within the same message the old members are informed that the tree increased with one level and the indexes of their keys changed, such that

$K_{2^{d-i}*j.2^{d-i}*(j+1)-1}$ becomes $K_{2^{d-i+1}*j.2^{d-i+1}*(j+1)-1}$. The whole new right sub-tree of the LKT will then be available to newcomers. Observe that LKT can grow more than one level at once making this process more efficient. Go to step 2.3.

Step 2.3. Re-key and include each new leaf Y into the LKT by sending the new session key SK^{new} as well as the auxiliary keys associated with LKT encrypted with its key K_Y. Y and all its ancestors will understand this message so the key propagation is re-established.

Step 3. The algorithm ends.

The number of transmissions used to exclude a category is:

$$2*\log(card(leafs_{CAG})) - 1 + newleafs(sn) + 1 \qquad (2)$$

where *newleafs* is a function, denoting the number of new leafs in CAG at session number *sn*. The last term 1 comes from the worst case assumption that any application of the exclusion algorithm will require expansion of the LKT.

The number of keys per user varies from $\log(card(leafs_{CAG})) + 1$ for the leafs in the CAG to $M + card(leafs_{CAG}) - 1$ for the root of CAG. The total number of keys is $M + card(leafs_{CAG}) - 1$ which is also the number of keys per controller. The solution has good performance for transmissions, but the number of keys per user as well as the number of keys per controller increases due to the propagation of keys.

For a given number of categories M the number of transmissions and the number of keys per controller depends on the number of leafs in CAG. Fewer leafs result in better numbers. On the other hand the number of keys per user depends not only on the number of nodes M and the number of leafs $card(leafs_{CAG})$ but also on the mapping between nodes from $leafs_{CAG}$ and the slots in LKT. According to equation 1, the set of keys depends on the union of keys propagating from its descendants, and therefore it has fewer elements in the case where the propagated keys are the same.

5. EVALUATION

We analytically compare the efficiency of our solution strategy with our reference schemes and then present experimental results obtained through simulation.

5.1 Comparison

The comparison is given in Table 1. We observe that the performance of the exclusion algorithm is dependent on the term newleafs(sn), see equation (2). We note that for a given number of categories M each category will sooner or later become a leaf in CAG. Also there will be at least as many sessions as M. Therefore, on average newleafs(sn) ≤ 1. We also note that card($leafs_{CAG}$) ≤ M and that M = N denotes the worst case where every category has exactly one user.

Table 1. Comparison with our reference schemes

		Our scheme	RKS	UKS
Transmissions to exclude	one user	NA	logN	2*logN – 1
	one category	2*log(card($leafs_{CAG}$)) + newleafs(sn)	NA	NA
Keys/user		log(card($leafs_{CAG}$)) + 1 .. card($leafs_{CAG}$) + M –1	logN + 1	logN + 1
Keys/controller		Card($leafs_{CAG}$) + M – 1	2*logN + 1	2*N – 1
Collusion resistance		Collusion requirement is configurable	Collusion can occur uncontrolled	Perfect resistance

NA = not applicable

5.2 Experimental results

We evaluate the performance of our proposed solution by simulating different configurations of the CAG in the case where the CAG is a tree. We motivate choosing a tree for CAG by the following facts: the tree is a worst case with respect to memory needed for the LKT; further, it is also a worst case with respect to number of keys per user; finally, there already exist random tree generators that have been used in benchmarking multicast protocols.

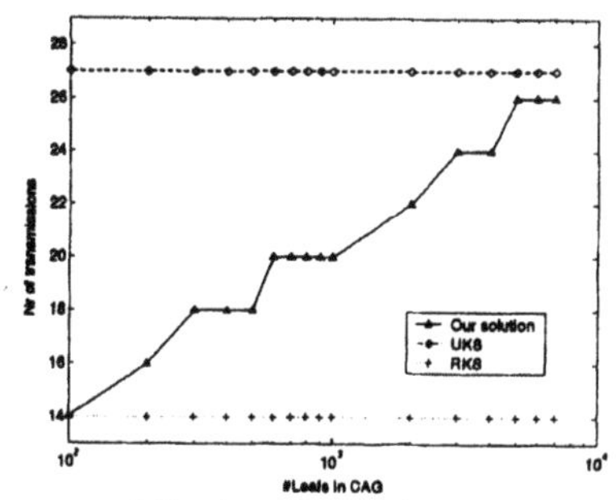

a) Number of transmissions

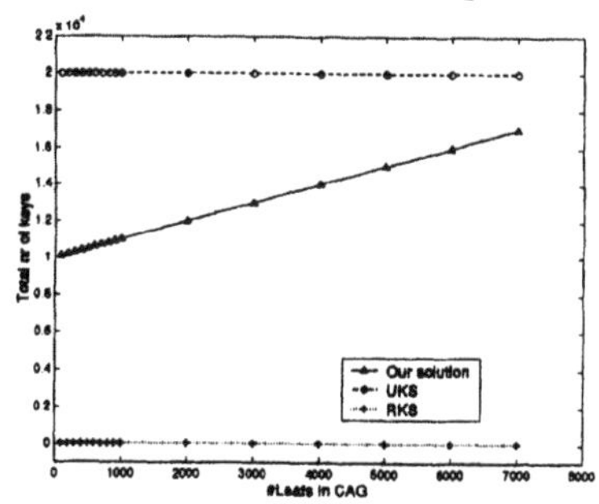

b) Number of keys/controller

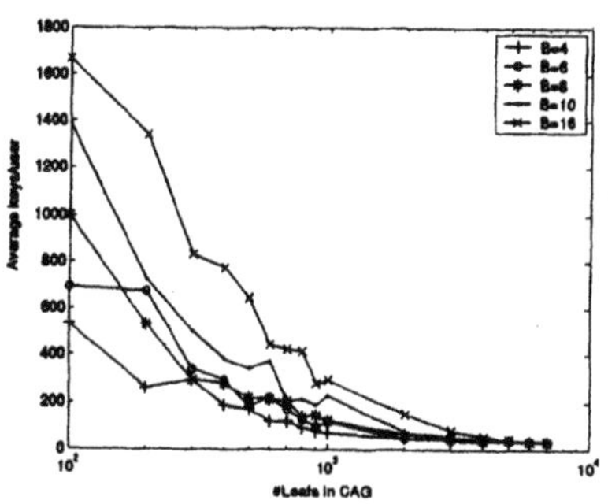

c) Average number of keys/user

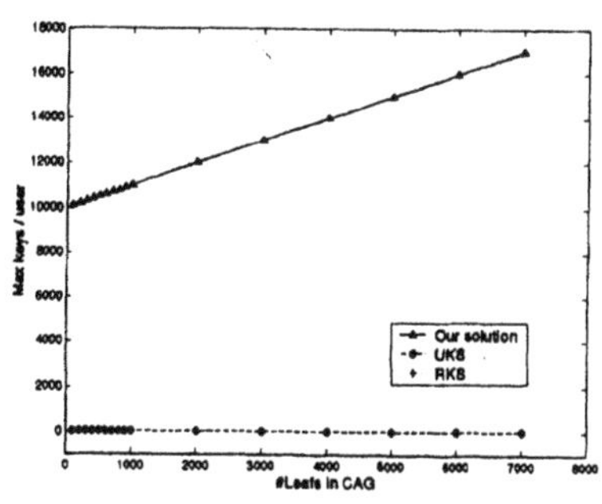

d) Maximum number of keys/user

Figure 2. Experimental results

A specific configuration of the CAG models a certain collusion requirement. We randomly generate such configurations by using a random tree generator with three degrees of freedom [14] - the maximum number of nodes, the maximum number of leafs and the maximum branching factor. In the experiments, the number of categories (nodes in CAG) has been kept to 10000, and the number of leafs has been varied from 100 to 7000. Each combination of nodes and leafs has been repeated with a branching factor of 4, 6, 8, 10, and 16.

As shown by the experiments, and as expected from equation (2), the number of transmissions depends solely on the number of leafs, see figure 2.a. Fewer leafs result in fewer transmissions, more leafs in more transmissions. Since the number of leafs is related to the degree of collusion, this result confirms our hypothesis – the more constraints are put on collusion the more transmissions we need. Our solution gives the possibility to balance the collusion requirement and the number of transmissions. The number of keys per controller, figure 2.b, is less than in the UKS, but it increases with the number of leafs in the CAG. Actually the number of transmissions and the number of keys per controller from the UKS are upper bounds for the number of transmissions and the number of keys per controller in our scheme.

Because the keys from child nodes are given to their parents, the fewer leafs we have the more keys per user we get, as shown in figure 2.c (on average) and figure 2.d. Note that we have computed the average number of keys per user in the conditions of only one user per category. If there are more than one user per category the distribution of keys per user can change very much and can greatly influence the average. If categories towards the root have many users, the average would become high. If on the contrary most of the users are concentrated in categories towards the leafs the average goes down.

6. RELATED WORK

An overview of various issues regarding multicast security is given in [1]. The topic of key management for multicast communication has been studied before. The GKMP [9] introduces a centralized controller that distributes session keys by unicasts to each group member. This approach does not scale well for large groups and frequent member changes. To provide scalability, Iouls [12] decentralizes the controller by using a hierarchy of trusted key distribution servers.

The scalability problem associated with frequent key change in large groups has been addressed in [15, 16, 17] by using logical key hierarchy (LKH) of auxiliary keys that balance the number of transmissions and the key storage. OFT [11] halves the communication for re-keying by introducing dependencies in the logical key structure that allows keys to be derived from other certain keys. More precisely, in OFT the key of one node is derived from the two keys of its child nodes. OFC [3] applies a similar principle to LKH, but only when re-keying, and halves its communication. In OFC, there exists a path from one of the leafs to the root of the tree such that the session key corresponding to the root can be obtained by iterative hashing of that key leaf. The hybrid scheme [2] reduces the storage requirement for the controller at the price of increasing communication and computation overhead. [10] finds the optimal hybrid scheme when constraints on communication and storage are given. More recently, ELK [13] allows trading communication overhead with security and computation. The idea is to avoid the transmission of the whole key when re-keying, by sending only smaller hints of the updates that would enable an authorized receiver to compute the key, partially by brute search.

Logical tree structures with reuse of keys, such as the BFM [4] and Flat [15] improve the efficiency by decreasing the number of keys stored by the controller as well as reducing the number of transmissions for cumulative member removal [4]. However, these schemes are susceptible to collusion. To reduce the probability of collusion the number of leafs of the tree is increased. If collusion still occurs the only way to successfully exclude the colluding group is to collectively remove the corrupted users. The algorithm proposed in [15] for such case suffers from the fact that it also expunges innocent users who happen to share keys with the colluding users. By using the scheme proposed by us the possible colluding users can be securely excluded by expunging the category to which they belong.

More close to our work is the family of broadcast encryption schemes from [6] that allows for flexibility with respect to the collusion requirements as defined there. The schemes allow a controller to broadcast a secret to any set of privileged users so that coalitions of k users not in the privileged set cannot learn the secret. Therefore, the collusion requirement is specified by the parameter k that is the maximum size of a corrupt coalition to which the scheme is still resistant. However, their work has mostly a theoretical value since the overhead of such scheme is very large. Moreover, they use a static distribution scheme with predefined slots.

7. CONCLUSIONS AND FUTURE WORK

This paper adds the collusion constraints as a requirement for designing key management systems. A formalization of the collusion requirement is given in terms of categories of users and constraints among these categories. A solution is proposed for the general case of collusion requirement. A scalability analysis is given in terms of the number of the transmissions for re-keying and the storage requirement (number of keys). We find that in general there is a tight dependency between the exact settings of the collusion requirement shown in the form of CAG and the performance of the solution. In general the solution has good performance for the number of transmissions needed to re-key in case a category must be excluded. However, the number of keys per user may become large due to the propagation principle.

Future work can be invested in designing smarter key management schemes that bring the best balancing between scalability and security, including collusion as a given requirement. We are currently investigating [5] how to alleviate the explosion of keys due to propagation by using hash dependencies among the keys similar to [3, 11]. This would minimize the storage requirement. However, the hash function would probably amend the computation resources of the end users.

REFERENCES

1. R. Canetti, B. Pinkas, "A Taxonomy of Multicast Security Issues", Internet Draft, 1998.
2. R. Canetti, T. Malkin, K. Nissim, "Efficient Communication-Storage Tradeoffs for Multicast Encryption", *Eurocrypt'99*, 1999.
3. R. Canetti, J. Garey, G. Itkis, D. Micciancio, M. Naor, B. Pinkas, "Multicast security: A taxonomy and efficient constructions", *Infocom '99*, March 1999.
4. I. Chang, R. Engel, D. Kandlur, D. Pendarakis, D. Saha, "Key Management for Secure Internet Multicast using Boolean Function Minimization Techniques", *IEEE Infocom '99*, March 1999.
5. C. Duma, N. Shahmehri, P. Lambrix, "Efficient Storage Requirement for Category-Based Key Management for Multicast", Internal Technical Report, Linköpings universitetet, Sweden, November 2002.
6. A. Fiat, M. Naor, "Broadcast encryption", *Crypto '92*, Springer-Verlag LNCS 839, 1994, pp. 257-270.
7. L. Han, N. Shahmehri, "Secure Multicast Software Delivery", *9th IEEE International Workshop on Enterprise Security (WET-ICE)*, June 2000.
8. L. Han, *Secure and Scalable E-Service Software Delivery*, Licentiate Thesis No. 906, Linköpings universitetet, Sweden, September 2001.
9. H. Harney, C. Muckenhirn, "Group Key Management Protocol (GKMP)", RFC 2093 and RFC 2094, July 1997.
10. M. Y. Li, R. Poovendran, C. Bernstain, "Optimisation of Key Storage for Secure Multicast", *Conference on Information Science and Systems 2001*, March 2001.
11. D. A. McGrew, A. T. Sherman, "Key Establishment in Large Dynamic Groups Using One-Way Function Trees", Technical Report No. 0755, TIS Labs at Network Associates, May 1998.
12. S. Mittra, "Iolus: A Framework for Scalable Secure Multicasting", *ACM SIGCOMM'97*, 1997.
13. A. Peering, D. Song, J. D. Tyger, "ELK, a New Protocol for Efficient Large-Group Key Distribution", *IEEE Security and Privacy Symposium 2001*, May 2001.
14. S. Ratnasamy, S. McCanne, "Inference of Multicast Routing Trees and Bottleneck Bandwidths using End-to-End Measurements", *Infocom '99*, March 1999.
15. M. Waldvogel, G. Caronni, D. Sun, N. Weiler, B Plattner, "The VersaKey Framework: Versatile Group Key Management", *IEEE Journal on Selected Areas in Communications*, Vol. 17, No. 8, August 1999.
16. D. Wallner, E. Harder, R. Agee, "Key Management for Multicast: Issues and Architectures", RFC 2627, June 1999.
17. C. K. Wong, M. Gouda, S. S. Lam, "Secure Group Communications Using Key Graphs", *ACM SIGCOMM '98*, 1998.
18. Y. R. Yang, S. S. Lam, "A Secure Group Key Management Protocol Communication Lower Bound", The University of Texas at Austin, Department of Computer Sciences, Technical Report TR-00-24, September 2000.

CONTENT, CONTEXT, PROCESS ANALYSIS OF IS SECURITY POLICY FORMATION

Maria Karyda[1], Spyros Kokolakis[2], Evangelos Kiountouzis[1]
[1]*Athens University of Economics and Business, 76 Patission Str., GR-10434 Athens, Greece. Email: {mka,eak}@aueb.gr, voice: +30-210-8203555, fax: +30-210-8237369.*

[2]*University of the Aegean, GR-83200 Karlovassi, Samos, Greece. Email: sak@aegean.gr, voice: +30-22730-82233, fax: +30-22730-82009.*

Abstract: Security management is now acknowledged as a key constituent of Information Systems (IS) management. IS security management traditionally relies on the formation and application of security policies. Most of the research in this field address issues regarding the structure and content of security policies; whereas the context within which security policies are conceived and developed remains rather unexplored. However, security policies that are formed without taking into account the specific social and organisational environment within which they will be applied, are often proven to be inapplicable or ineffective. In this paper we explore the issues pertaining to the formation of security policies under the perspective of *contextualism*. Within the framework of contextualism, we study the context, content and process of IS security policies development. This paper aims to contribute to IS security research by bringing forth the issue of context-dependent formation of security policies. In addition, it provides a contextual framework, which we expect to improve the effectiveness of IS security policies development.

Key words: Information systems, information systems security, contextualism.

1. INTRODUCTION

In the last decade security issues have emerged to the top of the Information Systems (IS) management agenda. Practice has shown that security tools and mechanisms alone cannot provide adequate protection to modern ISs. Tools and mechanisms should be incorporated into a comprehensive *IS security policy*, i.e. a structured set of principles, strategies and detailed guidelines for the protection of an IS.

Several approaches have been proposed for the design of security policies, with *risk analysis* [ISO, 1996] being at present the most frequently used. Most of the research in this field is concerned with issues regarding the structure and content of security policies, whereas the context within which security policies are conceived and developed remains rather unexplored. However, security policies that are formed without taking into account the specific social and organisational environment within which they will be applied, are often proven to be inapplicable or ineffective.

In this paper we consider the development and application of security policies in their social and organisational context. Under this perspective we propose a framework with three dimensions, i.e. *context*, *content* and *process*, to support the development and application of security policies. Moreover, based on the experience gained from several security policy development cases we identify specific factors in the social and organisational context that play an important role in the development and application of security policies.

2. INFORMATION SYSTEMS SECURITY MANAGEMENT AND SECURITY POLICIES

2.1 IS Security Management: What kind of problem is it?

Security concerns have been of primary importance for firms and organisations, since most organisational activities have come to depend heavily on information and communication technology. Moreover, current reports show that the number of security related incidents and consequent financial losses increase in magnitude, as well as in severance [CSI/FBI, 2002]. Security problems, in most of the cases, have been addressed by means of technical solutions, i.e. tools and mechanisms, such as intrusion detection and access control mechanisms.

An IS, however, should not be studied with a focus on its technical dimension only. ISs comprise a set of diverse elements, namely information, software, hardware, procedures and people, all of which interact with each other. IS security, therefore, aiming to protect all its comprising elements, as well as its entity and unobstructed functionality, involves a wide range of actions, which are of quite different nature. For example, training and awareness programs can be part of an IS security policy, to ensure that people involved in the operations of the IS take all appropriate actions to prevent disclosure of sensitive information and to reduce the probability of unauthorised use of software or hardware. Similarly, installation of special purpose software, such as anti-virus or network monitoring tools, could also be a part of the activities aiming to protect an IS.

It is evident, therefore, that technical methods on their own can neither adequately nor sufficiently provide for the security of an IS. Information systems security management, therefore, should also encompass other means of action, i.e. managerial activities, such as auditing and control, and human resource development activities, such as education and training, besides the employment of technical methods. The need for abandoning a 'pure' technical viewpoint in favor of a 'socio-technical' or even 'social' standpoint has, in the recent years, been acknowledged by a significant number of authors in the area of IS security research [Dhillon, 1997 and 2001, Dhillon and Backhouse 2001, Hitchings, 1995, Trompeter and Eloff, 2001, von Solms 2001]. We argue that the socio-technical analysis should not be restricted to the process of security policy formulation and its content. It should also include the analysis of the IS context.

2.2 Security policies as a major IS security management instrument

With regard to security, management at the IS level faces a complicated and ill-structured problem domain. Most widely-adopted security management methods and tools (such as firewall systems, network monitoring tools, risk analysis methods, security evaluation criteria, encryption mechanisms) share a common 'technical' point of view, thus overlooking, most of the times, the social and organisational aspects of IS security.

Faced with a great variety of security threats, organisations develop and put in action security policies. A security policy, in general, might have a different meaning for different people. Nevertheless, for the purposes of our research, we consider a security policy to be a high-level statement of the goals and objectives with regard to security, as well as the description of the general means for their attainment.

In this way, the formulation of security policies constitutes one of the most important 'tools' IS management employs, in order to address the issue of IS security. However, whereas needs and problems regarding the security of individual IS components (such as servers, workstations, files or networks) may be easy to identify and evaluate, there is no single security solution, nor a single security policy that can fit all organisations, since many security issues are organisation-specific and emerge in the organisational environment at a certain point of time.

There exist many ready-made, skeleton-type security policies, as well as standards that can be used as a reference guide or compliance target [ISO 17799]. However, researchers [Wood, 2000] as well as industry, i.e. [Control Data Systems Inc., 1999] still face the issue of 'why security policies fail'. A great variety of reasons and explanations have been put forth, such as that security controls constitute a 'barrier to progress' [Control Data Systems Inc., 1999], or that security policies are very likely to be circumvented by employees in their effort to perform efficiently their tasks [Wood, 2000].

3. THE SOCIO-TECHNICAL NATURE OF IS SECURITY POLICIES DEVELOPMENT

Despite the fact that security policies at the organisational level are a well-considered issue by a great number of organisations, there are still a number of factors that pertain the formulation and application of security policies and ultimately affect their success, which remain open issues and are still unexplored. Some of these issues, are presented in the following list:

a) What is the area of responsibility for the organisation with regard to IS security? In other words, who is responsible for the security of the IS?
b) Which management practices should be employed when developing and implementing an IS security policy?
c) What are the 'drivers' behind the formulation of security policies; who are the stakeholders and which factors should the author of the security policy take into consideration?
d) Which are the factors that may affect the implementation of a security policy and how can they be managed, so as to result to a 'successful' implementation?

We believe that one of the reasons that a great number of issues related to the formulation of security policies, still remain unresolved, is that current approaches to IS security policies mainly focus on the *content* of a security policy, but overlook two other aspects: the *context* and *process* of the formulation of a security policy, which are further analysed in Section 5.

4. CONTEXTUALISM IN INFORMATION SYSTEMS AND IS SECURITY RESEARCH

Information Systems is an interdisciplinary academic field, drawing from both systems engineering and social sciences, that is characterised by methodological pluralism [Avgerou, 2000]. Having in mind that IS security is a 'socio-technical' problem [Dhillon, 1997], we argue that it is well justified to enrich our approaches by employing an approach widely used in the area of IS research, which is *contextualism*.

Contextualism [Pettigrew, 1985] is an interpretive approach, which provides a framework for understanding, within the realm of subjectiveness [Dhillon and Backhouse 2001]. In the IS field, contextualism has been adopted by several researchers. Walsham [1993] applies this methodological approach, combined with structuration theory, in order to explore the context and process of organisational change. Symons [1991] uses the framework of contextualism to build a categorization of the IS evaluation literature. Pettigrew and Whipp [1993] apply the same framework to capture a holistic image of the link between strategic change and competition, with regard to British firms. As depicted in Figure 1, the contextualist point of view acknowledges the importance of the content in all organisational activities, but also gives emphasis to the process that has resulted to these activities, as well as on the context, the surrounding environment, within which these activities are formulated and carried out. From the contextualist perspective the process, content and context are closely interrelated and they should be studied jointly, in order to understand issues, such as organisational change.

Hence, employing contextualism in the formulation of IS security policies aims to enhance our understanding, which has been intrigued by questions like the ones listed in Section 3, but not to provide explanations.

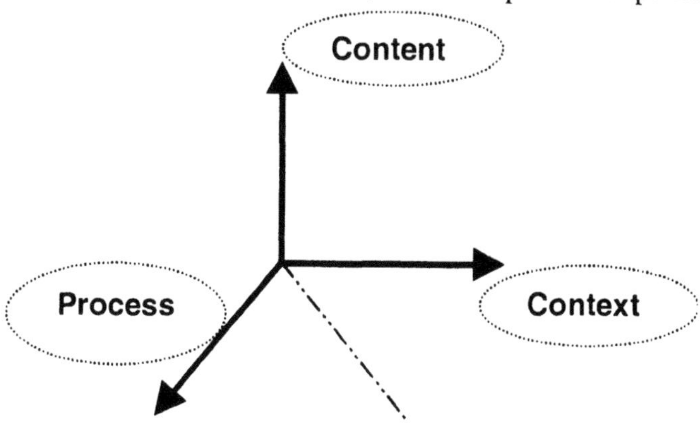

Figure 1. The framework of Content, Context, Process

5. CURRENT APPROACHES TO IS SECURITY POLICIES

Though most approaches used for the formulation of security policies address principally the technical aspects of security, a significant stream of research acknowledges also the importance of human-related and organisational-dependent dimensions of the process of security policy development. Research in this stream stresses the need for considering IS security management from a 'socio-technical' point of view and encourages further investigation under this perspective (e.g. Siponen [2000], Baskerville and Siponen [2002], Peltier, [1999].) Other researchers, in order to offset the technical bias, propose a systemic-holistic approach, e.g. Yngstrom [1995], Kiountouzis and Kokolakis [1996].

Siponen [2000] classifies security policies into two categories, namely 'technical' and 'organisational', stating that the level of maturity of research regarding 'people-oriented/non-technical' policies is quite low, compared to research on computer-oriented policies. The vast majority of currently employed approaches to security policy place great emphasis on the content of the policy; this mostly has to do with the description of procedures that provide for the security of the 'target' system, may it be a network, an operation system, a computer etc. Little or no attention at all, is paid however to other factors that could affect the formation and application of the policy and which are related to the social or organisational surrounding of the 'security target'. Moreover, with the exception of some training and educational activities that are usually included in the security policy, no mention is made of the ways the policy is communicated to the users and other personnel involved with the operations of the IS.

Modern organisations however, which rely heavily upon their informational infrastructure, need a comprehensive security policy, that will address all issues concerning IS security, by taking into account both their technological environment and the specific features of the organisational domain they operate in, as well as their unique culture.

It is evident that current approaches to the formation of security policies fail to face issues that affect the formation and application of the policy and stem from the organisational and social context, thus failing to meet current organisational needs for integrated IS security management.

6. APPLYING THE CONTEXTUALIST FRAMEWORK

In the following paragraphs we analyse the three dimensions of the framework presented above. In order to achieve this we have examined nine cases of organisations that have developed a security policy in the period 1997-2002 [Lambrinoudakis et al., 2001]. These include six government organisations, one non-governmental organisation and two private enterprises, in the areas of petroleum trade and pharmaceutics.

In these cases the authors were involved as consultants assigned the task of developing an IS security policy. Several variations of risk analysis were employed gradually adding elements of contextual analysis to the rather technical risk analysis methodology.

This was the first phase of the empirical research. In the second phase, the authors surveyed the security policy implementation in the above organisations. Several interviews were conducted with key persons that were involved in the implementation stage with the aim to identify the factors that affect the success of the security policy. Consequently, these factors were categorised in the three dimensions of the contextual framework presented in Figure 1.

6.1 IS Security Policies: Context

Context can be distinguished into social, organisational and technical. The majority of the currently employed methods for developing security policies provide the means for the analysis of technical context. However, the organisational and social contexts are equally important for the effective application of security policies. The main issue remains to identify the elements of the social, organisational and technical context, which are critical for the successful development and application of a security policy.

In order to identify these elements we have relied on the empirical study presented above. Throughout these nine cases, the authors have interviewed key persons in the operational, tactical and strategic managerial level. Through these interviews, several key issues with regard to the effectiveness of IS security policies have emerged. Then, reflecting upon the empirical evidence we have elicited a set of generic elements, which are presented in the following tables.

Table -1. Social context

Contextual elements	Description
Ethical considerations	Users would not accept policies that contradict to their ethical principles. Policy developers should be aware of any such conflicts and seek for consensus.
Legal and regulatory constraints	In the last decade there has been a plethora of laws concerning data processing and ISs in general, e.g. regulation on personal data protection, intellectual property protection etc. Thus, the legal and regulatory framework may be quite complex and need thorough examination before a security policy is launched.
Power structure and politics	Security policies control the access to and use of information, which is a significant source of power. It should be expected that the security policy would be at the center of the political arena. No matter how technically brilliant it may be, it is bound to fail, unless it finds political support.
Communication structures	For a security policy to succeed, it needs to be properly communicated to stakeholders. If it is expressed in a too technical language, it may be received with doubt.
External stakeholders	With this term we refer to stakeholders which are outside the organisational boundaries. They may be clients, consumers' organisations, data protection authorities etc. It is often the case that stakeholders exercise significant influence to policy making.

Table -2. Organisational context

Contextual elements	Description
Management structure	Management structure is usually depicted in the organisational chart. Policy developers should examine whether the current management structure is able to support the application of the security policy. Otherwise, re-structuring may be required.
Organisational culture	Norms and practices prescribed within a security policy usually require some sort of change in the way people perform their organisational activities. Flexibility to change, however, is closely related to the organisational culture that may or may not favour changes.
Motivation	Policy developers should consider the motives, which have led to the decision to develop a security policy.
Structures of responsibility	Policies should address the question: who will take responsibility for the implementation of the policy? Without unambiguous allocation of responsibilities, policies run the risk of remaining inactive.
Internal stakeholders	Stakeholders within the organisation, IS users in particular, may resist the implementation of a security policy. Therefore, their acceptance is also important.

Table -3. Technical context

Contextual elements	Description
IS technical elements	Hardware, software and data, with their relationships, lie at the core of the technical context.
Plans for future developments	Since ISs rarely remain static, policies should take into account any plans for future modifications to the current system or the development of new systems.
Threats and vulnerabilities	Threats exploit vulnerabilities to cause damage to the assets of the IS. Threats may be of human origin, or they may be related to physical disasters, technical failures etc.
Technology trends	Since technology evolves continuously, current technology trends need to be taken into account, in order to expand the life period of the security policy.
Currently available security technology	The selection of technical countermeasures should consider the current state-of-the-art.

6.2 IS Security Policies: Content

A wealth of resources, including sample policies, baseline policies and lists of measures, is available to policy developers. In the following table, we delineate the issues that should be covered by a security policy.

Table -4. Content

Categories	Description
Organisational re-structuring	In most of the cases a new organisational framework needs to be established, in order for the security policy to be implemented successfully.
Administrative procedures	A broad category of procedures is included in security policies, comprising personnel related procedures, system administration procedures etc.
Terms and concepts	Establishing and elucidating the conceptual framework of the security policy appears as a prerequisite for the effective communication of the policy.
Awareness, education, training	Awareness, education and training constitute an important element in a security policy, since the levels of security awareness in the public remain low.
Technical measures and tools	Security goals stated within a security policy are achieved by applying a set of technical measures and tools, which are prescribed within the security policy.
Policy evaluation, monitoring and review	Procedures and criteria for the evaluation, continuous monitoring and reviewing in designated time, should also be part of a security policy.

6.3 IS Security Policies: Process

6.3.1 Development process

Several methodologies for the development of security policies are currently available. It is not within the scope of this paper to review them or to propose yet another methodology. However, we may suggest that regardless of the methodology adapted, the process of developing a security policy should employ a contextualist view, by including the following tasks:

- Define the problem.
- Obtain stakeholders' support and resources for the development and implementation of the policy.
- Analyse the social, organisational and technical context by recognising the aforementioned factors (see Tables 1 to 3).
- Define the content of the policy.
- Define evaluation criteria, monitoring processes, review and update procedures.
- Develop an implementation plan.
- Evaluate impact on social, organisational and technical factors due to planned changes introduced by the security policy.

6.3.2 Implementation, monitoring and maintenance

It is often the case that security policies remain inactive or are rendered ineffective. This justifies the need for a strategy that will guide the implementation of the policy, also covering issues such as monitoring and maintenance of the policy. Although there are currently no methods to guide this process, we may provide an indicative list of factors to be considered.

- **Implementation**: Who will have the responsibility to implement the security policy (e.g. Security Officer, System Administrator)? What means will be employed for this purpose? When is the appropriate time for the implementation of each module of the policy? What are the priorities for the implementation?
- **Acceptance**: How will the policy be communicated and acceptance will be obtained?
- **Contextual integration**: How to overcome hindrances stemming from the social, organisational and technical context?
- **Evaluation and monitoring**: Which are the criteria and the processes that will be used for the evaluation and monitoring of the effectiveness of the policy?

- **Review**: Which are the procedures for reviewing and updating the policy?

7. SUMMARY AND CONCLUSIONS

In this paper we have explored the relationship of the security policy formation with the environment within which the policy shall be applied. For this reason we applied the perspective of contextualism to a set of nine cases of organisations (including government and non-government organisations, as well as private companies) that have developed a security policy in the period 1997-2002. In these cases, at which the authors were involved as consultants, several variations of risk analysis were employed, gradually adding elements of contextual analysis to the rather technical risk analysis. In the aftermath, the authors studied the implementation of the security policy in the above organisations, by conducting several interviews with key persons that were involved in the implementation stage, aiming to identify the factors that affect the success of the security policy. These factors were then categorised in the three dimensions of the contextual framework presented in Figure 1. The conclusions resulting from our research include the following:

- the relationship between a specific organisational context and the security policy formation should not be overlooked when developing the policy;
- research and practice should pay equal attention to factors that characterise all three dimensions, namely the content, the context and the process of the policy formulation;
- most widely used approaches currently overlook the context of the policy, thus resulting in inapplicable and inefficient security policies.

This paper aims to contribute to IS security research by bringing forth the issue of context-dependent formulation of security policies. In addition, it provides a contextual framework, which we expect to improve the effectiveness of IS security policies development.

8. REFERENCES

Avgerou C. (2000), 'Information systems: what sort of science is it?', *Omega*, Vol., 28, pp.567-579, Elsevier Science Ltd.

Baskerville, R. and Siponen M. (2002) 'An Information Security Meta-policy for Emergent Organizations', forthcoming in *Journal of Logistics Information Management*.

Control Data Systems Inc. (1999) 'Why Security Policies Fail - White Paper' available at http://www.cdc.com

Dhillon G. (1997) *Managing Information System Security*, Macmillan Press Ltd.

Dhillon G. (2001) *Information Security Management: Global Challenges in the New Millennium*, Idea Group Publishing.

Dhillon G. and Backhouse J. (2001) 'Current directions in IS security research: towards socio-organizational perspectives', *Information Systems Journal*, Vol. 11, pp. 127-153.

Hitchings J. (1995) 'Deficiencies of the Traditional Approach to Information Security and the Requirements for a New Methodology', *Computers and Security* Vol.14, No.5, pp.377-383.

ISO 17799 Directory: Services and Software for ISO 17799 Compliance, ISO 17799 Audit, ISO 17799 Implementation and Security and Risk Analysis (also available at: http://www.iso17799software.com).

ISO/IEC/JTC1 (1996) Information Technology - Security Techniques - Guidelines for the Management of IT Security, GMITS, ISO/IEC DTR13335.

Kiountouzis E.A. and Kokolakis S.A. (1996) 'An analyst's view of information systems security', in *Proc. of the 12th International Information Security Conference (IFIP/SEC '96)*, Samos, Greece, May 1996, Chapman & Hall.

Lambrinoudakis C., Kokolakis S., Gritzalis D. (2001) 'Recurrent IT security issues and recommendations: learning from risk assessment reviews', in *Proc. of the Security and Control of IT in Society (SCITS-II), IFIP Conference*, Bratislava, Slovakia, June 2001.

Lindup K.R. (1995), 'A New Model for Information Security Policies', *Computers and Security*, Vol. 14, pp. 691-695.

Peltier T. (1999) *Information security policies and procedures: a practitioner's reference*, CRC Press.

Pettigrew A.M. (1985), *The Awakening Giant: Continuity and Change in ICI*, Blackwell, Oxford.

Pettigrew A.M. and R. Whipp (1993) *Managing Change for Competitive Success*, Blackwell.

Siponen M. (2000), 'Policies for Construction of Information Systems' Security Guidelines', *Information Security for Global Information Infrastructures*, Qing S., Eloff J.H.P. (eds.), pp. 112-120, Kluwer Academic Publishers.

Symons V. J. (1991), 'A review of information systems evaluation: content, context and process', *Journal of Information Systems*, Vol. 1, No 3, pp205-212.

Trompeter C. and Eloff J. (2001) 'A Framework for the Implementation of Socio-ethical Controls in Information Security', *Computers and Security*, Vol. 20, No 5, pp.384-390.

von Solms B. (2001) 'Information Security – A Multidimensional Discipline', *Computers and Security*, Vol. 20, No 6, pp. 504-508.

Walsham, G. (1993) *Interpreting Information Systems in Organisations*, J. Wiley & Sons Ltd.

Wood C. (2000) 'An Unappreciated Reason Why Security Policies Fail', Computer Fraud and Security, 10, pp. 13-14.

Yngstrom, L. (1995) 'A Holistic Approach to IT Security', in *Information Security - the Next Decade* (eds. Eloff, J. and S. von Solms), Chapman & Hall, London, pp.98-109.

INTEGRATING SECURITY INTO SYSTEMS DEVELOPMENT

Ulrika Evertsson, Urban Örthberg, and Louise Yngström
Department of Computer and Systems Sciences
Stockholm University/Royal Institute of Technology
Sweden

Abstract: There are suggestions that security may be an integrated part of any systems development method. One way to do this is to use a meta-methodology. With this theory as a leading star, a model, called the Pentagon Model is built as a bridge between The Systems Lifecycle (SLC) method and a company's security tools. The model describes what to do in order to develop more secure information systems, rather than a detailed description on how to do to succeed in this work. The level of security in the systems is determined by the context and will differ from case to case. This demands a flexible tool for integrating appropriate security solutions for each system. The Pentagon Model is designed to work together with the SLC, an approach used by most developers today. This way we eliminate the re-engineering of the model to fit in different projects, which might be necessary with a fixed and static model.

Key words: secure information system development, security awareness in development processes

1. INTRODUCTION

This paper is part of an action-oriented research carried out in a local division of a global IT-company mainly dealing with information systems development. Our mission was to improve the security awareness among the staff and to integrate this awareness in the whole system development process. The full report [Evertsson&Örthberg, 2002] includes organizational considerations and introduces a communication role to link the development and security departments. Our work was mainly influenced by researchers suggesting security aspects need to be taken account of already in the process of developing IS-systems [Baskerville, 1988, 92, 94, 2001, Siponen, 2001a-d, Siponen&Baskerville, 2001], and the facts that security needs to take account of business needs, stakeholder interests, and system contexts in a holistic approach [Magnusson, 1999, Yngström,1996, Fillery-James, 1999]. Our model, the Pentagon Model, can be deduced in particular from the IDEAL Approach within the SSE-CMM [SSE-CMM, 1999] and Fillery-James' Orion Strategy [Fillery-James, 1999] with some sub steps influenced by the local System Life Cycle, SLC, method. Even if Orion and IDEAL do not concern systems development in particular, they contribute essential steps in the process of creating secure systems. Together they complement each other in the Pentagon Model, as can be seen from table 1.

Table 1: The steps of the Pentagon Model derived from the Orion Strategy and the IDEAL Approach. Input and Output illustrates different areas to apply each method.

Systems Project/ Changes IN	Input concerning Information Security IN	Stimulus for change IN
The Pentagon Model	The Orion Strategy	The IDEAL Approach
0 – Reconnaissance	1 – Possible Security Vulnerability	1 – Initiating
1 – Current State	2 – Analyze Current Security Situation	2 – Diagnosing *Characterize Current and desired states*
2 – Ideal Solution	4 – Model Ideal Information Security Solution	
3 – Establish Solution	3 – Analyze Information Classes and sensitivity 5 – Compare Ideal Solution with Current Security 6 – Identify & Analyze Measures to Fill Gaps	2- Diagnosing *Develop Recommendations* 3 – Establishing
4 – Design & Produce	7 – Establish and implement Security Plan	4 – Acting
5 – Evaluate		5 – Learning
OUT Secure Information Systems	OUT Secure Information in Organizations	OUT Systems Security Engineering

The Pentagon Model is a compact model compared to the forerunners. This way we believe it to be easy to grasp and more user friendly. This approach was chosen since our sponsor required a tool to be used on a daily basis, not one that will be ignored due to its' complexity.

Simplifying the predecessors' outline may be understood as we are trying to take shortcuts, which may damage the scope of the models. This also implies a deteriorated quality of the Pentagon Model. We have considered this and feel that we incorporate all essential parts in a way suited for systems development. From table 1 it is also obvious that we have not left anything out, all steps of the Orion Strategy and the IDEAL Approach are included and influence the Pentagon.

2. VISUAL DESIGN

The visual design of the Pentagon Model as seen in Figure 1 is strongly influenced by the Orion Strategy. Some of the differences are that we have chosen a more symmetric shape and turned the steps around in a clockwise direction. The steps of The Pentagon Model are also fewer than in the Orion Strategy, which is an intellectual, rather than visual, influence from the IDEAL approach.

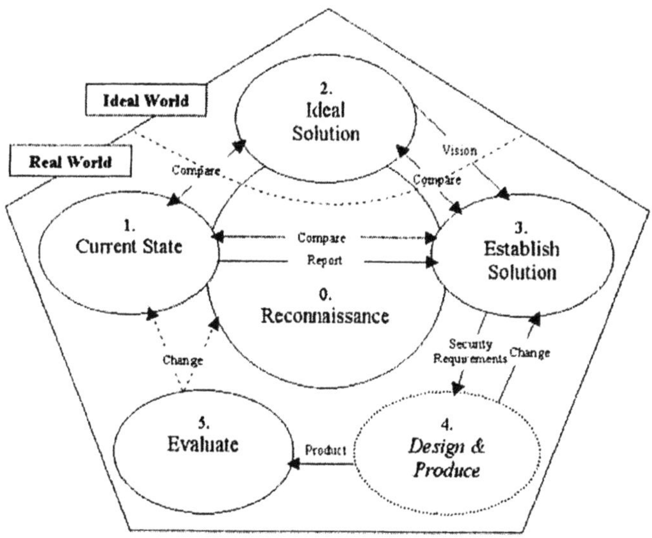

Figure 1. The Pentagon Model

One strong influence from the Orion Strategy is the concepts of an Ideal and a Real World, the visions produced in the Ideal world are essential to generate a well thought out security solution [cf. Fillery-James, 1999 p.138f]. Fillery-James also illustrates the iteration between the Real World and the Ideal World in her model. In the Pentagon we have tried to clarify this iteration by double pointed arrows between the steps 1,2 and 3. The rest of the arrows illustrate the output from each step as the input for the next. Steps 1,2 and 3 are also directly influenced by the findings in step 0, Reconnaissance, which is shown by the overlap of these steps. The fourth step *Design & Produce* is an inactive step, which consists of support for the designers and developers. A dashed border illustrates this.

3. THE STEPS OF THE PENTAGON MODEL

Below, each step of the Pentagon Model will be presented in detail. We use a systems approach where the inputs, processes and outputs of each step are described. This way we capture all the sub steps in each step and visualize the building blocks of the Pentagon Model and the connections between them.

As indicated in Figure 1, an indispensable approach is to iterate the model in general and the steps 1 through 3 in particular. We recommend that the steps 2 and 3 be completed at least twice, but ideally three times. This since it may be hard to grasp all important information in a single session [Modeling Specialist, 2001]. While performing this iteration, an on going comparison to the results of step 1 is essential in order not to loose focus on the current state and its' potential restrictions. There may also occur some iteration between the inactive step 4 and the previous steps and also between step 5 and the steps 0 and 1, in these cases the iteration will always be due to changes. Another general issue of importance is that the steps of the Pentagon Model have to be fixed at some point, in order to continue with the process. When this fixation occurs is dependant of the situation, but the iteration may generate a sense of when this should be done.

3.1 Step 0 - Reconnaissance

The thought behind this naming is that by reconnoitering the customers *Business Needs* and the *Systems Context* and conducting a *Risk Analysis* based on a *Security Policy*, a *Security Base* will be outlined. The security base must be anchored with the project management and the customers by

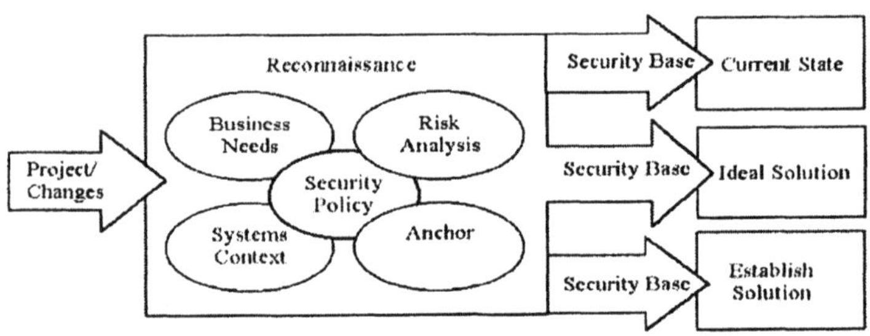

Figure 2. The Reconnaissance Step

convincing them of the severity of the risks in the thought system. The Reconnaissance step, see figure 2, is the minimum security work that has to be done in every systems development project.

The result, the Security Base, is the foundation for the rest of the process of using the Pentagon Model. It directly influences the steps *Current State*, *Ideal Solution* and *Establish Solution*. These steps formulate the *Security Requirements* that is the input to the *Design* step, which determines how the secure system will be built.

This reasoning is illustrated in Figure 3, where the Reconnaissance step is the foundation on which the Pentagon steps are built and the Security Base is the beam that holds it.

Figure 3. The Stairway to Security

By introducing this step in the initiation of a systems development process the developing company can highlight the risks of information systems in general and the thought system in particular. It is then up to the customers to decide whether to live with the risks and the potential damage or to take measures to prevent them from occurring. *Business Needs*: This step is inherited from the studied company's SLC and has the aim to determine the actual needs to be filled within the scope of the commission. A Business Need is a problem or opportunity within the business, which consists of one or more needs. These determine the type of system needed to fulfil the needs. The identification of the Business Needs will also aid in understanding the impact of the thought system on these needs. The focus in this step should be on security implications of the business needs. The step is carried out in cooperation with an analyst responsible for the overall business needs analysis.

Systems Context: The main goal of this step is to describe the information within the system. This description includes the different types of information, how it is communicated and who has access to it. The results define a high level description of the existing system and its environment along with their mutual influences on each other. To succeed with the reconnoitring of the systems context, a systemic approach may be useful.

Security Policy: In order to succeed in the work of developing secure IS it is imperative that the customer has a sufficient Security Policy, which is also the foundation of the next sub step Risk Analysis. The security policy determines the levels of the information security to be implemented in the information system. The step identifies if there is an existing security policy that is sufficient. If there is no security policy or if the existing is insufficient, a new policy has to be created.

Risk Analysis: The input to this step is the findings of the previous steps Business Needs, Systems Context and especially the Security Policy. The aim of the step is to identify the threats to and the risks of the thought IS. This is best performed with a scenario method for risk analysis, such as the SBA-Scenario [DFS, 2000, Lundqvist 2001]. The result of the risk analysis is one of the main characteristics of the Security Base, but also the basis for the Anchor step. Both Orion and IDEAL introduces the risk analysis in their second steps. Since the results of the risk analysis influence every later step in the Pentagon, we have chosen to incorporate it in the Reconnaissance step.

Anchor: This is where the results of the previous steps will be mediated to the customer for decisions on further action. It is essential that the results are presented in a well formed, categorized and realistic way to convince the audience. This activity is defined as its own sub step since it is of great importance that the customer is aware of the importance of IS security [cf. Fillery-James, 1999, p.146]. The customer is also the one who decides whether or not to proceed with the Pentagon Model.

3.2 Step 1 – Current State

In this step, see figure 4, an exploration of the existing IS security is performed. Every entity of the IS, such as hardware, software and roles, are explored. The result of the exploration is analyzed and compared to the Security Base in order to locate deficiencies.

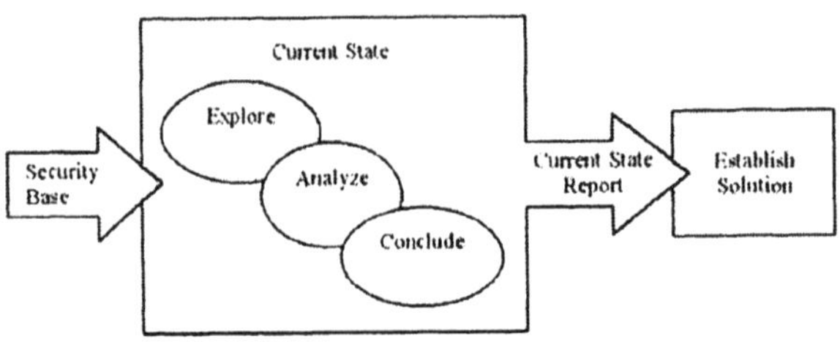

Figure 4. The Current State Step

The conclusions, regarding both sufficient and insufficient security in the existing IS, are then compiled into a Current State Report. This report is an important document, which must be considered throughout the following steps, Ideal Solution and Establish Solution. Current State may be performed with a tool for current state analysis, like the SBA-Check [DFS 2000,

Lundqvist 2001], where the Security Base is one of the parameters. The importance and rigidity of this step may vary. In new systems, where there is no previous IT, the process of this step is minimal. On the other hand, when the commission is to integrate existing and/or new systems with one another the process will be more rigid and of greater importance.

3.3 Step 2 – Ideal Solution

The input into this step, see figure 5, is the Security Base. The aim of this step is to generate a vision of an ideal security solution, without limit or constraints. The Ideal solution step should be viewed as a puzzle where all parts are needed to form a whole, which implies that no parts can stand-alone. All information derived and used should always be considered in light of how the demands for integrity, availability and confidentiality along with accountability, legitimate use and non-repudiation will affect it as required by the puzzle piece *C.I.A*. Furthermore, applying the piece *System Thinking* implies a holistic view of the situation, which is important in order to improve the solution.

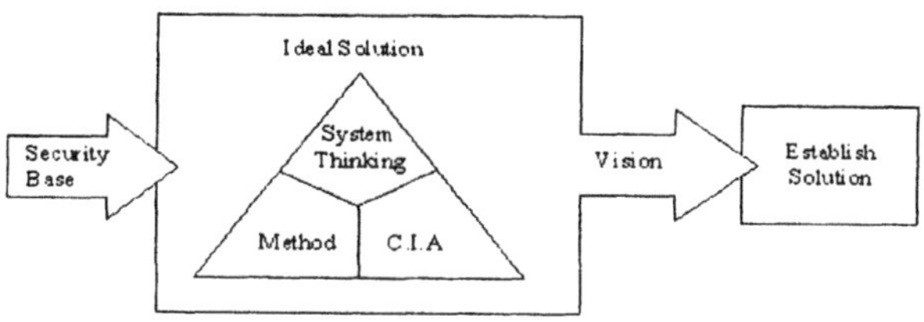

Figure 5. The Ideal Solution Step

Along with the pieces of this puzzle there are two other main ingredients that must be considered, user participation and creativity. The users hold the information on how the company in question is organized, how the work is performed, and what information should be protected within the company and, most importantly, users perceive a fixed situation differently. The users are not always aware that they possess this information and in order to retrieve as accurate and diversified information as possible, a high degree of creativity is needed by the analysts responsible for this step.

The third piece of the puzzle is *Method*. In order to complete this step it is essential to have a method that stimulates creative thinking. There are a number of different approaches of which we have chosen to suggest using *brainstorming, futuristic workshop,* or *functionality analysis* [Löfgren et al]. A common feature of these methods is that they all demand a high level of user involvement. As the step is completed, one or several visions of the ideal system solution are produced. The vision includes both the functionality of the thought system and its security solutions. The system is described in each vision through for example, use cases that handle the different parts of the system and their subsequent functionality.

3.4 Step 3 – Establish Solution

In this step, see figure 6, four sub steps are to be performed to generate the requirements specification for an optimized solution. This involves all requirements of the thought system, including those regarding security. The order of the steps is not fixed but using the recommended order is thought to be the most appropriate.

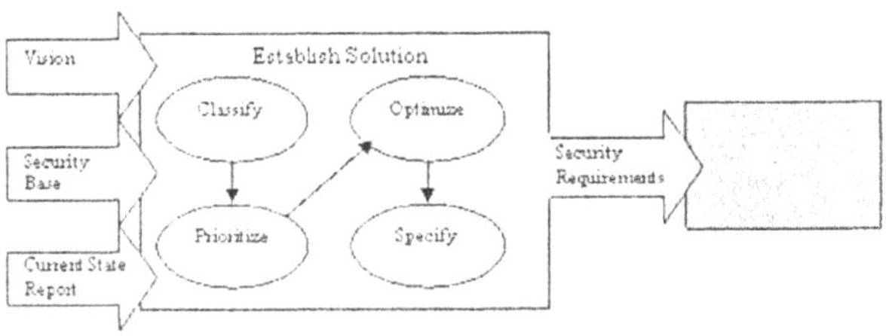

Figure 6. The Establish Solution Step

Classify: The sensitivity of information varies, which implies that different types of information need to be protected on different security levels. In order to be able to protect the information at an appropriate level, it is essential to classify each type of information.

Prioritize: In order to structure the results of the former steps of the development process it is essential to prioritize the cluster of sub-solutions generated in Ideal Solution. How this is done depends on the context. The business needs determine what solutions are the most significant. The Current State also affects prioritizing, regarding both guidance and constrains, but not to the same extent. In addition, there are a number of other constrains which have to be considered during this step. Examples of such constrains may be economical, technical and constrains of competence. These components are used to attain a reasonable ranking of the solutions.

Optimize: Optimizing the requirements involves finding the best possible solution to meet the business needs within the boundaries of the commission. To obtain this, the Security Base, the Current State Report and the Visions must be regarded and compared to each other to assure that the requirements will work together in a cooperative way. It is important to be aware of the risk that some requirements will be left out in this sub-step due to conflicts with the system. In such a case, it is crucial to have in mind that the main functions of the thought system must be fulfilled, which also includes the protection of the most important information of the IS.

Specify: In this sub-step the requirement specification is specified. This may be done in any appropriate way. Some recommendations are that the specification is clear enough to avoid misunderstandings, that the requirements are grouped in an orderly fashion and that the specification is complete.

3.5 Step 4 – Design & Produce

At this stage, the requirements of the product are defined and guide the rest of the process. In the ideal case this will be an inactive step of the Pentagon Model, a black box. On the other hand, an Information Security Analyst must be available to meet questions from designers and developers and changes to the product.

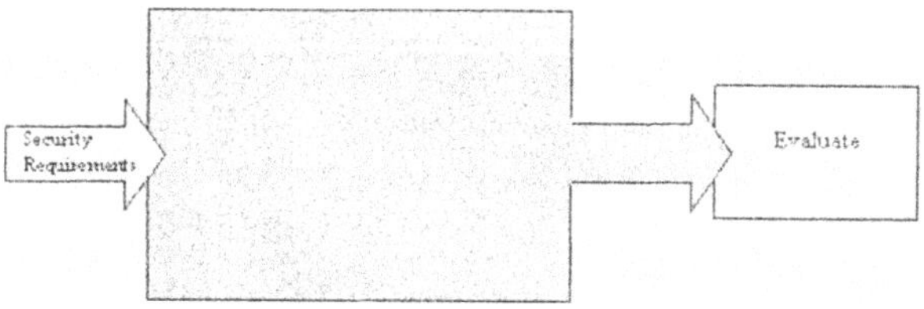

Figure 7. The Design & Produce Step

3.6 Step 5 – Evaluate

The Evaluation step may seem to be a bit misplaced, since it does not follow immediately from the other steps in the model. This is an illusion though, as the previous steps are the foundation of the products to be evaluated. It is necessary to perform evaluations throughout the systems lifecycle. The Evaluate step is applicable during or after the produce, optimize, implement, as well as the operations and maintenance, and termination-phases of the lifecycle. The sub-steps of the Evaluate step are to be executed in the order illustrated in Figure 8.

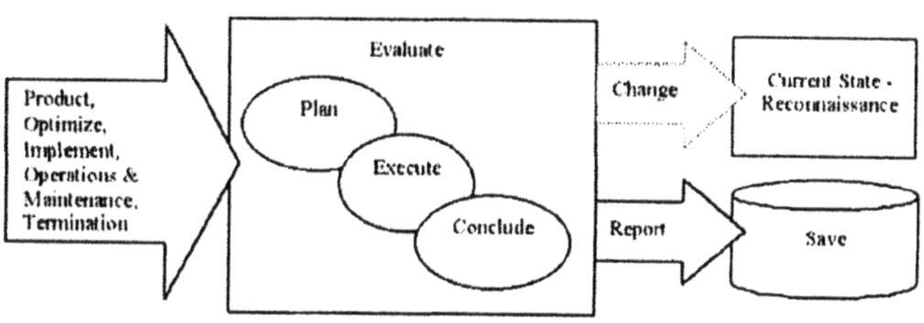

Figure 8. The Evaluate Step

In the sub-step *Plan* it needs to be determined what should be evaluated and also how this evaluation will be performed. The base for what is to be evaluated is the documentation of the preceding steps. How to perform the evaluation may be inspired by using an evaluation method available on the market, such as the Common Criteria [CC].

During the *Execute* sub-step the evaluation is performed according to the guidelines acquired in the sub-step *Plan.* Finally, during the *Conclude* step, the results of the evaluation should be compared to the initial requirements of the system. If the results concur with the requirements then the evaluated segment is ready for release to the next phase of the system life cycle. However, if the results and requirements are not in accordance with each other, then the segment needs to be re-iterated through the Pentagon Model, either starting at step 0 or at step 1.

4. PENTAGON IN SYSTEMS LIFECYCLE

The Pentagon Model is designed to fit into the entire systems lifecycle. In this case this means the Systems Lifecycle (SLC) and the other methods in our sponsor's Framework for Global Systems Solutions, FGSS. However, since the SLC is more or less compatible with the standard Life Cycle Model, the Pentagon Model is thought to fit with any such lifecycle model.

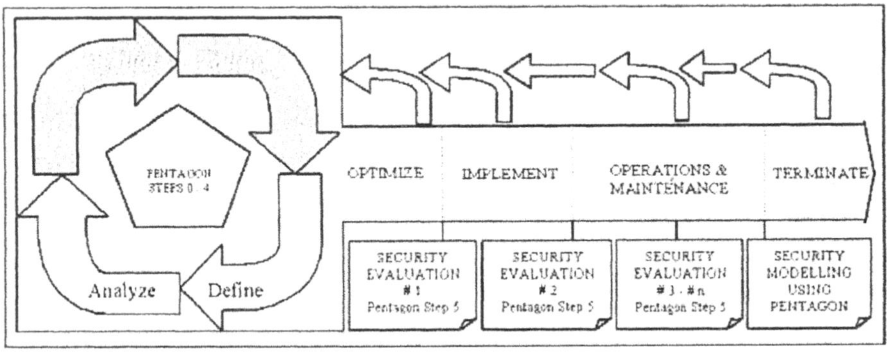

Figure 9. The Pentagon Model incorporated in the entire Systems Lifecycle

Figure 9 illustrates how the steps of the model fit with the framework and any other systems lifecycle. This figure shows the first five steps of the model are parts of the SLC that contains the steps Define, Analyze, Design and Produce. The emphasis of the Pentagon Model first four steps is to use them in the first two steps of the SLC, while step five of the model is connected to the rest of the lifecycle. The fifth step of the Pentagon Model, Evaluate, has the aim to detect insufficiencies in the security controls of the system, to report deficiencies and to evaluate corrections. This work must be done throughout the lifecycle to assure that the right level of security is applied. There are four checkpoints where this step must be performed. After the Produce step the first mandatory evaluation should be conducted to find out if the general security requirements are met. Connected to the optimization of the system is an evaluation of the entire security solution. So far, the system and its security solutions have been tested in a developmental environment.

Now it is time to implement the system into its real environment, which may cause unforeseen problems. The third evaluation is therefore performed to investigate this. The fourth mandatory checkpoint consists of a complete session with the Pentagon Model and is performed in connection with the termination of the system. This has to be done to assure that all assets of the system are treated in a secure manner during and after the termination of the system. During the operations and maintenance phase of a systems lifecycle, evaluations should be performed with regularity. What this means exactly is dependant of the complexity of the system and available budget, its environment and the confidentiality of the handled information. Any evaluation may call for changes in the system, which is illustrated with the left-pointing arrows in Figure 9. However, every change does not imply a full session with the Pentagon Model. Small problems in the system might be corrected with minor interference. When major or medium changes are called for, we recommend entering the Pentagon Model. The stage of the lifecycle decides in what part of the model to enter.

5. CONCLUSIONS

The Pentagon Model is a meta-model derived from several predecessors designed to work with a general systems lifecycle model. Our model combines the use of the aforementioned tools with a high level of user participation, to ensure that the security requirements of the system are in accordance with the security needs. The Pentagon Model also features an evaluation step to be used, not only during the development of a system, but throughout the entire systems lifecycle. However, the emphasis is on that the model is activated in the beginning of the developmental process. This ensures that the security requirements are incorporated into the entire system and also that the duality in systems development is reduced.

References

[Baskerville 2001] – Baskerville, R.: E-mail interview. 2001/10/04

[Baskerville, 1988] – Baskerville, R.: Designing Information Systems Security, John Wiley & Sons, Chichester, 1988

[Baskerville, 1992] – Baskerville, R.: "The Developmental Duality of Information Systems Security", J of Mgm Systems 4 (1) 1992, pp. 1-12

[Baskerville,1994] – Baskerville, R.: "Information Systems Security Design: *Implications for Information Systems Development*", Computing Surveys 25 (4), December 1994 pp. 375-414

[CC] – Common Criteria, http://www.commoncriteria.org, 2001/10/23

[DFS 2000] SBA Scenario 4.0, SCS 2000

[Evertsson&Örthberg, 2002] – Evertsson, U& Örthberg, U: "Bringing Security to Software. Introducing the Pentagon Model", DSV, 2002

[Fillery-James, 1999] – Fillery-James, H: "A Soft Approach To Management of IS", PhD, School of Public Health, Curtin University of Technology, Perth, 1999

[Lundquist 2001] – Lundquist, Mats: Interview and demonstration of SBA Scenario, Dataföreningen, 2001/10/31

[Magnusson 1999] – Magnusson, C: Hedging Shareholder Value in an IT-dependent Business Society – *the Framework BRITS*, PhD, DSV, 1999

[Modelling Specialist 2001] – In dept interview regarding the Pentagon Model, the FGSS and the methods used in modeling, 2001/09/28

[Siponen 2001a] – Siponen, M.: "On the Scientific Background of Information Security Management Standard: a Critique and an Agenda for Further Development", 2nd Annual Int. SSE Conference, 28 Feb – 2 March 2001, Orlando, Florida, USA

[Siponen & Baskerville 2001] – Siponen, M&Baskerville, R: "A New Paradigm For Adding Security Into IS Development" in Advances in Information Security Management & small Systems Security. Eloff, J., Labuschange, L., von Solms, R., and Dillon, G. (Eds), Kluwer Academic Publishers, 2001

[Siponen 2001b] – Siponen, Mikko T.: "A Paradigmatic Analysis of Conventional Approaches for Developing and Managing Secure IS – *Implications for Research and Practice*", 6th International Conference on Information Security, 11-13 June 2001, Paris, France

[Siponen 2001c] – Siponen, Mikko T.: "An Analysis of the Recent IS Security Development Approaches, In G. Dhillon: IS Mgt – Global Challenges in the Next Millennium, Idea Group Publishing, 2001

[Siponen 2001d] – Siponen, M: E-mail interview, 2001/10/04

[SSE-CMM 1999] – "*SSE-CMM – Model Description Document, Version 2.0*", CMU/SEI, Carnegie Mellon University – Software Engineering Institute, Pittsburgh, 1999

[Yngström 1996] – Yngström, L: "A Systemic-Holistic Approach to Academic Programmes in IT Security", PhD, DSV, Kista, 1996

INTEGRATING INFORMATION SECURITY INTO CORPORATE GOVERNANCE

Kerry-Lynn Thomson and Rossouw von Solms
Port Elizabeth Technikon,South Africa, s9942984@student.petech.ac.za, rossouw@petech.ac.za

Abstract: Information is an important asset of any organisation and the protection of this asset, through information security is equally important. This paper examines the relationship between corporate governance and information security and the fact that top management is responsible for high-quality information security.

Key words: Corporate Governance, Information Security, Accountability, Responsibility

1. INTRODUCTION

Corporate governance relates to the responsibilities of the Board of Directors and top management of a company. Corporate governance states that an effective Board that can both lead and control the company should head all companies. The Board has a collective responsibility to provide effective corporate governance (von Solms, 2001, p 505). The question is, to what extent is information security part of corporate governance?

Information security is that discipline concerned with the implementation and support of security and control procedures to protect the confidentiality, integrity and availability of electronically stored information (British Standards Institute, 1999, p 1). *Confidentiality* of electronic assets is concerned with ensuring that information of a specific classification is not circulated to persons outside the category for which it is classified. In other words, sensitive information must be prevented from being disclosed to unauthorised parties (Krige, 1999, p 8; Bruce & Dempsey, 1997, p 36). *Integrity* of electronic assets is concerned with the quality and reliability of information, such that management can be assured that information on which decisions are based has not been modified dishonestly or otherwise. Integrity means that an asset or information can only be modified by authorised parties or only in authorised ways (Krige, 1999, p 9; Bruce & Dempsey, 1997, p 37). *Availability* of electronic assets is concerned with guaranteeing the availability of systems and data on a timely basis such that strategic and business decisions can be effected as rapidly as possible (Bruce & Dempsey, 1997, p 41).

Information and information security has grown in importance in our ever-changing world. The well-being of an organisation depends principally on quality information and the security thereof. Taking the importance of information and information security into account, it can be argued that currently information security forms the weakest link in corporate governance.

The purpose of this paper is to investigate the accountability and responsibility of the top management of an organisation with regard to information security. It will be explored who is responsible and who can be held accountable if there are breaches in information security. This will help accentuate the link between corporate governance and information security.

2. CORPORATE GOVERNANCE

According to Bob Garratt, author of "The Fish Rots from the Head", corporate governance states that Boards of Directors is not there only to manage a company through its day-to-day operations, but also to lead it through "direction giving" and strategy implementation (Planting, 2001, online).

2.1 Importance of Corporate Governance

First-rate corporate governance is extremely important to shareholders, as is demonstrated in a survey conducted by McKinsey & Co., released in June 2000. McKinsey & Co., working with Institutional Investors Inc., found that more than 84% of the approximately 200 global institutional investors, showed a readiness to pay a premium for the shares of a well-governed company over one deemed poorly governed, but with a equivalent financial record. Three-quarters of these investors specified that Board practices were at least as imperative as financial performance, when assessing companies for possible investment. So by simply developing good governance practices, managers can potentially add considerable shareholder value (King Report, 2001, pp 14-15).

2.2 Pillars of Corporate Governance

There are four central pillars of corporate governance, namely; accountability, responsibility, fairness and transparency (King Report, 2001, p 17), which are needed to ensure effective corporate governance.

Accountability means that those individuals or groups in a company who make decisions and take actions on specific issues are accountable for their decisions and actions. Mechanisms must be in place to ensure accountability. This provides investors with the means to question and evaluate the actions of the Board and its committees (King Report, 2001, p 14). The modern approach is for a Board to identify the company's stakeholders and to agree to policies that determine how the affiliation with those stakeholders should be controlled in the interests of the company (King Report, 2001, p 8).

Responsibility, with a view to management, relates to the behaviour that allows corrective action to be taken and penalising mismanagement and misconduct. Responsible management would, when required, put in place what it would take to set the organisation on the right path. While the Board is answerable to the company, it must act responsively to and with responsibility towards all shareholders of the company (King Report, 2001, p 14).

The difference between accountability and responsibility is that, one is liable to provide an account when one is accountable and one is liable to be called to account when one is responsible. In corporate governance terms, one is accountable by law to the organisation if one is a director and one is responsible to the shareholders identified as relevant to the organisation (King Report, 2001, p 8).

Fairness must be in practice to ensure balance in the organisation. The rights of various groups have to be recognised and valued. For example, minority shareholder interests must receive equal consideration to those of the dominant shareholders (King Report, 2001, p 14).

Transparency is the ease with which an outsider is able to make significant assessment of a company's actions, its economic fundamentals and the non-financial aspects relevant to that business. This is a measure of how good management is at making necessary information available in an open, precise and timely manner – not only the audit data but also general reports and press releases (King Report, 2001, p 13).

These four pillars of corporate governance must be put into practice by those responsible for the well-being of an organisation. The next section deals with identifying who exactly is responsible for corporate governance and its implementation.

2.3 Structure of Corporate Governance

The company is run by a Board, which consists of the chairperson, managing director, executive directors and non-executive directors. This is the commonly used Board structure in South Africa. An executive director is involved in the everyday management and could be in the full-time employment of the organisation. A non-executive director is not involved in the everyday management and is not a paid employee of the organisation. The Board has a joint responsibility to provide effectual corporate governance, which involves a set of relationships between the management of the company, its Board and its shareholders (King Report, 2001, pp 45, 56).

The Board must set or approve policies for the guidance of the management appointed by it. The duty of the management or directors is to give effect to the policy prescribed by the Board and to attend to the daily conduct and administration of the business of the organisation (Leveson, 1970, p 52).

The Board is subject to the firm and objective leadership of a chairperson. The most important function of the chairperson is to supervise meetings of directors and to ensure the smooth functioning of the Board in the interests of good governance. The chairperson will also preside over the company's shareholders meetings and acts as the informal link between the Board and management (King Report, 2001, p 51).

Now that corporate governance has been discussed in general, it can be discussed in relation to information security. This discussion will explore the current management duties of the Board of Directors and their accountability and responsibility towards information security.

3. CORPORATE GOVERNANCE AND INFORMATION SECURITY

Since 1994, information technology has emerged as a key driving force for an organisation's decisions and strategies (King Report, 2001, p 11). Commercial organisations and governments rely heavily on information to conduct their daily activities. For this reason, it is of extreme importance to protect these information resources from loss of confidentiality, integrity and availability. Protection alone is not sufficient, because the security of the information needs to be managed and controlled properly. Information is an organisational asset, and consequently the security thereof needs to be integrated into the organisation's overall management plan (Lane, 1985, pp 2-3; Smith, 1989, p 193). The process of protecting these information organisational assets is called information security.

Other important organisational assets are the financial resources, required for the successful operations of an organisation. An external auditor is appointed to examine annual financial statements of an organisation. The external auditor ensures that the company has kept proper accounting records and that the annual financial statements are in agreement with its accounting records and returns (Botha, Oosthuizen & De La Rey, 1987, pp 357-358). The external auditor will give their independent opinion on the organisation's financial statements to the shareholders (King Report, 2001, p 77). The role of the internal auditor is to provide a service to the company and report any problems or discrepancies to management (King Report, 2001, p 77).

For years, this financial culture has been nurtured in organisations – nearly everyone knows how important the financial assets are to an organisation. It is time for this culture to be extended to information security and just as the financial state of an organisation is properly governed and protected, so should the informational state.

"The information possessed by an organisation is among its most valuable assets and is critical to its success. The Board of Directors, which is ultimately accountable for the organisation's success, is therefore responsible for the protection of its information. The protection of this information can be achieved only through effective management and assured only through effective board oversight" (A Call to Action for Corporate Governance, March 2000, online).

The problem with protecting information assets, in most cases, is that senior management does not take responsibility for information security or information security is given low priority in the organisation, because the seriousness of protecting information is not emphasised. Looking at the following statistic highlights this fact. According to Datamonitor's eSecurity analyst, Ian Williams, more than 50% of businesses worldwide spend 5% or less of their IT budget on security (13 April 2002, online).

The lack of attention given to information security is also stressed with a comment from KPMG in their Global Information Security Survey – "Without Board level commitment and drive, security will always be seen as a technology issue and not give the necessary resources and attention to ensure that risks are effectively minimised" (CD-ROM, 2002).

3.1 Effect of Poor Information Security

Poor or no information security has a negative effect on the welfare of an organisation. The integrity of information is essential to the business. If unauthorised parties modify the information used by managers, for example, any decisions made by management could be based on inaccurate information. In the event that systems or data is unavailable, opportunities may be lost, deadlines missed or commitments defaulted. Work progress could be impacted if the information is not available when it is needed.

Even if the information is exactly what is needed to meet business requirements, it must be available to complete the task in a reasonable time (Bruce & Dempsey, 1997, p 41). To attempt to avoid a breach in the confidentiality, integrity and availability of the information of an organisation, a carefully planned corporate information security policy is essential.

3.2 Corporate Information Security Policy

A good understanding of the risks accepted by a company in the pursuit of its objectives, together with the strategies employed to lessen those risks, is essential to the approval of its affairs by the Board and relevant stakeholders (King Report, 2001, p 96). This process of planning, arranging and controlling activities and resources to minimise the impacts of all risks to levels that are acceptable to shareholders is called risk management (King

Report, 2001, p 97). Internal control is the mechanism used to control risk management. Even though risk management should be practised throughout the company, it is ultimately the responsibility of the Board (King Report, 2001, p 96).

The Board is responsible for risk management and the system of internal control, including the establishment and communication of risk and control policies for the entire organisation (King Report, 2001, p 105). Risk management is essentially about protecting the assets of an organisation and, as has already been said, information is an important asset of the organisation. Therefore, the level of information security that the Board of an organisation is willing to recommend and implement, and the level of information security that is acceptable to the shareholders must be combined in the corporate information security policy created between them (King Report, 2001, p 96).

The chairperson of the Board will delegate implementation and maintenance of the information security policy to the Information Security Officer (ISO), who is responsible to the Board, should there be any security breaches or other problems related to information security. This, however, does not mean that the board is no longer responsible for the information security policy.

When directors delegate part of their duties to the ISO, or other managers, these directors should firstly take their duties towards the organisation into account. This is for the reason that directors may only circumvent liability in a court of law if they can prove that they have acted in the *bona fide* interest of the organisation and with the obligatory care, skill and diligence (Coetzee, 2002, online).

If the shareholders are dissatisfied with the level of information security that is being applied in the organisation, then it is the Board that should be responsible to take corrective action. In addition, if legal action is to be taken against the organisation due to a breach in confidentiality, integrity or availability, it should be the Board that is held accountable.

If legal action is taken against an organisation because of information security breaches, it is imperative that the Board of Directors has a 'defence' to protect itself from prosecution. This 'defence' must show that the Board of an organisation is taking steps to address information security to avoid legal liability. It is becoming increasingly evident that a court of law may go behind the 'corporate personality' of the company and find individuals, particularly members of management, who can be held accountable for breaches in the information security policy. The basis for this liability could be negligence, breach of fiduciary duty or failure to take corrective action once there was a compromise in security (Wood, 1999, p 4).

The corporate information security policy should be used as this 'defence' for the Board of Directors. The corporate information security policy should be based on the agreed corporate security objectives and strategy and is there to provide management direction and support for information security (British Standards Institute, 1993, p 17). The policy should identify all those controls that need to be in place in an organisation to ensure effective information security. Once the policy has been created, the Board must ensure that the necessary resources and manpower are available to enforce those controls identified in the policy.

However, it is not enough for an information security policy to simply be created and implemented in an organisation. If this policy is created internally and not compared to other policies that are effectively working in other organisations or countries, then the policy may not be successful. The organisation should be required to ensure that the policy meets specific requirements and that a certain level of information security is provided. This can be achieved by guaranteeing that the policy complies with certain codes of practices or standards, such as ISO/IEC 17799. If there is breach in security, it is important for the management of the organisation, which is held accountable for the breach, to be able to demonstrate that the procedures and statements outlined in the corporate information security policy adhere to international standards. These international standards ensure that most information security risks are addressed, through internationally accepted means, in the organisation's policy. However, fulfilment of a standard does not provide immunity from legal obligations (BS 7799-1, 1999, p iii).

The FBI's Chief Information Officer (CIO) Darwin John, gives his opinion on the role that information technology should play in an organisation. Darwin says that "I have always believed that an IT plan is not standalone but a plank in the larger plan for the enterprise" (15 July 2002, online). This relationship between the Board, the shareholders, the Information Security Officer (ISO) and the court of law and the policy that should bind them is represented in Figure 1.

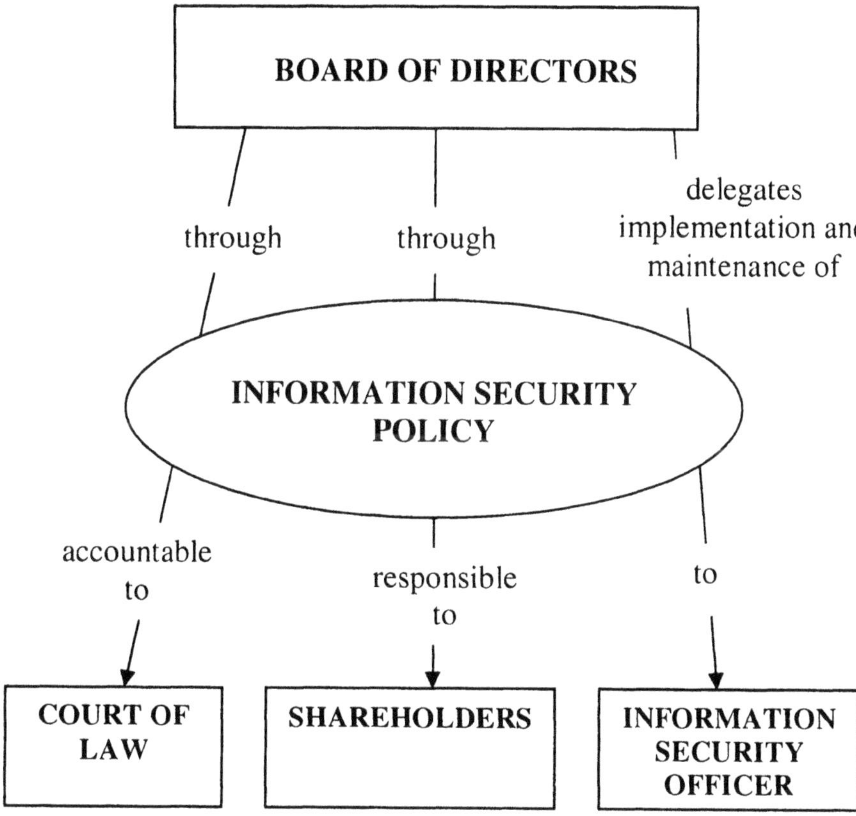

Figure 1. Flow of relationships involving the information security policy

The relationship between the Board of Directors, the court of law and the shareholders through the corporate information security policy should be strengthened if the policy adheres to an international code of practice. The Board must provide the necessary resources to the information security officer to enable the officer to fulfill security tasks. Once successful information security relationships between the Board of Directors and the various parties have been established through the security policy, the entire information security implementation and process needs to be audited. The information security auditing process of any organisation is of extreme importance in guaranteeing that information security controls are achieving their purpose and is continually evolving (National State Auditors Association and US General Accounting Office, 2001, p 8). The Board of Directors must make certain that the information security auditing process is functioning properly and that the information they receive as a result of this process is put to good use.

Michael Cangemi, President of Etienne Aigner Group Inc., has the following to say about the level of consideration that must be given to information security. Cangemi says that, "In today's economy, and with reliance on IT for competitive advantage, we simply cannot afford to apply to our IT anything less than the level of commitment we apply to overall governance" (14 July 2002, online).

Increasingly, trends around the world are moving in the direction that laws are being passed to protect, for instance, client information. The Healthcare Industry Privacy and Accountability Act (HIPAA) from the USA, protects the confidentiality and integrity of health information during both, storage and transmission. Legal action can be taken against those organisations that do not adhere to the conditions of the act. This would mean that the Board of Directors would, at least, have to explain the breaches in information security in a court of law (Von Solms, 2002, online).

4. CONCLUSION

Even though information is an important organisational asset and is essential to the continuance of organisations, information security is not given the attention it deserves. In many situations it is still seen as the responsibility of the Information Technology department and not a management concern.

From the discussion above, it is evident that information security is a direct corporate governance concern. The Board of Directors of an organisation can be held responsible by the shareholders or accountable by a court of law for a lack of information security.

5. REFERENCES

British Standards Institute. (1993). *Code of practice for information security management (CoP).* DISC PD 0003. UK.

Bruce, G. & Dempsey, R. (1997). *Security in distributed computing – did you lock the door?.* Upper Saddle River, New Jersey : Prentice Hall.

Botha, D.H., Oosthuizen, M.J., De La Rey, E.M. (1987). *Corporate law.* Durban, South Africa: Buttersworth.

BS 7799-1. (1999). *Code of practice for information security management (CoP).* DISC PD 0007. UK.

Coetzee, J. (2002). Presentation on King II at ISSA 2002. [online]. [cited 31 July 2002] Available from Internet: URL http://csweb.rau.ac.za/ifip/issa2002/presentations/Johan%20Coetzee.doc

Corporate Governance Institute (2002). [online]. [cited 14 July 2002] Available from Internet: URL http://csweb.rau.ac.za/ifip/issa2002/presentations/Basie%20von%20Solms.ppt

Datamonitor (2001). [online]. [cited 13 April 2002] Available from Internet: URL http://www.datamonitor.com/viewnewsstory.asp?id=1375

Farber, D. (2002, July 15). Unplugged: FBI CIO Darwin John. *ZDNet* [online]. [cited 25 July 2002] Available from Internet: URL http://techupdate.zdnet.com/techupdate/stories/main/0,14179,2874158-2,00.html

Global Information Security Survey [CD-ROM]. (2002). South Africa: KPMG.

IIA, AICPA, ISACA, NACD. (March 2000). A call to action for corporate governance [online]. [cited 16 July 2002] Available from Internet: URL http://csweb.rau.ac.za/ifip/issa2002/presentations/Basie%20von%20Solms.ppt

Krige, W. (1999). *The usage of audit logs for effective information security management.* Unpublished master's thesis. Port Elizabeth Technikon, Port Elizabeth, South Africa.

Lane, V.P. (1985). *Security of computer based information systems.* London: Macmillan.

McKinsey & Company (USA) (2000, June). Investor Opinion Survey. [online]. [cited 22 April 2002]. Available from Internet: URL http://www.gcgf.org/docs/72CGBrochure.PDF

National State Auditors Association and US General Accounting Office (2001, December 10). *Management planning guide for information systems security auditing* [online]. [cited 11 October 2002] Available from Internet: URL http://www.gao.gov/special.pubs/mgmtpln.pdf

Planting, S. (2001, March 9). Giving boards a workout - the fish rots from the head. *Future Company* [online]. [cited 27 April 2002] Available from Internet: URL http://www.futurecompany.co.za/2001/03/09/reviewb.htm

Smith, M.R. (1989). *Commonsense computer security.* London: McGraw-Hill.

South Africa. King Committee on Corporate Governance. (2001). *King report on corporate governance for South Africa 2001.*

Von Solms, B. (2002). *Corporate governance, IT governance and information security.* [online]. [cited 16 July 2002] Available from Internet: URL http://csweb.rau.ac.za/ifip/issa2002/presentations/Basie%20von%20Solms.ppt

Von Solms, B. (2001). Information security – a multidimensional discipline. *Computers & Security*, Vol. 20, No. 6, pp. 504 – 508.

Leveson, G. (1970). *Company directors – law and practice.* Durban, South Africa : Buttersworth.

Wood, C.C. (1999). *Information security policies made easy.* Baseline Software.

BUILDING AN ENTERPRISE IT SECURITY MANAGEMENT SYSTEM

Meletis A. Belsis, Leonid Smalov
Data Knowledge Engineering Research Group, Coventry University, Coventry, U.K.
Tel. +44 24 76 631313, Fax: +44 24 76 888052
E-mail: {Belsis,l.smalov}@coventry.ac.uk

Abstract: Moving towards a knowledge economy, managing effectively and safely the corporate data is the key to an organisation's survival and success. Corporative employees that technologies like computers, mobile and portable devices to access the information. Safeguarding corporate information that flows in unprotected land lines and airwaves is critically important. Adversaries attack information systems, their tools and techniques are numerous and widely available. Analysis of various security incidents has shown that the corporative attempt to achieve and maintain "absolute" security is not always effective and usually is far too expensive. To provide adequate protection for the modern enterprise, security architectures need to be build. These include security mechanisms, tools and policies that provide an acceptable level of protection for the enterprise. This paper presents the work in progress in developing an enterprise information security data model. The proposed prototype aims at presenting security specialists with more effective ways of managing existing security architectures implemented by the enterprise.

Keywords: Security Model, Enterprise Security Architecture, Security Management.

1. Introduction

Information is currently one of the greatest asset corporations have. Information about internal performance and the outside world allows an enterprise to take strategic decisions and expand into different markets. Accurate information allows a company to expand and increase its income, but misinformed enterprises could lose their share of the market [1].

Examples of valuable information to an organisation include: customer details; prototype designs; announcements of new regulations, instabilities in world events; etc [2].

To achieve a better acquisition and processing of information, enterprises spend large budgets in developing Information Technology architectures. These architectures use computer and communication technology for the acquisition, storage and local distribution of information. Some companies go even further, developing decision support systems based on technologies such as Data Warehouses and Data Mining [3]. These systems allow companies to obtain decisions based on special types of information and on performing '*what-if*' analysis. The importance of dealing effectively with information can be established by the existence of organisations whose main product is information management systems.

As corporations decide to connect their IT systems to the Internet to take advantage of the new market, the flow of electronic information has consequently expanded the need for Information Enterprises.

Enterprises are complicated systems and so include complicated IS/IT infrastructures. These infrastructures come from different environments and cover different requirements, which may change daily. Their IS/IT infrastructures must be able to adapt to these changes. To produce secure enterprises it is necessary to ensure that their security infrastructure will be able to follow the enterprise's future changes. The application of security in business environments is discussed in [4-5]. In addition to that security must be applied to fulfil the CIA (*C*onfidentiality, *I*ntegrity and *A*vailability) requirements without neglecting other requirements like system usability, efficiency and flexibility.

To develop such systems security cannot be functionality that is added as an afterthought. It must be an integral part of the overall system. Securing such complicated IS/IT infrastructures can be an extremely difficult task. Mechanisms such as encryption, integrity and access control can be bought off the shelf and installed by anyone on a computer system(s). But these programs are only one part of the solution. In order to provide secure business environments security architectures need to be constructed. These include technologies, processes and policies that need to collaborate in order to provide total protection.

To develop such architectures the security manager and/or analyst will have to review the enterprise's structure. The business processes and goals have to be analysed to produce the security requirements and security policy statements. In addition to this, the company's geographical locations, departments and employees need to be analysed in order to produce the requirements for information classification and employees' access privileges. As with any system investigation, all the previous have to take place alongside with support from the management and system users.

2. Enterprise Security Management

To manage such a dynamic architectures security managers need to be informed about the precise location of the security measures that are installed; who has access on what enterprise data, and, why. This information must be provided in a clear and precise form, of the whole enterprise plan.

Providing such an informational base, especially for large enterprises, is complex. Security technologies, tools, methods and processes have to be analysed in quite a fine detail. Based on this the security experts will be able to provide better advice to the management for security issues, on possible new technologies, and consequently affect the business decision stages.

In more detail some of the positive points of using such a database can be summarised below [6]:

- They promote more consistent and efficient collection of data from any number of diverse sources.
- They inherently force users to follow work processes that have been adopted by the company's best practices.
- They provide much needed information (often data compilations from diverse sources) to decision makers in appropriate formats and in a timely manner.
- They generate performance measures (metrics) for judging the success/health of activities and for making relative comparisons between various activities.

Products that provide such ability are called *Enterprise Security Management* (ESM) software and examples of such include: The *Enterprise Security Manager* by Axent Technologies, the *bv-Control and bv-Admin* by BindView Development Corporation, the *eTrust* by Computer Associates and the *Enterprise Security Architecture System*, by PRICEWATERHOUSECOOPERS ltd. These products utilise an enterprise security data model that is able to hold a detailed description of the enterprise's security architecture and a piece of code that is able to mirror the changes of the security architecture to the data model. ESM utilise the TCP/IP protocol to offer central management of the security products installed in the enterprise.

Unfortunately existing ESM products, with exception the Enterprise Security Architecture System, are concentrate on modelling parts of security architecture (i.e. security policy, authentication mechanisms) and do not represent or manage the totality of the security mechanisms implemented in an enterprise. An example of security information that is usually neglected is the enterprise security incident history, which is a vital part of the informational framework security experts need to have

A second problem found in the current ESM products is that due to the way their data models are designed it is very difficult to attach them to the enterprise's modelling framework. This can have the result that the security model is used decreasingly and is finally outdated.

3. Enterprise IT security data model

The model proposed in this research can be used by security managers to check and review their corporate security policies. Security experts will be able to understand the structure not only of the security mechanisms but also of the rest of the services that run on the systems (i.e. to answer who can access what data and which web servers run on which host). Users will be able to understand the corporate security policy and become aware of the things they can or cannot do as well as the penalty for bypassing specific policies.

The new model records information coming from the application of international security initiatives like *CCTA Risk Analysis and Management,* and *ISO 17799.* In order to be common across different sizes of enterprise the model can not follow, at the detailed level, specific security standards and guidelines. This is what makes the model dynamic and allows enterprises that follow different initiatives to use the same top level model.

In addition to the previous the new model provides solutions to the problems described earlier by incorporating the security history of an enterprise and by clearly describing the links of it with the rest of the enterprise models.

The context model of the proposed structure has four entities. Each one of those entities will be decomposed to form the next level of the proposed structure. The four main entities (figure 1) are the *Enterprise Organisational Infrastructure,* the *Enterprise Information and IT Infrastructure,* the *Enterprise Security Infrastructure,* and the *Enterprise Security Management Infrastructure.*

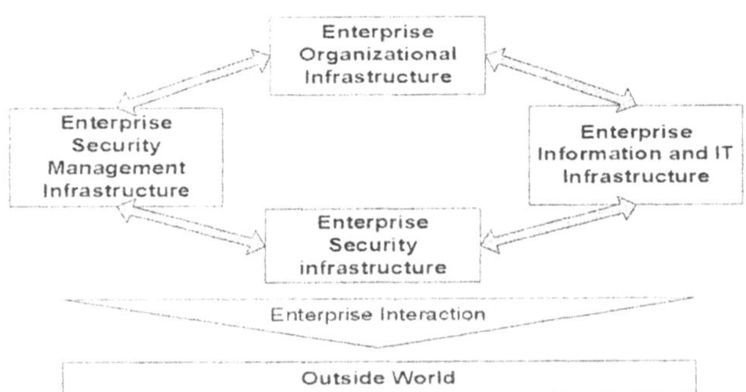

Figure 1 Context Model

The four main entities discussed previously are decomposed further to produce the context model of the proposed data model (figure 2):

Enterprise Organisational Infrastructure:

- *Enterprise Departmental Structure*: The ways the different departments are interconnected and operate are vital to security analysts. This information can be used to identify critical points in the enterprise.
- *Enterprise Employee Infrastructure*: This entity is assigned the job of describing the way the enterprise's employees are organised. Using this entity the security manager can classify employees depending on the security clearance they have.

Enterprise Information and IT Infrastructure:

- *Enterprise Information Infrastructure*: This entity describes the information vital to the enterprise. It classifies the information, describing the level of security that each element needs.
- *Enterprise IT infrastructure*: The number of network hosts, their type and the domain to which they belong are described here. In addition to that the entity describes the hardware specifications, the vendor and the services (i.e. open ports) run by each one of the hosts. The network devices that an enterprise network includes can be categorised using high level terminology in to the following: *Public enterprise server; private enterprise server; internal host; Internal Router; External Router*, and, *Miscellaneous*

Enterprise Security Infrastructure:

- *Enterprise physical security:* Information on the way the enterprise's buildings and offices are protected is stored by this entity. The IT offices and buildings physical protection is vital information for the security manager.
- *Enterprise IT Security*: The software and hardware procedures that protect the IT infrastructure are listed here. Examples of such include encryption and authentication mechanisms, intrusion detection systems and firewalls. The IT security mechanisms are organised according to their functionality into the following: *Firewalls; Secure Communications; Secure Storage; Antivirus; Software patches/ updates; User and Software Management; Security Policy; Load Balancing; Antisniffing; IDS*, and *System Penetration testing.*

Enterprise Security Management Infrastructure:

- *Enterprise Risks*: This entity describes the outcome of the risks analysis process. The risks and threats are stored here. This entity will allow for a number of different risk analysis processes to be used.

- *Enterprise Security History:* It is vital to keep a record on the security history of an enterprise. This record includes the details of security incidents that took place in the past and details of the changes that took place in the overall *Enterprise Security Infrastructure.*
- *Enterprise Security Policy:* This entity is used to capture the information associated with the enterprise's security policy. Every security mechanism and employee must follow the enterprise's security policy. The security policy describes the security mechanisms that are in place to enforce the policy and the penalties that will be applied for those not following the policy.

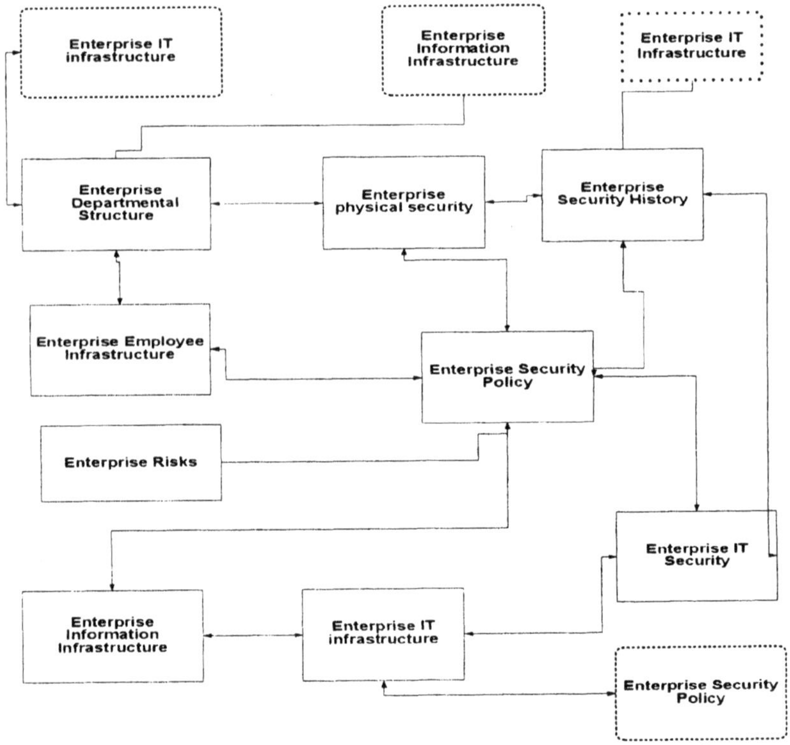

Figure 2 Context Model

During the decomposition of the proposed model the *Zachman framework* [7] is used to provide the next lower level model. In that way each entity will be analysed against most of the aspects that the Zachman framework includes. Describing such a decomposition process in one paper is impossible. Follows is one example of such decomposition for one of the entities the model includes:

Enterprise Departmental Structure: This entity provides a composite to encapsulate the organisational structure of the enterprise. The Data simply provides the lists of departments, the Function lists the tasks that each department performs, the Network shows the interfaces between departments and for departments to the outside world, the People simply shows the posts and roles in the department and their general responsibilities (not the actual people in the roles), the Time shows the possible sequence constraints for task and data elements, the Motivation provides a statement of purpose for the tasks, interfaces, roles and data. The refinement of these elements relates to the Owner, Architect, Designer, and Builder Views

4. Enterprise Security Incident History.

Keeping records of the past security incidents is vital for every enterprise [8]. These records can assist security specialist to avoid incidents from happening again, to educate users, and assist management in assigning the appropriate funds for information security. Currently much research has been done in delivering data models able to store information coming from past security incidents [9-11]. Unfortunately these models store only the technical information associated with an incident neglecting any managerial information that could be of help to the management. These models have been developed to assist Computer Security Incident Response Teams (CSIRTs) and so do no include any clear links with the enterprise's models.

Decomposing further the proposed enterprise IT security data model, an incident model was created. This model is able to store information coming from the security incident that took place on the enterprise's information systems and correlate this information with the rest of the enterprise IT security data model. The model was first published in [12]. An illustration of this model showing some of the links of it to the rest of the enterprise security data model is given in figure 3.

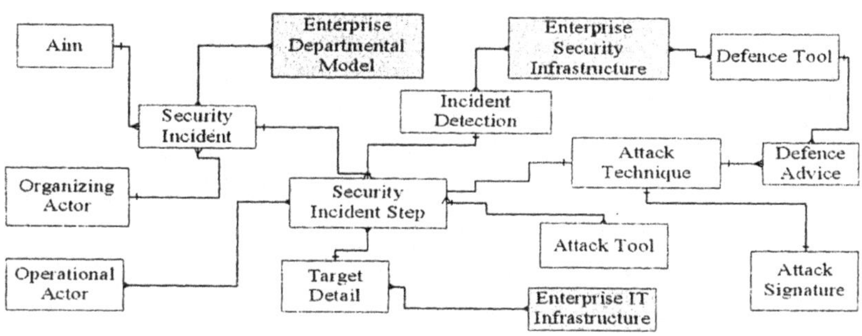

Figure 3 Enterprise Incident History Model

5. Implementing the proposed structure

Two issues regarding deployment of a security related database are the security of the data stored and the way this data will be accessed by the system's users.

Due to the nature of its data, such a database could be an invaluable tool for all kinds of hackers and/or criminals. Adversaries might be able to identify precisely the hardware and software that an enterprise uses. The database might be used as a hacking tutorial to advice adversaries on how to bypass specific systems. The problem becomes more apparent if the database is going to be accessed via the Web. In order to ensure the authorised use of the database, there must be security procedures in place to protect the stored data. The system that maintains the data model must be able to safeguard it against the *CIA* requirements.

The second problem concentrates on the way security related information are going to be accessed and is more difficult to handle. Current systems are localised for security specialists forgetting that managers are the ones that assign the budget for information security. Corporate managers need to identify the managerial information related to an incident. Examples of such are: an average cost to the enterprise; the time the company needed to recover from the incident, and, statistical data. The statistics will relate to the frequency of the attack and/or the type of companies this incident targets. This information will assist managers in identifying potential weak points and allow them to calculate a budget and/or extended the organisation *high level* security policy. For the security manager it would not be helpful to display a huge amount of technical information on the screen when data incidents are retrieved. The need for security, limits the utility of the current systems. At the same time security technicians are not interested in the architectural details of the security mechanisms. They are interested at the configuration information of the specific security tools they are assigned to. Enterprise employees would need an easy way to access their private security related information (i.e. passwords and encryption keys) as well as to identify specific parts of the corporate security policy. To enhance awareness users should be presented with an easy way of accessing some of the information coming from the past security incidents.

The above requirements raise issues in relation to the operation of such data structures. In addition to having a data model that provides sufficient scope, the way the content is accessed must be user friendly. Each user of the database must be able to see details that are closely related to the line of his work. The system supporting the model must allow for *smart queries* to be executed. Examples of smart queries that would be useful to a security expert include:

- Which incident targeted corporate confidential information?

Examples of smart queries that would be useful to a manager include:

- How many incidents cost more than $100?

Currently a number of research publications have proposed the use of the Common Object Request Broker Architecture (CORBA) to access Internet based databases [13-15]. CORBA with its security service can provide adequate security to fulfil the CIA requirements of the data stored in the incident database [16]. The system discussed here uses the CORBA model to allow registered users to fully access an incident database. The new system allows access through the TCP/IP protocol. In addition to this the new system automates the process of recording an incident by providing the ability to implement the client of the system as part of the overall company's security management console.

Every user of the system is assigned an X.509 digital certificate. This certificate can be the one that the enterprise had assigned when employed by the corporation.

Users will access the system by using the corporate intranet and authenticating with their digital certificate. They will then download a java applet. After setting up the applet, it will open a connection to the database server. From there the user will be able to update his security records and/or perform queries to the database (Figure 4). To allow more security the digital certificate will contain the privileges that this user has over the database.

To provide friendly access a Natural Language Interface DB (NLIDB) system [17-18] is used. Such systems provide the ability to use regular English expressions to search the database instead of SQL queries. The system is responsible for translating the English expression into an appropriate SQL statement and for formatting the search output into an acceptable form. Initial designs for the MS SQL Server and MS English Query have been constructed and the examples have been shown to be relevant to the proposed architecture. Using an NLIDB server provides a much more friendly way to search security related records than the traditional keywords search. It will allow non technical users to access and search the database easily. Along with that it allows the construction of smart questions that can be answered by the database.

The NLIDB server can create different views depending on the type of the user (i.e. manager or technical personnel). Using specific views, we avoid filling a manager's screen with lots of technical information or an administrator's screen with managerial information. This makes the output of a database search much more structured and readable. This also adds a second layer of security to the system due to the fact that the server can be programmed to hide the search results from 'confidential' fields.

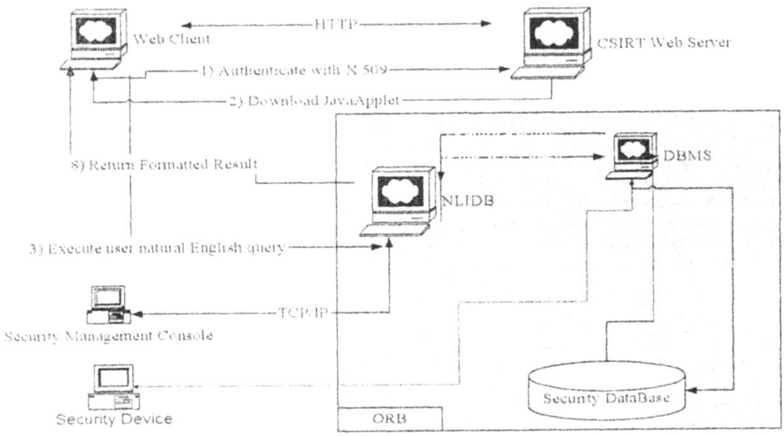

Figure 4 Proposed System

Security experts can use their existing security managing consoles or the intranet to access security related records. Due to the open architecture that the CORBA model provides security vendors are able to incorporate functions that will allow their product to access the database. This will enable security managers to maintain distributed records of their systems security history. This provides security systems with the ability of automatically registering a security incident when it occurs (i.e. intrusion detection sensors can record an anomaly as soon as the detect one). In addition to that security experts could update the intrusion detection sensors and firewalls of the enterprise to detect and stop the new anomaly. To be able to provide this functionality there are a number of problems that need to be solved first. Examples of such are: deciding on a common incident structure, and, ensuring that the detected incidents are not false.

The client software, either Java applets or embedded in security products, will be able to use CORBA's *DII* to identify and locate new services. CORBA will allow incident management teams to add new functionality on demand.

6. Conclusion

In this paper a novel contextual model of the enterprise security has been discussed. The CORBA based architecture for practical evaluation of the model has been developed. From the overall model the security incident decomposition was provided. To retrieve or exchange the security incident related information the developed architecture incorporates a natural language interface to the data stored. By using such integrated approach the authors have attempted to make process of handling security related information in more efficient and secure way. We relay on the following important facts:

- Firstly, that CORBA standards are Web Consortium (W3C) controlled and no single software vendor (in comparison Java-RMI is proprietary Sun's technology and COM/DCOM is one of Microsoft technologies) or a governmental body are responsible for developing CORBA protocols. That could make the proposed architectural approach very reliable and secure – as specific as needs of a particular enterprise;
- Secondly, there major web sites or even vendor's portals dedicated to the describing security related information, incidents and vulnerabilities as well as supplying security updates and recommendations. We found that all of them are not easy to use, required continuous attention of security administrators, managers or simply too generic for the needs of a particular enterprise. The embedded natural language interface could significantly simplify and streamline the process of retrieving the related information.

Finally as all work in progress there is a certain element of future development involved. In particular, the idea to use Web services, based on XML-SOAP approach appears as very attractive one. The powerful feature to supply and maintain application-to-application communication may be used to develop a Web service containing the details on security architectural descriptions, security incidents, security updates, costs, risks, vulnerabilities etc working together with a group of intelligent autonomous agents to retrieve and supply the related information. The web client may present the information to the end-user and could be tailored to the specific corporative needs. We consider this as next step in our research and looking for possible collaboration.

7. References

1. Donald L. Pipkin, 200, *Information Security: Protecting the Global Enterprise.* Hewlett-Packard Professional Books.
2. Kostantin Beznosov, *Information Enterprise Architectures: Problems and Perspectives.* Florida International University technical report 2000-06.2000
3. Rimvydas Skytius, *Business Decision Making, Managerial Learning and Information Technology.* Proc. Of the Informing Science: Challenges to Informing clients: A Transdisciplinary approach Conference. 2001
4. Ethan Sanderson and Karen A. Forcht, 1996, Information Security in Business Environments. Information Management and Computer Security, 4/1, pp. 32-37.
5. D. Spinellis, S. kokolakis and S. Gritzalis,1999, *Security requirements, risks and recommendations for small enterprise and home-office environments,* Information Management and Computer Security, 7/3, pp.121-128.

6. Tonda R. Henning, 1996, *Use of the Zachman Architecture for Security Engineering*, 19th National Information systems Security Conference. Baltimore
7. Zachman, J. A., *A framework for Information Systems architecture*. IBM Systems Journal, vol.26, No.3, pp.276-292. 1987
8. Anderson R. *Why Cryptosystems fail*. Technical Report. University Laboratory, Cambridge University. January 1994
9. IDWG. *Intrusion Detection Exchange Format Data Model (IDEFDM)*. 15 June 2000
10. Commission of the European Communities Security Investigations Projects. Project S2003-Incident Reporting a European Structure "Final Feasibility and Strategy Report". Report No19733.Version 1.0. 1992
11. Demchenko Y. *Incident Object Description and Exchange Format Data Model and Extensible Markup Language (XML)*. Internet Draft. July 2001
12. Belsis A. Meletis, Godwin Nick and Smalov Leon, *A Security Incident Data Model*, Proceedings of the 17th International Conference on Information Security (IFIP/Sec 2002), Cairo, Egypt, May 2002
13. Athman Bouguettaya, Boualem Benatallah, Mourad Ouzzani and Lily Hendra. Using Java and CORBA for Implementing Internet Databases. Proceedings of the 15th International Conference on Data Engineering, 1999, pp.218-227.
14. Athman Bouguettaya, Boualem Benatallah, Lily Hendra, James Beard and Kevin Smith and Mourad Ouzzani. World Wide Database- Integrating the Web, CORBA and Databases. Proceedings of the SIGMOD Conference 1999 ,pp. 594-596.
15. Ebru Killic, Gokhan Ozhan, Cevdet Dengi, Nihan Kesim, Pinal Koksal and Asuman Dogac, Experiences in using CORBA for a Multidatabase Implementation. In Proc. Of 6th Intl. Workshop on Database and Expert System Applications, London, Sept. 1995
16. Belsis A. Meletis, Nick Godwin, Leon Smalov. *Delivering Secure Manufacturing IT Systems within the CORBA Security Framework*. 14th International Conference on Systems Engineering (ICSE), Coventry, UK, 12-14 September 2000
17. Androutsopoulos I., Ritchie G.D., and Thanisch P. Natural Language Interfaces to DBs - An Introduction. Natural Language Engineering, vol. 1, part 1. Cambridge University Press, pp.29-81, 1995.
18. Ott N., Aspects of the automatic Generation of SQL Statements in a Natural Language Query Interface, Information Systems, 17(2),pp.147-159,1992.

INFORMATION SECURITY MANAGEMENT SYSTEM: PROCESSES AND PRODUCTS

M.M. ELOFF[1], J.H.P. ELOFF[2]

[1]eloffmm@unisa.ac.za
Department Computer Science & Information Systems,
University of South Africa,
PO Box 392, Unisa, 0003
South Africa
Telephone: + 27 (0) 12 429 6336
Facsimile: + 27 (0) 12 429 6655
[2]eloff@cs.up.ac.za
Department of Computer Science,
University of Pretoria,
Pretoria, South Africa
Telephone: +27 (0) 12 420-3120
October 2002

Key words: certification, certified products, code of practice, controls, evaluation criteria, guideline, Information Security Management System, process evaluation, product evaluation, protection classes, self-assessment, standards,

Abstract: The executive and operational management of organisations today realise that the successful protection of information assets depend on a holistic approach towards the implementation of safeguards. A holistic approach requires that the focus of management should rather be on minimising overall risk exposure as opposed to "tick-off" security safeguards on a checklist. The holistic management of information security requires a well-established Information Security Management System (ISMS). An ISMS addresses all aspects in an organisation that deals with creating and maintaining a secure information environment. Aspects such as policies, standards, guidelines, codes-of-practice, technology, human, legal and ethics issues all from part of an ISMS. Organisations can opt for different approaches to establishing an ISMS. One way is to implement the controls as contained in a standard or code-of-practice, such as ISO17799. In this case information security is driven from a management process point of view and referred to as "process security". Another approach that also complement or add to process security, is to use certified products in the IT infrastructure environment when possible. The approach here focuses on technical issues and is referred to as "product security". The 'process' ISMS and the 'product' ISMS approaches are only two ways to address information security, each from a different perspective. The question that arises is whether the 'process' ISMS and the 'product' ISMS can be combined into a more holistic ISMS and what the impact of the one will be on the other. The aim of this paper is to propose an ISMS that combines "process security" and "product security".

1. INTRODUCTION

Management who want to address any information security-related issues in their organisation, need to follow some form of an Information Security Management System. An Information Security Management System (ISMS) can be defined as a management system used for establishing and maintaining a secure information environment. This ISMS must address the implementation and maintenance of processes and procedures to manage Information Technology security. Information Technology (IT) security includes all aspects related to defining, achieving and maintaining the five security services of identification & authentication, authorisation, confidentiality, integrity and non-repudiation as specified by the ISO 7498-2 standard. [ISO02]

An ISMS can be approached from various perspectives. One way of establishing an ISMS is from a strategic perspective, addressing amongst others corporate governance, policies and management issues. Another approach can be from a 'human' side, addressing issues such as security culture, awareness, training, ethics and other human related issues. The technology ISMS may focus on software products. Another ISMS, the technical ISMS may focus on physical issues such as hardware. The processes ISMS promotes the implementation of the controls as contained in a standard or code-of-practice, such as ISO17799 and compliance to these controls. It is important to note that an ISMS need to take a holistic approach, requiring a combination and integration of all the abovementioned ISMSs.

In this paper the authors will combine two of these approaches, namely the process ISMS and the product ISMS and determine the influence of the one on the other.

The remainder of this paper is structured as follows:

- Section 2 contains definitions of the process ISMS and the product ISMS.
- Section 3 contains a high-level overview of the concept of 'protection classes'

- Section 4 defines and explains the requirements for the different protection classes

2. PROCESS AND PRODUCT ISMS

2.1 Process ISMS

Process ISMS is defined as a two-phase information security management system focussing on planning and implementing management practices, procedures and processes to establish and maintain information security. The Information Security Policy will form the basis of the process ISMS. [HONE02]An organisation firstly needs to implement the controls or guidelines as contained in a standard such as ISO17799. [ISO17799] Secondly, these implemented controls need to be assessed to determine whether they comply with the specific standard. An independent third party, who may be an individual or an organisation, that has the approval of a national or an international body, performs this assessment process.

Information security managers using this approach by will first plan the processes to be implemented, such as the screening of new employees; then implement the processes to ensure screening. The next step is to check if all new employees are indeed screened. Depending on the outcome, action can be adjustments or additional processes. The process ISMS is an iterative system with feedback and continuous improvements.

This paper focuses on the second tier of the process ISMS by checking the processes implemented and requires that the organisation has planned and implemented management processes and procedures such as the controls contained in ISO17799 standard [ISO17799] or something similar.

2.2 Product ISMS

Product ISMS is the management system where the organisation opts to use evaluated software products as far as possible in their IT infrastructure in order to establish and maintain information security. These evaluated software products and systems forms the basis of the product ISMS. Product evaluation is the process whereby a specific product or system is subjected to a detailed series of tests to determine whether it satisfies a predefined set of requirements.

Normally an independent third party expert technically reviews the design and implementation of a software product or system. If it satisfies the requirements, it will be classified at a specific level, for example the C2 level under TCSEC. [NGI 95] These software products are also termed certified products. Trusted Oracle8i was evaluated EAL4 under the Common Criteria. [CC02] It should be noted that the scope of product ISMS is limited to products or systems, and does not currently have any references to an organisation's information security management processes. [ELOF00] However, evaluated software products can also form part of the process ISMS, but then the focus will not necessarily be on the product ISMS.

In a previous article by the authors, [ELOF00[1]], the influence of evaluated products on the implemented controls from a code-of-practice were illustrated. Evaluated or certified products can be categorised in a number of different generic product categories, such as Communication systems, Databases, Networks and Operating systems. Each of these different categories can be potentially linked and mapped onto the sections of a code-of-practice, such as ISO17799 standard. The remainder of this paper is based on the ISO17799 standard. The reader should notice that any other code-of-practice can also be used as part of the illustration that follows.

A suggestion on how the relationship between the product categories and the ten sections of ISO17799 can be modelled, are summarised in the next table. Note that this table is not necessarily complete, but adequate to illustrate the concept of protection classes which is discussed the next section of this paper. The proper relationship modelling between controls of a code-of-practice and the product categories is a comprehensive task and requires functional as well as technical expertise. The entries in the table show the strengthening of a control area in case certified products are used in implementing and managing the processes of that specific control area. Asset classification and control will gain from using a certified DBMS as the repository of information.

ISO17799 Sections	Commu-nication systems	Data-bases	Net-works	Operating systems
3. Security policy				
4. Security organisation	Y		Y	
5. Asset classification and control		Y		
6. Personnel security	Y	Y		
7. Physical and environmental security			Y	
8. Communications and operations management	Y	Y	Y	Y
9. Access control	Y	Y	Y	Y
10. Systems development and maintenance	Y	Y	Y	
11. Business continuity management		Y	Y	Y
12. Compliance				

3. OVERVIEW OF PROTECTION CLASSES FOR COMBINING CERTIFIED PRODUCTS WITH EVALUATED PROCESSES

The primary focus in process ISMS is on management processes and procedures, therefore compliance to each one of the ten sections of ISO17799 will be categorised into one of four classes. This classification will be done on Section level for ISO17799, firstly to take cognisance of the fact that not all the sections may be of equal importance to organisations and secondly, certified products will not impact equally on all the sections of ISO17799. Classifying the sections of ISO17799 allows an organisation to initially focus on specific sections and expand to address subsequent sections at a later stage. Full compliance with ISO17799 may be 'a bridge too far' for many companies, and may, in fact, also be inappropriate.

The authors have decided to define four distinct protection classes, with increasing levels of protection. The implementation of the controls in each one of the ten sections of ISO17799 will be categorised into one of these four classes, firstly depending on the level of compliance to the controls of ISO17799, the process ISMS and secondly, influenced by the use of certified products associated with each section, the product ISMS. [ELOF00[1]], [ELOF00[2]]

The four protection classes, in ascending order, are:

- Inadequate protection
- Minimal protection
- Reasonable protection
- Adequate protection

The following protection classes may, for example, be associated with each of the ten sections of ISO17799 [ISO17799]: This can be given in a graphic format, as illustrated in Figure 1.

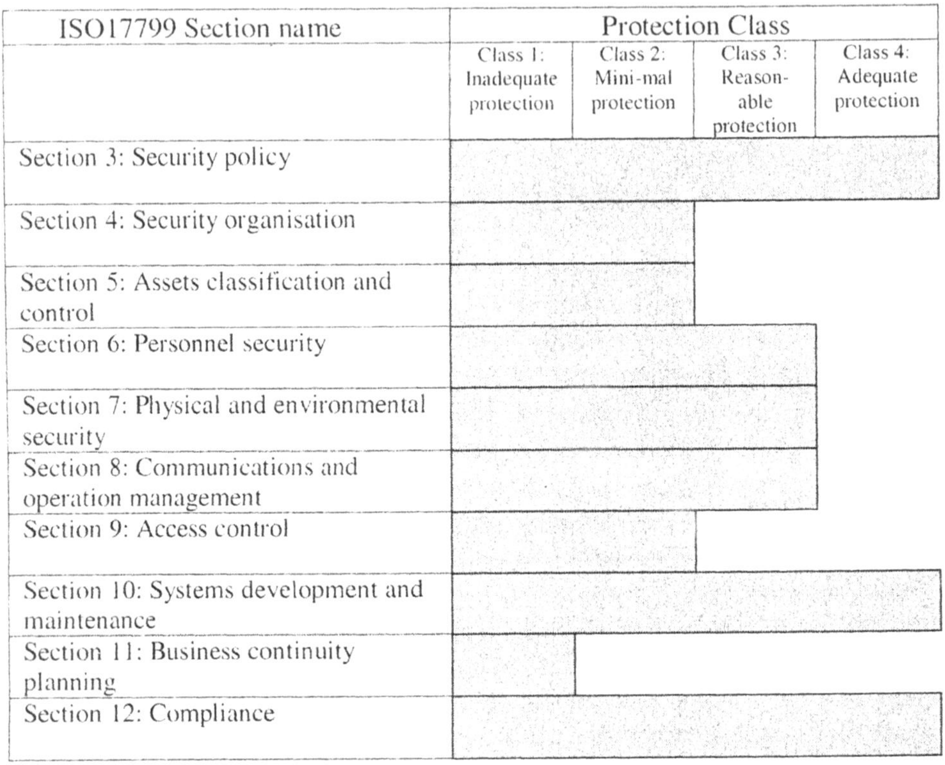

Figure 1. The Graphic illustration of Protection classes

From a graphic summary like this it will be easy for an organisation to determine weak areas that needs improvement.

A brief explanation of each protection class follows:

3.1 Class 1: Inadequate protection

Sections of ISO17799 will be classified in this class if no effort was made by the organisation to implement any of the recommended controls for their specific requirements. This is the lowest class.

Certified products do not have any influence on the classification of sections on this level.

3.2 Class 2: Minimal protection

If minimal effort was put into implementing some of the recommended controls, it will be possible to classify some sections in this class. The same requirement as for Class 1 is applicable for the ISO17799 controls in some of the sections.

Certified products do not have any influence on the classification of sections on this level either.

3.3 Class 3: Reasonable protection

The same requirement as for Class 2 is applicable for the ISO17799 controls in some of the sections. The majority of the sections must satisfy additional requirements based on implemented processes and procedures to prove that the recommended controls from ISO17799 are implemented on a reasonable level.

Some sections have an additional requirement for certified products to be used.

3.4 Class 4: Adequate protection

For a section to be classified as adequately protected, it must be verifiable that considerable effort was made to implement the complete set of recommended controls for the section. This implies full compliance to ISO17799 for that specific section.

Furthermore, the majority of sections have an additional requirement that certified products, in all the product categories, must be implemented to illustrate adequate protection.

If there are no related product categories for a ISO17799 section, it is possible for that section to advance to this class in the absence of certified products.

4. REQUIREMENTS FOR THE DIFFERENT PROTECTION CLASSES

4.1 Requirements for Class 1: Inadequate protection

If no effort was made by the organisation to implement any of the recommended controls for their specific requirements, the appropriate Sections of ISO17799 will be classified in this class. This is the lowest class.

The use of certified products on their own do not have any influence on the classification of ISO17799 sections, it can only enhance the implemented processes and procedures.

The following example illustrates this: An organisation are using only certified products associated with for example Section 9: Access Control, but have not implemented any of the controls contained in this section. Section 9 can only be classified into the class of Inadequate protection.

Table 2 summarises the requirements for Class 1 for all the sections of ISO17799.

Table 2: Security Requirements for Class 1

ISO17799	**Class 1: Inadequate protection**
3. Security policy	
4. Security organisation	
5. Asset classification and control	
6. Personnel security	
7. Physical and environmental security	
8. Communications and operations management	
9. Access control	
10. Systems development and maintenance	
11. Business continuity management	
12. Compliance	

Legend:

no requirement

All sections of ISO17799 can be classified in Class 1 if no effort was made to implement any of the controls.

4.2 Requirements for Class 2: Minimal protection

If minimal effort was put into implementing some of the recommended controls, it will be possible to classify some sections in this class. The same requirement as for Class 1 is applicable for the ISO17799 controls in some of the sections. The actual compliance of the implemented processes and procedures for the applicable sections should be at least 75% of the recommended controls before a specific section can be allocated in Class 2.

Certified products do not have any influence on the classification of sections on this level either. Take the same illustration as for Class 1, except that the implemented processes and procedures comply 80% with the controls contained in Section 9. Section 9 can therefore now be classified as minimally protected.

Table 3 summarises the requirements for Class 2 for all the sections of ISO17799.

Table 3: Security Requirements for Class 2

ISO17799	**Class 2: Minimal protection**
3. Security policy	
4. Security organisation	
5. Asset classification and control	
6. Personnel security	☒
7. Physical and environmental security	☒
8. Communications and operations management	☒
9. Access control	☒
10. Systems development and maintenance	
11. Business continuity management	
12. Compliance	

Legend:

no requirement

☒ additional requirement based on implemented processes and procedures

From this table it is clear that for Sections 6 to 9 to be classified as Minimally protected, an organisation need to prove that the implemented processes and procedures should comply with at least 75% of the controls as prescribed in ISO17799. The other sections can be classified as Minimally protected without proving any compliance.

4.3 Requirements for Class 3: Reasonable protection

The same requirement as for Class 2 is applicable for the ISO17799 controls in some of the sections. The majority of the sections must satisfy additional requirements based on implemented processes and procedures.

Some sections can advance to this class if actual compliance of the implemented processes and procedures comply with at least 75% of the recommended controls.

Some sections have an additional requirement for certified products to be used. Certified products for at least half of the appropriate product categories per section in ISO17799 should be implemented. A minimum of 75% of the implemented products within a specific product category, i.e. IT products already installed, must be certified products before it can influence the classification of a specific section.

These requirements will allow Section 9: Access Control, as used in the example for Class 2 to now be classified in the Reasonably protected class. Implemented processes and procedures comply 80% with the recommended, and all products used in both product categories applicable to this section, are certified products, satisfying the minimum 75% requirement for implemented products.

Table 4 summarises the requirements for all the sections of ISO17799 for Class 3.

Table 4: Security Requirements for Class 3

ISO17799	Class 3: Reasonable protection
3. Security policy	☒
4. Security organisation	☒
5. Asset classification and control	☒
6. Personnel security	☒☒
7. Physical and environmental security	☒☒
8. Communications and operations management	☒☒
9. Access control	☒☒
10. Systems development and maintenance	☒
11. Business continuity management	☒
12. Compliance	☒

Legend:

no requirement

☒ additional requirement based on implemented processes and procedures

☒☒ additional requirement based on implementation of certified products in at least half of the applicable product categories

From this table it is clear that all sections have additional requirements to be classified as Reasonably protected.

4.4 Requirements for Class 4: Adequate protection

For a section to be classified as adequately protected, it must be verifiable that considerable effort was made to implement the complete set of recommended controls for the section. This implies full compliance to ISO17799 for that specific section.

Furthermore, the majority of sections have an additional requirement that certified products, in all the product categories, must be implemented to illustrate adequate protection.

If there are no related product categories for an ISO17799 section, it is possible for that section to advance to this class in the absence of certified products.

If we take the example of Section 9: Access Control as used in this explanation, this section can now be classified as adequately protected, as all products used are certified products, satisfying the requirement of certified products, in all the product categories, to be implemented.

The following table, table 5, summarises all the protection requirements for the ten sections of ISO17799.

Table 5: Protection requirements for ISO17799 sections

ISO17799	**Protection class**			
	Class 1: Inadequate protection	Class 2: Minimal protection	Class 3: Reasonable protection	Class 4: Adequate protection
3. Security policy			☒	☒
4. Security organisation			☒	☒☒
5. Asset classification and control			☒	☒
6. Personnel security		☒	☒☒	☒☒☒
7. Physical and environmental security		☒	☒☒	☒☒☒
8. Communications and operations management		☒	☒☒	☒☒☒
9. Access control		☒	☒☒	☒☒☒
10. Systems development and maintenance			☒	☒☒☒
11. Business continuity management			☒	☒☒☒
12. Compliance			☒	☒

Legend:

no requirement

☒ additional requirement based on implemented processes and procedures

☒☒ additional requirement based on implementation of certified products in at least half of the applicable product categories

☒☒☒ additional requirement based on implementation of certified products in all of the applicable product categories

5. CONCLUSION

It has become manifest from this paper that management will, in future, have to follow a holistic approach when establishing an Information Security Management System, so that such issues could be addressed not only in the electronic domain but also in the procedural and process domains. In addition, it has become abundantly clear that the mere use of products certified under, say, the Common Criteria, or any other formal product-evaluation scheme, will by no means guarantee the Information Security status of an organisation. Following guidelines such as those contained in ISO17799 will, however, not ensure adequate Information Security status in an organisation either.

The combination of a process ISMS and a product ISMS into this one classification model allows management to implement a standard such as ISO17799 as well as certified products such as Oracle 8i to the best benefit of the information security status of the organisation.

This article illustrates how the process ISMS and the product ISMS can be combined and further visualised by the proposed protection classes.

If two identical organisations were to implement the exact same ISO17799 controls to the same exacting standards, but one company elected to use only certified products in so doing, whilst the other elected not to, the Information Security status of the former would be bound to outrank that of the latter!

6. LIST OF SOURCES CONSULTED

[CC02] Common Criteria http://niap.nist.gov/cc-scheme/iccc/TrackC/Smith/sld004.htm, October 2002

[ELOF00] Eloff MM, Von Solms SH, 2000, Information Security management: a hierarchical framework for various approaches, Computers & Security, Volume 19 Number 3, pp 243-256

[ELOF00[1]] Eloff MM, Von Solms SH, 2000, Information Security management: an approach to combine process certification and product evaluation, Computers & Security, Volume 19 Number 8, pp 698-709

[ELOF00[2]] Eloff MM, 2000, A Multi-dimensional Model for Information Security Management, PhD thesis, RAU

[HONE02] Höne, K, Eloff, JHP (2002), What makes an Effective Information Security Policy? Network Security, Vol. 2002 (6), pp. 14-16

[ISO02] ISO 7498-2, International Standards Organisation, Nov 1999 http://www.iso.ch, October 2002

[ISO17799] ISO/IEC 17799 Code of practice for Information Security Management, International Organization for Standardization/ International Electrotechnical Commission, 01-Mar-2000, http://www.iso.ch/iso/en/ISOOnline.openerpage

[NGI95] Evaluatie Kriteria voor IT-beveiliging, 1995, Nederlands Genootschap voor Informatica Afdeling Beveiliging, Edited by Dr Ir PL Overbeek, Kluwer BedryfsInformatie

DETECTING MALICIOUS USE WITH UNLABELLED DATA USING CLUSTERING AND OUTLIER ANALYSIS

G.S. Knight
Dept of Electrical and Computer Engineering, Royal Military College of Canada

L. Carosielli
Department of National Defence, Canada

Abstract: Most commercial intrusion detection systems (IDSs) presently available are signature-based network IDSs. Organisations using these IDSs are still experiencing difficulties in detecting intrusive activity on their networks since novel new attacks are consistently being encountered, and analysts can miss legitimate alarms when reviewing large alarm logs that contain a high number of false positives. There has been research investigating the use of data mining techniques to effectively detect malicious activity in an enterprise network. The results of many of these projects have demonstrated that these techniques can be effective when trained/calibrated using labelled datasets. Labelled datasets identify and characterize normal and malicious traffic for use in training/calibrating the detection sensor. However, the creation of labelled datasets is resource intensive. It requires a significant effort by security analysts to create a data set that characterises the traffic in a specific enterprise network environment. This research simulates and analyses malicious activity on an enterprise network to explore the detection of malicious activity with data mining techniques using unlabelled datasets. Semi-discrete decomposition (SDD) is used as a clustering and outlier analysis technique to characterize network traffic as either normal or anomalous.

1. INTRODUCTION

Signature-based network IDSs currently make up the greater part of deployed IDS sensors. Organisations using these IDSs are still experiencing difficulties in detecting intrusive activity on their networks since novel new attacks are consistently being encountered, and analysts can miss legitimate alarms when reviewing large alarm logs that contain a high number of false positives. Additionally, the original network attack may not have been prosecuted over the network and been visible at the IDS sensor. However, network traffic characterizing the malicious use of the compromised machine may be visible on the network as the attacker uses the machine for his/her own purposes. Often there is more traffic associated with this malicious use than there is associated with the original attack.

Anomaly-based intrusion detection techniques characterize normal network traffic and use this model of normality to identify abnormal, malicious traffic. This can allow an anomaly-based sensor to identify new types of malicious activity, which is difficult for signature-based IDSs.

Previous results [Blo01, Lee00] have demonstrated that data mining techniques can be effective when trained/calibrated using labelled datasets. Labelled datasets identify and characterize normal and malicious traffic for use in training/calibrating the detection sensor. However, the creation of labelled datasets is resource intensive. It requires a significant effort by security analysts to create a dataset that characterizes the traffic in a specific enterprise network environment. Moreover, the effort may have to be repeated at regular intervals as the network traffic patterns change with the changing use patterns of the users of the network and the applications that they use. This research simulates and analyses malicious activity on an enterprise network to explore the detection of malicious activity with data mining techniques using unlabelled datasets. In this project network data collected in normal daily usage is combined with known malicious traffic to create training and validation datasets. Semi-discrete decomposition (SDD) is used as a clustering and outlier analysis technique to characterize network traffic as either normal or anomalous.

Sections 2 and 3 of the paper provide some background information on clustering, outlier analysis, and SDD. Section 4 describes how to use SDD-based anomaly detection to detect malicious traffic in a network environment. The results of the work are presented in section 5 and section 6 provides discussion and conclusion.

2. CLUSTERING AND OUTLIER ANALYSIS

Cluster analysis is a data mining technique that groups objects into classes in an effort to maximize the intraclass similarity and minimize the interclass similarity. Similarities or dissimilarities are assessed based on attribute values describing the objects. The similarity or dissimilarity can be assessed using distance measures, partitioning methods, hierarchical methods, density methods, grid-based methods, or model-based methods [Han01]. Cluster analysis has been used to build customer profiles as well as in electronic fraud detection.

Outlier analysis tries to identify which data objects do not comply with the general behaviour of the dataset. Hawkins defines an outlier as an observation that deviates so much from other observations as to arouse suspicion that it was generated by a different mechanism [Haw80]. Outliers can be detected using statistical, distance-based, or deviation-based tests. For example, a statistical model might define outliers to be observations that lie three or more standard deviations from the mean. Deviation-based tests identify outliers by examining differences in the main characteristics of objects in a group. Objects that are significantly different (i.e. exceed the specified threshold) from the expected values are considered outliers [Han01]. Outlier analysis has been extensively used to detect the fraudulent use of credit cards and cellular telephone service.

3. SEMI-DISCRETE DECOMPOSITION

Semi-discrete decomposition (SDD) [Ole83, Zyt00] is a useful dimension-reduction and clustering technique. SDD has proved itself useful in applications involving storage compression, data filtering, and feature extractions. It has been used for image compression [Ole83, Zyt00], chromosome classification [Kol99], and latent semantic indexing of documents [Kol97]. The use of SDD as a deviation-based outlier detector was first suggested by McConnell and Skillicorn [Con01] when they were able to obtain outlier clusters that other outlier techniques were not able to find in a complex and highly correlated geochemical dataset.

3.1 SDD Description.

Given an m x n matrix A, the semi-discrete decomposition of A of dimension k is:

$$A_k = X_k D_k Y_k^T$$

Where X_k is an m x k matrix, D_k is an k x k matrix and Y_k is an k x n matrix. The entries of X_k and Y_k are from {-1, 0, 1} and D_k is a diagonal matrix of elements of **R**. The m x n decomposition matrix A_k is an approximation of the matrix A. This decomposition does not reproduce A exactly even if k = n, but uses very little storage with respect to the observed accuracy of the approximation [Kol97]. The matrix A represents a dataset with m rows representing records, and n columns representing attributes. Each record can be considered as a point in the n-dimensional feature space represented by the attributes. The SDD transforms the n-dimensional space into a new k-dimensional space. This in essence generates a faithful representation of the original data in a lower dimensional space. The rows of X_k are the coordinates of the corresponding rows of A in the space defined by the k new axes described by the rows of Y_k^T. The axes are ordered Y_k^T such that the variation in the original data is concentrated along the earlier axes [Con01]. That is, the axes associated with rows at the top of the matrix define dimensions along which there is a greater variance in data; there is less variance in the original data along the axes associated with rows lower in the matrix.

The columns of X_k are approximately ordered by decreasing variation among the records. Therefore, if we divide the rows of A according to whether they have a –1, 0, or 1 in the first column of the corresponding row of X_k, we have separated them into three classes which McConnell and Skillicorn expect captures the most important differences between them. The intuition here is that the 1 and –1 cases identify records/rows that have attributes significantly different from the normal data represented by the 0 case. The second and subsequent columns can be used to further subdivide the rows of A. In each case 1 and –1 values in the row of X_k for that column isolate classes of records that deviate from the norm. This produces a ternary decision tree. The further down the tree (i.e. the longer the sequence of leading zeros in a record in X_k) the more "normal" the records become.

The SDD approximation is formed iteratively. An efficient algorithm for the decomposition can be found in [Con01]. Matlab and C code for this SDD algorithm is available on O'Leary's website [OLEARY].

The SDD algorithm tries to select new axes along which the data exhibits considerable variance. The algorithm begins by selecting the values of the left most column of X_k ,the first axis vector of Y_k^T and the multiplier in D that give the least amount of error between the current approximation, A_x, and the original matrix A. Column values, axes, and multipliers are iteratively selected for successive columns of X_k. Therefore at each iteration the error between the approximation, A_x, and the original matrix A is reduced.

3.2 SDD as an Outlier Detector.

The general effect of SDD is to find regions of the matrix in which variation in the magnitude of the values is relatively large. During the approximation iterations, large variations are removed first followed by smaller variations. Since SDD tends to emphasize the most unusual patterns in a dataset it can be considered an outlier detector.

The algorithm used to calculate the SDD is sensitive to the initial parameters used in the iterative algorithm. Therefore, the algorithm does not always choose at each step a new axis that will remove the largest amount of error between the decomposition approximation and the actual matrix A. Hence later steps can find a more significant axis that was missed on previous steps. It is therefore possible that the weight the axis has in reducing the amount of error between A_x and A does not always decrease monotonically with the order of the axes in the matrix.

McConnell and Skillicorn [Con01] suggest a reordering scheme for the columns of the SDD matrices. This modification ensures that the strongest outliers appear closest to the top of the decision tree since it reorders the axes so that those with the largest weight appear first.

4. ANOMOLY DETECTION

For the proposed SDD technique to effectively detect malicious use of compromised systems, there are several assumptions that this method relies upon:

a. the number of normal elements in the dataset is significantly larger than the number of anomalous elements (typically 98% and 2 % respectively),
b. data instances of the same type will be close to each other in feature space, and
c. normal data of different sub-types will cluster together, while sub-types of malicious data will not be near the normal region of feature space.

In para a. above, the anomalous traffic is required in the training dataset so that the SDD analysis can differentiate between what normal and anomalous traffic attribute values are. The amount of anomalous traffic to interleave, 2%, was chosen to maintain consistency with the malicious to normal traffic ratios used in research by Portnoy et al. [Por01]. In this analysis anomalous traffic is considered to be malicious traffic. The assumptions of paras b. and c. are required if the data is to be suitable for clustering and outlier analysis.

4.1 Detection Procedures

In order to verify the proposed malicious use detection theory, the following procedures will be followed:

a. create the training model,
b. analyse independent network traffic, and
c. conduct network diversity validation.

To create the training model an example of normal network traffic is collected on the live target network. Malicious traffic is also collected in a closed lab network by using actual malware tools. This normal usage and malicious usage traffic is interleaved to form the training and validation datasets.

The raw network traffic is then processed using a connection analyser to produce network connection records containing the basic attributes of the network connections.

In the next step in the process, these attributes are normalized by calculating the Z-score of each attribute value [Han01]. The normalized connection data is then analysed using SDD. The code used to perform this analysis is a version of the SDD code provided by O'Leary [OLEARY], which has been modified by the researchers to implement the modifications suggested by McConnell and Skillicorn [Con01]. The resulting SDD X matrix is then used to create a ternary decision tree. The detection threshold is chosen such that the records that have a leading –1 or 1 in the first 50% of the k columns are labelled as anomalous. The value of 50 % of k was chosen empirically as a result of a series of experimental trials.

The training model is then used to analyse previously unseen network traffic. The validation datasets are constructed by interleaving new normal usage data, the malicious traffic data used to create the training model, and malicious traffic data that was not previously used to create the training model. The validation dataset includes malicious traffic data that was not used to create the training model in order to verify how well the proposed technique identifies new malicious use examples. The following procedures are followed to classify the connections in the validation dataset as either normal or anomalous:

a. convert/normalize the network traffic based on the statistical information of the training set,
b. compute the validation dataset's SDD values by appending additional records to the training model's SDD X matrix, and
c. use the newly appended rows of the SDD's X matrix to create a ternary decision tree where records that have a leading –1 or 1 in the first 50% of the k columns are labelled as anomalous.

5. RESULTS

The KDD Cup 1999 (KDD99) dataset is commonly used to verify the effectiveness of IDSs as it contains a wide variety of intrusions simulated in a military network environment [KDD99]. The KDD99 dataset consists of approximately 4,900,000 records. Early in the project two subsets of the KDD99 dataset were analysed to determine if it was worthwhile to continue investigating the feasibility of using the SDD technique. The promising results obtained by analysing the KDD99 dataset were used to further develop the malicious use detection methodology.

In further proof-of-concept trials of the malicious use detection methodology, representative data of daily usage network traffic was required to produce training and validation datasets. Examples of intranet and Internet network traffic were collected on RMC's LAN in order to verify how the proposed methodology performs with varying degrees of data complexity. A more complete presentation of the results is presented in [Car02].

5.1 KDD Results

Due to the large size of the KDD99 dataset, two randomly selected subsets of the overall KDD99 dataset were created for analysis. The KDD 37084 and KDD 98770 datasets respectively contain 37084 and 98770 connection records. 41 attributes were used in the SDD analysis of KDD99.

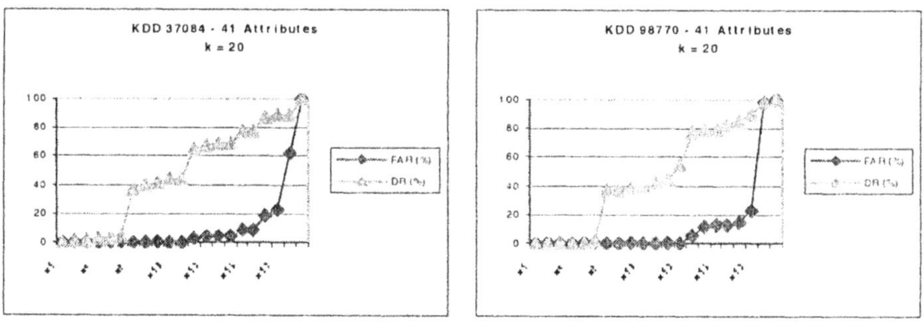

Figure 1: KDD99 Analysis Results

The X-axes of the graphs in Figure 1 represent the columns of the SDD X matrix (i.e X1 = first column, X2 = second column, etc.). These X-axes values are thresholds that correspond to the graph branches in the related ternary decision tree. The detection rates (DRs) represent how many malicious records are classified by the scheme to be abnormal when a given X-axes value, i, is used as a detection threshold. Recall that a –1 or a 1 any leading column (column 0 to i) classifies a record as abnormal. . The false alarm rates represent how many normal records are misclassified by the scheme to be abnormal when a given X-axes value is used as the detection threshold. From Figure 1, we can see that k = 20 returned the best results with a 43% DR and 0.1% FAR for KDD 37084 and 39% DR and 0.12%

FAR for KDD 98770 if the first 10 columns are selected (X10) in the resulting SDD X matrix.

5.2 RMC Intranet Results

The normal usage traffic was collected from a live LAN segment. The machines and applications run on this network segment are fairly homogeneous. Malicious traffic was collected in a closed lab network by using actual malware tools. This normal usage and malicious usage traffic was interleaved to form the training and validation datasets.

This raw network traffic is then processed using a connection analyser called Argus [ARGUS] to produce network connection records containing the basic features of network connections. Of the 14 basic features provided by Argus, the 11 features listed in Table 1 are used for further analysis to determine if the connection is normal or anomalous. Note that SrcRatio and DstRatio are derived from SrcBytes/SrcPkt and DstBytes/DstPkt respectively. These 11 features were selected for this research since they represent a combination of the intrinsic features used for the KDD99 dataset and the basic connection features used by Iguchi and Goto [Igu99].

Table 1: Eleven Basic Connection Features

Feature	Description
Duration	Total duration of a connection
Type	Type of protocol, e.g. TCP, UDP, etc.
Sport	Port number connection is coming from
Dport	Port number connection is going to
SrcPkt	Total numbers of outbound packets sent through a connection
DstPkt	Total numbers of inbound packets received through a connection
SrcBytes	Total numbers of outbound bytes sent through a connection
DstBytes	Total numbers of inbound bytes received through a connection
SrcRatio	Overall bytes per packet rate outbound through a connection
DstRatio	Overall bytes per packet rate inbound through a connection
State	Basic state of a transaction and how it is terminated

The malware tools selected for this research were installed on a stand-alone experimental network. Linux and Windows-based malware tools were used. For every experiment, there were typically two or three hosts involved with one collecting the network data using a packet-sniffing tool. Table 2 provides an example of the malware tools used.

The intranet training dataset analysed contained 115,925 daily usage and 3003 malware usage records. Figure 2 provides the results from one of the SDD analysis decompositions of the training dataset. If the threshold for malicious use detection is set at X3 then the expected false alarm rate is 0.697% and the detection rate is 33.5%.

Table 2: Malware Tools Used to Create Datasets

Backdoors	Scanning	Denial of Service	Covert Tunnels
BO2K	Netcat	TFN2K	Covert-tcp
Cd00r	Nmap	Winnuke	Httptunnel
Cgiback	Nessus		Rwwwshell
Netcat			Itunnel
Bindshell			
NetBus			
Pingback			
Subseven			

The SDD technique was validated for the intranet by using the matrices that were produced by the training decomposition to analyse another dataset. The validation dataset was prepared in the same way as the training dataset. The new dataset was prepared from different daily traffic logs from the target network, and included a different set of malware traffic data.

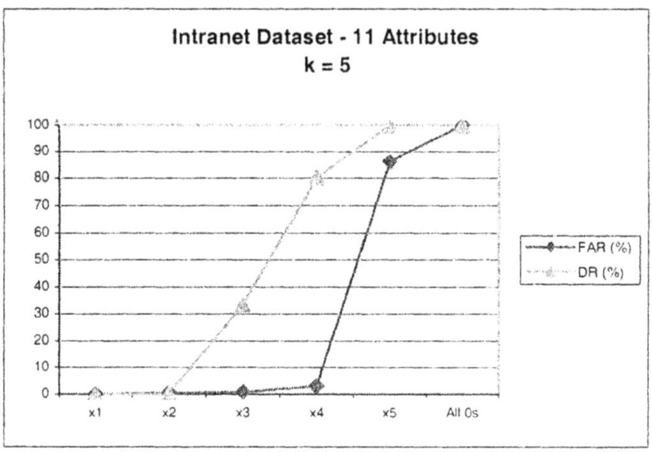

Figure 2: Intranet Training Dataset Analysis Results

The intranet validation dataset analysed contained 179,554 daily usage and 4888 malware usage records. The results obtained by computing the decomposition with k = 5, shown in Figure 3, demonstrate that the SDD methodology has a classification DR of 39.4% and a FAR of 0.70% at the X3 threshold. These results are comparable to the 33.3% DR and 0.7% FAR obtained for the intranet training dataset. The SDD analysis of the intranet validation dataset correctly classified 1926 malware records. This includes those that were also present in the training dataset as well as 960 previously unseen records. This demonstrates that the SDD methodology can detect certain types of previously unseen malware.

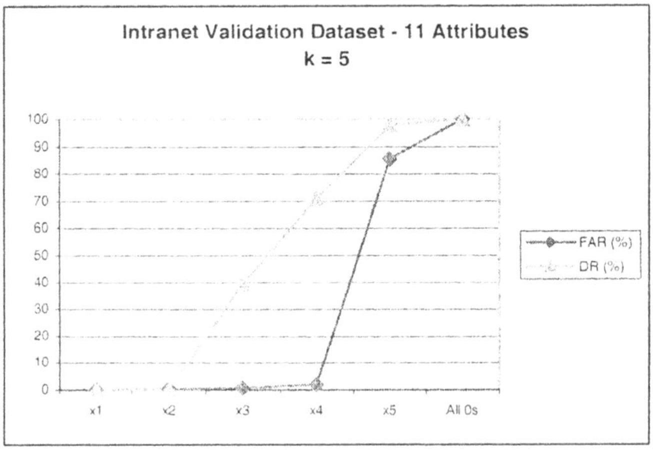

Figure 3: Intranet Validation Dataset Analysis Results

5.3 RMC Internet Results

In other experiments to explore the efficacy of the SDD technique, training and validation datasets were prepared for a sensor located at the RMC Internet firewall. This sensor monitors the much richer, heterogeneous network communications associated with the entire university campus network. This traffic also includes a significant volume of peer-to-peer traffic associated with the university dormitory. The training datasets and the validation datasets were prepared in the same way as for the intranet experiments. The results of the analysis technique when applied to this broad-spectrum network traffic were poor. The technique did not provide useful results in this mode. However, if the data at this sensor is filtered into several data streams in order to isolate specific kinds of network traffic, e.g. selections based on port number, interesting results are observed. Four datasets selected to filter traffic for ports 21, 23, 53, and 1000-6000 produced results similar to those for the intranet and KDD99 experiments. These results demonstrated that the analysis method would be useful in the reduction of a dataset for a specific protocol for further protocol analysis. The majority of the normal connections can be removed while keeping a large number of the malicious connections in the reduced dataset. This simplifies further protocol analysis by enabling the analysts to concentrate on the most interesting connections. The analysis method also detected an actual malicious scan of the RMC network that was coincidentally taking place at the time that the data for the validation dataset was being collected.

6. DISCUSSION & CONCLUSION

The SDD methodology's effectiveness is comparable to the effectiveness of existing methodologies. Labelled dataset techniques [Blo01, Lee00] generally obtained better DRs and FARs, but these improvements have to be weighed against the cost of producing the labelled datasets. The results from KDD 98770 and intranet test datasets had lower DRs than those obtained by Portnoy et al.'s clustering technique [Por01] but the FARs were better. Increasing the detection threshold to higher values of X could increase the DRs to 77.29% and 80.15% respectively for the KDD 98770 and the intranet test datasets, but their respective FARs would increase to 6.09% and 3.02%.

The effectiveness of the SDD methodology for the intranet dataset is further supported by the fact that the intranet dataset contained only 11 intrinsic TCP/IP connection attributes. The KDD99 dataset contained 41 attributes, of which 9 were intrinsic TCP/IP network connection attributes, 13 were content or packet payload based connection attributes, and 19 were time based connection attributes. These 41 attributes would be extremely resource intensive to produce since the analyser has to review each packet's payload and keep the state of numerous connections to produce the required attributes.

An interesting area of future work is the identification of additional attributes or features of network connections that will improve the performance of SDD based anomaly detection. The 11 basic features used in this work may be supplemented with measurements such as: timing latencies on either end of the network connection, recurring use of addresses/ports, or the overlap and interleaving of connection events.

This research has shown that an anomaly detection sensor trained using unlabelled data can be used to detect the malicious use of compromised systems. The SDD methodology obtained acceptable FARs and DRs when analysing intranet datasets. Systems can become compromised in many ways, some not yet known. An unknown compromise is difficult to detect using a signature-based system. This technique is therefore a useful part of a layered security suite. The SDD methodology can also be used to reduce Internet datasets for further specific protocol analysis. This would enable the analysts to concentrate on the most interesting connections.

REFERENCES

[ARGUS] Argus 2.0.2, http://www.qosient.com/argus/

[Blo01] E. Bloedorn, L. Talbot, C. Skorupka, A. Christiansen, B. Hill, J. Tivel, "Data mining Applied to Intrusion Detection: MITRE Experiences", MITRE Technical Report MTR01W0000103, September 2001.

[Car02] L.Carosielli, "Detecting Malicious Use With Unlabelled Data Using Clustering And Outlier Analysis", Masters Thesis, Department of Electrical and Computer Engineering, Royal Military College Of Canada, Kingston, Canada, April 2002.

[Con01] S. McConnell, D.B. Skillicorn, "Outlier Detection Using Semi-Discrete Decomposition", External Technical Report ISSN-0836-0227-2001-452, Department of Computing and Information Science Queen's University, Kingston, Canada, November 2001.

[Han01] J. Han, M. Kamber, "Data Mining: Concepts and Techniques", Morgan Kaufmann, San Francisco, 2001.

[Haw80] D. Hawkins, "Identification of Outliers", Chapman and Hall, London, 1980.

[Igu99] M. Iguchi, S. Goto, "Detecting Malicious Activities through Port Profiling", IEICE Transactions on Information and Systems, E82-D(4), April 1999, 784-792.

[KDD99] KDD Cup 1999 Data, http://kdd.ics.uci.edu/databases/kddcup99/kddcup99.html

[Kol99] T.G. Kolda, D.P. O'Leary, "Computation and Uses of the Semidiscrete Matrix Decomposition", ACM Transactions of Information Processing, 1999.

[Kol97] T.G. Kolda, D.P. O'Leary, "A Semi-Discrete Matrix Decomposition for Latent Semantic Indexing in Information Retrieval", ACM Transactions on Information Systems, 16, 1997, 322-346.

[Lee00] W. Lee, S. Stolfo, "A Framework for Constructing Features and Models for Intrusion Detection Systems", ACM Transactions on Information and System Security, 3(4), 2000, 227-261.

[Ole83] D.P. O'Leary, S. Peleg, "Digital Image Compression by Outer Product Expansion", IEEE Transactions on Communications, 31, 1983, 441-444.

[OLEARY] SDDPACK, Software for the Semi-Discrete Decomposition, http://www.cs.umd.edu/users/oleary/SDDPACK/

[Por01] L. Portnoy, E. Eskin, S.J. Stolfo, "Intrusion Detection With Unlabeled Data Using Clustering", To Appear in Proceedings of ACM CSS Workshop on Data Mining Applied to Security (DMSA-2001), Philadelphia, USA, 5-8 November, 2001.

[Zyt00] S. Zyto, A. Grama, W. Szpankowski, "Semi-Discrete Matrix Transforms (SDD) for Image and Video Compression", Technical Report, Department of Computer Science, Purdue University, 2000.

E^2XB: A DOMAIN-SPECIFIC STRING MATCHING ALGORITHM FOR INTRUSION DETECTION

K. G. Anagnostakis*, S. Antonatos, E. P. Markatos, M. Polychronakis†
Institute for Computer Science (ICS)
Foundation for Research and Technology - Hellas (FORTH)
P.O. Box 1385 - Heraklio, Crete, GR-711-10 GREECE
{kanag,antonat,markatos,mikepo}@ics.forth.gr

Abstract We consider the problem of string matching in Network Intrusion Detection Systems (NIDSes). String matching computations dominate in the overall cost of running a NIDS, despite the use of efficient general-purpose string matching algorithms. Aiming at increasing the efficiency and capacity of NIDSes, we have designed E^2xB, a string matching algorithm that is tailored to the specific characteristics of NIDS string matching. We have implemented E^2xB in `snort`, a popular open-source NIDS, and present experiments comparing E^2xB with the current best alternative solution. Our results suggest that for typical traffic patterns E^2xB improves NIDS performance by 10%-36%, while for certain ruleset and traffic patterns string matching performance can be improved by as much as a factor of three.

Keywords: network security, intrusion detection, string matching, network monitoring, network performance

1. Introduction

Network Intrusion Detection Systems (NIDSes) are receiving considerable attention as a mechanism for shielding against "attempts to compromise the confidentiality, integrity, availability, or to bypass the security mechanisms of a computer network" (2). The typical function of a NIDS is based on a set of *signatures*, each describing one known intrusion threat. A NIDS examines network traffic and determines whether any signatures indicating intrusion attempts are matched.

The simplest and most common form of NIDS inspection is to match string patterns against the payload of packets captured on a network link. The use

* Author is with the CIS Department, University of Pennsylvania, Email: *anagnost@dsl.cis.upenn.edu*
† Authors are also with the Computer Science Department, University of Crete

of existing efficient string matching algorithms for this purpose, such as (3, 1), bears a significant cost: recent measurements of the `snort` NIDS (13)on a production network show that as much as 31% of total processing is due to string-matching (6). The same study also reports that in the case of Web-intensive traffic, this cost is increased to as much as 80% of the total processing time. At the same time, NIDSes need to be highly efficient to keep up with increasing link speeds, and, as the number of potential threats (and associated signatures and rules) is expected to grow, the cost of string matching is likely to increase even further.

These trends motivate the study of new string matching algorithms tailored to the particular requirements and characteristics of Intrusion Detection, much like domain-specific algorithms were developed for efficient routing lookups and packet classification in IP forwarding (10, 7).

In this context, we present E^2xB, a string matching algorithm that is designed specifically for the relatively small input size (in the order of packet size) and small expected matching probability that is common in a NIDS environment. These assumptions allow string matching to be enhanced by first testing the input (e.g., the payload of each packet) for *missing* fixed-size sub-strings of the original signature string, called *elements*. The false positives induced by E^2xB, e.g., cases with all fixed-size sub-strings of the signature showing up in arbitrary positions within the input, can then be separated from actual matches using standard string matching algorithms, such as the Boyer-Moore algorithm (3). Experiments with E^2xB implemented in `snort`, show that in common cases, E^2xB is more efficient than existing algorithms by up to 36%, while in certain scenarios, E^2xB can be three times faster. This improvement is due to an overall reduction in executed instructions and, in most cases, a smaller memory footprint than existing algorithms.

2. Background

The general problem of designing algorithms for string matching is well-researched. One of the most widely used algorithms was first proposed in (3). The Boyer-Moore algorithm compares the search string with the input starting from the rightmost character of the search string. This allows the use of two heuristics that may reduce the number of comparisons needed for string matching (compared to the naive algorithm). Both heuristics are triggered on a mismatch. The first heuristic, called the *bad character heuristic*, works as follows: if the mismatching character appears in the search string, the search string is shifted so that the mismatching character is aligned with the rightmost position at which the mismatching character appears in the search string. If the mismatching character does not appear in the search string, the search string is shifted so that the first character of the pattern is one position past the mismatching character in the input. The second heuristic, called the *good suffixes heuristic*, is also triggered on a mismatch. If the mismatch occurs in the middle of the search string, then there is a non-empty suffix that matches. The heuristic then shifts the search string up to the next occurrence of the suffix in the string. Horspool (1980) improved the Boyer-Moore algorithm with a simpler and more efficient implementation that uses only the bad-character heuristic.

Aho and Corasick (1975) provided an algorithm for concurrently matching multiple strings. The set of strings is used to construct an automaton which is able to search for all strings concurrently. The automaton consumes the input one character at-a-time and keeps track of patterns that have (partially) matched the input.

Fisk and Varghese (2002) were the first to consider the design of NIDS-specific string matching algorithms. They proposed an algorithm called Set-wise Boyer-Moore-Horspool, adapting the Boyer-Moore algorithm to simultaneously match a set of rules. This algorithm is shown to be faster than both Aho-Corasick and Boyer-Moore for medium-size pattern sets. Their experiments suggest triggering a different algorithm depending on the number of rules: Boyer-Moore-Horspool if there is only one rule; Set-wise Boyer-Moore-Horspool if there are between 2 and 100 rules, and Aho-Corasick for more than 100 rules. This heuristic has been incorporated in `snort` and provides the baseline for our comparison in Section 4. Independently of Fisk and Varghese, Coit et al. (2002) implemented a similar algorithm in `snort`, adapting Boyer-Moore for simultaneously matching multiple strings, derived from the exact set matching algorithm of Gusfield (1977) .

Recently, we have proposed ExB, a precursor of E^2xB, providing quick negatives when the search string does not exist in the packet payload (11). E^2xB provides several improvements on ExB , the most important being a faster pre-processing phase, removing much of the overhead associated with initializing the occurrence map, and a wider set of experiment results, that also highlight NIDS properties that are interesting beyond the scope of the specific algorithm.

3. E^2xB: Exclusion-based string matching

We present an informal description of E^2xB, first in its simplest and most intuitive form and then in its more general form. E^2xB is based on the following simple observation:

> Suppose that we want to check whether an input string I contains a small string s. If there exists at least one character of string s that is not contained in I, then s is not a substring of I.

The above simple observation can be used to quickly determine several cases where a given string s does *not* appear in the input string I: **if s contains at least one character that is not in I, then s is not a substring of I.** However, this observation cannot be used to determine the cases where s *is* a substring of I. Indeed, if every character of string s belongs to input string I, then we should use a standard string matching algorithms (e.g., Boyer-Moore-

Horspool) to confirm whether s is actually a substring of I or not. The cases where every character of s is in I, but s is not a substring of I are called *false matches*, or *false positives*.

This method is effective only if there is a fast way of checking whether a given character c belongs in I or not. We perform this check with the help of an *occurrence map*. Specifically, we first *pre-process* the input string I, and for each (8-bit) character c that appears in string I, we mark the corresponding (i.e. c_{th}) *cell* on the (256-cell) map. Although we could use a binary value to mark the mentioned cells (i.e. if the c_{th} position of the cell map is 1, then the character c appears in I, otherwise it does not), our experiments in (11)suggest that the cost of cleaning (i.e. filling with zeros) the cell map for each new packet can be very high. To reduce this cost, we decided to mark the cell with the (index) number of the current network packet. Thus, if the c_{th} position of the cell map contains the number of the current network packet, the character c appears in I, otherwise it does not [1].

In order to reduce the percentage of false matches, the above algorithm can be generalized for *pairs* of (8-bit) characters: instead of recording the occurrence of single characters in string I, it is possible to record the appearance of each *pair* of consecutive characters in string I. In the matching process, instead of determining whether each character of s appears in I, the algorithm then checks whether each pair of consecutive characters of s appears in I. If a pair is found that does not appear in I, E^2xB knows that s is not in I.

Generalizing further, instead of using 8-bit characters, or 16-bit pairs of characters, E^2xB can use bit-strings of arbitrary length (hereafter called *elements*). That is, E^2xB records all (byte-aligned) bit-strings of length x. The element size exposes a trade-off: larger elements are likely to result in fewer false matches, but also increase the size of the occurrence map, which could, in turn, increase capacity misses and degrade performance.

The pseudo-code for pre-processing `input` and for matching a string `s` on `input` is presented in Figure 1.

The main difference between E^2xB and ExB is the use of cells: ExB assumed an occurence *bitmap* where each element was marked by setting the 1-bit cell to 1. This required the bitmap to be cleared for each packet, adding unnecessary overhead. A second difference lies in the way the two bytes forming an element are *hashed* together. E^2xB uses OR while ExB uses XOR. Although in theory XOR does provide a better hash than OR, the difference in the number of collisions was found to be negligible. The value of using XOR lies more in that XOR instructions were found to result in slightly better performance. Finally, an important implementation detail that has been addressed in E^2xB is support for *case-insensitive matching*, as many NIDS signatures

[1] To reduce the number of bits needed to store the cell map, the numbers of network packets are limited to a predefined number of bits, which we call *cell_size*. If the number of network packets exceed 2^{cell_size}, then the next packet gets the number 0.

```
pre_process(char *input, int len)
{
  pktid=pktno & (1<<cellsize - 1);

  for (int idx = 0 ; idx < len-1 ; idx++) {
       element = s[idx]<< ( elementsize-8 ) ^ s[idx+1];
       occurence_map [ element ] = pktid;
  }
}
search(char *s, char *input, int len_s, int len)
{
  for (int idx = 0 ; idx < len_s-1 ; idx++) {
      element= s[idx]<< ( elementsize-8 ) ^ s[idx+1];
      if ( occurence_map [ element ] != pktid)
          return DOES_NOT_EXIST ;
  }
  return boyer_moore(s, len_s, input, len);
}
```

Figure 1. Pseudo-code for E^2xB pre-processing and search.

are case-insensitive. This is done by modifying the *search* procedure to test for the occurence of all four combinations of upper- and lower-case for each of the two bytes used to compute the element index.

4. Experimental evaluation

Using trace-driven execution, we evaluate the performance of E^2xB against the heuristic of (6)(denoted as FVh in the rest of this paper) and the implementation of (3)in snort .

4.1 Environment

For all the experiments we used a PC with a Pentium 4 processor running at 1.7 GHz, with a L1 cache of 8 KB and L2 cache of 256 KB, and 512 Mbytes of main memory. The measured memory latency is 1 ns for the L1 cache, 10.9 ns for the L2 cache and 170.4 ns for the main memory , measured using lmbench (12). The host operating system is Linux (kernel version 2.4.14, RedHat 7.3). We use snort version 1.9.0 (build 205) compiled with gcc version 2.96.

Each packet is checked against the "default" rule-set of the snort distribution. The ruleset is organized as a two-dimensional chain data-structure, where each element - called a *chain header* - tests the input packet against a packet header rule. When a packet header rule is matched, the chain header points to a set of signature tests, including payload signatures that trigger the execution of the string matching algorithm. The default rule-set consists of 187 chain headers with a total of 1661 rules, 1575 of which are string matching rules.

We use packet traces from four different sources:

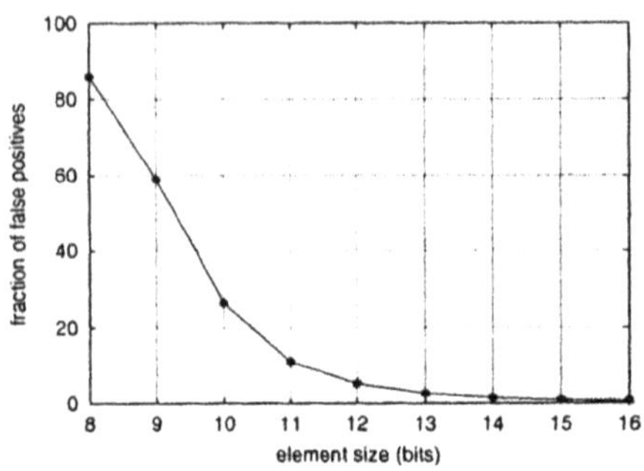

Figure 2. Effect of element and cell size parameters on the fraction of false positives

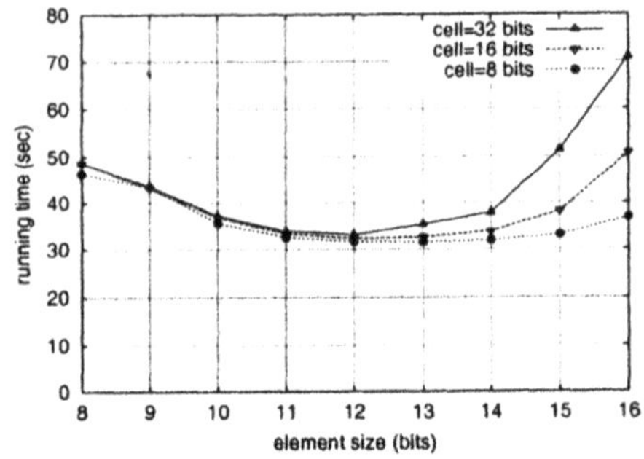

Figure 3. Effect of element and cell size parameters on running time

- A set of full-packet traces from the DEFCON "capture the flag" dataset. [2] These traces contain numerous intrusion attempts.
- A full packet trace containing Web traffic, generated by concurrently running a number of recursive `wget` requests on popular portal sites.
- Three header-only traces from the NLANR archive. These packet traces were taken on backbone links. Because these are header-only traces, for our experiments we added random payloads. We argue that the results are representative after determining that random payloads do not significantly alter NIDS performance.
- A set of header-only traces collected on the OC3 link connecting the University of Crete campus network (UCNET) to the Greek academic network (GRNET)(5), with random payloads.

For the experiments of Sections 4.2 and 4.3, we use the DEFCON `eth0.dump2` trace containing 1,035,736 packets. For simplicity, traces are read from a local file by using the appropriate `snort` option, which is passed to the underlying `pcap(3)` library. (Replaying traces from a remote host provided similar results.)

4.2 Element and cell size

We first determine the optimal size for E^2xB elements and cells. In Figure 2 we show the fraction of false positives for different element and cell sizes, and in Figure 3 the corresponding running time of `snort`, obtained using the `time(1)` facility of the host operating system. We observe that the fraction of false positives is well below 2% when using elements 13 bits or more. Completion time decreases with increasing element size, as the fraction of false

[2] Available at http://www.shmoo.com/cctf/

positives that have to be searched using Boyer-Moore is reduced. However, it is not strictly decreasing: it is minimized at 13 bits but exhibits a slight increase for more than 13 bits, apparently because of the effect of data-structure size (8 KB for 13-bit elements, 64 KB for 16 bits, for a cell size of 8 bits) on cache performance. For our specific configuration, 13-bit elements and 8-bit cells appear to offer the best performance.

4.3 Experiments with the default rule-set

We determine if E^2xB offers any overall improvement compared to FVh and BM using the `eth0.sump2` trace. The completion time for E^2xB , BM and FVh are 30.20, 47.31 and 47.36 seconds, respectively. We observe that using E^2xB , `snort` is 36% faster than both known algorithms. E^2xB is faster because, in the common case, it can quickly decide that a given set of strings is not contained in a packet. More specifically, in this experiment, the string matching function was invoked 22,716,676 times. Out of those, E^2xB was able to quickly state that the considered string was not a substring of the input packet in 22,395,210 of the invocations (or 98.4%). Thus, in 98.4% of all invocations, E^2xB was able to deliver the correct answer without actually searching for the pattern in the packet. In the remaining 1.6%, E^2xB used the Boyer-Moore string searching algorithm to find whether the string is really in the packet.

4.4 Other packet traces

We repeated the experiments with the three algorithms on the full set of traces. The results are summarized in Table 1. We first confirm that random payloads behave similarly to real payloads for the DEFCON `eth0.dump2` trace: the difference in performance between the original trace and the trace with the payload replaced with random data is negligible for all three algorithms. Based on this observation, we can argue that using random payloads on the NLANR and UCNET traces provides a reasonably accurate estimate on how the algorithms would perform with real payloads.

Comparing the performance of the string matching algorithms, we observe that E^2xB performs better than FVh and BM on all traces except for one and that the relative improvement varies. It is also interesting to see that FVh, reported in (6)to perform better than BM, sometimes performs worse for the traces examined. Although the improvement of E^2xB is typically between 25% and 35%, and can be as high as 36.17%, there are cases where the gain is only around 8% or, even in the case of the NLANR AIX trace, worse than BM by 8%. This appears to relate, at least in part, to differences in the packet size distribution: the average packet size is 835 bytes for the DEFCON `eth0.dump2` trace and 364 bytes for the NLANR AIX trace. For larger packets, `snort` spends more time in string matching, and E^2xB offers significant benefits, while for smaller packets, `snort` spends less time in string match-

Trace characteristics				Running time			
trace name	ID	nr. of packets	avg.pkt (bytes)	BM (sec)	FVh (sec)	E^2xB (sec)	%
eth0.dump2	D.02	1035736	835	47.31	47.36	30.20	+36.17
eth0.dump2.r	D.02.R			46.35	46.60	29.77	+35.77
eth0.dump4	D.04	595267	1481	14.11	56.24	9.81	+30.47
eth0.dump8	D.08	497302	1111	9.79	41.51	6.74	+31.15
webtrace	W.0	1188660	761	345.60	300.86	274.51	+8.76
NLANR IND	N.IND	2254931	703	93.53	83.8	62.04	+25.97
NLANR MRA	N.MRA	2760531	760	137.39	122.40	89.07	+27.23
NLANR AIX	N.AIX	1624223	364	13.17	14.00	14.26	-8.28
UCNET 0000	UC.00	1564131	422	103.93	82.35	66.84	+18.83
UCNET 0100	UC.01	2245938	413	108.69	84.20	62.54	+25.72

Table 1. Completion time of `snort` with different string matching algorithms – all traces

trace	rules	% pkts	% bytes	avg pkt
D.02	60	21.13	35.53	1336
	62	21.18	36.20	1358
	66	54.09	26.45	388
D.04	13	24.71	24.90	1472
	32	73.98	74.60	1473
D.08	13	24.82	24.84	1093
	32	74.83	74.91	1092
N.AIX	28	87.63	92.20	330
	36	5.56	2.84	160
N.IND	36	4.98	5.25	692
	38	40.07	30.31	495
	60	30.82	36.90	785
	62	8.38	9.22	721
N.MRA	60	43.72	44.04	713
	61	9.82	9.96	718
	62	13.89	14.17	722
	63	14.04	13.90	701
	101	6.16	5.80	667

trace	rules	% pkts	% bytes	avg pkt
W.0	103	56.47	33.41	419
	107	0.53	0.31	410
	820	42.99	66.28	1092
UC.00	36	15.81	13.52	316
	38	7.44	6.42	320
	60	18.85	16.63	326
	62	5.35	6.58	456
	68	12.71	10.13	295
	101	16.89	24.86	545
	102	9.62	10.47	402
	820	4.79	3.76	290
UC.01	36	11.54	9.51	296
	38	5.75	4.78	299
	60	42.71	39.91	336
	61	5.35	4.76	320
	68	7.35	5.70	279
	101	10.42	17.33	599
	102	7.68	10.09	473

Table 2. Analysis of rule-set invocations (rules rarely triggered are not presented)

ing, and E^2xB is less useful. On the other hand, results can be very different for traces with similar packet size statistics. For example, the average packet size for webtrace and MRA are 761 and 760 bytes, respectively, but the gain of E^2xB is 8.76% and 27.23%, respectively. More detailed analysis is therefore needed to understand the benefits of our approach.

We obtain processor-level statistics of executed instructions and L2 data cache misses for each trace using the `brink/abyss` toolkit which collects data from the Pentium performance counters (14). The results are presented in Figures 4 and 5. We observe that the number of instructions for E^2xB is significantly smaller in all cases except for the AIX trace. The reduction in

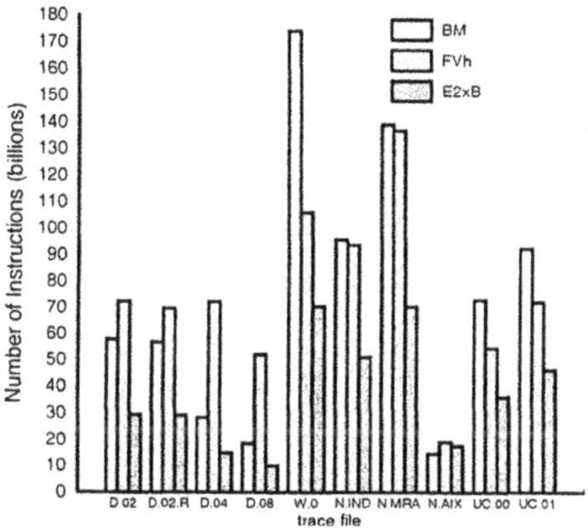

Figure 4. Executed instructions.

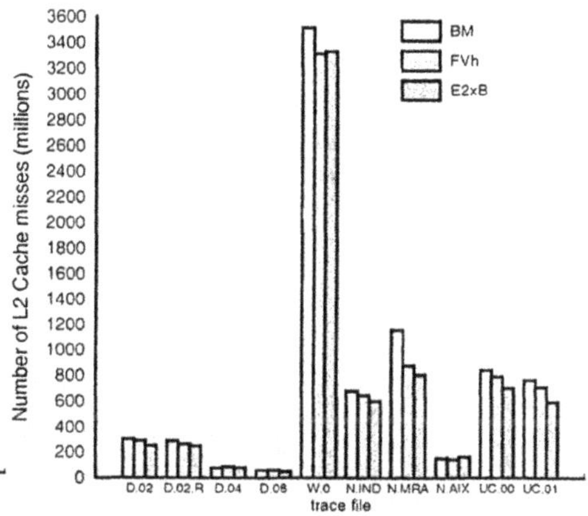

Figure 5. L2 data cache misses.

L2 data cache misses is relatively small compared to the reduction in executed instructions. For example, for the *W*.0 trace (Web-traffic) E^2xB has 30% less instructions but a slighly higher number of cache misses. This explains the relatively small overall performance gain (rougly 8%) for E^2xB on this trace.

To further understand the differences in the results, we instrumented `snort` to provide a trace of the chain headers and content rules invoked for each packet. The results for all packet traces are presented in Table 2. We observe that the string matching workload for different traces varies significantly. For instance, for the AIX trace 87.6% of the packets are checked against only 28 rules, while for the Web trace 56.4% of the packets are checked against 103 rules, and 43% against 820 rules. Considering these statistics, it appears that E^2xB offers larger improvements in cases where a large fraction of packets are checked against 30 to 100 content rules (as in the IND, MRA and all DEFCON traces). This also indicates that it may be necessary to consider hybrid algorithms, especially in cases where there is either a very small or very large number of rules applying to a significant fraction of packets. In such cases, E^2xB may not perform as well as BM when the number of content rules in a chain header is very small or the Aho-Corasick algorithm used in FVh when the number of content rules per chain header is large.

Although the details of such a hybrid algorithm are beyond the scope of this paper, we run a simple experiment to confirm that the cost of E^2xB is higher than BM for small sets of content rules and higher than Aho-Corasick for large sets of content rules. For this, we measure algorithm performance *off-line* e.g., as an isolated standalone program, with random inputs checked against a set

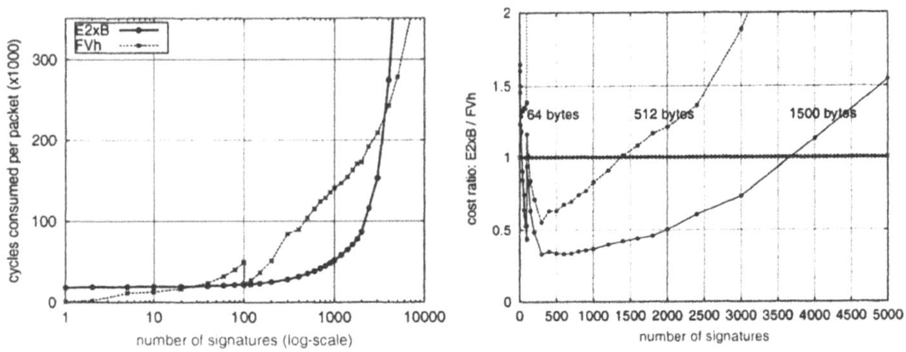

Figure 6. Off-line performance measurements of E^2xB and FVh.

of random rules. We fix the input size at 1500 bytes and obtain the average number of cycles for each input "packet" for different numbers of rules. Each rule is assumed to be a 20-bytes string. The results are presented in Figure 6 (left). We see that E^2xB is indeed more expensive than FVh for less than 20 rules, and that the relative performance benefits are maximized at around 700-1000 rules. After a certain point, the cost of E^2xB rises sharply, possibly due to the joint effect of increasing false-match rates *per-packet* and capacity misses (due to the size of the rule-set). We also run the same experiment with the input size set to 64 and 512 bytes, and compute the ratio of the average number of cycles consumed per-packet of E^2xB over FVh. These results are presented in Figure 6 (right). As expected, the relative benefits of the two algorithms and the ranges in which they perform better depend a lot on packet size. Experimentation with the actual NIDS and a more realistic traffic model and rule-set (or rule-set model) is, therefore, required to obtain the right thresholds for such a hybrid algorithm. Beyond the hybrid algorithm, these results also provide some insights on the scalability of different algorithms: E^2xB appears to cover a reasonable range of rule-set sizes that is likely to be sufficient as NIDS rulesets continue to increase in size.

4.5 Different architectures

We repeat the experiments on a system with a 1 GHz Pentium 3 processor and a 512 KB L2 cache. The results for the Pentium 3 are presented in Figure 7. We see that the gain for E^2xB is slighly higher on the Pentium 3 compared to the Pentium 4, with the proportion of the gain roughly consistent for the different traces. When comparing the performance of the P3 vs. the P4 system, the results may appear somewhat surprising: the P3 is almost always faster than the P4, as shown in Figure 8. This happens because the P3 has a 512 KB cache and the P4 we used has a 256 KB cache. For the Webtrace which has the highest memory usage among all traces, the P3 is almost 4 times faster than the P4. Besides highlighting the importance of considering the underlying

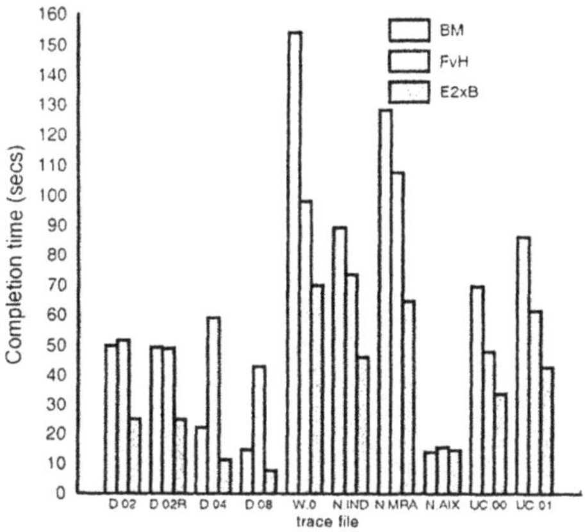

Figure 7. Performance on P3 processor.

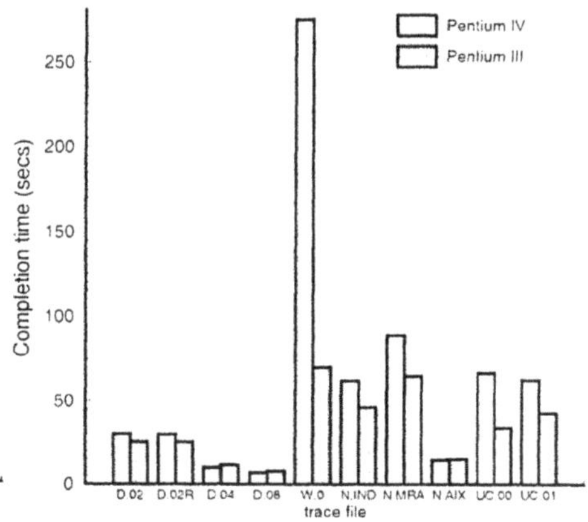

Figure 8. Performance on P3 vs P4.

system architecture when designing (and deploying) NIDSes, this experiment also demonstrates the great care needed in evaluating NIDS performance, as the results can be very sensitive to the environment.

5. Summary and concluding remarks

We have studied the performance of NIDS string matching algorithms, and presented the design E^2xB , a new algorithm for NIDS string matching. Using an extensive set of packet traces, we have evaluated E^2xB against existing algorithms. Our results show that in most cases E^2xB offers significant overall improvement in NIDS performance. We have shown realistic cases in which our approach improves performance by as much as 37%. The impact of E^2xB appears to relate to the packet size distribution and the number of string matching rules invoked per packet: small packets and very small or very large sets of rules per packet reduce the effectiveness of E^2xB . For medium-size rule-sets, E^2xB appears to be much faster than existing algorithms. These results point to the need for a hybrid algorithm, with E^2xB covering a range of medium-size rulesets. Determining the details of such a hybrid algorithm, including exact thresholds will be the subject of future work.

Our results also allow for some more general observations to be made on the performance as well as modelling, analysis and benchmarking of NIDSes: we have found that results are very sensitive to traffic and NIDS host processor and that random payloads behave similarly to real payloads. We expect these results to be useful towards more effective NIDS benchmarking and design.

Acknowledgments

This work was supported in part by the IST project SCAMPI (IST-2001-32404) funded by the European Union. Work of the first author is also supported in part by the DoD University Research Initiative (URI) program administered by the Office of Naval Research under Grant N00014-01-1-0795, and by the USENIX/NLnet Research Exchange Program (ReX). We would also like to thank Dionisis Pnevmatikatos for his constructive comments, and Vasilis Siris for providing the UCnet traces.

References

[1] A.V. Aho and M.J. Corasick. Fast pattern matching: an aid to bibliographic search. *Communications of the ACM*, 18(6):333–340, June 1975.

[2] R. Bace and P. Mell. *Intrusion Detection Systems*. National Institute of Standards and Technology (NIST), Special Publication 800-31, 2001.

[3] R.S. Boyer and J.S. Moore. A fast string searching algorithm. *Communications of the ACM*, 20(10):762–772, October 1977.

[4] C. Jason Coit, S. Staniford, and J. McAlerney. Towards faster pattern matching for intrusion detection, or exceeding the speed of snort. In *Proceedings of the 2nd DARPA Information Survivability Conference and Exposition (DISCEX II)*, June 2002.

[5] C. Courcoubetis and V. A. Siris. Measurement and analysis of real network traffic. In *Proceedings of the 7th Hellenic Conference on Informatics (HCI'99)*, August 1999.

[6] M. Fisk and G. Varghese. An analysis of fast string matching applied to content-based forwarding and intrusion detection. Technical Report CS2001-0670 (updated version), University of California - San Diego, 2002.

[7] Pankaj Gupta and Nick McKeown. Packet classification on multiple fields. In *Proceedings of the conference on Applications, technologies, architectures, and protocols for computer communication*, pages 147–160. ACM Press, 1999.

[8] Dan Gusfield. *Algorithms on Strings, Trees, and Sequences: Computer Science and Computational Biology*. University of California Press, 1997.

[9] R.N. Horspool. Practical fast searching in strings. *Software - Practice and Experience*, 10(6):501–506, 1980.

[10] T. V. Lakshman and D. Stiliadis. High-speed policy-based packet forwarding using efficient multi-dimensional range matching. In *Proceedings of the ACM SIGCOMM '98 conference on Applications, technologies, architectures, and protocols for computer communication*, pages 203–214. ACM Press, 1998.

[11] Evangelos P. Markatos, Spyros Antonatos, Michalis Polychronakis, and Kostas G. Anagnostakis. ExB: Exclusion-based signature matching for intrusion detection. In *Proceedings of the IASTED International Conference on Communications and Computer Networks (CCN)*, pages 146–152, November 2002.

[12] L. McVoy and C. Staelin. lmbench: Portable tools for performance analysis. In *Proc. of the 1996 Usenix Technical Conference*, pages 279–294, January 1996.

[13] Martin Roesch. Snort: Lightweight intrusion detection for networks. In *Proceedings of the 1999 USENIX LISA Systems Administration Conference*, November 1999. (available from *http://www.snort.org/*).

[14] Brinkley Sprunt. Brink and abyss: Pentium 4 performance counter tools for linux, February 2002. Available from *http://www.eg.bucknell.edu/~bsprunt/*.

INTRUSION MASKING
FOR DISTRIBUTED ATOMIC OPERATIONS

Meng Yu, Peng Liu, Wanyu Zang *
School of Information Science and Technology
Pennsylvania State University, University Park, PA 16803. USA.
{myu, pliu, wzang}@ist.psu.edu

Abstract Distributed database transactions are treated as atomic operations. This paper considers intrusion masking atomic operations among replica groups. The paper proposes two Byzantine fault tolerant two-phase commit protocols (BFT-2PC) to tolerate both malicious coordinator and malicious participants. When the total number of malicious replicas is no more than a specific threshold the protocols can mask attacks. Even if the number of faulty replicas is more than the threshold our protocols are still survivable in some cases. We analyzed the expected survivability and efficiency of our protocols. The analytic results demonstrate that our protocols are practical.

Keywords: Distributed systems, intrusion masking, survivability, atomic operations

1. Introduction

Intrusion tolerance is commonly achieved by replications [2, 6, 11, 14, 4]in distributed systems. Most of those techniques adopt the state machine approach [13]which ensures that replicated servers that start consistent will remain consistent as long as they apply the same deterministic actions in the same order. In the configuration of state machine approach a client sends requests to a group of replicated servers (a replica group) to obtain services.

State machine approaches can tolerate usually no more than one third malicious replica group members, a few lost or delayed messages, and those malicious clients that send inconsistent requests to different replica servers.

* We gratefully acknowledge funding support for this research. This research is supported by the Defense Advanced Research Projects Agency (DARPA) and Air Force Research Laboratory, Air Force Material Command, USAF, under agreement Number F30602-00-2-0575, by DARPA and AFRL, AFMC, USAF, under award number F20602-02-1-0216, by NSF CCR-TC-0233324, and by Department of Energy Early Career PI Award. This paper represents the opinions of the authors and does not necessarily represents the opinions or policies, either expressed or implied , of the United State government, DARPA, AFRL, AFMC, USAF, DOE, any of agencies.

At the same time, a hacked system may present arbitrary behaviors that can be modeled as Byzantine faults. So, Byzantine-fault tolerant algorithms can resist some malicious attacks. Applying Byzantine agreement algorithms to replicated database system for Byzantine fault tolerance has been discussed in [5], which suggests replicate both processing and data of whole data base system, namely full replication. Furthermore, the only necessary application of Byzantine agreement algorithm is submission of transactions to all replicas for resisting malicious attacks. This idea is essentially the same as the state machine approaches. Thus, the intrusion masking problem is often mistakenly considered easy to achieve by just using the total order services provided by group communication systems that are Byzantine-fault tolerant.

But both the state machine approach and others do not supply a directly solution of intrusion masking for distributed atomic operations, which are usually implemented by the two phase commit (2PC) protocol.

In the situation where neither coordinator nor participants are replicated, C. Mohan et al. proposed a Byzantine fault tolerant distributed transaction commit and recovery protocol [10]. They applie the Byzantine agreement algorithm in the second phase of 2PC to prevent the coordinator from sending inconsistent voting result to different participants. This protocol can only tolerate malicious coordinator in the second phase. But it obviously cannot tolerate malicious participants in the first phase of 2PC. Even a single malicious participant can paralyze the whole system by simply voting 'NO' to force the coordinator making a wrong 'abort' decision. Besides, the cost of Byzantine agreement algorithm is too expensive to be practical.

While more and more critical servers are replicated to replica groups the problem becomes more complex. For example, many banks could replicate their servers to replica groups to achieve high availability and survivability. There are already some qualified state machine approach based algorithms to guarantee the intrusion masking property when the client is a single host and makes a invocation to a replica group. The distributed transactions among banks are treated as atomic operations, which are either wholly committed or wholly aborted. When a replica group of one bank wants to have a transaction with other replica groups of other banks, we hope these distributed transactions are also intrusion masking. Therefore, we need new atomic commit protocols that can not only offer the capability of intrusion masking but also handle the replications.

The solution is not trivial. A normally functioned system should be able to abort distributed transactions due to resource contention, such as dead locks. We cannot simply grant a node as the delegate of a replica group to carry out the atomic commit protocol because such delegate nodes may be malicious and may work as we mentioned before to paralyze the system while we cannot distinguish it from good nodes.

The main contributions of this paper are as follows. As an example, we revised BFT [4]to demonstrate how to handle clients that are replica groups. Furthermore, we proposed two practical Byzantine-fault tolerant 2PC protocols for the distributed intrusion masking system. We analyzed the survivability and efficiency of these protocols.

2. Handling clients that are replica groups

2.1 Message Passing between Replica Groups

A replica group with n replicas is a n-size-group. Suppose there are m n-size-groups $\mathcal{G}_1, \mathcal{G}_2, \cdots, \mathcal{G}_m$ in the system. For all $\mathcal{G}_i, 1 \leqslant i \leqslant m, \mid \mathcal{G}_i \mid = n$. We can construct *working group set* $\mathcal{D}$ according to the following rules. Each element d of $\mathcal{D}$ is a *working group.*

$$\mid \mathcal{D} \mid = n$$

$$\forall d \in \mathcal{D}, \mid d \mid = m$$

$$\forall d_i \in \mathcal{D}, d_j \in \mathcal{D}, i \neq j \Rightarrow d_i \cap d_j = \phi, 1 \leqslant i, j \leqslant n$$

$$\forall a, b \in \mathcal{G}_i, a \in d \Rightarrow b \notin d, 1 \leqslant i \leqslant m$$

$$\bigcup_{1 \leqslant i \leqslant n, d_i \in \mathcal{D}} d_i = \bigcup_{1 \leqslant k \leqslant m} \mathcal{G}_k$$

For all $\mathcal{G}_i, 1 \leqslant i \leqslant m$, we say $\mathcal{D}$ *contains* $\mathcal{G}_i$. Every replica in a n-size-group is assigned to a working group. Each element in a working group comes from different replica groups.

In Figure 2, $\mathcal{G}_1 = \{A_1, A_2, \cdots, A_n\}$, $\mathcal{G}_2 = \{B_1, B_2, \cdots, B_n\}$ and $\mathcal{G}_3 = \{C_1, C_2, \cdots, C_n\}$ are three n-size-groups. We can construct $\mathcal{D} = \{\{A_1, B_1, C_1\}, \{A_2, B_2, C_2\}, \cdots, \{A_n, B_n, C_n\}\}$. Each element in $\mathcal{D}$, $\{A_i, B_i, C_i\}, 1 \leqslant i \leqslant n$, is a working group. Please note the construction of set $\mathcal{D}$ is not unique according to our rules.

When a m-size-group $\mathcal{F}$ wants to send a request r to a n-size-group $\mathcal{G}$ there are two typical methods.

One method is *symmetric sending* when m is equal to n. A working group set $\mathcal{D}$ that contains $\mathcal{F}$ and $\mathcal{G}$ must be constructed. For all $a \in \mathcal{F}$, a sends $\langle r \rangle_{\sigma_a}$ to b if and only if $\exists d \in \mathcal{D}, a \in d, b \in d$ and $b \in \mathcal{G}$. The σ_a means r should be signed by a. Note the r in all messages should be the same because they are the same request and just sent by different replicas.

Another method is *asymmetric sending* whatever m is equal to n or not. For all $a \in \mathcal{F}$, a send $\langle r \rangle_{\sigma_a}$ to all replicas in $\mathcal{G}$. Then totally mn messages are sent. Each replica in $\mathcal{G}$ will receive m messages signed by different replicas in $\mathcal{F}$ and choose $f + 1$ consistent messages of them as the message they received provided $m = 3f + 1$. Like BFT we adopt $f + 1$ consistent messages as the weak certificate.

Two examples of symmetric sending and asymmetric sending are shown in Figure 1. Note that the two different methods have different efficiency and

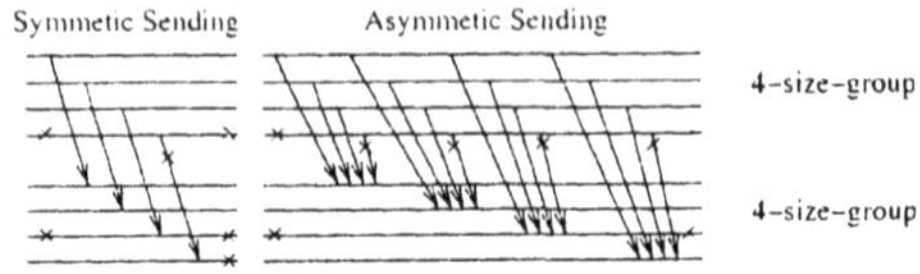

Figure 1. Examples of symmetric sending and asymmetric sending

capability of fault tolerance. In the examples, replicas marked with checks are faulty replicas and messages marked with checks are faulty messages. The symmetric sending has less communication cost but worse capability of fault tolerance than those of asymmetric sending. A fault in a replica group will be propagated to the receiver in symmetric sending while asymmetric sending can resist such propagation of faults.

A distributed intrusion masking system consists of some replica groups, which can be organized in many different ways according to the method of message sending among them. We focus on two ways that we called *symmetric configuration* and *asymmetric configuration* in this paper.

In symmetric configuration a working group set must be constructed, which contains all replica groups in the system. Every two interactive replica groups in the system send messages by symmetric sending. An example of symmetric configuration is shown in Figure 2. The management of working groups, such

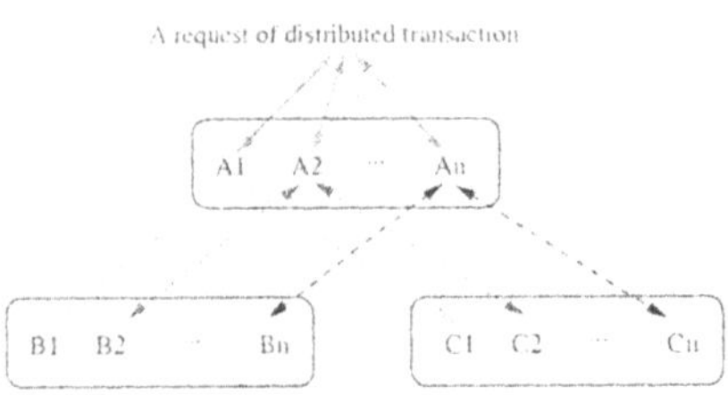

Figure 2. An example of symmetry configuration

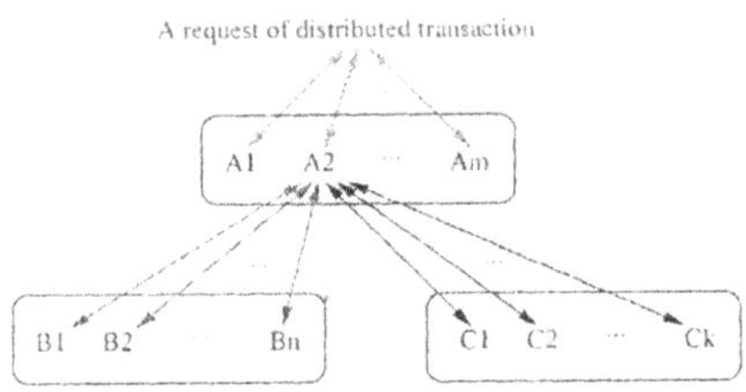

Figure 3. An example of asymmetric configuration

as static assignment or dynamic management is beyond the scope of this paper.

In asymmetric configuration every two interactive replica groups in the system send messages by asymmetric sending. The number of replicas in each replica group may be different. An example of asymmetric configuration is shown in Figure 3. A_2 interacts with all replicas in other replica groups, such as $B_1, B_2, \cdots, B_n$ and $C_1, C_2, \cdots, C_k$. The asymmetric configuration does not need management of working groups. So, asymmetric configuration is scalable and easy to be configured and managed.

2.2 Replica group as client

Based on BFT [4], we introduce a new Byzantine-Fault Tolerant protocol named BFT-S to meet the requirement of our communication schemes among replica groups. Please note our techniques are not limited on BFT. Our techniques can be applied to other similar protocols based on state machine approach.

We assume the client interacts with a $3k+1$-size-group. k is the maximum number of Byzantine-faulty replicas in the group that can be tolerated. In our architecture, either a single node or a replica group could be a client.

Phase request and reply. When the client is a $3k+1$-size-group and the system is under symmetric configuration the client symmetrically sends the $\langle \text{SYMMETRIC-REQUEST}, o, t, c\rangle_{\sigma_c}$ message to the $3k+1$-size-group. In the request t is the timestamp and o is the operation. c is a replica in the client. At the end of BFT-S each replica i in $3k+1$-size-group symmetrically sends reply $\langle \text{SYMMETRIC-REPLY}, v, t, c, i, r\rangle_{\sigma_i}$ to the client, where r is the result of request and v is the view number.

Otherwise, when the system is under asymmetric configuration (client is a single node or a replica group), or the client is a single node and the system is under symmetric configuration, the client asymmetrically sends the $\langle \text{ASYMMETRIC-REQUEST}, o, t, c\rangle_{\sigma_c}$ message to the $3k+1$-size-group. c is the client or a replica in the client. If the client is $3j+1$-size-group and the system is asymmetric configuration each replica in $3k+1$-size-group should wait $j+1$ matching requests as the request. When the BFT-S finishes the reply $\langle \text{ASYMMETRIC-REPLY}, v, t, c, i, r\rangle_{\sigma_i}$ will be asymmetrically sent to the client. Client waits a weak certificate as the result, which is $k+1$ matching replies that have the same v, t, r and valid signature as BFT.

Phase pre-prepare. The primary assigns a sequence number n to the request and multicasts the request to other replicas in the pre-prepare phase. Each replica will accept the request if and only if the request from client matches the request from primary. Otherwise, it will simply discard the request.

The prepare phase and commit phase are the same as BFT. They can be simply described as follows. In the prepare phase and commit phase, each replica broadcasts signed request to others and collects $2k+1$ matching requests as a certificate to continue the following operations. For more information about

BFT please refer to [4]. A normal BFT-S procedure with single client is shown in Figure 4.

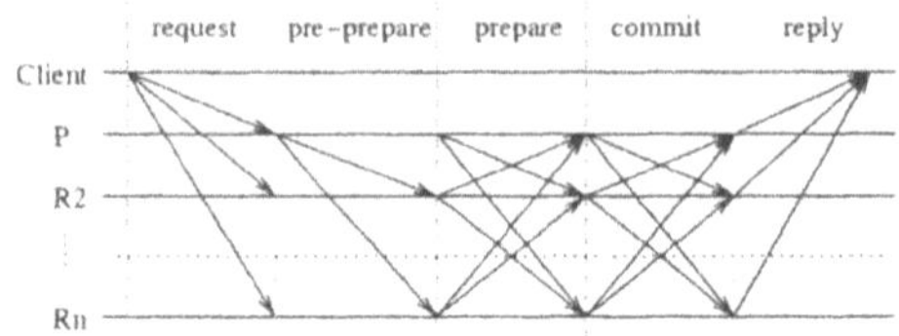

Figure 4. An normal BFT-S procedure

BFT-S improves BFT in three aspects. Firstly, a replica group can be a client of BFT-S. Secondly, in BFT-S all requests from the same replica group can be processed in parallel. This property will greatly reduce the unnecessary message cost in BFT-2PC protocols. Finally, clients have no necessary to know the primary of a replica group. We have the following theorem directly from BFT.

THEOREM 1 *BFT-S can tolerate no more than $\lfloor \frac{n-1}{3} \rfloor$ faulty members of a n-size-group.*

3. Distributed Atomic Operations

Two Byzantine fault tolerant atomic commit protocols (BFT-ACP) are introduced in this section. Our BFT-ACP protocols can be combined with 2PC or 3PC protocols and named as BFT-2PC and BFT-3PC respectively. We discuss BFT-2PC under Symmetry Configuration (BFT-2PC-SC) and BFT-2PC under Asymmetry Configuration (BFT-2PC-AC) protocols in this section.

3.1 Two BFT-2PC Protocols

During the execution of a distributed transaction, the replica group that received the requests from clients is called *coordinator group* and the others are called *participant groups*.

After accepting a distributed transaction from a client, the coordinator group carries out the phase pre-prepare, prepare and commit of BFT-S to achieve an agreement. After that, the request will be logged into the stable storage for further recovery in case of malicious transactions. Then, BFT-2PC-SC or BFT-2PC-AC will be carried out according to the system configuration.

The BFT-2PC-SC protocol is described as follows.

Phase one: request to prepare. Coordinator group symmetrically sends $\langle$SYMMETRIC-REQUEST, REQUEST-TO-PREPARE, $t, c\rangle_{\sigma_c}$ to all participant groups. Each participant group starts a BFT-S for the request to prepare.

Note t in the request should be same, which can be implemented by selecting the same one as that of the original distributed transaction. Because the t is used to guarantee the semantic of 'exactly once so it will not be confused even if two different requests have same timestamps.

Phase two: voting on commit. Participant groups symmetrically send the reply $\langle$SYMMETRIC-REPLY, v, t, c, i,PREPARED$\rangle_{\sigma_i}$ or $\langle$SYMMETRIC-REPLY, v, t, c, i, NO$\rangle_{\sigma_i}$ to the coordinator group in terms of the transaction can be prepared or not.

Each replica in coordinator group makes a decision for 'commit' if all replies received from all participant groups are PREPARED. Otherwise, it decides 'abort'. In both cases, all replicas should achieve agreement on their decisions to provide consistency, which is implemented by multicasting the decision of each replica and collecting $2f + 1$ matching decisions if the coordinator group is a $3f + 1$-size-group.

The coordinator group notifies all participant groups to 'commit' or 'abort' the transaction by symmetric sending the request $\langle$SYMMETRIC-REQUEST, COMMIT, $t, c\rangle_{\sigma_c}$ or $\langle$SYMMETRIC-REQUEST, ABORT, $t, c\rangle_{\sigma_c}$ to all participant groups respectively. Participant groups start another BFT-S procedure for the notification. Finally participant groups symmetrically send the reply $\langle$SYMMETRIC-REPLY, v, t, c, i,DONE$\rangle_{\sigma_i}$ to the coordinator group.

After the coordinator group receives DONE, the coordinator group sends replies to the client.

The BFT-2PC-AC protocol can be exactly described as the same as BFT-2PC-SC by replacing all symmetric sending with asymmetric sending and replacing all SYMMETRIC-REQUEST, SYMMETRIC-REPLY with ASYMMETRIC-REQUEST and ASYMMETRIC-REPLY.

3.2 Survivability

In this paper, we define that the *survivability* of a system is the probability that the system can function correctly under a given condition.

A working group d is *correct* if and only if every replica in d is not faulty and the communication among them is not faulty. Otherwise, the working group is a *faulty working group* because the operation among them cannot obtain right results.

THEOREM 2 *Provided in a distributed transaction the coordinator group is n-size-group and interacts with other participant groups, then, BFT-2PC-SC can survive no more than $\lfloor \frac{n-1}{3} \rfloor$ faulty working groups.*

PROOF SKETCH.Derived from Theorem 1. □

Please note in the Theorem 2 the number of faults are quantified by the number of faulty working groups but not the number of faulty replicas in each replica group. This is because the faults can be propagated in working groups. As shown in Figure 1, before the symmetric sending, each 4-size-group have one faulty replica that all of them can survive. After the symmetric sending, the fault of sender was propagated to the receiver, which leads to the receiver cannot survive such faults.

COROLLARY 3 *Provided there are m n-size-groups in the system under symmetric configuration, if the probabilities that f faulty replicas occur at any place are equal, then, BFT-2PC-SC can survive at least k faulty replicas. If $k < f \leqslant mk$, the survivability P of system can be described with equation (1). BFT-2PC-SC cannot survive more than mk faulty replicas.*

$$P = \frac{\binom{n}{k}\binom{mk}{f}}{\binom{mn}{f}} \tag{1}$$

where $k = \lfloor \frac{n-1}{3} \rfloor$.

PROOF. Omitted. □

THEOREM 4 *BFT-2PC-AC can survive no more than $\lfloor \frac{n-1}{3} \rfloor$ faulty replicas in each n-size-group in the system.*

PROOF SKETCH. Derived from Theorem 1. □

COROLLARY 5 *Provided there are m n-size-groups in the system under asymmetric configuration, if the probabilities that f faulty replicas occur at any place are equal, then, BFT-2PC-AC can survive at least k faulty replicas. Beside this, If $k < f \leqslant mk$, the survivability P of system can be characterized with equation (2). BFT-2PC-AC cannot survive more than mk faulty replicas.*

$$P \geqslant \max\left(0, \frac{\binom{mn}{f} - m\sum_{i=k+1}^{\min(f,n)}\binom{n}{i}\binom{(m-1)n}{f-i}}{\binom{mn}{f}}\right) \tag{2}$$

where $k = \lfloor \frac{n-1}{3} \rfloor$.

PROOF. Omitted. □

The Corollary 5 gives a lower bound of survivability of BFT-2PC-AC. When m is small enough (e.g. $m = 2$ or $m = 3$) the corollary gives the accurate survivability.

When there are m n-size-groups in the system, we compared the expected survivability of BFT-2PC-SC and BFT-2PC-AC. The expected survivability

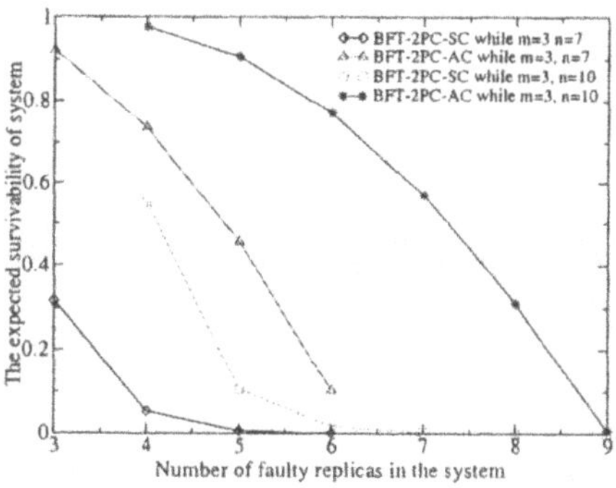

Figure 5. Comparing the survivability of BFT-2PC-SC and BFT-2PC-AC

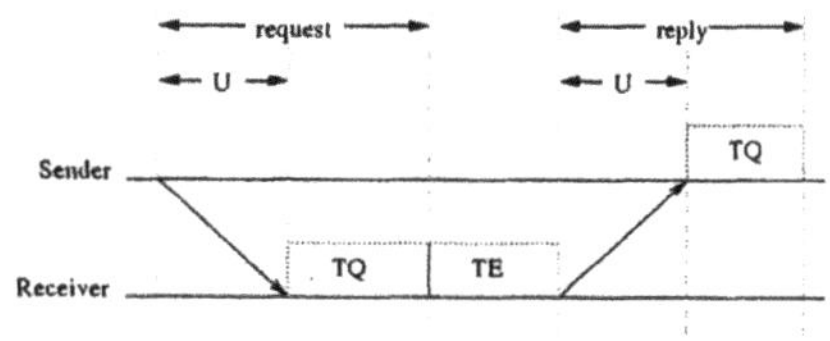

Figure 6. Time model

when m and n have different values is shown in Figure 5. We observed that BFT-2PC-AC always has better survivability than that of BFT-2PC-SC. We believe this is because the asymmetric sending has better capability of fault tolerance. The asymmetric structure of BFT-2PC-AC also contributes to its survivability.

3.3 Efficiency

The efficiency of protocols can be characterized in many aspects. We focus mainly on the communication cost and the latency in this paper.

The communication cost can be quantified by the number of messages, which depends on the implementation of the communication layer. For example, multicast could be implemented by unicast or broadcast in the lower layer. The communication costs of two methods are totally different. So we count for the messages for both two cases.

As for the latency of processing, we adopt the time model as shown in Figure 6, which is similar to BFT's.

In the figure U is the time of multicasting. All messages received by receiver are queued in the buffer of receiver. The receiver needs time TQ to process the message queue. Finally, the receiver needs time TE to execute the request.

Based on our time model, the latency of a procedure can be described as equation (3) in its critical path.

$$L = \sum U + \sum TE + \sum TQ \tag{3}$$

Because all participants can execute in parallel, so in the critical path, TE can be denoted by equation (4).

$$\sum TE = T_T + T_C + 2 \max T_P + T_V + t_\sigma N_{sig} \tag{4}$$

In the equation, T_T is the executing time of the transaction, T_C is the time of executing one BFT-S by coordinator group, T_P is the time of executing one BFT-S by participant group, T_V is the time of voting in coordinator group, t_σ is the signature time for a single message and N_{sig} is the total number of messages that need be signed in the critical path.

Regardless the topology of network and the detail of implementation, for simple analysis we just assume the multicast time U is in proportion to the total number of messages N and TQ is in proportion to the total length of message queue N_q in the critical path. Then we have equation (5).

$$\sum U + \sum TQ = t_m N + t_q N_q \quad (5)$$

In the equation t_m is the unit time to transmit a message and t_q is the unit time to process a message in the queue. So, we have the latency described with equation (6).

$$L = T_T + T_C + 2\max T_P + T_V + t_\sigma \sum N_{sig} + t_m N + t_q N_q \quad (6)$$

Suppose we have m n-size-groups, they can be configured in either symmetry or asymmetry. We compared their communication costs and latency. The parameters for latency evaluation is shown in Table 1. Some default values

Table 1. The parameters for latency evaluation

Symbol Definitions	*Default Values*
T_T: executing time of a transaction	1.2 second
T_C: time of one BFT-S by coordinator	0.1 second
T_P: time of one BFT-S by participant	0.1 second
T_V: voting time of coordinator	0.04 second
t_σ: signature time of a single message	0.1 second
t_m: time for transmitting a message	0.02 second
t_q: time to process a message in the queue	0.005 second

about transactions and communication in the table are chosen based on [8]. When the multicast is implemented by unicast communication the latency of two BFT-2PC protocols is shown in Figure 7. According to the results, BFT-2PC-AC is not a pragmatic scheme due to its poor latency while BFT-2PC-SC demonstrates better results. Also the total number m of replica groups has great impact on the latency of BFT-2PC-AC.

When the multicast is implemented by broadcasting the latency of two BFT-2PC protocols is shown in Figure 8. In the figure, the latency of BFT-2PC-SC and BFT-2PC-AC do not deviate too much. Both of them have reasonable latencies and are practical.

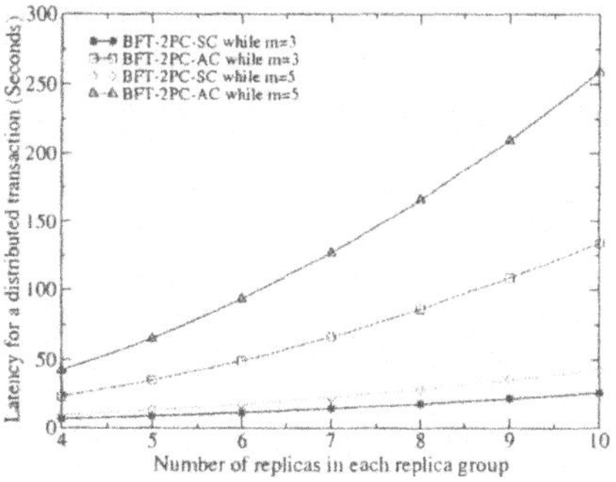

Figure 7. Latency when multicast is implemented by unicasting

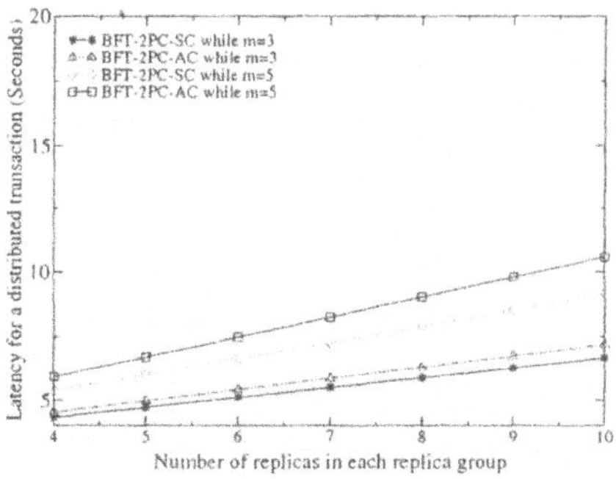

Figure 8. Latency when multicast is implemented by broadcasting

4. Discussion

Our two BFT-2PC protocols demonstrated how to carry out distributed operations among replica groups while offering the capability of intrusion masking. Other distributed operations, such as termination protocol, failure handling and optimization [3](e.g. Presumed Abort or Presumed Commit) can be constructed in similar approach.

Quorum replication [9]can also have the capability of intrusion masking. But quorum replications usually restrict operations (read and write) and needs locks to access variables. State machine approach based algorithms has no limitation on operations and could have better performance as BFT does.

Because our approaches bases on state machine approach they cannot handle consistent malicious requests sent by malicious clients. The techniques of recovery from malicious transactions [1]have been studied in recent years. These techniques can be integrated into our scheme because we can store accepted requests into stable storage. When the Intrusion Detection System (IDS) recognized the malicious requests, the system should isolate and confine the destroyed data, then start a consistent recovery request to recover from malicious transactions. If the malicious transactions are distributed, the recovery can be carried out with our BFT-2PC protocols.

Distributed operations implemented by reliable multicast and voting have been suggested in [12, 7]. Their communicating costs and voting cost are much more than ours.

5. Conclusions and Future Work

We proposed two intrusion masking 2PC protocols for distributed operations. The survivability and efficiency of two protocols have been studied. According to our analytic results both of two BFT-2PC protocols can survive Byzantine faults and are practical. No Byzantine agreement algorithm is needed in our protocols. We will apply our techniques into other distributed operations and investigate the impact in the future researches.

References

[1] P. Ammann, S. Jajodia, and P. Liu. Recovery from malicious transactions. *IEEE Transaction on Knowledge and Data Engineering*, 14(5):1167–1185, September/October 2002.

[2] Anish Arora and Sandeep S. Kulkarni. Designing masking fault-tolerance via nonmasking fault-tolerance. *IEEE Transactions on Software Engineering*, 24(6):435–450, June 1998.

[3] Philip A. Bernstein and Eric Newcomer. *Principles of Transaction Processing*. Morgan Kaufmann Publishers, Inc., San Francisco, California, 1997. ISBN 1-55860-415-4.

[4] Miguel Castro and Barbara Liskov. Practical byzantine fault tolerance. In *The Third Symposium on Operating Systems Design and Implementation (OSDI '99)*, New Orleans, USA, February 1999.

[5] Hector Garcia-Molina and Frank Pittelli. Applications of byzantine agreement in database systems. *ACM Transactions on Database Systems*, 11(1):27–47, March 1986.

[6] Felix C. Gärtner. Fundamentals of fault-tolerant distributed computing in asynchronous environments. *ACM Computing Surveys*, 31(1):1–26, March 1999.

[7] Bettina Kemme, Fernando Pedone, Gustavo Alonso, and Andr Schiper. Processing transactions over optimistic atomic broadcast protocols. In *Proc. 19th IEEE International Conference on Distributed Computing Systems*, pages 424–431, Austin, TX, USA, 31 May - 4 June 1999.

[8] Xiangning (Sean) Liu and Weimin Du. Multiview access protocols for large-scale replication. *ACM Transactions on Database Systems*, 23(2):158–198, June 1998.

[9] Dahlia Malkhi and Michael Reiter. Byzantine quorum system. *Distributed Computing*, 11(4):203–213, November 1998.

[10] C. Mohan, R. Strong, and S. Finkelstein. Method for distributed transaction commit and recovery using byzantine agreement within clusters of processors. In *Proceedings of the second annual ACM Symposium on principles of distributed computing*, 1983.

[11] G. Morgan and P.D. Ezhilchelvan. Policies for using replica groups and their effectiveness over the internet. In *Proc. 2nd International COST264 Workshop on Networked Group Communication (NGC 2000)*, Palo Alto, California, 2000.

[12] P. Narasimhan, L. E. Moser, and P. M. Melliar-Smith. Strong replica consistency for fault-tolerant corba applications. In *Sixth International Workshop on Object-Oriented Real-Time Dependable Systems (WORDS'01)*, pages 10–, Rome, Italy, January 08 - 10 2001.

[13] Fred B. Schneider. Implementing fault-tolerant services using the state machine approach: a tutorial. *ACM Computing Surveys*, 22(4):299–319, December 1990.

[14] Ciprian Tutu Yair Amir. From total order to database replication. In *22 nd International Conference on Distributed Computing Systems (ICDCS'02)*, pages 494–, Vienna, Austria, 1992.

USING FUZZY SYSTEM TO MANAGE FALSE ALARMS IN INTRUSION DETECTION

Mehdi Shajari*
National Research Council
46 Dineen Drive
Fredericton, NB, E3B 9W4, Canada
Mehdi.Shajari@nrc.ca

Ali A. Ghorbani
Faculty of Computer Science
University of New Brunswick
Fredericton, NB, E3B 5A3, Canada
ghorbani@unb.ca

Abstract The Fuzzy Adaptive Survivability Tools (FAST) is an intelligent multi-agent based intrusion detection system that survives the network in the face of large scale intrusion problems. The proposed system is based on automated detection and response approach for survivability. It identifies anomalous host and system variables and uses them to detect known attacks and events of interest. The system uses different intelligent agents to identify normal and abnormal patterns automatically and adaptively. Fuzzy logic is used to discover the underlaying structure of normal and misuse patterns. The simulation results obtained with KDD CUP 1999 data set indicates that the proposed system can effectively manage false alarms.

Keywords: Intrusion Detection, intelligent agent, false positive, false negative, fuzzy system, network survivability.

Introduction

One of the biggest problems facing Intrusion Detection Systems (IDS) is the number of false positives. Each false alert has a cost associated with it. Moreover, it keeps the security operation from focusing on the

*The first author is a Ph.D. student at the Faculty of Computer Science, University of New Brunswick, Fredericton, NB, E3B 5A3, Canada.

true alerts. The main difficulty is the fact that it is not always easy to tell the difference between a true and a false alarm.

There are two types of false positives. The first type of false positives are generated when an attack detection algorithm misclassifies normal traffic as an attack. This is normally due to a loophole in the detection algorithm. The second type of false positives (referred to as false alarms in (ISS01)) are generated when a detection algorithm correctly identifies a given pattern, but the pattern does not represent a true threat. This is mainly due to misconfiguration and constitutes the majority of false positives generated by an intrusion detection system. The second type of false positives is usually dealt with at the client sites where security operators configure IDS to reduce false alarms. In this paper we refer to both types of false positives simply as false positives. The term *false alarm* refers to all kinds of false alerts including false positives and false negatives.

Computer systems and networks continue to grow in size and complexity and even top experts are too slow to analyze the problems and react to them. This is simply impossible. It is therefore desirable to design a system that can simulate the experts knowledge and quickly react to the attacks. Fuzzy logic can best be applied to problems that rely heavily on human experience and intuition.

Currently, we are developing a multiagent-based intrusion detection and response system called Fuzzy Adaptive Survivability Tool (FAST). The system is based on automated detection and response approach for survivability. It identifies anomalous host and system variables and uses them to detect known attacks and events of interest. FAST consists of a knowledge-base and five different types of autonomous agents, namely: monitor agent, detection agent, decision agent, action agent and interface agent. The knowledge-base part of the system includes top security expert's knowledge, common sense reasoning and reactions to attack. This paper present the management of false alarms by FAST.

The remainder of this paper is organized as follows. Section 1 describes fuzzy partitioning of host and network variables. Design components are introduced in Section 2. The experimental results of a prototype implementation of FAST are presented in Section 3. Finally, the conclusions of the present study are summarized in Section 4.

1. Fuzzy partitioning of host and network variables

Fuzzy sets and probability theory are two most powerful tools to overcome uncertainty. Fuzzy membership functions represent similarities of

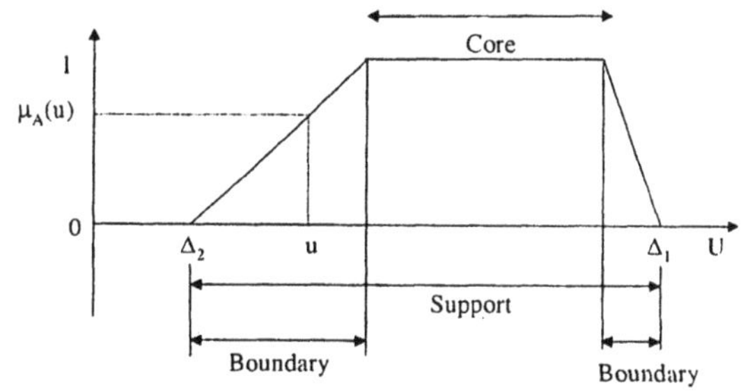

Figure 1. Core, support and boundaries of a fuzzy set, adapted from (Ross00).

objects to imprecisely defined properties, while probabilities convey information about relative frequencies (Dubois93). False alarms are the results of uncertainties in the detection of attacks. The uncertainties are mainly due to the inherent fuzziness of the host and networks variables. We propose to use fuzzy set theory as a mathematical framework for managing false alarms.

The core of a membership function for a fuzzy set A, $core(A)$, is defined as those elements of the universe, u, where $\mu_A(u) = 1$. The support of a membership function for a fuzzy set A, $supp(A)$, is defined as $0 < \mu_A(u) \leq 1$. The boundaries of a membership function is decided by $0 < \mu_A(u) < 1$. Figure 1 illustrates the regions for the core, support and boundaries of a typical fuzzy set.

Building membership functions is the most important part of the fuzzy modelling. The first method that may come to mind especially for the anomaly detection is converting frequency histograms or probability curves to membership functions. However, it should be remembered that the membership functions are not probabilities. In FAST, monitor agent monitors network variables and builds a fuzzy partition for each variable. Let $Q = \{A_1, .., A_n\}$ be a family of fuzzy sets on U. Q is a fuzzy partition of U when (Dumitrescu93)

$$\sum_{i=1}^{n} A_i(u) = 1, \quad u \in U. \tag{1}$$

Monitor agent's primary job is to find the $core(normal)$ and its boundaries in order to build normal membership function. *normal* is a membership function that describes the normal behavior of a variable. Monitor agent uses different definitions for building membership functions. The following are defined for each variable:

1 Number of membership functions: 2 partitions (*normal* and *abnormally-high*) or 3 partitions (*normal* and *abnormally-low* and *abnormally-high*).

2 A method for avoiding the anomalous observations in the training, so that the monitor agent can accurately learn the normal behavior of the variable.

3 A method for determining core of a normal membership function.

As part of their observations, monitor agents collect five different statistics (without considering the frequencies): the minimum value, the first quartile, the median, the third quartile, and the maximum value (see box plot in Figure 2). Any of these values as well as the range between any two values can be selected as $core(normal)$.

To build normal membership function, monitor agent starts with values, x's, that are normal (i.e., $\mu_{normal}(x) = 1$). Experts commonly choose median of the monitored values as the best representative of a normal situation. In such case, we have $\mu_{normal}(median) = 1$. Minimum, first or third quartiles values are also possible choices. Any range between any two of these values is also a reasonable choice in different situations. To avoid false positives, monitor agent assigns 0.5 as the degree of membership to the normal partition for the highest and lowest observed values that are believed to belong to normal operation (i.e., $\mu_{normal}(min) = 0.5$ and $\mu_{normal}(max) = 0.5$). Then, the positions of Δ_1 and Δ_1 (see Figure 2) can be decided to satisfy this assignment.

Figures 2(a) and 2(c) show normal membership functions for variables with three and two fuzzy numbers, respectively. Figures 2(b) and 2(d) show fuzzy partitions that are built based on Equation 1. When a variable is partitioned to *normal* and *abnormally-high*, only one of the values from five-number summary will be selected. Figure 2(d) shows the membership functions of the fuzzy set pair *normal* and *abnormally-high* and $normal(u) + abnormal(u) = 1$ for any u of observed values.

2. Design Components

2.1 Rule-base

A set of fuzzy rules representing the security experts' knowledge is defined. The rules are represented as

```
IF Condition (Premise) THEN Action (Conclusion)
```

In each rule, the condition and the conclusion consist of the statements in the form of:

```
(Variable) is (Term)
```

and are connected together by the standard logic operators. The representation of knowledge using fuzzy sets allows us: a) to apply a rule

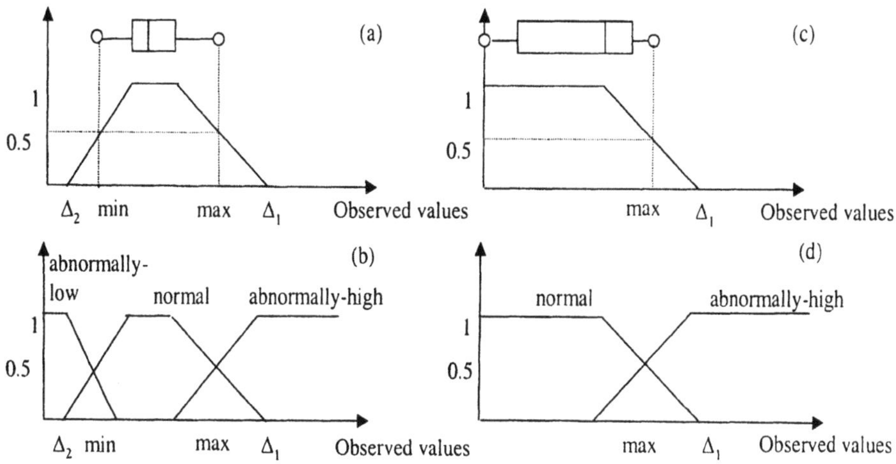

Figure 2. (a) and (c) Building normal membership functions, (b) and (d) fuzzy partitioning of a variable (note that the 5-number summary is shown by the box-and-whiskers plot).

even when the data does not match exactly the premise of the rule, b) to avoid the difficulty of determining the strict intervals for each linguistic term and c) to prevent the increase in the number of rules due to interval division. Moreover, a fuzzy rule system provides an interpolation mechanism for the different knowledge introduced. Thus, with a minimum number of rules, the system is able to respond to incomplete situations (Jaulent00).

In FAST, each detection agent is responsible for detecting an event of interest. This event can be very general, like probing in general or a specific event such as probing by one of the known probing tools. Table 1 shows examples of rule sets for detection agents.

2.2 Membership Functions

The shape of any particular membership function is often depends on the application. In FAST, the membership functions can be of linear, triangular or trapezoidal shapes. Figure 3 shows the membership functions for *same-host-diff-srv-in-time-window* variable. Figure 3(M1) illustrates the case where an agent uses the minimum value. Figure 3(M2) shows the membership functions where monitor agent uses the first quartile as the normal range for the variable. Figure 3(M3) illustrates membership functions when median of the observations indicates the normal range for the variable.

Each detection agent uses fuzzy inference to categorize a record in one of the three categories (no similarity to an attack, suspicious to be

Table 1. Examples of Rule sets for detection agents.

Type of Attack	*Rules in the rule-base of detection agent*
General Probing Attack	**Rule 1:** IF (same-host-diff-srv-in-time-window IS normal) AND (same-srv-diff-host-in-time-window IS normal) AND (same-host-diff-srv-in-recent-connections-window IS normal) AND (same-srv-diff-host-in-recent-connections-window IS normal) THEN probing IS not-detected
	Rule 2: IF same-host-diff-srv-in-time-window IS abnormally-high THEN probing IS certain
	Rule 3: IF same-srv-diff-host-in-time-window IS abnormally-high THEN probing IS certain
	Rule 4: IF same-host-diff-srv-in-recent-connections-window IS abnormally-high THEN probing IS certain
	Rule 5: IF same-srv-diff-host-in-recent-connections-window IS abnormally-high THEN probing IS certain
Neptune (Synflood)	**Rule 1:** IF S0 AND same-host-syn-error-in-time-window IS normal THEN neptune IS not-detected
	Rule 2: IF S0 AND same-host-syn-error-in-time-window IS abnormally-high THEN neptune IS certain
Smurf	**Rule 1:** IF ecr-i AND count IS normal AND srv-count IS normal THEN smurf IS not-detected
	Rule 2: IF ecr-i AND count IS abnormally-high AND srv-count IS abnormally-high THEN smurf IS certain

an attack, similar to an attack). For example, probe detection agent examines each record to see if it is similar to a probing attack or not. It may then label the record as a suspicious probing attack. Neptune detection agent does the same to see if the record belongs to neptune attack or not. A record may be labelled as both probing and neptune by two different agents.

The shapes of the output functions for a detection agent is configurable. Figure 4 shows different output functions used in our experiments. FAST can manage and control the rate of false negatives by tuning the output functions. The number of false negatives is decreased by increasing the range of suspicious membership (see Figure 4(O1)). At the same time, this output function generates more false suspicious alarms. As we narrow down the suspicious membership function (see Figure 4(O2-O5)), the number of false negatives is increased, but less false suspicious alarms are generated. Suspicious function can further be divided to demonstrate more levels of suspicion. Figure 4(O6) shows an output function with three suspicion levels.

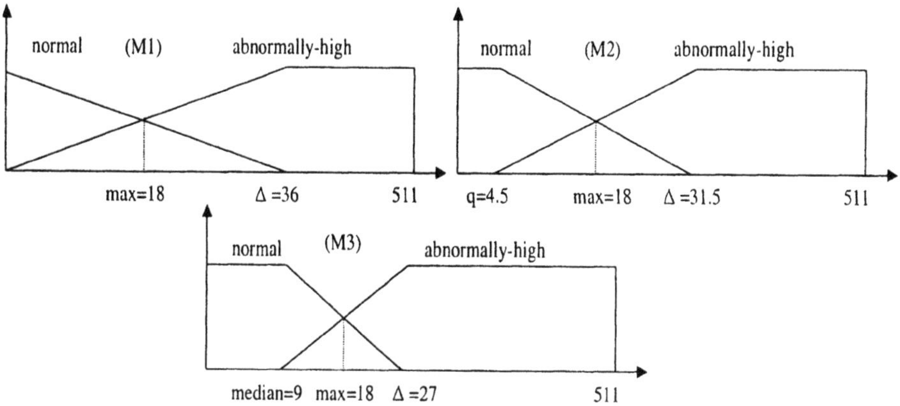

Figure 3. Membership functions for *same-host-diff-srv-in-time-window* variable. **M1**: minimum method **M2**: first quartile method **M3**: median method.

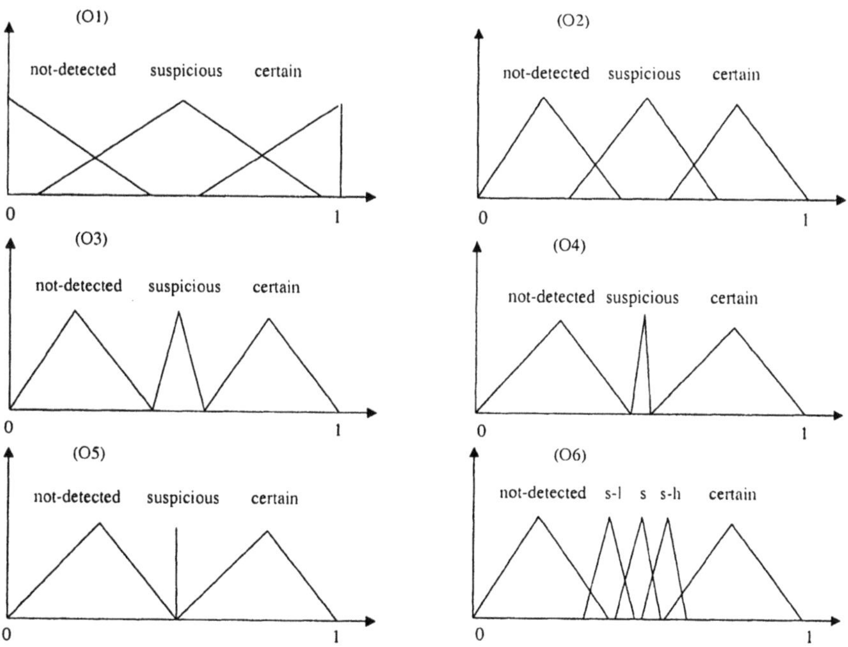

Figure 4. Output variable.

3. Simulation

We have carried out simulation studies using some of the features of the KDD CUP 1999 data set (KDD99). As an example, to obtain the *same-host-syn-error-in-time-window* we have used all the records with flag *S0* during normal operation. These records show all instances of SYN packets. Feature 25 of the data set is used to obtain the percentage of packets with SYN error received by a host in a time window of 2 seconds. The number of connections to the same host with SYN error is obtained by multiplying each rate by the value of feature number 23. Note that feature 23 shows the total number of connections to the same host in the past 2 seconds. A monitor agent uses these statistics to build the normal membership function for *same-host-syn-error-in-time-window.*

3.1 Experimental Results

Table 2 shows the results of detecting general probing, smurf and neptune attacks. The results shown in Table 2 are based on using input and output membership functions similar to those shown in Figures 3(M1) and 4(O3), respectively.

The primary goal of monitor agent is to build the membership functions so that false positives can be avoided. False positives that are reported in Table 2 are due to the similarity among different types of attacks. For example, the 1900 no-neptune records reported by neptune detection agent as neptune are in fact probing records. There are no normal records among these 1900 records. No-smurf records (36 records) reported by smurf detection agent as smurf are Ping of Death (PoD) attack records. Due to the fragmentation error in these records, PoD detection agent reports these records as PoD attack with higher confidence. This will convince the decision agent that this in fact is a PoD attack and not a smurf one. Meanwhile, it is possible that a record belongs to two different attack groups with the same degree. Decision agent takes care of both and updates its belief based on the future reports from the detection agents.

Table 3 shows the results of our experiments using the output functions shown in Figure 4(O6) and different membership functions shown in Figure 3. It is seen that the relative population of probe records increases as we move from suspicious(low) to suspicious and suspicious(high) membership functions. The decision agent uses this information to detect the escalation of an attack. If the level of suspicion of a detection agent increases continuously, it causes a decision agent to believe that an attack is underway. On the other hand, steady suspicion even in the same level can be a sign of some unknown malicious activity in the system.

Table 2. The results of detecting general probing, neptune and smurf in the KDD CUP data.

Probe Detection Agent	*Label on the Data Set*	*Number of Matches*
not-detected	no-probing	4197474
not-detected	probing	6494
suspicious	no-probing	659845
suspicious	probing	13099
certain	no-probing	9
certain	probing	21509

Neptune Detection Agent	*Label on the Data Set*	*Number of Matches*
not-detected	no-neptune	473+4028601[a]
not-detected	neptune	880
suspicious	no-neptune	10
suspicious	neptune	440
certain	no-neptune	1900
certain	neptune	866126

Smurf Detection Agent	*Label on the Data Set*	*Number of Matches*
not-detected	no-smurf	3701+2086770[b]
not-detected	smurf	42
suspicious	no-smurf	37
suspicious	smurf	71
certain	no-smurf	36
certain	smurf	2807773

[a]records without $S0$ flag.
[b]non ecr-i records.

Table 3. The results of probe detection with three levels of suspicions (Figure 4(O6)).

Probe Detection Agent	*Label*	*M1*	*M2*	*M3*
not-detected	no-probing	3684238	4082315	4259872
not-detected	probing	3988	5700	8002
suspicious(low)	no-probing	724019	443298	403913
suspicious(low)	probing	6102	4719	2774
suspicious	no-probing	449062	331706	193534
suspicious	probing	8905	8382	7830
suspicious(high)	no-probing	0	0	0
suspicious(high)	probing	1203	810	599
certain	no-probing	9	9	9
certain	probing	20904	21491	21897

3.2 Evaluation

Detection and false positive rates are the two major criteria for evaluating the performance of an intrusion detection system. To evaluate FAST, we have used a new criterion called false suspicious rate as well as a new definition for the detection rate. Let I, DI and DS represent the total number of intrusion instances in the test data, the number of intrusion instances correctly detected and the number of intrusion instances detected as suspicious, respectively. Let N represent the total number of normal instances in the test data, IN denote the number of normal instances incorrectly classified as intrusions, SN represent the number of normal instances incorrectly classified as suspicious and NI represent the number of intrusion instances that incorrectly classified as normal. System's performance is measured using the following ratios:

Conventional detection rate	$\mathcal{D}_1 = DI/I$
New detection rate	$\mathcal{D}_2 = (DI + DS)/I$
False positive rate	$\mathcal{F}_p = IN/N$
False suspicious rate	$\mathcal{F}_s = SN/N$
False negative rate	$\mathcal{F}_n = NI/I$

To evaluate the system, we examine the results obtained from the simulation of probe detection agent (see Table 4). Two different approaches are used to detect probes: time based and connection based. Time based window is used to detect fast probes. The second approach is based on a window of fixed number of recent connections (slow probe). We converted the relevant features in the KDD CUP data from the percentage format to the integer values and used them during training and test.

Table 4. The number of probing and no-probing in the KDD CUP data set.

Record Type	*Number*
probing records (*nnmap*, *portsweep*, *ipsweep*, *satan*)	41102
no-probing records (including all of the other intrusion records)	4857328
total	4898430

Figure 5 shows the conventional detection rate D_1 and the new detection rate D_2 of the system with different membership and output functions. It demonstrates the trade-off between D_1 and D_2. Membership functions with wide boundaries make the system more sensitive to suspicious activity and increase the new detection rate, D_2. At the same time, confidence of system for labelling the suspicious activities as attack decreases.

Figure 6 illustrates the false suspicious and false negative rates. It is seen that there is a trade-off between false negative and false sus-

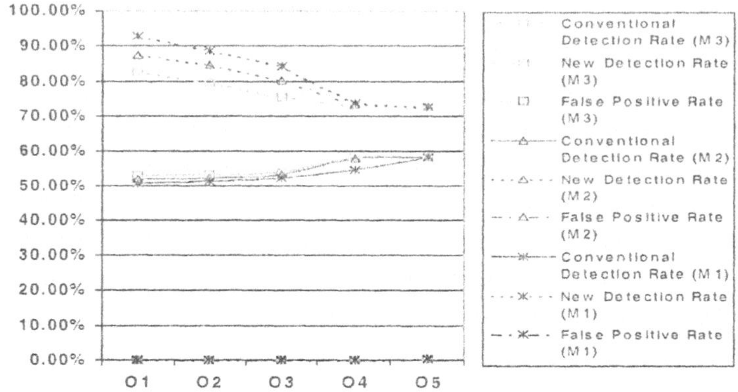

Figure 5. Trade-of between the conventional detection rate, $\mathcal{D}_1$, and the *new* detection rate, $\mathcal{D}_2$.

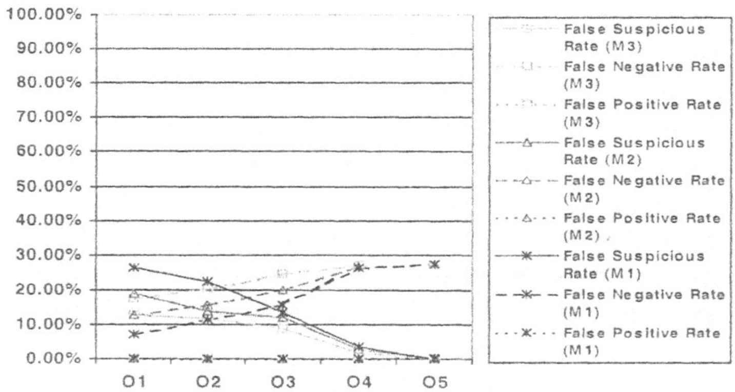

Figure 6. Trade-of between the false negative rate, $\mathcal{F}_n$, and the false suspicious rate, $\mathcal{F}_s$.

picious rates. In other word, to avoid false negatives, agents have to be suspicious to more records. The number of false positives increases slightly when we narrow down the suspicion interval. This is due to the fact that some attacks have similar effects and cause the rules from different detection agents to fire. These false positives don't label any benign connection as an attack, instead, they mistakenly label one type of attack with another one. When the suspicious interval is wide, most of these alarms are categorized as false suspicious. As we narrow down the suspicious interval, these records move from suspicious interval to the attack interval and increase the false positive rate. Decision agent solves this problem by assigning the record to the most possible attack category.

4. Conclusions

The main drawbacks of the current intrusion detection systems are: 1) large number of false positives, 2) inability to detect unknown attacks and 3) inability to properly assess the relative danger of the misuse and provide appropriate response. A new intrusion detection system for avoiding false positives and managing false negatives is proposed in this paper. The key elements of the proposed system are intelligent agents and fuzzy reasoning. Intelligent agents are capable of analyzing a situation, making decisions and communicating with other agents and users whereas fuzzy reasoning is used to identify and prioritize different attacks.

A prototype of the proposed multiagent-based intrusion detection system is simulated. The results obtained from the simulation studies using KDD CUP data set show that, through the selection of suitable membership functions for network variables, false positives can be avoided. Similarly, suitable output functions can significantly reduce false negatives at the cost of increasing the false suspicions. The system's performance on the KDD CUP data set as illustrated in Section 3, indicates that the proposed system can successfully manage false alarms.

Acknowledgments

Mr. Shajari's work is supported by the National Research Council, Fredericton, NB, Canada. Dr. Ghorbani's work is partially supported through grant RGPIN 227441-00 from Natural Science and Engineering Research Council of Canada.

References

Dubois, D. and Prade, H. (1993). Fuzzy sets and probability: Misunderstandings, bridges and gaps. *Proc. of the Second IEEE Inter. Conf. on Fuzzy Systems*, 2:1059-1068.

Dumitrescu D. (1993) Fuzzy Measures and Entropy of Fuzzy Partitions. *Journal of Mathematical Analysis and Applications*, 176:359-373.

Internet Security Systems Co. (2001). The Truth about False Positives. Available at http://documents.iss.net/whitepapers/TheTruthAboutFalsePositives.pdf

Jaulent M., Bombardier V., Cherrak I. and Perez-Oramas O. (2000). Fuzzy Quantification of Artery Lesions in Renal Arteriographies. In Szczepaniak, P. S., Editor, *Fuzzy Systems in Medicine*, pages 470-428. Physica-Verlag Company.

KDD CUP 1999 dataset Available at http://kdd.ics.uci.edu/databases/kddcup99/kddcup99.html

Ross T. J. (2000). Membership Functions, Fuzzification and Defuzzification. In Szczepaniak, P. S., Editor, *Fuzzy Systems in Medicine*, pages 48-77. Physica-Verlag Company.

AN EXPERIMENT IN SOFTWARE DECOY DESIGN

Intrusion Detection and Countermeasures via System Call Instrumentation

J. Bret Michael, Georgios Fragkos, and Mikhail Auguston
Naval Postgraduate School, Department of Computer Science, Monterey, California USA[1]
Hellenic Army General Staff, Holargos, Athens, GREECE[2]

Abstract: This paper presents an implementation of integrated intrusion detection and system response based on system call instrumentation. We introduce the notion of an intelligent software decoy as a means for detection and response to patterns of suspicious behavior. A prototype of such a system has been developed using NAI Labs' Generic Software Wrapper Toolkit. We present a case study of an ftp-based intrusion.

Key words: Automatic instrumentation, Deception, Intrusion detection, Intrusion response

1. INTRODUCTION

Two types of strategies for defending against attacks in cyberspace are in wide use: identifying and fixing known vulnerabilities of an information system, and detecting attacks before they inflict significant damage on an information system or legitimate users of the system.

These strategies are not sufficient to ensure either the survivability or the intrusion tolerance of critical information systems, such as those comprising the information infrastructure of a nation state. These systems have to both survive and tolerate attacks perpetrated by highly trained aggressors, known as information warriors, who unlike script-kiddies, continually customize their existing arsenal of attack programs and create new ones in order to both avoid detection and achieve the maximum desired effect.

Michael *et al.* introduced in [7] a different approach to defending information systems, founded on the notion of *intelligent software decoys*, to counter the attacks of information warriors. The approach has both a protection and counterintelligence component. The decoy consists of one or more software wrappers placed around a unit of software (*e.g.*, component or method), with each wrapper consisting of a set of rules for detecting and responding to suspicious behavior. Instead of indicating to the attacker that he has been detected, the decoy keeps the attacker occupied by creating the illusion for the attacker that the attack is progressing as expected, using techniques ranging from fake error messages to redirecting the interaction with the attacking computer process to a virtual sandbox (*e.g.*, via "dazzlement" [2]). The goal is threefold: to gather information about the nature of the attack, adjust the system's defenses based on the intelligence information, and cause the attacker to experience an opportunity cost (*e.g.*, waste attack resources that could have been better applied, or expose sources and methods).

There are two basic requirements for this approach to be successful: being able to detect the attack, and responding without human intervention. Michael *et al.* in [6] propose the use of an event-based language to meet these two requirements. This language uses event patterns to define suspicious behavior and the actions to be taken when the events occur.

In this paper, we describe the next step, which was to design a prototype system and then select an exemplar attack, use our high-level language to specify the decoys to be used to counter the attack, manually translate the high-level specifications into a representation that could then be automatically converted into executable kernel modules via NAI's Generic Software Wrapper Toolkit [5], and test the decoys against the attack program. [3]

2. CHAMELEON SPECIFICATION LANGUAGE

Our high-level decoy specification language, called CHAMELEON and introduced by Michael *et al.* in [6], provides for defining detection-and-response actions based on computations over event traces; it encompasses the characteristics of a cross section of the six classes of attack languages identified by Vigna *et al.* [11]. [4]

An *event* is any action that can be detected during program execution. An example of an event is a system call, such as `read`. Events can have attributes. For instance, the following statement declares that the `read` event has two attributes: `buf` (the buffer) and `nbyte` (the size of the buffer).

```
event read (buf, nbyte)
```

If we want to refer to one of these attributes we use the syntax `buf(read)`.

Two binary relations are defined for events, precedence and inclusion. An event may occur before another event or an event may be included inside another event. For example, the following axiom specifies that an event of type `open_running_processes` contains an event of type `EnumProcesses` followed by a set of one or more unordered events of type `OpenProcess`.

```
open_running_processes::(EnumProcesses {OpenProcess}+)
```

These two relations suffice to describe a program execution as a partially ordered set of events, that is, an *event trace*. The set of all events during a program's execution is contained in an event called `execute-program`.

An expression containing events and conditions on their attributes is an event pattern. The following event pattern matches any `read` system call with a buffer size larger than 1000.

```
x: read & nbyte(x) > 1000
```

In the above example the name `x` is associated with the specific instance of the event `read`.

Events have duration, a beginning, and an end. We can select from a trace only those events that match a specific pattern using the keyword `detect`. For example, the following statement selects a `read` event that has a buffer size larger than 1000 from the set of events that occur during the program execution.

```
detect x: read & nbyte(x) > 1000 from execute-program
```

A `detect` statement can also contain a *probe*. A probe is a Boolean expression containing event attributes, subroutine calls, or a combination of the two and is executed immediately after the previous event pattern has been successfully matched. Probes can be used to specify additional conditions for filtering events. For example, the following expression specifies that a user other than root attempts to write to the password file.

```
x: write & filename(x) == '/etc/passwd'
  probe (user != 'root')
```

An event pattern combined with an action forms a rule. When an event that matches the event pattern is detected, the action is performed. The action part of the rule is specified with the keyword `do` and contains C-like statements. The following rule specifies that each time a read event is detected, and the buffer contains the string "SITE EXEC", then the value "NOOP" should be assigned to the buffer.

```
detect x: read & post (buf(x) == "SITE EXEC")
  from execute-program  do buf(x) = "NOOP"
```

A sequence of decoy rules comprises a decoy specification; the sequence determines the order in which events will be detected and responses will be generated. The complexity of the attacks and the intricacy of deception tactics make it impractical to develop decoy specifications using only a plain sequence of rules. The following statement specifies that first we detect `rule_1` and then either `rule_2` or `rule_3`.

```
rule_1 (rule_2 | rule_3)
```

In the statement shown below, we expect `rule_1` first, then one or more occurrences of the sequence `(rule_2 rule_3)`, then `rule_4` might be detected, and finally `rule_5` might be detected zero or more times.

```
rule_1 (rule_2 rule_3)+ rule_4? rule_5*
```

In our approach, the decoy specifications are transformed into kernel modules. These modules run in kernel space and have unrestricted access to the entire operating system. The compilation of the decoy specifications produces wrapper definitions for the Generic Software Wrapper Toolkit, which in turn produces the kernel modules.

3. CASE STUDY

We demonstrate how we would instrument system calls to try to detect and respond to an attack. We start with a description of a variant of a well-known attack script, and then walk through the specification of actions we would like the software decoys to take to try to both detect and respond to the attack while simultaneously deceiving the attacker about the true nature of the effects of the attack on the decoy-enabled units of software.

3.1 Attack

Certain versions of Washington University's ftp server (wu-ftpd) contain an input-validation vulnerability associated with the `SITE EXEC` command (*vid.* [13]), which if exploited, can give root privileges to a remote user. Due to the widespread use of wu-ftpd, many programs have been developed that automate the exploitation of this vulnerability. Information warriors would also create their own variants of wu-ftpd attack programs, for instance to improve the speed of execution of the attack or to make it difficult for the adversary to link the attack program back to its creator. One of these programs is autowux.c [1], which via a series of specially formatted `SITE EXEC` commands overwrites the return address on the stack and executes arbitrary commands as root. The attack itself consists of eight steps.

Logging In (Step 1)

The attacker logs anonymously into the ftp server. Anonymous ftp does not require a specific password from the user, so when asked for a password the attacker sends a special string called *shellcode* that is treated as a series of machine language instructions, which if executed by the ftp server, can spawn a shell. Commands executed through this shell will have root privileges. The two steps are to first store the shellcode somewhere in the memory of the targeted computer (the anonymous user's password is stored in the server's memory) and then try to force the target to execute the shellcode.

Checking Vulnerability and Finding Buffer Address and EIP Location (Steps 2 - 6)

Next, the command "`SITE EXEC %.f`" is sent to test whether the server is vulnerable; if the server is not vulnerable, the attack script terminates itself.

The attacker sends a series of specially formatted "`SITE EXEC`" commands to find the location in the stack where the shellcode and the execution instruction pointer (EIP) reside. When a program calls a subroutine, this address is stored in the stack. After the subroutine ends, the EIP value is fetched from the stack. By changing this value before it is fetched, the attacker can execute the instructions stored in the location pointed to by the new value.

Exploiting and Starting the Shell (Steps 7 - 8)

Based on the information collected in the previous steps, the attacker sends a "`SITE EXEC`" command that substitutes the value in the location where the EIP is stored with the address where the shellcode is stored; the shellcode will be executed spawning a shell with root privileges. If the attack is successful, the attacker interacts with the shell instead of the ftp server. To confirm success, the attacker sends the "`id`" command. This command should be executed giving back the expected result.

At this stage the attack is considered to be complete. The attack program enters an infinite loop sending the user input to the server and handling the responses.

3.2 Foiling the attack via deception

We applied a simple deception strategy for the purpose of demonstrating our approach to specification and instrumentation: make the attacker believe that the attack proceeds as expected, while simultaneously protecting the server from executing any dangerous commands. We first specify, using the

CHAMELEON language, the detection and response actions to be performed by the software decoy. We then demonstrate how these specifications would be mapped from the high-level specification to the equivalent representation that the NAI Generic Software Wrapper Toolkit needs to generate the wrappers around system calls (*i.e.*, kernel modules) for the underlying operating system; we intend to implement a compiler to automate the translation process.

Since this is a remote attack, the targeted system only has access to the network traffic exchanged between the ftp server and the attacker: commands and responses. The only means by which a decoy can intervene during the attack is by intercepting and modifying this traffic. The ftp server communicates with the attacker with the help of two system calls: `read` and `write`. The wrappers can give access to these system calls and their parameters. The decoy can intercept these two calls and change the contents of the buffer passed as a parameter, substituting simulated commands and faked responses. The decoy must both substitute the commands before they reach the ftp server and the responses before they are transmitted over the network. One of the wrapper's features is the ability to intercept system calls either just before they are executed or after execution is complete, indicated by the keywords `pre` and `post`, respectively.

As mentioned above, the attack starts with the shellcode being sent as the password. We assume that each time the decoy detects the shellcode during a read operation, it needs to treat the corresponding slice of the event trace as an attack; it is unlikely that a benign user would submit a shellcode as a password. If the event slice is not detected, then the decoy does not proceed to the next step. The following is the wrapper definition code.

```
/* STEP 1 */
op{read} && step (((char *)$iobuf) =~ m|shellCode| )
  post {wr_printf("FTP Wrapper: STEP 1.\n");
  attackStep = 1; };
```

In the second step, the attacker sends the command `"SITE EXEC %.f"` to test if the ftp server is vulnerable to the attack. When executed, this command returns two lines of response, which the decoy must emulate. The decoy must also modify the value of `$sizeret`, which is the value that `read` returns, indicating the number of characters read: this value must include an extra newline character at the end.

```
 /* STEP 2a */
op{read}&& step((((char *)$iobuf)=~
  m|"^SITE EXEC %.f"| ))  post {char * newbuf;
  wr_printf("FTP Wrapper: STEP 2\n");
  attackStep = 2;
```

```
/* Replace SITE EXEC command w/ a harmless command */
/* that causes the server to respond w/ two lines  */
newbuf = wr_strdup("NOOP\n\n");
delete $iobuf;  $iobuf = newbuf;
$sizeret = 6; /* Change the return value of the  */
              /* read system call to reflect the */
              /* changes we made to the buffer  */  };
```

Once the decoy has intercepted the `read` system call, and substituted the buffer, the decoy must intercept the response from the ftp server and modify it before it reaches the attacker. The substitution must be done in such a way that the attack program receives exactly what it expects. The decoy rules we created to do this are shown in steps 2b and 2c.

```
/* STEP 2b */
op{write}  &&  step  ((((char  *)$iobuf)  =~  m|"^200"|)
           &&  (attackStep == 2)) pre {char * newbuf;
/* Replace the error message with what the attacker
   expects. */
newbuf = wr_strdup("200--2\r\n");
delete $iobuf;  $iobuf = newbuf; $sizeret = 8;  };

/* STEP 2c */
op{write} && step ((((char *)$iobuf) =~ m|"^500"|)
          && (attackStep == 2)) pre { char * newbuf;
/* Replace the error message with what the attacker
   expects. */
newbuf = wr_strdup("200  (end of '%.f')\r\n");
delete $iobuf; $iobuf = newbuf; $sizeret = 21; };
```

Steps 3 to 5 work in a way similar to step 2. The decoy intercepts the ftp commands before they reach the ftp server and substitute them. Likewise, the decoy intercepts the response from the ftp server and substitutes it with what the attack program expects. This way, the ftp server never executes any commands that could compromise it, and the attack program is deceived into believing that the attack proceeds as expected.

Step 6 poses a challenge, because, during this phase of the attack, the server is expected to crash several times. One way of simulating the crash is to make the ftp server close the connection. If during a `read` operation the decoy changes the value of `$sizeret` to zero, the ftp server will determine that it has reached the end of file (EOF) and close the connection.

```
  /* STEP 6a */
case op{read} && step (((char *)$iobuf) =~ m|"^SITE EXEC
%"| ) post { char * newbuf;
  if ((((char *)$iobuf) =~ m|"^SITE EXEC %3093$x"|)
          || (((char *)$iobuf) =~ m|"^SITE EXEC %3094$x"|)
          || (((char *)$iobuf) =~ m|"^SITE EXEC %3127$x"|)
          || (((char *)$iobuf) =~ m|"^SITE EXEC %3144$x"|)
          || (((char *)$iobuf) =~ m|"^SITE EXEC %3145$x"|)
          || (((char *)$iobuf) =~ m|"^SITE EXEC %3150$x"|)
          || (((char *)$iobuf) =~ m|"^SITE EXEC %3151$x"|)
          || (((char *)$iobuf)=~m|"^SITE EXEC %3152$x"|)){
        $sizeret = 0; /* EOF */
  } else {
/* Replace SITE EXEC command with a harmless command */
   newbuf = wr_strdup("NOOP\n\n");
   delete $iobuf; $iobuf = newbuf; $sizeret = 6; } };
```

3.3 High-level specification

The high-level specification follows exactly the sequence of steps of the low-level wrapper specification. The most important parts of the specification are discussed here; the complete specification is given in [4].

We declare two events: `read` and `write`.

```
event read(iobuf, sizeret)
event write(iobuf, sizeret, nytes)
```

Next, we specify a rule for each step in the wrapper definition. Step 1 is a rule with no action part. It only has a `detect` part. When the specified event pattern is detected, the decoy proceeds to the next step waiting for the next event to be detected.

```
step_1:: detect x: read & post (iobuf(x) == shellcode)
  from execute-program
```

Step 2 contains three rules. The logic in these rules is the same as in the wrapper definition.

```
step_2a:: detect x: read
  & post (iobuf(x) == "SITE EXEC %.f")
  from execute-program
  do {iobuf(x) = "NOOP\n\n"
    sizeret(x) = 6  }
```

```
step_2b:: detect x: write & pre (iobuf(x) == "^200")
  from execute-program
  do {iobuf(x) = "200--2\r\n"
    sizeret(x) = 8 }

step_2c:: detect x: write & pre (iobuf(x) == "^500")
  from execute-program
  do {iobuf(x) = "200  (end of '%.f')\r\n"
    sizeret(x) = 21 }
```

Steps 3 through 8 are specified in a similar manner. The part of the decoy specification that does the actual work is the last one, where we specify a composite rule, named `ftp_decoy`, consisting of all the previous rules.

```
ftp_decoy::
step_1 step_2a step_2b step_2c
(step_3_4_a step_3_4_b step_3_4_c)*
step_5 (step_5a step_5b step_5c)*
step_6_I (step_6a_I step_6b_I step_6c_I)*
step_6_7_II (step_6a_II step_6b_II step_6c_II)*
step_8a step_8b step_8c step_8d
```

Although this wrapper deceives the attacker into believing that the attack was successful, the deception ends when the attacker tries to interact with the shell. The shell functionality is not simulated and so the attacker will discover that something went wrong and possibly suspect that the targeted ftp server utilizes a deception mechanism. There are solutions to this problem. For instance, a library could provide all of the shell functionality, and be used to maintain the deception. Alternatively, the decoy could carry on the deception by transferring the attacker to another virtual machine where everything is simulated (*e.g.*, an *ante chamber* as described in [7]).

We submitted the low-level specification to the Generic Software Wrapper Toolkit, which produced a decoy for use with the Linux operating system. We then ran the attack script against the decoy-enabled ftp server; the decoy handled all of the system calls, as expected.

4. RELATED WORK

Sekar *et al.* [8] and Vankamamidi [10] developed the high-level Auditing Specification Language (ASL), with the aim of making information systems survivable. Their goal was to make systems capable of operating and offering their services even in the presence of vulnerabilities. This is achieved by detecting attacks in real-time and isolating them before they can cause significant levels of damage.

A program's intended behavior is described in ASL as a set of assertions. Any behavior not conforming to these assertions is treated as an intrusion. A process' behavior is observed through the system calls that it makes. An ASL specification involves a series of rules. Each rule consists of an event pattern and an action. The ASL specifications are compiled into C++ classes, which are then used to generate detection engines.

Eckmann *et al.* in [3] designed the STATL language to be extensible; it can be expanded via extension modules that contain domain-specific types, variables, and events. STATL supports the State Transition Analysis Technique [12] for detecting intrusions. Attack scenarios are described as a series of states and transitions. Each transition has an action associated with it. In order to abstract away the details of the modeled attacks, only the events without which the attack would fail are used. Further abstraction is achieved by describing the actions using higher-level representations, so that actions with the same effect, but different implementations, can have the same representation. The attack scenarios are compiled into dynamically linked modules called "scenario plugins."

Ko *et al.* [5] used the Generic Software Wrappers Toolkit to integrate intrusion detection and response functions into the kernels of operating systems. They treat software wrappers as state machines that intercept system calls. Wrappers are defined using the Wrapper Definition Language (WDL). The language describes the events that are going to be intercepted and the actions that the wrapper will take when these events are detected. The WDL specifications are compiled with the help of the Wrapper Compiler (WrapC) into native code.

The Wrapper Support Subsystem (WSS) facilitates the configuration and management of the wrappers. The wrapper modules are inserted into the kernel dynamically. Once a wrapper is loaded into the kernel it can wrap any process according to activation criteria defined by the administrator. Wrappers can be layered. Additionally, more than one wrapper can be associated with a program at the same time, each one implementing a different detection technique.

Finally, Templeton *et al.* in [9] argues that current intrusion detection techniques fail to detect multi-staged attacks, unknown attacks, or variations of known attacks. Their approach treats attacks as a set of capabilities. An attack is described as a set of abstract attack concepts. Their language, called JIGSAW, can be used to model the abstract concepts. Their approach can be used to discover new attacks or coordinated attacks across many systems.

5. CONCLUSION

The notion of intelligent software decoys has only begun to be explored. Nevertheless, their potential value, in protecting critical information systems, is apparent. The work presented in this paper addresses one aspect of decoy technology: the automatic instrumentation of software with detection-and-response capabilities.

New constructs and new concepts were added to the CHAMELEON language, improving its richness and expressiveness. The case study serves as the basis for demonstrating the expressiveness of the language for specifying decoy actions. The results of this experiment were satisfactory, since the kernel modules respond to the attack program as specified.

The Generic Software Wrapper Toolkit proved to be a valuable tool for controlling the interaction, in the form of system calls, between the autowux.c program and the decoy-enabled ftp server. The problem is that the wrapper definitions are low level, and implementing them requires knowledge about system calls and their parameters. The CHAMELEON language reduces the complexity of the definitions, making it easier for people to write and understand these definitions. We are currently working through more case studies to identify additional language features before beginning work on building a compiler that will automatically create wrapper definitions (in NAI's Wrapper Definition Language) from specifications written in the CHAMELEON language.

NOTES

1. Profs. Michael and Auguston can be contacted at {bmichael | maugusto}@nps.navy.mil

2. CPT Fragkos can be reached at gfra@softhome.net

3. Conducted under the auspices of the Naval Postgraduate School's Homeland Security Leadership Development Program, this research is supported by the U.S. Department of Justice Office of Justice Programs and Office for Domestic Preparedness. The views and conclusions contained herein are those of the authors and should not be interpreted as necessarily representing the official policies or endorsements, either expressed or implied, of the U.S. Government. The U.S. Government is authorized to reproduce and distribute reprints for Government purposes notwithstanding any copyright annotations thereon.

4. We chose the name "Chameleon" because, just as a the lizard of the genus *Chamæleo* can change both its color and behavior to deceive its predators and catch prey, our high-level language is meant to be used to formally specify how an intelligent software decoy is to adapt both its signature (*e.g.*, via the use of polymorphic argument types as described in [7]) and actions (*e.g.*, pretend to be vulnerable) to deceive and catch attackers.

REFERENCES

[1] Anonymous. Software program named autowux.c - wu-ftpd remote root exploit for x86/linux up to version 2.6.0, dated May 4, 2001.

[2] Cohen, F. and Koike, D. Leading attackers through attack graphs with deceptions. Unpublished manuscript, Sandia National Laboratories, Livermore, Calif., May 29, 2002.

[3] Eckmann, S. T., Vigna, G., Kemmerer, R. A. STATL: An attack language for state-based intrusion detection. *J. Computer Security* 10, 1/2 (2002), 71-104.

[4] Fragkos, G. An event-trace language for software decoys. M.S. thesis, Dept. of Computer Science, Naval Postgraduate School, Sept. 2002.

[5] Ko, C., Fraser, T., Badger, L., Kilpatrick, D. Detecting and countering system intrusions using software wrappers. In *Proc. Ninth USENIX Sec. Symp.*, USENIX Assn. (Denver, Colo., Aug. 2000), 145-156.

[6] Michael, J. B., Auguston, M., Rowe, N. C., and Riehle, R. D. Software decoys: Intrusion detection and countermeasures. In *Proc. Workshop on Inf. Assurance,* IEEE (West Point, N.Y., June 2002), 130-138.

[7] Michael, J. B. and Riehle, R. D. Intelligent software decoys. In *Proc. Monterey Workshop: Eng. Automation for Software Intensive Syst. Integration*, Naval Postgraduate School (Monterey, Calif., June 2001), 178-187.

[8] Sekar, R., Bowen, T., and Segal, M. On preventing intrusions by process behavior monitoring. In *Proc. Workshop on Intrusion Detection and Network Monitoring*, USENIX Assn. (Santa Clara, Calif., April 1999), 29-40.

[9] Templeton, S.J., Levitt, K. A requires/provides model for computer attacks. In *Proc. New Security Paradigms Workshop*, ACM (Cork, Ireland, Sept. 2000), 31-38.

[10] Vankamamidi, R. ASL: A specification language for intrusion detection and network monitoring. M.S. thesis, Dept. of Computer Science, Iowa State University, Ames, Iowa, Dec. 1998.

[11] Vigna, G., Eckmann, S. T., Kemmerer, R. A. Attack languages. In *Proc. Inf. Survivability Workshop,* IEEE (Boston, Mass., Oct. 2000).

[12] Vigna, G., Eckmann, S. T., Kemmerer, R. A. The STAT tool suite. In *Proc. DARPA Inf. Survivability Conf. and Exposition*, vol. 2, IEEE (Hilton Head, S.C., Jan. 2000), 46-55.

[13] Widespread exploitation of rpc.statd and wu-ftpd vulnerabilities. Incident note IN-2000-10, CERT Coordination Center, Carnegie Mellon University, Pittsburgh, Penn., Sept. 15, 2000.

A USER FRIENDLY GUARD WITH MOBILE POST-RELEASE ACCESS CONTROL POLICY

Douglas E. Williams, Amgad Fayad, Sushil Jajodia, Daniel Calle
The MITRE Corporation

7515 Colshire Boulevard, McLean, VA 22102-3481, USA

{dewillia,afayad, jajodia, dcalle}@mitre.org

Abstract: Information security guards perform an important function in multilevel security (MLS) environments. To perform their functions correctly, guards must contain data release and sanitization rules that accurately reflect the reclassification or declassification requirements to move data across information security boundaries. The current guards, however, require considerable technical skill to express release and sanitization rules, which data producers typically do not possess. Another limitation of the current guards is that once the data passes through a guard, all access control requirements to that data is lost. In this paper, we propose a high-level language to express release and sanitization rules, as well as post-release access control rules. We also describe a prototype that demonstrates the applicability of our approach.

1. INTRODUCTION

Information security guards regulate the transfer of data across security boundaries in multilevel security (MLS) environments. In addition to an allow or deny release decision, guards frequently perform operations such as sanitization of data by removing portions that are still considered too sensitive to be released. While some complex data will always require manual review, the ability to have automated review capability has the potential for being very cost effective when considering the large quantities of classified data that government organisations are reclassifying or releasing from classification over a period of time.

Traditionally, the source of data that passes through the guard is called the high side and the destination of the data the low side [5, 8]. On the high side, security guard operations generally involve two groups. The first group, which we will refer to as *Data Producers,* is responsible for producing the data and establishing associated release and sanitization rules. The second group, which we will refer to as *Guard Administrators,* is responsible for interpreting the Data Producers' rules to generate accredited executable release and sanitization rules on the guard. This relationship is a weakness of the current system. It requires accurate, rapid, effective, and consistent communication between the Producers and Administrators. If the Data Producers miscommunicate with the Guard Administrators about the correct policy rules to apply to a data object, the guard will not function correctly. This is further exacerbated in the current trend in dynamic multinational coalitions, where communication is even more difficult. It is therefore a necessity that guard rules must be communicated quickly and accurately between the Producers and Administrators.

Another challenge for writing software security guards is their certification for a formal evaluation of trust. Since guards become the responsible parties for information declassification, they must operate with a very high degree of reliability. To achieve this, the software code must be meticulously inspected for correctness and, if confirmed, certified correct. Therefore, the simpler the guard source code is, the more confident one can be to its reliability to perform correctly.

Finally, in addition to release control rules, Data Producers may wish to request that certain access control rules be enforced after the data is released beyond the guard to the low side. We refer to this capability as *post-release access control*, and could consist of both access provisions and access obligations [1, 6]. Unfortunately, existing guard mechanisms do not provide such a capability, and once a document is released, all control over that document is lost. Providing such control could enhance the security and flexibility of an information system.

Doshi et al. [4] propose a *mobile policy* framework that allows policies to move through the distributed system, accompanying the data it is intended to protect. In this framework, policy administration is separated from policy enforcement: policy is specified and administered at only those elements of the distributed system authorized to do so (frequently the "owner" of the data), whereas any trustworthy component in the distributed computing environment can enforce the policy.

In this paper we build on the idea presented by Doshi, et al. [4] and Felt, a Guard language currently in use [5, 8], and propose a high-level tool that acts as a front-end to legacy guard systems. We will also explore the use of mobile policy to implement post-release access control.

This paper is organized as follows. Section 2 describes current approaches to guards and their limitations. Section 3 outlines the architecture of our proposed solution. Section 4 describes our proposed guard language. Section 5 provides examples of guard rules using our language. Section 6 describes our prototype implementation. Finally, section 7 outlines conclusions and future directions for this work.

2. CURRENT APPROACHES AND THEIR LIMITATIONS

In this section, we give an overview of current guard systems. As outlined in the Director of Central Intelligence Directive (DCID) 6/3 [3], a guard is defined as a process (or set of controls) that function as a "controlled interface" mediating transfers across security boundaries. Guards typically control the flow of data from a "high" domain to a "low" domain, where the "high" domain is at a higher level of security classification than the "low" domain. However, this is not always the situation, because Guards may also control the "horizontal" flow of data between two domains of equal security classification levels. Finally, a Guard can also control the flow of data to more than one domain as in a one-to-many relationship. The guard is considered part of a domain's security architecture and it enforces a well-defined security policy.

Many variations of software security guards are in existence today. They provide services at security boundaries that include filtering, sanitization, transliteration, and integrity checks. Guard types range from low-to-high, high-to-low, manual review, and fully automated. As expected, many guards today consist of computer software, and one such guard development environment is *Felt* [5, 8] currently used by two popular guards: the Information Support Server Environment (ISSE) and the Command and Control Guard (C2G) of the U.S. Department of Defense.

Felt is a software development environment that was developed by The MITRE Corporation under funding from the Rome Laboratory of the United States Air Force Electronics Systems Command, and the Defense Information Systems Agency (DISA). Felt partly consists of a computer programming language with a special notation for defining data structures. This language has a special-purpose notation for defining message structures and it provides operations that can be used in writing constraint-checking procedures to determine whether a structured message is releasable, or to sanitize portions of it [5, 8]. The other part of Felt consists of an executable pre-processor that converts Felt code into the C programming language code. The code is then inspected by the guard administrators for correctness, is certified if it is, and then compiled with a regular C compiler.

While Felt provides a powerful mechanism for building guard filters and has proven to be quite successful, it has two disadvantages. First, it requires considerable expertise to use because of its power and flexibility. While Guard Administrators typically have the required expertise to use Felt, guard rules frequently originate from the Data Producers who often do not have the necesssary skills or training to accurately define policy for a document. A good solution to this problem is to develop a high-level language that is easier to use by the Data Producers.

Another limitation that Felt has pertains to release rules. In many situations release rules are sufficient, but at times it is useful to be able to control access to a document after it is released by the guard. For example, the Data Producer may wish to specify Role-Based Access Control (RBAC) rules that limit access to the data within the low side to individuals with particular role or rank credentials. Current guard tools, such as Felt, provide good release control, but do not provide any post-release access control functionality. For this additional flexibility a more comprehensive and extendable guard language is needed.

Before using a guard in a Department of Defense (DoD) environment, the guard and its rules must be officially certified to provide assurance that the guard will function properly and protect sensitive data from leaking to less secure domains. The Felt environment has gone through the rigorous, lengthy, and expensive verification program using formal methods and is consequently known to be correct. To replace an existing tool that works, in spite of its limitations, is an undesirable choice. Therefore, we chose to build on the existing Felt system.

3. OUR APPROACH

In this section, we outline our proposed solution to the limitations of usability and post-release access controls that we identified with current guard tools in Section 2 of this document. Figure 1 shows the data and policy flow between Data Producers and Guard Administrators. In order to improve this communication, we propose a high-level tool to bridge the gap between the Data Producers and the Guard Administrators. Using the tool, Data Producers can use a high-level language, called MoPEd, to specify the release and sanitization rules. See Section 4. The tool then translates these rules into Felt so that the Guard Administrator can produce the accredited executable release and sanitization rules to be applied by the guard. In addition to the release and sanitization rules, Data Producers can also use MoPEd to specify post-release access control rules. These rules are attached to the data in the form of a mobile policy [2, 4, 7].

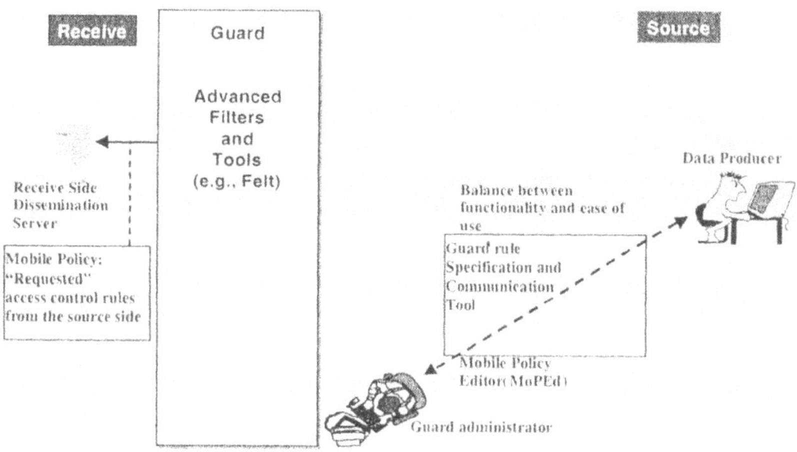

Figure 1. The Guard Policy Tool

The benefits of this approach include the following: First, communications between Data Producers and Guard Administrators about guard rules is easier and faster to use because the policy language more closely approximates human languages than Felt does. A result of this rule simplification should be that guard rule generation is also less prone to human error. Second, guard rule certification can be pipelined. This can be advantageous in two different ways. First, rather than being a wrapper, if a pre-processor approach is used there is no compelling need for the pre-processor to be certified, because all output from the pre-processor must next be processed by Felt before being put into operation. Second, if one does elect to certify the system using the pre-processor, this is more easily done because the pre-processor is separate and distinct from Felt and consequently can be considered alone. This is especially advantageous in dynamic environments that require quick changes to the software guards, or in environments where cost is an issue.

4. GUARD LANGUAGE

As we have indicated, one of the difficulties in implementing software guards is the problem of constructing reliable and accurate filtering rules for data crossing security boundaries. The ideal language used to describe the filtering rules must be sufficiently powerful to accurately apply security policies, yet also must be user-friendly enough to help, and not hinder, the correct operation of the guard. This is indeed one of the fundamental challenges of information security: making security as transparent to the users as possible.

Earlier we described the Felt language and compiler as a means of generating release filtering code for a guard. While FELT is a powerful and flexible language, it has two shortcomings. First, Felt is a relatively low-level language so it requires well-trained personnel because all details must be explicitly stated. Second, Felt expresses only filtering rules for release control, and does not provide any access control or rule provisions for the data after it is released. To overcome these shortcomings, we first developed a high-level and user-friendly language for generating Felt source code. Next, we extended our language by adding post-release access control features.

It is worth noting that since our language is at a higher level and a lower complexity, it does not provide all the functionality that Felt provides. Our intent is to strike a balance between functionality and ease of use. We do not consider our language is a replacement for Felt, but rather an enhancement to the Felt rule composition process. We believe this is justified, because the majority of guard rules are very similar and we intend to provide constructs in the language to describe these common rules.

The style chosen for this high-level language was similar to that proposed by Doshi, et al. [4], which in turn was similar to the grammar and syntax of the Structured Query Language (SQL) developed by IBM in the 1970s. Our language, named Mobile Policy Editor (MoPEd), was designed to satisfy the majority of needs for typical guard configuration and can be considered a high-level meta-language for Felt. MoPEd was deliberately kept simple to handle the majority of situations that occur in normal operations, but because it generates Felt code any filtering rule that can not be described using this language can instead still be written in Felt. The syntax of MoPEd is described in a Backus-Naur Form (BNF) style in Figure 2. This language should be considered as under development and may evolve in future releases.

Figure 2. MoPEd Language BNF

```
POLICY          ::=  "RELEASE" <OBJECTS> "AT" <CLASS> "APPLY" <FILTER> "WITH" <PRAC>
<OBJECTS>       ::=  <obj_regex> <OBJECTS> | <obj_regex>
<CLASS>         ::=  "UNCLASSIFIED" | "CONFIDENTIAL" | "SECRET" | "TOPSECRET"
<FILTER>        ::=  <SANITIZING> < EXCLUDING> ...
<SANITIZING>    ::=  "SANITIZE" <san_regex> | <empty>
<EXCLUDING>     ::=  "EXCLUDE" <exc_regex> | <empty>
<PRAC>          ::=  <GRANTING> | <REVOKING> | <empty>
<GRANTING>      ::=  "GRANT" <ACCESS> "TO" <SPATTR> "WITH" <PROVISIONS>
<REVOKING>      ::=  "REVOKE" <ACCESS> "TO" <SPATTR>
<ACCESS>        ::=  <READ> <WRITE>
<READ>          ::=  "READ" | <empty>
<WRITE>         ::=  "WRITE" | <empty>
<SPATTR>        ::=  <USERS> <ROLES> <RANKS> ...
<USERS>         ::=  "USER" <user_list> | <empty>
<ROLES>         ::=  "ROLE" <role_list> | <empty>
<RANKS>         ::=  "RANK" <rank_list> | <empty>
```

A description of the MoPEd language semantics is given below.

- "RELEASE" - A flag denoting the start of a policy statement.
- <OBJECTS> - A list of objects the policy it to affect. It is designated by a regular expression, but in its simplest form could simply be limited by the operating systems file naming constraints.
- "AT" – A flag denoting the start of the security classification the released object is to have.
- <CLASS> - The permitted security classifications
- "APPLY" – A flag denoting filtering to be applied before release of the object.
- <FILTER> - The set of possible release filters. Currently there are only "SANITIZE" and "EXCLUDE", but this list will probably grow in the future. The difference between the two types of filters is that "SANITIZE" means to replace a specific expression with a word such as

"censored", while "EXCLUDE" deletes any paragraph containing a specified expression.

- <san_regex> - The list of expressions to be sanitized from the object. Currently this is interpreted as simply omitting the sanitized part of the object.
- <exc_regex> - The list of expressions to be sanitized from the object. Currently this is interpreted as omitting the part of the object.
- <PRAC> - Post-Release Access Control (PRAC) rules, or those that apply to the object after the object leaves its security domain when a security principal attempts to access it. Currently the two options are "GRANT" and "REVOKE."
- <ACCESS> - The current attributes for the released object. Currently there are only "READ" and "WRITE," but this list will probably grow in the future.
- <SPATTR> - Security Principal ATTRibutes, or people or processes that may interact with the released object. Currently these may be a list of specified users, roles, and ranks.
- "USER" – A flag denoting the start of the list of users affected.
- <user_list> - A user, a delimited list of users, or the empty set of users.
- "ROLE" - A flag denoting the start of the list of roles affected.
- <role_list> - A role or a delimited list of roles, or the empty set of roles. Some examples are "radio operator", "system administrator", or "coalition members only".
- "RANK" - A flag denoting the start of the list of affected ranks.
- <rank_list> - An organisational rank or a delimited list of ranks, or the empty set of ranks. Some examples are "Colonel", "department manager". Whether ranks include those above the specified level, or only those at the specified level, depends on the environment's security policy.
- <prac_regex> - The post-release access control list is a delimited list of environmentally specific restrictions placed on access control outside the object originating boundary. Some examples might be "delete after reading" or "access only after a specified date".

Finally, definitions for release rules, and post-release access control Grant and Revoke rules in MoPEd are given.

Definition 1 (Release Rule): A guard policy release rule is a rule of the following form:

RELEASE <*OBJECT*>
AT <CLASS>

APPLY *<FILTER>*
WITH *<PRAC>*

Definition 2 (Post-Release Access Control Grant Rule): A post-release access control (PRAC) grant rule is a rule that is applied when access to the object is made after its release from the guard. Consequently, the post-release access control grant rule, if one exists, is inserted into the *<PRAC>* field of Definition 1 above. It has the following form:

GRANT *<ACCESS>*
TO *<SPATTR>*
WITH *<PROVISIONS>*

Definition 3 (Post-Release Access Control Revoke Rule): A post-release access control (PRAC) revoke rule is a rule that is applied when access to the object is made after its release from the guard. Consequently, the post-release access control revoke rule, if one exists, is inserted into the *<PRAC>* field of Definition 1 above. It has the following form:

REVOKE *<ACCESS>*
TO *<SPATTR>*
WITH *<PROVISIONS>*

5. LANGUAGE EXAMPLES

In this section some guard policy rules are presented to illustrate the power of the MoPEd system. First, an example demonstrating the economy and user friendliness of the language is given. This is followed by an example demonstrating the power of MoPEd has in integrating release rules and post-release access control rules into a single policy rule.

Consider, for example, that the words "cat" and "dog" must be removed from data and replaced with the word "censored" before the data can be declassified. In Felt, the following lines of program would be required.

```
%{
#include <stdio.h>
#include <string.h>
#include <sys/types.h>      /* Required for regex */
#include <regex.h>
%}

struct main {                    /* This filter */
  fields {                       /* rejects lines */
```

```
    string "\n" line;            /* that contain one */
  }
  action check_line              /* of four words */
};

%{
/* line_checker returns true if its arg matches
   the given regular expression. */
felt_regex_gen(line_checker,
               "cat|dog",
               REG_EXTENDED)
void check_line(ffInstance i)
{
  f_main d = (f_main)i->data;
  if (strstr(d->line->str, "cat")) {
    d->line->str = "censored";
    d->line->len = strlen(d->line->str);
    d->ffattributes.line.string = d->line;
  }
}
void check_line(ffInstance i)
{
  f_main d = (f_main)i->data;
  if (strstr(d->line->str, "dog")) {
    d->line->str = "censored";
    d->line->len = strlen(d->line->str);
    d->ffattributes.line.string = d->line;
  }
}
%}
```

Using the MoPEd language proposed in this paper, the entire previous policy would become:

RELEASE FILE
AT UNCLASSIFIED
APPLY SANITIZE CAT DOG.

Next, a more complex example showing the combination of guard release rules and post-release access control is presented. For given collection of classified data, a Data Producer might create the following guard filtering rule:

RELEASE FILE
AT SECRET
APPLY SANITIZE OVERLORD
WITH GRANT READ
    TO CAPTAINS 82AIRBORNE
    WITH NOPRINT

This guard release policy states that the object file may be released at a secret level, and the codeword "OVERLORD" is sanitized from it. In addition, the post-release access control rules state that only Captains of the 82nd Airborne Division are permitted to read the file, but they may not print the file. The voluminous Felt code that would be generated from the release control portion of this policy is omitted due to space limitations of this paper.

6. IMPLEMENTATION

As a prototype to process the MoPEd language, we are developing the MoPEd tool. MoPEd functions in the following manner: A Graphical User Interface (GUI) is presented to the Data Producer allowing him or her to specify release and sanitization rules for a data object. The MoPEd tool translator then "translates" the guard release rules into Felt code and in turn the Felt translator converts it into C code, which it attaches along with the post-release access control rules to the data object. The Guard Administrator reviews the attached policy and applies any other relevant global release and sanitization rules. The Guard Administrator then compiles the Felt generated C code into an executable guard, which in turn processes the data object to determine whether it is releasable. If releasable, the data object is released after stripping it of the Felt release rules and leaving attached only the post-release access control rules.

Users have options available for specifying policy using the MoPEd language. For standalone use by a Data Producer (i.e., an environment that does not provide a MoPEd web server), a simple command-line translator is available to transform a policy specified in MoPEd into Felt. This policy can then be sent to the Guard Administrator along with the data itself.

For extended use, the MoPEd Server presents a web-based interface to Data Producers allowing them to specify release and sanitization rules for data items. The server allows users to upload data and to specify additional policy in one of three ways: (1) Upload a text file containing a MoPEd policy specification; (2) Type lines of MoPEd directly into the web interface; or Use the provided GUI to define the policy via "point and click".

For the receiving end, our prototype system uses a Microsoft SharePoint portal to handle the post-release access control requirements. For proof of concept purposes, each receiving realm is represented by a workspace in SharePoint. Each workspace has its own body of Windows users and groups. The post-release access control specifications are implemented with operating system level access control by using groups corresponding to the various ranks, roles, and other access levels.

7. CONCLUSIONS AND FUTURE WORK

We have proposed a high-level tool that will provide a front-end to low-level guard tools, such as Felt. We defined a language to express release, sanitization, and post-release access control rules. We also developed a prototype to demonstrate the applicability of our approach to Felt-based guard systems. We succeeded in striking a balance between ease of use, and functionality in our language. We plan additional features for our language in order to broaden its power and functionality. Another direction for future work involves the actual binding of the post-release access control policy to the protected object.

REFERENCES

1. Claudio Bettini, Sushil Jajodia, X. Sean Wang, Duminda Wijesekera, "Obligation monitoring in policy management," *Proc. 3rd International Workshop on Policies for Distributed Systems and Networks (POLICY 2002)*, Monterey, CA, June 2002, To appear.
2. S. Chapin, S. Jajodia, and D. Faatz, "Distributed Policies for Data Management Making Policies Mobile," *Proc. 14th IFIP 11.3 Working Conference on Database Security*, Schoorl, Netherlands, August 2000.
3. DCID 6/3. Available at: http://www.fas.org/irp/offdocs/DCID_6-3_20Manual.htm
4. V. Doshi, A. Fayad, S. Jajodia, and R. Maclean, "Using Attribute Certificates and Mobile Policies in Electronic Commerce Applications," *Proc. 16th Annual Computer Security Applications Conf.*, 2000, pages 298-307.
5. Joshua D. Guttman, John D. Ramsdell, and Vipin Swarup, "Felt: A Security Filter Compiler," Revision 2, Technical Report,The MITRE Corporation, 1999.
6. Sushil Jajodia, Michiharu Kudo, V. S. Subrahmanian, ``Provisional authorizations," in *E-Commerce Security and Privacy*, Anup Ghosh, ed., Kluwer Academic Publishers, Boston, 2001, pages 133-159.
7. K. Smith, D. Faatz, A. Fayad, and S. Jajodia, "Propagating Modifications to Mobile Policies," *Proc. 17th IFIP 11 international conference on Information Security*, Cairo, Egypt, May 2002, To appear.
8. V. Swarup, "Automatic generation of high assurance security guard filters," *Proc. 17th National Computer Security Conference*, Baltimore, Md., October 1994.

SECURITY MODEL FOR HEALTH CARE COMPUTING AND COMMUNICATION SYSTEMS

Anas Abou El Kalam — Yves Deswarte
LAAS-CNRS, 7 avenue du Colonel Roche, 31077 Toulouse cedex 4, France.
anas@laas.fr, deswarte@laas.fr

Abstract Health Care Computing and Communication Systems (HCCS) are characterized by the complexity of the organizations to take into account and the richness of properties that are required. To address this complexity and richness, we propose a security policy based on roles, groups of objects and context. Indeed, similarly to roles that structure the subjects, we introduce the new concept "group of objects„ which structures objects. Our major aim is to facilitate the security policy management, to cope with access right complexity, and to reduce administration errors. Then we develop a security model that covers the diversity of HCCS while achieving a good compromise between the respect of the least privilege principle and the flexibility of the access control. Following a logical approach, we design a formal system that extends the deontic logic, and we express the security policy in our language.

Keywords Security policy and models, RBAC, Context aware computing, deontic logic.

1. PROBLEM DEFINITION

Recent progress in telecommunications has influenced in various levels the medical processes while this imposes stronger requirements on systems and networks to achieve various dependability attributes: reliability, safety, maintainability, confidentiality, integrity and availability. The aim on this section is to describe the HCCS, to identify the information to protect as well as the threats these systems are facing, and to describe security requirements that can counter the identified risks.

1.1 Identification of sensitive information

A HCCS can be defined as a large network dedicated to healthcare, connecting clinicians, patients, healthcare and social security organizations and interfaces to other systems (e.g., disease data banks). The system should possess reliable means assuring the communication, the processing, as well as the backup of medical, paramedical, administrative and financial information. Ethical obligations aim to protect the privacy of personal data. Unfortunately, even when identities are hidden, it is often possible to identify a person by combining some information, like telephone numbers, medical history or health insurance data. In addition to sensitive data, laws aim at protecting other HCCS resources and services. Indeed, the resolution 45/95 of the General assembly of the United Nations adopted guidelines for the regulation of computerized personal data files [1]. The European Commission has qualified the protection of the medical records as a priority: the Council of Europe has established recommendations concerning the automated medical data banks [2]; the European Parliament and the Council of Europe have adopted diverse directives: on these topics [3, 4, 5].

1.2 Some identified risks

Risk analysis can help to evaluate the consequences of existing vulnerabilities on the system security. This section identifies which entities to protect and enumerates some threats. But first, let us recall some definitions [6]: a *vulnerability* is a weakness in the system (an accidental fault, or a malicious or non-malicious intentional fault in the requirements, the specification, the design or the configuration that can be exploited to provoke a security failure); an *attack* is a malicious interaction fault exploiting a vulnerability and aiming to intentionally violate one or more security properties; an *intrusion* is a malicious, externally-induced fault resulting from an attack that has been successful in exploiting a vulnerability. Some of the laws mentioned above identify several threats. For example, [5, art 4] specifies that the supplier of an electronic service (e.g., a data warehouse) must take technical and organizational measures to guarantee the security of its services. It should also inform the subscribers (e.g., patients) about risks. On the same way, [1, guideline 7] lists some threats: accidental loss; destruction; human risks; non-authorized access; data diversion; viruses. HCCSs have to face specific threats such as patient's privacy violation by illegitimate means (e.g., exploiting vulnerability on the anonymisation process or on the socio-technical system), linking information (e.g., the knowledge of two of a woman's childbirth dates is sufficient to identify her), denial of HCCS critical services (emergencies, payment), illegitimate modification of data (e.g., allocation rules for social rights), etc.

The US government's Office of Technology Assessment [8] and the UK audit Commission [9] confirmed that healthcare appears to be one of the most attractive targets of attacks: both internal and external abusers attempt to harm the HCCS security (invasion of privacy, hacking, virus, fraud, theft of data or software). The threat against privacy is increased by data aggregation that networked computer systems encourage. In HCCS, an intrusion has a very critical aspect, because: if medical information is disclosed illegitimately, besides the violation of the privacy, it may cause a catastrophic damage to the patient (e.g., insurances might refuse to insure persons who have fatal diseases); if information is corrupted, clinicians may take incorrect decisions, which may harm or even kill patients; if information may occasionally be unavailable due to system failure or sabotage, both clinicians and patients will loose confidence in the system.

To sum up, if a HCCS is not secure, its value as a basis for clinical decisions is diminished. Moreover, clinicians called to justify their actions may not be able to rely on computer records for evidence [10].

1.3 HCCS Security requirements

Having identified the risks that HCCS have to face, we can define their security requirements according to confidentiality, integrity, and availability.

Confidentiality can be defined as the capacity to protect sensitive information from being disclosed to unauthorized recipients. In HCCS, confidentiality has two meanings: *privacy* founded on the rights of the patient to control the access to his data; *secrecy* of sensitive information maintained by the organisation (e.g., hospital).

Integrity is defined as the non-occurrence of inadequate information alterations. The system must ensure that patient records, as well as applications, are changed only in an authorized manner. The problem is more complex here because a HCCS is a largely distributed system. But at the same time, it must ensure the consistency and the accuracy of data stored even in case of system failures. Data integrity might also include verification of the data-entry validity. For instance, for a personal pseudonym-code to be always the same for a given patient, it is crucial to use methods to minimise the consequence of spelling mistakes (e.g., when nominative information is transformed by a compression or anonymisation algorithm).

Availability corresponds to readiness for usage. We distinguish: *(1) Short-term availability*: the system resources must be available to authorized users with reasonable response-time (process or data may have timeliness constraints). In emergency cases, clinicians must be able to access the medical data in a reasonable delay. *(2) Long time availability*: regulations impose that some records must be kept for a very long time: cancer records must be kept for the patient's lifetime, and records of genetic diseases have to be kept even longer. Only some well-identified users should have the ability to delete those data, and only after the appropriate time period has expired. It may also be desirable for clinicians to have at their disposal a longitudinal patient record, covering different periods and providers.

2. TRADITIONAL SECURITY MODELS

2.1 Security policy based on the RBAC model

The basic concept of Role Based-Access Control (RBAC) [11] [12] is that roles are assigned to users, permissions are assigned to roles and users acquire permissions by playing roles. A user's role may reflect his tasks in the organization. Hierarchical RBAC supports the role hierarchies, while constrained RBAC enforces the separation of duties. RBAC is used to alleviate user and resource administration: since permissions to access resources are associated with roles rather than users, an update in the users list has no effect on the managed resources, and vice versa.

2.2 Security policy based on the TMAC model

A TeaM-based Access Control (TMAC) was originally proposed in [13]. TMAC uses Teams to resolve some access control problems in collaborative environments. A concrete use of the team concept has been presented in C-TMAC (Context TMAC) [14]. C-TMAC gives a framework to deduct user permissions by combining roles and teams permissions. It also extends original TMAC to use other contextual information.

2.3 Discussion

RBAC is a good model that could be applied to most of actual organizations. To remain as general as possible, RBAC does not detail actions realized on the objects. One of the principal RBAC limits is that all the users having the same role possess the same permissions. However, even if two clinicians have the same role, they do not have necessarily access to the same patient records: only the attending clinician of a patient can consult his medical record. Indeed, in HCCS context, RBAC should be extended to cover other aspects, like the existing relation between the clinician and the patient; the involvement of the clinician, at the moment of the request, and in the process of care; and other contextual information such as location, time, emergency, etc. Our model extends RBAC with such notions.

The notion of team will also take part in our model because in HCCS users are indeed assigned to various teams. In C-TMAC, team permissions are deducted from the combination of the permissions of different users participating in the team. The combination can be an *aggregation*, a *maximum* or a *minimum*. We believe that this approach has certain weaknesses: (1) if the combination is an *aggregation*, the set of team permissions is the sum-up of the permissions of all team members. The derivation of permissions will assign the same set of permissions to every member of the team. But even if users belong to the same team, they do not play the same roles, so they should not have the same permissions. (2) If the combination is a *maximum* or a *minimum*: the permissions will have no sense in this application and does not resolve any particular problem of the HCCS. Moreover, contrary to C-TMAC where a user can activate any one of his roles in any one of his teams, in our model, the user can play different roles in different teams. In other words, C-TMAC consider separately two binary relations (user, role) and (user, team) but, as we will explain later, our model consider a ternary relation (user, role, team). Our proposal is more flexible since, for example, a physician can participate to two teams (*Ti* et *Tj*) but he can play the role "*team manager*" only in *Tj*.

3. CONCEPTS FOUNDING OUR MODEL

In the first step of this study, we opted for a cross use of roles and teams. We perceive the team as an entity grouping together a set of users having various roles and collaborating to realize a specific task. As mentioned in the previous section, in accordance with the relation *(user, role, team),* a user can activate a subset of his roles in each of the teams which he participates in. Sometimes, it is useful to impose *constraints* on team administration, like the max/min number of users in a given team (e.g., the surgery team should be constituted by at least: a surgeon, a nurse and a medical secretary); the max/min number of users activating a specific role in the team; a max/min number of users, playing a specific role, who may/must realize a certain task (e.g., in team *X*, every morning, at least one of the nurses should take the patient's temperature).

In the rest of this chapter, we present the novel concept of "group of objects" and we detail the various types of HCCS contexts. Active entities (which manipulate the information; e.g. users) are denoted as *subjects*, and passive entities (which essentially contain the information, and on which subjects realize actions; e.g. medical record) as *objects*.

3.1 Group of objects

Group of objects is the most novel concept of this paper. It is natural because, on the one hand, it is extracted from the real functioning of several organizations and, on the other hand, it contributes to facilitate comprehension, expression and management of the security policy.

In fact, a HCCS is a set of organizations that interact (e.g., hospitals, insurance companies, etc.). The hospital is a structure associating several organizations (e.g., units, services, departments). Every organization is a structure that establishes the link between a team and the objects that it manipulates (e.g., a healthcare unit implies the presence of a medical *team* that provides care to the patients of the unit). It is thus essential to build *groups of objects* (such as patient records) associated to units and to define the access rights for the teams of the unit and for the other users which interact with it. Furthermore, the specification can identify different classes of objects (e.g., record, equipment, etc.). But, from the access control point of view, this classification is insufficient and it is necessary to distinguish the different objects (of the same class) on which subjects can have different permissions. We propose that permissions be broken down into: a deontic operator (authorization, interdiction, obligation or recommendation); an action (e.g., read, write); and a group of object (e.g., all the records of the patients treated by the team T_i). So, instead of concentrate our model on role permissions, we focus it on actions to realize on groups of objects. It is important to note that groups of objects are constructed according to *logical criteria based on access rights*. Intuitively, the groups G_{di} (resp. G_{dj}) can designate the records Rec_{i1} ... Rec_{in} (resp. Rec_{j1} ... Rec_{jm}) handled by the team T_i (resp. T_j). Records Rec_{in} and Rec_{jm} are both instances of the class *record*, but they belong to two different groups. In oriented-object language, this can be interpreted by the creation of the method *ChangeTeam()* of the class *patient*. This method allows changing the attending team of a patient, by changing the value of the variable *AttendingTeam*, so as to give to the new team the permission to access to the medical record of the patient. Patients having the value of the attribute *AttendingTeam* equal to T_i, constitute the group of objects "*Patients treated in T_i*". From a relational database point of view (SQL), the elements of this group are the answer to the request: SELECT *AttendingTeam*, *RecNum* FROM *Record* WHERE *Record.AttendingTeam*=T_i. To clarify this point, let us detail how to construct groups of objects:

Step 1: according to a *logical view*, group together objects so as to distinguish between objects on which various groups of subjects realize different actions. In HCCS, the semantics could be some criteria such as: being part of a hospital, of a project, of a process, etc.

Step 2: establish the links between each group and the actions made on the group objects. *Steps 1 and 2* can be done by grouping together objects on which a subject (e.g., team) realizes the same actions. By playing a given role, a user obtains permissions allowing him to realize actions, not on all the objects of a class, but on the instances belonging to the group.

Step3: establish the *inheritance* of classes of objects and the *composition* of groups of objects. For examples, a resource of the emergency unit *is a* resource of a patient ward (inheritance); resources of the surgical ward C_5 can be made up from three groups: *rooms of the surgical unit C_5*, *workstations of the surgical unit C_5* and *records of the surgical unit C_5*.

This leads us to discuss the usefulness of other groups of objects. Indeed, inheritance and composition relations reduce the complexity of administration: they favour the distribution of the values of subclasses attributes towards the super-classes, and the actions on the aggregate towards constituents. In addition, the cost of associations {action, object} (without using groups) is of the order N_A*N_O, (N_A: number of actions; N_O: number of objects) while by using the groups, the cost is N_A+N_O. Moreover, the entities (roles, classes and groups), as well as associations {Role, team}, {Permission, action}, {action, groups} remain relatively stable in the information system; they can so be managed by the administrator. The association {objects, group}, for example (Marie, *patient in the ward* C_5), changes more often and it can be managed locally (assignment of patients to wards can be done by the reception staff). Thus, the new concept *group of objects* contributes to reduce the risk of errors and the cost of administration.

3.2 Context

Our model takes into account the context in which the access request is made. A context can be defined as any information that can be used to characterize the situation of an entity (person, place, physical or computational object) [20]. Several existing access models have used the notion of context: Covington et al. [21] expands the RBAC model by incorporating environment roles to capture environmental attributes; Bertino et al. [22] have examined temporal authorization in database systems, etc. For a potential oriented-object implementation, our work distinguishes different types of context and associates each type to the corresponding entity. Our interpretation considers the context as an attribute of classes such as: role, object, team, etc. For example:

The *context of a role* identifies the values that certain variables should have when a user requires to play a given role. For example: the role *ward physician* is valid during the normal hours of work whereas the role *duty physician* is valid at night. Constraints can be associated to roles. For examples, cardinality (the maximal number of users authorized to play this role); static mutual exclusion (the same user cannot be authorized for different roles, e.g., clinician and accountant) and dynamic mutual exclusion (the same user cannot be simultaneously in two given roles, e.g., physician at the hospital and expert for an insurance company) [15].

The *context of objects* defines specific contextual attributes of objects or groups of objects. For example, a duration attribute for the storage of certain data; a location attribute: healthcare units have their own files (stored and managed locally) and their own workstations whose use is authorized only to the unit members.

Users attributes describe characteristics that can influence access control: age, specific authorization, temporary rights, etc. For example, the membership of a national/international professional union; the experience in the practice of certain types of care; specific knowledge, etc.

The *context of use* is a novel concept that helps to realize a good trade-off between the respect of the least privilege principle and the needed flexibility of access control, in order to facilitate the healthcare professional work while preserving patient interests. We are partially inspired by the notion of *purpose* introduced in [16]. In HCCS, we think that if a user requires access to a resource, the context must belong to one of the two following cases:

(1) the user's team participates in a *process treating the patient*. In this case, the activity of care (process) has been already defined by authorized persons (e.g., the consulting physician) and registered into the server. For example, let us take the case of a patient that has heart problems; his consulting physician makes a first evaluation and initializes *the process of care* (he registers the activity of care into the server). Then he sends the patient to the hospital where specialists complete the diagnosis. The members of the team C_5 of the cardiology care unit take over the care of the patient and access, each one according to his role, the parts of the shared records (that contain the current medical history of the patient as well as temporary results and opinions) and archival records that interest them. The sharing of the data, belonging to this patient, among these various clinicians is made through the framework of the process of care declared by the consulting physician.

(2) Sometimes, even if there is no current process, certain users can declare a *purpose* (e.g., only the consulting physician is permitted to create a process, but in case of emergency, another doctor can declare the purpose "emergency„ and so provide care to the patient). Security rules should precisely specify which user/role has the right to declare which purpose, in which conditions (*upstream control*). For instance, for the purpose "emergency„, the access must be validated by values of certain environment variables: request made by an emergency ward; patient wounded in a vital organ; lack of personnel, etc. Permissions for a normal use in the framework of a process of care differ from permissions in emergency situations, and both differ from permissions for research/statistical purposes. Certain uses require the patient's consent; others, sometimes more urgent, take into account the purpose mentioned and grant the access with a higher responsibility and auditability (*downstream control*). For example, to favour flexibility, a security rule can authorize the physician who has formerly treated the patient to access the patient's current medical record, provided that he specifies as purpose *diagnosis revision*. This purpose will be the essential point of the authorization and will activate automatically a high-level audit or the automatic sending of a notification to the patient. To summarize, the aim of *purpose of use* is to assure flexibility while determining the responsibility of the user and to provide evidence in case of

problem or abuse of privilege. Furthermore, we notice that in addition to access control, our model takes into account the obligation to provide some measure such as accountability and replication (for increasing availability). Obligation can concretely be implemented by automating certain actions.

There are several means that can implement our approach, especially, the capabilities proposed by MAFTIA [19] or a language interpreted by access control mechanisms. For example, the use of XML documents to support authorization-based access control for web applications [17].

4. FORMAL SYSTEM

In this section, we propose a model able to formally express the security policy, the operational rules and the security requirements. The use of a formal approach allows to: manipulate the specification by using logical proofs; verify the security policy consistency; and verify that access control mechanisms satisfy the security requirements. Deontic logic [18] is a formal framework that is adaptable to specify security policies by means of modal operators such as obligatory "*O*„, permitted "*P*„ and forbidden "*F*„. The specification language we present in this section relies on deontic logic.

4.1 Alphabet of the language

The alphabet of our language is made up of the following sets: constants, functions, variables, predicates and actions.

(1) Constants: designate the entities: users (e.g., Bob), roles (e.g., physician), teams (T_i), patient wards (e.g., radiology), files (f_i), data (d_j), group of objects (g_j), patient (p_i), purpose (e.g., scientific research).

(2) Variables: u∈*User*, r∈*Role*, t∈*Team*, d∈*Data*, o∈*Object*, go∈*group of objects*, w∈*ward*, p∈*Patient*, rec∈*record*, *f*∈File, *proc*∈Process, etc.

(3) Function: is an element of the language that permits to build the terms. For example, a shared-record can be expressed by the function $shared-record(patient \times File \times File \times File \times File \times File \times File) \rightarrow Record$, arguments are respectively: patient identity; motive of the consultation; medical examination report; anaesthesia data; operating reports; prescriptions; and nursing report. Furthermore, any constant or variable is also a term.

(4) Predicate: relations are denoted by predicates, e.g., AURT(*u*,*r*,*t*) associates the roles that a user can play in each of his teams; AWard(*t*,*go*,*w*) associates the teams and the groups of objects to their patient ward; AObj(o,go) indicates the membership of objects to groups; ARec(*p*,*rec*) allows to establish the link between the patients and their records; etc.

(5) Actions: e.g., TRANSMIT*(u,f,u')*, CREATE_t *(u,t)*: the user *u* creates a new team *t*, $\text{ADD}_{u,t}$ *(u,t,u',r)*: *u* adds *u'* to *t* and assign him the role *r*.

4.2 The language

By means of predicates and actions, we can define the atomic formulas: if "A" is a *predicate* or an *action* of type $\lambda_1 \ldots \lambda_n$ and if $t_1 \ldots t_n$ are terms of type $\lambda_1 \ldots \lambda_n$, then $A(t_1 \ldots t_n)$ is an atomic formula. For example: AR(*Bob*, *clinician*) or READ(*Bob*, *record*$_i$). The language is generated by the following grammatical rule, given in notation EBNF (Extended Backus Normal Form), where f is a formula: $f ::= A(t_1,\ldots t_n) \mid \neg f \mid f \vee f \mid f \wedge f \mid \mathbf{O}f \mid \mathbf{P}f \mid \mathbf{F}f$

4.3 The semantics

The language semantics is defined by the model $M = \langle W, \Re, V, D\rangle$ where W is a set of possible worlds; $\Re$ is a binary relation over W called *accessibility relation*; D is a domain (non-empty set of values); V is a function that gives truth values to the elements of the language: $V(w,A) \subseteq D^n$, $V(w,\pi) \subseteq D^n$, $V(x) \in D$ and $V(a) \in D$ (A: predicate, π: action, x: variable, a: constant). Intuitively, *(Bob, doctor)* $\in$ *V(w,AR)* means that in the world w, *Bob* plays the role doctor; (*Sam*, *record*$_X$) $\in$ *V(w, READ)* means that in the world w, *Sam* executes the *READ* action on *record*$_X$.

4.4 Truth conditions

In a modal logic language, the notation $M,w \models p$ signifies that p is true in a world w of model M; our language truth-values, which extend usual propositional calculus, are as follow: $M,w \models A(t_1,\ldots t_n) \Leftrightarrow (V(t_1),\ldots,V(t_n)) \in V(w,A)$; $M,W \models \neg f \Leftrightarrow$ *we do not have* $(M,w \models f)$; $M,w \models f \vee g \Leftrightarrow M,w \models f$ *or* $M,w \models g$; $M,w \models f \wedge g \Leftrightarrow M,w \models f$ *and* $M,w \models g$; $M,w \models \mathbf{O}f \Leftrightarrow \forall w' \in W / w\Re w' \rightarrow M,w \models f$; $M,w \models \mathbf{P}f \Leftrightarrow \exists w' \in W / w\Re w' \rightarrow M,w \models f$; $M,w \models \mathbf{F}f \Leftrightarrow \forall w' \in W / w\Re w' \rightarrow (M,w \models \neg f)$

The formulas $\mathbf{O}f$ (it is obligatory that f), $\mathbf{P}f$ (it is permitted that f) and $\mathbf{F}f$ (it is forbidden that f) mean respectively: f is true in every world w' which w is in relation with; it should be possible to reach a world in which f is true; none of the accessible worlds should allow to conclude that f is true.

5. SPECIFICATION OF THE SECURITY POLICY

5.1 System description

The system described by means of the propositional logic operators (non modal). We represent essentially the functional aspects of the system that are relevant for security. At the level of semantics, the operational rules define the internal structure of the worlds ($q \rightarrow r$ means in any world w where q is true, r is also true). For example, take the role hierarchy: $\text{AR}(u, On-callPhysician) \vee \text{AR}(u, WardPhysician) \vee \text{AR}(u, ServicePhysician) \vee \text{AR}(u, nurse) \rightarrow \text{AR}(u, ClinicalStaff)$ or take the role activation: $\text{PROVIDE}(u, HPC(\_,\_,r,\_,t,\_)) \rightarrow \text{AURT}(u,r,t)$: if the user provide his HealthCare Professional Card (*HPC*), then he plays the role in the team mentioned on the card (the function *HPC* has as parameters: identification number, name, role, mode of duty, team, rate).

5.2 Security properties

Security properties are expressed by using modal operators. These operators allow modifying the properties of the accessibility relations between the various worlds of the model. They indicate if two worlds are accessible from one to the other. $\mathbf{F}[\mathrm{AR}(u, pharmacist) \wedge \mathrm{CREATE}(u, prescription)]$ is a rule that forbids a pharmacist to create prescriptions.

5.3 Security rules

A security rule is a modal formula with at least a non-modal clause (e.g., $r \rightarrow \mathbf{P}q$). It describes the link between the permissions, interdictions or obligations, and the state of the system. $\mathrm{ARec}(p, record_i) \rightarrow \mathbf{P}[\mathrm{READ}(p, record_i)]$ means: every patient is permitted to read his medical record; $\mathrm{APurpose}(u, emergency, p) \wedge \mathrm{AR}(u, Physician) \wedge \mathrm{AR}(s, system) \wedge \mathrm{ARec}(p,d)$ $\rightarrow \mathbf{P}[\mathrm{READ}(u,d)] \wedge \mathbf{O}[\mathrm{APPEND}_f(s, ConnectionData(u, emergency, p, r), AuditFile)]$ signifies that the user who plays the role *physician* and declares the purpose *emergency* can read the patient record. Simultaneously, the system saves connection data; the security rule $\mathbf{P}[\mathrm{PROVIDECARE}(u, \_)] \rightarrow \mathrm{AR}(u, ClinicalStaff)$ indicates that the action "provide care,, is only permitted to the clinical staff (necessary condition). So, the sufficient condition requires that the user play the role "clinical staff,, in the team where the patient is treated. The rule is: $\mathrm{AURT}(u, clinicalStaff, T) \wedge \mathrm{AWard}(t, go, \_) \wedge \mathrm{AObj}(p, go) \rightarrow \mathbf{P}[\mathrm{PROVIDECARE}(u,p)]$.

6. CONCLUSION

This paper describes a security model that covers the particularities of HCCS. It also achieves a good trade-off between respect of the least privilege principle and flexibility of the access control. This logical model can be exploited to verify the consistency of the security policy.

7. ACKNOWLEDGMENT

This work was supported in part and is experimented in the RNRT project "MP6,, where partners are: Ernst & Young Audit, ENST-Bretagne, ETIAM, France Telecom R&D, LAAS-CNRS, MasterSecuritY, ONERA-DTIM, Supélec-Rennes, and UPS-IRIT. We thank particularly Philippe Balbiani from IRIT for his contribution to the logic section.

8. REFERENCES

[1] Resolution A/RES/45/95 of the General Assembly of United Nations: *"Guidelines for the Regulation of Computerized Data Files"*, 14 December 1990.

[2] Recommendations R(81) of the Council of Europe: *"on Automated Medical Data Banks"*, Strasbourg, January 23, 1981.

[3] Directive 95/46/CE of the European Parliament and the Council of the European Union: *"On the protection of individuals"*, October 24, 1995.

[4] Directive 97/66/CE of the European Parliament and of the Council of 15 on: *"the treatment of the personal data and privacy protection on the telecommunications sector"*, December 15, 1997, Official Journal L 24, 30-1-1998, p. 1-8.

[5] Directive 2002/58/EC of the European Parliament on: *"the processing of personal data and the protection of privacy in the electronic communications sector"*, July 12, 2002, Official Journal L 201, 31-7-2002, p. 37-47.

[6] D. Powell and R. Stroud (Eds.), *Malicious and Accidental-Fault Tolerance in Internet Applications: conceptual model and architecture*, MAFTIA project Deliverable D2, November 2001, <http://www.research.ec.org/maftia/deliverables/index.html>

[8] B. Woodward, "The computer-based patient record and confidentiality,,, *New England Journal of Medicine*, v 333 N° 21, 1995, pp 1419-1422.

[9] Audit Commission, *Ghost in the Machine - An Analysis of IT Fraud and Abuse*, Audit Commission Publications, United Kingdom, ISBN 1-86240-05603, 1998.

[10] R. Anderson, *Personal Medical Information Security, Engineering, and Ethics*, Personal Information Workshop proceedings, Cambridge, UK, June 21-22, 1996, Springer ISBN 3-540-63244-1.

[11] S.I. Gavrila, J.F. Barkley "Formal Specification for Role-Based Access Control,,, *Third ACM Workshop on Role-Based Access Control*, Fairfax, VA, USA. 22-23, October 1998.

[12] D.F. Ferraiolo, R. Sandhu, S. Gavrila, D.R. Kuhn and R. Chandramouli "A Proposed Standard for Role-Based Access Control,,, *ACM Transactions on Information and System Security,* Volume 4, Number 3, August 2001.

[13] Roshan K.Thomas, "TMAC: A primitive for Applying RBAC in collaborative environment,,, *2nd ACM, Workshop on RBAC*, Fairfax, Virginia, USA, November 1997.

[14] Christos K. Georgiadis, Loannis Mavridis *et al.*, "Flexible Team-Based Access Control Using Contexts,,, *ACM Symposium on Access Control Models and Technologies (SACMAT'01)*, Chantilly, Virginia, USA, May 3-4, 2001, pp. 21-27.

[15] M. Willikens, S. Feriti, M. Masera, "A Context-related authorisation and access control method based on RBAC,,, *ACM Symposium on Access Control Models and Technologies (SACMAT'02)*, California, USA, June 3-4, 2002, pp. 117-124.

[16] P. Bonatti, E. Damiani, S. di Vimercati, P. Samarati, "An access Control Model for data archives,,, *16th IFIP TC11 International Conference on Information Security (IFIP/Sec'01)*, Paris, France, June 11-13, 2001, pp. 261-276.

[17] E. Damiani, S. De Capitani di Vimercati, S. Paraboschi, P. Samarati, "A Fine-Grained Access Control System for XML Documents,,, in *ACM Transactions on Information and System Security (TISSEC)*, vol. 5, n. 2, May 2002, pp. 169-202.

[18] B.F. Chellas, *Modal Logic: An Introduction*, 295p., Cambridge University Press, 1980, ISBN 0-521-29515-7.

[19] Y. Deswarte, N. Abghour, V. Nicomette, D. Powell, "An Intrusion-Tolerant Authorization Scheme for Internet Applications,,, in *Sup. of the Proceedings of the 2002 International Conference on Dependable Systems and Networks (DSN2002),* Washington, D.C. (USA), 23-26 June 2002, pp. C-1.1 - C-1.6.

[20] A.K. Dey, G.D. Abowd (1999). *Towards a better understanding of context and context-awareness.* GVU Technical Report GITGVU-99-22, College of Computing, Georgia Institute of Technology.

[21] M. Covington, W. Long, S. Srinivasan, A.K. Dey, M. Ahamad, G.D. Abowd, "Securing Context-Aware Applications Using Environment Roles,,, *ACM Symposium on Access Control Models and Technologies (SACMAT'01)*, Chantilly (Va), USA, May 3-4, 2001, pp.10-20.

[22] E. Bertino, C. Bettini, E. Ferrari, P. Samarati, "A Temporal access control mechanism for database systems,,, *IEEE Transactions on Knowledge and Data Engineering*, v8, 1996.

CONSTRAINED ROLE-BASED DELEGATION

LONGHUA ZHANG

NuTech Solutions, Inc
Charlotte, NC 28262, USA
Longhua.zhang@nutechsolutions.com

GAIL-JOON AHN

Dept. of Software and Information Systems
University of North Carolina at Charlotte
Charlotte, NC 28223, USA
gahn@uncc.edu

Abstract: Delegation is a promising alternative to traditional role administration paradigms in role-based systems. It empowers users to exercise discretion in how they use resources as it is in discretionary access control (DAC). Unlike the anarchy of DAC, in role-based access control (RBAC) higher-level organizational policies can be specified on roles to regulate user's action. Delegations and revocations are thus governed by these authorization policies. In this paper, we propose a policy approach for specifying and enforcing delegation authorizations. We present a mechanism for constructing authorization policies using a set of rules. Our rule-based language is flexible and powerful to specify and enforce authorization constraints. In addition, rules can also be used to define the exceptions for future actions and resolve possible conflicts.

Key words: Role-based delegation, authorization constraints, access control.

1. INTRODUCTION

Access control model must include an administration policy that regulates the specification of authorizations. In current role-based systems [1, 2], security officers handle this function. This approach is appropriate in centralized systems as well as distributed systems where users, roles, and their assignments are relatively static and stable. However, current dynamic and collaborative work environment often requires users to change their role memberships frequently. It could raise tremendous overhead because of the continuous involvement from security officers. One promising approach is to empower individual user to delegate authorizations. Through delegation, users are trusted to exercise their privileges in how they use resources as it is in discretionary access control (DAC) [4]. We have presented a delegation framework focusing on user-to-user delegation in role-based systems [5].

The framework consists of a delegation model called RDM2000 and a rule-based policy specification language. RDM2000 is our first attempt to address administration of roles through delegation. And the rule-based language is used to specify delegation policies. Administration of roles through delegation is quite feasible and practical. We have demonstrated how RDM2000 can support those features in several role-based systems [19]. However, the original rule-based policy language lacks capabilities to specify and enforce constraints, which are highly desirable features in RBAC. As constraints are a powerful mechanism for laying out organizational policy, constraints enforcement is an important component to administer role-based delegations [1].

In this paper, we enhance the rule-based language to support constraints specification and enforcement. We present a policy approach to implement role-based delegation authorization. We also demonstrate that our authorization policy is flexible and powerful for role-based delegation. We believe that our work provides a flexible mechanism for administration of roles in role-based systems.

The rest of this paper is organized as follows. Section 2 describes delegation requirements and reviews related works. Section 3 describes the RDM2000 model and role-based constraints. Section 4 presents a policy approach for the specification and enforcement of delegation authorizations. We discuss other issues and future directions in section 5. Section 6 concludes this paper.

2. BACKGROUND AND RELATED WORK

Delegation is an important factor for secure distributed computing environment. It has been studied by a number of researchers [5, 8, 9, 10]. In general, it is referred to as one active entity in a system delegates its authority to another entity to carry out some functions. In role-based systems, the delegated authorities are roles. The requirements related to role-based delegation have been identified in the literature [5, 9, 11].

There are many groups working on constraints specification [1, 12, 13]. Sandhu et al. [1] described several types of constraints in RBAC96. Ahn et al. [12] specified role-based separation of duty constraints using RCL2000 language and identified various classes of role-based authorization constraints. Bertino et al. [13] explored authorization constraints in workflow management systems. Bandmann et al. [18] illustrated how to impose controls on handling the delegation tree. However, the enforcement of these constraints has not received much attention. Lupu et al. [6] studied specification of policies in the context of role management. They consider roles as a set of policies and use policies to specify permissions of each role.

In their approach, authorization policies and roles are highly coupled, because roles cannot exist without policies. In our approach, permissions assigned to roles are specified by permission assignment (PA) and authorization policies specify whether a delegation (or revocation) is allowed. So policies and roles are loosely coupled. Another difference is to define a policy as a set of declarative rules instead of a single object. Since rules are easy to understand, create, and modify, it provides flexibility to meet different authorization requirements.

3. RDM2000 – THE DELEGATION MODEL

RDM2000 was originally introduced for user-to-user delegation in role-based systems. It formalizes the relationship between two user assignments (UAO/UAD) that form a delegation relation (DLGT), as shown in figure 1. Basic elements and system functions from the RDM2000 model are summarized in definition 1.

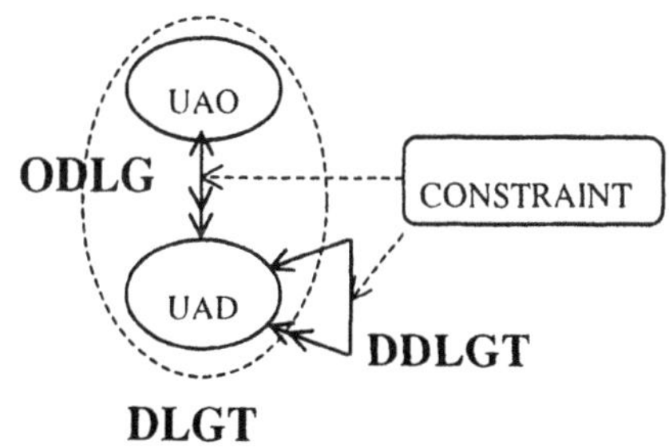

Figure 1. RDM2000

Definition 1. The following is a summary of components defined in RDM2000 model:

- $UA = UAO \cup UAD \subseteq U \times R$
- $UAO \subseteq U \times R$ *is an original user to role assignment relation.*
- $UAD \subseteq U \times R$ *is a delegated user to role assignment relation.*
- $DLGT = ODLGT \cup DDLGT \subseteq UA \times UA$.
- $ODLGT \subseteq UAO \times UAD$ *is an original user delegation relation.*
- $DDLGT \subseteq UAD \times UAD$ *is a delegated user delegation relation.*
- $DLGT = ODLGT \cup DDLGT$.
- *Prior:* $UA \rightarrow UA$ *is a function that maps a user assignment to another subsequent user assignment that forms a delegation relation.*
- $DP \subseteq UA \times UA$ *represents a delegation path.*
- $DT \subseteq UA \times UA$ *represents a delegation tree.*
- *Path:* $UA \rightarrow DP$ *is a function that maps a UA to a delegation path.*

In RDM2000, a set of authorization policies is defined. These authorization policies are represented in our policy language as basic authorization rules [5].

Constraints are an important component of RBAC since it can be used for laying out higher-level organizational policies in role-based systems [1,12]. Our objective is to specify and enforce constraints in role-based delegation authorizations. First, we overview some identified constraints in role-based systems [1, 12, 13, 14]: 1) *Static separation of duty*

(SSOD)/Incompatible roles assignment. This constraint states that no common user should be assigned to conflicting roles. A frequently used example is a user cannot be a purchase manager while at the same time being an account payable manager for the same organization. We denote a set of incompatible role assignments as IRA. 2) *Incompatible users.* This constraint states that two conflicting users cannot be assigned to the same role. For example, it might be a company's policy that members from same subdivision should not be assigned to the same steering committee. We denote a set of incompatible users as IU. 3) *Incompatible permissions.* This constraint states that conflicting permissions cannot be assigned to the same role. We denote a set of incompatible permissions as IP. 4) *Cardinality constraints.* This constraint states that a role can have a maximum number of members or a user may belong to a maximum number of roles. For example, there may be only one person in the role of CEO in an organization. As stated in [1], the role cardinality is difficult to implement since the system may not know exactly how many users are still "alive" – some may leave without notifying security officers. We denote the cardinality of x as $cardi(x)$, where x is a role term or a user term.

It is futile to enumerate all role-based constraints, as there are too many possibilities and variants [12]. In the subsequent sections, we show that the enhanced rule-based language is expressive enough to specify a wide range of constraints.

4. AUTHORIZATION POLICIES IN DELEGATION

4.1 Functions, Rules, and Policies

The fundamental element of the policy language is a set of functions. We categorize these functions into three groups: 1) a set of specification functions, expressing information of the RBAC and RDM2000 components; 2) a set of authorization functions, describing an authorization information or decision. We further divide them into a set of basic authorization functions (BAP), a set of derived authorization functions (DAP), and a set of negative authorization functions (NAP); and 3) a set of utility functions, providing supportive functionalities, e.g. comparison and aggregation. These functions and their semantics are listed in appendix.

We borrow the notion of two non-deterministic functions from RCL2000 [12]: *one_element* and *all_other* (originally as *OE* and *AO*). These functions are introduced to replace explicit quantifiers, thus keep the language simple and intuitive. The *one_element(X)* function allows us to get one element x_i from set X. Multiple occurrences of *one_element (X)* in a single rule statement select the same element x_i. With *all_other(X, x_i)* we can get a subset of X by taking out one element x_i.

The policy language is a rule-based language with a clausal logic [5]. A rule is the form:

$H \leftarrow B.$

Where H stands for rule head and B stands for rule body.

A successful inference of B triggers H to be true. This provides the mechanism for constraints specification and enforcement. A constraint is similar to an assertion. If the condition defined in the constraints is true, then it triggers some actions (restrictions). Thus, the condition information of a constraint can be encoded in a rule body; and the restrictions can be encoded in the rule head.

Since it is natural to represent restrictions as negative authorizations, we include the negative authorization concept in the rule-based policy language. A negative authorization defines what a user is forbidden to do. Given an authorization *can_do* that defines what can do, there can always be a negative authorization *cannot_do* that defines what cannot do. Although negative authorization has been introduced in discretionary access control for a long time, it has not been studied in role-based context. In [14], Bertino et al. explored negative authorization in relational data management systems (RDMS). They proposed strong and weak enforcement for positive and negative authorizations. Their approach provides a flexible mechanism to express a number of DAC policies. Because of the existence of role hierarchies, negative authorizations in RBAC are more complex than in DAC. For example, a negative authorization on a role needs to consider an impact on its senior roles. In this paper, we consider negative authorization can be inherited in role hierarchies: if a user cannot be assigned to a role *r*, he cannot be assigned to any roles that are senior to *r*. We do not distinguish a strong or a weak enforcement of authorization for the brevity. An override rule determines whether positive or negative authorization needs to be enforced. In this paper we limit the application of negative authorizations to constraints enforcement and exception handling. In our future work, we would general use of negative role-based authorizations in depth.

There are three sets of rules in RDM2000: basic authorization rules, authorization derivation rules, and override rules. Bodies of basic authorization rules are empty. In other words, they are always true. Basic authorization rules are predefined security policies or facts specified within RBAC components. An authorization derivation rule expresses authorization on an individual user. The rule body describes an inference logic that consists of basic authorization, specification and utility functions. The result can be either true (authorized) or false (denied). However, the result might be overridden by other rules in certain situations. An override rule specifies exceptions and conflict resolution policy. Having discussed different functions and rules, we define the following authorization policy:

Definition 2. (**Authorization Policy**) An authorization policy consists of a finite number (possibly zero) of rules.

An authorization policy is a logic program that defines authorization for individual users to exercise privileges in role-based systems. Each authorization policy has one or more authorization derivation rules representing the goal. The conclusion of a goal is the result of the logic program execution.

4.2 Constraints Specification

In order to represent constraints, we define rules that are extremely suited for constraints specification as well as enforcement. We articulate several constraints and specify them using our rule-based language.

A **static separation of duty (SSOD): incompatible roles assignment constraint** states that no common user can be assigned to conflicting roles in the incompatible role set $ira = \{r_1, r_2, \ldots\}$. This constraint can be represented as:

cannot_assign(u, r) ← senior(r, one_element(ira)) &
member_of(u, one_element(all_other(ira, one_element(ira)))).

where cannot_assign, equals, one_element, member_of, all_other are functions defined in our rule-based language; $u \in U$, $r \in R$, *and* $ira \in IRA$.

The rule says if *r* equals one element of a set of the incompatible role assignments *ira*, and a user *u* is already member of another role other than *r* in the incompatible role set, then *u* cannot be assigned role *r*.

An **incompatible users constraint** states that two conflicting users in the incompatible user set $iu=\{u_1, u_2, \ldots\}$ cannot be assigned to the same role. This constraint can be represented as:

cannot_assign(u, r)←
equals(u', one_element(all_other(iu, u))) & member_of(u', r).

An **incompatible permissions constraint** states that two conflicting permissions in the incompatible user set $ip=\{p_1, p_2, \ldots\}$ cannot be assigned to the same role. This constraint can be represented as:

cannot_assignp(r, p)← equals(p', one_element(all_other(ip, p))) &
in(p', permissions_role(r)).

A **role cardinality constraint** states that a role can have a maximum number *N* of user members. This constraint can be represented as:

cannot_assign(u, r)← greater_than(cardi(r), maxcardi(r)-1).

A **user cardinality constraint** states that a user can be member of a maximum number *N* of roles. This constraint can be represented as:

cannot_assign(u, r)←greater_than(cardi(u), maxcardi(u)-1).

We have demonstrated how different constraints can be specified using rules. Next we show how exceptions can be specified and how to resolve possible conflicts in rules.

4.3 Exception Handling and Conflict Resolution

Exceptions allow users to state overridden policies for previous specified and enforced authorizations in some cases. For example, a security officer may need to suspend Bob's role membership of account manager role *AcctMgr* without revoking him from the role. This can be achieved by issuing following rule:

cannot_activate(Bob, AcctMgr, _)←.

where _ stands for anonymous variable. An anonymous variable can be anything. In this case, it can be any session.

This rule enforces *Bob* cannot activate his role *AcctMgr* in any session.

Another exception example could be the duration-triggered revocation. Revocation using duration-restriction constraints was proposed by Barka and Sandhu [9]. In such a revocation, a duration constraint is attached to each delegation such that the delegation expires when the assigned time expires. Duration-restriction revocation is a simple self-triggered process that ensures the revocation of role membership. Suppose there is a delegation relation *(Linda, AcctMgr, Alice, AcctPart)* ∈ *DLGT* with an associated duration constraint *t*. The duration-triggered revocation can be represented as:

der_can_revokeGD(Linda, AcctMgr, Alice, AcctPart, rvk_opt)
← expires(Alice, AcctPart, t).

Therefore, role-based systems can revoke Alice from the *AcctPart* role, which is a part-time worker in an accounting department based on the duration *t*.

It is worth emphasizing that negative authorizations are the main mechanism to specify constraints and exceptions. Enabling negative authorization may inevitably cause inconsistency: whenever a user holds both a positive and a negative assertion for the same authorization, conflicts arise. A conflict resolution policy is then needed to determine whether the negative or positive assertion should be enforced. There are many different approaches that could be taken [16]: 1) *No conflicts allowed.* The presence of a conflict is considered as an error; 2) *Negative authorization takes precedence.* The negative always overrides the positive; 3) *Positive authorization takes precedence.* The positive always overrides the negative. 4) *A mixed approach.* Neither authorization is considered as prevailing over the other.

In our approach, we specify the override rules to resolve possible conflicts. The decision on whether a negative or a positive authorization takes precedence is determined by an override rule.

override(can_activate(Bob, AcctMgr, _), false)←
can_activate(Bob, AcctMgr, _)&
cannot_activate(Bob, AcctMgr, _).

This rule explicitly states that *Bob* cannot activate *AcctMgr* if conflict exists. Override rules themselves may have conflicts. Although another override rule can be defined to resolve the conflict, this may cause a loop in override rule definition. A default organizational policy can be specified to solve it. For example,

override(X, false)← override(X, true)&override(X, false).

It means that if there exist conflicting override rules, the negative takes precedence.

4.4 Delegation Authorization Policies

As defined in section 4.1, authorization policies are a set of rules regulating whether or not a user is allowed to exercise privileges. To support constraints and exceptions, the delegation authorization includes a single rule. For example, a user-to-user delegation is authorized by the user-user delegation authorization derivation rule in [5]:

der_can_delegate(u, r, u', r', dlg_opt) ←can_delegate(r'', cr, n)&
active(u, r, s)&delegatable(u, r)&
senior(r, r'')&satisfy(u', cr)&
junior(r', r'')&in(depth(u, r), n). (1)

To enforce constraints and exceptions, more rules are needed for authorizing the delegation. For example, if we consider SSOD, incompatible users, incompatible roles, and cardinality constraints, we need to add the following rules:

der_cannot_delegate(u, r, u', r', dlg_opt) ←cannot_assign(u', r'). (2)

cannot_assign(u', r')←senior(r', one_element(ira)) &
member_of(u', one_element(
all_other(ira, one_element(ira)))). (3)

cannot_assign(u', r')←equals(u'', one_element(
all_other(iu, u'))) & member_of(u'', r'). (4)

cannot_assignr(r', r'')←senior(r'', one_element(
all_other(irr, r'))). (5)

cannot_assign(u', r')←greater_than(cardi(r'), maxcardi(r')-1). (6)

cannot_assign(u', r')←greater_than(cardi(u'), maxcardi(u')-1). (7)

override(der_can_delegate(u,r,u',r' dlg_opt), false))←
der_can_delegate(u,r,u',r' dlg_opt) &
der_cannot_delegate(u,r,u',r' dlg_opt). (8)

where u, u', and u" are elements of users; r, r', and r" are elements of roles; cr and s are elements of prerequisite condition and sessions respectively; dlg_opt is a Boolean term, if it is true, then delegatable (u', r') is true; ira is any conflict role assignment set that contains r'; iu is any incompatible user set that contains u'; irr is any incompatible role set that contains r'; maxcardi(r') and), maxcardi(u') are maximum allowed cardinalities for r' and u' respectively.

Rule 2 specifies that if there is any constraint that forbids the user assignment (u', r') then the delegation should be denied. Rule 3, 4, 5, 6, and 7 specify constraints. Rule 8 deals with the resolution of conflicts. These rules authorize a user-to-user delegation. Next, we consider handling exceptions in the delegation authorization policy. The basic authorization rule allows users to delegate roles only if users satisfy the prerequisite condition. Otherwise, the authorization decision should be reconsidered. Since there may be multiple basic authorization rules that could be applied to infer the delegation authorization, we may specify the following exception handling rule:

der_can_revokeGD(u, r, u', r', rvk_opt) ← can_revokeGD (r') & not(satisfy(u', cr)) & not(der_can_delegate(u, r, u', r', dlg_opt)). (9)

This rule says whenever user *u'* cannot satisfy the prerequisite condition *cr* after an authorized delegation, the system needs to re-infer *der_can_delegate(u, r, u', r', dlg_opt)*. If the inference fails, then *u'* is revoked from *r'*.

The delegating user can also specify a duration-triggered revocation:

der_can_revokeGD(u, r, u', r', rvk_opt) ← can_revokeGD (r') & expires(u', r', t). *(10)*

The exception handling rules do not affect the initial decision of a delegation authorization. Rather, they define the actions that would be taken if the conditions embedded in the rule bodies are triggered after the delegation.

We summarize the delegation authorization policy as follows: a *goal*, which is specified by an authorization derivation rule; *rules* that enforce role-based constraints; *override rules* to resolve possible conflicts; and *exception handling rules* to specify sub-goals that process post-delegation authorizations.

Similarly, we can construct revocation authorization policies for grant-dependent (GD) and grant-independent (GI) revocations. The revocation authorization policies only consist of goals. Although we mainly illustrated specification of delegation and revocation authorization policies using rules in this section, the concept of building a policy is equally applicable to any other authorization scenarios in role-based systems.

5. DISCUSSIONS AND FUTURE WORK

We are attracted by some virtues of the rule-based language: they are highly expressive; they can easily be extended to facilitate additional requirements; and they can handle conflicts during creating and updating of rule sets. However, there are several challenges in rule-based policy implementation. One difficulty is the validation of semantics. Although the rule declaration is intuitively simple that non-experts can feel comfortable in specifying the rule sets, a formal definition and proof of soundness and completeness are still necessary. Another difficulty is the complexity of implementing inferences in the authorization policy. As an ongoing effort, we have been developing security architectures for delegation in distributed role-based systems. Policy service is one of the major components in this architecture. It consists of a rule compiler and a policy engine: the compiler runs as a preprocessor to convert declarative rules to logic program, the output is fed to the policy engine, which may infer the authorization decision and process exceptions for post-delegation actions.

6. CONCLUSIONS

In this paper, we presented a policy approach for constrained delegation authorization. We have shown that our authorization policy is flexible and powerful to regulate role-based delegation. Not only can it enforce role-based constraints, but also be used to define the exceptions for future actions. We reiterate that our work makes it easier to administer roles through delegation in role-based systems. By specifying authorization policy, the delegation is adapted to meet users' needs, while organizational policies can still be specified to impose restrictions. We believe that specifying and implementing complex delegation authorization policies are critical and challenging tasks in large, distributed role-based systems.

REFERENCE

[1] R. Sandhu, E. Coyne, H. Feinstein and C. Youman. Role-based access control model. IEEE Computer, 29(2), Feb. 1996.

[2] D. Ferriaolo, J. Cugini, and R. Kuhn. Role-based access control (RBAC): Features and Motivations. Proceeding s of 11th Annual Computer Security Application Conference, pages 241-248, New Orleans, LA, Dec 11-15 1995

[3] R. Sandhu, V. Bhamidipati, and Q. Munawer. The ARBAC97 Model for Role-based Administration of Roles. ACM Transactions on Information and System Security. Vol.2, No.1, Feb. 1999, pages 105-135

[4] S. Osborn, R. Sandhu and Q. Munawer. Configuring Role-Based Access Control to Enforce Mandatory and Discretionary Access Control Policies. ACM Transactions on Information and Systems Security, Vol.3, No. 2, (2000).

[5] L. Zhang, G. Ahn, and B. Chu. A Rule-Based Framework for Role-Based Delegation. Proceedings of ACM Symposium on Access Control Models and Technologies, pages 153–162. Chantilly, VA, May 3-4, 2001

[6] E. Lupu, D. Marriott, M. Sloman and N. Yialelis. A Policy Based Role Framework for Access Control. Proceedings of the First ACM Workshop on Role Based Access Control, Gaithersburg, Maryland, USA, Nov. 1995, ACM, ISBN: 0-89791-759-6.

[7] E. Lupu and M. Sloman. Towards a Role Based Framework for Distributed Systems Management. Journal of Network and Systems Management, 5(1):5-30, Plenum Press Publishing, 1997.

[8] N. Li and B. N. Grosof. A practically implementation and tractable delegation logic. Proceedings of IEEE Symposium on Security and Privacy. May 2000.

[9] E. Barka and R. Sandhu. Framework for Role-Based Delegation Model. Proceedings of 23rd National Information Systems Security Conference, pages 101-114, Baltimore, Oct. 16-19, 2000

[10] M. Gasser, E. McDermott. An Architecture for Practical Delegation a Distributed System. Proceedings of IEEE Computer Society Symposium on Research in Security and Privacy. Oakland, CA, May 7-9,1990

[11] A. Hagstrom, S. Jajodia, F. P. Presicce, D. Wijesekera, Revocations - a classification. Proceedings of 14th IEEE Computer Security Foundations Workshop, Nova Scotia, Canada, June 2001, pages 44-58.

[12] G. Ahn and R. Sandhu. Role-based Authorization Constraints Specification. ACM Transactions on Information and System Security, pages 207-226, Vol. 3, No. 4, ACM, November 2000

[13] E. Bertino, E. Ferrari, V. Atluri. The specification and enforcement of authorization constraints in workflow management systems, ACM Transactions on Information and System Security (TISSEC), Vol.2 No.1, p.65-104, Feb. 1999

[14] E. Bertino, S. Jajodia, P. Samarati, "A Flexible Authorization Mechanism for Relational Data Management Systems", ACM Trans. Information Systems, Vol. 17, No. 2, April 1999, pages 101-140.

[15] S. Jajodia, P. Samarati, M. L. Sapino, V. S. Subrahmanian, ``Flexible support for multiple access control policies," ACM Trans. on Database Systems, June 2001, pages 214-260

[16] S. Jajodia, P. Samarati, V. S. Subrahmanian, E. Bertino, A unified framework for enforcing multiple access control policies, ACM SIGMOD Record, Vol.26 No.2, pages 474-485, June 1997

[17] A. Herzberg, Y. Mass, J. Michaeli, D. Naor, and R. Ravid. Access control meets public key infrastructure, or: assigning roles to strangers. Proceedings of IEEE Symposium on Security and Privacy, Oakland, May 2000

[18] O. Bandmann, B. S. Firozabadi, and M. Dam. Constrained Delegation. Proceedings of IEEE Symposium on Security and Privacy. May 12 - 15, 2002. Berkeley, California

[19] Longhua Zhang, Gail-Joon Ahn, Bei-Tseng Chu: A role-based delegation framework for healthcare information systems, Proceedings of ACM Symposium on Access Control Models and Technologies, pages 153–162, June 2002.

APPENDIX

Some functions and their semantics are listed in table 1, 2, and 3. We use UT, RT, PT, ST, UAT, PAT, DLGTT, DPT, CRT, IRAT, IUT, IRRT, BT, DT, and NT to indicate set of users, roles, permissions, sessions, user assignments, permission assignments, delegations, delegation paths, prerequisite conditions, incompatible role assignments, incompatible users, incompatible roles, booleans, durations, and natural numbers, respectively.

Table 1. Utility functions

Predicate	Arity	Argument	Return	Meaning
All_other	2	set of XT, XT	set of XT	all_other(X, x) = X-{x}.
equals	2	XT, XT	BT	If equals(x, y) is true, then x = y.
In	2	XT, set of XT	BT	If in(x, y) is true, then x ∈ y.
Not	1	BT	BT	not(true) = false and not(false)=true.
one_element	1	set of XT	XT	oneelement(X) returns one element in set X.
satisfy	2	UT, CR	BT	If satisfy(u, cr) is true, then user u satisfies cr.

Table 2. Specification functions

Predicate	Arity	Argu.	Return	Meaning
cardi	1	RT	NT	cardi(r) returns current number of users in role r.
delegatable	1	UAT	BT	If delegatable(ua) is true, then ua can further delegate.
expires	3	UT, RT, DT	BT	expires(u, r, t) returns true if duration t assigned to (u, r) expires.
maxcardi	1	RT	NT	maxcardi(r) returns the maximum cardinality allowed for role r.
parent	2	UAT, UAT	BT	parent(ua, ua') ← equals(ua, prior(ua')).
predecessor	2	UAT, UAT	BT	predecessor(ua, ua') ← predecessor(ua, ua"), parent(ua", ua'). predecessor(ua, ua') ← parent(ua, ua').
revoked_cascade	1	UAT	BT	If revokedcas(ua) is true, then ua will be revoked cascadingly.

Table 3. Authorization functions

Predicate	Arity	Argu.	Type	Meaning
override	2	Rule head, BT	BAP	override(H, b) means let H=b. It states conflict resolution policy for H←B.
cannot_assign	2	UT, RT	NAP	cannot_assign(u, r) means user u cannot be assigned role r.
cannot_assignr	2	RT, RT	NAP	cannot_assignr(r, r') means role r' cannot be assigned to role r.
cannot_activate	3	UT, RT, ST	NAP	cannot_activate(u, r, s) means u cannot activate r in sessions. If session s is an anonymous variable, cannot_activate(u, r, _) means u cannot activate r in any session.
der_cannot_delegate	5	UT, RT, UT, RT, BT	NAP	der_cannot_delegate(u, r, u', r', b) means user u with role r cannot delegate role r' to user u'.

CSAP - AN ADAPTABLE SECURITY MODULE FOR THE E-GOVERNMENT SYSTEM WEBOCRAT

Fredj Dridi, Michael Fischer and Günther Pernul
Department of Information Systems,
University of Regensburg
Universitätsstr. 31, D-93053 Regensburg, Germany
{fredj.dridi,guenther.pernul}@wiwi.uni-regensburg.de,michael.fischer@gmx.de

Abstract In this paper we present a generic and adaptable security module called CSAP (Communication, Security, Authentication, and Privacy) which may be used in order to make e-government and e-commerce systems secure and trustworthy. CSAP is service-oriented and offers programming interfaces to core security services such as user identification, authentication, access control, auditing, and security management. We discuss the conceptual architecture, the layered design, and the object-oriented implementation of CSAP. The layered design of CSAP allows the application developer to exchange or enhance security mechanisms via a plug-in concept based on abstract classes and appropriate design patterns. As a consequence, CSAP becomes maintainable and adaptable.

Among other services, CSAP provides an implementation of a role-based access control subsystem that conforms to the Core RBAC model as defined in the proposed NIST standard. Currently, CSAP is almost fully implemented and integrated in the WEBOCRAT system which – in the framework of e-government – provides services supporting direct participation of citizens in democratic processes in a secure way.

Keywords: Security architecture and services, adaptable security systems, software design, role-based access control (RBAC).

1. Introduction

E-government is the term reflecting the use of Information and Communication Technologies in public administration in an attempt to ease access to governmental information and services for citizens, businesses, and government agencies. Furthermore it is always a target to improve the quality of the services and to provide greater opportunities for participating in democratic institutions and processes.

It is essential for e-government and e-commerce that information and services are adequately protected and that the citizen's/customer's privacy is maintained. Sensitive government, business, and citizen data need to be fully secured when stored, processed or transmitted across institutional, regional, national, and possibly international networks. The problem of developing security policies and services in such environments becomes critical [Joshi et al., 2001]. Today developers are faced with building (web-based) systems to serve an unknown, large number of concurrent users with a virtually unpredictable usage patterns. As a result, these systems must deploy a security architecture providing security services which are easily adaptable to changing security requirements.

In this work, we present a generic security architecture and its design and Java implementation. The implementation is called *CSAP*. This has been done within the context of the EU-funded *Webocracy*[1] project, whose aim is the innovative use of state-of-the-art web technologies in order to support direct participation of citizens in democratic processes [Dridi et al., 2001; Paralic et al., 2002]. In this project a system called WEBOCRAT is modularly designed and implemented. The WEBOCRAT system is an e-government system focusing on functions like discussion management, publishing on the web, opinion polling, intelligent retrieval of information, reporting and limited public procurement.

CSAP is an integral module within the WEBOCRAT system and its system requirements are specified by our user partners (three local authorities). However, CSAP is designed in a generic way so that it can be used by other types of web-based applications as well. Currently, CSAP is almost fully implemented and integrated in the WEBOCRAT system to make it secure and trustworthy. The key features of CSAP are: (a) The CSAP architecture is service-oriented, providing just the right level of abstraction and encapsulation to fulfill user requirements. (b) The layered design of CSAP allows the application developer to exchange or enhance security mechanisms via a plug-in concept based on abstract classes and appropriate design patterns [Gamma et al., 1995]. As a consequence, CSAP becomes maintainable and adaptable. (c) The CSAP module is easily deployable via standard Java technology (e.g., JSP/Servlets). (d) Among other services, CSAP implements a role-based access control subsystem that conforms to the *Core RBAC* model as defined in the proposed NIST standard [Ferraiolo et al., 2001].

These features of CSAP allow system designers to implement manageable and extensible security platforms. Such platforms can be deployed

[1]The project's full title is "Web Technologies Supporting Direct Participation in Democratic Processes". The acronym "Webocracy" means "Democracy on the Web".

to experiment flexibly with emerging "pluggable" security services, as well as to build scalable and secure web-based applications. This claim will be justified in the remainder of this paper which is structured as follows. Section 2 presents a generic service-oriented security architecture, the key security services and the requirements concerning its realization. Section 3 presents the layered design, implementation and use scenarios of CSAP. The presented use scenarios, focusing on the user authentication and access control processes, demonstrate the integration of CSAP into web-based applications. Section 4 discusses related work and Section 5 concludes the paper and gives an outlook on future work.

2. Generic Security Architecture

Generally, the following basic security objectives have been determined for web-based application (for example, see [Dridi and Neumann, 2000]): confidentiality, integrity, availability, authenticity of data, non-repudiation, proof of identification. Figure 1 illustrates the service-

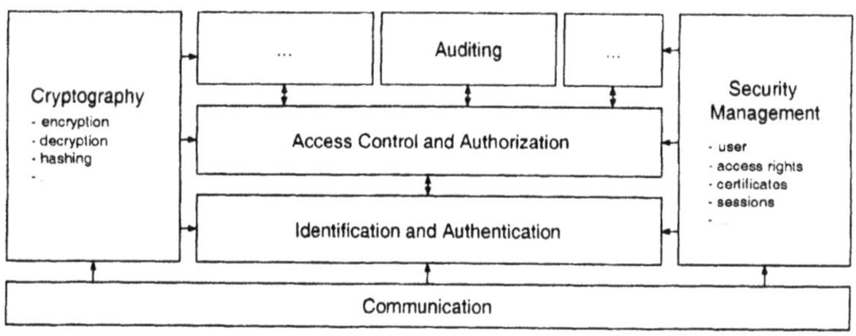

Figure 1. Generic, Service-Oriented Security Architecture. Necessary key security services to be provided and their interdependencies.

oriented security architecture we identified for achieving these security objectives. It is generic and service-oriented in the sense that it provides standard security services for a large array of applications.

2.1 Security Services

The key security services are: (1) *Identification and Authentication* is needed in order to get and verify the identity of the users attempting to access the system. (2) *Access Control and Authorization* is needed in order to verify what actions the users are able to perform and what information the users are able to access. (3) *Auditing* is needed to log all security relevant actions in order to make users accountable for their transactions. Audit trails are used to find patterns of abnormal use which are often a sign of (attempted) compromise. (4) *Security Management* is needed to manage (create, update, storage, etc.) global security information used within applications. Such management services are essential in order to customize and administrate security for applications.

All these services may require standard cryptographic services (such as encryption, decryption, hashing, etc.) and communication services. Such services are usually provided by existing software packages (e.g. Java 2 Platform) and therefore they do not need to be implemented again. The focus of our work is the *usable integration* of the key security services. As a consequence, several key realization requirements have

2.2 Realization Requirements

Several security systems implementing the generic security architecture discussed above have been built, but they all have their own restrictions that often do not correspond with the specific requirements of e-commerce and e-government applications (compare [Win et al., 2000], for a recent discussion of requirements [Lambrinoudakis et al., 2002]). Therefore, we need to implement an adaptable security system which can be deployed in different environments. In our case, the internationally dispersed project partners imposed different requirements on CSAP (the implementation of the generic security architecture) [Paralic and Sabol, 2001]. For example, the cooperating local authority from UK plans to use a PKI which will be developed to build secure forms of user authentication, including digital signatures. The Slovak local authorities want to use a user-password scheme. All the user partners have agreed to use RBAC. But we can imagine that, if CSAP will be used within another environment, different access control services (e.g. using access control lists) may be required. As a result the need to design a system where the security services are completely *changeable* is identified. The solution we provide is *"pluggable"* security services (to be explained below).

In order to realize *interoperation* with underlying backend systems it may be required that existing data (e.g. user data), which are relevant for the security system, have to be used regardless where it is stored. This way the decision about the storage system (files, databases, directory services) must not be hard-coded and has to remain *configurable*. Furthermore, security systems have to be *application independent* and *scalable*.

In order to achieve these requirements we deployed state-of-the-art software engineering techniques. We used appropriate design patterns [Gamma et al., 1995], UML (*Unified Modeling Language* [Booch et al., 1999]) specifications and the object-oriented language Java. Next we describe our CSAP module in more detail and show how those techniques have been used.

3. The CSAP Module

During the development of CSAP our overall goal was to develop a general, flexible and extensible module in which applications can selectively and dynamically access security services. As security requirements in large scale systems are changing constantly, CSAP should allow the developer to integrate new security services or to enhance existing ones. This should not require modification, recompilation, or even notification of client code unless there is a significant change in the specification. The term "client" refers to a user request or to any WEBOCRAT module which wants to use the CSAP services. For example, a CSAP client may be the Discussion module requesting user authentication or the Publishing module requesting access to a sensitive document.

3.1 Design

Figure 2 depicts the layered design of CSAP. It offers separation of concerns, because we can deal with parts of the source code in isolation, with minimal or no side effects in other layers. The design consists of three layers:

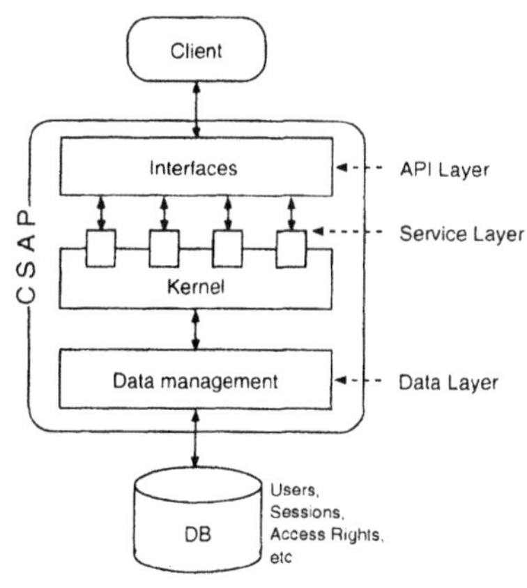

Figure 2. CSAP Layered Design.

The *API Layer* provides unified access to the security services implemented by CSAP. This layer separates the usage of a given security service from its implementation. Applications request security services only through the CSAP API.

The *Service Layer* is built upon the kernel of CSAP and provides the infrastructure for changing an existing security service or for plugging-in new services. All the security services discussed above are integrated in this layer. The clients use a service via the API layer. The data needed by the service are provided by the data layer.

The *Data Layer* provides the flexibility to access and manage user security information (e.g. access rights, passwords, session-ids, etc.). This layer defines a generic interface in order to access the security information independent of how they are stored. In CSAP the security information may be stored in XML files, in LDAP directory services [Wahl et al., 1997], or in SQL databases (e.g. MySQL). How these data is actually stored depends on the application and can be configured within CSAP. The data layer uses the security services implemented in CSAP to avoid non-authorized modifications of the security inforamtion. In other words the access to the CSAP databases is controlled with CSAP itself.

An example should illustrate the functionality of the layered CSAP design: Consider the RBAC service. On the API Layer, the authenticated user requests a certain role from the RBAC service at the Service Layer. Based on the role data accessed on the Data Layer the RBAC service presents the set of available roles. After the user has chosen a certain role, the RBAC service verifies, based on the permission data from the Data Layer, whether the user is allowed to activate the role. In case he is allowed the corresponding permissions are derived from the Data Layer.

By using such a layered design, we made CSAP adaptable so that we can easily exchange or enhance the security services according to changing requirements. The service and the data layer are configured by using an XML file. The structure of this configuration file is simple and will not be discussed here. In the next section we focus on the implementation issues of the authentication (user-password scheme) and access control services (Core RBAC).

3.2 Implementation Issues

The *API Layer* is implemented by means of Java interfaces and the design pattern "Facade". The concept of a Facade [Gamma et al., 1995] was chosen in order to hide the complexity of the CSAP security services from the clients by presenting a high-level, easy-to-use interface to them. This way a clear separation of implementation and usage aspects of the security services is achieved. The facade pattern forces the clients to use a single entry point to perform in an uniform way the calls to the security services. Due to space limitations this will not be described in this paper. The *Data Layer* is modeled by using the design pattern "Abstract

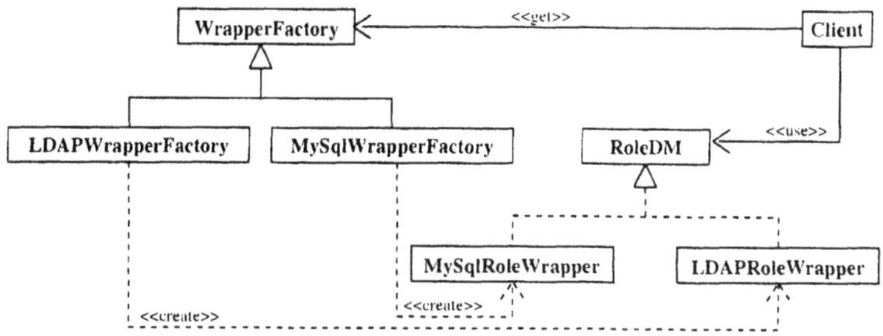

Figure 3. Abstract Factory within CSAP. A client is able to access data regardless of where it is stored. The WrapperFactory creates concrete wrapper implementing the access methods to the used database. The RoleDM is responsible for managing role data.

Factory" [Gamma et al., 1995]. The purpose of the Abstract Factory is to provide a generic interface for creating families of related wrapper objects without specifying their concrete classes, compare Figure 3.

Figure 4 depicts the core classes implementing the *Service Layer* and the kernel of CSAP. The abstract classes shown in this figure form the kernel of CSAP. We distinguish two kinds of classes: service classes and product classes. Service classes are responsible for creating products. A product is an instance of a class modeling low level objects within CSAP, like User, Object, Operation, Permission, Session and Role. The common service and product properties are defined in the classes `AbstractService` and `AbstractProduct` respectively. The CSAP clients mainly use the product classes User and Session. The remaining product classes are used for administrating the Core RBAC system. Basically, a CSAP client gets products from the corresponding service classes and uses the interfaces the products implement. The user/password service and the Core RBAC service are implemented within the two service classes `PasswordService` and `RBACService` respectively. The password service mainly implements a `login` method and creates an authenticated user object which can be used, for example, by the RBAC service. The RBAC service of CSAP implements a `checkAccess` method which determines whether an access is allowed or denied. In addition, it implements all the necessary methods as proposed by NIST to administer the RBAC system. This functionality is used for a servlet-based implementation of the CSAP administration console, which in itself is a GUI to administer RBAC.

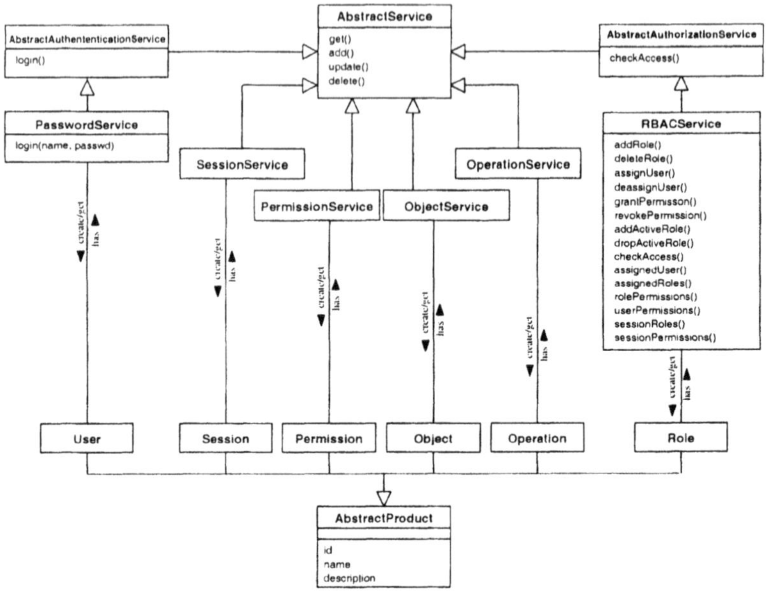

Figure 4. CSAP Service and Product Classes. New security services can be implmented by subclassing the corresponding absract classes.

CSAP can be tailored to different situations in which other security services may be needed. For example, in order to implement a certificate-based authentication service, a new service class (e.g. `CertService`) has to be defined as a subclass of the class `AbstractAuthenticationService`. This new service class could be used alternatively to the `PasswordService`. Both classes `AbstractAuthenticationService` and `AbstractAuthorizationService` can be used to define new subclasses implementing alternative authentication and access control mechanisms respectively.

3.3 Use Scenario

In this section, we describe how to use the CSAP module focusing on authentication and access control. Assume a situation in which CSAP is configured to use both the `PasswordService` and the `RBACService`. The authentication process consists of the following steps:

- *Get plugged services:* A request starts with a client asking the CSAP system which kind of authentication and access control services are available. In this example the client gets a reference to the `PasswordService` and `RBACService`.

- *Login:* The `PasswordService` implements a `login` method which accepts a username/password as parameters. If the authentication process is successful a user object will be created.

- *Select roles:* Due to the RBAC policy at least one role has to be selected as active role. The `RBACService` and the `RoleDM` (see Figure 3) will determine the set of the roles assigned to the user. The active role specifies the set of permissions a user may posses.

- *Create session:* As a result of the client request, a session object will be created in order to store the user object and the activated role for further use. After a session is established the session data are stored by the `SessionDM`. Sessions usually have a limited life time, after this time a session becomes invalid and will be deleted automatically by the `SessionDM`.

Before an access can be checked the user must be correctly authenticated and a valid session object must exist. In the example shown in Figure 5 we assume that the above sequence has been performed and that the client holds a valid session-id. The access control process is determined as follows:

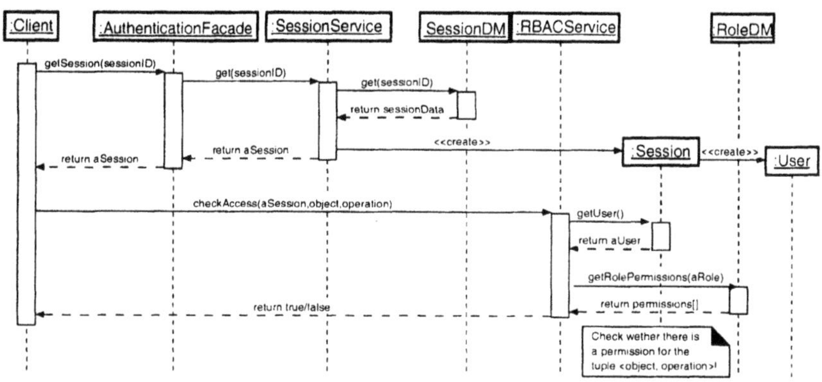

Figure 5. Sequence Diagram - Role-based Access Control.

- *Use Session:* The client gets the session object from the `Session-Service` using the assigned session-id. If the session is no longer valid, the user has to be asked by the client to re-authenticate and thereby to establish a new valid session.

- *Check Access:* The method `checkAccess` accepts three arguments: a session-id, operation name and object name. The user object that is stored within the session object is used by the `RBACService` in order to get the user's active role within this session. The user's permissions are determined by retrieving all the permissions assigned to the active role. Finally, the `RBACService` checks whether there is a permission for the tuple `<object,operation>`. In the positive case, the access will be granted otherwise denied.

4. Related Work

In this section we discuss some related work which have influenced the design and implementation of the CSAP module.

In [Park et al., 2001], Sandhu et al. present several implementation approaches for role-based access control. For this purpose well-known technologies with smart extensions such as cookies, X.509 certificates, SSL, and LDAP, providing compatibility with current Web technologies, have been used. For example, X.509 certificates have been extended in order to include the roles assigned to a particular user. In contrast to the CSAP approach their work is mainly restricted to a singular access control service only and not embedded into a large scale application.

Gutzmann [Gutzmann, 2001] introduces a security service architecture for HTTP-based environments. He describes an approach that uses RBAC and Web session management to prevent network security breaches. He uses LDAP and a ticket-based management service to realize an RBAC service. His work is focusing on session management, with CSAP we take a broader approach.

The Java Authentication and Authorization Service (JAAS) [Lai et al., 1999] augments JDK with support to authenticate the principal who runs the code and to enforce new access controls on the authenticated principal. It provides a flexible control of downloaded executable content and it has been extended with roles based on Java Servlets in [Giuri, 1999]. Although related to our work, their focus is mainly on mobile code and mobile agent authorization. Moreover, their focus was on extending the Java functionality while CSAP is building on the existing standard.

The Pluggable Authentication Modules (PAMs) [Samar and Lai, 1996] provide a well structured architecture for the integration of multiple authentication mechanisms. By using PAM, users who need access to certain network resources or who log in from outside the firewall may utilize strong authentication mechanisms. The main advantage of PAM is that administrators are able to select one or multiple authentication technologies without modifying applications or utilities. This is similar to our approach, however, CSAP is not realized at the operating system level nor does it depend on certain operating systems.

5. Conclusion

We have presented the architecture of CSAP, an autonomous software module offering programming interfaces to core security services such as authentication, access control, auditing, and security management. It is currently developed as part of the ongoing EU-funded Webocracy project which – in the framework of e-government – provides services supporting direct participation of citizens in democratic processes in a secure way.

The key design objective adaptability has resulted in a layered design including an Application Programming Interface Layer, a Service Layer and a Data Layer. The *Application Programming Interface* Layer provides unified access to the security services. At the *Service Layer*, different security mechanisms can be changed by using an easy-to-use plug-in technique. The *Data Layer* provides the flexibility to access and manage user security information independent of the storage platform. The current implementation of CSAP provides a password service subsystem and a role-based access control subsystem that conforms to the *Core RBAC* model as defined in the proposed NIST standard. CSAP is expected to provide a viable framework for addressing a wide range of security requirements for large scale applications like WEBOCRAT.

CSAP is available as a platform for implementing or extending existing security services, for experimenting with different security service alternatives, and for building secure and manageable large scale web-application. Our experience has shown that the chosen software design of CSAP is suitable for server-side integration.

In future work, the implementation will be extended to include alternative plug-in security services, like certificate-based authentication and access control. A graphical (web-based) user interface to the RBAC service within CSAP is currently under development. In addition we will improve the configuration functionality of CSAP to manage several applications with different storage requirements. Finally, after CSAP will have been tested in real settings by the user partners, some optimisations (e.g. performance) will be considered.

Acknowledgments

We would like to thank Wolfram Conen and our project partners for helpful comments and stimulating discussions. This work is done within the Webocracy Project which is supported by European Commission DG INFSO under the IST programme, contract No. IST-1999-20364.

References

Booch, G., Rumbaugh, J., and Jacobson, I. (1999). *The Unified Modeling Language Reference Manual.* Addison Wesley.

Dridi, F. and Neumann, G. (2000). Managing security in the World Wide Web: Architecture, services, and techniques. In Janczewski, L., editor, *Internet and Intranet Security Management: Risks and Solutions*, pages 106–139. Hershey PA: Idea Group Publishing.

Dridi, F., Pernul, G., and Sabol, T. (2001). The Webocracy project: Overview and security aspects. In Schnurr, H.-P., S. Stabb, R. Studer, G. S., and Sure, Y., editors, *Professionelles Wissensmanagement: Erfahrungen und Visionen*, pages 401–408, Aachen, Germany. Shaker Verlag.

Ferraiolo, D., Sandhu, R., Gavrila, S., Kuhn, D., and Chandramouli, R. (2001). Proposed NIST standard for role-based access control. *ACM Transactions on Information and Systems Security*, 4(3):224–274.

Gamma, E., Helm, R., Johnson, R., and Vlissides, J. (1995). *Design Patterns: Elements of Reusable Object-Oriented Software.* Addison-Wesley.

Giuri, L. (1999). Role-based access control on the web using java. In *Proceedings of the 4th ACM workshop on Role-based access control*, pages 11–18, Fairfax, Virginia.

Gutzmann, K. (2001). Access control and session management in the http environment. *IEEE Internet Computing*, 5(1):26–35.

Joshi, J., Ghafoor, A., Aref, W., and Spafford, E. (2001). Digital government security infrastructure design challenges. *Computer*, 34(2).

Lai, C., Gong, L., Koved, L., Nadlin, A., and Schemers, R. (1999). User authentication und authorization in the java platform. In *Proceedings of the 15th Annual Computer Security Application Conference*, pages 285–290, Phoenix, Arizona.

Lambrinoudakis, C., Gritzalis, S., Dridi, F., and Pernul, G. (2002). Security requirements for e-government services: A methodological approach for developing a common PKI- based security policy. *Comupter Communications, Special Issue on PKI.*

Paralic, J. and Sabol, T. (2001). Implementation of e-government using knowledge-based system. In *Proc. of the 2nd Int. Workshop on Electronic Government within DEXA 2001*, pages 364–368, Munich, Germany.

Paralic, J., Sabol, T., and Mach, M. (2002). A system to support e-democracy. In *Proc. of the 1st eGovernment Conference within DEXA2002*, pages 288–291, Aix-en-Provence, France.

Park, J., Sandhu, R., and Ahn, G. (2001). Role-based access control on the web. *ACM Transactions on Information and Systems Security*, 4(1).

Samar, V. and Lai, C. (1996). Making login services independent of authentication technologies. In *Proceedings of the 3rd ACM Conference on Computer Communications and Security.*

Wahl, M., Howes, T., and Kille, S. (1997). Lightweight directory access protocol (v3). *RFC 2251, Standards Track.*

Win, B. D., den Bergh, J. V., Matthijs, F., Decker, B. D., and Joosen, W. (2000). A security architecture for electronic commerce applications. In *IFIP TC11 16th Annual Working Conference on Information Security: Information Security for Global Information Infrastructures*, pages 491–500, Beijing, China.

PERCEPTIONS OF SECURITY CONTRIBUTING TO THE IMPLEMENTATION OF SECURE IS

Theodore TRYFONAS and Evangelos KIOUNTOUZIS
Dept. of Informatics, Athens University of Economics and Business
76 Patission Street, GR-10434, Athens, GREECE
{tryfonas, eak}@aueb.gr

Key words: Information systems implementation, IS security integration, Security perceptions, Metaphors.

Abstract: Contemporary information systems (IS) development within organisations involves multiple interconnected systems, a variety of development practices and also outsources responsibilities to third parties. It hence introduces new threats, new vulnerabilities and in consequence new security problems for the IS. In this paper we propose a theoretical framework to facilitate the implementation of secure IS into this contemporary, particularly complex, organisational environment. We start our study by examining organisational and systems development issues, such as the involved stakeholders and their security requirements. We then relate this theory to practice by identifying all those concepts that materialise the stakeholders' security understanding to specific security objectives and the tools in which they are manifested. Finally, we inspect various published cases in order to examine the use of these tools within organisations, so as to realise our theoretical design and prescribe its further use.

1. INTRODUCTION

The information systems (IS) literature has little so far to present in terms of frameworks, methodologies or techniques that consistently integrate

The authors would like to thank the Hellenic Ministry of Development for its kind support in this research work, through the research programme YPER97.

security with IS development (ISD). Researches however have been arguing that this is the most appropriate way of introducing security in the complex context of an IS for some time now (e.g. Baskerville, 1993). It seems that there exist significant barriers for such a task, as there are factors that lead practitioners first to implement a system and then to secure it. This can happen because during its development phase a system is not fully known in terms of its final attributes, hence the difficulty in protecting it. In addition, prior to its use a system's adding value might not be completely clear to its stakeholders; therefore valuation of its assets might not be accurate.

Most of the researchers who approach the problem propose ways of incorporating security within particular development steps, e.g. requirements collection, data modelling etc. (Siponen, 2001). Such approaches however are usually proprietary for specific development methodologies, techniques or tools. This is a problem though, as practitioners tend to customise or mix a wide range of ISD methodologies, techniques and tools, of the plethora being offered today (Fitzgerald, 1998).

Thus, the existing approaches for *embedded* IS security restrict the ability of the developers to use the development practices they prefer. This is a significant obstacle in the design of a methodological construct to achieve security integration with development. Siponen and Baskerville (2001) try to resolve this conflict by moving their proposed theoretical construct in the level of meta-methodology. They describe foundational concepts that could be embedded in any development methodology and facilitate the security design within the system design process. Their approach implies that the agent of the IS security enrichment is the developer, responsible for the design and the implementation of the system. It is possible however to create a theoretical construct to guide, in a similar manner, the security practitioner involved in the process (consultant, risk analyst etc.).

In this paper we try to produce a framework to assist the security expert in the selection of the appropriate security practices and tools, given an organisational context and a case of a system under development. In section two we present our research approach. Section three introduces theoretical aspects important for IS security (such as the stakeholders, the development approaches etc.) and also extends our reasoning based on an analysis of empirical data. Section four presents our proposed framework, whilst section five concludes with a summarising discussion.

2. RESEARCH APPROACH

IS researchers have pinpointed many important factors facilitating the development of secure systems. Those factors are a mixture of technical, social and managerial concerns, all important for building systems that can meet the security expectations of the involved parties. As it largely addresses 'soft' factors apart from the technicalities, the research approach should be capable of interacting between the two. For such an inquiry it is rather appropriate to use empirical observation and interpretive research (Walsham, 1995).

Following the research principles of analysis of empirical data and of the interpretive approach we develop a theoretical construct to facilitate the integration of security practices and tools to IS implementation. We inspect secondary empirical data, as it appears in published case studies concerned with IS securing projects or computer abuse cases. We then employ *stakeholder analysis*, IS theory, with regard to *ISD approaches* and the *tools to secure* information systems, and finally *metaphors*, as theoretical constructs in order to consolidate our analysis findings. Therefore we initially observe the related theory elements emerging through the empirical data and eventually we try to theorise those findings that can be generalised.

3. REFLECTIONS ON THEORY AND PRACTICE

3.1 Theoretical contextualisation of systems security

Several researchers have employed metaphors as mental models in order to understand the organisation and the phenomena within it (Morgan, 1997). There is a variation of the used ones, but they could all be summarised in three major categories: those describing the organisation as a (mindless) machine, those that describe it as an (individually minded) organism or a part of it, and those that describe it as a social (collectively minded) system.

It is interesting to note that the implicit adoption of any of such an understanding leads the analysts to focus on qualities that emerge from it (Walsham, 1991). This holds true for the security experts as well; in the machine analogy for example, as the workforce, material and informational resources are treated as interchangeable parts, it is important for the practitioner to locate, evaluate and assure those elements, in other words the organisational *assets*.

In a similar manner, the living analogy emphasises on the system's *processes*, because it is difficult to locate discrete assets due to the systems' emergence property (for example in an organism a 'leg' is not separable nor interchangeable as such, thus it is difficult to be treated as a concrete element, but 'health' can be treated as such). We believe that this observation is crucial for the subject matter of our study as such concepts imply what is important for the organisation, hence what needs protection.

Tryfonas and Kiountouzis (2002) use this as a starting point to draw comments on a theoretical discussion about important factors affecting the integration of systems development with systems security. The major factors they identified were:

- The expert's perception of the organisation.
- The stakeholders involved plus their expectations about the outcomes of the securing venture.
- The concept(s) that mediate those expectations and communicate them to the experts.

We think that this last issue is particularly important. Further illustration of the way those concepts mediate the communication between organisational stakeholders and security experts and become objects of discourse is therefore necessary.

3.2 Organisational constructs facilitating an IS view on the practice of systems security

The stakeholders' implicit understanding of IS security is realised as explicit security requirements through supportive concepts that mediate the communication between them and the security experts. Those elements embody the security objectives and become objects of discourse between the stakeholders and the experts. The most popular of them seem to be the concepts of the *asset*, the *process* and the *stake* of an individual or a group of people. We claim here that each such concept can be also a driver for the security methods and tools to be used.

3.2.1 Emerging approaches

As organisations operate in an uncontrolled environment, elements that, for whatever reason, could deviate from their expected state become a major issue of concern. Such a potential deviation can be perceived through the concept of accidental or deliberate *risk*, interpreted as the uncertainty that organisational elements might get exposed to, usually described in quantified and measurable terms.

In the following paragraphs we present a rudimentary classification of security approaches based on the organisational element of concern they focus on and discuss them in further detail.

Asset-based approach

As information adds value through its processing to the organisation, it is considered to be an organisational *asset*. It lives in the form of data that are accessed through information technology (IT) facilities. Potential threats against those data and facilities can be identified and their impact can be 'calculated' in terms of cost. This leads to the association between *assets*, *threats* and *impacts*. This is an approach widely employed in the field of IS security, influenced by a resource-based view of the organisation (e.g. Finne, 1998; Baskerville, 1993 etc.). An example of a risk analysis (RA) method utilising the concept of the asset, giving particular emphasis in asset identification and valuation, is the CCTA Risk Analysis and Management Method (CRAMM).

Process-based approach

Various researchers have signified the importance of process-modelling for the understanding of the organisation. For security scholars, a process model facilitates audit and control because it makes it easier to focus on points that could destabilise the system due to accidental or deliberate incidents. Researchers observed that a number of security issues arise from mistakes, omissions or failures within the systems development process (e.g. Wood & Snow, 1995; Anderson, 1993). The result is a defected product/system that its defects could be abused, so as to compromise an information system. Other researchers proposed ways of inspecting and evaluating process security (Eloff & von Solms, 2000) as a means to increase the assurance of a system.

Stake-driven approaches

Stake-driven approaches emerge in order to cope with the 'softer' factors (ethics, legislation, training, familiarization, user satisfaction etc.) involving individuals or groups of individuals that affect or are affected by the system.

We can identify two different streams:

- The *stakeholder* approach, where the involved individuals and their interactions with the system are identified and studied, for example including users' security responsibilities in job descriptions, concerns for human involvement etc. (e.g. Backhouse & Dhillon, 1996). *And*
- The *systemic* approach, where the involved parties are described in terms of groups, institutions or other organisational formations ('systems') that socio-politically interact (e.g. Hitchings, 1995b).

Ideally, the identified stakeholders shall pinpoint themselves the organisational assets and processes and the risks against them. Such systemic and largely participatory approaches need however to be guided by skilled analysts that can facilitate the entire process. In addition, the involved users of the IS must have a significant level of awareness, motivation and willingness to partake in this venture, which prerequisites a substantial effort in training and related preparation.

Other approaches

A number of other approaches are currently under research, as all previous approaches alone cannot ensure the secure state of a system under inspection. Such approaches introduce new organisational concepts that can be exploited and produce tools for embedding security into a system. There is for example the concept of the 'transaction' that could be utilised (Smith & Eloff, 2001). Rules can be defined per identified type of transaction and monitored in any transaction instance.

Another concept is that of the 'trust' between components (e.g. Chadwick & Basden, 2001 etc.). When properly quantified, it could be assigned as an attribute to different interoperable components and regulate their interaction. However the quantification of trust is still an obstacle for this approach, as it is very difficult to design globally accepted formal trust models.

As such approaches are currently under research, we shall not include those concepts (transaction, trust etc.) in our framework, taking into consideration only the approaches that have been rigidly exploited throughout literature and practice.

3.2.2 Tools in use

In the following Table 1 we have summarised the discussion on the theoretical constructs that introduce security in the IS and their associated tools.

Table 1: Theoretical constructs used to introduce security to the IS.

	Principal construct	*Approach*	*Example practices&tools*	*Example references*
Risk against	Asset	Asset-based	RA, baseline controls, best practices	Baskerville, 1993; Finne, 1998
	Process	Process-based	Assurance, standards, audit, contracts, insurance, business continuity	Eloff & von Solms, 2000; Wood & Snow, 1995; Anderson, 1993
	Stake of the - - Individual	Stake-driven Stakeholders	Training, security responsibilities in job descriptions, chains of command, job satisfaction	Backhouse & Dhillon, 1996
	- Group	Systemic	General awareness, ethics, legal/regulatory frameworks	Hitchings, 1995b
	Trust, Transaction etc.	Other (under research)	Digital certificates, fuzzy logic	Chadwick & Basden, 2001; Smith & Eloff, 2001

The tools used to secure a system come to a variety of platforms and applications and could assist methods and techniques used anywhere within the development lifecycle. Hence it seems that concepts employed to introduce IS security to the organisation, can imply suitable practices to be used to secure its IS. As we discussed previously, most of them depend on an organisational concept that introduces the idea of security within the organisation. RA methods and assisting tools, IT security standards, access control mechanisms, data encryption facilities, biometrics etc. are all based on concepts such as assets, processes, responsibilities etc.

3.3 Reflections on practice: Analysis of published cases

In Table 2 we present the selected cases from the literature that we will investigate in order to extract feedback and facilitate our theoretical design. The sample we use is profiled in terms of the organisational context, the IS/IT infrastructure and its development approach, the study's objective, the security tool used and the formal project outcomes. The inspected cases concern both private and public sector organisations of a variant size.

In Table 3 we present further outcomes of our data analysis, discussing issues that are not directly quoted from the actual articles' text, but rather derived against the theoretical parameters we have discussed elsewhere in this paper. As the lengthy, detailed per-case analysis is beyond the objective of this research paper, we shall only discuss in this section summarising points that we think are important.

Our primary observation is that the empirical data verify the constructs we have identified as mediating the introduction of IS security into the organisational environment. Risks, assets, processes, stakes, are all used to highlight security problems and design solutions in each case.

The interesting outcome here is the association of those with the authors' (explicitly or implicitly) adopted organisational perception. For example *risks* and *assets* are usually used when the organisational perception is mechanistic. On the other hand *assets* and *processes* are concepts emerging through the biological metaphor, whereas *processes* and their involved *stakeholders*, or *systems* in general, emerge when the environment is explored through societal metaphorical mechanisms.

The empirical data also highlight the fact we draw in Table 1, that the 'security-facilitating' concept determines the nature of the securing method/tool to be used for the project. For example, the use of RA presupposes an emphasis given on the data viewed as organisational assets, or that auditing approaches requires particular understanding of the business processes.

Table 2: A profile of the empirical data investigated.

Case	*Organisational context*	*Study's objective*	*IS/IT infrastructure & development*	*Security tool used*	*Project outcome*
Frosdick & Odell, 1996	England and Wales Police	To describe Police's IS-related risk management standard in England and Wales	Proprietary, loosely coupled	Risk analysis & management	National Policy for IS/IT risk management
Dhillon & Moores, 2001	Stock exchange (US)	To draw theoretical arguments on why the IS-related risk can come from 'inside'	Product-based or component-based, centralised	Law enforcement	n/a
Liechtenstein, 1996	Travel (AU)	To draw theoretical arguments on the selection of a risk assessment method	Component-based, centralised	Baseline protection	Baseline controls implementation
Spurling, 1995	Heavy industry (AU)	To propose guidelines for security awareness	Product-based, centralised	Security awareness	Organisational change
Muir, 1997	Education & research – Library (US)	To propose actions against student hackers	Component-based, centralised	Legal actions, code of student conduct	Organisational change
Spinellis *et al.*, 1999	Small business/Home-Office (GR)	To pinpoint the surprisingly high-risk exposure of the home-office environment and propose a best practice	Component-based, centralised	Risk analysis	Baseline controls recommendations

Table 3: Further data analysis.

Case	*Driver(s) for security requirements*	*Metaphors reflecting Authors' organisational perception*	*Security seems to be introduced through*	*Non-tangible outcome(s)*
Frosdick & Odell, 1996	Policing job requirements	Shifts from mechanistic to societal	Risk	n/a
Dhillon & Moores, 2001	Inefficiency of the 'traditional' models to explain breaks from 'within'	Societal	Process	Organisational awareness
Liechtenstein, 1996	Criticality of the informational assets	Biological	Asset	n/a
Spurling, 1995	Organisational awareness	Biological	Process	Cultural change
Muir, 1997	Organisational awareness	Societal	Stake of the individual/Stakes of interrelated groups	Organisational change
Spinellis *et al.*, 1999	The 'real' level of risk	Biological	Process	Increasing awareness

4. A FRAMEWORK FOR THE INTERPRETATION OF SECURITY UNDERSTANDING

In the following paragraphs, we shall investigate how a consolidation of the theoretical factors discussed, such as the development approach, security requirements expressed by the involved stakeholders, the theoretical constructs mediating their realisation etc., can facilitate the implementation of secure systems. To achieve such a consolidation, we first grouped all inspected cases as per their corresponding understanding of organisation. Then we grounded each group on the analysis data, partly presented in Table 2 and Table 3. The result, as we see it in Table 4, is that specific patterns emerge, representing the basic interpretations of IS security perceptions. The latter can be of key importance for the security expert.

We argue that the organisational context dictates the security approach that is mostly appropriate. For example, it seems that in case the target organisation is perceived mechanistically and the information system is expected to retain certain behaviour and nature at any cost whatever the circumstances, formal, systematic tools are primarily suitable. On the other hand, systems that deal with a changing environment and must adapt to it, tend towards a mixture of systematic and systemic security approaches. Last but not least, systems characterised by their strong social character seem to tend to purely systemic approaches.

The perceptions of security that have emerged through our theory drawing and the analysis of empirical data are distinguished amongst the following (we have attributed a 'suitable' code title to each emerged category):

- **"Fortress security"**, applicable whenever the organisational approach is mechanistic, the key concept is the risk against the system's valuable assets and the IS is usually built from scratch. Very common amongst governmental infrastructure systems, the military, the banking sector etc.
- **"Shelter security"**, applicable when the organisational approach is mostly biological, the key concept is usually the risk against the system itself and/or the adding-value process or service (and its continuity) and the IS is usually built by combining multiple independent applications or by deploying enterprise-wide customisable cores. Representative for service provision-oriented civil authorities and private firms.
- **"Web security"**, applicable for small home-office environments or research institutes, where the organisational approach is mostly societal, the key concept is the interacting uncontrollable elements or groups of elements and the IS are usually a combination of multiple components and services.

We think of the previous categories as of not being exclusively 'normative'. Concepts can span rows, especially those that neighbour.

However, practice dictates that many times security failures occur because of a misunderstanding of the contextual security requirements, expressed through un-appropriate 'images' for the case, which leads to the adoption of un-appropriate security approaches and eventually results in the deployment of controls that are not suitable for this environment.

Table 4: Basic interpretations of security understanding.

Organisational view	*Development approach*	*Security focuses on*	*Suitable security practises*	*Metaphor in use*	*Example cases*
Mechanistic	Primarily **custom**	Asset / Process	• Risk analysis • Security requirements analysis • Codes of practice, best practices	**Fortress** 	Frosdick & Odell, 1996
Biological	Primarily **configuration** or component-based **(systems integration)**	Process / the organisation as a whole	• Embedded security-features exploitation • Audit • Process assurance • Standard compliance • Contractual assurance • Insurance	**Shelter** 	Dhillon & Moores, 2001 Liechtenstein, 1996, Spurling, 1995
Societal	Primarily component-based **(multi-application)**	Stakeholder / System	• Responsibilities definitions in job descriptions • Education • Training • Ethics • Legal framework	**Web** 	Spinellis *et al.*, 1999, Muir, 1997

5. CONCLUSIONS

There are currently very few disciplined approaches to integrate security with systems implementation, mainly because there seems to be a lack of understanding that it is a problem to be faced from a problem-solving perspective and not as a traditional IT security problem (Anderson, 1993; Hitchings, 1995a; Yngström, 1996).

It is not easy for an implementer or a user to have such an expert knowledge of the particulars of the available security practices/tools, so as to choose the most appropriate ones for a system under development. Therefore, there is a need for a mechanism to indicate the most appropriate security practices and tools per case. The framework we present in this paper provides reasoning to investigate the suitability of security tools within a given organisational environment and a development practice in mind.

Security within IS comes through discourse and final agreement on what is important for the system, within which operations, what risks are there for the system and for its stakeholders. Thus, we believe that our approach is contributory to a new, more 'natural' view of IS security within organisations. Such a view is required so as to reveal the real social and organisational related character of IS security that nowadays seems to be locked behind the technicalities of the field.

We adopted the use of metaphors in order to stimulate the reader to re-examine assumptions underlying security, by imagining different combinations of organisational and development variables. IS security can be perceived in terms of required system states and fall under imagery descriptions. Each one of those descriptions signifies a different area of applicability and is based on different key-concepts, implying a different security approach and hence tools that are suitable for it.

Such use of metaphors is particularly recommended for interpretive-based IS intensive research (Walsham, 1991). However, we know that such an approach undergoes inefficiencies, as metaphor-based analogies can provide mind-trapping 'explanations of the world' (Boland, 1989). Used though as an analytical tool and a rough guide, we believe that they can significantly contribute to the implementation of secure information systems.

6. REFERENCES

Anderson, R.J. (1993), "Why cryptosystems fail", Communications of the ACM, Vol. 37, No 11, pp. 32-44.

Backhouse, J. and Dhillon, G. (1996), "Structures of responsibilities and security of information systems", European Journal of Information Systems, Vol. 5, No 1, pp. 2-10.

Baskerville, R. (1993), "Information Systems Security Design Methods: Implications for Information Systems Development", ACM Computing Surveys, Vol. 25, No. 4, pp. 375-414.

Boland, R.J. (1989), "Metaphorical traps in developing information systems for human progress", in Klein, H.K. and Kumar, K. (Eds.), Systems Development for Human Progress, Elsevier Science Publishers, pp.277-290.

Chadwick, D.W. and Basden, A. (2001), "Evaluating Trust in a Public Key Certification Authority", Computers & Security, Vol. 20, No 7, pp. 592-611.

Dhillon, G. and Moores, S. (2001), "Computer crimes: theorizing about the enemy within", Computers & Security, Vol. 20, No 8, pp. 715-723.

Eloff, M., and Von Solms, B. (2000), "Information Security: Process Evaluation and Product Evaluation", in Qing, S. and Eloff, J. (Eds.), Information Security for Global Information Infrastructures, Kluwer Academic Publishers, pp. 11-19.

Finne, T. (1998), "A conceptual framework for information security management", Computers & Security, Vol 17, pp. 303-307.

Fitzgerald, B. (1998), "An empirical investigation into the adoption of systems development methodologies", Information & Management, Vol. 34, pp. 317-328.

Frosdick, S. and Odell, A. (1996), "Practical management of programme risk: the case of the National Strategy for Police Information Systems for England and Wales", Information Management & Computer Security, Vol. 4, No 5, pp. 24-33.

Hitchings, J. (1995a), "Deficiencies of the traditional approach to information security and the requirements for a new methodology", Computers & Security, Vol. 14, pp. 377-83.

Hitchings, J. (1995b), "Achieving an Integrated Design: The Way Forward for Information Security", in Eloff, J. and von Solms, S. (Eds.), Information Security – the next decade, Chapman & Hall, pp. 369-383.

Liechtenstein, S. (1996), "Factors in the selection of a risk assessment method", Information Management & Computer Security, Vol. 4, No 4, pp. 20-25.

Morgan, G. (1997), Images of Organization, 2nd Ed., SAGE Publications, California.

Muir, S. (1997), "After the break-in occurs: How to handle the student hacker", Library High Tech, Vol. 15, No 1&2, pp. 92-95.

Siponen, M. (2001), "An Analysis of the Recent IS Security Development Approaches: Descriptive and Prescriptive Implications", in Dhillon, G. (Ed.), Information Security Management: Global Challenges in the New Millennium, Idea Group Publishing, pp. 101-124.

Siponen, M. and Baskerville, R. (2001), "A New Paradigm for Adding Security Into IS Development Methods", in Eloff, J.H.P. et al. (Eds.), Advances in Information Security Management & Small Systems Security, Kluwer Academic Publishers.

Smith, E. and Eloff, J.H.P. (2001), "Transaction Based Risk Analysis – Using Cognitive Fuzzy Techniques", in Eloff, J.H.P. et al. (Eds.), Advances in Information Security Management & Small Systems Security, Kluwer Academic Publishers.

Spinellis, D., Kokolakis, S. and Gritzalis, S. (1999), "Security requirements, risks, and recommendations for small enterprise and home-office environments", Information Management & Computer Security, Vol. 7, No 3, pp.121-128.

Spurling, P. (1995), "Promoting security awareness and commitment", Information Management & Computer Security, Vol. 3, No 2, pp. 20-26.

Tryfonas, T. and Kiountouzis, E. (2002), "IS security and the IS development project: Towards a framework for their integration", in Ghonaimy, M. et al. (Eds.), Security in the Information Society: Visions and Perspectives, Kluwer Academic Publishers, pp. 347-356.

Walsham, G. (1991), "Organisational metaphors and information systems research", European Journal of Information Systems, Vol. 1, No. 2, pp. 83-94.

Walsham, G. (1995), "Interpretive case studies in IS research: nature and method", European Journal of Information Systems, Vol. 4, pp. 74-81.

Wood, C.C. and Snow, K. (1995), "ISO 9000 and Information Security", Computers & Security, Vol. 14, pp. 287-288.

Yngström, L. (1996), "A holistic approach to IT security", in Eloff, J. and von Solms, S. (Eds.), Information Security – The Next Decade, Chapman & Hall, London.

NEW DIRECTIONS ON IS SECURITY METHODS

The process view

MIKKO T. SIPONEN

University of Oulu, Department of Information Processing Science, Linnanmaa, P.O.BOX 3000, FIN-90014 Oulu university, FINLAND. E-mail:Mikko.T.Siponen@oulu.fi

Abstract: Information systems (IS) security (ISS) methods can be broken down into process (what steps developers should take) to develop IS and modeling notation (how to model reality). Of these, modeling notation has attracted a lot of attention. Whereas process has been largely ignored. As a step towards remedying the situation, this paper first analyzes the limits of the processes of the existing ISS approaches in the light of the analytical framework. Second, the implications of the results for research are suggested.

Key words: ISS methods

1. INTRODUCTION

Several ISS methods have been nominated (Dhillon & Backhouse, 2001; Siponen, 2002). In recent years, increasing interest has been shown in making sense, comparing and exploring the underlying theoretical assumptions of these different ISS methods (Baskerville, 1993; Dhillon & Backhouse, 2001). These studies have improved our understanding of different ISS methods and their limits, and have suggested important avenues for future research on ISS.

Following Hirschheim and Klein (1992), IS development methods can be broken down into *process* (how, and in which order, IS development is carried out) and *modeling notation* (how things are presented). The waterfall model (Royce, 1970), suggesting a step-by-step process from requirement analysis to testing and maintenance, is an example of process. Object-oriented notations, such as UML (Fowler & Scott, 1999), are examples of modeling notation.

Malouin and Landry (1983) initiated the debate on nature of process in the area of IS development methods by showing that practitioners do not apply IS methods as prescribed by the method developers. This idea that there cannot be a universal "fit-one-fit all" method, but that IS methods need to be modified to suit different contexts, was later deployed by the method engineering (Brinkkember, 1996; Kumar & Welke, 1992) and amethodological community (e.g., Truex *et al.*, 2000).

However, although practitioners commonly modify IS methods in practice (Truex *et al.*, 2000), it is odd that considerations regarding the applicability and modifiability of processes of ISS methods have not entered the ISS area. The existing analyses on ISS methods (e.g., Baskerville, 1993; Dhillon & Backhouse, 2001) do not address this dimension. The aim of this study is to generate discussion on this issue in the area of ISS methods. To do this, we need first to analyze the assumptions underlying the process of the alternative ISS methods. Second, on the basis of this analysis, we propose requirements for future ISS methods.

The rest of the paper is organized as follows. In the second section, the theoretical framework is presented. In the third section, the alternative assumptions are analyzed. The fourth section discusses the results and implications of the study. Finally, the key results of this study are summarized in the fifth section.

2. AN OVERVIEW OF THE EXISTING ISS METHODS, AND ANALYTICAL FRAMEWORK

An overview of the existing ISS paradigms and approaches. Scholars have found alternative ISS paradigms, and their respective approaches (Baskerville, 1993; Dhillon & Backhouse, 2001; Siponen, 2001, 2002), including: *checklists*, *management standards*, *maturity criteria*, risk management, *self-reflected security mgt. cookbooks*, *information modeling approaches*, *responsibility approaches*, *business process*, *the security-modified IS development approaches* and *viable Information Systems*. These approaches are briefly described next; for details see (Siponen, 2002).

Checklists (e.g., AFIPS, 1979; Wood *et al.*, 1987) list the ideal means of protection found by practitioners, from which the developers tick off those relevant for their organizations. *Management standards* (BS7799, 1993; GASSP, 1999; Sanders *et al.*, 1996) in turn endeavours to capture the best industrial practices in standards and prescribes these standards for all organizations. *Maturity criteria* (Murine & Carpenter, 1984; SSE-CMM,

1998; Stacey, 1996) are similar to ISS checklists and security mgt standards, as these three are practitioner-driven aiming at improving ISS processes. However, maturity criteria have a distinct feature: they assess the maturity level of ISS. *Risk management* (e.g., Saltmarsh & Browne, 1983; Bennett & Kailay, 1992; Halliday *et al.*, 1996) calculates the occurrence of risks and the justification of controls. ISS approaches, which are 1) self-reflective (do not relate their work to existing research) and 2) do not use any research methods, form the paradigm of *self-reflected security management cookbooks* (e.g., Nitzberg, 1997; Sherwood, 1996). *Information modeling approaches* (Ellmer *et al.*, 1995; Pernul *et al.*, 1998) add modeling notations for expressing security constraints in structural and object-oriented IS development methods. *Responsibility approaches* (Backhouse & Dhillon, 1996; McDermott & Fox, 1999; Thomas & Sandhu, 1994) see the identification of workers' role responsibilities as the key question in designing ISS. *Business process security* approaches (Herrmann & Pernul, 1999; Röhm *et al.*, 1998) build security constraints into business processes. *The security-modified IS development* approaches (Baskerville, 1993; Booysen & Eloff, 1995; Hitchings, 1996; James, 1996) comprise a variety of ISS methods which have in a common interest in making use of the ideas of IS development methods. *Viable Information Systems* approaches (Hutchinson & Warren, 2000; Karyda *et al.*, 2001) suggest that the key issue is not on how to build secure, but how to create viable/survivable IS.

Analytical framework. Even though IS scholars have debated the nature of processes, they have not used any comprehensive framework, or intellectual map, which could be utilized for scrutinizing the assumptions underlying ISS processes. Hence, in this article a framework is synthesized from the Western philosophical literature.

We suggest that the debate on normative theories in philosophy is an excellent candidate for identifying the nature of ISS processes; e.g., for identifying whether a predefined universal process fitting all ISS development settings exists? Were found three intellectual assumptions in ISS methods: *monistic deontological*, *pluralistic deontological* and *consequentialism*.

According to *monistic deontology*, there is one predetermined, "engraved in stone", set of actions that fits all organizations and problems, i.e., one ISS method fits all development settings. Predetermined means that the developer applying the ISS method needs not to pay attention to the consequences of applying the method in an organization. This also means that monistic deontological methods hold that developers need not modify the methods as a result of negative consequences or experiences. In fact, such a situation is impossible for the monistic deontologist, because monistic deontological view holds that one method *per se* fits to problems. The philosophical background of *pluralistic deontology* stems from the *prima-facie* principles developed by W. D. Ross (1877-1971). *Prima-facie* in the IS development context means that we any not bound absolutely by any ISS development principles, but rather that they generally hold. Pluralistic deontologist would agree with the monistic deontologist in the respect that ISS methods are predetermined. The difference between pluralist deontology and monist deontology is that pluralist deontology insists that one predefined method, or one predefined set of ISS actions, is not enough. Hence pluralist deontology contends that different problems need different cures, and thus we need different ISS methods for different development situations.

Consequentialism: There are no prefixed rules - the consequences matter! So, in addition to the need to ponder the applicability of methods on a case-by-case basis in different situations (as in the case of pluralistic deontology), consequentialism stresses that no predetermined ISS methods or process can exist. The concept of consequentialism was first introduced by G.E.M. Anscombe, and later made famous by the utilitarians (Bentham, Mill).

3. AN ANALYSIS OF THE ISS PARADIGMS AND METHODS

Checklists. Wood *et al.* and AFIPS take a pluralistic deontological view. Wood *et al.* recognize a shortcoming of the monistic deontological view, namely it is impossible to put forward an all-encompassing list of actions: "*no checklist will ever be truly complete*" (Wood *et al.*, 1987 p. 8). Yet, they see that "*all control ideas described here need to be adapted to the environment being examined.*" (Wood *et al.*, 1987 p. 8). These extracts have a pluralist deontological flavor, i.e., there does not exist one predetermined set of actions that would fit all ISS problems, but different problems need different cures. They also see that we should approach ISS problems with certain predefined principles in mind (pluralist deontology).

AFIPS prescribes clear security imperatives, which organizations generally should follow: "*The following tasks are necessary...* " (AFIPS, 1979 p.11) and "*it is necessary to avoid the following management fallacies...*" (AFIPS, 1979 p.11). And yet, AFIPS recognizes that the checklist is not all-encompassing: "*Not all the questions in this manual can be used directly. It is essential to apply judgment, logic, analysis, and hard thinking.*" (AFIPS, 1979 p. 11). This implies that the checklist cannot be applied blindly as given, but according to the security expert's own judgment. *Management Standards*: BS7799, GASSP and Baseline security guidelines by Sanders *et al.* subscribe to the deontological view. Underlying BS7799 are both monistic and pluralistic deontological views.

As a whole in its philosophy for securing organizations BS7799 has adopted a very typical deontological position. It holds that there exist a predetermined set of ISS actions (controls, etc) that fits all organizations. However, BS7799 states that "*some controls are not applicable to every IT environment and should be used selectively, according to local circumstances*" (BS7799, 1993 p. 1). On the one hand, this passage indicates that BS7799 does not subscribe to monistic deontology. On the other hand, BS7799 maintains that "*however, most of the controls documented are widely accepted by large, experienced organizations as recommended good practice for all situations...*" (ibid p. 1). This latter passage ("*for all situations*") stresses monistic deontological thinking. This view is expressed more clearly in the concept of key controls, which "*apply to all organizations and environments*" (BS7799, 1993 p. 2). Thus the key controls are seen in monistic deontological terms; they prescribe a predetermined set of controls, which are universally applicable – every organization should use them.

Similar to BS7799, the approach taken by Sanders *et al.* (1996) is deontological as the guidelines are predetermined. This approach includes elements which draw on both monistic and pluralistic deontology. With respect to monistic deontology, the guideline states that "*the security guideline...should be applied in any European Health care Establishment...*" (Sanders et al., 1996 p. 87). The guideline provides two hints that it takes a pluralistic deontological view. First, it states that its aim is to provide a minimal protection (Sanders *et al.*, 1996 pp. 82, 84). Second, it declares that "*some of the guidelines may not be totally suited to all systems*" (Sanders *et al.*, 1996 p. 87). These two aspects suggest that the guideline entails pluralistic deontological thinking.

The overall approach of GASSP is deontological: an objective authority (GASPP) predefines the principles. This reflects the main motive of GASSP: to build an authoritative standard (GASSP, 1999 pp. 29-33). We further interpret GASSP as monistic deontological. The overall idea of three level ISS principles and the three-stage process are valid for every organization. Thus, we label the view of GASSP on the nature of processes as monistic deontological.

Maturity criteria. All three maturity criteria (SSE-CMM, Stacey's and Murine-Carpenter maturity criteria) engage in monistic deontology. SSE-CMM holds that there is one objective maturity criterion (SSE-CMM, 1998), which is able to indicate the maturity of all IS. The nature of the processes of this criterion is clearly seen from a monistic deontological perspective. SSE-CMM suggests that certain predetermined processes need to be in place, and which of those processes are in place or are missing in organizations, determines the ISS maturity level of that organization (monistic deontological view).

Stacey's process is monistic deontological: the maturity stages are prefixed and universal, i.e., argued to be valid for assessing the maturity of all organizations (Stacey, 1996 p. 22). Also the list of "musts" (cf., ibid pp. 31-33) for each maturity level supports the conclusion that this approach is monistic deontological (there are predefined and objective (= monistic deontology) lists of "musts" for each maturity level).

The Murine-Carpenter maturity criterion is monistic deontological in the sense that their criterion fits all organizations. However, even though they have adopted monistic deontology at the highest level of abstraction (the criterion itself), they have favoured pluralistic deontology at the lower levels of abstraction. This conclusion is drawn as one can freely select any technique to measure the quality of ISS security (cf., Murine-Carpenter, 1984 p. 213-214).

Self-reflected security management cookbooks. TIPS (Nitzberg, 1997) consists of six stages (1 security policy, 2 risk assessment, 3 security evaluation, 4 security awareness, 5 re-evaluation, 6 crisis management). The TIPS process is a typical waterfall one. According to TIPS, one should start by making a "security policy" and then follow the rest of the stages in order. After reaching the final stages, "re-evaluation" and "crisis management", one can start again or make iterations. The structured waterfall orientation with its fixed stages suggests that the TIPS process is monistic deontological: the stages and their order in development are predetermined.

SALSA engages in monistic deontology: "*the model is generic… for any organization*" (Sherwood, 1996 p. 501) and "*it is universally applicable*" (ibid p. 506). The expressions "*generic*" and "*universally*" suggest that the process of SALSA is applicable as such to every organization.

Risk Management. The Saltmar-Browne generic risk management approach, which consists of seven stages, subscribes to both monistic and pluralistic deontology. Monistic deontology can be seen in the injunction that the seven stages should be carried out in sequential order. The approach is also pluralistic deontological as it suggests the use of a predetermined list of assets in risk mgt. But this list is only valid in general sense, and can be modified, if regarded as irrelevant or unnecessary. Halliday *et al.* present a few possible ways (processes) of using their risk management techniques. Thus, these ways are not the only possibilities, but rather *prima-facie* type suggestions (hence pluralistic deontology). Monistic deontology is behind the Bennett-Kailay risk analysis: they put forward a prefixed seven-stage process valid for all organizations. The stages seem to be carried out in a sequential order from 1 to 7 (cf., Bennett & Kailay, 1992 p. 68) – hence the label monistic deontology.

Information modeling. Only one information modeling approach by Ellmer *et al.* presents a process. This process is monistic deontological as it proposes predetermined stages for ISS development. As the other information modeling approaches did not concern themselves with processes, one may object to our conclusion by arguing that other approaches may equally regard the process as irrelevant or consequentialistic. Our counter-argument would be that because the existing information modeling approaches are expounded by the same research group, we have reason to belief that they hold the very same view as expressed in (Ellmer *et al.*, 1995).

Responsibility approaches. Strens-Dobson (1993) and Backhouse-Dhillon (1996) do not propose any process. As they do not present any predetermined stages we speculate that they might regard the process guiding the use of modeling techniques/notations as consequentialistic, i.e., left to the developers to decide. Thomas-Sandhu's (1994) process is clearly deontological: it consists of five predefined steps. Yet, we see, on the basis of their design methodology stages (Thomas & Sandhu, 1994 Figure 6), that the stages should be carried out in a predetermined sequential order.

McDermott-Fox (1999) present a prefixed (deontological) process for identifying the abuse cases. It is impossible to ascertain whether this process is monistic deontological (i.e., are these only possible stages for sketching abuse cases), or pluralistic deontological. Nevertheless, the deontological five stage includes sub-rules of thumb, which are pluralistic deontological. This is the case, as for each stage McDermot-Fox (1999 p. 59-60) do not provide an explicit list of principles, but rather loose rules of thumb.

Business process. Similar to certain approaches within the responsibility paradigm, the business process approaches concentrate solely on modeling techniques without giving any consideration to the process guiding this notation. For these reasons, our interpretation of the nature of the process in the business process approaches is that they are consequentialistic.

The security-modified IS development approaches. Their descriptions of the nature of processes range from monistic deontological (Baskerville, Booysen-Eloff, Hitchings), monistic deontological and consequentialistic (James). Baskerville proposes five predetermined design phases, which he calls "*the five security design phases*" (Baskerville, 1988 p. 93). We understand that these stages should be followed in the order of 1 through 5. Yet, we interpret his approach to mean that the five phases should be followed in all cases. For these reasons, we conclude that the approach is monistic deontological.

Hitchings' approach is a deontological one. It proposes seven predetermined phases for ISS development. Although the process of virtual methodology is described in a step-by-step manner (Hitchings, 1995 p. 371,

372 and 374), the stages can be undertaken in a free order. Yet, these seven stages are valid for all organizations: "*VM* [virtual methodology] *has been designed to be applied to any IS within any type of organization.*" (Hitchings, 1995 p. 382). This gives reason to suggest that the core process of virtual methodology (consisting of seven stages) has adopted monistic deontological thinking. However, Hitchings (1995 p. 369) also states that the methodology can be adapted by different organizations. But it is not clear whether the term 'adapt' (understood as adjustment to different environments) refers to the models of this method, or to the whole process of virtual methodology, and to what extent one can adjust the virtual methodology.

Booysen-Eloff (1995) suggests that there are four quadrants (cf., spiral model) and 14 stages for developing secure IS. The 14 stages they put forth are predetermined; hence, they hold a deontological view. Booysen-Eloff (1995) do not state explicitly if these stages are the only relevant way of doing things. However, we understand that the stages are pretty much the sa as the stages for ISS development. This interpretation was made as they justified each stage using the formula "it [the stage in question] is necessary because...". Such statements give a strong hint that all 14 stages are necessary. In the light of this interpretation, the approach of Booysen and Eloff is monistic deontological. However, they make one statement, which suggests a different kind of thinking. When they describe the stages they state "*a typical example of the security spiral*" (Booysen and Eloff, 1995 p. 260). If "a typical" means that this is an example of one possible way of doing things, the Booysen-Eloff approach entails a pluralistic deontological view.

Viable Information Systems. Karyda *et al.* (2001) propose a three-stage process: Diagnosis, Re-design and Transformation. The nature of the processes in these stages seems to be monistic deontological. Although this process is iterative, the authors imply that the order of the stages is fixed: first, the stage of diagnosis; second, the stage of re-design and third, the stage of diagnosis (Karyda *et al.*, 2001 p. 459). Yet, they also give four-stage sub-processes for the re-design stage (they do not do the same for the other stages). This four-stage sub-process also hints at a deontological view (Karyda *et al.*, 2001 p. 464). As to the Hutchinson-Warren approach, we did not find any mention of the process. This led us to guess that they subscribe to consequentialism.

4. DISCUSSION AND IMPLICATIONS FOR RESEARCH

This paper scrutinized the assumptions underpinning the processes of ISS methods.

Monistic deontology. The strength of monistic deontology lies in the step-by-step process given to ISS developers. The ideal situation would be one where an optimal universal process, which fits all ISS development problems perfectly, existed.

The foundational weakness of monistic deontology stems from a belief in the uniformity of all ISS development situations. Clearly, several conflicts arise on the conceptual-theoretical and empirical level. To start with the former, let us assume that two ISS methods subscribing to a monistic deontological view propose two different processes. A conflict arises, given that both monistic deontological methods provide different "fits-one-fits all ISS problems", as to which one is the right one. The situation regarding different maturity criteria is a case in point. All ISS maturity criteria (SSE-CMM, Stacey's and Murine-Carpenter maturity criteria) differ – yet they all propose objective, predefined universal criteria. For the sake of argument, imagine for a moment that there are monistic deontological maturity criteria capable of determining the ISS maturity of every organization. It would follow that the 'right one' will be one of these three (and the other two false measured in terms of objectivity), or will be none of these, but one yet-to-be-found. In the former case, the problem that remains is how we recognize which one of these is the only and right one. In the latter case, it would mean that none of the existing ISS maturity criteria could label themselves as objective (or monistic deontological), and anyone seeking the objective criterion would need to wait for the one-to-be-discovered.

Another argument against monistic deontology is to claim that for certain predetermined and all applicable (monistic deontological) processes to exist, all development situations need to be predetermined. This argument is associated with the dispute between 'determinism' and 'indeterminism'. A critique of determinism (e.g., Peirce, 1935; Popper, 1985) may start from the claim that as we cannot exactly predict phenomena, unexpected situations may arise in which the existing methods may not be of any help, or be irrelevant. The critique would maintain that the relevance of processes are dependant on the context and situation in which they are used. And the situations they are used in are so multifarious that a predetermined method fitting all cases is either impossible to formulate or is irrelevant. Nevertheless, even if we were able to sketch a fit-one-fit-all list of ISS actions covering all situations, the list would become far too long to be of use (cf., Hare, 1981). Moreover, the monistic deontological ISS method, by prescribing certain hard-and-fast processes, shows less respect for developers' freedom, autonomy, creativity and competence.

There seems to be no empirical evidence for the relevance of monistic deontology (i.e., one prefixed process fits all problems) as it bears on ISS methods. However, there is empirical evidence to show that IS development methods, at least certain IS methods, are not *per se* applicable to each and every situation (Hardy *et al.*, 1995; Malouin & Landry, 1983).

Despite the fact that it is hard to believe in the utility of monistic deontology, this way of thinking might have an educative purpose – in addition to learning the weakness of the idea. Monistic deontological ISS methods may be good candidates for consideration as the first method students will learn about in ISS education (cf., Checkland & Holwell, 1998). Clearly, empirical studies are needed to assess the relevance of this idea further.

Pluralistic deontology. It is common for ISS approaches subscribing to a pluralistic deontological view that, while acknowledging that every approach needs to be tailored to different organizations and settings, they do not provide any guidance on how this may be achieved. The different "method engineering" approaches (Brinkkember, 1996) to developing IS have attempted to address this problem. However, similar approaches have been not presented in the arena of ISS methods. Thus, following the lead of "method engineering" is a possible avenue for ISS methods that adhere to pluralistic deontological thinking. In this case, the ultimate challenge arises: to what extent are our previous ISS development knowledge and skills are and valid in new ISS development situations?

Consequentialism. The strengths of the consequentialistic ISS approaches rest on the freedom and autonomy they provide for developers. The main weakness of the present consequentialistic ISS approaches is that they leave developers without any guidance on the ISS process. This may mean that consequentialistic approaches require more skill from developers than other approaches.

5. CONCLUSIONS

ISS methods can be divided into process and modeling. Modeling has gained a lot of attention in ISS literature, while process has not. To fill this gap, this paper analyzed and compared the assumptions underlying the processes of ISS methods in the light of a framework drawn from the philosophical literature. Three alternative views - monistic deontological, pluralistic deontological and consequentialism - were found. The implications of the findings for research on ISS methods were presented.

REFERENCES

AFIPS, (1979), Security: Checklist for Computer Center Self-Audits. AFIPS, USA.

Backhouse, J., and Dhillon, G., (1996), Structures of responsibilities and security of information systems. European Journal of Information Systems. 5(1): 2-10.

Baskerville, R., (1993), Information Systems Security Design Methods: Implications for Information Systems Development. Computing Surveys 25, (4) December, pp. 375-414.

Bennett, S. P., and Kailay, M. P., (1992), An application of qualitative risk analysis to computer security for the commercial sector. Proceedings of the Eighth ACM Annual Computer Security Applications conference.

Booysen, H.A.S., & Eloff, J.H.P. (1995). A Methodology for the development of secure Application Systems. Proceeding of the 11th IFIP TC11 international conference on information security.

Brinkkember, S., (1996), Method engineering: engineering of information systems development methods and tools. Information and software technology, 38(4): 275-280.

Checkland, P., and Holwell, S., (1998), Information, systems and information systems: making sense of the field. Wiley, cop.

BS7799, Code of Practice for Information Security Management, (1993), Department of Trade and Industry. DISC PD003. British Standard Institution, London, UK.

Ellmer, E., Pernul, G., Kappel, G., (1995), Object-Oriented Modeling of Security Semantics. In: Proceedings of the 11th Annual Computer Society Applications Conference.

Dhillon, G. & Backhouse, J. (2001) Current directions in IS security research: toward socio-organizational perspectives". Information Systems Journal, 11(2): 129-156.

Fowler, M. and Scott, K., (1999), UML Distilled: A Brief Guide to the Standard Object Modeling Language. Second edition, The Addison-Wesley.

GASSP, (1999), Generally Accepted System Security Principles (GASSP). Version 2.0. Information Systems Security. June, vol. 8, no. 3.

Halliday, S., Badenhorst, K., and von Solms, R., (1996), A business approach to effective information technology risk analysis and management. Information Management and Computer Security Vol. 4, No, 1, pp. 19-31

Hardy, C.J., Thompson, J.B., Edwards, H.M., (1995), the use, limitations and customization of structured systems development methods in the United Kingdom. Information and software technology, vol. 37, no, 9, pp. 467-477.

Hare R.M. Moral Thinking, Its Levels, Method and Point. Oxford University Press, 1981.

Herrmann, G., Pernul, G., (1999), Viewing Business-Process Security from Different Perspectives. International Journal of electronic Commerce, Vol. 3, No. 3, pp. 89-103.

Hirschheim, R. and Klein, H., (1992), A Research Agenda for Future Information Systems Development Methodologies. In: in W.W. Cotterman and J.A. Senn (eds): Challenges and Strategies for research in systems development, pp. 235-269.

Hirschheim, R., Klein, H. K., and Lyytinen, K., (1995), Information Systems Development and Data Modeling: Conceptual and Philosophical Foundations. Cambridge University Press, UK.

Hitchings, J. (1995). Achieving an Integrated Design: The Way forward for Information Security. Proceedings of the IFIP TC11 11th international conference on information security.

Hutchinson, W. and Warren, M., (2000), Using the Viable Systems Model to Develop an understanding information system security threats to an Organisation. Proceedings of the 1st Australian Information Security Management Workshop.

James, H.L. (1996). Managing information systems security: a soft approach. Proceedings of the Information Systems Conference of New Zealand.

Karya, M., Kokolakis, S., Kiountouzis, E., (2001), Redefining Information Systems Security: Viable Information Systems. Proceedings of the IFIP TC11 16th International Conference on Information Security (IFIP/SEC'01), June 11-13, Paris, France.

Kumar, K. and Welke, R.J. "Methodology engineering: A Proposal for situation-specific Methodology construction", in W.W. Cotterman and J.A. Senn (eds): Challenges and Strategies for research in systems development, pp. 257-269, (1992).

Malouin, J.L., and Landry, M., (1983), The Miracle of Universal Methods in Systems Design, Journal of Applied Systems Analysis, 10: 47-62.

McDermott, J. & Fox, C. (1999). Using abuse case models for security requirements. Proceedings of the 15th Annual Computer Security Applications Conference (ACSAC).

Murine, G.E. and Carpenter, C. L., (1984), Measuring Computer System Security Using Software Security Metrics. In Computer Security: A global challenge, J.H. Finch and E.G., Dougall (eds.). Elsevier Science Publisher.

Nitzberg, S.D., (1999), The Cyber Battlefield: Is This The Setting for the Ultimate World War? Proceedings of Military Communications Conference (MILCOM). Vol. 1.

Pernul, G., Tjoa A. M., and Winiwarter, W., "Modelling Data Secrecy and Integrity", Data and Knowledge Engineering. Vol. 26, pp. 291-308. North Holland (1998).

Peirce, C.S., (1935), "Collected Papers", Vol. 6, USA.

Popper, K., (1985), "Indeterminism and human freedom", In: Popper Selections (eds): D. Miller, Princeton University Press, USA, pp. 247-264.

Royce, W.W., (1970), Managing the development of large software: concepts and techniques. Proceedings of the IEEE WESTCON, Los Angeles, CA, USA.

Röhm, A.W., Pernul, G., Herrmann, G., (1998), Modeling Secure and Fair Electronic Commerce. Proceedings of the 14th Annual Computer Security Applications Conference.

Sanders, P.W., Furrell, and Warren, M.J., (1996), Baseline Security Guidelines for Health Care Management. In the SEISMED Consortium (eds): Data Security for Health Care: Volume 31: Management Guidelines, Baseline Security Guidelines for Health Care Management, pp. 82 - 107, IOS Press, The Netherlands.

Sherwood, J., (1996), SALSA: A Method for Developing Enterprise Security Architecture and Strategy. Computers and Security. Vol. 15, no. 6, pp. 501-506.

Siponen, M.T., (2001), An analysis of the recent IS security development approaches: descriptive and prescriptive implications. In: G. Dhillon (eds:) Information Security Management - Global Challenges in the Next Millennium, Idea Group (2001).

Siponen, M.T., (2002), Designing secure information systems and software: Critical evaluation of the existing approaches and a new paradigm. Academic Dissertation, Acta Universitatis Ouluensis A 387, Oulu University Press.

SSE-CMM, (1998), The Model and the Appraisal Method (v2.0). http://www.sse-cmm.org.

Stacey, T.R., (1996), Information Security Program Maturity Grid. Information Systems Security. Vol. 5, No.2., pp. 22-34.

Strens, R. and Dobson, J., (1993), How responsibility modelling leads to security requirements. Proceedings of the 1992 and 1993 ACM New Security Paradigm Workshop.

Thomas, R.K. & Sandhu. R.S. (1994). Conceptual Foundations for a Model of Task-based Authorizations. Proceedings of the 7th IEEE Computer Security Foundations Workshop.

Truex, D., Baskerville, R. & Travis, J. "Amethodical Systems Development: The Deferred Meaning of Systems Development Methods", Accounting, Management & IT, 10: 53-79, (2000).

Wood, C.C., Banks, W.W., Guarro, S.B., Garcia, A.A., Hampel, V.E., Sartorio, H.P., (1987), Computer Security: A Comprehensive controls Checklist. John Wiley and Sons.

SECURE VICKREY AUCTIONS WITHOUT A TRUSTED THIRD PARTY

A Prototype

Bart De Decker
K.U.Leuven, Dept. Computer Science, DistriNet,
Celestijnenlaan 200A, 3001 Heverlee, Belgium
Bart.DeDecker@cs.kuleuven.ac.be

Gregory Neven*
Gregory.Neven@cs.kuleuven.ac.be

Frank Piessens
Frank.Piessens@cs.kuleuven.ac.be

Abstract Secure distributed computing addresses the problem of performing a computation with a number of mutually distrustful participants, in such a way that each of the participants has only limited access to the information needed for doing the computation. Over the past two decades, a number of solutions requiring no trusted third party have been developed using cryptographic techniques. The disadvantage of these cryptographic solutions is the excessive communication overhead they incur. In this paper, we examine a case study: a Vickrey auction without a trusted third party. The design is explained and the communication overhead studied. Several techniques to reduce or alleviate this overhead are discussed.

Keywords: Secure Vickrey Auction, Secure Distributed Computing, SDC, Agents, Multiparty computation

---

*Research Assistant of the Fund for Scientific Research — Flanders, Belgium (F.W.O.)

Introduction

Most auctions are organized as follows: participants gather at a certain date and place, and make bids for a certain good. When the auction closes, the participant with the highest bid receives the good at the offered price.

Vickrey auctions differ in two essential points from traditional auctions:

- the participants deliver their bid in a *sealed envelope* to the bailiff; hence, the bid is not disclosed to the other participants. When the auction closes, the bailiff opens the envelopes and announces the winner.
- the winner (the participant with the highest bid) will have to pay the second highest bid.

The bailiff is the trusted third party (TTP). He should enjoy the confidence of every participant. The paper deals with a Vickrey auction[1] *without a TTP*.

The structure of this paper is as follows. In the next section, we start with a brief introduction to the secure distributed computing problem (SDC). In section 2, we show how SDC can be used to organize a Vickrey auction without a trusted third party. We discuss the design of the boolean circuit that implements the auction. The experimental results are discussed in section 3. Especially the communication overhead is assessed and optimizations are proposed in section 4. Finally, in section 5, we summarize the major outcomes of this article.

1. Secure Distributed Computing

Secure distributed computing (SDC) addresses the problem of distributed computing where some of the algorithms and data that are used in the computation must remain private. Usually, the problem is stated as follows, emphasizing privacy of data. Let f be a publicly known function taking n inputs, and suppose there are n parties (named $P_i, i = 1 \dots n$), each holding one private input x_i. The n parties want to compute the value $f(x_1, \dots, x_n)$ without leaking any information about their private inputs (except of course the information about x_i that is implicitly present in the function result) to the other parties. An example

[1]Although Vickrey auctions may not seem very important, small variations on this scheme are used by many public institutions: e.g., a call for tenders, where the contract is given to the lowest offer (or the second lowest).

is voting: the function f is addition, and the private inputs represent yes ($x_i = 1$) or no ($x_i = 0$) votes. In case an algorithm has to be kept secret, instead of data, f can be an interpreter for some (simple) programming language, and one of the x_i can be the encoding of the algorithm.

In descriptions of solutions to the secure distributed computing problem, the function f is often encoded as a boolean circuit, and therefore secure distributed computing is also referred to as *secure circuit evaluation.*

It is easy to see that an efficient solution to the secure distributed computing problem would be an enabling technology for a large number of interesting distributed applications across the Internet. Some example applications are: auctions ([15]), charging for the use of algorithms on the basis of a usage count ([16–17]), various kinds of weighted voting, protecting mobile code integrity and privacy ([17, 12]), ...

Secure distributed computing is trivial in the presence of a globally trusted third party(TTP): all participants send their data and code to the TTP (over a secure channel), the TTP performs the computation and broadcasts the results. The main drawback of this approach is the large amount of trust needed in the TTP.

However, solutions without a TTP are also possible. Over the past two decades, a fairly large variety of solutions to the problem has been proposed. An overview is given by Franklin [8] and more recently by Cramer [5] and Neven [14]. These solutions differ from each other in the cryptographic primitives that are used, and in the class of computations that can be performed (some of the solutions only allow for specific kinds of functions to be computed). The main drawback of these solutions is the heavy communication overhead that they incur.

In [9], Franklin and Haber propose a protocol for secret circuit evaluation. The boolean circuit is evaluated on encrypted data with a homomorphic probabilistic encryption scheme.

- An encryption technique is *probabilistic* if the same cleartext can encrypt to many different ciphertexts. To work with encrypted bits, probabilistic encryption is essential, otherwise only two ciphertexts (the encryption of a zero and the encryption of a one) would be possible, and cryptanalysis would be fairly simple.

- An encryption technique is *homomorphic* if it satisfies equations of the form $E(x \,\mathbf{op}\, y) = E(x) \,\mathbf{op}'\, E(y)$ for some operations $\mathbf{op}$ and $\mathbf{op}'$.

Recently, Cramer, Damgard and Nielsen have proposed in [6] a similar protocol that requires fewer encrypted bits per AND-gate. These optimizations are applied in the description of the Franklin-Haber protocol.

The modified Franklin-Haber protocol. The protocol is based on a joint encryption scheme. All participants know the public key K_{pub} while each participant $P_1, \ldots, P_n$ has his own private key $K_1, \ldots, K_n$. Using the public key, anyone can create an encryption $E_S(m)$ of some message m, where $S \subseteq \{P_1, \ldots, P_n\}$, such that the private key of each participant in S is needed to decrypt the message. More formally, if D_i denotes the decryption with P_i's private key, the relation between encryption and decryption is given by: $D_i(E_S(m)) = E_{S \setminus \{P_i\}}(m)$. The plaintext m should be easily recoverable from $E_\emptyset(m)$.

In the joint encryption scheme used by Franklin and Haber [9], a bit b is encrypted as

$$E_S(b) = \left[g^r \mod N,\ (-1)^b \Big(\prod_{j \in S} g^{K_j} \Big)^r \mod N \right]$$

where $N = pq$, p and q are two primes such that $p \equiv q \mod 4$, and $r \in_R Z_N$. The public key is given by $[N, g, g^{K_1} \mod N, \ldots, g^{K_n} \mod N]$. This scheme has some additional properties that are used in the protocol:

- *XOR-Homomorphic.* Anyone can compute a joint encryption of the XOR of two jointly encrypted bits. Indeed, if $E_S(b) = [\alpha, \beta]$ and $E_S(b') = [\alpha', \beta']$, then $E_S(b \oplus b') = [\alpha\alpha' \mod N, \beta\beta' \mod N]$.

- *Blindable.* Given an encrypted bit, anyone can create a random ciphertext that decrypts to the same bit. Indeed, if $E_S(b) = [\alpha, \beta]$ and $r \in_R Z_N$, then

$$\left[\alpha g^r \mod N,\ \beta \Big(\prod_{j \in S} g^{K_j} \Big)^r \mod N \right]$$

  is a encryption of the same bit.

- *Witnessable.* Any participant can withdraw from a joint encryption by providing the other participants with a single value. Indeed, if $E_S(b) = [\alpha, \beta]$, it is easy to compute $D_i(E_S(b))$ from

$$W_i([\alpha,\ \beta]) = \alpha^{-K_i} \mod N$$

First of all, the participants must agree on a value for N and g, choose a secret key K_i and broadcast $g^{K_i} \mod N$ to form the public key. To start the actual protocol, each participant broadcasts a joint encryption of his input bits.

For an XOR-gate, every participant simply applies the XOR-homomorphism. The encrypted output of a NOT-gate can be found by applying the XOR-homomorphism with a default encryption of a one, e.g.

$[1, -1]$. However, it is the AND-gate that causes some trouble. Suppose the encrypted input bits for the AND-gate are $\hat{u} = E(u)$ and $\hat{v} = E(v)$. To compute a joint encryption $\hat{w} = E(w) = E(u \wedge v)$, they need each others' help. The protocol proceeds as follows [6]:

1 Each P_i chooses a random bit b_i and broadcasts $\hat{b}_i = E(b_i)$.

2 Each participant repeatedly applies the XOR-homomorphism to calculate $\hat{u}' = E(u') = E(u \oplus b_1 \oplus \ldots \oplus b_n)$ from the received values of the first step. Each participant broadcasts a decryption witness for $\hat{u}'$, i.e. $W_i(\hat{u}')$.

3 Everyone can now decrypt $\hat{u}'$ into u'. Next, every partipant can calculate $\hat{w}' = E(u' \wedge v) = E((u \oplus b_1 \oplus \cdots \oplus b_n) \wedge v)$.

If u' is 0, then $u' \wedge v = 0$, and $E(u' \wedge v) = E(0)$. However, if u' is 1, then $u' \wedge v = v$, and $E(u' \wedge v) = E(v)$.

4 Every participant P_i calculates and broadcasts $\hat{w}_i = E(b_i \wedge v)$. Since P_i chose b_i, he knows the outcome of $b_i \wedge v$ (either 0 or v). Note that when b_i is 1, the participant should blind $E(v)$, thus ensuring that b_i remains secret to the other participants.

5 Every participant repeatedly applies the XOR-homomorphism to calculate $\hat{w} = E(w) = E(w' \oplus w_1 \oplus \cdots \oplus w_n)$ from the values received in the previous step. Note that $\hat{w}$ is an encryption of wanted $u \wedge v$. Indeed:

$$\begin{array}{rccccccc} w & = & u & & & & & \wedge v \\ & = & (u \oplus b_1 \oplus \cdots \oplus b_n & \oplus & b_1 & \oplus \cdots \oplus & b_n) & \wedge v \\ & = & (u' & \oplus & b_1 & \oplus \cdots \oplus & b_n) & \wedge v \\ & = & (u' \wedge v) & \oplus & (b_1 \wedge v) & \oplus \cdots \oplus & (b_n \wedge v) & \\ & = & w' & \oplus & w_1 & \oplus \cdots \oplus & w_n & \end{array}$$

When all the gates in the circuit have been evaluated, every participant has a joint encryption of the output bits. Finally, all participants broadcast decryption witnesses to reveal the output[2].

In this protocol, the evaluation of an AND-gate requires that every participant broadcasts two encrypted bits ($E(b_i)$ and $E(b_i \wedge v)$) and one decryption witness (which is half the size of an encrypted bit); hence, the total communication overhead amounts to 2.5 encryption bits per AND-gate (4 encryption bits in the original protocol [9]).

[2]Note that at this stage, some of the participants might try to cheat and broadcast wrong witnesses or broadcast nothing at all. However, this is noticeable to the honest participants.

2. Design of a Vickrey Auction without TTP

We assume that there are n bidders. The item will only be sold if the bid of one participant is strictly higher than the other bids. In all other cases there is no winner. The clearing price is the second highest bid. The requirements for this type of auction are the following:

- if there is no winner, nothing else (but the fact that there is no winner) is revealed;
- if there is a winner:
  - reveal the identity of the highest bidder, but hide the highest bid;
  - reveal the 2nd highest bid, but hide the identity of the 2nd highest bidder;
  - do not reveal any other information.

In the modified Franklin and Haber protocol, the participants evaluate a boolean circuit on enciphered data; the data being the participant's bid. Hence, the first task is to design a boolean circuit that implements these requirements.

2.1 Boolean Circuit for the Auction

For three participants x, y and z, the boolean circuit is shown in figure 1. The inputs to the circuit are b-bit bids (X, Y and Z). The output is the identity of the winner, represented by the bits $R1$ and $R0$ ($R1R0 = 00$ no winner, 01 winner is x, 10 winner is y, 11 winner is z), and the clearing price. If there is no winner, the clearing price is set to zero. To determine the winner, the circuit uses three comparators and a number of AND and OR gates. To determine the clearing price, four multiplexers are used. Consider the situation where X makes the highest bid. In this case $G1 \wedge G2 = 1$, $L1 \wedge G3 = 0$, $L2 \wedge L3 = 0$ and $R1R0 = 10$, so the second input to the final multiplexer will be chosen. The input on this line is determined by the bids made by y and z. If $Y > Z$ then $G3 = 1$ and Y will be selected as the clearing price. In the other cases ($Y < Z$ or $Y = Z$) Z will be the clearing price.

It is rather straightforward to extend the circuit for more than three participants.

The circuits for comparators and multiplexers are designed in such a way that the number of AND-gates are minimized. OR-gates can be transformed into AND-gates using the "De Morgan" laws. Figure 2 illustrates the circuit for a comparator that compares two 2-bit numbers.

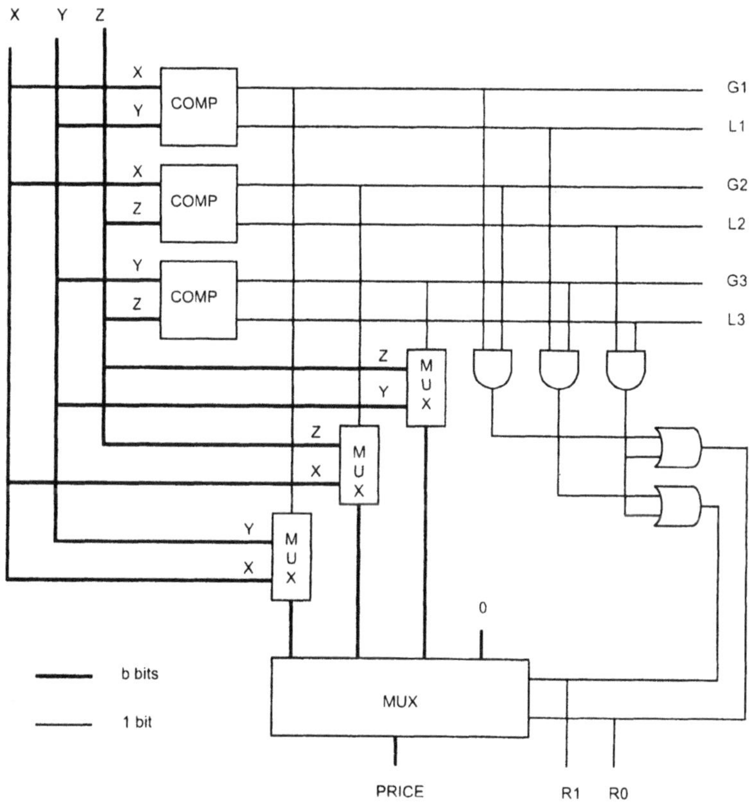

Figure 1. Boolean circuit of the Vickrey Auction for 3 bidders.

It is not difficult to extend the circuit for longer numbers. However, there is no general design strategy for minimizing the number of AND-gates.

2.2 The prototype

The prototype has been written in Java. All bidders in the auction run as a separate thread within one Java application. Broadcast communication was simulated through the use of shared buffers.

In all experiments the length of the modulus (N) was set to 512.

The platform for running the application was a Pentium III (450 MHz) processor.

3. Experimental results

Table 1 lists the execution time for basic operations (with a 512-bit modulus) . The table does not show the time necessary for the evaluation

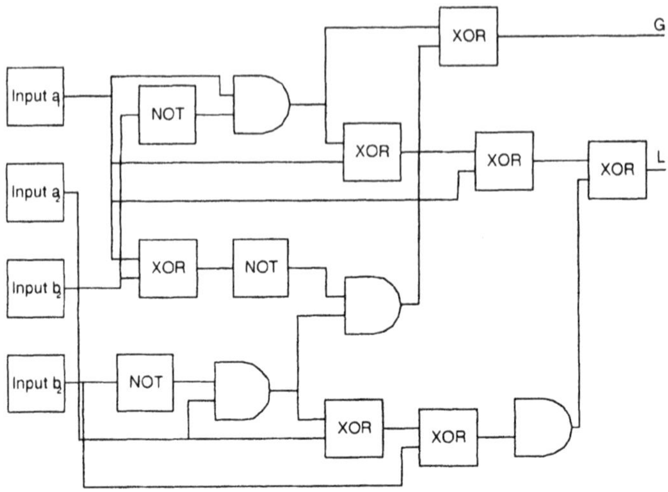

Figure 2. Boolean circuit for a two-bit comparator.

Operation	**Time (ms)**
Encryption of 1 bit	65
Evaluation of XOR gate	0.28
Calculation of witness	35
Usage of witness	0.13
Evaluation of NOT-gate	0.09

Table 1. Execution time for basic operations on Pentium III processor (450 MHz) with 512-bit modulus.

of an AND-gate, since it depends on the number of participants and is affected by the network latency time. The evaluation of an AND-gate requires the computation of several encryption bits and witnesses.

Table 2 lists the number of AND-gates in the boolean circuit as a function of the number of bits in the bid and the number of participants. These numbers represent about one fourth of the total number of gates in the circuit.

The total number of broadcasts can be calculated as $n.(3a + 2b + 1 + \lceil log_2(n+1) \rceil)$, where n is the number of participants, a the number of AND-gates and b the number of bits in the bid. After all, every participant broadcasts its b inputs, its part of the public key, 3 values per AND-gate, and $b + \lceil log_2(n+1) \rceil$ witnesses for the outputs.

Not all the broadcast messages have the same size: encrypted bits have twice the size of a witness or public key. Table 3 shows the communication overhead (the total amount of bytes sent over the network) as a function of the number of bits in the bid and the number of participants.

# participants	# bits/word 1	2	3	4	5	10	20
3	28	53	81	109	137	277	557
4	60	108	162	216	270	540	1080
5	102	179	266	353	440	875	1745
6	158	270	397	524	651	1286	2556
7	231	384	558	732	906	1776	3516
8	328	528	756	984	1212	2352	4632
9	439	682	981	1270	1559	3004	5894
10	572	884	1241	1598	1955	3740	7310
15	1642	2339	3141	3943	4745	8755	16775
20	3577	4809	6231	7653	9075	16185	30405

Table 2. Number of AND-gates in the complete circuit in function of the number of participants and the wordlength.

# participants	# bits/word 1	2	3	4	5	10	20
3	28.0k	52.6k	80.1k	107.5k	135.0k	272.2k	546.8k
4	78.6k	140.7k	210.7k	280.6k	350.5k	699.8k	1.3M
5	165.5k	289.6k	429.7k	569.8k	710.1k	1.3M	2.7M
6	306.0k	522.2k	767.2k	1012.2k	1.2M	2.4M	4.8M
7	520.6k	864.6k	1.2M	1.6M	1.9M	3.8M	7.7M
8	843.7k	1.3M	1.8M	2.4M	3.0M	5.8M	11.6M
9	1.2M	1.9M	2.7M	3.5M	4.3M	8.4M	16.6M
10	1.7M	2.7M	3.8M	5.0M	6.1M	11.7M	22.8M
15	7.7M	10.9M	14.7M	18.4M	22.2M	41.0M	78.6M
20	22.3M	30.0M	38.9M	47.8M	56.7M	101.2M	190.1M

Table 3. Total network overhead (in bytes) in function of the number of participants and the wordlength.

Note that the chosen modulus was 512 bits in length. A modulus of 1024 bits would double the amounts.

If there is no broadcast mechanism available, then the participants will have to use point-to-point communication. In that case, the amounts have to be multiplied by $n - 1$ where n is the number of participants.

The number of bits is linear with the number of bits in the bid and proportional with the cube of the number of participants (power of four without a broadcast mechanism).

4. Discussion

From the figures, it is clear that a secure Vickrey auction without a TTP is only feasible when the number of participants is limited. For 10 participants, 1.7 MB .. 22.8 MB of data is sent over a broadcast network

(17 MB .. 228 MB when point-to-point communication is used). The number of bits in the bid can most often be kept small, since the bid might be scaled by an agreed-upon constant.

If the number of participants increases, then the auction could be run in several rounds. E.g. all participants are grouped per four, and run the protocol in each group, the winners will then bid against each other in another round. (Some modifications are necessary, since the outcome of the first round should not be decyphered and both the highest and second highest bids must be kept for the next round.)

In an Internet setting, this huge amount of communication overhead would probably prohibit the organization of such an auction. The communication overhead could be remedied by introducing semi-trusted execution sites and mobile agents. In this approach, every participant P_i sends its representative, agent a_i, to a trusted execution site E_j. The agent contains a copy of the private keys and bid of the participant, and is capable of running the auction protocol. It is allowed that different participants send their agents to different sites. The only restriction being that the sites should be located closely to each other, i.e. should have high bandwidth communication between them. Of course, every execution site needs a mechanism to safely download an agent. However, that can be easily accomplished through conventional cryptographic techniques. The amount of large distance communication is moderate: every participant sends its agent to a remote site, and receives the result from its agent. The agents use a SDC-protocol, which unfortunately involves a high communication overhead. However, since the agents are executing on sites that are near each other, the overhead of the SDC-protocol is acceptable. No high bandwidth communication between the participants is necessary, and there is no longer a need for one single trusted execution site. P_i for example, does not need to trust site E_k, used by the agent of another participant. The agents that participate in the secure computation are protected against malicious behaviour of other (non-trusted) execution sites by the SDC-protocols. That is sufficient to make this approach work.

Moreover, in contrast with the approach where one uses an unconditionally trusted third party, the trusted sites are not involved directly. They simply offer a secure execution platform: the trusted hosts do *not* have to know the protocol used between the agents. In other words, the combination of mobile agent technology and secure distributed computing protocols makes it possible to use *generic* trusted third parties that, by offering a secure execution platform, can act as trusted third party for a wide variety of protocols in a uniform way.

Finally, the question remains whether it is realistic to assume that participants can find execution sites that are close enough to each other. Given the fact however that these execution sites can be *generic*, we believe that providing such execution sites could be a commercial occupation. Various deployment strategies are possible. Several service providers, each administering a set of geographically dispersed "secure hosts", can propose their subscribers an appropriate site for the secure computation. The site is chosen to be in the neighbourhood of a secure site of the other service providers involved. Another approach is to have execution parks, offering high bandwidth communication facilities, were companies can install their proprietary "secure site". The park itself could be managed by a commercial or government agency.

A modified version of the prototype could be used for a public "call for tender". The job would be assigned to the participant with the (second) lowest bid, without revealing the other bids. Participants can have a higher degree of confidence that their bid will be treated correctly. Colluding local authorities cannot manipulate the assignment process, neither leak bids to other parties.

One final remark about the used protocol: it requires the usage of a large modulus N of which the prime factors are unknown. It seems reasonable to use a TTP for generating this modulus. However, since the TTP does not participate in the protocol otherwise, it could be an independent body that is monitored by the government and others. Organizations that would like to organize a Vickrey auction, could buy a certified modulus from this TTP.

5. Conclusion

Secure Vickrey auctions without a TTP are possible if the number of participants is limited. The complexity of the boolean circuit is $O(b.n^2)$, where b is the number of bits in the bid, and n the number of participants. The message complexity is $O(b.n^3)$ if a broadcast mechanism is available, and $O(b.n^4)$ otherwise. The use of mobile agents might alleviate the communication overhead, by running the protocol on hosts that are located closely together.

Acknowledgements

The authors wish to thank Johan Daems, MSc in engineering, for building this prototype as part of his master's thesis project. The tables in this paper were extracted from [19].

References

[1] M. Abadi and J. Feigenbaum, "Secure circuit evaluation, a protocol based on hiding information from an oracle," Journal of Cryptology, 2(1), p. 1–12, 1990

[2] C. Cachin, J. Camenisch, J. Kilian and J. Müller, "One round Secure Computation and Secure Autonomous Mobile Agents", submitted to ICALP 2000.

[3] D. Chaum, I. Damgård and J. van de Graaf, "Multiparty computations ensuring privacy of each party's input and correctness of the result," in *Advances in Cryptology—CRYPTO '87 Proceedings* (Lecture Notes in Computer Science, Vol. 293), ed. C. Pomerance, p.87–119 , Springer-Verlag, New York, 1988

[4] B. Chor, O. Goldreich, E. Kushilevitz and M. Sudan, "Private information retrieval," Proc. of 36th IEEE Conference on the Foundations of Computer Science (FOCS), p. 41–50, 1995

[5] R. Cramer. "An intro. secure computation", in LNCS 1561, pp 16–62, 1999.

[6] R. Cramer, I. Damgard, J. Nielsen, "Multiparty computation from Threshold Homomorphic Encryption", BRICS Report Series, ISSN 0909-0878, 2000

[7] S. Even, O. Goldreich, A. Lempel. "A randomized protocol for signing contracts." Communications of the ACM, vol. 28, 1985, pp. 637–647.

[8] M. Franklin, "Complexity and security of distributed protocols," Ph. D. thesis, Computer Science Department of Columbia University, New York, 1993

[9] M. Franklin and S. Haber, "Joint encryption and message-efficient secure computation," Journal of Cryptology, 9(4), p. 217–232, Autumn 1996

[10] O. Goldreich, S. Micali and A. Wigderson, "How to play any mental game," Proc. of 19th ACM Symposium on Theory of Computing, p. 218–229, 1987

[11] O. Goldreich, R. Vainish. "How to solve any protocol problem: an efficiency improvement", Proceedings of Crypto'87, LNCS 293, pp. 73–86, Springer, 1987

[12] S. Loureiro and R. Molva, "Privacy for Mobile Code", Proceedings of the workshop on *Distributed Object Security*, OOPSLA '99, p. 37–42.

[13] G. Neven, F. Piessens, B. De Decker, "On the Practical Feasibility of Secure Distributed Computing: a Case Study", to appear in Proceedings of WCC2000.

[14] G. Neven, E. Van Hoeymissen, B. De Decker, F. Piessens, "Enabling Secure Distributed Computations: Semi-trusted Hosts and Mobile Agents", Networking and Information Systems Journal, Numro spcial Mobile agents for telecommunication applications, Ed. E. Horlait, 2000, pp. 649-666

[15] N. Nisan, "Algorithms for selfish agents", *Proceedings of the 16th Annual Symposium on Theoretical Aspects of Computer Science*, Trier, Germany, March 1999, p. 1–15.

[16] T. Sander and C. Tschudin, "On software protection via function hiding", *Proceedings of the 2nd workshop on Information Hiding*, Portland, Apr. 1998.

[17] T. Sander and C. Tschudin, "Towards mobile cryptography", *Proceedings of the 1998 IEEE Symposium on Security and Privacy*, Oakland, California, May 1998.

[18] T. Sander, A. Young, M. Yung, "Non-Interactive CryptoComputing for NC^1", preprint.

[19] J. Daems, "Veilige Vickrey veiling zonder vertrouwde derde partij", Master's Thesis, K.U.Leuven, 2001.

INTEGRATING LOGICS AND PROCESS CALCULI FOR CRYPTOGRAPHIC PROTOCOL ANALYSIS

Mauricio Papa *, Oliver Bremer, John Hale, Sujeet Shenoi
University of Tulsa, Center for Information Security, Computer Science Dept.
{mauricio-papa, oliver-bremer, john-hale, sujeet}@utulsa.edu

Abstract This paper describes a formalism for cryptographic protocol simulation and analysis that integrates logic and process calculus components. Novel features include the comprehensive modeling of encrypted and unencrypted messages, an expressive message passing semantics and sophisticated constructs for modeling principals. Moreover, the seamless integration of inference rules for communication, reduction and information analysis supports formal proofs about the knowledge and behavior of principals, and about the properties of protocols.

Keywords: Formal methods, authentication, encryption, process calculi, cryptographic protocols

1. Introduction

The comprehensive analysis of cryptographic protocols requires modeling the messages exchanged by principals, the knowledge held by principals and the behavior of principals [4,10,14,15]. Logic-based techniques, e.g., BAN logic [5,6] and its derivatives [7,16], model messages and the beliefs of principals. However, they do not provide mechanisms for capturing and reasoning about the behavior of principals. Also, protocols must be idealized, i.e., abstracted, before analysis. Idealizing a protocol is difficult and prone to misinterpretation and errors.

Process calculus techniques, e.g., Spi calculus [2,3], on the other hand, focus on the behavior of principals (agents in a process calculus [1,13]). But they lack constructs for modeling the knowledge held by principals and reasoning about this knowledge. Thus, only limited properties can be proven about protocols.

*To whom correspondence should be addressed (email: *mauricio-papa@utulsa.edu*).
Research supported by MPO Contracts MDA904-96-1-0114, MDA904-96-1-0115 and MDA904-98-C-A900.

The integrated approach described in this paper draws features from process calculus and logic based approaches. Process calculus components are used to formally model the behavior and evolution of principals using concurrent communicating agents. Logic components are employed to simulate protocols and reason about the knowledge and behavior of agents (principals), and about the properties of protocols. The integrated approach can prove that protocols are vulnerable to attacks, thereby complementing state enumeration techniques [11,12] used to identify protocol vulnerabilities.

The following section defines communication syntax and semantics. Next, principals are formally modeled as concurrent agents, as in process calculi. Sections 4 and 5 present inference rules for agent and protocol analysis. In Section 6, the Needham-Schroeder Protocol [8,9,15] and a "middle person" attack are used to illustrate the power of the formalism. Finally, Section 7 presents our conclusions.

2. Modeling Communication

Communication between principals in protocols is modeled as synchronous message passing between agents. The sender outputs a "message" that matches a "pattern" exposed by the receiving agent. This section describes the syntax and semantics of agent communication. The synchronous model can express asynchronous communications and complex, encrypted messages.

<u>**Definition 2.1:**</u> A *key* ($key \in KEY$) is a public/private key (K_n/K_n^{-1}), a shared or secret key (K_n^s), the concatenation of two keys ($K_n\colon K_m$), a placeholder for a key that is not yet known ($key?$), or nil, for an unencrypted message:

$$key \ ::= \ K_n \mid K_n^{-1} \mid K_n^s \mid K_n\colon K_m \mid key? \mid nil$$

We assume the existence of a basic type $NAME$ comprising an infinite set of *names.* This basic type is used to create unique keys, and data for messages and patterns. For example, n and m in Definition 2.1 are of type $NAME$ ($n, m \in NAME$). Note that the concatenation of keys can be used to model k of n protocols, e.g., Clipper Key Escrow.

<u>**Definition 2.2:**</u> The key matching operator ($\overset{K}{\sim}$) is defined by the following rules:

$$K_a \overset{K}{\sim} K_b^{-1} \text{ iff } a = b \qquad K_a^s \overset{K}{\sim} K_b^s \text{ iff } a = b \qquad nil \overset{K}{\sim} nil.$$

Messages are defined as nested tuples of "values" encrypted under a key. Values can be keys, messages, names (representing data) or "fresh names" (representing nonces and time stamps).

$$
\begin{aligned}
message &::= lstv_{key} \\
pattern &::= lstp_{key} \mid key \mid n? \mid n \\
lstv &::= \{\, value^{*} \,\} \\
lstp &::= \{\, pattern^{*} \,\} \\
value &::= key \mid message \mid n \mid \#n \\
key &::= K_n \mid K_n^{-1} \mid K_n^{s} \mid K_n : K_m \mid \\
&\quad\;\; key? \mid nil
\end{aligned}
$$

Figure 1. Message and pattern syntax

Definition 2.3: A *message* ($message \in MSG$) is a list of values $\{v_1, v_2, ..., v_j\}$ encrypted under key and denoted by $\{v_1, v_2, ..., v_j\}_{key}$. A *value* ($value \in VAL$) is a key ($key$), a message ($message$), a name ($n \in NAME$) or a fresh name ($\#n$ where $n \in NAME$):

$$message ::= \{v_1, v_2, ..., v_j\}_{key} \qquad value ::= key \mid message \mid n \mid \#n$$

Patterns permit the capture of messages and (possibly) their contents. A pattern exposed by a receiver expresses the knowledge it possesses about the format and content of the message.

Definition 2.4: A *pattern* ($pattern \in PAT$) is a list of patterns $\{p_1, p_2, ..., p_j\}$ encrypted under key ($\{p_1, p_2, ..., p_j\}_{key}$), a key ($key$), a wildcard or placeholder ($n?$) for capturing values, or a name (n):

$$pattern \;\; ::= \;\; \{p_1, p_2, ..., p_j\}_{key} \mid key \mid n? \mid n$$

A BNF syntax for messages and patterns is presented in Figure 1. We now define the matching of messages and patterns, fundamental to agent communication.

Definition 2.5: The *message-pattern matching operator* ($\sim$) is defined by the following rules ($v, v_i \in VAL$, $p, p_i \in PAT$, $key, key_i \in KEY$, $m \in MSG$ and $n \in NAME$):

$$
\begin{aligned}
\{v_1, v_2, ..., v_j\}_{key_1} &\sim \{p_1, p_2, ..., p_j\}_{key_2} \text{ iff } key_1 \overset{K}{\sim} key_2 \wedge v_i \sim p_i \\
m &\sim n? \\
v &\sim n? \\
v &\sim n \text{ iff } v = n \\
key &\sim key? \\
key_1 &\sim key_2 \text{ iff } key_1 = key_2
\end{aligned}
$$

3. Modeling Principals

Modeling the behavior of principals is required for the comprehensive analysis of protocols. Most conventional techniques [5,6,7,16] concentrate on messages exchanged in protocols, but do not model the behavior of principals. Our approach, with its richer semantics, models messages and the behavior of principals. A "system" is defined as the concurrent composition of communicating "agents" that represent principals.

Definition 3.1: A *system* is defined as zero or more concurrently executing agents (& denotes the concurrency operator):

$$system \ ::= \ agent \,\&\, system \mid nil$$

Definition 3.2: An *agent* is characterized by its id, $id \in Name$, a list of values, $[lstv]$, representing its knowledge, and a list of concurrent communication sequences, $(cseq)$:

$$agent \ ::= \ id[lstv](cseq)$$

An agent engages in concurrent "communication sequences." Each sequence, called an "annotated sequence," represents a distinct protocol run. An annotated sequence comprises a "sequence" of message outputs and/or pattern exposures and an "annotation" that contains the fresh names (nonces or time stamps) associated with the particular sequence.

Definition 3.3: Let $m \in MSG$, $p \in PAT$ and $lstn$: List of $n \in name$, then a *concurrent sequence* $(cseq)$, *annotated sequence* $(aseq)$ and *sequence* (seq) of messages and/or patterns are defined by:

$$\begin{aligned} cseq \ &::= \ aseq \diamond cseq \mid nil \\ aseq \ &::= \ [seq].[lstn] \mid [seq]_\infty \\ seq \ &::= \ \hat{}m\ seq \mid \rightarrow p\ seq \mid nil \end{aligned}$$

where $\diamond$ is the commutative concurrency operator for sequences.

The definition above defines a sequence (seq) as empty (nil) or a sequence with an output message $(\hat{}m seq)$ or an exposed pattern $(\rightarrow p seq)$. An annotated sequence $(aseq)$ is a sequence of messages and/or patterns followed by a list of names $([seq].[lstn])$; the list $[lstn]$ stores fresh names for the corresponding sequence $([seq])$. The term $[seq]_\infty$ for an annotated sequence denotes a sequence that has to be executed repeatedly, e.g., to model a server. Note that when unfolding an infinite sequence, an unmodified copy is always maintained, i.e., $[seq]_\infty \equiv [seq].[nil] \diamond [seq]_\infty$. A concurrent sequence $(cseq)$ is the concurrent composition $(\diamond)$ of an annotated sequence and a concurrent sequence. The syntax for specifying systems of concurrent, communicating agents is presented in Figure 2.

To illustrate the expressive power of the approach, we formally model the Needham-Schroeder Protocol [5,15] shown in Figure 3. Note that the conventional notation only describes the contents of messages and indicates the message senders and intended receivers. It does not specify the behavior of principals as the protocol progresses.

Figure 4 presents formal definitions of the three participating agents. The *system* is defined as the concurrent composition (&) of agents a, b and s. Note that corresponding principals and agent ids are written in upper case, i.e., A, B and S, respectively.

Agent a is defined by its id A, its list of values $[lstv_A]$ and a single concurrent sequence comprising five actions and a null list of fresh names $(lstn)$: $([\hat{}\{\cdot\} \rightarrow \{\cdot\}\,\hat{}\{\cdot\} \rightarrow \{\cdot\}\,\hat{}\{\cdot\}].[\,])$ The five actions are: (i) an output to send $\{A, B\}$ to S (Step 1 in Figure 3), (ii) a pattern exposure to

system	::=	*agent* & *system* | *nil*
agent	::=	*id*[*lstv*](*cseq*)
cseq	::=	*aseq* ◇ *cseq* | *nil*
aseq	::=	[*seq*] . [*lstn*] | [*seq*]$_\infty$
seq	::=	^ *message seq* | → *pattern seq* | *nil*
lstn	::=	{ n^* }

Figure 2. Agent system syntax

1.	A	$\longrightarrow$	$S:$	$\{A, B\}$
2.	S	$\longrightarrow$	$A:$	$\{K_b, B\}_{K_s^{-1}}$
3.	A	$\longrightarrow$	$B:$	$\{N_a, A\}_{K_b}$
4.	B	$\longrightarrow$	$S:$	$\{B, A\}$
5.	S	$\longrightarrow$	$B:$	$\{K_a, A\}_{K_s^{-1}}$
6.	B	$\longrightarrow$	$A:$	$\{N_a, N_b\}_{K_a}$
7.	A	$\longrightarrow$	$B:$	$\{N_b\}_{K_b}$

Figure 3. Needham-Schroeder Protocol

receive $\{K_b, B\}_{K_s^{-1}}$ from S (Step 2), (iii) an output to send $\{\#N_a, A\}_{K_b}$ to B (Step 3), (iv) a pattern exposure to receive $\{N_a, \#N_b\}_{K_a}$ from B (Step 6), and (v) an output to send $\{N_b\}_{K_b}$ to B (Step 7). Agents b and s are defined similarly.

Note that as the agents evolve with each communication, their *lstv*'s and *lstn*'s are updated accordingly. For example, $lstv_A$, representing the knowledge held by agent a, initially contains *nil* key (for unencrypted messages), K_a^{-1} (a's private key), and K_s (s's public key), i.e., $lstv_A = \{nil, K_a^{-1}, K_s\}$. After Step 2, $lstv_A$ is updated with K_b. Likewise, agent a's $lstn_A$ is originally empty. It is updated with the fresh name (nonce) N_a after Step 3. Finally, note that bindings to wildcard variables occur when agents communicate. For example, when agent a sends the message $\{A, B\}$ to server s in Step 1, s's wildcards *id*1? and *id*2? are bound to the agent ids A and B, respectively.

4. Inference Rules

Inference rules specify a formal semantics of agent behavior. Three groups of inference rules are specified: (i) agent communication and reduction rules, (ii) agent knowledge rules, and (iii) system development rules.

Definition 4.1: Agent communication and reduction are defined by the following inference rules:

$$\textbf{In}: \frac{m \sim p}{id[lstv]([\rightarrow p\ seq].[lstn] \diamond cseq) \xrightarrow{m} id[lstv \cup m]([seq].[lstn] \diamond cseq\{p/m\})}$$

$$\textbf{Out}: \frac{}{id[lstv]([\hat{\ } m\ seq].[lstn] \diamond cseq) \xrightarrow{\bar{m}} id[lstv \cup m \cup fresh(m)]([seq].[lstn \cup fresh(m)] \diamond cseq)}$$

$$\textbf{Comm}: \frac{a_1 \xrightarrow{\bar{m}} a_1',\ a_2 \xrightarrow{m} a_2'}{a_1\ \&\ a_2 \Longrightarrow a_1'\ \&\ a_2'}$$

$$\begin{array}{lcl} system & ::= & a \ \& \ b \ \& \ s \\ a & ::= & A[lstv_A]([\hat{}\{A,B\} \rightarrow \{keyB?,B\}_{K_s}\ \hat{}\{\#N_a,A\}_{keyB} \rightarrow \{N_a, nonceB?\}_{K_a^{-1}}\ \hat{} \\ & & \{nonceB\}_{keyB}].[\,]) \\ b & ::= & B[lstv_B]([\rightarrow \{nonce?,id?\}_{K_b^{-1}}\ \hat{}\{B,id\} \rightarrow \{key?,id\}_{K_s}\ \hat{}\{nonce,\#N_b\}_{key} \rightarrow \\ & & \{N_b\}_{K_b^{-1}}].[\,]) \\ s & ::= & S[lstv_S]([\rightarrow \{id1?,id2?\}\ \hat{}\{K_{id2},id2\}_{K_s^{-1}} \rightarrow \{id2,id1\}\ \hat{}\{key_{id1},id1\}_{K_s^{-1}}]_\infty) \end{array}$$

Figure 4. Agent description (Needham-Schroeder Protocol).

The following notation is used. Agent communication offers are denoted by $\xrightarrow{\alpha}$, where α is m (for a pattern exposure) or $\bar{m}$ (for a message output). Single- and multi-step reductions are written as $\Longrightarrow$ and $\overset{*}{\Longrightarrow}$, respectively. The symbol $\equiv$ denotes agent equivalence.

The **In** rule defines the behavior of an agent that exposes a pattern and receives a message. The precondition $m \sim p$ requires the message m to match the pattern p exposed by the agent $id[lstv](\cdot)$. The postcondition states that, after the message is accepted, the annotated sequence $([\rightarrow p\ seq].[lstn]$ of the agent becomes $[seq].[lstn]$ and all free occurrences of wildcards in p in the remainder of the agent's concurrent sequences are replaced by m. Moreover, since the agent has gained new knowledge m, $lstv$ is augmented with m ($\cup$ denotes concatenation).

The **Out** rule specifies the behavior of an agent outputting a message m. On offering message m, the annotated sequence $([\hat{}m seq].[lstn] \diamond cseq)$ of agent $id[lstv]$ reduces to $([seq].[lstn \cup fresh(m)] \diamond cseq)$, where all fresh names in m are added to $lstn$. Similarly, the list of values $lstv$ held by the agent is updated with the offered message to produce $lstv \cup m \cup fresh(m)$. Note that the output message m and the fresh names contained in this message constitute potentially new knowledge that must be added to the agent's $lstv$.

The **Comm** rule defines reduction for a pair of communicating agents. Two preconditions must be satisfied for a_1 & a_2 to reduce to a_1' & a_2' after communicating message m. First, agent a_1 must be able to reduce to agent a_1' with output message $\bar{m}$. Second, agent a_2 must be able to reduce to agent a_2' with input pattern m.

Definition 4.2: The inference rules **Knows**, **Extract** and **Construct** are defined by:

$$\textbf{Knows}: \frac{(id[lstv](cseq) \equiv id[lstv'](cseq),\ id[lstv'](cseq) \text{ knows } v) \lor (v \in lstv)}{id[lstv](cseq) \text{ knows } v}$$

$$\textbf{Extract}: \frac{id[lstv](cseq) \text{ knows } \{v_1,\ldots,v_n\}_{k_1},\ id[lstv](cseq) \text{ knows } k_2,\ k_1 \sim k_2}{id[lstv](cseq) \equiv id[lstv \cup v_1 \cup \ldots \cup v_n](cseq)}$$

$$\textbf{Construct}: \frac{id[lstv](cseq) \text{ knows } v_1,\ldots,v_n,\ id[lstv](cseq) \text{ knows } k}{id[lstv](cseq) \equiv id[lstv \cup \{v_1,\ldots,v_n\}_k](cseq)}$$

The **Knows** rule expresses predicates of the form "agent $id[lstv](cseq)$ knows value v." The precondition states that an agent knows v if it can be transformed into an equivalent agent that knows v or if v is in the agent's $lstv$.

The **Extract** rule extracts values from inside a message held by an agent in its $lstv$. The precondition requires the agent to hold a matching key to access the message components. The agent's $lstv$ is augmented with the extracted components as specified in the rule conclusion.

The **Construct** rule creates new values from values that are known to an agent. The newly constructed values are concatenated to the agent's $lstv$. Note that changes to $lstv$ due to the **Extract** and **Construct** rules do not create new agents; they only change the representations of what the agents know. The remaining two inference rules, **Chain** and **ChainBase**, define reductions for systems of concurrent agents with multiple communication steps.

Definition 4.3: The inference rules **Chain** and **ChainBase** are defined by:

$$\textbf{Chain}: \frac{a_1 \,\&\, a_2 \Longrightarrow a_1' \,\&\, a_2',\; a_1' \,\&\, a_2' \,\&\, a_3 \,\&\, \ldots \,\&\, a_n \overset{*}{\Longrightarrow} a_1'' \,\&\, a_2'' \,\&\, a_3 \,\&\, \ldots \,\&\, a_n}{a_1 \,\&\, a_2 \,\&\, a_3 \,\&\, \ldots \,\&\, a_n \overset{*}{\Longrightarrow} a_1'' \,\&\, a_2'' \,\&\, a_3 \,\&\, \ldots \,\&\, a_n}$$

$$\textbf{ChainBase}: \frac{a_1 \equiv a_1'', a_2 \equiv a_2'', \ldots, a_n \equiv a_n''}{a_1 \,\&\, a_2 \,\&\, \ldots \,\&\, a_n \overset{*}{\Longrightarrow} a_1'' \,\&\, a_2'' \,\&\, \ldots \,\&\, a_n''}$$

The **Chain** rule models pseudotransitivity, i.e., $X \Longrightarrow Y \wedge YW \overset{*}{\Longrightarrow} Z \models XW \overset{*}{\Longrightarrow} Z$. The **ChainBase** rule serves as a base case for the recursive application of the **Chain** rule. It simply states that two systems containing equivalent agents can reduce to each other.

5. Protocol Analysis

The formal analysis of protocols involves modeling principals using the agent syntax, and applying the inference rules, **In**, **Out**, **Comm**, **Chain** and **ChainBase**, to simulate agent behavior and the inference rules, **Knows**, **Extract** and **Construct**, to reason about the knowledge held by agents as the protocol progresses.

As an example, we model and analyze Step 1 of the Needham-Schroeder Protocol where agent a sends agent s the unencrypted message $\{A, B\}$ (Figure 3). The first part of the analysis of Step 1 is to show that the concurrent system $a \,\&\, s$ evolves to the reduced system $a^1 \,\&\, s^1$ after a single communication. Then, we prove that s^1 knows the individual message values, i.e., "s^1 knows A, B."

We use the **Comm** rule to show that "$a \,\&\, s \Longrightarrow a^1 \,\&\, s^1$." According to this rule, the postcondition $a \,\&\, s \Longrightarrow a^1 \,\&\, s^1$ holds if $a \xrightarrow{\bar{m}} a_1$ and $s \xrightarrow{m} s_1$ are true. Thus, it has to be proven that agent a reduces to a^1 by outputting the message $m = \{A, B\}$ and agent s reduces to s^1 after receiving m. Figure 5 shows the sequence of rule applications.

On instantiating the **Out** rule for agent a, we obtain:

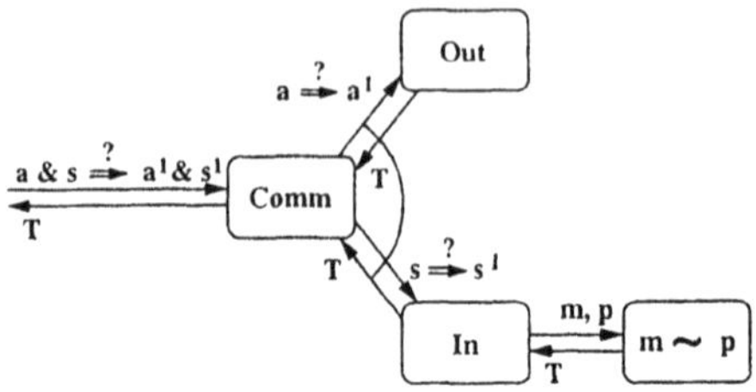

Figure 5. "a & $s \Longrightarrow a^1$ & s^1."

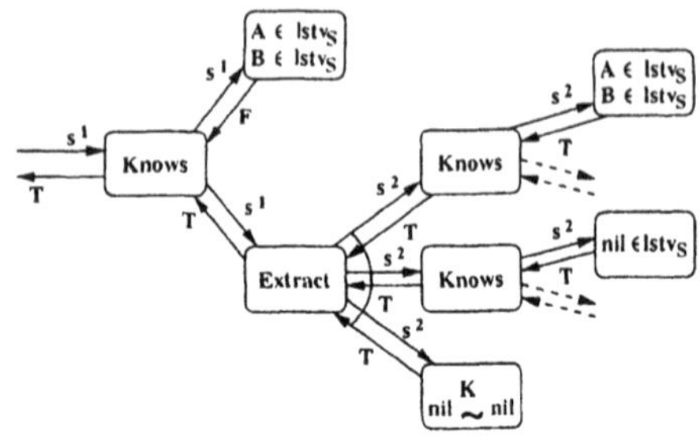

Figure 6. "s^1 knows A, B."

$$\textbf{Out}: \frac{}{A[lstv_A](\lceil\{A,B\}\ \ldots].[\,]) \overset{\overline{\{A,B\}}}{\longrightarrow} A[lstv_A \cup \{A,B\}]([\ \ldots].[\,])}$$

Thus, the reduced agent a^1 is given by $a^1 = A[lstv_A \cup \{A,B\}]([\ldots].[\,])$. The corresponding instantiation of the **In** rule for agent s is:

$$\textbf{In}: \frac{\{A,B\} \sim \{id1?, id2?\}}{S[lstv_S]([\rightarrow \{id1?, id2?\}\ \ldots]_\infty) \overset{\{A,B\}}{\longrightarrow} S[lstv_S \cup \{A,B\}]([\ \ldots]_\infty\{\{id1?, id2?\}/\{A,B\}\})}$$

According to the **In** rule's precondition, agent s must expose a pattern $p = \{id1?, id2?\}$ that matches $m = \{A,B\}$. Since $m \sim p$ according to Definition 2.5, the postcondition holds and agent s reduces to $s^1 = S[lstv_S \cup \{A,B\}]([\ldots]_\infty\{\{id1?, id2?\}/\{A,B\}\})$.

Since the **Out** and **In** rules evaluate to true, **Comm** also returns true. Thus, "a & $s \Longrightarrow a^1$ & s^1."

Now we show that "s^1 knows A, B" – equivalent to proving that "s^1 knows A" and "s^1 knows B." Figure 6 illustrates the proof for both parts. Note that proving "s^1 knows A" (resp. "s^1 knows B") requires testing the condition $A \in lstv_S$ (resp. $B \in lstv_S$).

First, the **Knows** rule is instantiated to show that "s^1 knows A."

$$\textbf{Knows}: \frac{(S[lstv_S \cup \{A,B\}]([\ldots]_\infty) \equiv S[lstv'_S]([\ldots]_\infty),\ S[lstv'_S]([\ldots]_\infty) \text{ knows } A) \vee (A \in lstv_S \cup \{A,B\})}{S[lstv_S \cup \{A,B\}]([\ldots]_\infty) \text{ knows } A}$$

The preconditions state that either $A \in lstv_S \cup \{A,B\}$ (A is already in the knowledge base of s^1) or s^1 is equivalent to some other agent s^2 which in turn knows A ($s^1 \equiv s^2 \wedge s^2 \text{knows} A$). The first precondition does not hold because $lstv_S \cup \{A,B\}$ contains $\{A,B\}$, and not A (and B). Therefore, the **Extract** rule is used to obtain A (and B) from $\{A,B\}$.

$$\textbf{Extract}: \frac{S[lstv_S \cup \{A,B\}]([\ldots]_\infty) \text{ knows } \{A,B\},\ S[lstv_S \cup \{A,B\}]([\ldots]_\infty) \text{ knows } nil,\ nil \overset{K}{\sim} nil}{S[lstv_S \cup \{A,B\}]([\ldots]_\infty) \equiv S[lstv_S \cup \{A,B\} \cup A \cup B]([\ldots]_\infty)}$$

3. A	$\longrightarrow$	B :	$\{N_a, A\}_{K_b}$
6. B	$\longrightarrow$	A :	$\{N_a, N_b\}_{K_a}$
7. A	$\longrightarrow$	B :	$\{N_b\}_{K_b}$

Figure 7. Simplified Protocol

1.3 A	$\longrightarrow$	I :	$\{N_a, A\}_{K_i}$
2.3 I	$\longrightarrow$	B :	$\{N_a, A\}_{K_b}$
2.6 B	$\longrightarrow$	I :	$\{N_a, N_b\}_{K_a}$
1.6 I	$\longrightarrow$	A :	$\{N_a, N_b\}_{K_a}$
1.7 A	$\longrightarrow$	I :	$\{N_b\}_{K_i}$
2.7 I	$\longrightarrow$	B :	$\{N_b\}_{K_b}$

Figure 8. Middle person attack.

Three preconditions must hold for **Extract**: the equivalent agent s^2 (i) must know the message, (ii) must know a decryption key and (iii) this decryption key must match the encryption key for the message. Obviously, s^2 knows the (unencrypted) message $\{A, B\}$. Furthermore, every agent, including s^2, knows the matching key (*nil* in Definition 2.2) needed to unlock unencrypted messages.

Extract creates the equivalent agent s^2 whose knowledge base ($lstv'_S = lstv_S \cup \{A, B\} \cup A \cup B$) contains $\{A, B\}$ as well as A (and B), i.e., $s^2 = S[lstv_S \cup \{A, B\} \cup A \cup B]([\ldots]_\infty)$.

Since "s^2 knows A (and B)" and $s^2 \equiv s^1$, it follows that "s^1 knows A (and B)."

6. Analysis of the Needham-Schroeder Protocol

This section analyzes the well-known "middle person attack" on the Needham-Schroeder Protocol [4,5,8]. The vulnerability in the original protocol is expressed in terms of a message secrecy property. Next, the corrected protocol is formally specified and verified.

The original Needham-Schroeder Protocol can be viewed as two separate, interleaved protocols [8]. The first is used to obtain the other principal's public key from the server (Steps 1 and 2 for K_b and Steps 4 and 5 for K_a). The second, comprising Steps 3, 6 and 7, handles the actual communication between A and B and is vulnerable to the middle person attack. To analyze the vulnerability and the correction, we concentrate on the second interleaved protocol (Figure 7).

6.1 Middle Person Attack

The middle person attack involves an intruder (I) who participates in two interleaved runs of the protocol, the first involving communication between I and A and the second between I and B [8]. Figure 8 labels the steps in the first (resp. second) interleaved protocol as 1.3, 1.6 and 1.7 (resp. 2.3, 2.6 and 2.7).

The middle person attack occurs when A initiates a communication with I. Intruder I then initiates a communication with B with the goal

Initial Description

$$a \equiv A[K_a, K_a^{-1}, K_i](([\hat{}\{\#N_a, A\}_{K_i} \rightarrow \{N_a, nonceI?\}_{K_a^{-1}}\ \hat{}\{nonceI\}_{K_i}].[\,])$$

$$b \equiv B[K_b, K_b^{-1}, K_a](([\rightarrow \{nonce?, id?\}_{K_b^{-1}}\ \hat{}\{nonce, \#N_b\}_{K_a} \rightarrow \{N_b\}_{K_b^{-1}}].[\,])$$

$$i \equiv I[K_i, K_i^{-1}, K_b]\ (([\rightarrow \{nonce_1?, id_1?\}_{K_i^{-1}}\ \hat{}msg \rightarrow \{nonce_2?\}_{K_i^{-1}}].[\,] \circ [\hat{}\{nonce_1, id_1\}_{K_b} \rightarrow msg?\ \hat{}\{nonce_2\}_{K_b}].[\,])$$

Step 1.3

$$a \equiv A[K_a, K_a^{-1}, K_i, \{N_a, A\}_{K_i}, N_a](([\rightarrow \{N_a, nonceI?\}_{K_a^{-1}}\ \hat{}\{nonceI\}_{K_i}].[N_a])$$

$$b \equiv B[K_b, K_b^{-1}, K_a](([\rightarrow \{nonce?, id?\}_{K_b^{-1}}\ \hat{}\{nonce, \#N_b\}_{K_a} \rightarrow \{N_b\}_{K_b^{-1}}].[\,])$$

$$i \equiv I[K_i, K_i^{-1}, K_b, \{N_a, A\}_{K_i}](([\hat{}msg \rightarrow \{nonce_2?\}_{K_i^{-1}}].[\,] \circ [\hat{}\{N_a, A\}_{K_b} \rightarrow msg?\ \hat{}\{nonce_2\}_{K_b}].[\,])$$

Step 2.3

$$a \equiv A[K_a, K_a^{-1}, K_i, \{N_a, A\}_{K_i}, N_a](([\rightarrow \{N_a, nonceI?\}_{K_a^{-1}}\ \hat{}\{nonceI\}_{K_i}].[N_a])$$

$$b \equiv B[K_b, K_b^{-1}, K_a, \{N_a, A\}_{K_b}](([\hat{}\{N_a, \#N_b\}_{K_a} \rightarrow \{N_b\}_{K_b^{-1}}].[\,])$$

$$i \equiv I[K_i, K_i^{-1}, K_b, \{N_a, A\}_{K_i}](([\hat{}msg \rightarrow \{nonce_2?\}_{K_i^{-1}}].[\,] \circ [\rightarrow msg?\ \hat{}\{nonce_2\}_{K_b}].[\,])$$

Step 2.6

$$a \equiv A[K_a, K_a^{-1}, K_i, \{N_a, A\}_{K_i}, N_a](([\rightarrow \{N_a, nonceI?\}_{K_a^{-1}}\ \hat{}\{nonceI\}_{K_i}].[N_a])$$

$$b \equiv B[K_b, K_b^{-1}, K_a, \{N_a, A\}_{K_b}, \{N_a, N_b\}_{K_a}, \mathbf{N_b}](([\rightarrow \{N_b\}_{K_b^{-1}}].[N_b])$$

$$i \equiv I[K_i, K_i^{-1}, K_b, \{N_a, A\}_{K_i}, \{\mathbf{N_a}, \mathbf{N_b}\}_{\mathbf{K_a}}](([\hat{}\{N_a, N_b\}_{K_a} \rightarrow \{nonce_2?\}_{K_i^{-1}}].[\,] \circ [\hat{}\{nonce_2\}_{K_b}].[\,])$$

Step 1.6

$$a \equiv A[K_a, \mathbf{K_a^{-1}}, K_i, \{N_a, A\}_{K_i}, N_a, \{\mathbf{N_a}, \mathbf{N_b}\}_{\mathbf{K_a}}](([\hat{}\{N_b\}_{K_i}].[N_a])$$

$$b \equiv B[K_b, K_b^{-1}, K_a, \{N_a, A\}_{K_b}, \{N_a, N_b\}_{K_a}, N_b]\ (([\rightarrow \{N_b\}_{K_b^{-1}}].[N_b])$$

$$i \equiv I[K_i, K_i^{-1}, K_b, \{N_a, A\}_{K_i}, \{N_a, N_b\}_{K_a}](([\rightarrow \{nonce_2?\}_{K_i^{-1}}].[\,] \circ [\hat{}\{nonce_2\}_{K_b}].[\,])$$

Step 1.7

$$a \equiv A[K_a, K_a^{-1}, K_i, \{N_a, A\}_{K_i}, N_a, \{N_a, N_b\}_{K_a}, \{N_b\}_{K_i}](([\,].[N_a])$$

$$b \equiv B[K_b, K_b^{-1}, K_a, \{N_a, A\}_{K_b}, \{N_a, N_b\}_{K_a}, N_b](([\rightarrow \{N_b\}_{K_b^{-1}}].[N_b])$$

$$i \equiv I[K_i, \mathbf{K_i^{-1}}, K_b, \{N_a, A\}_{K_i}, \{N_a, N_b\}_{K_a}, \{\mathbf{N_b}\}_{\mathbf{K_i}}](([\,].[\,] \circ [\hat{}\{N_b\}_{K_b}].[\,])$$

Step 2.7

$$a \equiv A[K_a, K_a^{-1}, K_i, \{N_a, A\}_{K_i}, N_a, \{N_a, N_b\}_{K_a}, \{N_b\}_{K_i}](([\,].[N_a])$$

$$b \equiv B[K_b, K_b^{-1}, K_a, \{N_a, A\}_{K_b}, \{N_a, N_b\}_{K_a}, N_b, \{N_b\}_{K_b}](([\,].[N_b])$$

$$i \equiv I[K_i, K_i^{-1}, K_b, \{N_a, A\}_{K_i}, \{N_a, N_b\}_{K_a}, \{N_b\}_{K_i}, \{N_b\}_{K_b}](([\,].[\,] \circ [\,].[\,])$$

Figure 9. Evolution of agents during attack (original protocol).

of impersonating A. In Step 1.6, I forwards the message $\{N_a, N_b\}_{K_a}$ received from B to principal A. At this point, I does not have access to the message components because it does not know A's private key (K_a^{-1}). However, in Step 1.7, A is unknowingly used as an oracle by I. It decrypts the message $\{N_a, N_b\}_{K_a}$ to obtain the components. Then, it encrypts N_b under I's public key (K_i) and sends $\{N_b\}_{K_i}$ to I. In Step 2.7, I is able to impersonate A in the communication with B because it knows the formerly secret nonce N_b.

Successful authentication in the Needham-Schroeder Protocol relies on the secrecy of the nonce N_b. The middle person attack occurs because N_b is known by I.

Definition 5.1: The Needham-Schroeder Protocol is *vulnerable* to the middle person attack if nonce N_b is known to the intruder i, i.e., i knows N_b is true.

3.	A	$\longrightarrow$	B:	$\{N_a, A\}_{K_b}$
6.	B	$\longrightarrow$	A:	$\{\underline{B}, N_a, N_b\}_{K_a}$
7.	A	$\longrightarrow$	B:	$\{N_b\}_{K_b}$

Figure 10. Revised protocol

1.3	A	$\longrightarrow$	I:	$\{N_a, A\}_{K_i}$
2.3	I	$\longrightarrow$	B:	$\{N_a, A\}_{K_b}$
2.6	B	$\longrightarrow$	I:	$\{\underline{B}, N_a, N_b\}_{K_a}$
1.6	I	$\longrightarrow$	A:	$\{\underline{B}, N_a, N_b\}_{K_a}$ (A expects $\underline{I}$)

Figure 11. Attempted attack.

Starting with the initial definitions of agents a, b and i in Figure 9, we prove that the Needham-Schroeder Protocol is vulnerable. Figure 9 shows the evolution of agents as the protocol progresses. The inference rules **In**, **Out**, **Comm**, **Chain** and **ChainBase** are applied, as illustrated in Section 5, to reduce the agents. Note that Figure 9 gives the agent descriptions after each communication step.

Examination of Figure 9 reveals that the nonce N_b (in boldface) is created by agent b in Step 2.6 and is stored in its *lstv*. After Step 2.6, agent i knows $\{N_a, N_b\}_{K_a}$ (boldface), but it does not know N_b because it does not know K_a^{-1}. These results are proved, as in Section 5, using the **Knows** and **Extract** rules.

After executing Step 1.6, the *lstv* of agent a contains $\{N_a, N_b\}_{K_a}$ (boldface). Since a knows K_a^{-1} (boldface), it also knows N_b; this is proved using the **Knows** and **Extract** rules.

However, after Step 1.7, agent i has $\{N_b\}_{K_i}$ (boldface) in its *lstv*. Since agent i already knows K_i^{-1} (boldface), on applying the **Knows** and **Extract** rules, we can show that it also knows N_b. Thus, "i knows N_b" is true, and the Needham-Schroeder Protocol is vulnerable to the middle person attack according to Definition 5.1. In Step 2.7, agent i exploits the vulnerability by sending $\{N_b\}_{K_b}$ to agent b, thereby impersonating a.

6.2 Revised Protocol

To prevent the middle person attack, nonce N_b must not be captured by intruder I. Therefore, the revised protocol [4,8,9] requires the identity of the contacted principal (B) to be included in the message sent in Step 6.

Note that the initiating principal A expects the identity of the principal to be included in the message it receives. If the identity that is received differs from what is expected, A rejects the message. Figure 10 shows the revised protocol. Note that the new information added to the protocol is underlined in Step 6.

Figure 11 shows the attempted attack by intruder I. Steps 1.3 and 2.3 proceed as in the original protocol. However, in Step 2.6, B sends its identity B embedded in the encrypted message $\{\underline{B}, N_a, N_b\}_{K_a}$ to I. Since intruder I does not know K_a^{-1}, it cannot unlock the message and insert its own identity $\underline{I}$ in place of $\underline{B}$. All it can do is replay $\{\underline{B}, N_a, N_b\}_{K_a}$ to

A. Since A expects $\{\underline{I}, N_a, N_i\}_{K_a}$, it rejects the message sent by I and the attack fails.

7. Conclusions

The integrated approach described in this paper supports formal, yet natural translations of cryptographic protocols, eliminating the need for protocol idealization as in BAN logic. It also improves on process calculus methodologies (e.g., Spi calculus) by permitting the exhaustive modeling of messages and principals, thereby supporting comprehensive protocol analysis and verification.

Novel features of the approach include an expressive message passing semantics, sophisticated concurrency constructs and seamless integration of inference rules for agent communication, reduction and information analysis. The approach facilitates the analysis of cryptographic protocols in open, potentially hostile environments by making no assumptions about the honesty of principals.

8. References

[1] Abadi, M. and Cardelli, L. (1995) An imperative object calculus. *Proceedings of the Conference on Theory and Practice of Software*, 471-485.

[2] Abadi, M. and Gordon, A. (1997) A calculus for cryptographic protocols: The Spi calculus. *Proceedings of the Fourth ACM Conference on Computer and Communications Security.*, 36-47.

[3] Abadi, M. and Gordon, A. (1997) Reasoning about cryptographic protocols in the Spi calculus. *CONCUR'97: Concurrency Theory, Springer LNCS, Vol. 1243*, Amsterdam, The Netherlands, 59-73.

[4] Anderson, R. and Needham, R. (1995) Programming Satan's computer. *Computer Science Today*, 426-440.

[5] Burrows, M., Abadi, M. and Needham, R. (1989) A logic of authentication. *ACM Operating Systems Review; Proceedings of the Twelfth ACM Symposium on Operating Systems Principles*, **23(5)**, 34-37.

[6] Burrows, M., Abadi, M. and Needham, R. (1990) A logic of authentication. *ACM Transactions on Computer Systems*, **8(1)**, 18-36.

[7] Gong, L., Needham, R. and Yahalom, R. (1990) Reasoning about belief in cryptographic protocols. *Proceedings of the IEEE Symposium on Research in Security and Privacy*, 234-248.

[8] Lowe, G. (1995) An attack on the Needham-Schroeder public key authentication protocol. *Information Processing Letters*, **56(3)**, 131-133.

[9] Lowe, G. (1996) Some new attacks upon security protocols. *Proceedings of the Ninth IEEE Computer Security Foundations Workshop*.

[10] Lowe, G. (1998) Casper: A compiler for the analysis of security protocols. *Journal of Computer Security*, **6**, 53-84.

[11] Meadows, C. (1999) Analysis of the Internet key exchange protocol using the NRL Protocol Analyzer. *Proceedings of the IEEE Symposium on Security and Privacy*.

[12] Meadows, C. (2000) Open issues in formal methods for cryptographic protocol analysis. *Proceedings of the DISCEX 2000 Conference*, 237-250.

[13] Milner, R. (1989) *Communication and Concurrency*. Prentice-Hall, New York.

[14] Neuman, C. and Ts'o, T. (1994) Kerberos: An authentication service for computer networks, *IEEE Communications*, **32(9)**, 33-38.

[15] Schneier, B. (1996) *Applied Cryptography*. John Wiley, New York.

[16] Syverson, P. and van Oorschot, P. (1994) On unifying some cryptographic protocol logics, *Proceedings of the IEEE Symposium on Research in Security and Privacy*, 165-177.

FLEXIBLE DELEGATION SECURITY FOR IMPROVED DISTRIBUTION IN UBIQUITOUS ENVIRONMENTS

Georgios Kalogridis[1], Chan Yeob Yeun[1] and Gary Clemo[1]
[1]*Toshiba Telecommunications Research Laboratory, England*
{georgios.kalogridis;chan.yeun;gary.clemo}@toshiba-trel.com

Abstract: Since one of the services that delegation offers is a more optimised distribution paradigm, reconfigurable terminals are envisaged to be able to show how security can negotiate and adapt itself in a flexible way, in favour of performance, without nevertheless compromising fundamental security requirements. So far we observe that protocols that enable cascade delegation and maintain end-to-end accountability among all the involved actors, demonstrate heavy computations or increased network usage and unnecessary redundant complexity. With a novel set of delegation algorithms we show that it is possible to maintain end-to-end accountability and at the same time have compact and lightweight cascade characteristics. This has been further enhanced with an innovative security mechanism that can be automatically optimised in various environments. Due to these attributes, the proposed delegation algorithms will additionally enable reconfigurable terminals to perform complicated tasks either when they enter an untrusted PAN or they use a slow communications link. These characteristics make our protocols suitable for ubiquitous environments as well as for diverse personalised services and mobile applications.

Key words: Flexible security, cascade delegation, multicasting delegation, ubiquitous distribution

1. INTRODUCTION

The main goal of this paper is to introduce systems that will be able to adapt some of their security mechanisms in a flexible way in favour of performance without nevertheless compromising sensitive security requirements. Distributed and wireless security considerations are mainly focused on delegation techniques which are considered to be a mechanism able to leverage richer mobile services for the benefit of the user. Personal Area Networks (PAN) are considered to be promising environments that will enable diverse applications to be realised in mobile devices in the future. These applications will mainly be highly distributed and in many cases services will dynamically be downloaded to terminals.

Delegation techniques so far either restrict themselves to specific systems and networks or do not present robust and efficient characteristics. In this paper we attempt to introduce a set of protocols that will enable delegation in diverse networks and will be suitable for a wide variety of services. At the same time we strive to reduce the complexity and specialised infrastructure dependencies. Our proposed delegation will be able to configure itself in a private or public PAN or in complex heterogeneous network topologies. In order to completely support ubiquity, our protocols will adapt in a dynamic environment by exploiting a proposed trust evaluation mechanism.

2. CONCEPTS

2.1 Delegation Background

The value of delegation in distributed environments is that it can significantly enhance the efficiency of usage of local or remote resources and provide end users with more qualitative services and richer applications. A delegation service could save a mobile terminal from expending large amounts of CPU, network interaction, battery as well as tedious and lingering human interactions with the terminal and the network. However, the introduced security implications impose quite challenging problems.

Various general-purpose delegation protocols that have been proposed so far seem not to be suitable for ubiquitous and diverse services. Some are either cryptographically heavy or do not provide robust accountability. A good introduction to various delegation schemes can be found in [4].

Cascade delegation described in [8] suggests quite efficient and secure protocols. However the requirement of authentication is met with an increased complexity and the usage of an authentication server. Similar techniques are used in [9] where either nested or chain delegation tokens are used, however tracing and accountability are not straightforward. In [3] fine grained levels of accountability and authentication are introduced. This offers optimum security but it has an undesirable effect on the performance, since it needs excessive network and computing resources.

Finally in [11] a very efficient delegation protocol is presented, ideal for terminals and capable to tackle demanding mobile agent applications that might include secure software download [10] or intelligent, personalised and localised mobile commerce. In this proposal cascade delegation is more compact and is suited for reconfigurable terminals and PAN applications.

2.2 Problems and Approaches

One main problem that delegation protocols [1], [3], [5], [8], [9] suffer from is unnecessary dependencies between authentication and delegation. This is not recommended because key management becomes cumbersome and there is no clarity for accountability of actions. On the other side of the spectrum, protocols that use role-based asymmetric or symmetric keys introduce high complexity. These issues have been tackled successfully in [11] by using only one message exchange from the grantor to the grantee.

On the other hand, delegation in [11] cannot support simultaneous migration to various mobile agents in a multicasting way. The success of the one message exchange depends of the usage of a short-lived delegation token and as a result a delegation broadcast in parallel is not applicable. Although this might not be a practical problem in certain networks, it is nevertheless envisaged that in future ubiquitous networks multicasting delegation might be required. In addition the protocol demands the terminal to both create the delegation keys as well as sign and encrypt the delegation token, which offers maximum security but has an impact on efficiency.

In this paper we will address the above issues and further improve current delegation protocols. This will be achieved with novel end-to-end design from the grantor to the final server and through the whole chain of delegates. More specifically we introduce for first time a kind of flexibility and multi-mode operation that will support ubiquitous delegation in different network configurations (PAN, Internet, ad-hoc, cellular) or a combination of them.

The main obstacle that we have to overcome is how to migrate the same delegation in different networks and how to leverage this with a compact mechanism. In order to achieve that, we have to facilitate dynamic selection of mode of operation in a single cascade delegation. In addition the problem of extending a terminal's capabilities in a multi-domain distributed environment is taken under consideration. With our novel approach we try to tailor the cryptographic burden to the specific environmental requirements but we never compromise fundamental security requirements.

2.3 Notation

Entities within the distribution system are denoted with capital letters. The principal that delegates will be denoted with the A_i letter and the principal that will perform the final transaction will be denoted with the *B* letter. Between A_1 and B there will always be A_2 that receives delegation from A_1. A_2 might further transfer some delegation rights, if applicable, to A_3 and so on. At the end an A_f will exercise the delegation rights by contacting B. At every single step the grantee will have to form a Delegation Token. The Delegation Token that A_i gives to A_{i+1} will be denoted as DT_i.

In addition, we denote SK_i and VK_i respectively as the Signing Key and the Verification Key that belong to A_i. Next, we denote DSK_i and DVK_i to be the Delegation Signing and the Delegation Verification keys respectively. This is a separate asymmetric key pair that A_i will use for delegation purposes. This will be created and maintained by A_i, but A_{i-1} will have to authorise it in order to give A_i the power to exercise roles that are defined in DT_{i-1}. This key pair does not lie within any network of trust and only A_i is responsible for keeping DSK_i private and sharing DVK_i.

At this point, we have to make clear that when asymmetric keys are used standalone then they indicate the actual keys but when they are followed by brackets *(data)* then they represent the actual cryptographic function that will either sign or verify the enclosed data. We also suggest that signing functions are performed on hash values. Hence $DSK_i(data)$ or $SK_i(data)$ will more explicitly represent $DSK_i(h(data))$ or $SK_i(h(data))$ respectively.

Finally, in equations (1), (2), (3) we define the Signed Delegation Token (SDT_i) that A_i transfers to A_{i+1}, a fresh random sequence and a series.

$$SDT_i = r_i \| SK_i(A_i \| A_{i+1} \| DT_i \| r_i \| DVK_{i+1}) \quad (1)$$

$$r_i = T_i \| N_i \text{ , or } r_i = T_i \text{ , or } r_i = N_i \quad (2)$$

$$C_i(a_{i-k}) = a_1 \| a_2 \| \cdots \| a_{i-k} \quad (3)$$

With || we symbolize concatenation. The fresh random sequence, r_i, represents a unique piece of information that could be either T_i, which is a time-stamp, n_i, which is a nonce, or a combination of both of them. As a nonce either a sequence number or random data could be used. It should be mentioned that r_i is produced by A_i, just before it creates and sends the SDT_i and it will be always bound to that. In any other cases r_i' will be used.

2.4 Design Issues and Architecture

In our delegation protocols the primary concerns are provision of authentication, integrity and accountability. Accountability is actually formal evidence that a specific actor made a specific action. Accountability of delegation enables detection of a fraudulent delegate that does not strictly comply with the delegated policy. Accountability will also enable an innocent actor to protect itself from allegations of misusing its rights.

For robust accountability, it is strongly recommended that the Delegation Token (DT_i) with include the following entries:

- An exact formation of sets of tasks to be delegated from a specific entity to another specific entity. Such a format has been proposed in [2].
- Indispensable component of every DT_i should be an absolute expiry date and time after which the delegation rights are automatically removed. Other policy and authorization restrictions and delegation issues should also be addressed like permanence, totality, levels of delegation, etc.
- Some requests inside the DT_i will need to be followed by suitable credentials in compliance with the delegate's policy. A formal approach towards such delegation logic has been proposed in [6].
- It should be clearly stated what exactly can be used as a legitimate delegation credential. This will be the Signed Delegation Token (SDT_i) as defined above. No other object can be legitimately used for that purpose.

The flexibility in the formation of the DT_i makes our protocols ideal for diverse architectures that have been proposed for distributed environments, mobile agent systems, authorization and access control systems and even other frameworks like MExE as it will be shown in section 4.1. However adaptation to specific models is not within the scope of this paper.

3. FLEXIBLE DELEGATION PROTOCOLS

3.1 Multi-Mode Levels of Trust

As previously mentioned, our protocols will adapt themselves to the environment. This flexibility will alleviate the computational burden but in no event will it compromise our basic security requirements which are authentication and accountability of delegation. Our approach depends on the trust of a specific migration that is defined as a function of the device's trust towards the communications medium and the delegate principal.

First we consider the communications medium and we define two different classes C1 and C2.

C1 classification will be adopted when delegation takes place in an environment that is supposed to have its communications links secured. For example this could be realised if one of the following scenarios are applied:

- The terminal connects to a computer with a direct cable or cable connection to a private trusted LAN.
- The terminal enters a trusted PAN or wireless LAN either in a home or office environment. Fundamental security is provided by the underlying technology (Bluetooth, 802.11, etc).

In contrast to this, C2 classification will be adopted when delegation takes place in an environment where communication is not secured and can be intercepted. This could be realised in one of the following scenarios:

- The terminal enters a public ad-hoc network that either offers no security or generally there are concerns of several security risks.
- The terminal uses a (wireless or fixed) access point or delegates through untrusted or unknown networks.

Next we separate delegates in four categories:

a) T1: In this category the mobile device blindly trusts the delegate. For example the delegate could be an agent service operating at a platform like a home PC or a private workstation.
b) T2: The terminal has high levels of trust for the delegate that could be a service or a site that is guaranteed to be indisputable. This could be a service running in a corporate PAN or a ubiquitous service that is certified by the terminal's manufacturer.
c) T3: The terminal has acceptable levels of trust for the delegate. In this case the delegate should bear an acceptable certificate.
d) T4: In this case the terminal does not trust the delegate. Such delegate might for example have a certificate that cannot be authenticated or is verified but has poor or expired attributes.

3.2 Terminal Delegation

All entities that get involved are expected to be or be able to become a part of a generally acceptable network of trust. This could for example be a Public Key Infrastructure (PKI). Every entity should maintain an asymmetric key pair (SK_i, VK_i) that will be registered with this network of trust and will serve the authentication and revocation requirements. We also assume that all entities are capable of dynamically creating new key pairs (DSK_i, DVK_i) in a decentralised and autonomous way and will be totally responsible for keeping safe the signing (private) keys.

Following the previous classification, the terminal delegation will have five different modes of operation to choose from. We define mode *{a}* to be case C1/T1 or case C1/T2; mode *{b}* to be case C1/T3; mode *{c}* to be case C2/T1 or case C2/T2; mode *{d}* to be case C2/T3; mode *{e}* to be case C1/T4 or case C2/T4.

1. First message $\langle A_1 \rightarrow A_2 \rangle$:

$$\{a\} or \{b\}: A_1 \| DT_1$$
$$\{c\} or \{d\}: A_1 \| DT_1 \| r_1' \| SK_{A_1}(A_2 \| DT_1 \| r_1')$$

2. Second message $\langle A_2 \rightarrow A_1 \rangle$:

$\{a\}: DVK_2$

$\{b\} or \{d\}: r_2' \| DVK_2 \| DSK_2(DVK_2) \| SK_{A_2}(A_1 \| DT_1 \| r_2' \| DSK_2(DVK_2))$

$\{c\}: r_2' \| DVK_2 \| SK_{A_2}(A_1 \| DT_1 \| r_2' \| DVK_2)$

3. Final message $\langle A_1 \rightarrow A_2 \rangle$:

$\{a\} or \{b\} or \{c\} or \{d\}: SDT_1$

In mode *{e}* the delegate is an untrusted party and delegation terminates or proceeds according to the user preferences or approved overruled actions.

The delegation in all cases is a protocol involving the exchange of three messages: a delegation request, an acceptance of the request and the actual delegation. The delegate is also required to create a new delegation key pair and send it back for getting its power to delegate authorised. This is achieved by binding the Delegation Token with the delegation key.

In mode *{d}* the request (DT_1) is accompanied with a signature and a timestamp. As a result A_1 is authenticated to A_2 and there is also prevention against reply attack. A_2 in advance creates DVK_2 and SDK_2 and sends back only DVK_2 for A_1 to authorize it. In order to prove the existence of DSK_2 he also uses that key in order to sign DVK_2. A_1 will never be aware of DSK_2 but will still have good reasons to believe that it exists and it is unique. However this knowledge will only improve security when this delegation mechanism is followed on (in a cascade scenario) by other delegation variations. This will be further analysed in section 4.3. A_2 in addition authenticates itself to A_1 by concatenating a signature of this message. The same signature can also be used as evidence by A_1 that A_2 has accepted the specific delegation.

The last part of the protocol is the same for all the modes and consists of A_1 sending A_2 the Signed Delegation Token. As discussed above this is the only token that gives A_2 the power to exercise this delegation.

Next, mode *{c}* is exactly the same with mode *{d}* apart from the delegate's response, which gives no clue about the nature of DVK_2. However, this is not necessary because it is assumed that A_2 does not have any reason for doing so since it belongs to the T1 or T2 domain.

Next we consider mode *{b}* which demands A_2 to send back a signed declaration that he accepts the delegation, in the same way that this happens in mode *{d}*, but now A_1 just sends an unsigned DT_1 in the first message. The reason for the former is that A_2 cannot be sufficiently trusted and the reason for the latter is again efficiency. The hypothesis of a potential man-in-the-middle attack is practically nonexistent as the communication medium can be trusted, for various reasons. One could also claim that in the first message A_1 does not authenticate himself to A_2. As a result A_2 formally accepts a delegation that might originate from a malicious party. However, A_1 is obliged to authenticate itself and authorise A_2 in the final message.

Finally in mode *{a}* we present the most lightweight version of the protocol during which all the cryptographic burden for the terminal is just the creation of a signature in the last message. In this case unilateral authentication is acceptable because A_2 is highly trusted.

3.3 Cascade Delegation

Cascade delegation will also be a three step message exchange. The first two messages will be exactly the same with the terminal delegation according to the new mode of operation. After that the delegate that wants to forward the delegation, will have to bind the new Delegation Verification Key that has been received with the new Delegation Token that has to be legally formed in line with the previous one. Finally the new Signed Delegation Token has to be accompanied by the previous ones. This third message will be the same for every mode and will be the following:

$$\langle A_2 \rightarrow A_3 \rangle : A_1 \| DT_1 \| DVK_2 \| SDT_1 \| SDT_2 \| DSK_2(SDT_2)$$

Cascade delegation can have arbitrary length and in the most general case this message will be the following.

$$\langle A_{i-1} \rightarrow A_i \rangle : C_i(A_{i-2}) \| C_i(DT_{i-2}) \| C_i(DVK_{i-1}) \| C_i(SDT_{i-1}) \| DSK_{i-1}(SDT_{i-1})$$

Please note that in our equations DVK_1 is null data. Also it is not necessary for A_i to verify the whole chain of $C_i(SDT_{i-1})$, except for SDT_{i-1}.

3.4 Delegation at End Point

The last delegate A_f that contacts the end point (B) that provides services has to prove to the latter that he holds a valid SDT_{f-1} and requests a specific service (SRV) to be granted to A_1. The server will have to verify that the service (SRV) complies with the last Delegation Token. In advance, the server will also have to verify that all the Delegation Tokens, which should be attached, comply with their previous ones. This process has to continue iteratively until the whole chain of Delegation Tokens is exhausted and the server finally reaches, verifies and parses DT_1. The message has as follows:

$$\langle A_f \rightarrow B \rangle : C_f(A_f) \| C_f(DT_{f-1}) \| C_f(DVK_f) \| C_f(SDT_{f-1}) \|$$
$$r_f \| SRV \| SK_f(A_f \| B \| SRV \| r_f) \| DSK_f(r_f \| SRV)$$

The delegation at the end point differs from all other steps in the fact that it is suggested to be accomplished with just one message. In terms of accountability, the final delegate is responsible for the proper usage of the SDT_{f-1} that receives from the previous entity as well as the DSK_f that has created. In addition, although A_f binds the *SRV* with A_1, this does not mean that A_1 is accountable for the SDT_{f-1}. This kind of responsibility is transmitted backwards until the entity that misused the received rules is detected. In the case that all delegates manage to demonstrate legitimate actions, then the chain of responsibility eventually ends in A_1.

The whole delegation ends successfully at the point where *B* will eventually directly serve the appropriate entity and will send straight back to it all the necessary data, in a secure way. This in most cases will be A_1, but also it can be an arbitrary entity that should be specified in *SRV*, in compliance with the specifications of DT_1 and the whole chain of $C_f(DT_{f-1})$.

4. ANALYSIS

4.1 Compatibility and Interoperability

The protocol does not require special architectures and it basically depends on the prerequisite of a network of trust (e.g. leveraged by public key identity based certificates). Delegation is decentralised; hence our protocol is scalable and compatible with diverse ubiquitous environments.

The terminal in most cases should operate either on mode *{d}* or *{c}*. These are safe solutions for every case and are thereafter preferable. In specific environments the device will probably be configured. Mode *{b}* could be enough for a trusted PAN. Finally the terminal could be initialised along with a personal mobile agent and probably choose either *{a}* or *{c}*.

Another case involves compatibility with cellular networks or similar networks offering wireless Internet services. At this stage we present compatibility with the MExE specifications [7], although we could also consider other platforms. MExE classifies downloaded material into four distinct domains according to the properties of the accompanying digital signature. For every domain specific permissions are given and the applications' functionality is constrained within a sandbox. Our mechanisms perfectly match with such framework, if we simply consider T2 to be the Operator/Manufacturer domain, T3 to be the trusted third party and T4 to be the untrusted third party. As a result, after initial authentication, the device will be able to adapt to a specific mode of delegation.

4.2 Performance Analysis

In aspects of data transmission, less data has to be exchanged in comparison with other proposals. There are three main reasons for that:

a) Redundant information that a principal is supposed to know about another principal are not resent. As a result even if there are three message exchanges, the total number of bytes is reduced to minimum.
b) Cryptographic data are not used when there is no practical risk for that.
c) The first modes of operation further reduce the messages' length.

In aspects of computational expense, the whole protocol is much more lightweight. The main reasons for that are the following:

a) The usage of cryptographic functions for signing and verifying offers a great advantage over other solutions that suggest heavier asymmetric or symmetric cryptographic computations.
b) The creation of delegation keys, which require expensive battery and CPU consumptions, is done by the delegate rather than the terminal.

Finally the whole model offers a better quality of service as a result of its compact multicasting features. A multicasting scenario can be envisaged when the mobile device enters a PAN that has access to the Internet. It might be desirable to make the same delegation request to a multitude of servers and choose the best one according to their responses. This is impractical with delegation schemes where only one specific agent can be used at a time.

4.3 Security Analysis

Whenever timestamps and/or nonce are used, freshness and uniqueness of the accompanying message is provided. This also prevents against reply and denial-of-service attack. However by just relying on time-stamps we assume that there is relative time synchronization between the two communicating parties. It is envisaged that it is not realistic for mobile terminals to just depend on that assumption. Consequently the usage of nonce is recommended either with or without the presence of a timestamp.

By default the protocol will mainly operate in mode *{d}* or *{c}* where denial-of-service and reply attacks will be prevented by the protocol itself. While operating in mode *{a}* or *{b}* one could argue the fact that either DVK_2 or DT_I are sent completely in plain text. Considering that the terminal will always bind the Delegation Verification Key with its own identity and the identity of A_2, the SDT_I will only have value in the hands of A_2 and only if the genuine DVK_2 has been signed. Although the potential man-in-the middle attack cannot be realised in such an environment, it will still however be easily detected since every entity is always accountable for every action it takes. This can be verified if we make the hypothesis that a fraudulent entity

A_2' manages to impersonate A_2 and further cascade the delegation. At the end point the server will be able to track down the fact that A_2' misused the SDT_1 that was intended for A_2.

Next we need to comment on the difference between mode *{c}* and mode *{d}* which consists of having the delegate explicitly prove that the DVK_i that he sends back for approval is indeed part of an asymmetric key pair. This proof will make the delegate accountable for using DVK_i only as it has been described in section 3.2 and not as a symmetric secret, which is supported by this delegation technique. However if the delegation mechanism is kept uniform then mode *{d}* offers little security improvement over mode *{c}*. On the choice of whether using asymmetric or symmetric delegation keys, it should be mentioned that generally the former should offer more robust accountability due to the fact that the secret key needs not to be shared.

Furthermore, we have to mention that the security of the whole protocol will heavily depend on the security of the public key network of trust and management, which is out of the scope of this paper. This only concerns the authentication part of the protocol, since the delegation is totally decentralised and separate. It is generally assumed that firm regulations govern certificate authorities and/or certificate storage and management.

Another important issue is revocation. This consists of two parts: The first one is revocation of SK_i for which one should refer to public key management background, such as Certification Revocation List (CRL), which is suited for PKI. The second one is revocation of DSK_i, which at this stage is considered negligible as SDT_i should generally be short lived. Hence we strongly recommend the DT_i to have a short expiry date (see Section 2.4). Also, delegation key strength should always be evaluated.

Finally it is recommended for accountability reasons all entities to store in a safe place audit trails for all the signed messages.

5. CONCLUSION

In this paper a first step has been made towards designing ubiquitous delegation algorithms. These algorithms demonstrate robust characteristics like multicasting efficiency and multi-mode operability. We have introduced end-to-end cascaded delegation protocols that demonstrate simplicity and flexibility to adapt to various networks and applications. In addition special care has been taken in order to preserve accountability of delegation.

The described characteristics make this protocol ideal for reconfigurable terminals and ubiquitous services since the proposed cascade delegation activities can take place in the PAN environment or in general purpose hostile networks in a compact way. However, extra work has to be done on detailed public key and trust management issues. In addition it is vital to develop a simulation environment in order to thoroughly evaluate the protocol in different scenarios that will quantify the actual benefit. Continuing this initial work, we expect to provide protocols with greater flexibility and further improve performance. Finding such solutions is considered of great importance for future secure ubiquitous services.

ACKNOWLEDGEMENTS

The authors would like to acknowledge the anonymous referees for their constructive comments and suggestions.

REFERENCES

[1] M. Abadi, M. Burrows, C. Kaufman, and B. Lampson, "Authentication and delegation with smart-cards", Science of Computer Programming, 21:91–113, October 1993.

[2] M. Abadi, M. Burrows, B. Lampson and G. Plotkin, "A calculus for Access Control in Distributed Systems", ACM Transactions on Programming Languages and Systems, Vol. 15, No 4, Pages 706-734, September 1993.

[3] B. Crispo, "Delegation protocols for electronic commerce", Proceedings of the 6th IEEE Symposium on Computers and Communications, July 2001.

[4] Y. Ding, Patrick Horster, Holger Petersen, "A new approach for delegation using hierarchical delegation tokens", Proc. 2nd Conference on Computer and Multimedia Security, Chapman and Hall, 1996, S. 128-143.

[5] M. Gasser, A. Goldstein, C. Kaufman, and B. Lampson, "The digital distributed system security architecture", Proceedings of the National Computer Security Conference, 1989.

[6] N. Li, B. N. Grosof, and J. Feigenbaum, "Delegation Logic: A logic-based approach to distributed authorization", ACM Transactions on Information and System Security (TISSEC), in press, February 2003.

[7] Mobile Execution Environment Forum, "MExE specifications", Available online from http://www.mexeforum.org

[8] K. R. Sollins, "Cascaded authentication", In Proceedings of the 1988 IEEE Symposium on Security and Privacy, pages 156–163, April 1988.

[9] V. Varadharajan, P. Allen, and S. Black, "An analysis of the proxy problem in distributed systems", In IEEE Symposium on Security and Privacy, pages 255–277, 1991.

[10] C. Y. Yeun, and T.Farnham, "Secure Software Download for Programmable Mobile User Equipment", IEE 3G Mobile Communication Technologies Conference, pages 505-510, 8-10 May 2002.

[11] C. Y. Yeun, G. Kalogridis, and G. Clemo, "Secure Mobile Delegation for Future Reconfigurable Terminals and Applications", In Proceedings of the 1st Software Defined Radio Technical Conference, November 2002.

COOPERATIVE DEFENSE FIREWALL PROTOCOL

Magdi M. S. El-Soudani [a] and Mohamed A. Eissa [b]

[a] National Telecommunications Institute (NTI), MCIT, Egypt, melsoudani@menanet.net
[b] Intel Corp., Canada, meissa3560@rogers.com

Abstract: Most of today's firewalls are standalone systems. This fact leads to some limitations in defending organized multi-point attacks. Therefore, communicating firewalls were introduced. This opens the door for a cooperative defending technique, capable of pushing and isolating attacks far from the targets. In this work, we propose a new firewall communication protocol that fulfills the cooperative defense model. In this protocol, a firewall node broadcasts its security policy to the surrounding firewall nodes. The security policy travels in the path towards the point of attack, so the firewall nodes enforce the security policy and cooperate in defending the targets and isolating the attack to the closest possible point to the source of attack. The security of the communication protocol is studied to ensure its strength against some network threats and to protect the network from using the protocol itself in denial of service attacks. The behavior of the protocol is studied using a protocol simulator. Using this simulator, we execute different experiments to observe the protocol behavior.

Keywords: Communication Firewall, Denial of Service, Border Gateway protocol.

1. INTRODUCTION

Smith and Bhattacharya in their 1999 paper [1] have proposed a Communicating Gateway Firewall Protocol (CGFW) as a tool for a distributed defending model. The main objective of that model is to stop the Denial of Service (DoS) attack, which is one of the major attacks on the Internet [2],[3]. The idea was to distribute firewalls across the Internet and to develop the firewall to be active in case of attack. Usually the firewall is placed on the perimeter of the network. The CGFW was built on top of one of routing protocol, the Border Gateway Protocol 4 (BGP-4).The CGFW uses BGP-4 as a transporting protocol and saves the cost of implementation from scratch [4]. Its main inefficiency is the fact that BGP-4 was designed to be a routing protocol and not a firewall communication protocol. In the following section, we briefly discuss their approach and its limitations. Afterwards, we present the proposed new cooperative defense firewall protocol (CDFP). The design objectives and assumptions are also considered in section three. The security of the protocol itself is discussed as well as the protection of the network from the denial of service attack using CDFP itself. An example is given in section four to describe the behavior of the protocol during an attack. We conclude our work with a comparison between the CGFW and the proposed CDFP.

2. DISTRIBUTED COMMUNICATING FIREWALLS PROTOCOL

The CGFW communicating firewall protocol [1] is a distributed defending model that is used to stop the Denial of Service (DoS) attack. The idea was to distribute firewalls across the Internet and to develop the firewall to be active in case of attack. In CGFW protocol, the originator requester is typically a node that has been under attack and wants to block the attack in a point nearer to the source of the attack. However, any CGFW node can initiate the protocol with any other CGFW node on behalf of the originator. In other words, any node can invoke other nodes in the effort to push the attacker near to the source of the attack. Since the CGFW is based on BGP-4 routing protocol, its disadvantages are mainly due to the limitations of BGP-4 protocol, which does contain security measures. The protocol also needs to continuously maintain a table containing full details of the network topology. This table consumes huge storage space and long search time to retrieve the required information while calculating the optimum nodes to be contacted in the defending process. It does not utilize the capabilities of application level proxy firewall for example. There is no conflict resolution mechanism to resolve the problem of receiving contradicting security rules at a given firewall node which tries to cooperate in the defending process.

3. COOPERATIVE DEFENSE FIREWALL PROTOCOL

The main objective of the proposed protocol is to enable a group of firewall systems to communicate and to work together to stop the traffic generated by an attacker at a earlier point as possible. This is achieved by broadcast security policies between firewalls to isolate the attacks. The protocol to follows the changes in network topology and security policy. It has also to resist IP spoofing. In the design of the protocol we assume that all nodes are under the same administration (autonomous system), firewall nodes will cooperate in the defending process, and all firewall nodes are aware of the proposed firewall communication protocol prior to defending the network. We also assume that there is a certificate authority server (CA) in the network that is accessible by all nodes.

3.1 CDFP Architecture

A firewall automatically decides its role according to either the information it receives from foreign networks, or through its detection of violation of its own network security policy. Firewalls within our proposed system can take two major roles; they can either act as a Defender Firewall (DFW), or as an Assistant Firewall (AFW). A defender firewall is physically connected to the target network. The DFW inspects each incoming packet against its security policy database. If a violation occurs, it will create a "deny" security rule, add it to its policy database and mark it as active. It will also log the incident's details into the database for historical reporting, and notification of the administration. The protocol also introduces a new process that is scheduled to run every interval $T_{broadcast}$. When this broadcast service is due, it will scan the policy database to extract all the entries marked as active. When an assistant firewall receives a broadcast message, it will inspect the message to make sure it has not been tampered. Then, it will extract the rules included in the message and check their security. If the message and the rules have proved to be valid, it will add them into its own policy database. Mark them as inactive initially and set their type as dynamic rules (DR). We can summarize the protocol rules as follows:

For "deny" rules:

- If "*deny*" rule is used, mark the rule as active and broadcast it to the surrounding nodes. When the rule is broadcasted mark it as inactive.
- Discard "*deny*" rule if it is inactive for time $t>=t_d$.

For "permit" rules:

- A "*permit*" rule is always broadcasted (always active) till it is discarded after time $t=t_p$ or if "*deny*" rule reaches a matching "*permit*", and replaces it.
- If "*permit*" rule reaches a matching "*deny*", it will replace it.

For all rules:

- Never discard *static* rules unless stated by the administrator
- Split horizon technique can be used also, which means not to broadcast the information came from a certain direction to the same direction again.

3.2 Security Policy Changes

Policy changes can occur from two major sources, administrative decisions, or decisions initiated by an Intrusion Detection System (IDS). These changes either permit denied rules, or deny allowed ones. If a "deny" rule was broadcasted previously to other firewalls, the traffic gets filtered from earlier nodes on the network. To change this, a "permit" rule must be created to reflect the policy change, and rebroadcasted again to the network in order for the change to take place.

The DFW is the source of policy changes. To change a "deny" rule, the DFW has to initiate a rule exactly the same as the previously issued denied rule, but with a "permit" action instead. Then the DFW broadcasts this rule to its neighbors, and by turn, they will do the same until the rule is permitted network wide.

3.3 CDFP Protocol Security

The proposed cooperative defense firewall protocol, like any other communication protocol can introduce new risks to the network, due to its existence in public, insecure media. The protocol would provide an attacker with a perfect tool to mount a Denial of Service (DoS) attack if he could alter/simulate the messages exchanged between firewalls to impose false policy. By achieving this, malicious intruders can deny a trusted node/user an authorized access to certain network resources. As examples of possible threats to CDFP are masquerading, message altering (Man-In-the-Middle attack – MIM), and message replay. To overcome these threats access control mechanism, authentication, integrity check are used. Based on RSA algorithm, a public-key certificate authority CA is also assumed tob part of the network. A given *firewall node n* should have the following components available prior to issuing a message; a public/private key pair (K_{npb}, K_{npr}) and a digital certificate C_n issued by CA.

Every firewall node generates a digital certificate enrollment request to CA. This enrollment request contains the public key of the firewall node, as well as its identity information, such as the nodes public name, its IP address, DNS name, etc. We also include the IP addresses and netmasks of the networks, which this firewall is held responsible for, within the request. After the verification process held by the CA concludes, the CA will approve and issue a digital certificate C_n for that node, containing information that verifies the identity of this firewall, and describes it to act as a DFW for that network. It will also contain information about the specific networks that this node is authorized to speak on their behalf as explained by the following equation.

$$IP_{addresses}\ IP_{address1} \| \text{Subnet mask}_1 \| \text{IP address}_2 \| \text{Subnet mask}_2 \| \ldots$$
$$\ldots \| IP_{addressn} \| \text{Subnet mask}_n$$
$$C_n = \text{IP addresses} \| K_{npb} \| E(H(IP_{addresses} \| K_{npb}), K_{capr})$$

where E(..) and H(..) are the encryption and hashing operation respectively. Every time the firewall broadcasts a rule, it attaches this certificate to it. On the other hand, when another firewall receives this message it checks the network addresses within the message, against the ones stated in the digital certificate to verify that the sender of the message is authorized to speak on behalf of the networks associated with the rule.

Every time a firewall broadcasts a rule R, it concatenates its digital certificate C_n to it. It then, calculates the hash value and encrypts the hash result using its private key K_{npr}. The output of the encryption process is the digital signature of the rule SIG.

$$SIG = E(H(R \| C_n), K_{npr})$$

Finally, the message M_n is constructed by concatenating SIG, R and C_n before it is ready in its final form to be broadcasted.

$$M_n = R \| C_n \| SIG$$

i.e. $M_n = R \| C_n \| E(H(R \| C_n), K_{npr})$

When a firewall receives an incoming message M_n, it extracts the rule R, the Digital Signature SIG, the digital certificate C_n from the message. Using the certificate C_n, it extracts the sender's pubic key K_{npb}. The digital signature SIG is decrypted using the public key K_{npb}, to produce the hash value H_1 that was calculated by the sender.

$$H_1 = D(SIG, K_{npb})$$

Afterwards, it hashes the concatenation of R and C_n to calculate H_2.

$$H_2 = H(R \| C_n)$$

The two hash values H_1, H_2 are compared; if they are identical, the sender is authenticated, the message integrity is not compromised, and the rule is accepted for further processing.

To resist the replay attack, the message generated before will be enhanced by adding a time-stamp field T_s to the rule at the originator. That field will take part of the message generation, as follows:

$$SIG = E(H(T_s \| R \| C_n), K_{npr})$$
$$M_n = T_s \| R \| C_n \| SIG$$

i.e. $M_n = T_s \| R \| C_n \| E(H(T_s \| R \| C_n), K_{npr})$

On the other hand, the receiver checks this time-stamp against its own clock; if this message was sent before or not. If yes, it will be discarded. By using those three techniques, the protocol is capable of withstanding the threats described earlier. Figure 1 shows the protocol message format and the access control and rule signature are parts of it.

The CDFP has three different rule formats. Rules of level one are concerned with router-based packet filtering firewalls, which contain simple packet filters. Level two rules are more concerned with circuit level proxies, and some router-based firewalls that understand transport layer TCP protocol. Level three rules are focused towards today's sophisticated firewalls that contain application layer proxy servers, and can filter application specific traffic. Figure 2 shows CDFP rule formats.

At the defender firewall, DFW, it is the administrator responsibility to insure the proper order of these rules. At the AFW, the order field is defined to resolve any conflicts when they receive rules from the same source. The DFW's are responsible for assigning the right value for this field based on its original table of rules. The AFW's will not be confused by the order of these rules and their priorities because the DFW has already sorted them out. Other mechanism also can be considered such as Hazelhust's algorithm [5].

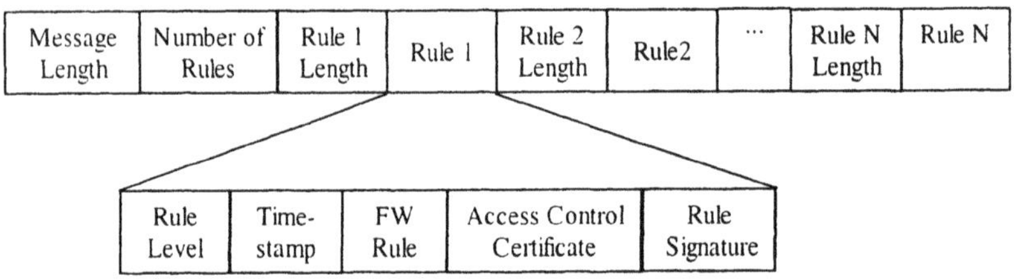

Figure1 CDFP Message Format

Rule Level 1	Order	Src IP	Dest IP	Action

(a) Rule format for network layer

Rule Level 2	Order	Src IP	Dest IP	Transport Protocol	Src Port	Dest Port	Action

(b) Rule format for transport layer

Rule Level 3	Order	Src IP	Dest IP	Transport Protocol	Src Port	Dest Port	Application Protocol	Application Sub-Command	Action

(c) Rule Format for application level

Figure 2 CDFP Rule Formats

4. SIMULATION AND EXPERIMENTAL RESULTS

4.1 Simulator Architecture

The network simulator we created for this experiment is a C++ application designed using the Object Oriented Programming (OOP) concepts [6-8]. It consists of 5 types of objects (classes). The main object is the node object, which simulates a physical firewall, router, or host node. Each node has a number of interfaces that can be linked to other interfaces on other nodes. These links represent the communication links between the nodes in real life. We also implement the Routing Information Protocol RIP [9] to provide the nodes with the capability to dynamically select their own routes between any two nodes without external guidance. We also created a link failure feature to drop any desired link. At that time, the RIP will help selecting an alternative route automatically.

We created a specific high-level configuration language that is used to describe the topology of the network we want to simulate. The simulator also has other types of object that represent different features to enhance the capabilities of each node. Figure3 shows the simulator architecture.

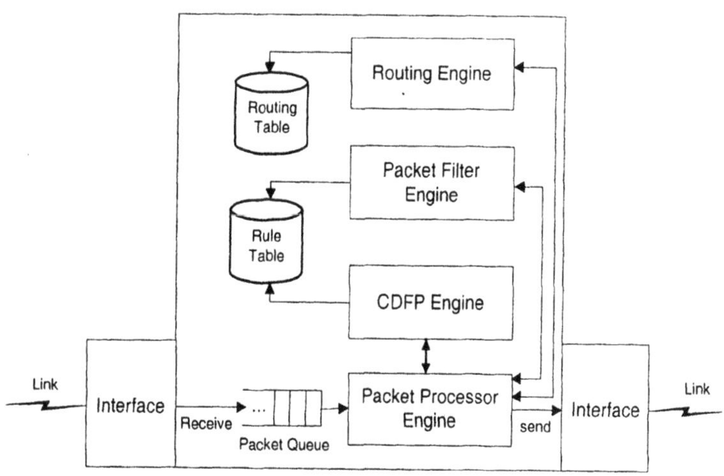

Figure 3 Simulator node object architecture

4 .2 CDFP in Operation

We conduct our experiment on a matrix of 16 firewalls/router nodes and 2 hosts. As shown in Figure 4-a, Node 17 represents the first host, which simulates the attacker. Node 16 represents the second host, which simulates the target we would like to defend. The DFW is presented in node 15. The rest of the nodes are AFWs. In all firewall nodes, the Routing Engine and the CDFP Engine are enabled and the routing tables are dynamically built and maintained over time. A packet generator within the node 17, which generates outgoing traffic to node 16, simulates the attack.

4.3 Example of CDFP Operation

Consider the above mentioned topology where node 17 represents the attacker, node 16 represents the target, and all other nodes have multiple interfaces so that they have routing and packet filtering capabilities. According to the simulator results, a packet travels from node 17 to node 16 can go through the path (17,0,1,6,7,11,15,16) as shown in Figure 4-a. When a packet arrives to node 15, it is filtered according to the "deny". This rule is marked as an active rule. The rule is broadcasted from node 15 to the surrounding nodes, nodes 11 and 14 through its interfaces.

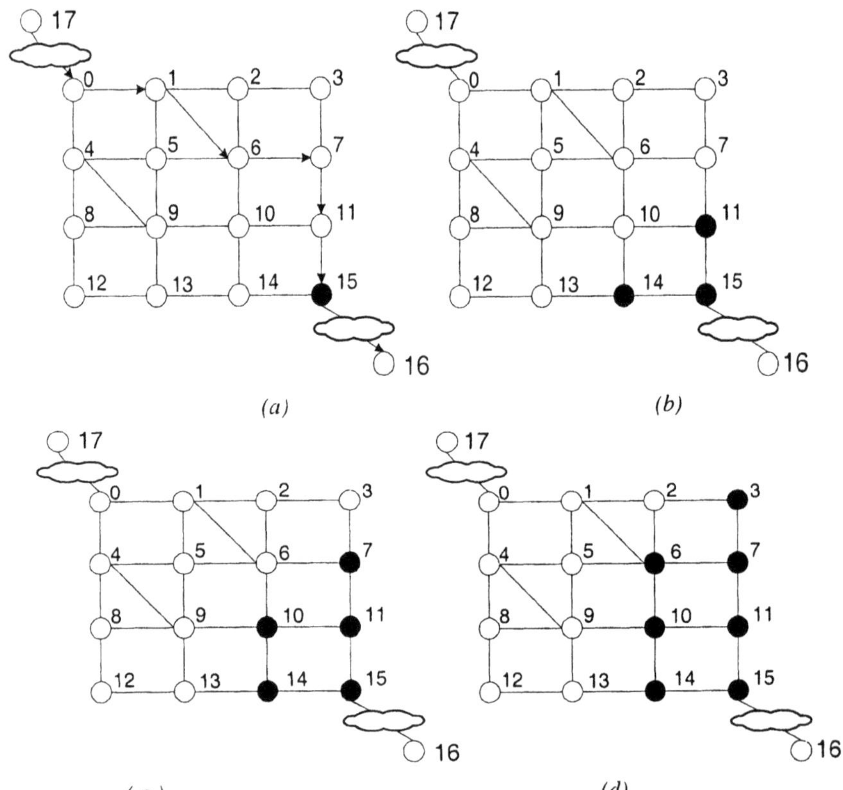

Figure 4 Experiment : Isolating Attack
(Solid nodes show the propagation of FW rules)

The rule continues to propagate towards node 17 as long as the traffic continues as shown in Figure 5. Node "0" keeps filtering the attack traffic as long as node 17 is attacking. It also broadcasts the rule to node 4 as shown in Figure 5-c. Other nodes hold the rule for certain time, after that they discarded the rule as shown in Figure 5-d. By filtering the traffic earlier at node "0", the attacker is isolated far from the target node 16. The CDFP is able to apply the security policy at further points within the path of attack and to isolate the attack at the nearest point to the attacker.

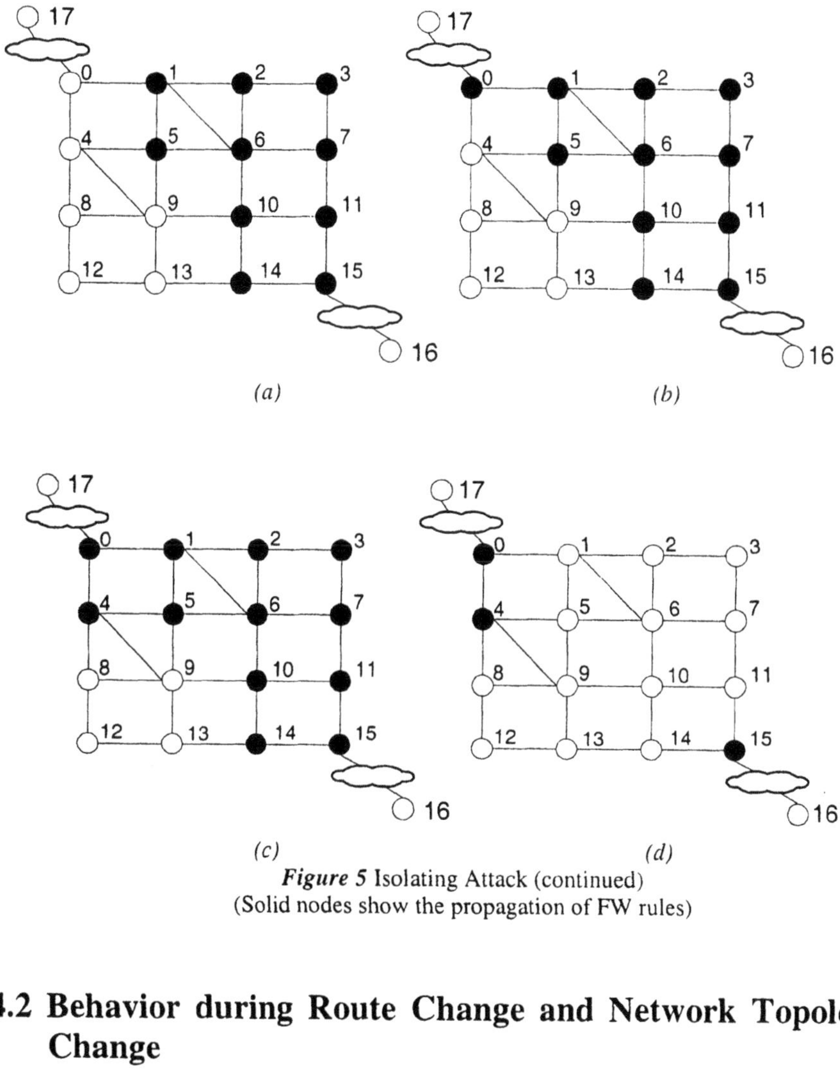

Figure 5 Isolating Attack (continued)
(Solid nodes show the propagation of FW rules)

4.2 Behavior during Route Change and Network Topology Change

The attacker can change the path of the attack by using the source route option within the IP protocol. If the route changes before the rule reaches the firewall at the attacker's network and isolates the traffic of the attack, the attack will take its route to the defender firewall. The defender firewall will detect the traffic from the new path and will start broadcast its messages towards the new path. The cooperation relations will be built with the firewalls within the new path. The same is true in case of a change in network topology.

4.3 Behavior during IP Spoofing Attack

During IP Spoofing attacks the attacker impersonates himself as a different node on the network. Within this attack, there are two different paths; one is the physical path of attack, which starts by the real source towards the target destination. The second one is the virtual path of attack, which starts by the impersonated node, towards the target destination. As before, the CDFP protocol will detect the real path of attack, and broadcast the "deny" rule towards that path. This will result in isolating the attacker by the nearest available firewall. Other experiments have been conducted to study the behavior of the proposed protocol. The details are given in [10].

5. CDFP VERSUS CGFW

Both CGFW and CDFP main goal is to isolate the attacker to the farthest possible point, each does this in a different manner. As mentioned before, the CGFW is built on top of BGP-4 routing protocol which has a database with details about the interconnected networks topology. This database is dynamically updated based on the network status. When a node is subject to an attack, the CGFW uses this information to calculate the optimum nodes that are used to partition the network into a secure zone and insecure zone. Then, it sends the filter request to these specific nodes to ask them to cooperate in the defense process. Although CGFW uses the same graph theory used in ATM networks [11], partitioning the network to isolate the attacker is a difficult task in case of a wide network such as the Internet with a very complex topology [1]. On the other hand, CDFP uses broadcasting to deliver the message to the surrounding nodes, which will hopefully create an immediate shell to protect it. In turn, those nodes will deliver the message to their neighbors in the path of attack and thus, CDFP reaches the optimum points.

Concerning the security features such as authentication, BGP-4 has an optional authentication feature, which can be turned on by administrators. The authentication feature is presented in using the Message Authentication Code (MAC). The technique uses a one-way hash function (usually MD5) with a key to generate a 16-bytes value at the sender to be transmitted with the message. The receiving end must have the same key to be able to verify the sender identity and the message integrity.

Both CGFW and BGP-4 specifications have not defined an access control mechanism [1]. So, if someone passes the authentication check, he is free to distribute information about other portions of the network. On the other hand, CDFP can use digital certificate and access control mechanism based on the RSA public key algorithm.

CGFW has a time limits in the filter request. The filter and monitor requests will begin based on a start time and last for a specified duration. CDFP has also a time-stamp field as a replay attack detection mechanism.

Concerning the operation requirements, CGFW processing power is mainly consumed in the search process to find the optimum points. That can be a lengthy search if the number of nodes is high. The calculation process will also depend on the attacker's source address, which could be easily spoofed in some attacks. The routing table could be huge if the network is too complex and a long processing time could be expected while calculating the optimum nodes to be contacted. Also, CGFW needs to maintain a table for the network topology and a second table for the firewall rules. It worth to mention that the CGFW processing could be used as a DoS by keeping the router node busy trying to calculate the optimum points. In the case of CDFP, most of the processing power is consumed in the cryptographic operations to sign or verify the messages. CDFP needs only one table to hold the firewall rules, the process of broadcasting is very light in comparison to the CGFW, but it requires more memory for the certificates and other security information.

CGFW has a network topology database that has to be updated through the exchange of messages between different nodes. These messages will be exchanged only when a change in the network occurs, and will be communicating to the calculated nodes directly during an attack. While CDFP does not need a lot of traffic to initialize, it will consume more bandwidth during an attack because of the broadcasting. It needs to retransmit the message to the nodes within the path of attack and their neighbors till it reaches the optimum point. Usually the number of retransmission for a filter request is proportional to the number of intermediate nodes between the attacker and the target.

6. DISCUSSION AND CONCLUSIONS

The proposed CDFP protocol is designed specifically to achieve cooperative communication between firewalls during attacks. This protocol enables firewalls to advise each other about current and potential malicious activities on the network, which provides firewalls with more intelligence to help withstand the increasing number of sophisticated attacks on today's networks. By acquiring this cooperative defense approach between firewalls, we can further isolate the attacker from reaching the target network by filtering its access from the nearest available firewall node to this network. Thus, this can help preventing unnecessary traffic and save bandwidth. On the other hand, hackers could use CDFP to perform a denial of service attack. To overcome this risk, security measures such as authentication, access control, message integrity, and replay detection, are added to CDFP. We use a network simulator, built using C++ , to study CDFP behavior during isolating a direct attack, IP Spoofing attack, network topology change and security policy change. In case of an attack within the CDFP own network, the protocol succeeded in filtering the traffic at the nearest node to the attacker, isolating it far from the target node. We also found that CDFP protocol is able to deliver the policy change to all the other nodes which are able to apply the "permit" rule. The same is true in case of network topology change since it can track the dynamically changing path of attack. Throughout the experiments conducted using our simulator, we strived to simulate as much as possible the real life environment where CDFP will exist. In simulation a single CA was used for simple illustration. In more complex network scenario, digital certificate chaining concepts of PKI could be employed. The PKI technology is designed to be scaleable. It allows Certificate Authorities to be chained. Finally, there were two objectives that we excluded from our experiments for the sake of simplicity. One is implementing the cryptographic portion within the CDFP protocol, and the second is running the protocol between firewalls with different levels of intelligence or within different autonomous systems. This will be the subject of future work.

7. REFERENCES

[1] Robert N. Smith and Sourav Bhattacharya, "A Protocol and Simulation for Distributed Communicating Firewalls", in Proceedings of IEEE 23rd Annual International Computer Software and Applications Conference, COMPSAC, pp:74-79,1999.

[2] Chris Hare and Karanjit Siyan, "Internet Firewalls and Network Security (Second Edition)", New Riders Publishing, Indiana Polise, IN, 1996.

[3] "Maximum Security: A Hacker's Guide to Protecting Your Internet Site and Network (Second Edition)", Book News, Inc., Portland, 1999.

[4] Rekhter, Y. and Wastson, T.J., Li., "A Border Gateway Protocol 4 (BPG-4), Internet Engineering Task Force", Network Working Group, RFC-1771, March 1995.

[5] Scott Hazelhust, Raymond Sinnappan and Adi Attar, "Algorithms for Improving the Dependability of Firewall and Filter Rule Lists", Proceedings of the International Conference on Dependable Systems and Networks (DSN 2000) , IEEE COMPSAC , pp:576-585, 2000.

[6] Jim Holmes, "Building Your Own Compiler With C++", Prentice Hall, Englewood Cliffs, NJ, 1995.

[7] John Lakos, "Large-Scale C++ Software Design", Addison-Wesley Publishing Company, 1996.

[8] Scott Meyers, "Effective C++ (Second Edition)", Addison-Wesley Publishing Company, 1997.

[9] Chuck Hedrick, "Routing Information Protocol", RFC 1058, June 1988.

[10] Mohamed A. Eissa, "Coperative Defence Firewall Protocol", M. Sc. Thesis, Faculty of Engineering, Cairo University, January 2002.

[11] Rainer, R., MacGregor, M.H., Grover, W.D., "Optimal Capacity Placement for Path Restoration in STM or ATM Mesh-Survivable Networks", IEEE/ACM Transactions on Networks, Vol.6, No.3, pp:325-336, June 1998.

HOW TO TURN A PIN INTO AN IRON BEAM

A patent-free and practical protocol for secure communication using a weak common secret

Stefan Lucks
Theoretische Informatik, Universität Mannheim, Germany
lucks@th.informatik.uni-mannheim.de

Ruediger Weis
Department of Computer Systems, Vrije Universiteit Amsterdam, Netherlands
ruedi@cryptolabs.org

Abstract It is a hazardous fact of life that users are hardly ever willing and able to memorise strong passwords or long personal identification numbers (PINs). This paper describes a variant of the "open key exchange" (OKE) protocol, a cryptographic scheme to provide high security even when using low-entropy passwords. The variant has been dedicatedly designed for slow devices, such as smart cards.

1. Introduction

Speak "friend" and enter! (J. R. R. Tolkien)

Consider two principals, Alice and Bob, trying to communicate via an insecure network. Think of Alice being a host and Bob being a smart card[1]. Alice, as the host, does not know whether she is connected to Bob or to a fake smart card, and Bob does not know whether he is connected to a fake host. Worse, Alice may be connected to a fake smart card, *and* Bob may be connected to a fake host *and* the adversary has simultaneously access to the fake smart card and to the fake host – i.e., the connection between Alice and Bob may be completely controlled by the adversary, whom we call Eve here[2].

If Alice and Bob use a *strong secret key*, or if one of them knows the other's *authentic public key*, standard cryptographic techniques for key agreement allow both sides to establish a session key and to use it for secure communication (i.e., to guarantee both confidentiality and authenticity of the messages). Many practical applications, however, suffer from the following problem: An authentic public key is not known, and if both sides agree on a secret key, it is a *weak secret key*, generated from a simple password to be entered by the user. [3] Since humans are quite bad at generating and memorising high-entropy secrets, searching for all likely (or even possible) keys - so-called *dictionary attacks* - is efficient and will probably reveal the secret key.

Fortunately, cryptographers have started developing "*password protocols*" to securely authenticate and exchange session keys, even if the participants only have agreed on a weak key in advance. The security of such protocols depends on counting how often an attempt to establish a secure connection fails. The failure may occur either because the other participant responds "wrongly", or because no response is given at all (some "time-out" event). We describe this by a *reject counter.*

Here, we reconsider the Protected OKE protocol from Lucks [15]. While the security assurance from the proof of security may be smaller, especially in comparison to protocols provably secure in the standard model [11, 13], we argue that for some practical applications, only Protected OKE is efficient enough. The reason is, that the competing protocols all use either the Diffie-Hellman key exchange or (in the case of [13]) the Cramer-Shoup Cryptosystem as their main cryptographic primitive. In contrast to this, Protected OKE uses RSA and allows the use of small fixed public exponents, such as 3. Let n be a security parameter. Given a group base g, both Diffie-Hellman and Cramer-Shoup require to compute some values g^x (modulo an n-bit number). This is computationally much more expensive than computing x^3 (modulo a composed n-bit number). In the case of Protected OKE, only one of the parties needs to compute the RSA-decryption operation (i.e., to compute x^d for a large d). Think of an application, where one of the parties is computationally impaired, e.g. by using a slow smartcard. In this case, computing x^3 can be fast enough, even if general exponentiations are too slow.

Sometimes, even Protected OKE with the public exponent 3 may be too slow. We describe a much more efficient variant, by trading *some security* for *greatly improved efficiency.*

2. The Security Model

In this section, we give an informal description of the security model.[4]

The Attack Model. As mentioned above, Eve has complete control over the connection between Bob and Alice, see below. She can

- read all messages,
- modify the messages, delay them or send them multiple times,
- create any message she wants on her own and send it to Alice as "Bob's message" and to Bob as a message seemingly from Alice.

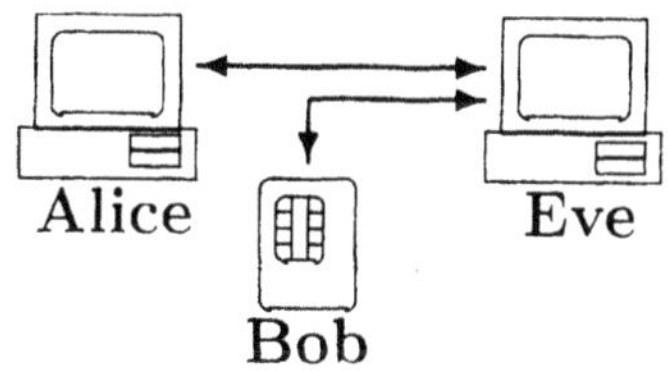

We consider protocols for *the authenticated key exchange (for weak keys)* between Alice and Bob. Such a protocol is *sound*, if both partners accept with overwhelming probability, assuming each message from Alice to Bob and each message from Bob to Alice is faithfully transmitted.

Both Alice and Bob can either send a reply, or accept the communication and create a session key, or reject the communication. They reject, if they either find out that a reply they get is "wrong", or if a connection is timed out when they are waiting for a reply. So, in order to avoid being rejected, Eve must give "correct" replies.

Eve's target is to learn a session key, which has been accepted by either Alice or Bob or both of them.

The Reject Counter. We assume that both Alice and Bob will not continue any communication after a fixed number $\mathcal{R}$ of *rejections.* [5] The number of allowed rejections is crucial for Eve's probability of success.

The Trivial Attack. Consider the following trivial attack:
Eve guesses the password and runs the protocol with either Alice or Bob. If her guess has been correct, her partner accepts and she learns the session key, i.e., she succeeds.
If she had guessed the wrong password, her partner rejects (hopefully!).

If the protocol is good, Eve learns nothing else about the correct password, except that it is different from her guess.

If the initial probability to guess the right password is $\leq \sigma$, if Alice stops communication after at most τ_a rejections, and if Bob stops communication after at most τ_b rejections, then Eve's complete probability of success by this *trivial* attack is $\leq \sigma(\tau_a + \tau_b)$. [6]

Secure key exchange protocol for weak keys. A protocol to do the authenticated key exchange protocol for weak keys is *secure*, if no attack is "much"[7] better than the trivial attack.

3. The generic open key exchange protocol

We fix two security parameters K and L with the following requirements: *K is large enough such that doing any 2^K operations is infeasible. Let $L > K$ be large enough such that factorising an L-bit RSA-modulus N, which has secretly been chosen as the product of two $L/2$-bit primes, is infeasible.* Currently, we recommend $K \geq 80$ and $L \geq 1024$.

For the protocol, we need hash functions $h_i : \{0,1\}^* \longrightarrow \{0,1\}^l$ ($i \in \{1,2,3\}$), an asymmetric key pair (E, D), such that E describes the encryption operation $E : S_E \longrightarrow S_E$, where S_E is a finite group, "$*$" denotes the group operation, and "$/$" its inverse, and a hash function $H : \{0,1\}^* \longrightarrow S_E$. [8]

The group operation needs to be compatible with the encryption function, i.e. for all $x, y \in S_E$: $E(x) * E(y) = E(x * y)$. Also, the encryption function must be invertible, i.e. $D(E(x)) = x$ must hold for $x \in S_E$. The group S_E can depend on the choice of E, as for RSA. The pair (E, D) and hence the group S_E can be chosen once by Alice and remains fixed during the experiment of running the protocol in the presence of Eve. D is kept secret. We use "$|$" to indicate the concatenation of bit strings.

3.1 Protocol Description

The generic OKE protocol works like this [15]:

0. *Both in advance:* Alice and Bob agree on a common secret π.
   Alice in advance: Alice generates a public/private-key pair (E, D).

1 Alice chooses $m \in_R \{0,1\}^l$ and sends E and m to Bob.[9]

2 Bob chooses $\mu \in_R \{0,1\}^l$ and $a \in_R S_E$, computes $p = H(E|m|\mu|\pi)$ and $q = E(a) * p$, and sends μ and q to Alice.

3 Alice computes p like Bob, $a' = D(q/p)$, and sends $r = h_1(a')$ to Bob. (Now $a' = a$.)

4 If $r \neq h_1(a)$, Bob rejects. Otherwise, he computes $k = h_2(a)$ and $t = h_3(a)$, sends t to Alice, and uses k as his session key.

5 Alice rejects if $t \neq h_3(a')$. Else, she uses $k' = h_2(a')$ as session key.

3.2 Security Theorem

We make the following two cryptographic assumptions:

A1: The hash functions H, h_1, h_2, and h_3 are treated as "random oracles" [4], i.e. Eve can send queries $x_1, x_2, \ldots$ to the random oracle h_i resp. H and receives answers $h_i(x_j)$, resp. $H(x_j)$, all independent random values. Only when a query $x_c = x_j$ is sent to the oracle h_i (or H) and Eve was given the oracle response $h_i(x_j)$ ($H(x_j)$) before, the result is predictable: $h_i(x_c) = h_i(x_j)$ (or $H(x_c) = H(x_j)$).

A2: Given a value x, randomly chosen from the set S_E, it is infeasible to find a value y with $y = D(x)$.

THEOREM 1 *Under the assumptions A1 and A2, the generic OKE protocol is a secure key exchange protocol for weak common secrets, i.e., it has the following properties:*

1 If all participants behave as specified, both Alice and Bob accept with overwhelming probability and compute identical session keys.

2 If Eve faithfully transmits all messages between Alice and Bob and only listens passively, her probability of success is negligible.

3 If Eve mounts any active attacks, her probability of success does not significantly exceed the trivial attack.

Proof: See [15].

4. When RSA comes into play

At a first look, the RSA public-key cryptosystem appears to be ideal for open key exchange. The public key is the pair $E = (e, N)$, where $N = PQ$ is the product of two huge primes P and Q and e is relatively prime to $\varphi(N) = \varphi(P)\varphi(Q) = (P-1)(Q-1)$. The encryption function is defined by $E(x) = x^e \bmod N$, the decryption function is $D(x) = x^d \bmod N$, where the secret exponent d is chosen such that $ed \equiv 1 (\bmod \varphi(N))$. The natural choice for the group operation $*$ is the multiplication mod N, the group S_E is the set of all numbers in $\{1, \ldots, N-1\}$ which are not divisible by P or Q, i.e. the size of S_E is $|S_E| = \varphi(N)$.

4.1 A Security Problem

Note that the function E must be invertible. We had required this above. This property is actually used in the proof of security [15].

If Eve, when impersonating Alice, chooses E such that it is not invertible, i.e., no function D exists at all, Theorem 1 is no longer applicable.[10] In the case of RSA, unfortunately, Eve may choose her public key such that encryption is not invertible (and thus, not really "encryption" any more, since decryption is impossible). Specifically, if N is the product of two distinct odd primes P and Q, the RSA-function $y = x^e (\bmod N)$ is invertible, if and only if e divides neither $P-1$ nor $Q-1$.

Even though it may seem counter-intuitive, it may be useful for Eve to choose a non-invertible function E. We describe an attack:
For all likely passwords π^*, *Eve computes* $p = H(E|m|\mu|\pi^*)$. *If the equivalence* $a^e \equiv (q * (p^*)^{-1}) \pmod N$ *has no solution, Eve concludes that* π^* *is wrong. By elementary group theory, we know that the number of such solutions is either 0 or a constant c, which depends on* N.[11]
Thus, if here had been $|\Pi|$ *passwords before the attack, this attack allows Eve to reduce the number of passwords down to* $|\Pi|/c$, *on the average.*

4.2 Protected OKE

To defend against the above attack, we need an additional *protection step* when using RSA-based OKE variants. Alice (or whoever communicates with Bob) must prove that the function E in use is actually invertible. If the proof fails, Bob rejects.

The basic idea for such a proof is to require Alice to sign a couple of random values, using N and her secret exponent d. Bob checks the validity of these signatures, using N and the public exponent e. Lucks [15] suggested to use K such signatures, i.e., Alice had to sign K random values, and Bob had to verify K signatures. Each random value can only be signed with probability $1/c$, and if Alice (or Eve) fails to sign any given random values, Bob rejects.

[15] also proposed a technique to save bandwidth, avoiding the transmission of $K - 1$ of these signatures. Eve's chances to trick Bob into accepting a non-invertible encryption function are negligible.

4.3 Fixing the Exponent $e = 3$

In the context of this paper, N is an RSA-modulus, and for the sake of efficiency, we suggest to use $e = 3$ as the public exponent. [12]

If Eve makes the attempt to "cheat" by using a non-invertible encryption function, this means choosing $N' = PQ'$ with $Q' - 1$ divisible by 3. Then no value d exists with $3d \equiv 1 \pmod{Q'}$, and, in fact, an equivalence $y = x^3 \pmod{N'}$ with $\text{lcm}(y, N) = 1$ has either none or at least three solutions for x. (E.g., set $N' = 35 = 5 * 7$: the equation $29 = x^3 \pmod{N'}$ has three solutions, namely 5, 9, and 29.)

4.4 A Trade-Off between Security and Efficiency

With $K \geq 80$, Protected OKE requires Bob (the smart card) to do more than 80 public-key operations. This is quite slow, even if all these operations are of the form $y = x^3 (\text{mod } N)$. The bandwidth-saving technique uses multiplications mod N, which slows down things additionally.

In order to speed up the protocol, we propose to do only $K' \ll K$ signatures. Eve's chance to convince Bob that she can decrypt mod N may then be small, but not negligible. Consider Eve having chosen a modulus N such that $y = x^e (\bmod N)$ is not invertible, i.e., $c > 1$.

- With K' signatures, and if Bob stops communication after having rejected τ_b times, Eve is accepted

$$\frac{\tau_b}{c^{K'}} \quad \text{times on the average.}$$

- Each time her "cheated" modulus N is accepted, the number of passwords (or PINs) still possible

$$\text{decreases from a value } |\Pi| \text{ down to } \frac{|\Pi|}{c} \text{ on the average.}$$

  Thus, $\log_2(c)$ bit of the Password- or PIN-entropy are lost.

Recall that c is under Eve's control. If Eve chooses a large c, her forged modulus N is unlikely to ever be accepted. If c is small, such as $c = 3$, she has some chance to reduce the password-space, but only by a moderate amount, such as decreasing the password-entropy by $\log_2(3) \approx 1.6$ bit. Consider, say, a random 6-digit decimal PIN. The initial entropy of such a PIN is $\log_2(1000000) \approx 20$ bit. In this case, the (unlikely but possible) loss of 1.6 bits of entropy may be tolerable.

How likely is the event, that Eve succeeds with her cheating, and some of the entropy of π is lost? We provide two examples:

- Consider $K' = 5$, and assume that Bob stops all communication after $\tau_b = 5$ rejections. In this case, Eve's probability of success is no more than $5/(c^5)$, i.e., even for $c = 3$ it is only about 2.1 %.
- With $K' = 7$ and $\tau_b = 10$, Eve's probability of success is less than 0.46 %, even for $c = 3$.

We stress that the security of the scheme against this type of attack only depends on the number K' of signatures required, and on the number τ_b of rejections Bob tolerates.

For most applications, $K' = 5$ and $\tau_b = 5$ seem to provide a reasonable compromise between security and efficiency. We stress that the event with probability 2.1 % is not "Eve succeeds in finding π", but only "Eve succeeds in reducing the entropy of π by 1.6 bit".

4.5 Description of Modified Protocol

Our modified RSA-based Protected OKE protocol works like this:

0. *Both in advance:* Alice and Bob agree on a common secret π. *Alice in advance:* Alice generates an RSA-modulus $N = PQ$, with the prime factors P and Q not being divisible by 3.

1 Alice chooses $m \in_R \{0,1\}^l$ and sends E and m to Bob.

1.1 Bob sends a random challenge x_0 to Alice.

1.2 For $i := 1$ to K', Alice calculates $x_i = H(x_{i-1})^d \pmod N$. Alice sends the values $x_1, ..., x_{K'}$ to Bob.

1.3 Bob checks $(x_{i-1}) = x_i^3$ (for $1 \le i \le K'$) and rejects if this fails for any such i.

2 Bob chooses $\mu \in_R \{0,1\}^l$ and $a \in_R \{1, \ldots, N-1\}$, computes $p = H(N|m|\mu|\pi)$ and $q = E(a) * p \pmod N$, and sends μ and q to Alice.

3 Alice computes p like Bob, $a' = (q/p)^d \pmod N$, and sends $r = h_1(a')$ to Bob.

4 If $r \neq h_1(a)$, Bob rejects. Otherwise, he computes $k = h_2(a)$ and $t = h_3(a)$, sends t to Alice, and uses k as his session key.

5 Alice rejects if $t \neq h_3(a')$. Else, she uses the session key $k' = h_2(a')$.

Note that the steps are numbered as their counterparts in the generic protocol. The additional "protection" steps are numbered as $1.x$.

5. Final Remarks and Conclusion

5.1 Communication Time ↔ Computations

We proposed a "reasonably secure" variant of RSA-based protected OKE, which improved on the original version [15] by reducing the amount of computations. The two *disadvantages* of this variant are:

1 the security is *somewhat* reduced (as quantified above), and

2 the amount of communication grows.

When implementing smartcard-based protocols in practice, the amount of computations dome the smartcards are not always the performance bottleneck. Sometimes, the performance is mainly determined by the amount of communication instead. In this case, we recommend to use the original RSA-based protected OKE protocol [15], which is more secure and even more efficient under such circumstances.

5.2 On Proofs of Security

The fact that the Generic OKE protocol is provably secure, but its seemingly natural instantiation with RSA can be insecure, raises some questions about "provably secure" cyptosystems. An application based on a "provably secure" cryptosystem may nevertheless be insecure, for one or more of the following reasons:

- The application fails to enforce some of the system's environmental requirements. This is the case for RSA-based generic OKE.
- An assumption made to prove the scheme's security is false.
- The "proven" security does not satisfy the application's needs.

Is "provable security" cryptography of no use, then? We do not think so. Providing a proof of security for a cryptosystem forces its author

- to explicitly describe the system's environmental requirements,
- to explicitly declare the assumptions made, and
- to exactly specify the what kind of "security" the scheme is supposed to provide.

A "provably secure" cryptosystem tells the security architect, what she has to watch for, when implementing it. This is different from "heuristic" cryptosystems, published without a proof of security. Note that the problems of RSA-based generic OKE have been described in the same paper as OKE and its proof of security [15], and are in fact quite obvious from the specification of the environmental requirements. On the other hand, security problems of variants of EKE, e.g. for RSA-based EKE [17] have been found years after the publication of these schemes.

5.3 The Random Oracle Model

Proofs of security in the *random oralce model* assume that the adversary treats hash functions like random oracles. The corresponding security results, showing the infeasiblity of some attacks, are thus only valid with respect to restricted, so-called *generic* attacks. All currently known and practically relevant attacks against cryptographic protocols are generic. But in theory, non-generic attacks could exist. So a proof of security in the random oracle modell is good, but a proof of security in the *standard model* is more assuring and better. See [9] for details.

5.4 Related Work

The formal verification of the security of all kinds of cryptographic protocols has been intensively studied before. We refer the reader to [8] for a "classical" example and to [2] and references therein for more up-to-date information.

The first password protocol has been developed in 1989 [14]. Some protocols with similar goals followed. An important step has been the "Encrypted Key Exchange" (EKE) protocol from Bellovin and Merritt 1992 [6]. The core idea behind EKE is to use the secret (symmetric) key π to encrypt the public key E of a randomly chosen asymmetric key pair (E, D), then to use E to encrypt the randomly chosen (symmetric) session key k and finally to decrypt $E(k)$ using D. The security of EKE depends on the fact that two parties using different values for π are likely to use different public keys E and E', and that knowing an asymmetric key pair (E', D') does not help to decrypt $E(k)$. It is important for EKE protocols, that every public key is used only once.

None of the early password protocols came with a formal proof of security, and in fact, some have been shown to be insecure [1, 10, 17]. Thus, researchers started to look for *provably secure* protocols. The *Open Key Exchange* (OKE) protocol by Lucks [15] has been the first such protocol. [13] The approach in [15] is based on the work of Bellare and Rogaway on key exchange protocols for *strong secret keys* [3]. In the sequel other protocols have been proven to be secure [16, 7, 5].

The proofs of security in [15, 7, 5] are all in the random oracle model. A proof in the standard model would be more meaningful and provide an improved security assurance. Quite recently, password protocols provably secure in the standard model have been developed. Goldreich and Lindell [11] described such a protocol and a proof of security based only on the assumption that trapdoor one-way permutations exist. The protocol from [11] borrows techniques from general multi-party computation and thus is quite impractical. Nevertheless, [11] can be seen as a theoretical break-through. Another recent protocol [13] is quite practical and provably secure in the standard model, but it is based on the Cramer-Shoup Cryptosystem and less efficient than our protocol.

5.5 On Smartcard Programmer Interfaces

When trying to implement new cryptographic schemes (such as OKE or other password protocols, or blinding for anonymous digital money, or ...) on smartcards with support for public-key cryptography, one may get disillusioned. Often, the interface for plain number-theoretic operations such as "given e, N, and x, compute $x^e \bmod N$" or "given N, x, and y, compute $xy \bmod N$" is just missing. This is, e.g., the case for the JAVA Card 2.0 API. This has two implications:

1 Without access to the raw number-theoretic functions, the application programmer may be locked into using the given primitives, making it very hard to implement new ones.

2 Some of the pre-defined primitives may turn out to be insecure (e.g., PKCS#1 v. 1.5 padding for public-key encryption). The application programmer may be locked into using an insecure scheme!

Of course, the application programmer may implement a "BigNum" library on her own. However, this is expensive, error-prone and terribly unnecessary. Also, a self-written "BigNum" library may be much less efficient than a pre-installed one, especially on a smartcard with a hardware accelerator for public-key cryptography.

5.6 Conclusion

We presented a new variant of the Protected Open Key Exchange password protocol, based on the provably secure Generic Open Key Exchange protocol. The goal is to enable secure communications using slow devices, low-entropy PINs or passwords and no PKI. A trade-off between security and efficiency allows the security architect to meet reasonable security requirements while outperforming other password protocols.

Notes

1. Cryptographers are very unhappy if they have to use other names.

2. All this scenarios can happen in the real world if we have a manipulated smart card reader or we have a scenario like the Internet Smart Card [12].

3. I.e., the password is stored on the smart card, and when needed typed in at the host.

4. A random oracle based formal security model can be found in [15].

5. This is consistent with a typical smart card application, where the smart card stops all operations if the wrong password has been typed in a fixed number of times and the user should not (and probably will not) type in her password hundreds or thousands of times.

6. As a concrete example, think of the password being a random 6-digit decimal number, i.e. $\sigma = 1/1\,000\,000$. If the smart card stops communication after 10 failed identification attempts, and the human user gives up after at most 90 failed attempts, then Eve's probability of success is at most $(1/1\,000\,000)(10+90)$, i.e. $\leq 0.01\,\%$.

7. See [15] for a more formal description.

8. The four *independent* hash functions can be implemented based on on single hash function, such as the well-known SHA-1.

9. Note that though the pair (E, D) can be chosen once, it does not make sense to assume Bob can remember E. If Bob already did know Alice's authentic public key E, he could simply choose the session key k_B and send $E(k_B)$ to Alice, instead of running the protocol.

10. This has some implications for the use of "provably secure" cryptosystems. We discuss this in Section 5.2.

11. If the public exponent $e = 3$ and $c > 1$, then $c \geq 3$.

12. Technically, $N = PQ$ is the product of two distinct large primes P and Q, and neither $(P-1)$ nor $(Q-1)$ is divisible by 3.

13. In the context of this paper, and in general when dealing with cryptographic protocols, any proof of security assumes the security of the cryptographic primitives in use. E.g., if the instantiation of a cryptographic protocol uses a 400-bit RSA key, this can hardly be secure, because 400-bit RSA is insecure. The protocol by itself may nevertheless be secure, such as an instantiation with, say, 2000-bit RSA.

References

[1] R. ANDERSON, S. VAUDENAY: "Minding your p's and q's", Asiacrypt 96, Springer LNCS.

[2] M. ABADI, P. ROGAWAY: "Reconciling Two Views of Cryptography (The Computational Soundness of Formal Encryption)", IFIP International Conference on Theoretical Computer Science, IFIP TCS2000, (2000).

[3] M. BELLARE, P. ROGAWAY: "Entity Authentication and Key Distribution", Crypto 93, Springer LNCS 773.

[4] M. BELLARE, P. ROGAWAY: "Random Oracles are Practical: A Paradigm for Designing Efficient Protocols", First ACM Conference on Computer and Communications Security, ACM, 1993.

[5] M. BELLARE, D. POINTCHEVAL, P. ROGAWAY: "Authenticated Key Exchange Secure against Dictionary Attacks", Eurocrypt 2000, Springer LNCS 1807.

[6] S. BELLOVIN, M. MERRIT: "Encrypted Key Exchange: Password-Based Protocols Secure against Dictionary Attacks", IEEE Computer Society Symposium on Research in Security and Privacy, 1992, 72–84.

[7] V. BOYKO, P. MACKENZIE, S. PATEL: "Provably Secure Password-Authenticated Key Exchange Using Diffie-Hellman", Eurocrypt 2000, Springer LNCS 1807.

[8] M. BURROWS, M. ABADI, R. NEEDHAM: "A logic of authentication", ACM Transactions on Computer Systems 8(1), Feb. 1990, 18–36.

[9] R. CANTTI, O. GOLDREICH, S. HALIEVI: "The Random Oracle Method Revisited", Proceedings of the 13th Annual ACM Symposium on Theory of Computing (SToC), 1998.

[10] Y. DING, P. HORSTER: "Undetectable on-line Password Guessing Attacks", Operating Systems Review, Vol. 29, No. 4, Oct. 1995.

[11] O. GOLDREICH, Y. LINDELL: "Session-Key Generation using Human Passwords Only", Crypto 2001, Springer LNCS 2139.

[12] N. ITOI, T. FUKUZAWA, P. HONEYMAN: "Secure Internet Smartcards", Proc. Java Card Workshop , Cannes, 2000.

[13] J, KATZ, R. OSTROVSKY, M. YUNG: "Efficient Password-Authenticated Key Exchange using Human-Memorable Passwords", Eurocrypt 2001, Springer LNCS 2045.

[14] M. LOMAS, L. GONG, J. SALTZER, R. NEEDHAM: "Reducing Risks from Poorly Chosen Keys", ACM Symposium on Operation System Principles, 1989.

[15] S. LUCKS: "Open Key Exchange: How to Defeat Dictionary Attacks Without Encrypting Public Keys", Security Protocols 1997, Springer LNCS 1361.

[16] P. MACKENZIE, R. SWAMINATHAN: "Secure Authentication with a Short Secret", Submission to IEEE P1363, `http://grouper.ieee.org/groups/1363/addendum.html`.

[17] S. PATEL: "Number-Theoretic Attacks on Secure Password Schemes", IEEE Symposium on Security and Privacy, 1997.

WORLD FRAMEWORK FOR SECURITY BENCHMARK CHANGES

Lech J. Janczewski, Andrew M. Colarik
The University of Auckland, New Zealand

Abstract: The paper contains presentation of a framework, which would significantly increase quality of information security products and procedures, and Commentary on difficulties of implementing such a model. Main idea behind the framework is creation of a body assessing quality of information security products and procedures, similar to the system the ISO 9000 certificates.

Key words: Information security management, quality assurance, security benchmarks

1. CURRENT QUALITY ASSURANCE OF THE SECURITY PRODUCTS AND METHODS

Current quality assurance of the security products and methods could be divided into four stages:

Stage 1; A researcher / research facility announces a new product, which according to them, solves a specific security problem, for instance offering a new, more powerful cipher, new security protocol, etc. In most cases the product was released after passing in-house testing.

Stage 2; World community implements the invention, or product.

Stage 3; Other researchers start evaluation of the product and announce their findings through their publication channels. They usually are very eager to publish their findings as that such critique inevitably improves their standing within the security community. Hackers start the same activities but not all their findings are published. There are many "official" hacker publications, like "2600, the Hacker Quarterly" magazine (Hackers, 2002) or hackers conventions, but in general, the knowledge is released to the wider community after they took advantage of their findings.

Stage 4; Upon receiving information about possible faults of the product the researches start developing mechanisms for blocking the discovered vulnerabilities of the systems. The process returns to stage 1.

What are the weak points of the process presented above? In our opinion there are several:

In the majority of cases, security products and procedures are not undergoing sufficient scrutiny of fellow researchers. Many software houses before releasing their products offer their product for free evaluation. However, the possible recipients of these packages are not in most cases chosen by their abilities to do a proper evaluation. There is no consistency with the critique of a new product. A publication with limited circulation could present the critique and the original developer would not have any opportunity to read it. Or even in the case of hackers, such critiques may never be published in a respected security forum.

Common Criteria are good as a presentation of general methodological assessment of the quality of security products but, for the obvious reasons, lacks details. Take for instance an issue of the physical protection of IT resources. It could be quite difficult to find direct instruction on how to evaluate system/devices falling into this category. Acceptance or rejection of a particular system could have significant financial consequences. The evaluation process should be set up in such a way that possible differences in the interpretation be eliminated to minimum.

2. MODEL CONCEPT OVERVIEW

There are three improvements to the above environment that we put forward.

1. The establishment of an independent, peer-based confirmation program that can validate specific capabilities and claims put forward by security vendors.

2. The creation of a certification program equivalent to Underwriters Laboratories (UL) and Canadian Standards Association (CSA) on products that carry liability insurance.

3. The establishment of security benchmark barriers for the purpose of disclosing the limitations of security products to the consumer similar in practice to Consumer Digest.

3. THE PROCESS

The validation/invalidation process consists of twelve (12) phases and is identified in the Table 1.

Table 1: Framework for security benchmark

Phase	Description
Classification	Apply a product to a classification system
Presentation	Apply standardized product presentation requirements to claims
Procedures	Develop revised verification procedures for each product based on original classification procedure
Validation	Product is submitted and evaluated by Verifiers
Reporting I	Initial reports generated by Verifiers - initial round
Reporting II	Exchanged reports allow re-examination by Verifiers
Final Report Generation	Reports are compiled and claims are validated/invalidated
Revised Claims	Manufacturer has opportunity to revise claims based on final report for certificate issuance
Certificate Issuance	Certificate is issued providing revised claims are consistent with final report
Certified Product Claims Published	Products invalidated by breaches may be revoked if not promptly addressed

4. ESTABLISHMENT OF SECURITY BENCHMARK BARRIERS

The first and second objectives are fulfilled through the validation and certification processes that have been outlined. However, as a security community of varying levels of expertise and understanding, there remains a need yet unfulfilled. The need is the dissemination of well-established issues about electronic security mechanisms. These issues are paramount to the establishment of procedures in the first and second objectives.

Authors, such as Bruce Schneier (2000), suggest that all security is based on social context and have identified fundamental weaknesses in the approaches to securing electronic based information systems. The Certification Granting Institution is positioned to accumulate and disseminate these fundamental concept weaknesses to all the Players. This is the first logical step in focusing developmental efforts by the security community for the improvement of the industry. It would also serve to educate a realistic approach by consumers for the implementation and maintenance of security within their respective organizations.

The final question is: which organisation should participate in the process, or rather, which organisation should be appointed as having rights to issue certificates and perform the validation tests? We think that the reverse question may be a bit more appropriate: which organisations should not play these roles? In the case of testing facilities, they should not be connected with any manufacturer of security products. That would eliminate claims of possible bias in their opinions and findings. On the other hand, the certificate granting bodies should have international recognition.

Many national standards organisations are issuing the ISO 9000 certificates. The verification process leading to ISO certificate issuance is carried out by the standard organisations themselves. Hence the national standards organisation could be a good candidate for issuing such certificates. Other possible candidates could be CERT-type centres or units attached to such bodies as TC-11 of IFIP.

5. CONCLUSIONS

Annual CSI/FBI (2002) report on status of the information security affairs clearly indicate that loses resulting from abusing information systems are on a constant rise. This indicates that despite all the claims the security industry is still behind the attackers. This is reflected in public perception that conducting business on Internet is not secure.

If that trend is to be reverse, the security industry must undertake some drastic measures to increase the quality of its services and products. We believe that the path we have outlined in this paper is a right way to go. We do not claim that this is the only way to solve the problem, but we think that the security industry must establish a testing and certification environment for their products and services in a trusted third party manner.

REFERENCES

Hackers, 2002, *2600, the Hacker Quarterly*, http://www.2600.com

Schneier, B., Fixing Network Security by Hacking the Business Climate, proceedings of the IIR 7th proceedings of the IIR 7th Annual National Summit on IT Security, 2002

CSI/FBI Computer Crime and Security Survey, http://www.gocsi.com/press/20020407.html, 2002

Schneier, B., Secret & Lies, Wiley, 2000

INFORMATION SECURITY: AUDITING THE BEHAVIOUR OF THE EMPLOYEE

Cheryl Vroom and Rossouw von Solms
Port Elizabeth Technikon,South Africa, cherylv@webmail.co.za, rossouw@petech.ac.za

Abstract: The following paper serves to examine the evolution of auditing in the organization from traditional financial auditing through the introduction of computers into daily transactions. It discusses the need for information security in business today and the methods that can be taken to verify that the security measures are properly utilized to ensure the safety of information systems. This paper hopes to enhance the future role of the auditor by including auditing the employee and his behaviour.

Key words: Information Security Policies, Operational Controls, Information Technology (IT) Auditing, Information Systems (IS) Security Auditing

1. INTRODUCTION

Many procedures are introduced and precautions are taken to ensure the safety of one of the organization's most crucial assets – information. The integrity, confidentiality and availability of vital company information is extremely important and needs to be protected at all costs.

Auditing plays a huge role in this protection by examining the current procedures that are in place to prevent the misuse of information and to ensure that these measures are effective and efficient. Conventional auditing methods are primarily technical in nature, examining the physical, technical and operational procedures of the business, yet one of the most crucial links to the security of information is often overlooked – the human factor. The people in the business are central to any organization, yet also the most serious threat to it, whether intentional or not. (Martins & Eloff, 2002, p1)

How can the behaviour of the employee be checked and verified to ensure that the individual is carrying out his duties to safeguard confidential and valuable information? Can conventional auditing techniques be used to achieve this aim or is a new type of approach needed to ensure the behaviour of the employee is compatible with the goals of the organization with regard to information security?

To answer these questions, auditing and the methods employed by the auditor needs to be investigated with a view to adapting the role of the auditor to incorporate behavioural auditing in information security.

2. TRADITIONAL AND IT AUDITING

Throughout history, the process of auditing has been necessary whenever humans have performed some form of transactions in order to control the accuracy and honesty of finances to a large extent.

The main objective of an audit is to enable a report that is truthful and fair regarding the financial position shown by the balance sheet of the organization. The role of the auditor is to examine the financial statements prepared and provided by the owners and management to ensure that, in his or her opinion, that it is an accurate and fair account of the company's financial position. (Cooper, 1979, p2)

Traditional auditing, however, concentrates solely on the financial records of the organization and the methods that protect these finances. With the introduction of computers to assist in business, the financial side of the organization is no longer the only means that business uses to interact.

Organizations often succeed or fail as a result of how efficiently and effectively they are able to process and convert data into useful and valuable information. (Chambers & Court, 1991, p12) Therefore, the controls and procedures relating to the handling of information in the organization have become extremely relevant and important. The need for auditing of the technology and tools used in business today became apparent, and therefore IT auditing developed.

However, although the advances in information technology have provided enormous benefits to companies and revolutionized the way that they operate, it also creates significant risks and challenges to the organization. (Langelier & Ingram, 2001, p4)

3. INFORMATION SECURITY AND AUDITING

The confidentiality, integrity and availability of the organization's valuable information could be compromised if proper and stringent security precautions are not in place and carried out effectively. Information security has become a cornerstone in the protection of information in virtually all organizations nowadays. To carry out effective information security, controls are used, namely physical, technical and operational controls.

The operational controls are those that concern the behaviour and actions of the employee with regard to information security. An organization has physical controls such as lockable doors, but if the employee does not lock the door, it renders the physical control ineffective. Likewise, technical controls, such as password systems, will be impotent if the user of the system writes the password down for all to see. Locking the door and not writing the password down are deemed operational controls.

Operational controls are considered extremely important as the conduct of the employee within the organization plays an increasingly vital role in securing information. In order to regulate this behaviour and conform to the objectives of the company, the employees of the organization need strict and proper guidelines. These guidelines are set out in the information security policies of the organization, detailing the procedures, rules and regulations that need to be followed by the employees in order to preserve the integrity and confidentiality of company information.

However, these security policies need to be audited to ensure that they are in the best interests of the company with regard to the protection of its information and assets. Therefore Information Systems (IS) security auditing has been introduced to ensure that these policies, procedures and regulations are indeed effective enough to meet their individual objectives.

The IS security audits are utilized to ensure that the measures taken by a company to protect their information resources are compliant with the requirements stipulated in the security policies of the organization and to verify that any security breaches of violations are properly recorded. (atsec Information Security GmbH, 2000) Audits on systems and network, security training programs, policies, etc. are performed to ensure that evaluations on virtually all aspects of the company are provided.

However, although traditional and IT auditing, as well as IS security audits all have their role to play, there is another facet to auditing that has not been addressed directly.

The three types of auditing, discussed in the previous sections, all concentrate on the technical aspects of the business – the financial records, information technology and the information security policies and procedures of the organization. Yet auditing is not performed on the employees who actually follow the operational controls that are prescribed. It is simply assumed the employee will adhere to these audited policies.

The actions of the employee are vitally important to the security of the organization. The behaviour of the personnel and how they react in situations is paramount to the information security aspect of the business and this issue needs to be addressed to ensure that the employees and their behaviour are not the weak link in the information security chain.

4. AUDITING THE EMPLOYEE

Human behaviour is only recorded in the actions that are the result of this behaviour. For example, information can be stolen due to the employee not logging off his computer or leaving the door of his office unlocked. Both the technical and physical controls are not effective in this case because the operational control was not followed, even though the audited policy procedure should be effective if followed.

Therefore, all that auditing results can prove is that although all controls were successfully audited and shown to be effective to the security of information, the information was still stolen. This is due to the human factor. Human behaviour is not performed according to a set of written rules, but according to the personality of the individual.

However, this behaviour can be categorized. Much well-documented research has gone into human psychology and the study of human behaviour. Personnel departments use personality testing during interviews to discover whether potential employees are compatible with the objectives and structure of the organization. In the same vein, can this type of behavioural psychology be used with regard to information security?

The potential for the use of behavioural psychology in the area of information security is enormous. The ability to assess the potential of an employee to violate security policies and procedures is beneficial to the company, but unfortunately it has its drawbacks. It is unethical, and currently unlawful, to target an individual and categorize him as a potential threat to the security of a company.

It may be an academic exercise currently, but the potential for it to become a basis for practical reality in future business is possible.

5. REFERENCES

[1] atsec Information Security GmbH. (2000). Security Auditing and Revision. [online] [Cited May 11, 2002] Available from Internet URL http://www.atsec.com/e/service_auditing.php3.

[2] Chambers, A.D. & Court, J.M. (1991). Computer Auditing 3rd Edition. London:Pitman Publishing.

[3] Cooper, V.R.V. (1979). Student's Manual of Auditing. London:Gee & Co (Publishers) Limited.

[4] Langelier, C. & Ingram, J. (2001). National State Auditors Association and the U.S. General Accounting Office : Management Planning Guide Information System Security Auditing. [online]. [Cited May 11, 2002] Available from Internet URL http://www.gao.gov.

[5] Martins, A. & Eloff, J.H.P (2002) Assessing Information Security Culture. 2nd Annual Information Security for South Africa Conference 2002. Muldersdrift.

PRIORITIES IN THE DEPLOYMENT OF NETWORK INTRUSION DETECTION SYSTEMS

Marcin Dobrucki & Teemupekka Virtanen

Nokia & Helsinki University of Technology, Finland.

Abstract: The purpose of this work is to study the priorities in the deployment of network intrusion detection systems (NIDS) in small corporate networks. The goal is to minimize costs while optimizing performance. Despite apparent benefits of automated intrusion detection systems (IDS), they are not widely deployed at this time. Our main research problem is defining key cost areas of NIDS deployment and then developing ways to achieve the required functionality with minimal costs. We present a concept of pre-ids stage, where small, isolated tools are used to target network security problems. The ease of deployment and low maintenance costs help of these tools allow to combat a large part of these problems at a fraction of the costs of a full IDS.

Keywords: Network intrusion detection, optimization and deployment.

1. INTRUSION DETECTION

By intrusion detection, we mean identifying potentially malicious or undesirable activity that may have occurred in a given environment as recorded in an audit trail (Amoroso, 1994) of a security system. Five steps make up this process: capture, analyze, classify, report, and possibly react (Bace, 1999; Heberlein et al., 1991; Lunt et al., 1988; Smaha, 1998) to the event. Our ability to automate the system, and benefit from it is highly dependent on our ability to collect quality data (Ptacek and Newsham, 1998) and our ability to extract useful information from that data.

2. DEPLOYMENT PRIORITIES

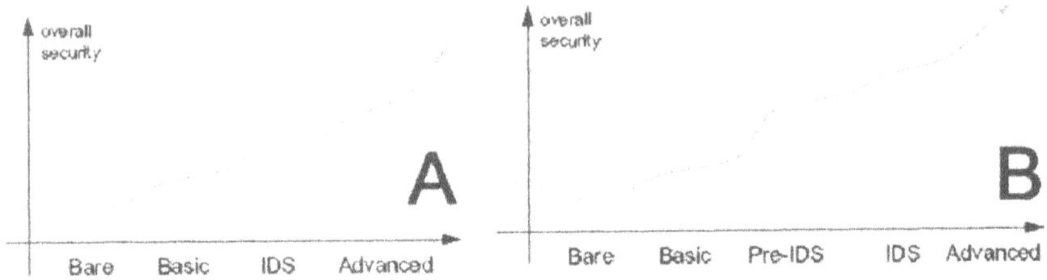

Figure 1. Original (A) and improved (B) security phases in small corporate network

We use the stages in Figure 1A to roughly represent the deployment of security measures in a network infrastructure. The *bare* stage represents computers directly connected to a larger network without any kind of security provisions. We define the *basic* phase when the company implements a firewall (FW), and possibly divides the network into separate zones such as de-militarized zone (DMZ) or extranets. Beyond the basic stage, companies begin to look for active defenses. This typically involves active monitoring of network traffic (NIDS), or host-based IDS, or both. Whereas the gap between the bare and basic functionalities is quite simple to close, the deployment of an IDS is a large and difficult project. Beyond the IDS phase we have defined an Advanced stage, where anything from large data-mining IDS systems to verified platforms can be found.

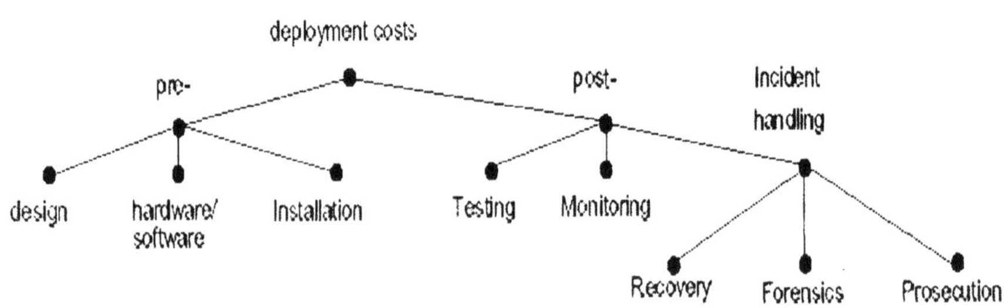

Figure 2. Costs layout for intrusion detection system deployment

In Figure 2 we present different cost areas and divide them into two parts: the pre- and post- deployment expenses. On the *pre-deployment* branch, we accumulate costs such as system evaluation, selection, software purchases, and system installations. At the *post-deployment* branch, we look at costs of actually running the IDS. Deployment of IDS for PR value is wasteful, and hence we should aim towards some return on investment

(ROI) from our system. The gain can vary from minimizing damage inflicted by the intrusions, to providing evidence which can be used in courts to seek compensation from the attackers (Berinato, 2002). In most cases we have studied, however, use of IDS is limited to helping track down and patch problems. If the IDS is expensive to deploy and maintain, this results in low ROI.

3. SECURITY PRIOR TO INTRUSION DETECTION

The costs and difficulties of IDS deployment lead to a question if there is some more cost-efficient way to improve network security? We introduce an idea of pre-ids phase (as shown in Figure 1B), a set of improvements which are designed to mitigate most of the common problems related to network intrusions. We assume that there is a proper FW and the network has been structured to isolate functionality and create zones (Sanchez, 2000). Recent studies have shown that up to about 70-80% of corporate security problems originate from within the companies. (Raili, 2002) Some of the typical events of interest which we would like to detect are: 1. Address spoofing, are there any packets on our network with interesting looking source address? 2.Are there any new bindings between IP addresses and MAC addresses? 3. Has any of our computers put any of their interfaces in promiscuous mode? 4. Has any of our computers started sending or receiving more traffic than usual? 5. Has any of our computers started to listen on a port which was previously closed?

Inside perimeter defenses, the false positive rate for detected spoofs is very low, because under normal circumstances, no legitimate action should require spoofing of any kind. This allows us to deploy a miniature tool, such as ARPWatch for instance, to monitor changes in address bindings on our network. Promiscous mode detection is more difficult, however it provides a clear indication of suspicious activity (Graham, 2000). Most currently utilized operating systems require administrative rights to put network interfaces into promiscous mode. Hence detection of an unknown promiscous interface should be treated as an intrusion. After a certain period of utilization, patterns of systems behaviour and network utilization should be possible to establish (focus.ids, 2002). Detection of new service ports, or abnormal traffic patterns for any trusted host should hence be viewed as suspicious. Typically such checks can be incorporated into network monitoring tools supplemented by periodic network or vulnerability scans. It might appear unclear at first why deploying a number of small, fairly limited tools might yield more benefits than deploying one solid IDS system. However, referring back to Figure 2, we can identify a number of cost-saving factors on both the pre- and post- deployment branches. At the *pre* stage, we almost completely eliminate the initial expenses associated with deploying IDS. The tools reviewed for this paper were evaluated within a few short hours, and their deployment was almost instaneous. They have also provided reliable information on the main events of interest mentioned above. The savings at the post stage relate mostly to limiting the responsibility of the system administrators to monitor and maintain yet another surveillance system, when a number of them have already been put into use.

4. CONCLUSIONS

The application of a pre-ids technique is limited to certain type of environments however, it can yield positive results. The deployment of a full-scale IDS can be expensive, and although the initial costs can be kept low, a proper maintenance of the system will be costly. We have identified the common events of interest which constitute the majority of issues that a typical IDS deals with. We have then provided a cost-effective solution to combating them through the use of small, dedicated, easily deployable tools.

REFERENCES

Amoroso, E. (1994). Fundamentals of Computer Security Technology. Prentice Hall, Englewood Cliffs, NJ.

Bace, R. (1999). An intro to intrusion detection assessment. Technical report, Infidel Inc.

Berinato, S. (2002). Finally, a real return on security spending. CIO Magazine. http://www.cio.com/archive/021502/security content.html.

focus.ids (2002). Focus-ids: Statistical anomaly analysis. http://www.securityfocus.com.

Graham, R. (2000). Sniffing faq, v.0.3.3. http://www.robertgraham.com/pubs/sniffing-faq.html.

Heberlein, L., Levitt, K., and Mukherjee, B. (1991). A method to detect intrusive activity in a networked environment. In Proceedings of the 14th National Computer Security Conference. Washington DC.

Lunt, T., Jagannathan, R., Lee, R., Listgarten, S., Edwards, D., and Ford, J. (1988). Ides: The enhanced prototype, a real-time intrusion-detection expert system. Technical report, SRI International.

Ptacek, T. H. and Newsham, T. N. (1998). Insertion, evasion, and denial of service: Eluding network intrusion detection. Technical report, "N/A", Suite 330, 1201 5th Street S.W, Calgary, Alberta, Canada, T2R-0Y6.

Raili, S. (2002). Tietoturvan syydetään raha heikoin tuloksin. ITViikko, (6).

Sanchez, S. C. (2000). Ids "zone" theory diagram. http://infosec.gungadin.com. referred 2.1.2002.

Smaha, S. (1998). Haystack: An intrusion detection system. In Proceedings of the IEEE Fourth Aerospace Computer Security Applications Conference. IEEE. Orlando, Florida.

BRIDGING THE GAP BETWEEN RISK ANALYSIS AND SECURITY POLICIES

Using Requirement Engineering Techniques

Paul Gaunard, Eric Dubois
Centre de Recherche Public Henri Tudor (CRP-HT)
Centre d'Innovation par les Technologies de l'Information (CITI)
6, rue Coudenhove-Kalergi. 1359 Luxembourg
{paul.gaunard,eric.dubois}@tudor.lu

Abstract: In the IT security management process, a methodological gap exists between the results of a risk analysis, the development of adequate security policies and the selection of appropriate operational controls. We believe that a number of methods and techniques developed by the Requirement Engineering community, and goal requirements modelling in particular, can be useful to bridge this gap by providing modelling frameworks that might support those processes.

Key words: IT Security, Risk Management, Requirement Engineering methods and modelling techniques

1. INTRODUCTION

IT insecurity results from a particular set of risks that should be properly evaluated and then minimized to a level acceptable regarding the organisation's goals and constraints.

While most of the bricks needed for the management of IT security exist, there are still some methodological gaps to be filled to achieve a rational process that will minimize the actual subjectivity involved in the translation of the risk analysis results into appropriate security policies and decisions for the selection of appropriate controls.

2. CONCEPTS OF A RISK-BASED SECURITY MANAGEMENT PROCESS

The information security management process is based on risk management principles and mixes risk analysis methods with technical and organisational practices. Although many variants exists, the process is almost always based on the following steps [1, 2, 3]:

- an analysis of the organisational context, and in particular, of goals set by the stakeholders and constraints imposed on the organisation;
- an identification of the assets (also called resources) to be protected;
- a security risk analysis, identifying threats vulnerabilities and impacts;
- the development of a security policy for the risk reduction;
- the selection, implementation and management of operational controls.

3. REQUIREMENT ENGINEERING AND RISK MANAGEMENT

Making explicit goals and constraints is vital to ensure a proper policy development and controls selection. The Requirement Engineering (RE) community has done a lot of work to provide adequate methodologies and tools to enhance the software requirement elicitation process, based on the integration of those goals and constraints. These tools have proven useful in various situations, even outside the software world.

Recent researches [4, 5, 6, 7] also present some attempts to integrate IT security concepts and risk management methods into the requirement engineering process. In the line of these efforts, we propose some extensions to a well established RE modelling framework in order to capture and reason on risks and security concepts.

Our proposal is based upon a modelling framework inspired from the Goal Requirement Language (GRL) [8], developed by the University of Toronto. According to its authors, GRL is "a language for supporting goal-oriented modelling and reasoning of requirement, based on the merge of two previously studied frameworks, namely:

- the NFR framework [9], dealing with non-functional requirements;
- the I* [10] framework, an agent oriented modelling framework.

Through several experiences and case studies, the GRL approach has been proven successful in helping in understanding organizational situations, in identifying stakeholders' goals and in reasoning about requirements alternatives.

4. ILLUSTRATION

Let's illustrate (fig.1) our proposal on a basic example presenting security problems and potential solutions associated to a database for which goals like confidentiality, integrity and availability are required.

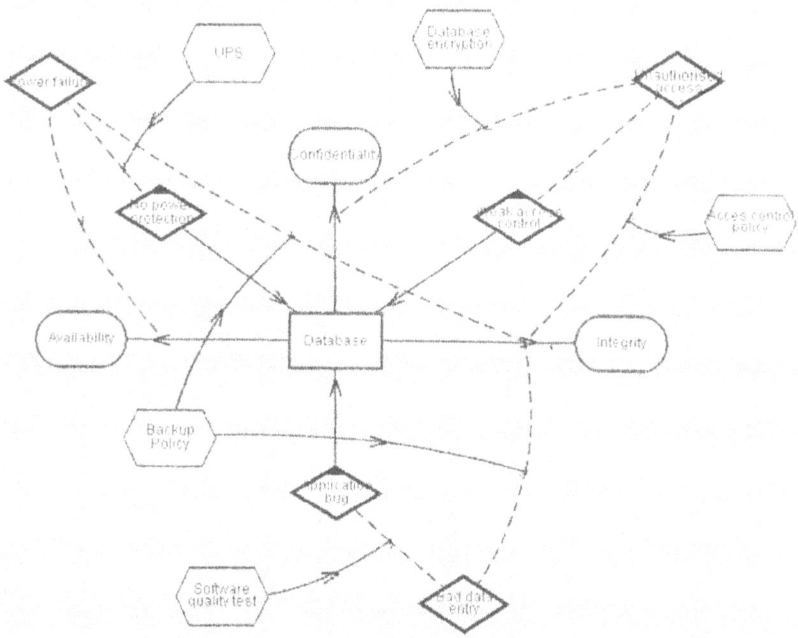

Figure 1. Database confidentiality, integrity and availability.

The database, modelled by a rectangle at the centre of the model, is a resource we wish to protect. Around it, our security goals are modelled by rounded rectangle. The database is affected by various vulnerabilities, like an application bug, a lack of power failure protection and weak access control, modelled by diamonds with black upper corners. These vulnerabilities can be exploited by various threats, modelled by diamonds, to results into various impacts modelled by dashed arrows linking those threats to the links between resources and related goals. Various controls and counter-measures, like UPS, backup, access control and encryption can be applied to counter those identified risks. entry, thus reducing the integrity risk associated to bad data entries.

This example emphasises the importance to get the "big picture" to fully understand the ins and outs of IT security risks, since many solutions exists for a given problems and one solution might be useful to several problems. We thus believe that such modelling framework, including various GRL concepts, would provide visual support helping practitioners during the security policy and control selection processes.

5. CONCLUSION

In this paper, we have suggested that the requirement engineering community had developed models from which various modelling ideas could be reused within the IT security management process. The next step in our research would be to determine the exact semantics required to build efficient models and to evaluate their practicability in real situations.

ACKNOWLEDGEMENTS

The work is partially supported by the Research National Fund of Luxembourg (Acces-PME project). Part of the research is performed within the context of the LIASIT (Luxembourg International Advanced Studies in Information Technologies) Institute.

REFERENCES

1. Stoneburner, G., Goguen, A., Feringa, A. Risk Management Guide for Information Technology Management, National Institue of Standard and Technology, October 2001
2. Octave Critical Threat, Asset and Vulnerability Evaluation (OCTAVE), Carnegie Mellon - Software Engineering Institute, June 1999
3. Expression des Besoins et Identification des Objectifs de Sécurité (EBIOS), Service Central de la Sécurité des Systèmes d'Information, Juin 1997
4. Chung, L.,"Dealing with Security Requirements During the Development of Information Systems,"; Proc. CAiSE '93, 5th Int. Conf. Advanced Information Systems Engineering, Paris, France. Berlin: Springer-Verlag, 1993, pp. 234-251
5. Eames, D. and Moffett J. D.,(1999), "The Integration of Safety and Security Requirements", Safecomp'99, 27-29 Sept 1999, Toulouse, France
6. Antón, A. I., Earp, J. B., "Strategies for Developing Policies and Requirements for Secure Electronic Commerce Systems", 1st ACM Workshop on Security and Privacy in E-Commerce (CCS 2000), Athens, Greece, unnumbered pages, 1-4 November 2000
7. Moffett, Johnatan. D. "Requirements and Policies", Position paper for Workshop on Policies in Distributed Systems, 15-17 November 1999, HP-Laboratories, Bristol, UK
8. Goal-oriented Requirement Language, http://www.cs.toronto.edu/km/GRL/ , University of Toronto, Canada
9. Chung, L. Representing and Using Non-Functional Requirements: A Process-Oriented Approach, Ph.D. thesis, Department of Computer Science, U. of Toronto, 1993
10. Yu, E., Modelling Strategic Relationships for Process Reengineering, Ph.D. thesis, Department of Computer Science, U. of Toronto, 1995

FRAMEWORK AND ARCHITECTURE FOR SECURE MOBILE BUSINESS APPLICATIONS

Jochen Haller, Philip Robinson, Thomas Walter, Roger Kilian-Kehr

SAP AG, CEC Karlsruhe
[jochen.haller | philip.robinson | roger.kilian-kehr]@sap.com

DoCoMo Euro-Labs
walter@docomolab-euro.com

Abstract: With the mobile telecommunication systems (GPRS, UMTS) enterprises have the possibility to better integrate their mobile employees into their backend business processes. However, from an enterprise perspective access to security-critical information from a mobile user's device requires appropriate and often enormous management efforts. This typically ranges from advanced firewall policies to special security components such as virtual private networks. These mechanisms are not suitable for the broad range of mobile business applications that require security properties independent from the properties guaranteed by the network layer. To achieve true security for these applications an appropriate application framework is presented that facilitates the development and deployment of secure mobile business applications.

Key words: mobility, business applications, security, security policies, smart cards

1. INTRODUCTION

In recent years the number of mobile users has steadily increased. Companies are seeking solutions to support their mobile workforce with online access to their corporate networks and applications. Traditional solutions like firewall policies [2] or virtual private networks (VPN) [3] are rather inflexible when used in an environment with mobile users.

The WiTness[1] [4][1] – Wireless Trust for Mobile Business – project looks into an application layer security framework for secure mobile business applications.

2. SECURE MOBILE BUSINESS APPLICATION

Traditional (client-server based) business applications are based on multi-tier architectures where client systems communicate with several servers to process business transactions. The expansion of mobile devices and consequent mobility of users adds another level of complexity with respect to heterogeneity and number of devices representing the "client side". The notion of a *secure mobile business application* is therefore a move towards coping with this complexity.

The term *secure* implies that particular policies must be satisfied with respect to accessing critical resources (data, processes, network equipment, etc.). The enforcement of these policies may include mechanisms for assurance of mutual authentication, authorization, integrity, and confidentiality.

Mobility is enabled by the dimensional properties of devices as well as the properties of the communications media and infrastructure. Consider small devices with limited resources like processing power, display and storage communicating over heterogeneous wireless networks, for instance GSM or 802.11 WaveLan.

Applications are the way that a business' productivity and processes are technically implemented. They therefore should reflect company policies, including security policies, through their implementation.

Application layer security represents true end-to-end security, independent from underlying network security mechanisms.

Furthermore, application layer security makes the integration of security into the application design process a more realistic and conceptually feasible task. There are also specialized applications explicitly referred to as *security services*. The foremost of these security services is the *security module* whose architectural properties are also further defined in this chapter.

[1] IST-Programme / KA2 / AL: IST-2001-2.1.3.

3. FRAMEWORK AND ARCHITECTURE

WiTness is concerned with a business-to-employee scenario with three identified main domains of interest: *corporate domain*, *personal domain*, and *network domain*.

3.1 Corporate domain

The corporate domain includes all systems, system components, either hard- or software required to run business applications. In particular, information provider and server systems and their respective interconnecting networks are meant. It is assumed that all connections within the corporate domain as well as every system is secure.

3.2 Personal domain

The counterpart of the corporate domain is the personal domain. It consists at least of a mobile device (e.g. a mobile phone) and a smart card. More complex personal domains can be generated by simply adding further (mobile) devices setting up so-called *federations of client devices*.

The essential requirements for federations are that communication between devices and between the federation and corporate domain runs over secured channels.

Within a federation, a smart card performs a specific role. It implements the before mentioned security module. A security module holds a set of user credentials which allow an employee to identify and authenticate with the corporate domain and to perform further security related tasks (e.g., session key generation or signing data hashes).

3.3 Network and Operator domain

Mobility of users and devices is best achieved and guaranteed with a wireless network infrastructure. Because all security related functions are implemented in the application itself, it is even of no relevance which security support is implemented in the network domain. Consequently, WiTness abstracts the heterogeneity of underlying networks, primarily with respect to their security provisions.

3.4 Core WiTness architecture

The core architecture comprises the following elements:

- Application modules are implemented as *partlets*. These are either pre-installed or dynamically downloaded to mobile devices. Partlets encode the business logic of an application.
- WiTness provides implementations and supporting libraries for handling of federations, security logic and communications handling.
- Additionally, a security service is implemented in the security module. It is a stand-alone security application providing services and functions such as key generation, document signing, en- and decryption with private key, certificate management etc.
- With regards to policies and policy management, WiTness also delivers methodologies and utilities for policy management. Policies are enforced by *security logic*, which again is implemented in the *partlets* complementing the business logic.

4. CONCLUSION

This contribution has provided an overview of the architecture for secure mobile business applications introduced by the WiTness project. The secure mobile business application itself was introduced and the different domains – personal, corporate and network – necessary to introduce the core WiTness architecture. The final chapter deals with the actual application, its design process, implementation and finally its deployment.

REFERENCES

[1] Sheila Frankel, *Demystifying the IPsec Puzzle*, Artech House, 2001.

[2] William Stallings, Cryptography and Network Security – Principles and Practice – Second Edition, Prentice Hall, 1999.

[3] William Stallings, *IP Security*, The Internet Protocol Journal, Volume 3, Number 1, www.cisco.com/warp/public/759/ipj_issues.html, March 2002.

[4] Thomas Walter, Peter Schoo, Jochen Haller, Philip Robinson, *WiTness – Wireless Trust for Mobile Business – Position Statement*, PAMPAS Workshop, Royal Holloway, University of London, www.pampas.eu.org/workshop.html, September 2002.

[5] WiTness consortium, *Wireless Trust for Mobile Business*, IST-2001-32275, www.wireless-trust.org, 2002.

ISO 17799 AND AUSTRALIAN HEALTHCARE ORGANISATIONS

W.J.Brooks[1], M.J.Warren[1] and W.Hutchinson[2]
[1]Deakin Univeristy, Australia and [2]Edith Cowan Univeristy, Australia

Abstract: Information security is now recognised as critical factor within the healthcare industry. With the gradual move from paper-based to electronic information there is an even greater need for protection. However, financial and operational constraints often exist which influence the practicality of developing a secure system. A new baseline security standard has been drafted which applies specifically to the unique information security requirements of the healthcare industry. The aim of this paper is to look at the effectiveness of the health information security standard and the development of information security within the Australian healthcare industry.

Key words: Security Healthcare, Baseline Security, AS/NZS ISO/IEC 17799.

1. INTRODUCTION

The Australian healthcare industry has undergone significant changes over the past 10 years. To deal with the issues of security within healthcare, the Health Information Security Management Implementation Guide (Deloitte Touche Tohmatsu 2002) was drafted. This is based on the Australian and New Zealand Standard (AS/NZS) 17799 (Standards Australia, 2000 & 2001), to apply specifically to the interests and unique information security requirements of the Australian healthcare industry. This standard provides a comprehensive set of controls comprising of current best information security practices that will provide assistance with the initiation, implementation, and maintenance of information security measures within a health business (Deloitte Touche Tohmatsu, 2002). Once a business has implemented the standard they can be certified against that standard by a certification authority. But will this standard actually offer a set of controls and safeguards that are suitable for the healthcare industry; is the healthcare industry willing to conform to the development of a national health information network? To answer these questions the Health Information Security Management Implementation Guide was critically analysed and a survey sent out to Victorian health establishments to determine the views of information security in the healthcare industry. The results of this survey will be discussed in this paper.

2. RESULTS OBTAINED FROM SURVEY

The survey objectives are to heighten awareness of the development of information security management systems; to seek an understanding of information security trends and issues; and, to determine the reactions and intention regarding certification against an information security standard, particularly the AS/NZS ISO/IEC 17799:2001, throughout health organisations in Victoria, Australia. The overall rate of response for the survey was 20% (similar rate of return to AusCERT and CSI/FBI security surveys) which included public and private hospitals, day procedure centres, bush nursing hospitals and other health services facilities; each response has been carefully reviewed.

Over 80% of the respondents rated the security of their health organisation's information as highest priority but this level of importance for security was contradicted by a number of answers to other questions within the survey, such as:

- 93% of the organisations that responded allow internet access to staff but only 62.5% of these organisations have a formal written policy concerning staff internet usage;
- 40% of respondents have performed a formal risk assessment to determine potential areas of risk, 49% have not performed a formal risk assessment but plan to in the future, and the remaining 12% have not performed a formal risk assessment and do not plan to. Of those organisations that have performed a formal risk assessment many chose to hire security consultants outside of their organisation, or other healthcare bodies.
- With regards to each organisation's current state of their information security policy the majority of respondents (26%) are still gaining information about security standards and considering action. Second to this, 24% of respondents are agreeing on internal standards, and only

14% of respondents are ready to implement their information security policy.

The majority of health organisations perceive the protection of business information to be the main benefit of implementing an information security policy, with secondary benefits of raising security awareness among staff, and, the development of an internal information security framework. The vast majority of organisations surveyed believe computer viruses to be the main risk to their information, closely followed by lack of security awareness among staff. Other risks noted were failure of data backups, lack of direct control due to using another hospital's network, staff's willingness to 'upgrade', and the financial issues of implementing an information security policy in smaller health organisations. Table 1 illustrates the results obtained.

Type of Security Risk	Percentage of Respondents
Computer Viruses	74%
Hackers	21%
Disgruntled Employees	12%
Data Integrity Corruption	54%
Human Failure	63%
Technical Failure	63%
Natural Disasters	14%
Denial of Service	9%
Lack of Security Awareness	65%
Other	9%

Table 1. The perceived security risks

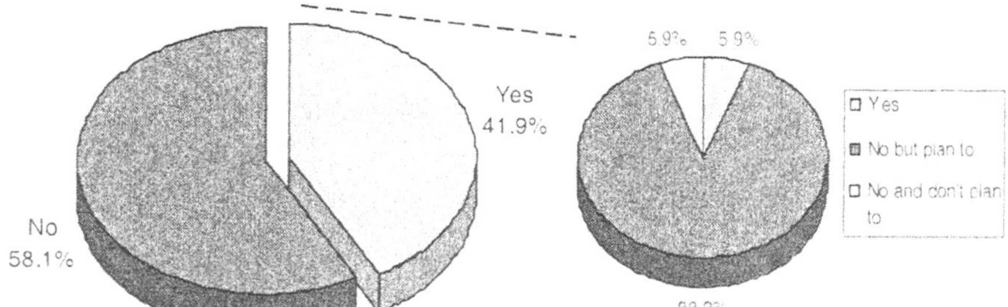

Figure 1. Awareness of AS/NZS and its implementation

Even though computer viruses are a major concern among Victorian hospitals, only 62% of respondents that allow staff Internet access have a formal written policy on internet usage in place. Within the health industry AS/NZS ISO/IEC 17799:2001 and certification against this standard is still in its early stages but there is clear evidence of gradual acceptance. It was a case that 41.9% of respondents are aware of the standard but only 5.9% have implemented AS/NZS ISO/IEC 17799:2001. The majority of organisations are planning to take action in the future as shown by figure 1.

3. CONCLUSIONS

The Australian healthcare industry handles very sensitive information, whether it is a patient's health record or scientific test data it is imperative to maintain data integrity as well as adhering privacy laws and legislation. This is particularly the case as more health information is being stored and transmitted in electronic format, and the simplicity of distribution of information has increased dramatically. A recent Australian computer crime and security survey jointly produced by AusCERT discovered 67% of respondents suffered a computer security incident in 2002, twice the level of 1999, and 35% of these experienced six or more incidents (AusCERT et al., 2002). These results provide enough evidence to suggest that it is imperative for health businesses to implement a set of security controls and safeguards that satisfy the very distinctive requirements of the healthcare industry. The survey has shown that, within Victoria, the Australian healthcare industry is not ready to certify itself against any information security standard.

REFERENCES

AusCERT, Deloitte Touche Tohmatsu, and NSW Police (2002) *2002 Australian Computer Crime and Security Survey*, The University of Queensland, Australia.

Deloitte Touche Tohmatsu (2002) *Health Information Security Management Implementation Guide to AS/NZS 17799.2*, Australia.

Standards Australia (2001) *Information Technology – Code of practice or information security management*, AS/NZS ISO/IEC 17799:2001, Standards Australia & Standards New Zealand.

Standards Australia (2000) *Information security management – Specification for information security management systems*, AS/NZS 7799.2:2000, Standards Australia & Standards New Zealand.

STATISTICAL DISCLOSURE ATTACKS

Traffic Confirmation in Open Environments

George Danezis
University of Cambridge, Computer Laboratory
William Gates Building, 15 JJ Thomson Avenue
Cambridge CB3 0FD, United Kingdom
George.Danezis@cl.cam.ac.uk

Abstract An improvement over the previously known *disclosure attack* is presented that allows, using statistical methods, to effectively deanonymize users of a mix system. Furthermore the *statistical disclosure attack* is computationally efficient, and the conditions for it to be possible and accurate are much better understood. The new attack can be generalized easily to a variety of anonymity systems beyond mix networks.

Keywords: Statistical disclosure attack, traffic analysis, anonymity

1. Introduction

Since the concept of a mix network was introduced in (Chaum, 1981) the field of anonymous communications has been growing as new systems and attacks are proposed. All mix systems require that messages to be anonymized should be relayed through a sequence of trusted intermediary nodes. These nodes, called mixes, hide the correspondence between their input and output messages.

Although originally it was proposed that all participants should act as mixes, subsequent systems developed and deployed (Möller and Cottrell, 2000; Gulcu and Tsudik, 1996; Danezis et al., 2002) make a distinction between clients simply using the network, and mix nodes that form its core. This distinction is observable by an adversary, that sets as his goal to trace the ultimate recipient of messages injected in the network or trace back the originators of messages coming out of the network. Using information present at the edges of the mix network, where messages are injected or received, the attacker can try to link senders and receivers.

Such attacks are sometimes called *traffic confirmation* attacks since they do not rely on tracing messages through the network.

Another family of well known attacks against mix systems are intersection attacks (Berthold et al., 2000). These rely on the fact that different messages use the same route through the network to perform traffic analysis. Kesdogan presents an interesting variant of this attack in (Kesdogan et al., 2002), where it is applied to a whole anonymity system. He assumes that a particular user, Alice, sends messages only to a restricted set of recipients. He then observes that it is possible by observing the recipient anonymity sets attributed to her messages to extract information about their ultimate recipients. The attack is generalized by viewing mix networks or other systems providing anonymity as abstract mixes, since the attack does not rely upon any particular properties of mixing other than the unlinkability it provides.

In this paper we are going to briefly describe the disclosure attack as originally presented. A more efficient attack, the statistical disclosure attack, will then be presented. It requires less computational effort by the attacker and yields the same results. An analysis of the applicability and efficiency of the statistical disclosure attack, and a discussion of its relevance to other systems beyond the formal model is included.

2. The Disclosure Attack Revisited

The formal model on which the disclosure attack is based is quite simple. A single mix is used by b participants each round, one of them always being Alice, while the other $(b-1)$ are choosen randomly out of a total number of $N-1$ possible ones. The threshold of the mix is b so it fires after each of the round's participants has contributed one message. Alice chooses the recipient of her message to be a random member of a fixed set of m recipients. Each of the other participants sends a message to a recipient chosen uniformly at random out of N potential recipients. We assume that the other senders and Alice choose the recipients of their messages independently from each other. The attacker observes $R_1, \ldots, R_t$ the recipient anonymity sets corresponding to t messages sent out by Alice during t different rounds of mixing. The attacker then tries to establish which out of all potential recipients, each of Alice's messages was sent to.

The original attack as proposed by Kesdogan (Kesdogan et al., 2002) first tries to identify mutually disjoint sets of recipients from the sequence of recipient anonymity sets corresponding to Alice's messages. This operation is the main bottleneck for the attacker since it takes time exponential in the number of messages to be analyzed. The underlying method used is equivalent to solving the Constrains Satisfaction Problem which is well known to be NP-complete.

The second phase of the algorithm proposed intersects the disjoint sets found with anonymity sets of messages. When this intersection generates a set of only one element it is assumed that it is a correspondent of Alice.

3. The Statistical Disclosure Attack

We wish to use the same model as above to show that a statistical attack is possible that yields the set of potential recipients of Alice. In turn this set can be used to find the recipients of particular messages sent out by Alice.

We define as $\vec{v}$, the vector with N elements corresponding to each potential recipient of a messages in the system. We also set the values corresponding to the m recipients that might receive messages by Alice to $\frac{1}{m}$ and the others to zero, therefore requiring $|\vec{v}| = 1$. Observe that $\vec{v}$ is the probability distribution that is used by Alice to choose the recipient of its message for each round of the abstract mixing as described in the formal model above.

We also define $\vec{u}$ to be equal to the uniform distribution over all potential recipients N. Therefore all elements of $\vec{u}$ are set to be equal to $\frac{1}{N}$ with $|\vec{u}| = 1$. This vector represents the probability distribution used by all other senders to select their recipients' for each round of mixing.

The information provided to the attacker is a sequence of vectors $\vec{o_1}, \ldots, \vec{o_t}$ representing the recipient anonymity sets observed corresponding to the t messages sent by Alice. Each of $\vec{o_i}$ is the probability distribution assigning potential recipients to Alice's message during round i. The adversary will therefore try to use this information in order to infer $\vec{v}$ that, as described above, is closely linked to the set of recipients that Alice communicates with.

The principal observation underlying the statistical disclosure attack is that for a large enough set of observations t it holds true that (by using the Law of Large Numbers):

$$\bar{O} = \frac{\sum_{i=1\ldots t} \vec{o_i}}{t} = \frac{\vec{v} + (b-1)\vec{u}}{b} \tag{1}$$

It is therefore possible, just from the knowledge of the observations $\vec{o_1}, \ldots, \vec{o_t}$, the batch size b of the mix and the model $\vec{u}$ of other senders to calculate $\vec{v}$, the set of recipients of Alice:

$$\vec{v} = b\frac{\sum_{i=1\ldots t} \vec{o_i}}{t} - (b-1)\vec{u} \tag{2}$$

When the vector $\vec{v}$ is reconstructed by the adversary it can then be used to give an indication on the particular communications partners of Alice in a round k. The attacker simply multiplies each element of the $\vec{v}$ vector with each element of the observation $\vec{o_k}$ of round k, and normalizes the resulting vector.

$$\vec{r_k} = \frac{\vec{v} \cdot \vec{o_k}}{|\vec{v} \cdot \vec{o_k}|} \tag{3}$$

The elements with highest probability out of $\vec{r_k}$ are the most likely recipients of Alice's message k.

The statistical disclosure attack therefore allows an attacker to identify all possible recipients m of Alice's messages and even further to establish the precise recipients of particular messages in the formal model, with an arbitrary degree of confidence that, as we will see, depends on the number of observations t.

3.1 Applicability and Efficiency of the Statistical Disclosure Attack

The main drawback of the original disclosure attack was its reliance on solving an NP-complete problem. The statistical disclosure attack only relies on collecting observations and performing trivial operations on vectors, and therefore is computationally cheap and scales very well. Therefore we foresee the collection of observations, and the calculation of anonymity sets corresponding to messages to be the main computational bottleneck of an attacker.

It is important to establish the limits of the statistical disclosure attack and calculate the number of observations that are necessary in order to reliably perform it. We observe that extracting the vector $\vec{v}$ is a typical signal detection problem. The problem therefore is to differentiate the signal of Alice from the noise introduced by the other senders. In this case the signal strength of Alice is $\frac{1}{m}t$ versus the noise strength of the other senders that is equivalent to $\frac{b-1}{N}t$. For the signal to noise ratio to be larger than one we require:

$$\frac{\text{Alice's Signal}}{\text{Noise Strength}} = \frac{\frac{1}{m}t}{\frac{1-b}{N}t} > 1 \Rightarrow m < \frac{N}{b-1} \tag{4}$$

The above bound on m provides the necessary condition for a mix system following the formal model to be susceptible to the statistical disclosure attack. It is interesting that Kesdogan arrives to the same result in (Kesdogan et al., 2002), but proves it in a different way, which means that any system that is vulnerable to the disclosure attack is also susceptible to the attack presented here.

Given that the signal to noise ratio allows for the statistical disclosure attack to be performed, it is important to calculate how many observations t are necessary to reliably retrieve $\vec{v}$. This depends on the variance of the signal $\vec{v}$ and the noise $(b-1)\vec{u}$.

The observations in $\bar{O}$ corresponding to Alice's recipients have a mean proportional to $\mu_{\text{Alice}} = \frac{1}{m}t$ and a corresponding variance of $\sigma^2_{\text{Alice}} = \frac{m-1}{m^2}t$ while the noise has a mean of $\mu_{\text{Noise}} = \frac{1}{N}(b-1)t$ and a variance of $\sigma^2_{\text{Noise}} = \frac{N-1}{N^2}(b-1)t$. We should require a number of observations t large enough for the mean of the signal to be larger than the sum of the standard deviations, multiplied by an appropriate factor to provide us with a satisfactory confidence interval.

$$\mu_{\text{Alice}} - l\sigma_{\text{Alice}} > l\sigma_{\text{Noise}} \tag{5}$$

$$t > \left[ml \left(\sqrt{\frac{m-1}{m^2}} + \sqrt{\frac{N-1}{N^2}(b-1)} \right) \right]^2 \tag{6}$$

With $l = 2$ we have a 95% confidence of correct classification, when determining if a recipient is associated with Alice or not, while $l = 3$ increases the confidence to 99%.

4. Conclusions

The statistical disclosure attack does not simply provide a computational improvement over the disclosure attack, but also presents important new features. The conditions for it to be possible can be expressed in closed algebraic form, as presented above, and therefore no simulations are required to decide when it is applicable and effective.

An important improvement over the previous work is also the fact that the statistical disclosure attack can be applied when the probability distributions described by $\vec{v}$, $\vec{u}$ and $\vec{o_i}$ are not uniform, but are skewed. This extends the attack from being applicable to anonymity systems that create discrete anonymity sets, to probabilistic systems that provide anonymity described by the entropy of the anonymity sets, as presented in (Serjantov and Danezis, 2002). As a result the entropy of the vector $\vec{r_k}$ represents the anonymity that a message still has after the attack has been performed. Therefore the statistical disclosure attack is more general than the simple disclosure attack, and can be applied to other models beyond the formal model presented here.

More work can be done on modeling different senders and their corresponding vectors $\vec{u}$, to construct a more realistic formal model. Even if all other senders besides Alice have their own small sets of recipients we foresee the statistical disclosure attack to still be applicable if different senders are involved in each round.

Acknowledgements. The author would like to thank Andrei Serjantov and Richard Clayton for their comments on this work.

References

Berthold, O., Pfitzmann, A., and Standtke, R. (2000). The disadvantages of free MIX routes and how to overcome them. In *Designing Privacy Enhancing Technologies, LNCS Vol. 2009*, pages 30–45. Springer-Verlag. http://www.tik.ee.ethz.ch/~weiler/lehre/netsec/Unterlagen/anon/disadvantages_berthold.pdf.

Chaum, D. (1981). Untraceable electronic mail, return addresses, and digital pseudonyms. *Communications of the ACM*, 4(2). http://www.eskimo.com/~weidai/mix-net.txt.

Danezis, G., Dingledine, R., Mathewson, N., and Hopwood, D. (2002). Mixminion: Design of a Type III Anonymous Remailer Protocol. Manuscript. http://seul.org/~arma/minion-design.ps.

Gulcu, C. and Tsudik, G. (1996). Mixing E-mail with Babel. In *Network and Distributed Security Symposium - NDSS '96*. IEEE. http://citeseer.nj.nec.com/2254.html.

Kesdogan, D., Agrawal, D., and Penz, S. (2002). Limits of anonymity in open environments. In *Information Hiding, 5th International Workshop*, Noordwijkerhout, The Netherlands. Springer Verlag.

Möller, U. and Cottrell, L. (2000). Mixmaster Protocol — Version 2. Unfinished draft. Available online on the World Wide Web. http://www.eskimo.com/~rowdenw/crypt/Mix/draft-moeller-mixmaster2-protocol-00.txt.

Serjantov, A. and Danezis, G. (2002). Towards an information theoretc metric for anonymity. In *Proceedings of the Privacy Enhancing Technologies Workshop 2002*, San Francisco, CA.

ON THE ANONYMITY OF TIMED POOL MIXES

Andrei Serjantov
University of Cambridge
Computer Laboratory
15 JJ Thomson Avenue
Cambridge CB3 0FD, United Kingdom
Andrei.Serjantov@cl.cam.ac.uk

Richard E. Newman
Department of Computer & Information Science & Engineering
PO Box 116120 University of Florida
Gainesville, FL 32611-6120, USA
nemo@cise.ufl.edu

Abstract This paper presents a method for calculating the anonymity of a timed pool mix. Thus we are able to compare it to a threshold pool mix, and any future mixes that might be developed. Although we are only able to compute the anonymity of a timed pool mix after some specific number of rounds, this is a practical approximation to the real anonymity.

1. Introduction

Many anonymity systems use the notion of a mix as introduced by Chaum (Chaum, 1981). The purpose of a mix is to hide the correspondence between incoming and outgoing messages, so that the attacker (who is not able to see the inner workings of a mix) cannot tell who sends messages to whom.

Thus, a mix is a proxy that collects some number of messages inside it (thus introducing a delay), "mixes them up" and forwards them on. There are two fundamental characteristics of a mix: the anonymity it provides, or roughly speaking, the number of messages it collects, and the time for which it delays messages. The former should be maximized while minimizing the latter.

Mixing can be done in a variety of ways. For example, a mix may wait for a particular number of messages to arrive (threshold mix) before forwarding the messages on, or a particular time interval (timed mix). Chaum's original system used a simple threshold mix, but over the last few years many mixes have been proposed in the literature (Kesdogan et al., 1998; Jerichow, 2000; Cottrell, 1994). A survey of some mixing strategies with an emphasis on their properties under active $(n-1)$ attacks has been presented by Serjantov et al. (Serjantov et al., 2002). Although the minimum and maximum anonymity of several mixes were presented there, the average anonymity of timed mixes was not. In fact, the authors stated that the anonymity of a timed mix depends on the entire history of message arrivals at this mix, but do not go further in exploring this idea. In this paper, we look at this issue in detail and show how working out the anonymity of timed pool mixes can be achieved.

First, we describe the timed pool mix itself. We then describe the threshold pool mix and give an outline of a method which will enable a comparison of the two. We then proceed to give a general outline of how to analyse the anonymity of the timed mix. Finally, we describe our implementation of the analysis and give some suggestions for a fair comparison of the two mixes.

2. Description of the Timed Pool Mix

Timed Pool Mix

Parameters: t, period; n, pool.

Flushing Algorithm: The mix fires every t seconds. If N_i messages have arrived since the last time the mix fired, then a pool of n messages[1] chosen uniformly at random from the $N_i + n$ is retained in the mix. The others are forwarded. If $N_i = 0$, the mix does not send out any messages.

It is interesting to compare the mixing strategy of this mix to that of a threshold pool mix.

Threshold Pool Mix

Parameters: N, threshold; n, pool.

Flushing Algorithm: The mix fires when $N + n$ messages accumulate in the mix (or when N messages have arrived since the last time the mix fired). A pool of n messages, chosen uniformly at random from all the messages, is retained in the mix. The other N are forwarded on.

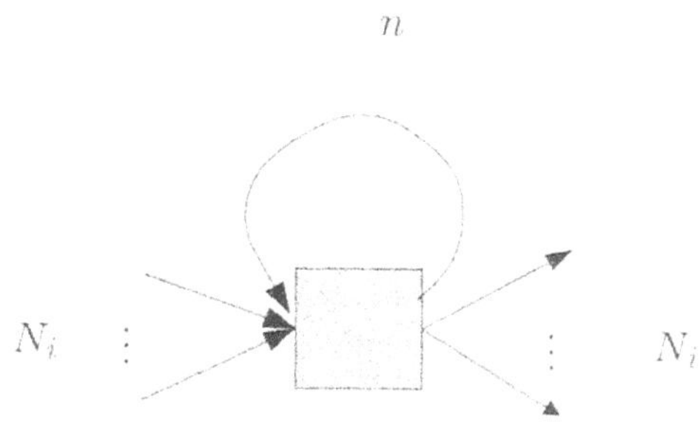

Figure 1. A Timed Pool Mix

It is clear that the anonymity set of the timed pool mix at round i (the set of senders that have a non-zero probability of having sent a message present in the mix at round i) includes the senders of all the messages that have passed through it since round 0. This is also the case for the threshold pool mix. Thus, using anonymity sets (or, to be more precise, the size of the anonymity sets) for measuring anonymity does not distinguish the two mix types.

Thus, we follow the approach taken in (Serjantov and Danezis, 2002)[2] and calculate anonymity of the timed pool mix using the information theoretic metric proposed in that paper. That work has already analysed the threshold pool mix, so that will not be repeated here.

3. Method

First of all, assume that all messages arrive at the pool mix directly from senders. Furthermore, for the purposes of comparison, assume that the senders of all the messages are distinct.

We proceed as follows:

Consider a message inside the mix at round r (we do not care whether this message leaves the mix or not). Now, calculate the probabilities that it had been sent by each of the senders who sent a message at round j, $j < i$. We now have a probability distribution of senders who could have sent the message. Taking the entropy, $\sum p \log p$, of this probability distribution, will give the anonymity. For a detailed (and a more general) definition of this information theoretic metric see Serjantov and Danezis, 2002.

Given the mix at round r and a history of message arrivals to the mix $[N_1, \ldots, N_r]$, let us calculate the probability of a message from rounds $1 \ldots r$ still being in the mix.

If the message was in the mix before the first flush (round 0), the probability of it staying until round r is:

$$p_0 = \prod_{i=1}^{r} \left(\frac{n}{N_i + n} \right)$$

The probability that a particular message that is in the mix at round r has entered the mix at round r is:

$$p_r = \frac{N_r}{N_r + n}$$

Thus, each of the senders (there were N_r of them) at round r sent this message with probability:

$$p_r = \frac{1}{N_r + n}$$

Similarly, the probability that a message that is in the mix at round r has entered the mix at round $r - 1$ is:

$$p_{r-1} = \frac{n}{N_r + n} \left(\frac{N_{r-1}}{N_{r-1} + n} \right)$$

Now we can calculate the anonymity of the entire probability distribution.

$$\begin{aligned} E_r = & -\frac{N_r}{N_r + n} \log \frac{1}{N_r + n} - \left(\prod_{i=1}^{r} \frac{n}{N_i + n} \right) \log \left(\prod_{i=1}^{r} \frac{n}{N_i + n} \right) - \\ & - \sum_{x=1}^{r-1} \left(\frac{N_x}{N_x + n} \left(\prod_{i=x+1}^{r} \frac{n}{N_i + n} \right) \log \left(\frac{1}{N_x + n} \prod_{i=x+1}^{r} \frac{n}{N_i + n} \right) \right) \end{aligned}$$

At this point it may be helpful to refer back to Section 5 of Serjantov and Danezis, 2002 and observe how the above expression follows on from the one for anonymity of the threshold pool mix.

We can also derive the anonymity of a timed pool mix in a different way. Recall the formula for composition of mixes from Section 3.2 of Serjantov and Danezis, 2002:

$$E_{total} = E_{mix} + \sum_{0 < x \leq n} p_x E_x$$

Intuitively, this says that the anonymity of a message in the mix is the inherent entropy of the mix (E_{mix}) plus the mean anonymity of all the messages inside the mix.

A message in a pool mix at round i could have come from two places: from the pool remaining after the previous round (call the probability of this p_i) or from a round i sender. So,

$$p_i = \frac{n}{N_i+n} \quad \text{and} \quad 1 - p_i = \frac{N_i}{N_i+n}$$

Then, the inherent entropy of the mix at round i is

$$E_{i_{mix}} = -p_i \log p_i - (1 - p_i) \log(1 - p_i)$$

Using the above formula we can now obtain the anonymity of a timed pool mix after r rounds:

$$E_r = E_{r_{mix}} + p_r E_{r-1} + (1 - p_r) \log N_r$$

This can be rewritten as:

$$E_r = E_{r_{mix}} + (1-p_r) \log N_r + \sum_{x=1}^{r-1} E_{x_{mix}} \prod_{i=x+1}^{r} p_i + \sum_{x=1}^{r} (1-p_x) \log N_x \prod_{i=x+1}^{r} p_i$$

It is important to notice that to calculate the anonymity of a timed pool mix (using either method), we need to know the number of messages that had arrived at the mix during each of the previous rounds.

Now suppose we wish to analyse the anonymity of a timed pool mix at round R. It is clear that messages which have passed through the mix a long time ago will not contribute much to the current anonymity.[3] Thus, we can approximate the total anonymity by pretending that only r of the R rounds contribute to the anonymity.

Suppose that message interarrival times during time period T follow some probability distribution (an exponential distribution, for example) and that N messages arrive in total. Furthermore, take T to be some multiple of t, the time parameter of the mix, so that the N messages arrive over $r = \frac{T}{t}$ rounds. Now we can simply enumerate all the possible ways (we call these histories) that N messages can arrive in r rounds, and calculate the probability of each one. Now all that is left to do is to calculate the anonymity of each one of the histories, the probability of each history occurring given the exponential (or in fact any other) distribution and compute the mean anonymity.

4. Implementation and Results

Naturally, this is far too tedious to do by hand, so a short program found in Haskell (Peyton Jones et al., 1999) was written to enumerate all the possible histories, calculate their probabilities using an exponential distribution and determine the anonymity of the pool mix. Our program calculates anonymity using both methods presented above, and gives the same results in all our test cases. We hope to make the source code available for download in the near future.

Note that this approach is not as precise as the one used for the threshold pool mix – we were unable to come up with a closed form for the anonymity of a timed pool mix as the number of rounds grows large. However, we consider the method used above satisfactory and practical. Unfortunately, it relies on the correctness of the implementation.

This program enables a comparison with a threshold pool mix. We take the same scenario and calculate the anonymity of a threshold pool mix after r rounds.

We performed the comparison in the following settings: we took a timed pool mix with a pool of 2 messages over 5 rounds and with 10 messages arriving to it during these 5 rounds. The mean interarrival time for the Poisson process was taken to be 1.

We then compared it to a threshold pool mix with the same volume of traffic flowing through it over 5 rounds. We took the threshold to be 2 messages. Note that this corresponds to the anonymity of the timed mix when the history of the timed mix is $[2, 2, 2, 2, 2]$. The anonymity of the threshold pool mix was 2.91 bits, whilst the anonymity of the timed pool mix was 3.012 bits. Interestingly enough, if we model the arrival of messages using a zipf distribution, the anonymity of the timed pool mix is 3.07 bits.

We do not currently wish to make any general claims about the anonymity of timed mixes versus threshold mixes. Such a statement would be much more a product of the various assumptions we have made than the batching strategies themselves. Indeed, a rigorous comparison of the two mixes would also have to take account of the average delay of the messages through the two mixes, and possibly other factors. In this paper, we merely illustrate that the method which we use to work out the anonymity of a timed mix is powerful enough to enable such a comparison.

5. Related Work

In our opinion, properties of mixes have not been well studied. Many mixes have been proposed (Cottrell, 1994; Jerichow, 2000; Kesdogan et al., 1998), but rigorous descriptions of their properties are lacking.

For instance, Jerichow (Jerichow, 2000) describes "time controlled mixes" and "event controlled mixes" (timed and threshold mixes in our terminology), but only goes as far as providing qualitative statements about their anonymity.

The idea of using a Poisson process to model message arrivals to a mix is due to Kesdogan; he uses it in the analysis of SG mixes (Kesdogan et al., 1998).

6. Conclusions and Future Work

In this paper we have presented an analysis of the anonymity of the timed pool mix. Although we were unable to come up with a simple expression for the anonymity and our methods enumerated all the possible histories of message arrivals, the method still enabled us to do a comparison of the timed and the threshold pool mixes. The sensitivity of timed pool mixes to the distribution of interarrival times of the message arrival process is also of interest.

In the future, we would like to consider more complicated timed pool mixes such as the Cottrell mix (Cottrell, 1994; Serjantov et al., 2002), and a generalised mix where the number of messages sent out onto the network is a function of the number of messages inside it at the time it flushes. A practical method (and an implementation of it) for analysing timed mixes is an important step towards this goal.

We would also like to perform a rigorous comparison of the properties of timed and threshold pool mixes, including details about how they interact with other features of anonymity systems such as dummy traffic.

Notes

1. When the mix starts operating, the pool is filled up with n dummy messages
2. It is worth noting that a very similar metric is proposed in Diaz et al., 2002.
3. Implementors of mixes have also suggested that including a timeout clause such as "message should note be delayed for more than 10 rounds" would make them feel more comfortable(!).

References

Chaum, D. (1981). Untraceable electronic mail, return addresses and digital pseudonyms *Communications of the A.C.M.*, 24(2):84–88.

Cottrell, L. (1994). Mixmaster and remailer attacks. `http://www.obscura.com/~loki/remailer/remailer-essay.html`.

Diaz, C., Seys, S., Claessens, J., and Preneel, B. (2002). Towards measuring anonymity. In *Privacy Enhancing Technologies*, volume 2482 of *LNCS*.

Jerichow, A. (2000). *Generalisation and Security Improvement of Mix-mediated Anonymous Communication*. PhD thesis, Technischen Universitat Dresden.

Kesdogan, D., Egner, J., and Buschkes, R. (1998). Stop-and-go-MIXes providing probabilistic anonymity in an open system. In *Proceedings of the International Information Hiding Workshop*.

Peyton Jones, S., Hughes, J., et al. (1999). Report on the programming language Haskell 98, a non-strict, purely functional language. `http://www.haskell.org/`.

Serjantov, A. and Danezis, G. (2002). Towards an information theoretic metric for anonymity. In *Privacy Enhacing Technologies*, volume 2482 of *LNCS*, San Francisco, CA.

Serjantov, A., Dingledine, R., and Syverson, P. (2002). From a trickle to a flood: Active attacks on several mix types. In *5th Workshop on Information Hiding*, volume 2578 of *LNCS*.

PRIVACY IN CONTENT DISTRIBUTION NETWORKS

A framework description

R.J. Hulsebosch
Telematica Instituut, PO Box 589, 7500 AN, Enschede, The Netherlands
e-mail: Bob.Hulsebosch@telin.nl; phone: +31 (0)53 4850498; fax: +31 (0)534850400

Abstract: A framework is proposed for secure delivery of personalized content in the presence of a transparent intermediary while the privacy of the user is being preserved. The framework includes delegation of authority to the intermediary content distributor allowing him to act on behalf of the content provider. To maximize privacy, the framework enables users to control their profile and the ability to manage which personal information gets disclosed in the presence of a transparent intermediary.

Key words: Privacy, Proxy Certificate, Content Distribution, Identity management.

1. INTRODUCTION

Network edge caching proxies have been successfully deployed to accelerate web content delivery towards the user and reduce the load on origin web servers of the content provider (CP). In these so-called Content Distribution Networks (CDNs [1]), the intermediary edge caching proxies act as a gateway between web users and CPs and are nowadays more and more utilized with intelligent services other than simple caching. User-demanded services like virus scanning, content adaptation for personalization, and insertion of advertisements are suitable for such proxy servers and fit very well in the CDN model. The increased need for intermediaries to acquire access to security-related information, personal information about individual users and organizations, and proprietary information belonging to users and CPs, however, introduces new risks.

Several problems have to be tackled for delivering personalized content to the user in a CDN. The intermediary CD is dealing with both the CP and the user. For personalized content adaptation the CD must obtain information about the user and must use this information in delivering and adapting the content and services that the user chooses. The main problem is related to the fact that the CD often operates transparently for the user and on behalf of the CP. The user does not have any knowledge of the existence of the CD. Normally, a user enters the URL of the CP in his web browser. If this CP has an agreement with a CD, the request will be (almost) transparently redirected to this intermediary. The user usually is not aware of this and shall only allow the CP insight in some of his profile attributes in return for content, not the CD. Therefore the CD requires credentials of the CP to convince the user he is acting on behalf of the CP in order to obtain the user credentials.

A solid framework for authentication and authorization is required to allow end-points to delegate authority to intermediaries so that they can adapt content on behalf of them. The framework must also facilitate secure handling of user information required for content adaptation services. In this communication we describe a certificate-based framework for secure content adaptation by the intermediary CD in a CDN. The framework enables delegation of authority to the CD allowing him to act on behalf of the CP. A Profile Manager (PM) is introduced for management and selective dissemination of the personal profile of the user. A scenario for anonymous browsing while personalized content is being delivered is discussed.

2. FRAMEWORK FOR SECURE PERSONALIZED CONTENT ADAPTATION AND DELIVERY

We propose a framework that is an extension of the IDsec concept for virtual identities on the Internet [2,3]. IDsec introduces a Profile Manager (PM) that allows the user to manage and control the distribution of personal credentials to the CP. Digital certificates are used as a tool for access to these credentials. Session Certificates (SCs) are introduced to provide for a pointer to the profile located at the PM. These SCs do not contain any other information. Access to profile information is based on the elements in the digital certificate of the CP. The high-level basic framework constituting the actors, their relations, and the most important attributes is shown in Figure 1.

The user logs in at the PM and alters his profile (1). When he logs off, a SC is returned (2). When the user requests for content, a SC is included in the request (3). The CD receives the request. Prior to sending the content, the CD wants to adapt the content he has obtained from the CP. In order to do this, the CD needs to know the preferences and capabilities of the user, i.e., his profile at the PM. For this reason the CD has to identify himself and reassure the PM that he is working on behalf of the CP (4). If this is true, the PM will grant the CD access to the credentials the user has given the CP access to (5). The CP provides the original content (6). Once the CD has obtained the credentials of the user, content adaptation can be performed (7). The adapted content is returned to the CD (8), and forwarded to the user (9).

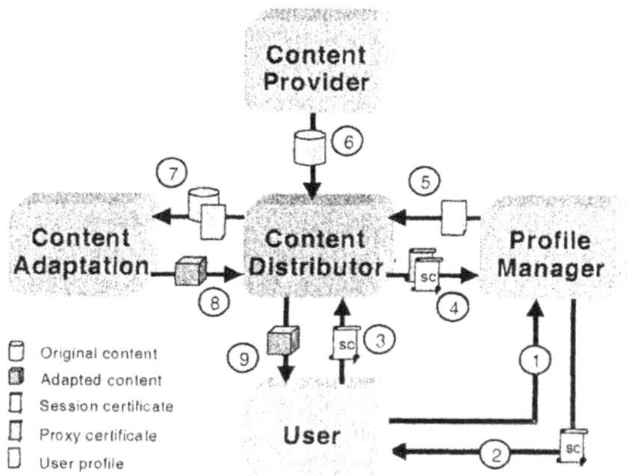

Figure 1: Framework for personalized content delivery in a CDN environment.

The fourth step in this scenario is the most critical one. Here the CD has to assure the PM he is operating on behalf of the CP in order to obtain access to the profile of the user. For this to work out we propose the use of proxy certificates (PC, [4]). The use of so-called proxy credentials for impersonation is a common technique to allow entity A to grant another entity B the right for B to authenticate with others as if it were A. In other words, entity B is impersonating entity A. The CD can use a PC to authenticate to the PM on behalf of the CP. The outcome is that the CD obtains access to the profile attributes of the user, which are stored at the PM. The Grid Security Infrastructure (GSI, [5]) for instance has proven the viability of impersonation as a basis for authentication. The delegation process and the X.509 PC profile used in our model have been extensively described in an IETF Internet Draft of the PKIX working group [6].

In the next sections we will have a closer look at the different processes that take place during content adaptation and delivery.

Profile Management

The PM allows the user to manage his profile attributes and the access to these attributes. The user - PM interactions are as follows (see Figure 2):

1. The user enters the PM via secure channel. Mutual authentication between the user and the PM is essential. Both the user and the PM need to be sure that they are dealing with the real party and not a bogus one.

2. Via the PM the user is able to structure his profile and to control access to his profile attributes. This means that the user can disclose a specific portion of his profile without revealing any other information.
3. A user-authenticated asymmetric session key pair is generated. This key is pair is used during the Internet session and has a short lifetime. The private key is securely stored while the public session key is sent to the PM via the secure connection. The PM generates a SC including the public session key of the user.
4. The PM returns the SC to the user. The SC identifies/represents the user on the current terminal but does not expose any user identification.

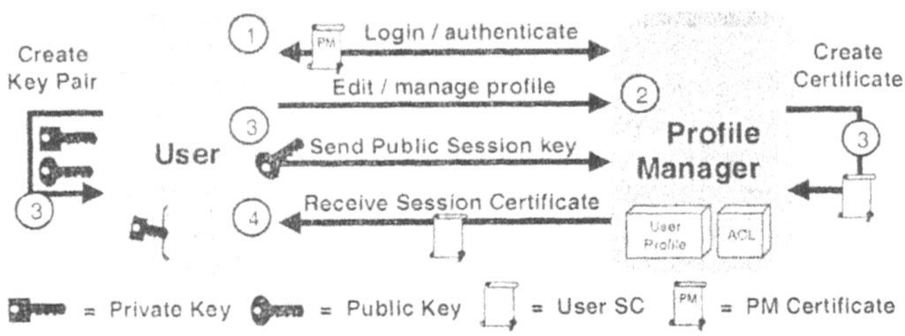

Figure 2: User profile management.

Users will be required to have multiple attributes for a number of different CPs. To assign CPs to the profile attributes they need the user is able to create Access Control Lists (ACLs). Access to the attributes is based on the distinguished name of the entity to which the certificate relates (e.g. the CP) *and* the digital signature of the certificate issuing party [2].

Delegation of content adaptation rights

The CD must be authorized by the CP in order to adapt the original content. In other words, the CP must delegate the content adaptation rights to the CD. Moreover, these delegation rights have to be used by the CD to obtain the profile of the user. Since access to the profile attributes is based on the distinguished name of the CP [2], the CD must convince the PM he is operating on behalf of the CP. The CD therefore must perform several operations that allow him to approach the PM server on behalf of the CP, i.e. the CD must obtain a PC of the CP. The delegation of content adaptation rights from the CP to the CD is depicted in Figure 3.

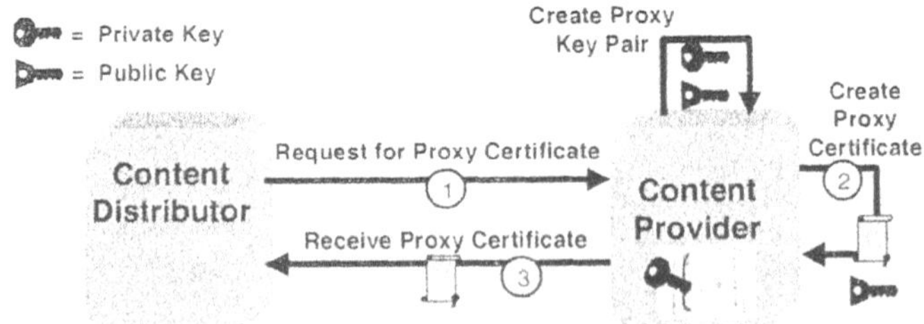

Figure 3: Delegation of content adaptation rights.

Content delivery

Figure 4 explains the process of personalized content delivery via the CD:

1. The SC is sent to the CD together with the URL request that the user makes.
2. To obtain the user profile attributes the CD must enter the PM. He uses his personal certificate for authentication at the server.
3. The PM authenticates to the CD and a secure channel is established.
4. The SC, PC and the CP certificate are sent to the PM via the secure channel. Both the SC and PC are used by the PM to determine the access rights of the CD. The CP certificate is used for verification of the PC signature. The signature of the CP certificate determines whether the PM trusts the CD - CP relation. If the PM trusts the signature, the SC allows him to perform a lookup for the session and user in order to retrieve the attributes of the user profile that the CP has access to. Access to attributes is controlled by the user and is based on the distinguished name of the PC since the ACL contains these names [2].
5. The profile is returned to the CD and is used to adapt the content. Naturally, the CP has stated the boundaries for the CD to adapt his content. A negotiation process between the limitations posed by the CP, the capabilities of the CD, and desires posed by the user for content adaptation is started.
6. The adapted content is sent to the user. If confidential information needs to be exchanged between the CD and user, the CD may use the public session key to encrypt the content sent. Only the user will be able to read the messages since he owns the private session key for decryption. If required by the CD, user authentication can be done via the private key of the SC. This would dynamically prove that the user is the owner of the SC.

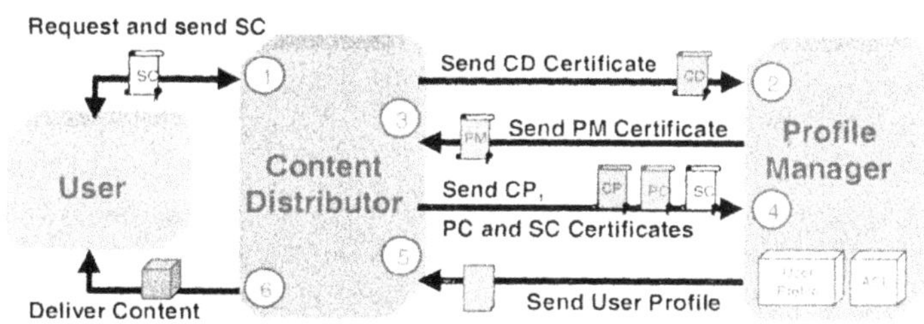

Figure 4: Personalized content delivery based on SCs.

Note that in this scenario the user has stayed anonymous for the CD and CP.

3. CONCLUSIONS

Personalized and localized content adaptation services are hot on the Internet. The rise of CDNs and the proposed value-added edge services fulfill and facilitate this need [7]. As a result, users on the Internet are often privy to large amounts of personal information, and should be very careful to prevent unintentional leakage of this information to other sources. Therefore, the parameters required for content adaptation need careful handling by an intermediary party. Though a CD typically operates transparently, the intermediary value-added services provided by a CD must therefore not be transparent: they have to be authorized by either the content requestor or the provider, corresponding to whom the service is being provided for. CPs may have a say on what adaptation is allowed, while on the other hand, the content consumers have the right to authorize services on their behalf. Authentication and (delegation of) authorization are two crucial aspects in establishing a trusted relationship in this complex situation.

We have presented a viable framework for a transparent intermediary CD to securely deliver personalized content to an anonymous user. The model allows a user to provide personal information while maintaining privacy by keeping control over its release. As a result the CD can offer services matching the need of each user. The model uses a PM for secure online management and administration of the private credentials of the user and issuing of SCs and encryption keys. The PM allows the user to determine what information gets released to which site. Thus, the responsibility of balancing access and privacy lies ultimately with the user. Since access is based on the distinguished name of the CP, delegation of authority is necessary to allow the CD access. Delegation of authority means that the authenticated identity of the CP must be carried over to the CD. This is accomplished by giving the CD a so-called PC to further perform operations on behalf of the CP.

REFERENCES

1. B. Hulsebosch, R. Brussee, H. Eertink, W. Huijsen, M. Rougoor, W. Teeuw, M. Wibbels, H. Zandbelt, Content Distribution Networks State of the Art, Telematica Instituut, 2001, https://doc.telin.nl/dscgi/ds.py/Get/File-15534/cdnsota.pdf.
2. H. Zandbelt, B. Hulsebosch, H. Eertink, IDsec: Virtual Identities on the Internet, Internet draft, http://idsec.sourceforge.net/draft-zandbelt-idsec-01.txt.
3. R.J. Hulsebosch, J.F. Zandbelt, E.H. Eertink, Virtual Identities on the Internet, submitted to the Proceedings of the Twelfth International World Wide Web Conference, 20-24 May 2003, Budapest, Hungary.
4. B.C. Neuman, Proxy-Based Authorization and Accounting for Distributed Systems, Proc. 13th International Conference on Distributed Computing Systems, Pittsburg, 1993.
5. Grid Security Infrastructure description: http://www.globus.org/security.
6. S. Tuecke, D. Engert, I. Foster, V. Welch, M. Thompson, L. Pearlman, C. Kesselman, Internet X.509 Public Key Infrastructure Proxy Certificate Profile, draft-ggf-gsi-proxy-03, 2002, http://www.gridforum.org/security/ggf5_2002-07/draft-ggf-gsi-proxy-03.PDF.
7. A proposed edge server technology can be found on the web site of the IETF OPES working group, http://www.ietf.org/html.charters/opes-charter.html.

SECURITY, FAULT-TOLERANCE AND THEIR VERIFICATION FOR AMBIENT SYSTEMS

Jaap-Henk Hoepman
Department of Computer Science, University of Nijmegen
P.O. Box 9010, 6500 GL Nijmegen, the Netherlands
jhh@cs.kun.nl

Abstract For the emerging ambient environments, in which interconnected intelligent devices will surround us to increase the comfort of our lives, fault tolerance and security are of paramount importance. In contrast to the computers in a normal distributed system, ambient devices are generally small (meaning they have little computing power or memory space), often battery operated and interconnected much more dynamically. In this paper we discuss the fundamental research issues that emerge while designing the distributed algorithms for such ambient systems that must be both fault tolerant and secure.

Keywords: Security, cryptography, fault tolerance, formal methods, program verification, dependability, autonomous systems, distributed systems, ambient intelligence, embedded systems.

1. Introduction

In order to reduce cost, and to make management and addition of new services easier, our critical infrastructures (like the energy grid, or telecommunication systems) are increasingly built on and interconnected with Internet technology. Because of the open and best-effort nature of the Internet, these infrastructures have become increasingly vulnerable both to malicious attacks and ordinary faults [PCC97], implying that not only security, but also fault tolerance should be a real concern [Eld01].

Similar problems trouble the vision of future ambient environments [RTD02], in which interconnected intelligent devices will surround us, at home or while travelling. With these intelligent devices integrated in all kinds of consumer electronics (ranging from light switches, thermostats to audio, television and kitchen equipment), people expect equivalent reliability levels. Hence, security (to protect the home environment from hostile interactions with the outside world) and fault tolerance (to gracefully handle unavoidable system and component failures) need to be incorporated into the ambient, autonomous, environment, as well as privacy enhancing technologies [Hor01].

The last few years more and more embedded systems have become remotely managed over Internet connections, without much consideration for security and fault tolerance issues [Ano02]. This is clearly of great concern. As explained by Wood *et al.* [WS02], even denial of service attacks in sensor networks may permit real-world damage to the health and safety of people, when these devices are deployed in health-care and safety critical applications.

Emerging research is addressing the combined treatment of both fault tolerance and security [MM99]. However, current research topics are scattered, and do not address the fundamental issues concerning a unified treatment of security and fault tolerance in protocol design, and the verification of these properties. Moreover, the proposed solutions do not scale very well to the ambient world, either because the complexity rises sharply with the number of nodes in the system (which in an ambient system may be in the order of billions), or because they do not consider the resource poorness inherent to the embedded devices.

In this paper we discuss the fundamental research issues that emerge while designing distributed algorithms for ambient systems that must be both fault tolerant and secure. For concreteness, we also briefly describe some of our specific research topics in this area.

2. Ambient systems: fundamental research issues

Ambient systems posses some unique characteristics that set them apart from current large scale distributed systems and networks, posing new fundamental research questions in the area of fault tolerance and security.

2.1 Characteristics of ambient systems

An ambient system consists of many small interconnected devices. On a global scale, the number of such devices may easily run into the billions. Devices may range from special purpose controllers to general purpose computers, with special purpose but programmable devices (like mobile phones) or other general purpose handheld devices somewhere in between. In general, these devices should be cheap and therefore kept as simple as possible. They contain just enough computing power and storage space to accomplish their tasks. Some may not even have a form of persistent storage. Many of them will not be powered directly, but instead are powered through e.g., batteries or (either because they are portable, or because they are in a location without access to the power grid). To summarise, an ambient device is *resource poor*: it has little memory, only a small CPU, and should consume little energy.

The devices in an ambient system are interconnected in many different ways. Many only have a simple short range wireless interface (e.g. Bluetooth or infrared). Others may be equipped with larger range wireless interfaces (e.g. GSM/UMTS, or WiFi) or a fixed network connection. With such diverse network connections, and the highly mobile nature of at least some of the devices, we see that the ambient network is highly dynamic in its topology and exhibits unpredictable availability. Moreover, there is no hope to achieve any kind of centralised control.

2.2 Fundamental research questions

These unique characteristics of ambient systems give rise to the following largely open new fundamental research questions.

The traditional measures to analyse distributed algorithms have been *message complexity* (either in the number of messages sent or in the number of bits transmitted) and *time complexity*. For mostly battery powered ambient systems, energy consumption is also great concern. Therefore, the *energy complexity* of an algorithm should be analysed as well. Clearly, energy complexity of an algorithm is strongly related to both its time and message complexity. But this relationship is not as straightforward as it may seem at first.

- Sending messages consumes more energy than receiving. For broadcast channels like wireless networks, broadcasting a message takes as much energy as sending it to any particular node within transmission range.
- Waiting for a message ("listening to the wire") consumes considerable energy, yet waiting for a message is usually not included in the total time complexity of an algorithm.
- In emerging energy conserving reconfigurable hardware platforms hardware reconfiguration may either speed up the computation or conserve energy.
- The size of the data structure used by the algorithm influences its energy consumption: they may require secondary storage (either discs, EEPROM, or auxiliary RAM) that could otherwise have been switched off.

A realistic yet generally applicable and future proof model of the energy consumption of a computing device – the "battery powered" Turing Machine – is required [LV92]. Within such a model, we can reason about and maximise *security and fault-tolerance per Joule*.

In cryptography, the strength of a cipher is most realistically measured in terms of its *security parameter* k [Gol97][Bel98]. Within this model, ciphers and protocols are shown to require at least $g(k)$ work to break by the adversary (where a protocol is considered secure iff g is super polynomial in k). In other words, the probability of the attacker to break the system in one particular instance is $o(1/g(k))$, i.e., negligible in k for secure protocols. This is a weaker condition than the usual requirement for fault tolerant algorithms that must remain operational whatever the actions and work spent by the adversary (a condition that can usually only be met by restricting the number of faulty nodes f to be significantly less than the total number of nodes n) [LSP82]. For probabilistic fault tolerant algorithms, the usual approach is to maintain impossibility of failure, and to use randomisation to improve the expected running time [Rab83].

When studying algorithms that need to offer both security and fault tolerance, it does not make sense to keep this strong notion of fault tolerance. Instead the level of fault tolerance should be comparable to the strength of the security measures, and should therefore be expressed in terms of the security parameter k as well. Moreover, the traditional Byzantine failure model assumes that the adversary has unlimited computing resources and can guess or modify any messages sent by the nodes. This is too strong because it would defy any cryptographic security protection. A model similar to the authenticated Byzantine agreement systems (where the adversary is unable to forge signatures) [DS83] appears to be more suitable. In any case, this approach to specifying the security and fault tolerance of protocols poses new challenges to their formal verification, where cryptographic primitives are usually considered as black boxes that offer absolute security.

Finally, the lack of any centralised control and the fact that the network is highly dynamic (both in overall structure and connectedness of individual nodes) has large ramifications for the design of secure protocols. For instance, many security protocols require the assistance of a trusted third party. In practice even in fixed networks with centralised control it turns out to be hard to find parties that most agree on to be trustworthy. For highly dynamic networks, this is even harder. Moreover, in such networks trusted third parties may often be unreachable. Also, Public Key Infrastructures (PKI) with their hierarchical structure of certification authorities appear to be inappropriate for ambient networks. This is not only caused by their dynamic network topology, but also because the concept of ownership of and control over the embedded ambient devices becomes much more diverse and diffuse.

3. Emerging research topics

We conclude this paper with the description of three concrete examples of emerging research topics that we plan to study in this area in the coming years.

A challenging topic to focus our research on is the design of a fault tolerant and secure Domain Name System (DNS) [AL01]. Because of the large dependence of many Internet applications on the DNS, proper functioning of the DNS is of vital importance, and in fact proposals for and first implementations of a secure version of DNS (called DNSSEC) are emerging [Eas99]. However, current DNSSEC proposals suffer from two shortcomings. Due to backward compatibility requirements, DNSSEC has to be compatible and interoperable with older, non-secure, DNS clients and servers. This has seriously limited the available design options, adversely influencing the security of the overall design. Apart from the existence in the traditional DNS of 13 root domain servers, and the use of caching to speed up serving requests DNSSEC does not address the issue of fault tolerance at all. By dropping the backward compatibility requirement, we aim to study the ideal design of a secure and fault tolerance DNS. An extra challenge is to make sure the design can also be used within resource poor ambient environments that will (just as much as the current Internet) rely on a stable domain name system [Gie01].

We are currently raising support to investigate fault tolerant privacy protection of users in an ambient world [EHL+02]. Here we aim at a two-tier approach. In order to prevent collection of data about the user a system that allows for pseudo-identities and secure computing mechanisms will be investigated. On the other hand, to control the dissemination of data of the user, a license-based system will be developed. The licensing system will be based on the premise that user data needs to be accompanied by a license that shows that a party obtained the data rightfully. A license prescribes the actions (such as viewing, linking or transferring) a party is allowed to perform on the data. This requires a careful drafting of the semantics (i.e. meaning) of such licenses, efficient structuring and encoding of licenses, as well as protocols to securely issue, verify, transfer, split, limit, and combine licenses. Throughout the project, solutions must be both fault tolerant and secure, and are constrained by the limited computing, storage and communication resources available on the ambient devices, while making use of the much larger resources available in the home gateways and beyond.

Another interesting avenue of research is the issue of key management and key distribution in faulty environments [SMF+02]. The goal here is to devise secure key distribution protocols (for example those used in group membership protocols), that can not only survive processor failures but also memory/state corruptions. The latter type of errors have been extensively studied in the area of *self-stabilisation* [Dij74]. Algorithms that are both self-stabilising and fault tolerant are much harder to design [AH93][HPT02], and this is even without any security requirements.

References

[AL01] Albitz, P., and Liu, C. *DNS and BIND*. O'Reilly & Assoc., Inc., 2001.

[AH93] Anagnostou, E., and Hadzilacos, V. Tolerating transient and permanent failures. In *7th WDAG* (Lausanne, Switzerland, 1993), A. Schiper (Ed.), LNCS 725, Springer-Verlag, pp. 174–188.

[Ano02] Anonymous. Embedded systems. Crypto-gram, December 15, 2002.

[Bel98] BELLARE, M. Practice-oriented provable-security. In *Proceedings of First International Workshop on Information Security (ISW 97)* (1998), E. Okamoto, G. Davida, and M. Mambo (Eds.), LNCS 1396, Springer, Berlin.

[Dij74] DIJKSTRA, E. W. Self-stabilizing systems in spite of distributed control. *Comm. ACM* **17**, 11 (1974), 643–644.

[DS83] DOLEV, D., AND STRONG, H. R. Authenticated algorithms for byzantine agreement. *SIAM J. Comput.* **12**, 4 (1983), 656–666.

[Eas99] EASTLAKE, D. Domain name system security extensions. Tech. Rep. RFC 2535, IETF, 1999.

[Eld01] ELDER, M. *Fault Tolerance in Critical Information Systems*. PhD thesis, Department of Computer Science, University of Virginia, 2001.

[EHL+02] ETALLE, S., HOEPMAN, J.-H., LUBBER, J. C. A. VAN DER, VERSCHUREN, J. H. S., AND HUIZENGA, J. PAW: Privacy in an Ambient World. GENCOM project proposal, 2002.

[Gie01] GIEBEN, R. Chain of trust: The parent-child and keyholder-keysigner relations and their communication in dnssec. Tech. Rep. CSI-R0111, University of Nijmegen, The Netherlands, 2001.

[Gol97] GOLDREICH, O. On the foundations of modern cryptography. In *CRYPTO '97* (Santa Barbara, CA, USA, 1997), B. S. K. Jr. (Ed.), LNCS 1294, Springer.

[HPT02] HOEPMAN, J.-H., PAPATRIANTAFILOU, M., AND TSIGAS, P. Self-stabilization of wait-free shared memory objects. *J. Parallel & Distr. Comput.* **62**, 5 (2002), 766–791.

[Hor01] HORN, P. *Autonomic Computing*. IBM Corp., 2001.

[LSP82] LAMPORT, L., SHOSTAK, R., AND PEASE, M. The byzantine generals problem. *ACM Trans. Prog. Lang. & Syst.* **4**, 3 (1982), 382–401.

[LV92] LI, M., AND VITÁNYI, P. M. B. Theory of thermodynamics of computation. In *PROC. IEEE Phys. of Comput. Workshop* (Dallas, TX, USA, 1992), pp. 42–46.

[MM99] MEADOWS, C., AND MCLEAN, J. Security and dependability: then and now. In *Computer Security, Dependability, and Assurance: From Needs to Solutions, 7-9 July 1998 & 11-13 November 1998, York, UK & Williamsburg, VA, USA* (1999), Los Alamitos, CA, USA : IEEE Comput. Soc, 1999, pp. 166–70.

[PCC97] Critical foundations: Protecting America's infrastructure. Report of the President's Commission on Critical Infrastructure Protection, 1997.

[Rab83] RABIN, M. O. Randomized byzantine generals. In *24rd FOCS* (Tucson, AZ, USA, 1983), IEEE Comp. Soc. Press, pp. 403–409.

[RTD02] The priorities of the sixth framework programme 2002–2006. RTD Info, DG Research, European Commission, 2002.

[SMF+02] STADDON, J., MINER, S., FRANKLIN, M., BALFANZ, D., MALKIN, M., AND DEAN, D. Self-healing key distribution with revocation. In *IEEE Security & Privacy* (Berkeley, CA, USA, 2002), IEEE, pp. 241–257.

[WS02] WOOD, A. D., AND STANKOVIC, J. A. Denial of service in sensor networks. *IEEE Comput.* (2002), 54–62.

HIDDEN LAYER AUTHENTICATION USING SMART CARD FOR WEP BASED WLANS

GIANNIS PIKRAMMENOS, GHASSAN SARKIS, JOHN SOLDATOS, VASILIOS ANAGNOSTOPOULOS

National Technical University of Athens,

Electrical Engineering and Computer Science Dpt.

GR 15753, Athens, Greece. *e-mail: gpik@telecom.ntua.gr*

Key words: Smart Card, WLAN, Security, WEP, IV, IVT, authentication.

Abstract: WEP has been criticized for vulnerabilities of the offered security services. Several factors contribute to this effect, as the wireless nature of IEEE 802.11 standards, the solid architecture of the deployed LAN components as well as the inflexible security algorithm of WEP. Secrecy is dependent on the synchronization of the peer encrypting processes and their proper authentication. By implanting a hidden layer to the architectural structure of the system, the complexity of the system is elevated. Such an implant could be a Smart Card containing secrets related to encryption and authentication of multiple components. The on demand introduction of Smart Card in the hosting system enables the pre-synchronization of the systems secrets as and two-way authentication.

1. INTRODUCTION

Layering principles are widely applied in IT world in order to classify the functional responsibilities and to monitor the operational characteristics of each layer mechanism. A well known layering application is the IEEE networking protocol stack with WLAN (IEEE 802.11) [1] as an example. Security layering is also widely accepted, separating accessibility to clusters depending on the privileges of the attached users. The file system structure of a Smart Card fits within this area.

Hidden layers of information processing are common in Neural Networks as well as in telecommunications' routing. These layers are intermediate layers of the processing procedure that are not directly noticeable from the user. Their lack to adapt to variable operational conditions could be bypassed by enabling real-time structural update, elevating in this way its complexity [2] and scrambling the picture to attackers.

The idea presented here is to introduce Smart Cards as a hidden layer as a secure storage area and an authentication gateway. Embedded processing capabilities of Smart Cards allow for the encryption and manipulation of information, making feasible the update of the contents without any degradation to the achieved secrecy, integrity and confidentiality level [3]. This hidden layer shall interwork with diverse layer protocols, computational environments and functional entities vertically as well as horizontally.

2. SMART CARD BASED HIDDEN LAYER

Wired Equivalent Privacy (WEP) is the security element which has been bundled to 802.11 directly and serves to provide confidentiality and authentication services to 802.11 networks. WEP uses the RC4 algorithm with 40 bit or 128 bit (symmetric) encryption keys to encrypt data at the link-layer (MAC layer). There are two fundamental flaws found in WEP security [4], [5]. The first (more mathematically proven than practically) is the way RC4 algorithm uses key scheduling and random number generation. The second lays in the way WEP handled the RC4 keys for encrypting the 802.11 payloads. Specifically, there is a problem with Initialization Vector (IV) being transmitted in the clear along with the cyphertext for the purposes of rapid decryption at the receiving end, and that it is repeated more or less frequently, depending on the amount of traffic.

The problem with key scheduling based on the random generation mechanism could be solved by centrally dictating the IV sequences. This would require a storage area where bundles of such sequences could be stored temporarily for immediate application in a table. The insecure transmission of these IVs over the air could be bypassed if initial values could be securely provided to the remote wireless terminal so as to be aware that it shares a secret with the AP without being obliged to transmit it. The integration of a Smart Card into the wireless terminal could be the solution to both problems. The transmitted information that represents IVs could be replaced by pointers to actual IVs stored in a table (Initial Vector Table - IVT) that is common between the two peers. Third parties could not then access the actual information in the clear and could possibly be discouraged from statistically revealing it by frequently updating the IVT contents with new values. The update could be realized downward (from the AP to the wireless terminal) once the connection is secured. It is preferable to involve another security mechanism for this transaction (different from the one under discussion) so as to disengage the control data from the controlled channel. IVTs could be transmitted in bursts or continually as and in one piece or concatenated, so as to elevate system's complexity and to moderate the traffic overhead imposed to the data transmission because of security information exchange.

Smart Cards could be a perfect place for the IVT information storage, as it is an autonomous, secure computational system that could interact with the host device at the wireless terminal under the supervision of the authorized person (the card holder). This scheme allows for a layered security mechanism that enhances the operation of the present WEP mechanisms with minor modifications while at the same time it increases the system complexity by incorporating multiple authentication dependencies. Keys for the encryption are produced under the co-operation of multiple mechanisms based on systems that work in different locations (Smart Card and Smart Card Authentication Server – SCAS).

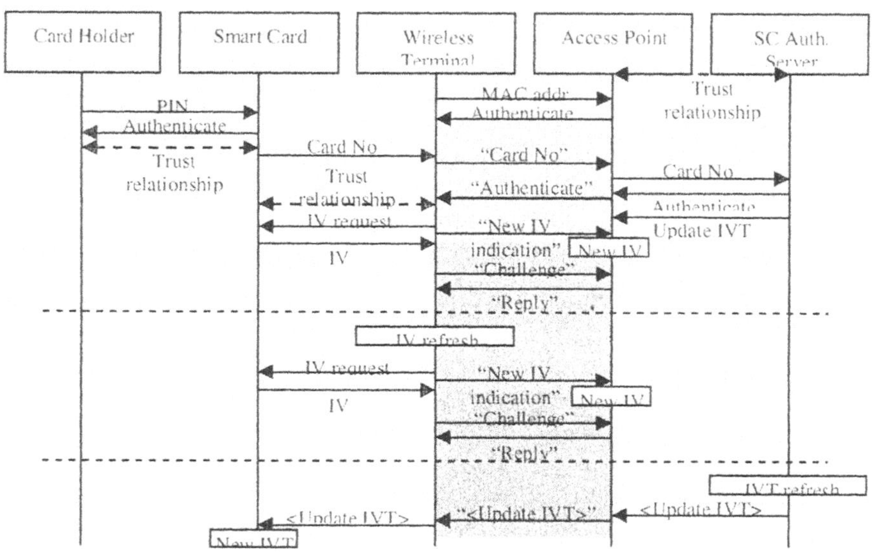

Figure 1 Authentication dependencies and security levels applied – light grey: plain WEP encryption, dark grey: enhanced encryption with dynamic IV update.

Until the enhanced method develops a key to encrypt the air channel (darker gray areas), the encryption mechanism is based on the classical WEP operation (light grey). The exchange of the pointers identifying the actual (kept secret) key value is hardening attackers' efforts to resolve and link keys to an attack attempt, while the co-operation of remote systems favors the involved parties synchronization and the monitoring of critical information exchange. Figure 2 depicts the architecture of the system with the enhanced security mechanism regarding the functional interworking among the components as well as the roles assignment regarding authentication. Note that potential multiple usage of the Smart Card for different applications allows for its interworking with higher layer mechanism to produce analogous security functions. In such a case, the User could be authenticated indirectly by the Smart Card or directly interworking with higher layer mechanisms. Resuming, a Smart Card could guarantee user's authority on the system operation (as the card holder), wireless terminal encryption logic secrecy and possibly higher layer encryption logic secrecy as well.

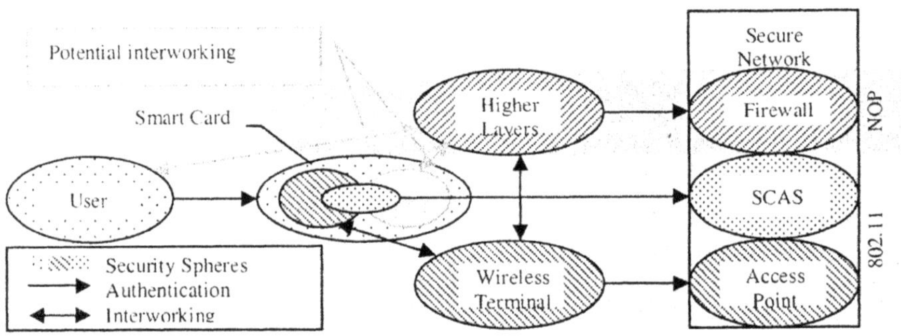

Figure 2 Architecture of a Smart Card enhanced WLAN system.

The modifications to the WEP mechanism in order to incorporate Smart Cards as IVT storage medium, as described in the previous, include:

- The adoption of an Initial Vector Table (IVT) logic that is not embedded but referenced,
- The introduction of a register that would point to IVT for the actual value of the WEP key to be fetched, being transmitted over the air in clear instead of the real value,
- A fetching mechanism that would apply interworking between Smart Card (referenced storage area) and MAC embedded WEP mechanism,
- The introduction of a Smart Card hosting device in the configuration of the wireless terminal,
- The introduction of a dedicated server (SCAS) that would validate Smart Cards in operational wireless systems and update them with IV values.

3. CONCLUSIONS

The added value offered by Smart Cards to the security mechanism of wireless systems as IEEE 802.11 is that it introduces a hidden layer that incorporates secrecy intelligence. This secret layer, that alters the operational model of the WLAN, is able to interwork with all the involved functional components as an authentication mediator. As such, secrecy is raised and the proper secrets are revealed only to the authorized procedures. This extra layer is not straightforwardly detected and this adds complexity to the system along with the capability to dynamically update the functionality of the encryption mechanism by refreshing with new keys dictated by a central repository monitoring their usage.

This paper proposes a new architecture in comparison with those proposed in [6], the hidden layer authentication based on removable media as Smart Cards. It is preferable method over fast packet keying [7] because it decomposes the information of the station from the secret information. Upper layer authentication [8] is supported through the smart card as well, as explained in the previous. Finally, Hidden Field Equations [9] proposal is cordial to the spirit of the presented proposal, strengthening its basis.

4. REFERENCES

[1] IEEE Std 802-2001, "IEEE Standard for Local and Metropolitan Area Networks: Overview and Architecture," IEEE Computer Society, LAN/MAN Standards Committee, 8 March 2002

[2] "Rapid Re-keying WEP recommended practice to improve WLAN Security", Nancy Cam-Winget (Atheros), Jesse Walker (Intel Corp), Bernard Aboba (Microsoft Corp), Joe Kubler (Intermec Corp), August 2001, http://www.drizzle.com/~aboba/IEEE/1

[3] "JAVA CARD MANAGEMENT SPECIFICATION," Java Card Management (JCM) Task Force, Version 1.0b, 06 October 2000.

[4] "WEPCrack is an open source tool for breaking 802.11 WEP secret keys" http://wepcrack.sourceforge.net/

[5] Fluhrer S., Mantin I., Shamir A., "Weaknesses in the key scheduling algorithm of RC4", Eighth Annual Workshop on Selected Areas in Cryptography, August 2001.

[6] "An IEEE 802.11 Wireless LAN Security White Paper", Jason S. King, October 22, 2001, http://www.llnl.gov/asci/discom/ucrl-id-147478.html

[7] "WEP Fix using RC4 Fast Packet Keying", RSA Security Inc, http://www.rsasecurity.com/rsalabs/technotes/wep-fix.html

[8] "Wireless LAN upper layer authentication and key negotiation", Håkan Andersson, RSA Laboratories, January 17, 2002, http://www.rsasecurity.com/rsalabs/technotes/wlanweb.doc

[9] "Security of Hidden Field Equations (HFE)", Nicolas T. Courtois, RSA'2001, San Francisco, April 10th 2001

PINPAS: A TOOL FOR POWER ANALYSIS OF SMARTCARDS

J. den Hartog[1], J. Verschuren[2], E. de Vink[3,4], J. de Vos[2], W. Wiersma[3]

Abstract This paper describes the PINPAS tool, a tool for the simulation of power analysis and other side-channel attacks on smartcards. The PINPAS tool supports the testing of algorithms for vulnerability to SPA, DPA, etc. at the software level. Exploitation of the PINPAS tool allows for the identification of weaknesses in the implementation in an early stage of development. A toy algorithm is discussed to illustrate the usage of the tool.

Keywords: Smartcard, Power Analysis, Side-Channel Analysis, Simulation

Introduction

Developers of smartcard algorithms are confronted, among others, with the question of the vulnerability of their final implementation to power analysis attacks (Kocher, 1996; Fahn and Pearson, 1999; Messerges, 2000). Typically, in a late stage of the development of the smartcard application some evaluating company is consulted. Over a period of several weeks this specialized company assesses the security level of the smartcard. In case a power analysis attack is successfully launched against the smartcard, re-design and patches should improve the actual code. Time-to-market and project deadlines seem not to allow for a different approach.

Central to the situation, in our view, is that power analysis vulnerability is tested on a physical smartcard in a late phase. It is possible to do this inspection earlier. The key observation is that the implementation is not needed in hardware to find an attack. For power analysis it is sufficient that the algorithm is available in software.

[1]Corresponding author, Eindhoven University of Technology, P.O.Box 513, 5600 MB Eindhoven, The Netherlands, jhartog@win.tue.nl
[2]TNO-TPD, Delft, The Netherlands
[3]Eindhoven University of Technology, Eindhoven, The Netherlands
[4]LIACS, Leiden, The Netherlands

An instruction level interpreter for the machine language of the smartcard and a physical model of the smartcard will do. The power consumption of an instruction with its data can be represented by a power consumption frame. Then, interpretation of a program leads to a trace of power consumption frames. The trace is in fact an abstraction of the power trace obtained when measuring the power consumption of a smartcard running the program with an oscilloscope.

The set-up sketched above brings several advantages compared to the physical approach: (i) Power analysis can be done in an early stage of the development of the application, say on the code of a skeleton version of the program. (ii) Immediate feedback can be given on the vulnerability to power attacks as time-consuming measurements by an evaluator can be avoided. (iii) As turn-around time has decreased significantly, iterative improvements of the code are feasible and the power analysis can be explored at leisure of the developer.

1. The PINPAS tool

Above we described a scheme for evaluating the vulnerability of a smartcard to power analysis attacks. The PINPAS (Program INferred Power Analysis in Software) tool is being developed to implement this scheme. Currently the tool consists of two major components: a simulator and an analyzer.

One part of the tool provides a simulator for programs to be run on a given smartcard. The simulation not only calculates the input/output behavior of a program, but also models the side-channel information that becomes available during the execution of the program. From this additional information the power consumption frames of the abstract power traces, as mentioned above, are generated. By incorporating only the information that leaks for the particular card, the abstract power trace is an accurate representation of a trace that would otherwise have been obtained physically. The simulator will in general deliver perfect traces without any sort of jitter or noise, although this is not essential in case of a sufficient signal-to-noise ratio; if noise is present more traces may be required but the same attacks can still be mounted.

The other main part of the tool supports the power analysis of the generated traces. Due to the modular software architecture it does not matter which program and simulator were used to generate these traces; only the traces have to be supplied to this part of the tool. In later sections we explain how the PINPAS tool can be used on a toy algorithm and leakage of Hamming weights over the bus. However, the tool has been successfully applied in experiments including DES, TEA and AES.

2. A simple example

To illustrate the PINPAS tool at work we discuss a toy algorithm, viz. `return Sbox[ input XOR key ]`. The algorithm takes the exclusive or of an 8-bit input and an 8-bit key and calculates their 4-bit signature. The function `Sbox[ x ]` selects one out of four S-boxes based on the first two bits of `x` and uses the remaining six bits as the usual S-box input. Further details of the S-boxes are omitted. Clearly this algorithm, as such, is not secure, but it handles the main ingredients of an algorithm like DES. As platform we assume some vanilla smartcard using some generic processor. The smartcard is assumed to leak information about values transported on the memory bus.

As a first step we translate the algorithm to the assembler code for our smartcard. A straightforward implementation is

```
MOV x,input; XOR x,key; MOV output,Sbox[x]; EXT
```

Here we have used the operations `MOV x,y` to move data to `x` from y, `XOR` for the exclusive or and storage of the result in the first operand, and `EXT` to end the program by returning the value `output`. The implementation of the program can be loaded into the simulator and run to test its functionality.

The next step is to evaluate the vulnerability to power analysis of the assembler code. A potential source for DPA is the value `input XOR key`, which can be calculated from the known value of the input and a guessed value of the key. After generating power traces with the simulator, the traces can be split into two groups using the 'trace condition' for the expected power consumption of `XOR x,key`. A difference trace is obtained by subtracting the average traces for each of the two groups. This is done for each possible value of the key. Exhibition of large amplitudes indicates that the correct value of the key has been found.

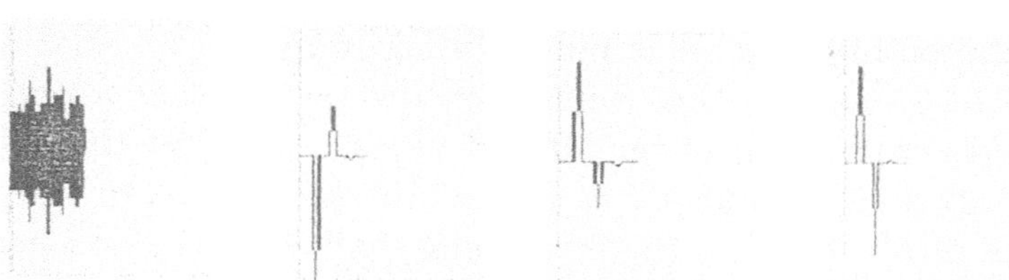

The images above show some of the output produced by the simulator. The first image shows an example of a generated power trace. The second trace shows the difference trace for splitting on the input only. The spikes indicate where the input can still be recognized. The third and fourth image show the difference trace for an incorrect and a correct guess of the key, respectively. The correct guess can be identified because it produces a large downward spike.

3. Flexibility of the PINPAS tool

The PINPAS tool is flexible in the selection of the algorithm that is being investigated, making it easy to check several algorithms for a given platform. One can choose any well-known algorithm, e.g. DES, IDEA, etc., or any proprietary algorithm but one can also switch between different implementations of the same algorithm. This makes it feasible to evaluate software defenses introduced in an implementation to protect against vulnerabilities that have been found. Another aspect of the flexibility of the PINPAS tool lies in the choice of the hardware platform. One can easily switch between different cards, for example cards based on well-known processors, based on specialized processors or even based on processors which have only been designed but not (yet) implemented in hardware. This flexibility in the choice of the card allows testing of an algorithm on several potential cards and assessing vulnerabilities of an algorithm irrespective of the precise platform.

In the remainder of this section we illustrate how both software and hardware defenses can be tested in the tool. This is done by introducing a DPA countermeasure for the vulnerability found in the example algorithm. The DPA attack above is based on the fact that information about the Hamming weights of certain values leaks in the power usage. Several techniques have been proposed in the literature to strengthen smartcard algorithms, e.g. (Chari et al., 1999; Messerges, 2000; Goubin, 2001). One possible defense is to protect important values by masking them with random values. Unmasked values are only used within the registers of the chip, which are assumed not to leak significantly. This defense protects against the attack described above, but is still not sufficiently safe. To render information about Hamming weight of values completely useless one can apply so called dual rail logic. When using dual rail logic the Hamming weight of values is always the same and thus cannot provide the attacker with any useful information. An implementation of this scheme purely in hardware can be efficient and transparent to the algorithm running on the card, but at a price; the hardware resources have to be doubled in size. To limit the cost one could include dual rail operations in the processor but leave the choice of when to invoke these to the programmer, allowing the non-sensitive data to be coded normally.

By using the dual rail operation `XORdr`, which calculates the exclusive or of numbers in dual rail format, we can easily implement our example program as `x = single2dual(input); y = Sbox2[x XORdr key2]; return dual2single(y)`. Here Sbox and key are stored in dual rail format (denoted by `Sbox2` and `key2`). The function `single2dual` converts an 8-bit number to its 16-bit dual rail equivalent. Finally, **dual2single** converts back from the dual rail format. The implementation of this algorithm on our generic smartcard is straightforward. The function **XORdr** is directly mapped to a dual rail operation implemented on the chip.

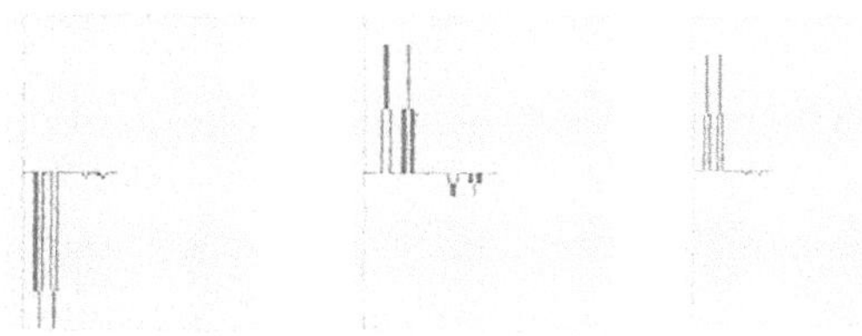

The first image shows the difference trace for splitting on the input only. The value of the input can only be recognized at the start (first two spikes), after this no leakage occurs. The other two images show that a wrong and a correct guess of the key can no longer be distinguished: The trace for the correct key guess is not significantly different from the traces for incorrect guesses.

4. Conclusion

We have introduced the PINPAS tool which can simulate a smartcards power consumption and a side channel attack on that smartcard. The software simulation done with the PINPAS tool can be profitable in the testing of existing cards and algorithms. The tool is especially useful as an aid in the design of both cards (hardware) and algorithms (software), allowing for an assessment of the risk of side channel attacks in a much earlier stage of development. This way the production cycle and time-to-market of a new smartcard product can be greatly reduced. We have illustrated how the development process can be supported by the PINPAS tool for a toy algorithm which, although being very simple, contains steps comparable to widely accepted encryption standards.

References

Chari, S., Jutla, C., Rao, J., and Rohatgi, P. (1999). Towards sound approaches to counteract power-analysis attacks. In Wiener, M., editor, *Proc. CRYPTO'99*, pages 398–412. LNCS 1666.

Fahn, P. and Pearson, P. (1999). IPA: A new class of power attacks. In Koç, C. and Naccache, D., editors, *Proc. CHES'99*, pages 173–186. LNCS 1717.

Goubin, L. (2001). A sound method for switching between boolean and arithmetic masking. In Koç, C., Naccache, D., and Paar, C., editors, *Proc. CHES 2001*, pages 3–14. LNCS 2162.

Kocher, P. (1996). Timing attacks on implementations of Diffe-Hellman, RSA, DSS, and other systems. In Koblitz, N., editor, *Proc. CRYPTO'96*, pages 104–113.

Messerges, T. (2000). *Power Analysis Attacks and Countermeasures for Cryptographic Algorithms*. PhD thesis, University of Illinois, Chicago.

ASSESSING SECURITY IN ENERGY-EFFICIENT SENSOR NETWORKS

Yee Wei Law, Sandro Etalle, Pieter H. Hartel
Faculteit Elektrotechniek, Wiskunde en Informatica, Universiteit Twente
Postbus 217, 7500 AE Enschede, The Netherlands
{ywlaw, etalle, pieter}@cs.utwente.nl

Abstract

In this paper, we describe why current research in ad hoc networks requires an effective assessment framework, and how our *system profile* proposal can be used for the purpose. With this tool at hand, we have managed to carve out manageable design spaces from the seemingly infinite possibilities of ad hoc mobile wireless networks.

1. Introduction

Wireless sensor networks combine the characteristic of ad hoc mobile wireless networks (ad hoc networks in short) at the system level, with the characteristics of sensors at the component level. Ad hoc networks are: (1) **ad hoc**: the network set-up is possibly short-lived; (2) **mobile**: the nodes are not attached to any fixed communications infrastructure as well as fixed energy supply; (3) **wireless**: the nodes communicate wirelessly. These three properties imply a series of constraints, that together with the constraints imposed by sensors (among which energy being the predominant), form the starting point of our security research.

In our opinion, the current research landscape lacks structure. Here, we show how prevalent (proposed) architectures are based on assumptions that are not only implicit but even conflicting at times. As an example of implicit assumptions, to curb selfishness, the Terminodes project introduces a virtual currency called *nuglets* [2]. To protect these nuglets from tampering, every node must be equipped with a tamper-resistant *security module*. At the same time, the proposed cross-certification architecture calls for public-key cryptography. In addition, as part of the Terminodes project, Hubaux *et al.* propose that each node maintains its own *certificate repository* [5]. These repositories store the public certificates the node themselves issue, and a selected set of certificates issued by the others. It is thus concluded, although the Terminodes project does not specify, that the implicit assumptions or requirements of Terminodes are that they have to be (1) tamper-resistant, (2) capable of performing resource-intensive public-key cryptography, and (3) have sufficient storage for a potentially large certificate repository.

In direct contrast to the above approaches are Basagni *et al.*'s *pebblenets* [1] and Perrig *et al.*'s SPINS [6] which specifically avoid public-key cryptography that sensors are ill-equipped to handle. The different assumptions in public-key cryptography present an insurmountable barrier in unifying the earlier proposals with Basagni *et al.*'s or Perrig *et al.*'s. Of further interest is that Basagni *et al.*'s *pebbles* are required to be tamper-resistant to ensure forward secrecy. Building tamper-resistance into a sensor can substantially increase the cost of the sensor depending on the intended FIPS 140-1 level (`csrc.nist.gov`). This presents a case of potentially self-contradicting requirements within a single proposal.

Our contribution to providing structure is *system profiles*. System profiles are an effective means for assessing and categorizing s system according to its actual specification and requirements. Under this framework, we make it possible for architectural designs to relate to a set of fine-grained properties they should comply with, instead of a hypothetical and often arbitrary set of assumptions. Keeping one system profile in perspective at a time helps to prevent oversight and underestimation.

2. System Profiles

The inspiration of system profiles comes from Sun's Java^{TM} 2 Platform, Micro Edition (J2ME) (`java.sun.com/j2me`), a Java platform targeted at low-end devices such as PDAs, cellphones etc. As the capabilities of these devices vary tremendously, Sun introduced the concept of *configurations*. Configurations map to Sun's two primary design targets: devices that can be held in the hand and devices that can be plugged into a wall. Hence there are two configurations: Connected Limited Device Configuration (CLDC) and Connected Device Configuration (CDC). CLDC targets resource-constrained devices with typically a 16/32-bit processor, and 128~512 KB of memory available for the Java platform and applications; whereas CDC is for more powerful devices. The strategy of J2ME attests to the fact that one size does not fit all. We are adopting a similar profiling strategy. The only difference is what we are profiling are not the nodes themselves, but the systems.

We categorize different ad hoc networks into different system profiles, each of which is defined by a set of boolean *critical system parameters*.

(The boolean nature of the papameters is really an abstraction of a more refined scale that we would like to investigate in the future.) The following critical system parameters have been defined:

1. Message Confidentiality (MC) specifies the requirement for encrypting all network messages. Rationale: Although encrypting network messages is useful for battling traffic analysis by attackers, not all types of system require this level of security. A brute force approach of encrypting all messages regardless of necessity does not necessarily provide the highest level of security, nor is it energy-efficient. In the case where MC=F(alse), the confidentiality of the payload data is considered an application-dependent (as contrasted to system) requirement .

2. Tamper Resistance (TR) speficies whether there is an allowance for using tamper-resistant hardware to protect every node in the network. Rationale: To entrust a node with a key, we have to make sure the node itself does not divulge the key to unauthorized parties upon tampering. If not all nodes in the network can be made tamper-resistant, it is insufficient to rely on cryptography alone to ensure the integrity of any node, since any node can be tampered, with its keys compromised and its program modified. For such networks, cryptographic material cannot be kept at any node for any extended period, and supplementary means are necessary. It is for simplicity that this parameter is represented as a binary scale instead of a multi-level scale as in FIPS 140-1.

3. Public-Key Cryptographic Capability (PKCC) refers to the capability of any node in the network to perform public-key cryptography. Rationale: This parameter determines whether public-key cryptographic technology can be employed. Note however that the fact that PKCC is true does not guarantee that public-key cryptography can or should be used extensively. It only indicates that the technology *can* be used, and the degree of usage depends on the architectural design. In general, to perform public-key cryptography, the processor speed is not the only issue, the deciding factor is the sufficiency of memory, therefore PKCC more or less translates to the sufficiency of memory.

4. Rich Uncles (RU) refers to the availability of Rich Uncle nodes, which are resourceful nodes, both in terms of computing resources and energy, that are suitable for the role of certification authorities, for example in the Rich Uncle Protocols [3]. These nodes might be floating or might be gateways to some external wired networks. If all nodes are equally "rich" (i.e. the network is homogeneous), we may assume that either every node is a Rich Uncle or no node is a Rich Uncle. Rationale: the existence of Rich Uncles confirms the possibilities of relegating resouce-intensive tasks and assigning important security roles to them, thereby facilitating the use of certain hierarchical architectures and possibly public-key cryptography.

This selection of parameters is not meant to be exhaustive or definitive and yet we find it an unambiguous way for categorizing the types of system we know so far. We give a few examples below of how we classify some typical ad hoc network systems:

- **Battlefield interpersonal communication** is a scenario where telecommunication devices, carried by vehicles and soldiers, communicate in an ad hoc fashion without the need as well as the danger of using a base station (whose compromise would jeopardize the entire mission). The requirement for MC and TR is obvious. The assumption for PKCC can also be justified, while RU may not be as readily assumed. Hence, MC=T, TR=T, PKCC=T, RU=F.
- **Battlefield sensor surveillance** is the class of systems in which minute wireless sensors (e.g. chemical sensors, seismic sensors etc.) are dispatched in military zones for critical surveillance. Signals Intelligence data are meant to be gathered from Unmanned Aerial Vehicles (UAVs) and relayed to the forward operating base for analysis and correlation. Because of the low cost and disposable design of sensor nodes, TR, PKCC and RU cannot be assumed. MC is undoubtably critical. Hence, MC=T, TR=F, PKCC=F, RU=F.
- **Spontaneous networking** is, as described by Feeney *et al.* [4], a technology that allows people to meet and use their laptops, PDAs, tablets etc. to start collaborating on some tasks through wireless networking, i.e. in the absence of a fixed infrastructure. For the same reason why IPsec is invented, MC is important. TR, as applied to consumer hardware, cannot currently be assumed. PKCC is generally available although the performance varies widely across the classes of device. By the psychological reasoning that nobody wants to spend more energy than the others, we can assume that nobody wants to be a RU. Hence, MC=T, TR=F, PKCC=T, RU=F.
- **SPINS-type sensor networks** refer to the class of networks with sensors deployed around a central base station. The presence of the base station immediately guarantees the existence of a RU. Hence, MC=T, TR=F, PKCC=F, RU=T.
- **EYES networks** is the class of networks we design for the EYES project (`eyes.eu.org`). We envision our prototype to be a congregation of sensor networks for intelligent buildings. The sensors are meant to collaborate to achieve some desired functions, but often in the course of performing such functions, privacy and security-sensitive data are transmitted, so MC is to be enforced. For economic reasons, TR is not assumed. We expect our node to have PKCC because each sensor

will carry a 1MB serial RAM, which is large enough for the purpose. We also do not want to rule out the possibilities of RU, since the office environment is largely under our control. Note that even with these assumptions in place, we are not restricting ourselves to any specific architecture, centralized or decentralized. What we have in mind of the topology is a sea of sensors, some of which mobile and some static, peppered by tiny islands of relatively resource-rich devices. Hence, MC=T, TR=F, PKCC=T, RU=T.

To wrap up, system profile is a means of classification and assessment, it does not dictate what architecture should be adopted for which particular profile.

3. Conclusion

Realizing that one size does not fit all, we have introduced a unified assessment framework based on the notion of system profiles, not only to remind ourselves of the valid set of assumptions and requirements, but also to allow ourselves to concentrate on one profile at a time. Our research exercise has testified it to be a useful tool in assessing ad hoc networks.

References

[1] S. Basagni, K. Herrin, D. Bruschi, and E. Rosti. Secure pebblenets. In *Proceedings of the 2001 ACM Int. Symp. on Mobile Ad Hoc Networking and Computing*, pages 156–163. ACM Press, October 2001.

[2] L. Buttyán and J.-P. Hubaux. Nuglets: A Virtual Currency to Stimulate Cooperation in Self-Organized Mobile Ad Hoc Networks. Technical Report DSC/2001/001, Department of Communication Systems, Swiss Federal Institute of Technology, 2001.

[3] D.W. Carman, P.S. Kruus, and B.J. Matt. Constraints and approaches for distributed sensor network security. Technical Report #00-010, NAI Labs, 2000.

[4] L. Feeney, B. Ahlgren, and A. Westerlund. Spontaneous networking: An application-oriented approach to ad hoc networking. *IEEE Communications*, 39(6):176–181, Jun 2001.

[5] J.-P. Hubaux, L. Buttyán, and S. Capkun. The quest for security in mobile ad hoc networks. In *Proc. of the ACM Symp. on Mobile Ad Hoc Networking and Computing (MobiHOC '01)*, pages 146–155. ACM Press, October 2001.

[6] A. Perrig, R. Szewczyk, V. Wen, D. Culler, and J.D. Tygar. SPINS: Security Protocols for Sensor Networks. In *Proceedings of the 7th Ann. Int. Conf. on Mobile Computing and Networking*, pages 189–199. ACM Press, 2001.

FROM FINITE STATE MACHINES TO PROVABLY CORRECT JAVA CARD APPLETS

Engelbert Hubbers, Martijn Oostdijk, and Erik Poll
Nijmegen Institute for Information and Computing Sciences, University of Nijmegen, P.O.Box 9010, 6500GL, Nijmegen, The Netherlands
{hubbers,martijno,erikpoll}@cs.kun.nl

Abstract This paper presents a systematic approach to developing Java Card applets and/or formal specifications for them, starting from descriptions in the form of finite state machines. The formal specifications are written in the specification language JML, and can be checked against Java Card source code using the static checker ESC/Java.

1. Introduction

Specification of software, let alone *formal* specification of software, is difficult, as is checking that source code actually conforms to a given specification. Often finite state machines (FSMs) provide a convenient notation for specification, for example for the life cycle of an applet or the access control it enforces. The aim of this paper is to show that, for the kind of software running on small devices such as smart cards, it is possible to automatically generate machine-checkable formal specifications from such FSMs, just as it is possible to generate (a skeleton of) the actual source code itself.

Our approach is to automatically generate prototype Java Card applets and formal specifications in JML [Leavens et al., 1999], starting from a description in the form of a FSM. Additional functionality is to be manually added to the generated applet source code afterwards. Also, more details can be added to the generated specifications.

Instead of contributing any grand new theories to the field of software engineering, this paper explores the above approach using mainly existing technologies and tools, as described in Section 2. How Java Card applets and JML specifications are automatically generated is described in Section 3. Possibilities for future work and some conclusions can be found in Section 4.

2. Applied Technologies

Several tools and languages are used in the transformation from FSM to Java code and JML specifications.

The Uppaal model checker [Pettersson and Larsen., 2000] is used to draw diagrams of FSMs which can be saved as XML documents. We do not use Uppaal's verification capabilities. An FSM in Uppaal consists of states (of which one is marked as initial) and transitions between these states. Every transition has a label and possibly additional attributes, such as guards and an assignments. Since Uppaal does not distinguish between normal and abnormal transitions, the labels in our diagrams have names ending with `Nor!` or `Exc!`.

The Java Modeling Language (JML) [Leavens et al., 1999] is a specification language tailored to Java. JML specifications consist of class invariants, global constraints, and pre- and postconditions for individual methods. These are all written as special comments in the Java source code, so that Java compilers do not notice them, but JML-aware tools can make use of them. One of the strengths of JML is that its syntax resembles normal Java syntax, so that Java programmers can easily understand it. Another strength of JML is that there are several tools available for it: the JML runtime assertion checker [Leavens et al., 1999], ESC/Java [Detlefs et al., 1998], and the LOOP tool [Van den Berg and Jacobs, 2001].

The F2J tool is a simple translator of our own creation which takes a Uppaal XML document as input and generates Java source code and JML specifications. This tool is described in Section 1.3.

The ESC/Java 'extended static checker' is a tool developed at Compaq SRC for automatically checking JML-annotated code. It detects, at compile time, possible violations of specifications by a program. ESC/Java is extremely good at spotting for example where one might potentially dereference a null pointer or access an array outside its bounds, which typically violates some postcondition or invariant. ESC/Java uses a theorem prover to verify assertions in code, without any user interaction. The tool is neither sound nor complete, which means that ESC/Java might complain about errors that will never arise when the program is run, and that ESC/Java might miss errors that may occur at runtime. However, this drawback usually only occurs in more complicated programs and specifications, whereas the applets and their properties we look at are relatively simple. Moreover, the bold step to give up on soundness and completeness is what makes ESC/Java such an effective tool, as attempting either of these two properties would probably result in a tool far too complicated and slow to be useful in practice.

3. Generating Applets and Specifications

Java Card applets have a very standard structure. They all implement a *process method* which deals with so-called *application protocol data units* (APDUs), instruction packets that are sent to the card by a terminal (and back). APDUs have a header which encodes the instruction to be performed by the applet, while the rest of the APDU is just data. Typically, the process method inspects the header, to determine which operation is to be performed, and calls dedicated helper methods to process the rest of the data. Depending on the state of the applet an instruction may be valid or invalid. A typical applet will throw an exception when it receives an invalid instruction.

In order to generate Java code from the FSM, a special `mode` field is introduced to encode the state of the FSM. The transitions in the FSM correspond to the possible instructions that are valid for the applet. The `mode` field implements a life cycle model for the applet, similar to those in [Marlet and Métayer, 2001; Mostowski, 2002]. The process method is generated as a nested switch. The outer switch is a case distinction on `mode`. The inner switches are case distinctions on the header of the incoming APDU. A dedicated helper method is generated for each possible instruction. The generated code ensures that, in case the corresponding guard is true in the FSM, `mode` is changed to the result state of the transition and all corresponding assignments are executed. Invalid instructions result in exceptions being thrown, leaving `mode` unchanged. The generated code is a legal Java Card applet with limited functionality. Typically one will want to manually add some code to the generated skeleton code. Our running example in this paper is a simple purse applet whose Uppaal specification is given in Figure 1.
The generated JML specification consists of a global *invariant*, a global *constraint*, and pre- and postconditions for all methods. The generated invariant enumerates the different possible values of `mode`.

```
/*@ invariant
  @  (mode==INIT || mode==ISSUED || mode==CHARGING || mode==LOCKED)
  @*/
```

An invariant is a predicate that has to be preserved by every method. A constraint in JML is a relation between pre- and post-states of methods that has to be respected by every method. Contrary to an invariant, a constraint can make use of JML's `\old` keyword to refer to the value of a

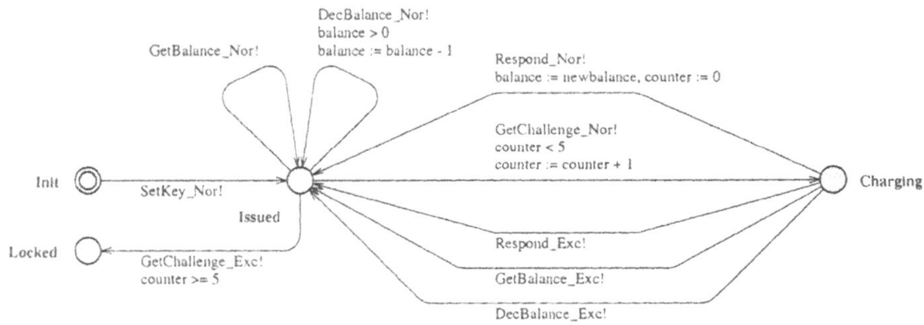

Figure 1. Life cycle model of simple purse applet.

field in the pre-state of a method. The generated constraint captures the flow of control throughout the applet's life, by listing logical implications describing the different transitions.

```
/*@ constraint
  @  (mode==LOCKED ==> \old(mode)==ISSUED || \old(mode)==LOCKED) &&
  @  (mode==INIT ==> \old(mode)==INIT) &&
  @  (mode==ISSUED ==> \old(mode)==INIT || \old(mode)==ISSUED
  @                    || \old(mode)==CHARGING) &&
  @  (mode==CHARGING ==> \old(mode)==ISSUED || \old(mode)==CHARGING) &&
  @  (\old(mode)==LOCKED ==> mode==LOCKED) &&
  @  (\old(mode)==INIT ==> mode==ISSUED || mode==INIT) &&
  @  (\old(mode)==ISSUED ==> mode==ISSUED || mode==CHARGING
  @                          || mode==LOCKED) &&
  @  (\old(mode)==CHARGING ==> mode==ISSUED || mode==CHARGING);
  @*/
```

The generated constraint only describes the control flow. Additional constraints could be added, for instance to relate `mode` to the other fields. For example, an interesting relation between `mode` and `balance` is that 'once the applet is `ISSUED`, the `balance` can only decrease'. It should not be very difficult to generate such additional constraints based on more advanced analysis of the FSM.

Verifying the kind of properties discussed above is well within the capabilities of ESC/Java, so it can be used to check that a Java Card applet behaves conform the generated JML specification. Applets will, of course, invoke methods from the Java Card API. Fortunately, JML specifications for all these methods are available [Poll et al., 2000]. Note that control flow, even in a simple Java Card program, can be hard to follow due to all the possible exceptions. So the verification performed by ESC/Java is more complicated than it may appear.

4. Discussion

We have discussed an approach to use FSMs to automatically generate Java Card source code, that can serve as the skeleton for a smart card applet, and to generate formal JML specifications, that are well-suited to automatic verification using ESC/Java. The F2J translation described in this paper is still under development, and is currently just a prototype. The invariant and constraint generation can certainly be improved through more advanced analysis of the FSM.

One obvious next step is to use Uppaal not just as a graphical editor, but to use it as a model checker. It could be used to check some interesting properties of an FSM (for example, for our running example, that the balance always remains non-negative) even before we generate source code or specifications. In addition to just modeling the smart card applet, one could also model the behavior of the terminal application that communicates with the smart card, and then check more interesting properties of the applet and the terminal interacting. Another possibility for further work is to extend the syntax allowed in FSMs, notably in the guards and assignments, so that more of the behavior of the Java applet can be described in the FSM. Finally, a more ambitious project for future work would be to extract an FSM from given Java Card source code, rather than the reverse as we do now.

References

Detlefs, D. L., Leino, K. R. M., Nelson, G., and Saxe, J. B. (1998). Extended Static Checking. Technical Report 159, Compaq Systems Research Center.

Leavens, G. T., Baker, A. L., and Ruby, C. (1999). JML: A notation for detailed design. In Kilov, H., Rumpe, B., and Harvey, W., editors, *Behavioral Specifications for Businesses and Systems*, pages 175–188. Kluwer Academic Publishers.

Marlet, R. and Métayer, D. L. (2001). Security properties and Java Card specificities to be studied in the SecSafe project. Technical Report SECSAFE-TL-006, Trusted Logic.

Mostowski, W. (2002). Rigorous development of JavaCard applications. In Clarke, T., Evans, A., and Lano, K., editors, *Proc. Fourth Workshop on Rigorous Object-Oriented Methods, London.*

Pettersson, P. and Larsen., K. G. (2000). UPPAAL2k. *Bulletin of the European Association for Theoretical Computer Science*, 70:40–44.

Poll, E., van den Berg, J., and Jacobs, B. (2000). Specification of the Java Card API in JML. In Domingo-Ferrer, J., Chan, D., and Watson, A., editors, *Fourth Smart Card Research and Advanced Application Conference (CARDIS'2000)*, pages 135–154. Kluwer.

Van den Berg, J. and Jacobs, B. (2001). The LOOP compiler for Java and JML. In Margaria, T. and Yi, W., editors, *Tools and Algorithms for the Construction and Analysis of Software (TACAS)*, volume 2031 of *LNCS*, pages 299–312. Springer-Verlag.

SECURITY CHARACTERISTICS OF E-COLLABORATION ENVIRONMENTS

Security architectures and recommendations

Bob Hulsebosch, Ernst-Jan Goedvolk, Wil Janssen
Telematica Instituut, P.O. Box 589, 7500 AN Enschede, The Netherlands
e-mail: {Bob.Hulsebosch, Ernst-Jan.Goedvolk, Wil.Janssen}@telin.nl

Abstract: To realize a trustworthy e-collaboration business environment more is needed than ICT-security tools only. One needs to understand the characteristics of such an environment, which have an impact on the overall security. Based on this observation we suggest architectures and recommendations for ICT-security in three different e-collaboration environments.

Key words: Security, E-collaboration, Characteristics, Architectures.

1. INTRODUCTION

Over the past years, the Internet has evolved into one of the most important means of communication. Businesses thrive on the increased efficiencies, reduced costs and expanded reach of the Internet [1]. Yet the full potential of modern Internet communication is often not utilized. Especially in the communication between enterprises, a certain reluctance to move to the Internet is present. An important reason for this is the perceived lack of security and trust [2]. Despite the availability of a wide variety of new ICT-security tools and techniques more is required to address the challenges of secure e-business environments on the Internet and to increase the trust level. In order to realize a trustworthy business environment for e-collaboration one first need to understand the characteristics of such a business environment, that might have an impact on the overall security.

Three models for e-collaboration environments where small and large ICT systems have to communicate with each other are distinguished [3]:

Bilateral model: all parties independently perform individual transactions with each other. The overall 'logical' transaction often comprises a number of bilateral transactions. The data is stored within the own domain of each party and is not accessible by others.
Decentralised model: all parties control and distribute the information/data they own/have. The data storage is within each party's own domain and each party offers services to allow controlled access to the information by others.
Centralised model: all parties make use of a central database or service provider, which is outside their domain.

In this paper, we study the different security characteristics of the three e-collaboration models. Recommendations for security architectures are given. These results were developed and validated in the Virtual Port project [4].

2. E-COLLABORATION SECURITY ASPECTS

Several aspects that typically arise in an e-collaboration environment and have an impact on the overall security can be recognized. The *autonomy* of the collaborating parties must often be respected. The differences between the autonomous actors make it difficult to impose network-wide security measures. Furthermore, in an e-collaboration environment it is important to know who is *responsible* for the physical goods and information and must take the necessary measures. If one is not made responsible for its actions, one can always deny having performed an action. Perhaps the most serious problem in managing security risks is the *absence of accepted network-wide systems that enable companies to judge the risks* embedded in their current e-business environments. Finally, one should also take into account that not all actors in the e-collaboration network have the same *level of system security*. Naturally, services like *confidentiality, integrity, authentication, authorization, non-repudiation* remain essential in each security architecture.

Bilateral e-collaboration model

This model for e-collaboration is currently applicable to most of the processes in many e-business environments. Several specific characteristics of the bilateral model concerning security can be recognized. Firstly, the *parties know each other*. Consequently, the temptation to use non-ICT channels (e.g. phone, fax) to communicate with the other party is high, since both parties know each other. Such heterogeneity of communication channels significantly reduces the level of security and complicates implementation of security measures. The absence of third parties, which are often viewed as undesired middlemen, gives a larger feeling of confidence. Secondly, a bilateral model typically *hampers chain/network-wide agreements* and use of standards. Lack of such agreements reduces the effectiveness and efficiency of all security measures. In a bilateral environment there is *little flexibility* concerning security services, i.e. processes are optimized for both parties only. As a result, management and control of encryption keys/certificates is often done locally. The conclusion of a new bilateral agreement with another party will subsequently result in more complex key management and interoperability problems. Finally, although information is always accurate for a sending and receiving party, other parties are not aware of their information exchange and are kept in *uncertainty*. Precautionary measures are difficult to plan and as a result the overall process is delayed.

In the bilateral model, all companies must decide for themselves which security measures they use. A logical approach as to whether the content of a message needs security measures must be made by each individual party and will largely depend on the infrastructure used. Use a virtual private network (VPN) for communication integrity, end-user authentication at the application level, and access control to information. To introduce some flexibility and reliability of the authentication process, we favor a PKI in which a central party co-ordinates the management of digital certificates.

Decentral e-collaboration model

The decentralized model is growing popular because it allows more efficient working practices. Many people from within and outside the secured domain may have access to process-related information, which demands greater *discipline* and sense of *responsibility*. In a distributed system, the players are *in control* of their own data, i.e. they can decide who has access to which information. Another advantage is that the system is more *flexible/scalable*, i.e. new parties can easily join the network. On the other hand, such flexibility makes it difficult to manage access control. For each new party joining the system, all other parties have to adjust their access control lists. Accidental operations such as lock-up checks, dealing with lost keys, and access control management make the model *expensive* and *time-consuming*.

The security characteristics of distributed systems are inherently different from those of centralized systems. These differences stem from the *lack of a central authority* responsible for data handling, security, and policy enforcement. Security models for distributed systems need to take these differences into account and must scale to a large number of users. The size of distributed systems and the fact that they tend to span organizational boundaries means that they are basically characterized by several security problems [5]. Firstly, it is difficult to provide the *same level of security* to all distributed systems (components, applications, and communication links). Secondly, organizations are *responsible* for enforcing security policies over the systems that are under their jurisdiction but used by others as well. Most organisations lack the experience and facilities to take this responsibility.

In this model, where parties have little knowledge about each other and flexibility is important, we recommend to use a VPN for secure transmission of data and for shielding of the party's own information systems. A centralized system for management of VPN server certificates is required. At the application level, each actor must be held responsible for his operations. Moreover, the actors will need to authenticate to the other party to gain access to information. This means that all parties in the decentral model must have knowledge of all actors/roles in the system. Such a knowledge system can only be based on actor/role-based certificates, which are controlled and issued by a central party. In other words, a fully functional PKI is required.

Central e-collaboration model

Today's e-business environments require a fail-safe, secure infrastructure. Availability of the data at all time is crucial and requires back-up and fail-over capabilities. Security in centralized systems depends on the ability of a trusted computing base to control access to protected resources and secure communication.

The designated key-holders guarantee that all data is placed properly and maintain close checks on loss or theft. Although reliable and proven, this is not the most *efficient* system. User profiles, roles, and rights are critical to creating a secure system and are easy to control in a central system. *Access control* to data in the central database is crucial. Therefore, roles, profiles and rights must be determined and agreed upon by all companies collaborating with the central party. Moreover, all companies must *trust* each other and the central party and must be willing to place their data in the central database. Centralization also allows for easier implementation of *standards*, which generally facilitates sharing of data across the organization.

Choosing for a central system has its advantages: it is relatively *easy* to manage authentication and access control, data will be more consistent for all parties in the network, parties can use specific information elements without having to wait until the whole (e.g. EDI) message is sent. Some disadvantages of the central system are: the *availability* of information, trust is not present, parties are not always willing to share their information, who is really in control of the data in the central database?

Based on these characteristics we propose the following security architecture for the central e-collaboration model. A central database, containing all relevant information, is easily accessed via a Web interface. The interface must be secured via an authentication check. Access to the information stored at the database is crucial. SSL is used to establish a secure connection to the Web site. A server site certificate authentication procedure is used to enable the SSL handshake. We prefer SSL above a VPN connection because of its simplicity and ease of use.

3. CONCLUSIONS

To realize a trustworthy e-collaboration business environment more is needed than ICT security tools. One needs to understand the characteristics of such an environment that have an impact on the overall security. Typical examples of these characteristics are the (desired) autonomy of the collaborating parties and their systems, the clear definition of responsibilities and accepted risks, and the differences in computerization between the collaborating parties. Security architectures must have the ability to support these aspects. Based on three models for e-collaboration, we have presented how various parties with a different level of computerization and a variety of systems can collaborate securely. When coupling various (small) systems one should take into account the relative advantages of each model:

- Bilateral model: simple, but not scalable;
- Decentral model: robust, flexible, but highly complex;
- Central model: simple for most parties, scalable, but may conflict with the business culture.

Finally, we want to state that the current ICT systems in most e-collaboration environments are based on existing business processes. Often, little attention has been paid to the aspect of security in these business processes. As a consequence, in order to protect the ICT systems, business processes have to be redesigned taking security policies into account. Only then a suitable architecture for ICT security can be developed that tightens the trust relationships that exist in e-collaboration infrastructures. We stress that it is of importance to first have a good insight in the business processes, their critical assets and the responsibilities. Only then proper security policies can be made up and suitable security measures can be implemented.

REFERENCES

1. R. Alt, E. Fleisch, & H. Österle,, *Business networking: Shaping enterprise relationships on the Internet*, H. Österle, E. Fleisch, & R. Alt (Eds.), p. 1-13, Berlin: Springer, 2000.
2. L. Ang, C. Dubelaar & B. Lee, *To trust or not to trust?* 14th Bled Electronic Commerce of Conference, Bled, Slovenia, June 25-25, 2001.
3. Hau L. Lee & Seungin Whang, *Information Sharing in a Supply Chain*, International Journal of Technology Management, Vol. 20, p. 373-387, 2000.
4. W. Janssen & H. van Raalte (eds.). *Blueprint for a virtual port.* https://doc.telin.nl/dscgi/ds.py/Get/File-23315/, see also www.virtuelehaven.nl.
5. See also: http://www.cs.utexas.edu/users/new_directions/Papers/ken_goldman.html.

ROADMAP FOR SECURING HANDHELD DEVICES

System Integrity and Confidentiality

Preetida Vinayakray-Jani
Nokia Research Center
P.O.Box 407, FIN-00045 NOKIA GROUP, Finland
preetida.vinayakray-jani@nokia.com

Abstract With increasing connectivity and data sharing possibilities with handheld devices, potential threats to device security, user privacy and home/corporate LAN have become very significant. Currently there is no prevention against malicious software and supported access control - if any at all - is lacking any security relevant attributes. Often when such countermeasures are designed, the security is traded for performance and battery power. Key security issues within handheld devices necessitate the mandatory security policies to be assigned and enforced. This paper creates the roadmap for securing handheld devices by identifying security relevant policies and discusses how such policies can be assigned and enforced[1].

Keywords: Malicious software, System security, Software development and execution

1. Introduction

While user takes an advantage of handheld devices with multi-interfaces e.g. WLAN, Bluetooth, UMTS etc. and increased computational power, there are significant security risks posing threats to user privacy, integrity of the device and network. Versatility of this device allows users to send and receive emails, to access corporate data, to surf Internet, and to sync and transfer stored data to home PC or PC within corporate LAN. Eventually when handheld devices due to their flexibility, compactness and usefulness have become prevalent in corporate environment, the encountered security risks include:

- Wireless Interception: Connecting handheld devices to vulnerable web sites, receiving/transmitting unencrypted emails or usage of flawed cryptographic tools will allow an attacker to create Man-in-the middle attack.

[1]Disclaimer: The views expressed are those of the author and do not represent an official view of Nokia Research Center.

- Probing: Probing in sensitive area and directing confidential information to unauthorized users can generate privacy threats to user/corporation.

- Malicious Software/Code: Installation of software without verifying its integrity and trustworthiness. Often this practice leads to malware [2] attack to home/corporate network.

- Weak/Null Authentication: Used authentication mechanism is either weak or disabled, allowing access to unauthorized users.

- Roaming in dangerous environment: Any device roaming in vicinity of the other handheld device can create intentional attack and deprive particular handheld device from providing/receiving any service.

- Lack of user initiative and awareness: Very frequent users do not take strong initiative to protect information stored within device. Also sometimes user does not recognize that sensitive information stored within the device is vulnerable and about to be compromised by the attacker.

Mitigation of such risks, through tools (e.g. antivirus, sandboxing, access control etc.) is unable to keep pace with the emerging new applications. Compared to conventional applications, current applications draw upon the services and resources from other applications and not just the operating system [1]. In fact, the successful impact of application specific security solutions very much hinges over the secure platform. Therefore, when system platforms of handheld devices are designed to be open and modular to support third party applications, the *integrity* and *confidentiality* of *system* as well as *software applications* cannot be overlooked.

Hence in this paper section 2 discusses the platform security including its inadequacy against malicious code and policies necessary to derive secure system for device. Section 3 examines existing software flaws in the application in terms of buffer overflow, lack of memory protection, system stability and mobile code. Section 4 provides conceptual framework for assigning and enforcing the security policies. Finally section 5 presents the concluding remarks.

2. Platform Security

Since the handheld devices are extended with capability like remote connectivity or access, the span of its authorization has also expanded; a malicious program can cause damage to any installed application, except that there is no authorization. Malicious software can easily override the user's access rights

[2] This includes viruses, Trojans and worms. Together they are also called *malware*.

for any particular objects, making malicious application indistinct from legitimate one. With lack of user authorization role it is difficult to identify which activities are permissible or not and this can lead to all types of attacks. Since there is no strong coupling between user and the code he executes, current handheld device platforms neither support integrity of the code nor provide logical means to classify roles of users so that sensitive information can be protected.

This can be prevented if the authorization is outside the control of typical user. This can be achieved by means of *mandatory security policies* in which authority is vested in some users - system administrators, but there are control on delegation and allocation of authority. Research efforts made by [3] have clearly emphasized the usage of mandatory security policy, classified into various kinds of policies such as:

- Authentication policy for users to prevent unauthorized access
- Differentiating policy for users with specific functional roles (e.g. security administrator for system and ordinary user) and process privileges
- Authorization policy for accessing confidential information and database
- Integrity policy for file access to prevent tampering of data/application

Any possible adversary action to invoke malicious software can override the access mechanism policies of the files belonging to the authorized user. Thus access control mechanism also requires the *trusted path* mechanism and that will allow authorized user to access trusted software only [3]. The practical means of assigning mandatory policy should be justified through suitable mechanisms where policy can be enforced with consistent cost.

3. Software flaws in Application: Development, Instillation and Execution

Today when evolution of system is reliant on applications, attackers are looking for gaining unauthorized access on system by exploiting vulnerabilities in application program through buffer overflow, depriving user from using any particular application or passing dangerous command to system subroutines.

Buffer Overflow

Sometimes the system vulnerability is exposed to the flaws in standard software coding techniques. Nonetheless, this vulnerability may be due to the inadequacy of the system or it may be inherent to coding method. Very frequent application developer is careless about examining the size of the arguments and stores them into a buffer of fixed size using standard functions causing buffer overflow. Application with buffer vulnerability often gives attacker an opportunity to inject and execute malicious software. An effective coding language and method should be used to prevent buffer overflow.

Lack of Memory Protection

With current device system all application/data reside within battery-backed RAM. It is very likely that residing bad applications stomp on themselves and also on other trusted/untrusted applications or the system itself. Encountered error in one application can reflect erroneous changes in subsequent trusted/untrusted application, eventually crashing system itself. Thus memory protection is needed for preserving integrity and privacy of applications. Implementing hardware-based memory management unit (MMU) in conjunction with secure and reliable bootstrap architecture is one possible solution to this problem as usage of ROM and Flash memory is not convincing [5].

System stability

Even if memory protection is encountered efficiently there are still risks if the command used to pass on malicious parameters to system subroutines. With this system does not know that it has been asked to do something that is pernicious. Since system does not access to the application memory, it is possible to break the system integrity without violating memory protection. Therefore mandatory policy like *sanity checking* is needed to verify parameters before executing them.

Mobile Code: Automate Execution

Another possible risk is the containment of untrusted mobile code. Neutral to any operating platform this code can be distributed seamlessly over Internet and is often received by a device with request to execute with user privileges. Apparently this automatic execution does not postulate any existing vulnerability, as system does not acquire such mechanisms evaluating the security implications of the executing code. Any failure to handle this code result in more serious damage like giving significant privilege to access sensitive information and system resources, creating denial of service (DoS) attack or penetrating in corporate LAN through downloaded Trojan or virus [2]. Although policy like implementing *sandboxes* can be useful to constrain mobile code but that is not enough as any implementation errors enable mobile code to circumvent the sandbox's security mechanisms. Solution like *Program shepherding* can be applicable but that also requires the un-circumventable sandboxing [6]. In brief, proper mechanisms are needed for system to prevent the harmful influence of the mobile code.

4. Security Administration: A Conceptual Framework

Having all mentioned above the risk mitigation through efficient security measures is not panacea for future security risks that are not feasible today. Despite the fact that future handheld device might be governed through the proper security measures, the corporate LAN will remain on the verge of security threats if prescribed security of corporate is bypassed. As a result following discussion provides the conceptual view of assigning security policy and enforcing it. A very similar but detailed approach proposed as a proof-of-concept in [4] for Palm OS. Over here proposed work does not emphasize any particular operating platform of handheld device.

Assignment of Proprietary Policy

Handheld device should contain the default security policy as well as proprietary policy assigned by the corporate system administrator. Default policies are rudimentary that confine the usage of device for a very limited applications. Proprietary Policy assigned by security administrator should handle the usage of assets and audit log of the device. Here asset means the confidential information specific to corporation/user. Policy should assign security attributes with program that will support system security configuration management and protect against malicious modification of program by malware. Also policy should assign other security attributes associated with program that will restrict specific operation permitted by specified program on specified objects when they are executed.

To maintain the integrity of the device against new attacks, assigned proprietary policies should be frequently updated. Moreover, assigned proprietary policies should be protected by means of theft protected proprietary certificate that can be validated by means of suitable mechanism.

Enforcement of Proprietary Policy

The policy enforcement mechanism on handheld device should be configured according to the assigned proprietary policies and its activation assures security administrator that device as well as user has complied with the assigned proprietary policies. Once device validates the proprietary policy certificate policy enforcement mechanism should monitor and govern any security relevant activities on device.

Enforced policies should update the audit log and restrict the external flow of the confidential information. The audit log should store fine grain (memory access) security events to high-level operations (process calls) to the operation that can change the security configurations. Enforcement mechanism may contain many mechanisms in terms of access control, installation of third party software, periodic syncing with the network, determent of theft etc. Monitoring and managing the periodic sync of audit log information on computer allows security administrator to analyze the collected log and take necessary actions if any anomalies are found.

5. Conclusion

This paper addresses the inadequacy of the current handheld devices against the malicious code. Privacy and integrity of the device not only requires the secure platform but also efficient software engineering and memory management. To gain acceptance of handheld device as *Trusted Device* in corporation or in enterprise a conceptual framework for assigning and enforcing the proprietary policies is presented. Overall paper provides the roadmap for securing handheld device stemming from the platform security to assignment and enforcement of proprietary policies.

6. Acknowledgement

Author is grateful to Markku Kylänpää and Kaisa Nyberg for providing helpful comments and feedback, Jani Suomalainen for updating and discussing mandatory security approaches, and Janne Mäntylä for supporting this work.

References

[1] Marshall D. Abrams and Michael V. Joyce. (1995). *Trusted System Concept.* Computers & security, Vol. 14 No.1, Pages 45-56, Copyright Elsevier Advanced Technology 1995, Oxford, UK.

[2] Matt Blaze, Joan Feigenbaum, John Ioannidis and Angelos D. Keromytis. (1999). *The Role of Trust Management in Distributed System Security.* Book: Secure Internet Programming: Security Issues for Mobile and Distributed Objects, *ed.* Jan Vitek and Christian Jensen, Springer-Verlag Inc., New York, NY, USA. Pages 185-210. 1999.

[3] Peter Loscocco, Stephen Smalley. (2001). *Integrating Flexible Support for Security Policies into the Linux operating system.* Technical Report, NSA and NAI Labs, February 2001.

[4] Wayne Jansen, Tom Karygiannis, Serban Gavrila, and Vlad Korolev. (2002). *Assigning and Enforcing Security Policies on Handheld Devices.* In Proceedings of the Canadian Information Technology Security Symposium, May 2002.

[5] Kingpin and Mudge. (2001). *Security Analysis of the Palm Operating System and its Weakness Against Malicious Code Threats.* In Proceedings of the 10th USENIX Security Symposium, Washington, DC, August 13-17, 2001, Pages 135-151, ISBN 1-880446-07-3.

[6] Vladmir Kiriansky, Derek Bruening and Saman Amarasinghe. (2002). *Secure execution Via Program Shepherding.* In Proceedings of the 11th USENIX Security Symposium (Security '02), San Fransisco, California, August 2002.

LAWFUL CYBER DECOY POLICY

James Bret Michael and Thomas C. Wingfield
Naval Postgraduate School, Department of Computer Science, Monterey, California USA
ManTech Aegis Research Corporation, Falls Church, Virginia USA

Abstract: Cyber decoys provide a means for automating, to a degree, counterintelligence activities and responses to cyber attacks. Like other security mechanisms for protecting information systems, it is likely that cyber decoys will in some instances be misused. In the United States, criminal law provides us with analogies for preventing or punishing improper state use of deception, and criminal and civil law give us a range of tools to use against private actors. However, in addition to states, nongovernmental entities and individuals can employ cyber decoys. In this paper we present a principled analysis of the use of cyber decoys. We explore the absolute minima in terms of customary principles for what might be considered to be acceptable use of deception.

Key words: Deception, Law, Computer security

1. DECEPTION IN CYBERSPACE

In [1], Michael *et al.* propose to use software-based deception as a means for hardening operational systems against attack. Critical units of software are wrapped with "decoying" rules, which are the cyber embodiment of both the policy (including doctrine) of an organization or individual for conducting counterintelligence and applying countermeasures against attackers. The wrappers are placed around critical units of software (*e.g.*, a component or method) to be protected. By critical, we mean units of software that are integral to the continued survivability of an information system and the correct enforcement of the policy embedded in the system.

When a wrapper detects a suspicious pattern of system calls by one or more computer processes, it begins to conduct counterintelligence tasks and initiates countermeasures; pattern recognition is performed at runtime. The wrappers, referred to as "decoys," conduct counterintelligence by allowing the interaction with suspicious processes to continue, collecting information about the nature of the processes' behavior. The wrappers respond to requests for service from the processes by applying countermeasures, with coordination of their responses provided by "decoy supervisors." The countermeasures include actions taken to shield the wrapped software from any ill effects of the interaction, and the responses to the processes that are needed to deceive the attacker into concluding that his or her computer processes are successfully carrying out their mission. As new patterns of suspicious behavior are discovered, the database of rules for counterintelligence and countermeasure actions is updated.

1.1 A potential "homeland security" application

Homeland security within the United States encompasses, among other things, the protection of public and private cybernetic property against espionage and sabotage, especially if such a compromise would have a significant adverse effect on the national security of the United States.[1]

Let's make the discussion of software decoys more concrete by considering how they can be used to protect a particular type of cybernetic property—a public-switched telephone network (PSTN). Within a PSTN, software units that authenticate subscribers to the network are necessary for enforcing policy against unauthorized eavesdropping on conversations. In addition, the survivability of a PSTN is contingent on the continued correct functioning of the software that implements the Signaling System 7 (SS7) protocol. Thus, by our definition, these software units are system-critical.

Software decoys can be created for both the subscriber-authentication and SS7 software units. For instance, these software units can be wrapped so that they discover patterns of system-level events that are indicative of attempts to cause exceptions to be raised in normally infrequently-called methods of these software units—such invocations of methods constitute a form of suspicious behavior. On detecting a sequence of invocations, such as one that would cause a buffer overflow, the decoys would begin gathering information about the nature of the calling processes' behavior. If a process continues to try to raise exceptions, the decoys could, for instance, fake error-handling messages with the aim of making it appear to the process that the exception was raised and not handled. The goal of the decoy at this point is to maintain interaction with the process, providing the decoy with the opportunity to gather more information about the nature of the interaction. If analysis of the interaction is indicative of an attack, the decoy may be able to discern the sources and methods of the attack, using this information to make decisions about whether to applying passive (*i.e.*, strictly defensive on the attacked system) or active (*i.e.*, counterattack) countermeasures. Likewise, the decoys may discover the interaction is non-malicious in nature, notifying the owner of the process of his or her egregious use of the software units; this addresses, to some extent, the need to correctly handle false positives.

1.2 Potential for misuse of decoys

The users of software decoys need to employ counterintelligence and countermeasures in a judicious manner, so as to prevent their misuse. For instance, software decoys, like any other software, can behave in unanticipated ways due to the presence of unknown software defects; defects can cause side effects that result in the generation of inappropriate responses. Similarly, the decoys may be poorly designed in terms of the breadth of responses, or in terms of the fidelity with which they implement the owning organization's policy. Alternatively, the decoys may not have built-in controls to prevent users or their decoys from inadvertently contravening an organization's policy on the use of countermeasures and counterintelligence; the foregoing examples exemplify the *technical misuse* of decoys.

Suppose that a public telephone company instructs the decoys used in conjunction with its SS7 software to provide deceptive responses, such as exaggerated delays, to the communication devices used by customers of competing telephone service providers, with the aim of providing those users with a degraded level of service. In the United States, injecting such delays is legal as there is no general duty on the part of nongovernmental entities to tell the truth: suboptimal performance is rarely, if ever, unlawful *per se*. In the eyes of some, the exaggerated delays represent a misuse of the technology in that the company might gain an unfair competitive advantage. We call this *intentional lawful misuse* of decoys.

Further, suppose the federal agencies within the United States employ software decoys. If the National Security Agency were to use the decoys to collect information about attackers who turn out to be U.S. citizens, this would be a violation of federal law. We refer to this as an example of *unintentional unlawful* use of decoys. One means proposed in [2] for countering this and the other types of misuse is to make the decoy supervisors responsible for checking whether the rules for conducting counterintelligence and applying countermeasures in a particular context do not contravene policy.

2. LAWFUL CYBER DECOY POLICY

Policy can be used to provide guidance within an organization on how to properly use software-based deception mechanisms. For instance, the telephone company in the preceding example could have a policy that all of its networks must require knowing intelligent waiver by the user of certain privacy rights after reasonable notice has been given to both legitimate users and intruders that software deception is in use would protect the company, absent any other egregious behavior on its part, from being held legally responsible for damage incurred by the user due to the user's interaction with the software decoys.

Criminal law already goes a long way toward giving us analogies for preventing or punishing improper state use, and criminal and civil law give us a range of tools to use against private actors. However, there are gaps in the law. For example, what if corporations start using software decoys within acceptable limits and contract out those aspects of deception that would cross the line (*i.e.*, be unlawful) while maintaining plausible deniability? (*N.B.*: Nations often contract out covert operations to civilians.)

2.1 The view of deception in society

Deception or "ruses of war" is permissible in military campaigns, and only runs afoul of the law when it rises to the level of "perfidy," the treacherous misleading of an enemy about his—or your—status under the law. However, there is a cultural bias in the United States against the use of deception by any level of government, as evidenced by the recent reluctance to institutionalize deception by quashing the effort to create the U.S. Office of Strategic Influence, whose charter was to conduct perception management across agencies, including disseminating misinformation to foreign journalists in support of the war on terrorism [3]; there is also a strong legal and cultural predisposition against using domestic U.S. journalists for active deception (vice selectively withholding information, which can be enormously effective in crafting the desired conclusion), including formal guidance within the intelligence community against using them in covert operations. It is possible that proposals by the Department of Homeland Security and other government agencies, to defend against terrorist attacks on cyber property, may also fall victim to negative public sentiment: there are enough mainstream concerns about civil liberties to render a potentially intrusive program politically unpalatable. Thus, we propose that individuals and organizations apply principled analysis in assessing the legality of using software-based deception.

2.2 Principled analysis of decoy usage

Principled analysis of the use of deception involves taking into account the value of the target, the nature and immediacy of the threat, the identity of the actors, the degree to which any state is supporting them, etc. For instance, consider the principle of proportionality, as it pertains to the *jus in bello*, or the law which operates between belligerents in time of war: "[t]he principle of proportionality requires the military commander to balance the collateral damage (against civilians and their property) of a planned attack against the concrete and direct military advantage expected to be gained" [4]. In other words, while civilians and their property may never be targeted as such, the amount of permissible collateral damage varies with the immediate importance of the military target. This applies to digital in cyberspace as certainly as it does to kinetic warfare in realspace. Beyond proportionality, there are three additional customary principles of the law of armed (and information) conflict: chivalry, which embodies the distinction between lawful ruses of war and unlawful perfidy, as mentioned above; discrimination, which allows military objectives, such as combatants and their equipment and facilities, to be targeted, but prohibits the intentional targeting of civilians or their property; and necessity, which has two components. Its quantitative component allows the use of all the force necessary to accomplish a lawful military mission, but no more; its qualitative component permits all means for accomplishing such a mission, with the exception of a small number of uncivilized weapons and techniques deemed too inhumane to be used to *any* degree. Such outlawed means include chemical weapons, biological weapons, x-ray transparent bullets, and blinding lasers. These four customary rules, described as they pertain to military use of software decoys to protect semantic webs, may be found in [2].

Let's proceed to the example of software decoys generating unwanted side effects due to the presence of software defects in the decoys. The principle of proportionality applies here: if the government fails to allocate adequate resources to test and validate its decoys, it would be difficult to conduct a proper proportionality analysis in the heat of information operations in a time of war. Numerous other legal problems, particularly under the principle of necessity, also arise, potentially generating legal liability up to and including the status of "war criminal" for information operators, mission planners, military commanders, and civilian approval authorities. With appropriate advance work, these potential consequences—certainly those due to advance negligence or recklessness—may be virtually eliminated.

3. CONCLUDING REMARKS

It is possible that software decoys can be used as an airlock between the technology and the law in that the decoys can be programmed with a wide spectrum of options for taking action. Software decoys provide for anticipatory exception handling. In other words, the decoy anticipates the types of inappropriate interaction between the calling process and the wrapped unit of software, providing in advance rules for learning about and evaluating the nature of the interaction, in addition to rules for response. One could envision developing policy that places boundaries on the extent and type of deception to be employed, but providing some degree of latitude to the user of decoys to inject creativity into deceptions so as to increase the likelihood that the deceptions will be effective. The boundaries could be used to delineate the thresholds that if breached could result in the misuse or unlawful use of decoys. That is, principled analysis can be used to meet all domestic legal criteria, and set absolute minima in terms of the four customary principles of discrimination, necessity, proportionality, and chivalry.

Lastly, the U.S. Department of Homeland Security will be responsible for coordinating the protection of both public and private cybernetic property using cyber weapons. There are gray areas in the law regarding how to coordinate counterintelligence activities and countermeasures that need to take place at the intersection of law enforcement, intelligence collection, and military activity. Principled analysis can help here too, but public policymakers will need technically and legally sophisticated advice to manage the best technological defense available within the framework of the law.

NOTES

1. Conducted under the auspices of the Naval Postgraduate School's Homeland Security Leadership Development Program, this research is supported by the U.S. Department of Justice Office of Justice Programs and Office of Domestic Preparedness. The views and conclusions contained herein are those of the authors and should not be interpreted as necessarily representing the official policies or endorsements, either expressed or implied, of the U.S. Government.

REFERENCES

[1] Michael, J. B., Auguston, M., Rowe, N. C., and Riehle, R. D. Software decoys: Intrusion detection and countermeasures. In *Proc. Workshop on Inf. Assurance,* IEEE (West Point, N.Y., June 2002), 130-138.

[2] Michael, J. B. On the response policy of software decoys: Conducting software-based deception in the cyber battlespace. In *Proc. Twenty-sixth Annual Computer Software and Applications Conf.*, IEEE (Oxford, Eng., Aug. 2002), 957-962.

[3] Pentagon closed besieged strategic office, *L.A. Times*, 27 Feb. 2002, A6.

[4] Wingfield, T. C. *The Law of Information Conflict: National Security Law in Cyberspace.* Falls Church, Va.: Aegis Research Corp., 2000.

ELECTRONIC SIGNATURE AS A PART OF INFORMATION SOCIETY INFRASTRUCTURE

Legal and Technological situation in Finland, the Republic of Croatia and the Czech Republic

Juhani Paavilainen, Suzana Stojakovic - Celustka, Dagmar Brechlerova

Abstract: This study describes and compares the use of Electronic Signature, Certificate Authorities, Public Key Infrastructure and Government to Citizen (G2C) and Citizen to Government (C2G) services in three European countries: Finland, the Czech Republic and the Republic of Croatia. These countries have built their own Information Society Infrastructure where public IT security issues were mostly based on Public Key Infrastructure. The Legislation is regularly coordinated with the one of the European Union and it very slightly differs between the countries. G2C and C2G services are under construction.

Key words: Electronic Signature, Certificate Authority, PKI

1. INTRODUCTION

The beginning of the 21st century is characterized by the massive growth of electronic communication. Important part of IT implementation at the moment is electronic government (G2C, C2G). New technologies have as well brought considerable IT security risks. This required suitable technologies like electronic signature and Public Key Infrastructure (PKI) to be established as a form of managing and mitigating these risks. Technology itself proved to be insufficient for adequate administration of IT security issues and the need for 'legal infrastructure' was set.

Finland is a Scandinavian country with one of the best economy ratings in the world and is a member of the EU. Czech Republic is Eastern European country, and is currently undergoing candidation for the EU membership. Republic of Croatia is Southern European country, one of the youngest in Europe. It started building democracy after a severe war. This study will compare current legal and technological situation of PKI in the context of information society situation among the three countries. Well known inadequacies of conventional PKI and its implementation are not taken into consideration. [18].

2. INTERNET USE STATISTICS

The use of Internet in Finland is quite widespread. In 1999 it was one of the most computerized countries in the world [15]. About 60 % of the population had computers at home, at work or in schools and around 44% used Internet constantly. In 2001 more than 90% of enterprises used Internet [16] [17]. In Finland there are about 65 Internet Service Providers (ISPs) [1]. The use of Internet in Czech Republic started in 1991. It became more common after 1996. In proportion 15 % of connections are done from home, 16% from libraries and 52% from work places. In Czech Republic there are many ISPs.

The use of Internet in Croatia started in 1992. It was mostly used in academic purposes. Currently there are about 200 000 Internet users and 9 ISPs.

	Czech Republic	Finland	Republic of Croatia	EU Average [21] [22]
Area (Km2)	78866	337030	56542	
Population (millions)	10,3	5,2	4,4	375
GPD ($/capita) (2001)	14400	25800	8300	22500
Fixed telephone connections (Per 100 persons) 2001, 1)1997	38	55 [1)]	39	46
Mobile phones (Per 100 persons) 2001, 2) 1997	53	57 [2)]	30	40
Internet users (% of population) (2000)	11	44	5	19
Number of Government Web-Sites (2000/2002)	83/168	198/198	60/75	
ISP Providers (in 2000)	More than 300	65	9	

Table 1. A summary of characterizations [1] [21] [22].

3. ELECTRONIC SIGNATURE SITUATION AND RELATED SERVICES

Electronic signature is well known application of PKI, therefore it is not described in more detail. In the following sections terms such as certificates, certificate providers, electronic signatures, advanced electronic signatures and other PKI related terms are used as they are defined in EU Directive 1999/93. [4]. The definitions are given in those cases where used terms differ.

3.1. Certificates and Certificate Service Providers

In the late 1990s Finland reformed and harmonized its laws according to EU legal regulations. Five new laws relating to information security and electronic administration were passed in 1999 (Acts 565, 723, 760, 1318, 189). This was a sign that the administration was trying to accommodate the recent advances in Internet use. A new identification card with electronic ID was issued by police in 1999. A person who wanted the new FINEID (Finnish Electronic Identity) card could use with (secret key is in the card) or without electronic identification. Thus the Finnish government defined that Finnish governmental PKI is grounded on the use of smart card based authentication. This means that a card reader is needed for on-line use. In the future, identification will be done from a mobile device such as a cellular phone equipped with a special chip. Currently the FINEID card cannot be used as a social security card and is more like an ID and travel document without general public administration use.

In Finland there are several Certificate Service Providers (CSP) but only the Finnish Population Register Centre is accredited. This is provided for in the Finnish laws 507/1993, 1318/1999 829/1999. CSPs in Finland do not have any hierarchical structure. The basic idea, under current legislation, is that certificate service provision is pure business. Every company that fulfils all the requirements for an accredited service provider can be such a provider. Thus, CSPs satisfy Finnish laws and also business laws.

In the Czech Republic the mode of action is quite similar to Finland. The PKI system is not hierarchical. The Electronic Signature Act of the Czech Republic (Act. 227/2000) [3] also defines requirements of CSPs [2]. This act differs slightly from the EU directive [3] and only use as a qualified certificate is under this Act. The Electronic Signature Act was amended in 2002 [6]. There are several CSPs in the Czech Republic but most of them are in business fields. Only one CSP is currently accredited. Certificates and keys issued by this CSP are only accepted by public administration authorities [3]. The qualified certificate from this accredited provider (with or without smart card) is expensive for ordinary people.

In Croatia public infrastructure is undergoing major development. Like other European countries Croatia is also constructing laws closer to EU legislation. PKI systems are in use, but mostly in the business field, i.e. banks and financial organizations. These systems are internal business systems and cannot be used in public transactions. Every system has its own certificate provider and is not officially accredited. The law on electronic signature was passed at the beginning of 2002 and its definitions of certificates and signatures are very similar to the EU directive [4][7][8][9][10]. The root certificate is in the possession of Ministry of Economy which is also the Bridge Certification Authority. It intrinsically defines the hierarchical structure of PKI. The first CSP is Croatian Financial Agency (FINA). Other possible providers are not yet known.

3.2. Accepted certificates in public administration

In Finland accepted certificates have been prescribed by the law "Act on Electronic Services in Administration" [13]. Every public authority has to give the opportunity for electronic transactions (under predefined conditions) and an accredited certificate must be accepted. In principle all public authorities are ready for G2C/C2G services regarding the law but technically the situation is not the same. Only a few public authorities offer services where certificates can be used.

The current situation in Finland is that the Act on Electronic Signature is still undergoing preparation. Current certificates can be divided to certificates and qualified certificates, which are officially accredited. Practically this is FINEID. In the draft legislation 197/2001 qualified certificate is defined as "a civil certificate" and every Finnish citizen will have one [14]. This creates the possibility for new G2C and C2G services.

According to the Czech Republic Act [3]: "In the area of organs of public authority, only advanced electronic signatures and qualified certificates issued by an accredited certification-service-provider may be used." Currently there is only one accredited CSP. In Croatia there is not yet exact definition what certifications are accepted by public authorities.

3.3. Existing G2C and C2G services

The Finnish government has been committed to information society and G2C and C2G services, but the information society is not yet in full swing. Nowadays there are more than twenty services which are using accredited certificates, but only 13 000 FINEID cards are in use. To improve the current situation the state has started several pilot projects where certificates have been used. One was the FEIDHE project (Electronic Identification in Finnish Higher Education) [11]. The purpose was to investigate and to plan possibilities for implementing a smart card based electronic identification system in institutions of higher education. One goal was to make a full scale PKI system and it was first in the world on this scale and with technology. Another was a project named Satakunta Macro Pilot where a new electronic social security card was introduced [12]. There were many technical problems in these projects caused by actors, vendors, problems in software and technical interfaces. Nevertheless, these projects demonstrated that electronic ID card and certificates can be used in public services but the infrastructure as a whole, established procedures and service processes are not ready for this.

In the Czech Republic there is only one public administrative application that currently uses advanced electronic signatures and qualified certificates [3]. This application is for social support, but only 3 people have used it because the required confirmation had to be also on paper. However, the new Ministry of Informatics has great new plans for the novel use of electronic signature in all public administration

Because laws and regulations have only recently been passed and legislative infrastructure has just been built in Croatia, the new services do not yet exists. The current PKI practice in Croatia after the Electronic Signature Act and its Regulations has not much changed from the practice before this act. Intensive efforts are in progress to make the proposed PKI work as soon as possible.

4. CONCLUSIONS

Finland was one of the first countries to produce electronic identity and related services. The first release of a national electronic identification card and related services was more or less unsuccessful. Therefore, Finland is now losing its position as a leading country in the information society. Czech Republic and Croatia started a little later with their own information societies, but have caught up with Finland and other European countries. The gap between these countries is becoming smaller all the time [20]. Even though technological and legal infrastructures in the information society differ, the practical situation is almost the same. Main obstacles for practical use of electronic signature and PKI are: the certificates are too expensive for ordinary people; the advantages of their use are not clearly explained to public; the use of Internet is not so widespread or is too expensive; the required forms are still complicated and there is no suitable knowledge about proper use of PKI and electronic signatures. As the situation in Finland shows, it seems to be a long way from building legal and technological infrastructure for the general use of G2C and C2G services. Countries which have started later, can learn from existing mistakes and failures and avoid wasting their resources.

REFERENCES

[1] The World fact Book 2002, http://www.cia.gov/cia/publications/factbook/index.html

[2] Brechlerová D. "IT and Law – The Situation in the Czech republic". In *Security and Control of IT in Society –II*, IFIP, p.173-181, 2001.

[3] Electronic Signature Act http://www.uoou.cz/eng/227_2000.php3

[4] EU Directive 1999/93, Community framework for electronic signatures, Official Journal L 013, 19/01/2000 p. 0012-0020.

[5] Hobley Christopher. Just numbers, Numbers on Internet use, electronic commerce, IT and related figures for the European Community. January 2001, Published by the European Commission' s Electronic Commerce Team

[6] Novel proposal for Czech Republic Electronic Signature law, www.uoou.cz/Z-226-2002.pdf, only Czech

[7] Croatian Electronic Signature Act, NN No. 10, 30.01. 2002, (in Croatian),

[8] Croatian Regulation about Evidence of Providers of Certification Services for Electronic Signatures, NN No. 54, 15.05.2002., (in Croatian)

[9] Regulation about Measures and Actions of Use and Protection of Electronic Signature, Advanced Electronic Signature, Equipment for Making Electronic Signature and [Croatian Act 5] Advanced Electronic Signature and Systems for Certification and Obligatory Insurance of Providers of Qualified Certificates, NN No. 54, 15.05.2002., (in Croatian)

[10] Regulation about Technical Rules and Conditions of Connection of Systems for Certification of Electronic Signatures, NN No. 89, 25.07.2002., (in Croatian)

[11] FEIDHE project report, https://hstya.funet.fi/

[12] Report of Satakunta macro project (http://www.makropilotti.fi/english/

[13] Finnish Act 1318/1999, Act of Electronic Service in the Administration, Also in English:

[14] HE 197/2001, Finnish Government's proposal for new Electronic Signature law.

[15] Internet Metrics: using Host and domain counts to Map the Internet. The International Journal on Knowledge Infrastructure Development, Management and Regulation Volume 24, No. 6/7 (July/August 2000), http://www.tpeditor.com/contents/2000/zook.htm

[16] Internet and eCom in enterprises in 2002 Tilastokeskus. (in Finnish)

[17] Nordic Information Society Statistics 2002, Nordic Council of Ministers, Yliopistopaino, Helsinki 2002 , ISBN 952-467-109-3

[18]Roger Clark, "The Fundamental inadequacies of Conventional Public Key Infrastructure". In Proc. Conf. ECIS. 2001 June; Bled Slovenia.

[19] Anzinger Gunnar. Governments on the WWW, www.gksoft.com/govt/en/world.html

[20] European Economy. Directorate-general for Economic and Financial Affairs, Supplement B, Business and Consumer Surveys results, No 12, December 2000.

[21] Straubhaar Thomas. Migration Policies and EU Enlargement, East-West Migration: Will It Be a Problem?. Intereconomics, July/August 2001. P 167-170.

www.ingramcontent.com/pod-product-compliance
Ingram Content Group UK Ltd.
Pitfield, Milton Keynes, MK11 3LW, UK
UKHW020130290926
15471UKWH00003B/391

* 9 7 8 1 4 7 5 7 6 4 8 8 8 *